The Longest Journey

The Longest Journey

*Southeast Asians and
the Pilgrimage to Mecca*

ERIC TAGLIACOZZO

OXFORD
UNIVERSITY PRESS

OXFORD

UNIVERSITY PRESS

Oxford University Press is a department of the University of
Oxford. It furthers the University's objective of excellence in
research, scholarship, and education by publishing worldwide.

Oxford   New York
Auckland   Cape Town   Dar es Salaam   Hong Kong   Karachi
Kuala Lumpur   Madrid   Melbourne   Mexico City   Nairobi
New Delhi   Shanghai   Taipei   Toronto

With offices in
Argentina   Austria   Brazil   Chile   Czech Republic   France   Greece
Guatemala   Hungary   Italy   Japan   Poland   Portugal   Singapore
South Korea   Switzerland   Thailand   Turkey   Ukraine   Vietnam

Oxford is a registered trade mark of Oxford University Press
in the UK and certain other countries.

Published in the United States of America by
Oxford University Press
198 Madison Avenue, New York, NY 10016

A copy of this book's Cataloging-in-Publication Data is on file with the Library of Congress.

ISBN 978-0-19-530828-0 (hbk)
978-0-19-530827-3 (pbk.)

1 3 5 7 9 8 6 4 2
Printed in the United States of America
on acid-free paper

CONTENTS

PART III. MAKING THE HAJJ "MODERN":
PILGRIMS, STATES, AND MEMORY

ACKNOWLEDGMENTS

I wrote a very long Acknowledgments section for my first book: some four single-spaced pages. Though I am happy to stand by my gratitude to so many people then, as now, one of the nice things about doing this all a second time is trying to learn a sense of brevity. I am deeply grateful to a large number of people who helped me over nearly a decade in getting this book to press. Seven scholars did me the huge favor of reading the entire manuscript, at different times in its preparation; to Michael Feener (NUS), Michael Gilsenan (NYU), Michael Laffan (Princeton), Bruce Lawrence (Duke), Merle Ricklefs (Monash), John Sidel (LSE), and Jean Gelman Taylor (UNSW/Sydney), I owe a large debt. Their in-depth questions and meticulous critique helped to make the final product significantly better than it would have otherwise been.

I also benefited enormously from close readings of my individual chapters by scholars who agreed to read work on their individual areas of expertise. For part I of the book, on the early Hajj, this included Ahmed Abushouk (International Islamic University), who read and commented on chapter 1; for chapter 2, "Mecca's Tidal Pull," Kerry Ward (Rice) was equally invaluable for her readings of the early modern Indian Ocean. For chapter 3, "Financing Devotion," Raj Brown (London/R.Holloway) was a guardian angel, as was Annabel Teh Gallop (British Library) for chapter 4 on religious manuscripts and politics. The second part of the manuscript, on colonial worlds of the Hajj, was also read by scholars who helped me enormously in their particular areas of specialty. Chapter 5 on Conrad received a tight reading by Andrew Francis (Cambridge), and chapter 6 on medical matters was critiqued by Nile Green and Jim Gelvin (both of UCLA). Chapter 7 on Snouk Hurgronje benefited from the close scrutiny of Nico Kaptein (Leiden), and Priya Satya (Stanford) helped me with chapter 8, on espionage and politics in Arabia. The last third of the book, "Making the Hajj 'Modern,'" was also read by a generous group of scholars. Chapter 9, on the postcolonial Hajj and the state, was critiqued by

Jeff Hadler (Berkeley), chapter 11 on Hajj memoirs was equally picked apart by Anna Gade (Wisconsin), and chapter 12 on oral history interviewing and the pilgrimage received the once-over by Mary Steedly (Harvard). Chapter 10, on the lands outside Southeast Asia's Muslim arc, needed the most help, and from the most people, all of whom weighed in on geographies less known to me than my normal academic terrain. For this help, I benefited greatly from Wen-Chin Chang (Academia Sinica, on Burma), Tamara Loos (Cornell, on Thailand), Emiko Stock (Phnom Penh, on Chams in Cambodia and Vietnam), and Jojo Abinales (Hawaii, on the Philippines).

Susan Ferber, my editor at Oxford University Press, was ever present in this project; she deserves a huge amount of thanks for the thought and care that she put into this manuscript. Several student assistants helped me at various points in the research and writing of this book, too; Mohamed Nawab Mohamed Osman for his help with some transcriptions in Singapore, Sze Wei Ang for help in Kuala Lumpur, Oiyan Liu for help in Jakarta, and Deborah Cheong and Michael Ying for help with typing or retyping parts of the book, when I just could not get enough time to do it on my own. A small army of librarians in a number of libraries and archives around the world, mentioned at the back of this book, also deserve great thanks. Mona Lohanda at the Arsip Nasional in Jakarta and Danielle Mericale at Cornell need to be especially thanked, though: Mona for her unfailing help with locating materials, and for her friendship over many years, and Danielle for the assistance she gave me in readying images for publication. A number of funding bodies made trips all over Eurasia possible, and this book would not have been written without their support: the Faculty Fulbright Program was important here, as was the CAORC Program in Washington, D.C., with its irrepressible director, Mary Ellen Lane (and her staff). The Asia Research Institute in Singapore, the Center for Southeast Asian Studies in Kyoto, and the Society for the Humanities at Cornell all gave me fellowships and time off to write, the former important and the latter indispensable to getting this project done. After eight years of shuttling between repositories scattered throughout Europe, the Middle East, and Southeast Asia, I can honestly say that this monograph would have been impossible to complete without all of this help. This book belongs to many people, therefore, and not just me.

Colleagues in the History Department and in the Southeast Asia Program at Cornell have contributed to this book in many ways. I have also been fortunate to serve as Director of the Comparative Muslim Societies Program and of the Cornell Modern Indonesia Project, where I learned much from fellow professors and from students in both places. Finally, many friends and family scattered in many places helped me along through life while this book was being researched and written. Again, I named so many people in my first time around writing a book that I will try to learn brevity here, but most of those same folks toward the end of the last acknowledgments had a hand in keeping me sane this time, too. My mother and sister are particularly important here; they are anchors in my world and know that they are this to me always. My immediate Ithaca family make life full, and are all things to me. This book is dedicated to them in gratitude and love.

Note on Translations:

All translations from Malay/Indonesian, Chinese (for interviews in mountain, mainland Southeast Asia), Dutch, French, and Italian are my own, unless otherwise specified. There are some vagaries in the spelling of vernacular words throughout the book, based on the different orthographical systems used by different governments, both colonial and post-colonial. I have tried as much as possible to maintain agreement in these cases.

The Longest Journey

Introduction

In the sepia-tinted photograph, the people on the ship look tired. They sit strewn across baggage and ropes on the deck of the vessel, staring out at a listless sea. Roughly a thousand pilgrims are stuffed into the gills of the steamer, a huge number of them baking on the deck in the equatorial sun.[1] They perch on wooden crates, sometimes two, three, or more crowded on each. There is no space at all to breathe.

This is just one ship among many vessels that will be making the voyage across the Indian Ocean this year early in the twentieth century, from the wet tropics of Southeast Asia to the arid wastes of the Arabian Desert. The pilgrims will crawl across the surface of the sea in ships such as these for weeks, moving imperceptibly toward Mecca to perform the rites. They are aspirants—Hajjis and Hajjas in waiting—and they have made this voyage to fulfill one of the five central commandments of the Muslim faith. Who can know if they will return to their villages in Java, Borneo, and islands even further afield? But returning is not essential; only arriving in Mecca is required. To die on a journey such as this bears no consequence and certainly bears no shame; indeed, it is seen as a blessing, if it should happen. The ship's European officers, attired in immaculate white uniforms, stare down at the sarong-clad multitudes. Every year the scene is more or less the same, with the coir ropes pulling, the sound of waves lapping against the rusted waterlines of the ships, and the murmur of pilgrims reciting prayers filling the stillness of the air. The sun sets in the west over the horizon, but the pilgrims continue their praying in the fading light. Thousands of their compatriots will already be over that horizon in the great white mosques of the desert, some murmuring their devotions in Malay, others in Arabic. Now the goal for these pilgrims is to get over that horizon, too, so that Allah and his commandments can be met in the holy cities.

This book writes a history of such voyages, the undertaking of the Hajj from Southeast Asia to Arabia from earliest times to the present. The pilgrimage to Mecca is one of the five so-called pillars of Islam. Every Muslim must try to perform the Hajj once in his or her lifetime, if he or she has the means to do so. (This

is different from Umrah, the so-called lesser pilgrimage, which also takes religious Muslim travelers to Mecca but is not compulsory, has fewer rites, and may
be performed at any time of the year.) The Hajj is performed annually only in the
month allotted to the pilgrimage, which changes yearly with the lunar calendar.
During the month of Hajj, pilgrims find their way to Jeddah, Saudi Arabia, the
feeder city of the Hajj, today usually by jet. They then begin the rites of the Hajj
once they have disembarked. Before heading to Mecca, they change their normal
garments to enter into a state of *ihram* (a sacred state of purity, simplicity, and
cleanliness), donning plain white cotton cloth to symbolize that all are equal
before God, regardless of their worldly stations. They then go to circumambulate seven times the great stone cube known as the Ka'ba in the center of Mecca's
most important mosque. This is the place, Muslims believe, that Abraham was
asked to sacrifice his son by God. The Ka'ba is covered with a huge black cloth,
and only a small portion of the building (encased in silver) survives from very
early times.

After doing this, pilgrims head to Mina, and from there to the Plain of Arafat,
where they stand on the Mount of Mercy and recite certain preordained prayers.
From here, the pilgrims head to Muzdalifah, where other prayers are said and
small stones are gathered for the next day's activities at Mina. For the next three
days, the pilgrims stay at Mina, where they perform a central rite, the famous
stoning of the three pillars, which is meant to represent Abraham's similar act of
rejection of Satan, who had sought to dissuade him from Allah's instructions.
Once this act is completed, pilgrims pay to have an animal sacrificed, to recog-
nize, in turn, Abraham's willingness to sacrifice his son for God. Thousands upon
thousands of sheep, goats, and camels are then slaughtered, with much of the
meat being distributed to the poor. The massive cortege then returns to Mecca.
In Mecca, the pilgrims have their hair shorn from their heads to symbolize a new
beginning in their lives, and the Ka'ba is visited one last time. The Hajj is now
complete. Many Hajjis then go to Medina, the Prophet's city, to see Muhammad's mosque and last resting place; others visit other places in Saudi Arabia, the
Middle East, or even Europe. Their pilgrimages finished, they return home from
one of the world's most unforgiving deserts, connected to the rest of the adher-
ents of their faith through these centuries-old rituals.

The Hajj is only one of the main episodes of pilgrimage still extant in the
world, but it is the most important across a range of indices. In 1927, some
100,000 pilgrims performed the Hajj globally, and by the end of the twentieth
century, the numbers approximated 2 million annually. This year, nearly 3 million will go. Over the course of the 1960s and 1970s, much of this traffic began
to move less by surface transport of land and sea, and more and more often by
air.[2] Jewish pilgrimages to the Western Wall; Christian pilgrimages to the Vati-
can, Jerusalem, and Santiago de Compostela; and even Hindu pilgrimages to

Benares and some of the other great pilgrimage sites of the Indian subcontinent cannot compare in complexity to the Hajj as a global phenomenon.[3] If this is so for the so-called world religions, then it is even truer for the smaller pilgrimages that mark out a number of other global geographies, such as Shinto pilgrimage shrines in Shikoku, Japan, or Elvis Presley's Graceland in the American South, for example.[4] The Hajj combines an ancient history with a global reach, and it also combines immense size with a cosmopolitan diversity that is simply unique in the history of the world. It makes good sense to study a phenomenon of this nature not because of "wars on terror" or anxieties over potential "plots in the desert," but because there is no more dynamic and vital agglomeration of human beings traversing large spaces in the world today. Southeast Asia makes up a particularly important part of the global whole of the Hajj, and the history of these movements is ancient and the number of pilgrims in transit is now larger than for most other parts of the planet. Indonesia is the world's largest Muslim country by population, and thus it sends more aspirants annually to Mecca than any other nation. Yet pilgrims come from Malaysia, Brunei, and all the other countries of the region as well—by the hundreds of thousands per annum, and by the millions if we include historical time.[5] Now—and perhaps especially now, with everything one sees coming across the global news wires—seems to be a good time to try to understand these journeys more fully.

From the Middle Eastern side of this transit, the Hejaz (the Red Sea coasts of Yemen and Arabia)—and not the more customary central Egypt and the Levant—becomes the main axis of the story told here. From the sixteenth century onward and to some extent even before, the Red Sea and the Arabian and Yemeni coasts were important way stations for travelers, of the religious sort or otherwise. The desert littoral here had a long history leading up to the contact age of 1500 CE or thereabouts, and the products of these coasts were sought far and wide, even in Europe and distant China.[6] By the sixteenth century, though, the Ottomans became the most important players in the Middle East, and numerous foreign sojourners, some of them African or Asian but for the first time (in any density at least) Europeans, too, began arriving in ever greater numbers, as the velocity of contact increased.[7] By the eighteenth and nineteenth centuries, Yemen and the southern Arabian coasts were becoming vital waterways in world history.[8] By the twentieth century, this state of affairs became even more noticeable, as imperial rivalries and transregional flows of human beings marked the Red Sea as crucial to a developing new world order.[9] It would not be an exaggeration at all to say that the Red Sea was one of the most important spaces on the planet by this time, with the Hajj pouring hundreds of thousands of people through this waterway annually by the turn of the twentieth century.

Southeast Asia was one of the places that began channeling human traffic toward the Hejaz over the course of the last six or seven centuries. Some scholars

have looked at these circuits from the vantage point of doctrine and ideas, primarily, summing up such religious and intellectual links from earliest times to
the present.[10] Other scholars have taken a more mixed intellectual-materialist
approach, emphasizing in roughly equal shares the movement and interplay of
ideas, concepts, religion, and commodities (including human commodities), as
all of these "things" pushed across the Indian Ocean over the past several hundred years.[11] Though many of the flows that have been studied have moved from
Southeast Asia westward toward the Arabian Peninsula, there have also been
other strands—especially in the study of Hadrami (Yemeni) populations—that
have transited primarily in the opposite direction. A number of scholars have
made this counterclockwise traffic the substance of important volumes of scholarship.[12] By the nineteenth and early twentieth centuries, the circuits had become
quite large and also quite complicated (figure I.1). Students, teachers, Sufi itin-
erants, and traveling families of merchants were all making the trip across the
Indian Ocean, connecting the far poles of the Indian Ocean's shores in an increasingly complex embrace.[13] By 1900, the Indian Ocean really did seem to have
"one hundred horizons," and all of these horizons were populated by a range of
human beings in constant motion.[14]

How old is the Hajj from Southeast Asia? How long has this massive con-
veyor belt of human beings been functioning, and how has it changed over time?
What is the nature of the pilgrimage to Mecca from the lands beneath the winds,
and how different is the conduct of the Hajj between the various landscapes and

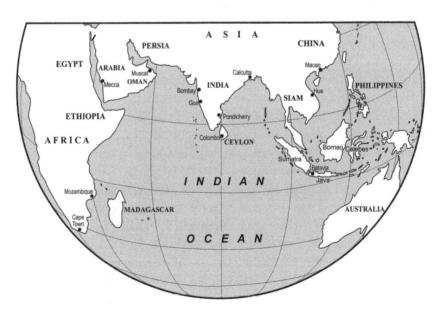

Figure I.1 The Indian Ocean basic map.
Credit: Map drawn by Lee Li-kheng, Geography Department, National University of Singapore.

seascapes that make up the panoramic diversity of Southeast Asia? What are the engines of the Hajj—religious, political, economic, and cultural—that have enabled this vast system to run year after year for so many centuries? This book is a history of this enormous phenomenon that draws in literally millions of people and spans the width and breadth of the Indian Ocean. Its approaches to this history are eclectic, making use of archaeology, archival history, literary criticism, sociology, epidemiology, political science, and ethnography. Telling a broad, inclusive story over many centuries, the book also has a central argument, or rather three intertwined arguments. First, I argue that the Southeast Asian Hajj started out as a more or less individual phenomenon, a practice undertaken by those who were able to pay and who gradually took along other Muslims via their own pecuniary means. This was not how all pilgrimages were accomplished in premodern times, but this model accounts for the majority of these early voyages. Second, in the colonial age, the pilgrimage became much more of a state-sponsored enterprise, one that could be ordered and adjudicated accordingly. Southeast Asian pilgrims took advantage of this system to go on Hajj in far greater numbers than ever before, but the price was performing a central tenet of Islam under the conditions and rubrics of non-Muslim powers. Third, the postcolonial age has seen a synthesis of these earlier two approaches, with states very much regulating the Southeast Asian Hajj, but individuals once again determining the kinds of journeys they are able to make to the Hejaz. This hybrid approach has become the hallmark of the modern Hajj in Southeast Asia—a religious ritual that is at once individual and profoundly communal at the same time.

The Nature of the Hajj and Transregional History

To give both breadth and depth to the study of the Southeast Asian Hajj from earliest times to the present, the book is organized into three roughly chronological parts. The first third of the book deals with the pilgrimage to Mecca as seen from the first centuries when there are records to track this institution's influence as an enormous mover of men. It examines the early influence of Mecca on the monsoon lands across the Indian Ocean, looking at how this embrace was instigated and then nourished over the course of the passing centuries. The second third of the book covers the high colonial period of both Southeast Asia and the Middle East, primarily spanning the second half of the nineteenth century and the first half of the twentieth. In this portion of the study, the avenues of vision onto the Hajj are also divided, with the chapters taking a number of different perspectives: one of a sailor on colonial pilgrim ships; a second on the medical and epidemiological dimensions of the pilgrimage; a third from the vantage of an important colonial statesman, whose utterances impacted policy on the Hajj from Southeast Asia; and a fourth on the dynamics of imperial espionage in the Hejaz. The last third of the book is on the modern Hajj, the pilgrimage in the age of independent Southeast Asian nation-states. These chapters explore sequentially the role of the state in the operation of the modern pilgrimage, the place of Hajjis from outside the Muslim-majority landscapes of Southeast Asia, the use of memoirs in telling regional experiences in the Hejaz, and what the contemporary experience of the pilgrimage is like, based on oral testimonies told to me by Hajjis from across a bandwidth of Southeast Asian societies. The book therefore encapsulates the lived experiences of a very large number of people, over many disparate centuries, all of them woven into one narrative.

The pilgrimage to Mecca offers fascinating opportunities to analyze both the internal and the external lives of human beings at the same time, in one syncretic attempt. Durkheim famously spoke of the five elementary forms of religious life and included Islam in his study, trying to show how the concept of the sacred and the profane, belief in spirits and divinities, and actualized religious rites came together in the consciousness of all of the world's principal faiths. Durkheim's analysis was particularly based on the sense of the "internal," in trying to make sense of the inner lives of human beings.[15] Yet we know, of course, from other noted scholars such as Erving Goffman that religion is not only internal or internalized but also a social process. Goffman called this dialectic the "presentation of the self," a phrase that he eventually used in the title of his most famous book.[16] The Hajj can certainly be seen as part of this discourse as well, as a pilgrim's life often changes in many ways when he or she returns home to the everyday sociality we all inhabit. Perhaps marrying concepts of Durkheim and Goffman, Anthony Giddens saw a trajectory in these processes, as he felt that modernity shaped such interactions differently as the centuries wore on.[17] For him, the Hajj would have been no timeless rite inherited from tribes in the desert more than a millennium ago, but rather a continually evolving institution, driven forward by the power of people to continually construct narratives of their own behavior. If all of this is true, then perhaps Habermas would be the capstone in this architecture of thought—a kind of summation of thinking about why people might do something as onerous and difficult as the Hajj. For Habermas, the Hajj might have been part and parcel of the concept of the public sphere, a space in which Muslims could make community in ways often unsanctioned by the modern state. Habermas never wrote directly about the pilgrimage to Mecca, but I would argue that in its annual passage one can see some of the deepest *geist* of Habermas's ideas—the Hajj as the ultimate nonstate space, open and channeled at the same time, and repeating itself in time year after year.[18]

What of thinkers who have written directly about pilgrimage, however? What can they tell us about the nature of such circuits that manage to continually reproduce themselves? Perhaps no scholar has been more influential in this respect than the anthropologist Victor Turner, whose formulations on the topic have become classic works on the study of the idea of pilgrimage generally. Turner was a specialist on Christian pilgrimages, and much of his scholarship focused on themes and discourses of sacred journeying within the confines of Christian Europe.[19] Yet he was also interested in the notion of pilgrimage per se anywhere in the world, and his ideas on death within pilgrimage ritual, and also the notion that pilgrimage sites *by necessity* had to be outside of the field of normal human existence, still carry great currency, even today.[20] Like Goffman, he saw the pilgrimage—any pilgrimage—as a social process, not just a spiritual quest. Pilgrimages were socially enacted and were completed not just for internal reasons, but very much for external ones, too.[21] Today, Turner's notions often act as bedrock in newer interpretations of how to look at pilgrimage both sociologically and through a number of other disciplines where new insights can be gained about the reasons people make such difficult journeys. Geographers now plot the details of pilgrimage to see what the data can tell them about correlations between prosperity, devotion, and conversion in the world's religions.[22] Others now look at pilgrimage through the lens of tourism, asking how the two traditions meet and differ across a range of global possibilities.[23] The Hajj is certainly part of this discourse of the evolution of tourism, as we will see later in this book. Anthropologists, historians, and political scientists all see important reasons to study this phenomenon as well, with theorists and Muslim intellectuals bringing particularly important recent perspectives to the table.[24] The idea of sacred travel holds out the promise of the attainment of deeper knowledge, yet it is clear that alongside the aspirants themselves, there has been an invisible army of researchers trying to figure out why people go in the first place, often at serious risk of life or limb.

To move from the internal to the external, in a provocative article some twenty years ago, the influential scholar of Islam Albert Hourani wrote, "How should we write a history of the Middle East?" and then sketched some intriguing possibilities for doing exactly that. Hourani was both bemused and (some might say) dissatisfied with the approaches he saw in print; the Middle East seemed fairly static in its scholarly representations, at least to him at the moment of his writing. I have taken Hourani's admonition seriously, and to my eyes at least, one of the best ways to help write *new* histories of the Middle East is to decenter the narrative away from that geography, so that the Arab corridor of these arid lands plays only a part in the history of the region. Southeast Asia, and the Indian Ocean more generally by this viewpoint, can therefore be a legitimate part of a wider Islamic history of the Middle East.[25] Hourani was not alone in his questioning of orthodoxies; other well-known scholars were also looking at the ways that Islam—and the interpretation of Islam, from a meta perspective—were changing in the modern world.[26] Much of this had to do with a shift away from Orientalism as the dominant paradigm for studying the Middle East, as area studies and other branches of knowledge were increasingly utilized to analyze a part of the world that had traditionally been interpreted via older methodologies.[27] Political economy approaches in particular started to become more important, with their insistence that even Islamic societies could and should be studied through social, economic, and political windows.[28] The study of the Southeast Asian Hajj over the *longue duree* seems to fit rather effortlessly into this change of paradigms, as any understanding of the pilgrimage by necessity involved (and still involves) all of these latter approaches. The pilgrimage is tailor made for such methods of inquiry; one might say, in fact, that it is the perfect vehicle in which such a new history can travel.

The Hajj became a hallmark of a developing world of linkages among Muslims, and arguably one of the most important of the strands that were helping to create a larger Indian Ocean ecumene. This history is beginning to be sketched in increasingly smaller sections and divisions of territorial space, so that we are starting to obtain an idea of how various these processes were over the long term. Some scholars have simply made Muslim voyaging itself a theme for their research, in all of the many avatars that this kind of journeying can mean. The Hajj, after all, is not the only kind of sacred travel for Muslims; there are also regional and even local variants.[29] Others have looked at the Hajj as a trans–Southeast Asian phenomenon, querying what the pilgrimage to Mecca has meant for the region as a whole as a concept and as a phenomenon lasting literally hundreds of years.[30] Dutch scholars have often been the leaders in narrowing this vision down to the Indonesian archipelago, the largest single source of Hajjis from Southeast Asia in all of the centuries described in this book.[31] And the inquiry does not stop at the colonial divide: the modern journey to Mecca has become the subject of more and more studies as well, including those of scholars who are themselves Muslim and who have access to holy spaces in the Hejaz that no outsiders can hope to obtain. This is crucial because these newer accounts often provide details that are very difficult to find and corroborate for those who (on religious grounds) are unable to take their studies into the heartland of Islam itself.[32] There is a continuum, therefore, in these accounts that links the pilgrims of the present to those of the past, all of whom crossed thousands of miles of ocean in their quest to satisfy one of the five most important dictates of their faith.

All of this knowledge is built on earlier foundations, however. One of the great ironies of colonial rule is that Christian powers left such profoundly detailed records on the Southeast Asian Hajj. Base suspicion and an often genuine desire to know the hearts and minds of their subjects at the same time made this possible. In addition to C. Snouck Hurgronje and J. Eisenberger, who wrote classic studies on nineteenth- and early-twentieth-century archipelago pilgrimages, a number of others weighed into these debates while colonialism was still an active reality in the region.[33] Dutch authors were pioneers in this regard, often writing in the mainstream Dutch Indies press, where their reports and opinions found avid audiences among colonial expatriate populations in the Indies (and at home in Europe).[34] Though English authors and civil servants wrote comparatively less about the pilgrimage from their evolving bases in Singapore, Penang, and Malaya, they also described the Hajj as they saw it, often in rather denigrating terms.[35] The writings left behind by bureaucrats give a real sense, collectively, of how the British Empire conceptualized the Hajj through the lens of the "official mind."[36] In smaller quantities, French, Spanish, and American writers also left records on the pilgrimage from the former Indochina and the Philippines, parts of Southeast Asia where the Hajj was a less common occurrence but still a recognizable phenomenon, year after year.

Yet to date there has not been a book written specifically about the pilgrimage to Mecca from Southeast Asia, a fact that seems fairly astonishing, given that this is a history of so many people over many centuries. In recent decades, there have been two very worthwhile studies of the global Hajj, but both of these books—by F. E. Peters and more recently by Robert Bianchi—spend only short amounts of time on the lands beneath the winds.[37] Peters's vision is resolutely global, and Bianchi budgets only two chapters to discussing the Southeast Asian Hajj, one each on Malaysia and Indonesia.[38] At least two good volumes of edited travelers' accounts of global pilgrims heading to Mecca have also appeared, yet Southeast Asian sojourners are mostly conspicuous by their absence in these tomes.[39] There have, however, been two good books produced on the Indian and the Ottoman early modern experiences of the Hajj, both of which have been useful in getting a sense of how this huge transit worked in the western half of the Indian Ocean over time.[40] In Southeast Asia itself, the pickings have been altogether less voluminous: a worthwhile doctoral dissertation on the Malaysian Hajj that appeared in 1986 (but was never published) and a slim edited volume presenting five Malay texts of Hajj (and excellent annotations of these texts) by two respected scholars of the genre.[41] Two very good statements on the Southeast Asian Hajj were produced in colonial times, though these tracts now date from 1928 and 1931, respectively.[42] Only two modern scholars have made the Southeast Asian Hajj a real research interest and subject of serious study during their lifetimes.[43] Though the pilgrimage to Mecca has appeared tangentially in the writings of a number of people, it certainly feels like it is time to attempt a history of this subject, given that the Hajj has been an active phenomenon in Southeast Asia for at least half a millennium, and also given that it is becoming more and more important—at least numerically, which we can track—every year.

If the Ottoman (and pre-Ottoman) lands of the Hejaz start us on an inquiry into the history of the Hajj in monsoon Asia, it is only appropriate that Southeast Asia, then, makes up the other terminus of the transoceanic story told here. Islam in Southeast Asia is fairly well-worn scholarly terrain by now; a number of writers (increasingly including indigenous scholars) have made Islam in the lands beneath the winds a well-catalogued research topic for some years now.[44] Many of these authors have presented regional visions of Islam throughout the Malay World, showing how the Islam that came to the archipelago developed its own impulses and histories in a diffuse culture area over time.[45] These histories included local pilgrimages (not just Hajj) to area shrines, offerings, sacrifices, and the quest for merit through meritorious deeds. Still other scholars have connected these histories to larger themes of pan-Islamism (among other currents of connection), which allowed the wellspring of Muslim discourse in Southeast Asia to bind itself to larger, regional conversations.[46] The Hajj allowed these conversations—whether based thematically, such as in Islamic law, or geographically, such as in studies on the Islamization of Java—to flourish.[47] By taking place once a year, every year, over hundreds of years, the connections that the pilgrimage wrought have allowed Islam to survive and evolve in Southeast Asia. This was a well that, once started, historically never ran dry, and one that still provides nourishment to the region today. The history of the Hajj is worth studying for all of these reasons, therefore, whether because of its longevity, cosmopolitanism, or the power of its annual influence on a broad stretch of the world.

The Architecture of This Book

Part I of *The Longest Journey* lays out the earliest beginnings of the Southeast Asian Hajj, as traced from the records of the fourteenth-century traveling jurist Ibn Battuta, wandering itinerant Sufis, and other sojourners along the transoceanic trade routes. Though much of the earliest information on the Hajj is textual, by looking at gravestones, mosque records, and the evidence from various sorts of archipelago architecture, we can also glean clues about early pilgrimages. The VOC (or Dutch East India Company) records include scattered notices of Hajjis on their way to Mecca as early as the seventeenth century, as do scattered examples of epigraphy, classical poetry, and British East India Company records in a pan–Indian Ocean context. Southeast Asians looked west and joined the stream of pilgrims beginning to make their way to Mecca from the rest of the world in early modern times. Hadrami wanderers from what is now Yemen moved in the other direction, spawning great networks of familial exchange, as did traders and religious mendicants, who set up brotherhoods of various Sufi orders in the archipelago. As these two-way contacts deepened over the centuries, the possibilities of pilgrimage became greater and greater. A thickening of traffic on the ocean's surface led to ever more contact between Southeast Asia and the Middle East. The rise of commerce in the Red Sea—originally trade of exotic stimulants but later of coffee and other tended crops—increased these possibilities still further. These first two chapters map out this early modern world of voyaging and exchange, which started to create an ecumene where none had previously existed in these transregional spaces.

Chapter 3 focuses on the economics of Hajj from precolonial to colonial times. Saving for the pilgrimage was usually a lifelong affair; the Hajj would almost always be the single longest trip that any Southeast Asian Muslim would take in his or her lifetime. Yemen and Java were key nodes in these far-flung networks, connecting either side of the Indian Ocean. Institutions such as waqf (financial investiture for religious purposes) and Hajj-related debt, the latter a problem that plagued generations of Southeast Asian pilgrims, also connected the two regions. Chapter 3 grounds the spiritual journey of the Hajj firmly in its material realities through these various institutions. Chapter 4 takes a very different tack, concentrating instead on the genealogy of Malay texts in regard to the pilgrimage. How did religion and politics intertwine in the *longue duree* history of the Hajj? This chapter examines Malay documents for clues about the beginnings of the Hajj in this part of the world. Terminology and syntax are important in showing how Southeast Asian sultanates first became aware of the pilgrimage and how this awareness was eventually used for very local purposes and designs. Far from being distant and obscure topics, notions of "Mecca" and "the Hajj" became vital in both religious and political discourse in Southeast Asia, as the courts of the region started to slowly see themselves as part of a larger Indian Ocean realm of Islamic interaction.

Part II of the book then looks at the Hajj from four different colonial perspectives. It begins with the most famous Muslim pilgrim ship in history: the *Patna*. En route from Singapore to Jeddah in the late nineteenth century with a cargo of hundreds of Southeast Asian pilgrims, the real-life basis for the ship *Patna* "sank" and was immortalized by Joseph Conrad in his fin de siècle novel *Lord Jim*. This chapter uses period newspapers, correspondence, and Conrad's surviving letters to explore what actually happened in the case of this ship. It also uses the case of the *Patna* to analyze how literature, when scrutinized for period facts, can say important things about history. Chapter 6 then focuses on the specter of disease on Hajj ships sailing between the Middle East and Southeast Asia. More than perhaps any other problem, controlling contagion—particularly cholera—presented a huge challenge to colonial pilgrims and to the colonial states that ruled them. This chapter delves into the medical mountain of disease control that was a yearly part of the voyage to Mecca. A small Red Sea island en route to Jeddah was commissioned as a cholera isolation station by the imperial powers, so that the disease would not run through the pilgrim populations of many nations during the height of Hajj season. French, English, Dutch, and Italian records from doctors and medical reporting bodies abound on this topic, showing how seriously all of the regional colonial powers took this threat. This literature highlights the danger that Southeast Asian ships carrying pilgrims represented in the expanding global order of late colonial times.

Chapter 7 then provides a bird's-eye view of the Hajj from a civil servant and scholar of Islam, C. Snouck Hurgronje, Holland's most famous Orientalist in the late nineteenth and early twentieth centuries. Snouck became a willing servant for the colonial regime in Indonesia and to this day is vilified by many Indonesians as the controlling force behind the history of Dutch expansion in parts of the country. Serendipitously, for our purposes, he left behind a large amount of private correspondence on how he saw the Hajj, both as a civil servant and as a scholar of Islam. His private letters are often at variance with his public pronouncements on the pilgrimage, revealing much about colonial mindsets during the fin de siècle period. Finally, Chapter 8 looks at the functioning of the Jeddah consulates of both England and Holland, the two powers that had significant numbers of pilgrims arriving in Arabia from their colonies in Southeast Asia. The Jeddah consulates kept tabs on suspicious troublemakers, smoothed the flow of devotees, and dealt with surveillance and control issues over a period of several decades around the turn of the twentieth century. The main source for this chapter is the 22,000 fiches of the Jeddah archives, only recently made available for easy public use. This archive provides an unparalleled view of the *mentalites* of the colonial regimes with regard to the Southeast Asian Hajj. The Red Sea and the pilgrimage to Mecca that passed through it became a space where espionage and devotion went hand in hand for decades during the high colonial age.

The final part of the book then explores the Hajj in the postcolonial period, after World War II and independence. Chapter 9, "Regulating the Flood," is centered on the coordination of the modern Hajj that regulates the hundreds of thousands of Southeast Asian pilgrims heading to Mecca on an annual basis. This chapter is based on source materials I have collected from the Hajj bureaus I visited in a number of countries in Southeast Asia's Muslim arc, including instructional books, statistical data, and newspaper clippings, which together detail how the Southeast Asian Hajj operates today. Though the bulk of this book deals with the Muslim-majority countries of Indonesia, Malaysia, and Brunei, other countries in the region—most notably Singapore, Thailand, and the Philippines but also the mainland states of Southeast Asia—are also home to significant Muslim populations. Chapter 10 focuses on those countries where Islam is the religion of only a minority of the population, but where Muslim lines of pilgrimage and the accompanying issues of movement, separatism, and even violence still loom large in delineating patterns of Hajj and its control. Based on my fieldwork among pilgrims and pilgrim aspirants in Burma (with the Rohingya in Arakan, Indian Muslims in Yangon, and Chinese Muslims in the north), in Thailand, among Cham populations in Vietnam and Cambodia, and in the Philippines, this chapter gives a textured sense of the Hajj in parts of Southeast Asia where its annual conduct is by no means a given.

Memoirs highlight the emotional experiences of pilgrims as they set out for the Hejaz, complete their religious obligations, and then begin their long journeys home. Chapter 11 looks at the memoirs of pilgrimage penned by literally hundreds of Southeast Asian Hajjis, mainly (but not exclusively) from the start of the postindependence period. These testimonials come from most countries in the region but are particularly numerous from Malaysia and Indonesia and are written in Malay and Indonesian. Although such life stories address different personal issues, they share a variety of themes—piety, hardship, and spiritual bliss among them. I have translated and analyzed these accounts to try to shed some light on what it means to write a memoir of the Hajj, as so many Southeast Asian Muslims have done over the years. Composing a memoir differs from telling one's story aloud, however; the former narratives are written to be read, but the spontaneous conversation of an interview can often yield very different kinds of information. The book's final chapter, based on seven years of intermittent fieldwork across Southeast Asia, lays out the shared (and often disparate) themes and concerns of more than one hundred Hajjis and Hajjas about their pilgrimages. They present the Hajj in all of its complexity: the poverty of some pilgrims, consigned forty-five to a room in outlying dormitories; the quiet power of the great mosques, both in Mecca and Medina; and the meaning of pilgrimage, both as a lived experience and as something remembered for the rest of a lifetime. I end with Muslims' own voices in this book, because it is, after all, *their* pilgrimage to Mecca—and they should have the last word. By retelling the stories of their travels to the holy cities and what these journeys have meant to them, I hope to include a last, living chapter of the book, one whose story is still evolving, even as this volume goes to print.

NOTES

1. I am indebted to Virgina Utermohlen for showing me this photograph from her private family collection. Now retired herself, her grandfather, Dr. Gerrit Paul Utermohlen, was a medical officer on shipping lines carrying pilgrims from the Dutch East Indies to Arabia in the early twentieth century. The photograph is undated, but is almost certainly from the first decade of the 1900s.
2. Gwyn Rowley, "The Pilgrimage to Mecca and the Centrality of Islam," in Robert Stoddard and Alan Morinis, eds., *Sacred Places, Sacred Spaces: The Geography of Pilgrimages* (Baton Rouge, LA: Geoscience, 1997), pp. 141–160, especially p. 150.

3. See Simon Coleman and John Elsner, *Pilgrimage: Past and Present in the World Religions* (Cambridge, MA: Harvard University Press, 1995); some Indian pilgrimage festivals are indeed huge, but getting to them does not compare to the organizational and infrastructural challenge of the global Hajj, which is of a completely different order.

4. Jean Dalby Clift and Wallace Clift, *The Archetype of Pilgrimage* (New York: Paulist, 1996).

5. As the Saudi government imposes a quota of 0.1 percent of the domestic Muslim population for pilgrims to determine how many can come in any one year, this equates to roughly 250,000 Hajjis per annum from Indonesia right now. Though the numbers recede as we go backward in time, the totals for sixty years postindependence certainly reach into the millions.

6. G. Rex Smith, "The Political History of the Islamic Yemen down to the First Turkish Invasion, 622–1538," in G. Rex Smith, *Studies in the Medieval History of the Yemen and South Arabia* (Aldershot, UK: Variorum, 1997), pp. 129–139.

7. Lein Oebele Schuman, "Political History of the Yemen at the Beginning of the Sixteenth Century: Abu Makhama's Account (1500–1521)" (PhD Dissertation, University of Groningen, 1960). This is one of the relatively few extant accounts available of a Yemeni view of this contact age in the Red Sea.

8. Abdulrahman Al-Shamlan, "The Evolution of National Boundaries in the Southeastern Arabian Peninsula, 1934–1955" (PhD Dissertation, University of Michigan, 1987).

9. Eugene Rogan, *Frontiers of the State in the Late Ottoman Empire* (Cambridge: Cambridge University Press, 1999).

10. Peter Riddel, *Islam and the Malay-Indonesian World: Transmission and Responses* (Honolulu: University of Hawai'i Press, 2001).

11. Patricia Risso, *Merchants and Faith: Muslim Commerce and Culture in the Indian Ocean* (Boulder, CO: Westview, 1995).

12. Huub de Jonge and Nico Kaptein, eds., *Transcending Borders: Arabs, Politics, Trade, and Islam in Southeast Asia* (Leiden: KITLV, 2002); Ulrike Freitag and William Clarence-Smith, eds., *Hadhrami Traders, Scholars, and Statesmen in the Indian Ocean, 1750s–1960s* (Leiden: Brill, 1997); Ahmed Abushouk et al., eds., *The Hadhrami Diaspora in Southeast Asia: Identity Maintenance or Assimilation?* (Leiden: Brill, 2009); Natalie Mobini-Kesheh, *The Hadrami Awakening: Community and Identity in the Netherlands East Indies, 1900–1942* (Ithaca: SEAP, 1999).

13. Michael Laffan, *Islamic Nationhood and Colonial Indonesia: The Umma below the Winds* (London: Routledge, 2003).

14. Sugata Bose, *A Hundred Horizons: The Indian Ocean in the Age of Global Empire* (Cambridge, MA: Harvard University Press, 2006).

15. Gianfranco Poggi, *Durkheim* (Oxford: Oxford University Press, 2000).

16. Erving Goffman, *The Presentation of Self in Everyday Life* (Edinburgh: University of Edinburgh Social Sciences Research Centre, 1959).

17. Anthony Giddens, *Modernity and Self-Identity: Self and Society in the Late Modern Age* (Cambridge: Polity, 1991).

18. Jürgen Habermas, *The Structural Transformation of the Public Sphere* (Cambridge: Polity, 1962).

19. Victor Turner and Edith Turner, *Image and Pilgrimage in Christian Culture: Anthropological Perspectives* (New York: Columbia University Press, 1978).

20. Victor Turner, "Death and the Dead in the Pilgrimage Process," in F. E. Reynolds and E. Waugh, eds., *Religious Encounters with Death* (University Park: Pennsylvania State University Press, 1976), pp. 24–39; Victor Turner, "The Center Out There: The Pilgrims Goal," *History of Religions*, 12/3, 1973: 191–230.

21. Victor Turner, "Pilgrimages as Social Processes," in Victor Turner, ed., *Dramas, Fields, and Metaphors* (Ithaca, NY: Cornell University Press, 1974), pp. 167–230.

22. Surinder Bhardwaj, "Geography and Pilgrimage: A Review," in Robert Stoddard and Alan Morinis, eds., *Sacred Places, Sacred Spaces: The Geography of Pilgrimages* (Baton Rouge, LA: Geoscience, 1997), pp. 1–24, especially pp. 11 and 16–17.

23. Erik Cohen, "Pilgrimage and Tourism: Convergence and Divergence," in Alan Morinis, ed., *Sacred Journeys: The Anthropology of Pilgrimage* (Westport, CT: Greenwood, 1992), pp. 47–64, especially pp. 48–49.

24. See Bruce Kapferer and Angela Hobart, eds., *Aesthetics in Performance: Formations of Symbolic Construction and Experience* (New York: Berghahn, 2005); and Abdellah Hammoudi, *A Season in Mecca: Narrative of a Pilgrimage* (New York: Hill and Wang, 2006).

25. Albert Hourani, "How Should We Write the History of the Middle East?" *IJMES*, 23, 1991: 125–136.

26. John Obert Voll, *Islam: Continuity and Change in the Modern World* (Syracuse, NY: Syracuse University Press, 1982).

27. Area Studies, of course, grew out of earlier Orientalist traditions; there was a continuity between the two. But Area Studies, as it is normatively practiced now, at least has been self-conscious of this parentage, in a way that Orientalism rarely was of its original methods and aims.

28. Peter Gran, "Political Economy as a Paradigm for the Study of Islamic History," *IJMES*, 1980: 511–526.

29. Willy Jansen and Huub de Jonge, "Islamitische Pelgrimstochten: Inleiding," in Willy Jansen and Huub de Jonge, eds., *Islamitische Pelgrimstochten* (Muiderberg, Netherlands: Coutinho, 1991), pp. 7–10; also D. A. Rinkes, *Nine Saints of Java* (Kuala Lumpur: Malaysian Sociological Research Institute, 1996). I briefly discuss *ziarah* and other forms of sacred visiting further on in this book.

30. William Roff, "The Meccan Pilgrimage: Its Meaning for Southeast Asian Islam," in Raphael Israeli and Anthony Johns, eds., *Islam in Asia* (II) (Boulder, CO: Westview, 1984), pp. 238–245.

31. Kees van Dijk, "Indonesische Hadji's op Reis," in Willy Jansen and Huub de Jonge, eds., *Islamitische Pelgrimstochten* (Muiderberg, Netherlands: Coutinho, 1991), pp. 37–56; Ernst Spaan, "Taikong's and Calo's: The Role of Middlemen and Brokers in Javanese International Migration," *International Migration Review*, 28/1, 1994: 93–128.

32. Zafarul-Islam Khan and Yakub Zaki, eds., *Hajj in Focus* (London: Open Press, 1986); Dick Douwes and Nico Kaptein, eds., *Indonesia dan Haji* (Jakarta: INIS, 1997).

33. S. Keijzer's monumental 1871 study, *De Bedevaart der Inlanders naar Makka*, is one of these foundational tomes; it was followed four years later by another important study by J. D. van Herwerden, *Toenmende Bedevaart naar Mekka*. See S. Keijzer, *De Bedevaart der Inlanders naar Makka: Volledeige Beschrijving van Alles wat op de Bedevaart-gangers uit Nederlandsch-Indie Betrekking Heeft* (Leiden: Gualt, Kolff, 1871); J. D. van Herwerden, *Toenemende Bedevaart naar Mekka* (The Hague: J. A. de la Vieter, 1875).

34. See, for example, Anonymous, "De Bedevaart naar Mekka, 1909/1910," *IG*, 2, 1910: 1638; Anonymous, "De Indische Bedevaartgangers," *TNI*, 1, 1874: 55–67; and E. Th. Van Delden, "Mekkagangers," *TNI*, 2, 1898: 639–661.

35. A. Wolluston, "The Pilgrimmage to Mecca," *Asiatic Quarterly Review*, 1, 1886: 408.

36. Anonymous, *Records of the Hajj: A Documentary History of the Pilgrimage to Mecca*, 10 vols. (Chippenham, UK: Archive Editions, 1993).

37. See F. E. Peters, *The Muslim Pilgrimage to Mecca and the Holy Places* (Princeton, NJ: Princeton University Press, 1994); and Robert Bianchi, *Guests of God: Pilgrimage and Politics in the Islamic World* (Oxford: Oxford University Press, 2004).

38. I treat in some detail in this book the functioning of the Tabung Haji in Malaysia and the sources and procedures of the Indonesian Hajj office in Jakarta—the two pilgrimage offices central to Bianchi's discussion in these chapters. See Chapter 9, "Regulating the Flood."

39. Michael Wolfe, *One Thousand Roads to Mecca: Ten Centuries of Travelers Writing about the Muslim Pilgrimage* (New York: Grove, 1997); Dale Eickelman and James Piscatori, eds., *Muslim Travellers: Pilgrimage, Migration and the Religious Imagination* (Berkeley: University of California Press, 1990).

40. Michael Pearson, *Pilgrimage to Mecca: The Indian Experience, 1500–1800* (Princeton, NJ: Markus Wiener, 1996); Suraya Farooqhi, *Pilgrims and Sultans: The Hajj under the Ottomans, 1517–1683* (London: I. B. Tauris, 1994).

41. Mary Byrne McDonnell, "The Conduct of the Hajj from Malaysia and Its Socio-Economic Impact on Malay Society: A Descriptive and Analytical Study, 1860–1981" (PhD Dissertation, Columbia University, 1986); V. Matheson, and A. C. Milner, eds., *Perceptions of the Haj: Five Malay Texts* (Singapore: ISEAS, 1984).

42. J. Eisenberger, *Indie en de Bedevaart Naar Mekka* (Leiden: M. Dubbeldeman, 1928); C. Snouck Hurgronje, *Mekka in the Latter Part of the Nineteenth Century: Daily Life, Customs and Learning of the Moslims of the East Indian Archipelago* (Leiden: Brill, 1931).

43. See William Roff, "Sociological Interpretations of Religious Practice: The Case of the Hajj," in Virginia Hooker and Noraini Othman, eds., *Malaysia, Islam, Society and Politics: Essays in Honor of Clive Kessler* (Singapore: ISEAS, 2002), pp. 37–54; William Roff, "Sanitation and Security: The Imperial Powers and the Haj in the Nineteenth Century," *Arabian Studies*, 6, 1982: 143–160; also William Roff, "The Conduct of the Hajj from Malaya, and the First Malay Pilgrimage Officer," in Anonymous, *Sari Terbitan Tak Berkala: Occasional Papers* (Kuala Lumpur: Institute of Malay Language and Culture, University of Malaya, 1975), pp. 81–112; and Michael Laffan, *Islamic Nationhood and Colonial Indonesia: The Umma beneath the Winds* (London: Routledge, 2003), as well as his new study, which also deals with the subject, at least partially, *The Making of Indonesian Islam: Orientalism and the Narration of a Sufi Past* (Princeton, NJ: Princeton University Press, 2011). See also an important collection of four essays, Nico Kaptein and Dick Douwes, eds., *Indonesia dan Haji: Empat Karangan* (Jakarta: INIS, 1997).

44. Azyumardi Azra, ed., *Perspektif Islam di Asia Tenggara* (Jakarta: Yayasan Obor Indonesia, 1989).

45. Mohamad Taib Osman, ed., *Islamic Civilization in the Malay World* (Kuala Lumpur: Dewan Bahasa dan Pustaka, 1997).

46. Anthony Reid, "Nineteenth Century Pan-Islam in Indonesia and Malaysia," *JAS*, 26/2, 1967: 267–283.

47. M. B. Hooker, ed., *Islam in South-East Asia* (Leiden: E. J. Brill, 1983); M. C. Ricklefs, *Mystic Synthesis in Java: A History of Islamization from the Fourteenth to the Early Nineteenth Centuries* (Norwalk, CT: Eastbridge, 2006); M. C. Ricklefs, *Polarising Javanese Society: Islamic and Other Visions, 1830–1930* (Singapore: Singapore University Press, 2007).

PART I

DEEP STRUCTURE, *LONGUE DUREE*

Charting the Hajj over the Centuries

1

Ancient Pilgrims

Southeast Asia's Earliest Muslim Pilgrims

> In the sixteenth century of our era, a visitor from Mars might well
> have supposed that the human world was on the verge of becoming
> Muslim.
>
> —Marshall Hodgson, "The Role of Islam in World History"

We will likely never know for certain when the first pilgrim from Southeast Asia
showed up in the Hejaz on his or her way to Mecca. No Malay text can be physically dated before the end of the fifteenth century, though a Yemeni biography
from this same period mentions for the first time a *Jawa* (a term applied univer-
sally to Southeast Asians in the medieval and early modern period) being in the
Hejaz sometime between 1277 and 1367 CE.[1] Whether this person completed
the Hajj is also unknown, but it seems highly unlikely that he would not have,
after crossing the vast space of the Indian Ocean in sailing ships to get to the
Middle East. References for this earliest period, which predate Dutch record
keeping that began around 1600, are tantalizingly few in number and often
incomplete. Other sources suggest that Muslim grave memorials were being
shipped in fair quantities from Gujarat to Indonesia in the fifteenth century, and
Hajjis were being commemorated in this manner (epigraphically, with the title
"Hajj") in north Sumatra and coastal Java during this very early period as well.[2]
We know for certain that Hamza al-Fansuri, a renowned Sufi poet who traveled
from Sumatra to Ayutthaya to Mecca (and even to Jerusalem), did make Hajj
sometime in the early sixteenth century. His poems (written in Malay but with
Arabic, Persian, and Javanese words scattered in the texts) tell us of his induction
into a Sufi order and of his travels along the maritime trade routes of Asia.[3] Acehnese Hajjis lived in groups in the Ottoman court in the early seventeenth century,
as well as in the Hejaz, and seem to have been there comfortably for some years
already at that point in time, stretching back into the sixteenth century.[4]

This chapter attempts to piece together the history of the earliest Hajjis to
Mecca from Southeast Asia, predominantly from the early seventeenth century

onward, when records in significant quantity first become available. It begins by looking at the Indian Ocean as a space for travel in the early modern world, one that was both an ecumenical and a religious terrain. The chapter examines how Southeast Asian Hajjis first began to be written about in extant records and sketches out the parameters of an expanding world system. It then focuses on the rising numbers of human beings, among them the important population of Hadramis from southeastern Yemen, who began crossing the Indian Ocean for religious and other purposes. Their travels linked Southeast Asia and the Middle East in increasingly important circuits, though they were only one among a number of groups whose passage contributed to an emerging dialogue between distant civilizations.

The Indian Ocean as a Field for Travel

Southeast Asian history prior to 1511, when the Portuguese sacked Malacca and set up a trading fort in the region, is very difficult to research: accounts do exist in Chinese, Arabic, Persian, and a few other languages, but they are extremely scattered and notoriously difficult to interpret. A number of Southeast Asian kingdoms, sultanates, and other protopolities, of course, also kept indigenous records that have survived to the present day, yet these chronicles (known as *hikayats, babads,* and *sejarahs* in the maritime world) are usually genealogical in nature, extolling the powers of rulers, and they frequently leave little by way of social history. There are exceptions: Zhou Daguan's description of Cambodia in 1253, for example, and the fifteenth-century *Undang-undang Melaka* immediately come to mind as pre-1511 texts that impart unusual stores of information. But as a rule, this assertion holds true. Only after the arrival of the Portuguese did rounder, more detailed records begin to appear on the social, mercantile, and religious customs of Southeast Asians, as told by the sailors of the first Western voyages to the region (figure 1.1). Scholars have combed many of these period indigenous and nonindigenous records to paint a picture of local life at the time.[5] Yet the most important and compulsive keepers of records about the early history of the Hajj were the Dutch, who followed the Iberians into Southeast Asia's waters in their own quest for spices.

Dutchmen began to notice the appearance of people called Hajjis soon after their arrival in the Indies archipelago at the end of the sixteenth century, though there was some confusion on their part about what this term actually meant. From as early as 1612, however, Hajjis were showing up in places like Banda in the spice-laden Moluccas, one of Holland's primary economic targets in the Indies, and by 1642 they were described in Dutch records in Bantam, West Java, as well.[6] The Dutch knew these people were well respected because of their journeys

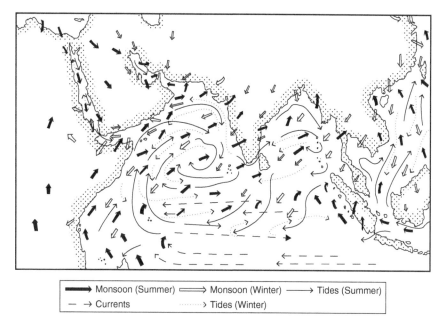

Figure 1.1 Indian Ocean Monsoon Winds, Tides, and Currents.
Credit: Hikoichi Yajima, *The Arab Dhow Trade in the Indian Ocean* (Tokyo: Institute for the Study of Languages and Cultures of Asia and Africa, 1976), p. 6.

to Mecca. That same year, they recorded Arabs in the Indies for the first time, and, ominously from the Dutch point of view, this first Arab "priest" arrived on an English ship.[7] As the seventeenth century wore on, the Dutch connected these personages with other Hajjis they were seeing on the rest of the Indian Ocean trade routes, including Indian Hajjis for the first time in 1656, the pilgrimages of royalty from the subcontinent in 1662, and Hajjis on the way to Yemeni ports in the Red Sea in 1679.[8] They also began to note that a certain number of Hajjis seemed to be implacably against the establishment and growth of a Dutch presence in the Indies and that these men propagated "hate" against the Dutch before fleeing the forces that Batavia had at its disposal in the islands.[9] Perhaps the most famous among them was Shaykh Yusuf of Makassar, whose long itinerant career between Sulawesi, Bantam, and Mecca eventually caused a wary Dutch East India Company (Vereenigde Oost-Indische Compagnie, or VOC) to exile him to South Africa.[10]

Even if Europeans in Southeast Asia knew fairly well by the end of the seventeenth century that Muslim pilgrims were moving back and forth across the Indian Ocean, they still had only a vague idea of what the Hajj was about. Many Dutchmen assumed that the great pilgrimage was to "Muhammad's grave in Mecca," and despite this inaccuracy, it eventually became the easiest way to explain a mass movement of human beings across still partially unknown global spaces.[11] Latent in much of this thinking was the implied threat of the Hajj, about which the Dutch, in particular, spilled much ink. In 1690, the Dutch commented on "troublemaking Hajjis" from Ternate, who had sprouted up in Rembang, East Java; in 1725, they noted again the secret movement of Hajjis to Semarang in Central Java, a matter of some concern, as the latter was by now a major Dutch commercial port.[12] This "threat" stretched all the way west to Sumatra as well. In 1726, the Dutch wrote about Hajjis leading armed resistance fighters against VOC forces in the mountains outside Padang; one of these men had been the subject of an intensive manhunt by Batavia for more than seven years.[13] These connections between Dutch outposts in the Indies and the religious connection of the Hajj all the way out to the Arabian peninsula conditioned much thinking about the nature of the early modern Hajj and set the stage for a set of interactions for many years to come.

This process was in keeping with European expansion east of the Cape during the sixteenth, seventeenth, and eighteenth centuries. Scholars have shown convincingly how much of the medieval world system was not in any way dependent on Europeans before this epoch started. Rather, it was unitary, or perhaps better segmentary, with corridors of interactions abutting and overlapping each other as one moved east into the Indian Ocean and eventually all the way out to East Asia itself.[14] Yet this world began to slowly change after the initial contact period in a number of ways, as Europeans began to assert pressures on these older arrangements and refashion them in more coercive directions.[15] Some of this had to do with new relationships between merchants and states, but military balances, the growth of state power, and changing transport and transaction costs all played parts as well. In short, the older attributes of the world system began to slowly dissipate in some ways into formalized new arrangements, only some of which were conducive to habitual freedoms of travel that had previously existed. Yet even if coercion was being felt more strongly after the sixteenth century commenced, some of the structures of the evolving system—including the maintenance and exploration of sea routes and travel—meant that an undertaking such as the Hajj might actually be facilitated rather than retarded by the growth of European power in Asian seas.

The transition from the Indian Ocean as a *mare liberum* in these initial centuries to a space of competing interests and situational repression by European ships helped the Hajj along in certain rather unexpected ways. The *cartaz* system adopted by the Portuguese meant that passports were needed for certain parts of the Indian Ocean, but it also meant that "piracy" was reduced in certain stretches of sea, which was, of course, useful to heavily laden pilgrimage ships. The vast increase in knowledge about Indian Ocean weather, current, and wind systems also made long blue-water voyages like the Hajj safer and easier, though storms and cyclones were common dangers of travel. Yet it was the rise in trade and shipping that really made the Indian Ocean a more hospitable place for the pilgrimage to Mecca, whether Hajjis were coming from East Africa, the Gulf, South Asia, or Southeast Asia to fulfill their religious obligations. Most pilgrims traded at the same time that they performed their Hajj, so improving commercial conditions along vast stretches of the sea was a boon for everyone and allowed people to earn money to pay (often along the way) for their journeys to the Hejaz. Wars, rivalry, coercion, and outright extortion still happened on the routes, rendering Hajj shipping dangerous and downright impossible at times. But the gradual upturn in trade conditions all along the Indian Ocean sea-lanes made the pilgrimage a surer bet than it once was, despite there being many more powers to placate on the increasingly congested routes to the Red Sea.[16]

None of this is to say that the Hajj did not happen earlier than 1500 or before the arrival of Europeans. It certainly did, though records of it on an oceanic scale are very difficult to come by. One of the few narratives is by Ibn Battuta, the enigmatic Moroccan jurist of the fourteenth century who traveled from Morocco to Mecca and, eventually (if his account is to be believed), all the way to Southeast Asia and even China.[17] He made the Hajj while he was on his travels and kept company all along his itinerary with fellow members of a cosmopolitan Muslim elite who passed along the trade routes (dragomans, merchants, princes-in-exile, and others), many of them across the vast latitudes of the Indian Ocean. Ibn Battuta saw the ulama (religious notables, of which he was a member) as the protectors of Islam, and his own travels show how respected he was in almost every society he visited.[18] The elites in these coastal courts knew to welcome him as a representative of a cosmopolitan learning that transited along the routes as a matter of course during this time. Likely other such figures were moving alongside him, though most of their accounts have been lost over time.[19] Hajjis would have been one of these classes of people in motion, hopping from Indian Ocean port to Indian Ocean port, picking up work along the way as jurists, *qadis* (judges), and interpreters of Muslim texts and allying themselves when they could with local princes who had powers of patronage (box 1.1). In return, men such as Ibn Battuta would have conveyed prestige on these same courts, marking them as centers of learning and religious interpretation for other wanderers passing on the routes.

Box 1.1 **The Southeast Asian Sea Route According to Arab Geographers and Travelers**

"The motion of the sea coincides with the course of the winds, for when the sun is in the north the air moves to the south, hence the sea is, during summer, higher in the south, for the northern winds are high and force water there.... The shifting of the water in the two directions for south to north and from north to south is called ebb and flow."

Al-Mas'udi, *Maruj al-dhahab* (ed. de Meynard) (Paris, 1862), Vol. I, pp. 252–253, quoted in S. M. Ziauddin Alavi, *Arab Geography in the Ninth and Tenth Centuries* (Aligarh, India: Aligarh University, 1965), pp. 61–62.

"The harbour of Malacca is between Pulau Ubi and Sabta. So enter the port successfully moving through five fathoms to four and then anchor. The people then come out to you—and what people. They have no culture at all. The infidel marries Muslim women while the Muslim takes pagans to wife. You do not know whether they are Muslim or not. They are thieves for theft is rife among them and they do not mind. The Muslim eats dogs for meat and there are no food laws.... Be always careful of them for you cannot mix jewels with ordinary stones."

Shihab al-Din Ahmad ibn Majid, in Hawiyat al-Ikhtisar fi 'Ilm al-Bihar, MS. 2292, quoted in G. R. Tibbetts, *A Study of the Arabic Texts Containing Material on South-East Asia* (Leiden: Brill, 1979), pp. 205–206.

"The Voyage from Malacca to Aden. When you leave Malacca you follow the land to Mount Pulau Basalar, and beware of the bank mentioned before. When you see Mount Pulau Basalar in the direction of east by south you turn northwest by west, until you see Pulau Jumar a short distance off. When you have left it behind you, turn due north until you sight the islands of Pulau Sanbilan, and when you come to these you turn for a little north by northwest, to Pulau Batagh, and from there you travel west by north to the islands of Naja bari (the Nicobars)."

Sulaiman b. Ahmad al-Mahri, in Kitab al-Minhaj al-Fakhir fi 'Ilm al-Bahr al Zakhir, MS. 2559, quoted in G. R. Tibbetts, *A Study of the Arabic Texts Containing Material on South-East Asia* (Leiden: Brill, 1979), p. 219.

"The Meccans are elegant and clean in their dress, and as they mostly wear white their garments always appear spotless and snowy. They use perfume freely, paint their eyes with *kuhl*, and are constantly picking their teeth with slips of green arak-wood. The Meccan women are of rare and surpassing beauty, pious and chaste."

Ibn Battuta, quoted in Ross Dunn, *The Adventures of Ibn Battuta, A Muslim Traveler of the 14th Century* (Berkeley: University of California Press, 1986), p. 75.

The histories of this sea may have been changed over time, but the ocean remained as the constant to be crossed, whether for religious or other purposes (table 1.1). A wide variety of people wrote about this maritime world in the medieval, pre-European period of roughly 1200 to 1400, including Marco Polo, Odoric of Pordenone, John of Montecorvino, and Fra Jordanus among the

Table 1.1 **The Dhow Trade and Commodity Distribution in the Indian Ocean World**

Persian Gulf to Red Sea, East Africa, and South Asia:

Wet and dry dates, grains (rice, wheat, barley, peas, millet), sugar, tea, salt, oils, dry fruits, cotton, textiles, medicinals, copper-, brass-, and earthenware, dried fish, pearls, mats, carpets

Red Sea to Persian Gulf, East Africa, South Asia, Southeast Asia:

Dried fish, salted fish, grains, salt, oils, coffee, *qat*, livestock, *murreh*, frankincense, textiles, spices, drugs, hides

East Africa to Persian Gulf, Red Sea, and South Asia:

Mangrove poles and coconut-wood, firewood, coconut oil, hides, tusks, dried lemons, medicinals, peas

South Asia to Persian Gulf, Red Sea, East Africa, and Southeast Asia:

Grains (rice, wheat, barley, peas, millet), tea, sugar, spices, textiles, woods (teak and coconut), tiles

Southeast Asia to Red Sea and South Asia:

Turbans, veils, sugar, books, medicinals, rice, spices, baskets, trinkets

Source: Compiled by the author.

Europeans; Ibn Battuta, Qazwini, Ibn Sa'd, and Maqrizi among the Arabs; and Chau Ju-kua and the Sung and Yuan official histories on the Chinese side. For the period from 1368 to 1500, there are Swahili traditions, Nicolo Conti's travels, and the Great Ming voyages of Zheng He from 1405 to 1433, as well as archaeological and numismatic evidence. A Russian potentially may have reached Burma in 1470, the Venetian Josephat Barbara washed ashore in Oman in 1471, and Pedro da Covilhao's voyage to the western Indian Ocean happened in 1487–1493.[20] The patterns of the monsoons and sailing times and directions can be tabulated from all of these journeys.[21] Their collective accounts provide information about the hulls of ships and how they were often stitched together with fibers (no nails); how masts and sails were constructed and fabricated out of coconut or palm trees, and sailcloths were made out of coarse cotton; and even details about navigation and life at sea, including astronomy and the development of novel navigational tools, such as the windrose.[22] All of these approaches help us map out the Indian Ocean as an increasingly known space, upon which the Hajj could be undertaken by larger and larger numbers of human beings.

Arab geographers were among the most important interpreters of the Indian Ocean sailing systems, and a number of such scholars contributed to this corpus of knowledge. Yet the salient figure among all of these medieval scholars was Ahmad Ibn Majid, who drew explicit connections in his writing between geographical knowledge and the pilgrimage to Mecca by sea. Most classical Arab geographies of the Red Sea stop in Jeddah, which, simply, was where everyone was going. Ibn Majid understood this rationale: "For how long a time have we sailed in ships from India…the coast of Africa and Persia, the Hijaz and the Yemen and other places, with the fixed intent of not being turned aside from the direct route to the Desired Land (Mecca), either by worldly possessions or by human agency."[23] He knew that these seas were particularly treacherous in terms of navigational dangers, and therefore, it was all the more important to get these measurements right. "For the sea of Qulzum al-'Arab is the most dangerous of all the seas of the world, and yet people use it more than all the seas of the world because of the 'Ancient House' and the pilgrimage of the Prophet."[24] Ibn Majid, like others among his fraternity, conveyed the Hajj, seafaring, knowledge of the world, trade, and politics as part of the same Indian Ocean project. In this, he was a man of his times but also a prescient historian of sorts. He understood that the maritime road to Jeddah was only truly useful in its full multidimensional context, which is to say a voyage that took in spiritual as well as earthly travels.[25]

The Indian Ocean therefore supported transoceanic travel even before the turn of the seventeenth century, when Dutch records became available in large numbers through the correspondence and detailed bookkeeping of the VOC. Isolated travelers had made their way across subsections of the ocean before this time, and a few intrepid souls had sailed larger distances, sometimes crossing the entire length of this encircled sea from Southeast Asia to the Middle East, or in the opposite direction. Along with Ibn Battuta were a sprinkling of Italians, Arabs, and Chinese, with the occasional Portuguese and other Europeans thrown in for good measure, who could claim to be pan–Indian Ocean travelers, moving between points along the rhythm of the tides. In the later sixteenth and early seventeenth centuries, however, European powers in particular began to police the ocean rather than just traverse it, jealously guarding the routes to certain commodities and trying to enforce commercial patterns that would suit their own interests. For the Hajj, such enforcement was not always detrimental, because it could mean protection from piracy and the vagaries of some of the more aggressive littoral states. The Dutch, in particular, quickly figured out that hindering the pilgrimage to Mecca was not in their business interests, and though there were periods of hesitation policy-wise, for the most part they facilitated the Hajj as best they could. Arab geographers of the medieval and early modern periods also took a great interest in these travels, though their vision tended to be less commercial and more knowledge based (either religiously or as a matter of geography) over the course of time. Both sets of onlookers were fascinated by the evolution of these ocean pathways and of the people who were traveling them from all of the various corners of the Indian Ocean.

People in Motion

The VOC records known as the *Generale Missiven* first start mentioning the Hajj as such (*bedevaart* ["pilgrimage"], as opposed to the title Hajji) in 1699, when the Dutch noted that the Emperor Aurungzeb in India had prepared a huge ship to help along the pilgrimage from his own Mughal lands to the Hejaz.[26] After this, the mentions come more numerously and regularly (table 1.2). In 1705, the Dutch were concerned that Muscati Arabs had imprisoned Persian Hajjis on their way back to their own country in the Persian Gulf and made notes on this situation for several years running in the *Missiven*.[27] The following year, Emperor Aurungzeb appeared again in the Dutch ledgers when he informed them he was going to commence his own Hajj as a ninety-year-old man with fifty-seven ships in attendance upon him, and he was in need of a Dutch sea-pass to make the journey.[28] The emperor, as it turned out, also wished to bring many of his women with him. Ten years later, fugitive Hajjis from the East Indies were being commented upon, and notes were being taken on the fact that Bantam Hajjis were proselytizing Islam in Cirebon, an observation that was echoed again in 1729.[29] The links with trade and profit were never far from VOC minds, however: in 1737, the Dutch expressed the hope that the ruler of Ceram would release more sappanwood for sale after he returned from his own Hajj to the Hejaz.[30] These notices underscore a world of Muslims in motion along the sea routes, often with economic or political undertones in the reporting, but with the Hajj as an important spoke of observation in Dutch record keeping in Asia.

Period records such as the *Missiven* emphasize a larger conceptual truth of these times: the Hajj acted as the perfect vehicle for building Muslim networks across the Indian Ocean and even beyond it. The history of Islam spilled out from Mecca and also came back to the same place; it did this through a very large number of networks, which brought human beings and institutions together through such associations, transforming both at the same time.[31] Indeed, Mecca began to exert an almost tidal pull on a huge range of societies. In the Indian Ocean alone, these included Yemen and the Gulf emirates, East Africa, Kutch, Gujarat, Southern India, Sri Lanka, and much of island Southeast Asia.[32] This is to say nothing of the radials running west to Egypt and the Maghreb, as well as south from there to the Horn and even to parts of Muslim West Africa. Muslim history, in very real respects, therefore, was one of the centers of world history, both geographically and qualitatively.[33] A kind of "Muslim space" developed

Table 1.2   **Bedevaart ("Pilgrimage") in Early VOC Notices of the Generale Missiven**

Notice of Aurungzeb's huge ship helping along the Indian Hajj (1699):

VOC, Gen Miss: Van Outhoorn, Van Hoorn, Pijl, De Haas, Van Riebeeck, XXIII, November 23, 1699 (Kol. Arch. 1503, fol. 12–237), p. 88.

Notice of Muscati Arabs Imprisoning Persian Hajjis in Persian Gulf (1705–1706):

VOC, Gen Miss: Van Hoorn, Van Riebeeck, Van Swoll, De Wilde, Douglas, IX, November 30, 1705 (Kol. Arch. 1588, fol. 16–381A), p. 380; VOC, Gen Miss: Van Hoorn en Raden van Indie, XIII, March 31, 1706 (Kol. Arch. 1608, folio 516–570), p. 409; VOC, Gen Miss: Van Hoorn, Van Riebeeck, Van Swoll, De Wilde, Douglas, XVI, November 30, 1706 (Kol. Arch. 1608, fol. 23–488), p. 458.

90-year-old Aurungzeb will perform Hajj again with 57 ships; needs passes (1707):

VOC, Gen Miss: Van Hoorn, Van Riebeeck, Van Swoll, Douglas, De Vos, XXI, November 30, 1707 (Kol. Arch. 1627, fol. 406–729), p. 504.

Hajjis as "Troublemakers" in the Indies, especially on the Java Pasisir (1719/29):

VOC, Gen Miss: Van Swoll, Castelijn, De Haan, Zwaardecroon, Timmerman, XV, November 30, 1717 (Kol. Arch. 1779, folio 14–600), p. 312; VOC, Gen Miss: Zwaardcroon, Castelijn, De Haan, Timmerman, Faes, VIII, November 30, 1720 (Kol. Arch. 1824, folio 472–954), p. 509; VOC, Gen Miss: Diderik Durven V, November 30, 1729 (Kol. Arch. 2005, VOC 2113., folio 2521–3260), p. 60.

Maluku trade to resume when Ceram ruler returns from Hajj (1737):

VOC, Gen Miss: Abraham Patras, IX, April 2, 1737 (Kol. Arch. 2257, VOC 2365, fol. 2030–2303), p. 815.

Credit: Abstracted from W. Ph. Coolhaas, ed., Generale Missiven van Gouverneurs-Generaal en Raden aan Heren XVII der Verenigde Oostindische Compagnie ('s Gravenhage, Netherlands: Martinus Nijhoff, 1960).

within the larger global context of world history, as these networks conveyed a centrality to Mecca through much of the known world.[34]

The Hajj in early modern times, to use the tidal metaphor one more time, moved with these oceanic rhythms of weather, currents, and winds. Yet it also moved with human rhythms. Although the Hajj is limited to one month, the same pilgrimage routes used by merchants, Sufis, and Muslim wanderers gradually started to function throughout the year.[35] Muslim merchant culture contributed to this expansion and to the maintenance of such pathways, usually via the lived economics of everyday life in the harbors of many Indian Ocean cities. Many Muslim port officials preferred to trade with coreligionists, further

enhancing the power of these networks.[36] This does not imply any kind of unitary quality to Muslims moving between such Indian Ocean port towns;
linguistic diversity even during mosque sermons in this part of the world was
almost taken for granted on the part of believers going to pray.[37] Those who
traveled were from many cultures and spoke multiple languages, underscoring
how flexible these diasporas and connections were in their orientation and
outlook.[38]

Perhaps the best example is the Hadrami diaspora, which reached from
Yemen all across the Indian Ocean, from East Africa and the Middle East to
South and Southeast Asia, with an impact far greater than their numbers would
suggest. The diaspora of these travelers helped to create and sustain vast networks that literally covered all of this ocean's shores. Maintaining these networks
was accomplished through many methods, from religious teaching to political
patronage and from emigration to entrepreneurship activities.[39] The Indian
Ocean arm of these human movements looks in only one direction; the Hadramis and their activities even reached westward into North Africa, where they
performed many of the same functions in the deserts that they did in the maritime world of monsoon Asia.[40] Period Arabic texts show this occurring before
the Portuguese ever showed up in Asian waters around the turn of the sixteenth
century, though it certainly happened afterward as well.[41]

The routes that the Hadramis blazed over the centuries made Yemen itself,
the homeland of these wanderers, a multiethnic place. There, one might hear
Malay or Telegu or Gujarati being spoken in Mukalla or Tarim, in addition to
the local dialect of Arabic. This was due to mixed marriages and a tendency for
many Hadramis to return to Yemen, sometimes for very long periods of time or
even permanently.[42] Although Hadrami society ended up being essentially
translocal in nature, with a base in Southern Arabia and Yemen and tendrils
peeling outward in a number of different directions, Hadrami factions often
sought to garner assistance from various foreigners in settling their own internal
conflicts. Especially in matters involving large amounts of money, such as the
Hajj from various parts of the extended diaspora, this was often an important
consideration.[43] Hadrami clans and branches settled over time in a number of
places and maintained strong ties with their homeland, allowing for routes between the nodes of the network to flourish and regenerate as new colonies of
migrants were continually established (figure 1.2). In India alone, there seem to
have been three major branches of Hadrami families, each of which sent sons
back for the Hajj and on visits to the Hadramaut: one in Gujurat, one on the
Malabar coasts, and one on the Deccan plateau, where they mixed with local
Muslim kings.[44]

Eventually, some 20 to 30 percent of the entire Hadrami population lived in
the diaspora, and estimates have put the share of these people in insular Southeast

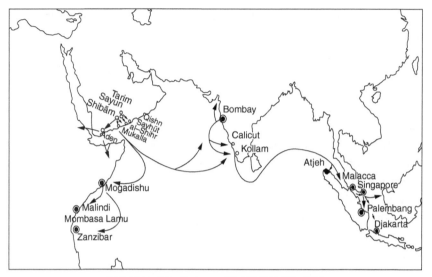

Emigrations of the Hadramawt Kathiri (A.D. 15th–19th)

Figure 1.2 The Hadrami Diaspora in the Indian Ocean.
Credit: Hikoichi Yajima, *The Arab Dhow Trade in the Indian Ocean* (Tokyo: Institute for the Study of Languages and Cultures of Asia and Africa, 1976), p. 13.

Asia at some 80 percent of the totals abroad.[45] The bulk of this migration pre-dated concerted European involvement in the politics of the Yemen in the nineteenth century.[46] Many Hadramis played a big part in transport, changing Muslim religious ideologies across the Indian Ocean, not only from the Middle East to Southeast Asia, often via the wings of returning Hajjis, but also in the other direction, in a kind of boomerang effect.[47] Hadramis also got involved in resisting British and Thai influence in the northern Malay states such as Kedah, Perlis, and Perak, and they also had a profound religious influence on eastern and southern states like Kelantan, Terengganu, and Johor.[48] Their presence was secular and economic, as well as doctrinal and religious; eventually, Hadramis came to own some 6 percent of the real estate of Penang and a full quarter of the real estate of Singapore, though this happened slightly later.[49] These connections were maintained and grown over a long period of time, in other words, and insti-tutions like the Hajj were the ideal vehicles to renew intellectual, religious, political, and economic ties with the homeland.

No place in Asia had stronger ties to the Hejaz than the Dutch East Indies, both from a numerical perspective and from the sheer weight of ideas, matériel, and human beings moving back and forth between the two places. L. W. C. van den Berg, writing in French in the mid-1880s, was among the first to try to chronicle this complicated relationship in *Le Hadhramout et les Colonies Arabes dans L'Archipel Indien.*[50] Residency patterns of Hadramis in the Indies have also been analyzed, and through this research, it has been found that migrants from Yemen eventually had no fewer than three dozen enclave-communities scattered throughout the Indies, each with connections to other nodes and many with connections back to the Hadramaut as well.[51] Travel between the Indies and Yemen took place on a large scale over the centuries, with the Hajj a vital part of these movements. Official passes were granted for this purpose but for few other reasons by a suspicious Dutch government.[52] The Hejaz was deemed to be an acceptable destination for Indies subjects, including those of Arab extraction, but only under certain circumstances and then in only the most controlled ways.

Southeast Asian writers themselves left behind records of such travels across the sea as well. Two early Bugis manuscripts from Sulawesi in the Indies discuss the teachings of Hajji Banktasi, the chief artillerist (or gunnery specialist) of Istanbul, who was the founder of the Bektashi order and the spiritual source of inspiration for the corps of Janissaries in the Ottoman Empire.[53] The fact that this Hajji appears in manuscripts a world away is revealing of how the fame of certain Hajjis traveled, even to the ends of the known earth within the *dar al-Islam* ("abode of Islam"). Malay-language manuscripts also reveal the movements of Hajjis within this wider Indian Ocean world, such as several extant versions of the *Hikayat Muhammad Hanafiah*, in copies from 1682, 1805, and 1814. This story also had a Middle Eastern provenance, yet circulated widely in Southeast Asia in different forms over a century and a half of literary and textual wandering.[54] A copy of the *Undang Undang Aceh* was written by another pilgrim to Mecca, one Hajji Muhammad Anak Bintan in either 1708 or 1747, showing that Hajjis were not just the stuff of legends, stories, and codes, but writing them as well.[55] Even mundane textual specimens, such as a letter from Hajji Yusuf to his younger brother Raja Mandandang, announcing the former's arrival to an island south of Selayar in the Sunda Sea, also survived. In all of these cases, the concept of the Hajji is somewhat incidental, but pertinent; the term's repeated appearance shows that early modern Hajjis used their titles widely, even in casual, everyday correspondence, such as when addressing other people as to their whereabouts or activities.[56] All of these different permutations for following Hajjis—either through texts, in texts, or as the authors of texts—provide a different dimension for thinking about the motion of human beings as early pilgrims to Mecca, either in literary or actual form.

Clearly, the Indian Ocean was a "networked place" in the early modern era and was becoming more so all the time. The Dutch only began to refer to the concept of *bedevaart* at the turn of the eighteenth century, but they referred to Hajjis far earlier than this, and they knew that such Hajjis were in fact going on pilgrimage and meeting each other in the cities of the Hejaz year after year. This was not considered to be a problem early on in Dutch eyes, but it became more of one after a while, though the VOC still saw in the transport costs of the journey a very profitable business enterprise. Yet if Hajjis were beginning to leave Southeast Asia for the Middle East in larger and larger numbers, then travelers from Arabia were also making the opposite journey, winding their way to the various sultanates and city-state kingdoms of Southeast Asia as well. The most significant community in this respect, as previously noted, was the Hadramis, but Omanis were also represented, and eventually a number of South Asian communities would claim a concerted presence across the face of the region, too.[57] The conditions of the network were set early on. The Hajj strengthened these burgeoning ties on a regular or semiregular basis, in the form of the contacts made between Southeast Asia and the Middle East with every passing trip.

Conclusion

It is clear that a trickle of Southeast Asian pilgrims started to sail west toward the Hejaz sometime around the sixteenth century. Prior to this time, there would have been a few Jawa (Southeast Asians) in the Muslim teaching and student circles of the Hejaz, but extant records about them are so fragmentary and incomplete that it is difficult to tell for sure who these men may have been, with whom they interacted, and how long they stayed in the holy cities. By the seventeenth century, we start to get a few more details. In the wake of Hamza Fansuri, the great Sufi poet, men such as 'Abd al Ra'uf al-Sinkili al-Jawi (1615–ca. 1693) forged a career by teaching in the Hejaz, and other scholars such as al-Kurani (1616–1690) made their living by lecturing the growing community of Southeast Asian religious students who were pursuing their studies in Mecca and Medina.[58] Still other figures, such as Nur al-Din al-Raniri, who made the pilgrimage to Mecca in 1621, traveled from Gujarat to Aceh to Mecca and back again to Southeast Asia, before settling down in Pahang on the Malay Peninsula.[59] His travels show a third type of early "Hajj possibilities" for these earliest centuries of contact. If Abd al Ra'uf was a Southeast Asian who became a religious teacher in the Hejaz, al-Kurani taught many others as a non-Southeast Asian, and al-Raniri transited between various outposts of Asian Islam, including the Middle East, South Asia, and Southeast Asia, all in one career. In the Indian Ocean world of the seventeenth century, Islam traveled on the wings of education and via formalized arrangements for distant religious study in spiritually powerful places.[60] It also traveled on the wings of the Hajj.

If the Hajj and religious study beckoned Southeast Asians to the Hejaz in larger and larger numbers from the seventeenth century onward, then these travels were part and parcel of larger movements of men and matériel passing in both ways across the Indian Ocean. Many immigrants and traders were in transit during this time—the Hadramis may have been the most visible community of human actors traveling these routes, but they were only one of many, as the early sources make clear. Arabs found their way to places such as Aceh and Palembang and Brunei, but Southeast Asians also found their way to the cities of the Hejaz, where they studied religious texts and made new contacts with other sojourners of the wider Muslim world. The Hajj linked these circuits of human travelers into a community of believers—an *ummah*—one in which members had a common frame of reference and a common set of experiences to draw upon in conversation. The Ka'ba stayed fixed in Mecca in the Arabian Desert, but the hope of circumambulating its mass traveled to nearly all of the distant points of the Indian Ocean via the journeys of the faithful. This notion of the pull of the Red Sea and its holy cities became important in the early modern world, and it is to this concept and the actualities of its history that we now turn.

NOTES

1. See Michael Laffan, "Finding Java: Muslim Nomenclature of Insular Southeast Asia from Srivijaya to Snouck Hurgronje," in Eric Tagliacozzo, ed., *Southeast Asia and the Middle East: Islam, Movement, and the Longue Duree* (Palo Alto, CA: Stanford University Press, 2009), p. 40; and especially R. Michael Feener and Michael Laffan, "Sufi Scents across the Indian Ocean: Yemeni Historiography and the Earliest History of Southeast Asian Islam," *Archipel*, 70, 2005: 185–208.
2. Elizabeth Lambourne, "From Cambay to Samudera-Pasai and Gresik: The Export of Gujarati Grave Memorials to Sumatra and Java in the Fifteenth Century CE," *Indonesia and the Malay World*, 31, 2003: 221–289.
3. Peter Riddell, *Islam and the Malay-Indonesian World: Transmission and Responses* (Honolulu: University of Hawai'i Press, 2001), p. 104–105.
4. Ibid., p. 104; Anthony Reid, "Sixteenth Century Turkish Influence in Western Indonesia," *Journal of South East Asian History*, 10/3, 1969: 395–414; Giancarlo Casale, *The Ottoman Age of Exploration* (New York: Oxford University Press, 2010).
5. See Anthony Reid, *Southeast Asia in the Age of Commerce: The Lands beneath the Winds*, 2 vols. (New Haven, CT: Yale University Press, 1988 and 1993); Victor Lieberman, *Strange Parallels* (Cambridge: Cambridge University Press, 2003); Barbara Watson Andaya, *The Flaming Womb: Repositioning Women in Early Modern Southeast Asian History* (Honolulu: University of Hawai'i Press, 2006).
6. W. Ph. Coolhaas, ed., *Generale Missiven van Gouverneurs-Generaal en Raden aan Heren XVII der Verenigde Oostindische Compagnie* ('s Gravenhage, Netherlands: Martinus Nijhoff, 1960; hereafter VOC, Gen Miss); VOC, Gen Miss: Pieter Both, Fort Mauritius Nabij Ngofakiaha op het Eiland Makean, VI, July 26, 1612, (961, 7 folios), p. 10; VOC, Gen Miss: Van Diemen, Caen, Van der Lijn, Maetsuycker, Schouten, Sweers en Witsen, XVIII, December 12, 1642 (1047, fol. 1–116), p. 180.
7. VOC, Gen Miss: Van Diemen, Van der Lijn, Maetsuyker, Schouten en Sweers, XX, January 13, 1643, (1050, fol. 1–13), p. 193.
8. VOC, Gen Miss: Maetsuyker, Hartzinck, Cunaeus, Van Oudtshoorn, Verburch en Steur, XII, December 4, 1656 (K.A. 1104, fol. 1–80), p. 96; VOC, Gen Miss: Maetsuyker, Hartsinck, Verburch, Steur en Joan Thijsz., December 26, 1662 (K.A. 1128, 1–467), p. 447; VOC, Gen

Miss: Van Goens, Speelman, Bort, Hurdt, Blom, Van Outhoorn, XI, 1q December 1, 1679 (1230 fol. 155–671), p. 356.

9. VOC, Gen Miss: Van Goens, Speelman, Bort, Van Outhoorn en Camphuys, VI, December 21, 1678 (1220, fol. 1–94), p. 248.

10. VOC, Gen Miss: Speelman, Bort, Hurdt, Van Outhoorn, Camphuys, VII, March 1 and 9, 1683 (1260 fol. 722–735), p. 496. His remains were eventually moved back to Sulawesi, though there is still a grave in Capetown.

11. VOC, Gen Miss: Van Outhoorn, Van Hoorn, Pijl, De Haas, Van Riebeeck, XV, November 30, 1697 (Kol. Arch. 1475, fol. 13–398), p. 855.

12. VOC, Gen Miss: Camphuys, Van Outhoorn, Pit, Van Hoorn, De Saint-Martin, XXI, March 14, 1690 (Kol. Arch. 1347, fol. 8–228), p. 351; VOC, Gen Miss: De Haan, Huysman, Hasselaar, Blom, Durven, Vuyst, IV, November 30, 1725 (Kol. Arch. 1911, fol. 541–965).

13. VOC, Gen Miss: De Haan, Huysman, Hasselaar, Blom, Durven, Vuyst, IV, March 27, 1726 (Kol. Arch. 1915, folio 2669–2858), pp. 49 and 50.

14. Janet Abu-Lughod, *Before European Hegemony: The World System, 1250–1350* (New York: Oxford University Press, 1989).

15. James Tracy, ed., *The Political Economy of Merchant Empires* (Cambridge: Cambridge University Press, 1991).

16. See K. N. Chaudhuri, *Trade and Civilisation in the Indian Ocean: An Economic History from the Rise of Islam to 1750* (Cambridge: Cambridge University Press, 1985); Kenneth McPherson, *The Indian Ocean: A History of People and the Sea* (Delhi, India: Oxford University Press, 1993); and Eric Tagliacozzo, "Underneath the Indian Ocean: A Review Essay," *Journal of Asian Studies*, 67/3, 2008.

17. Ross Dunn, *The Adventures of Ibn Battuta, a Muslim Traveler of the Fourteenth Century* (Berkeley: University of California Press, 1986), pp. 1–12, 56–80, 106–136; see also Ibn Battuta, *The Travels of Ibn Battuta, AD 1325–1354* (London: Hakluyt, 2000).

18. Vincent Cornell, "Ibn Battuta's Opportunism: The Networks and Loyalties of a Medieval Muslim Scholar," in Miriam Cooke and Bruce Lawrence, eds., *Muslim Networks from Hajj to Hip Hop* (Chapel Hill: University of North Carolina Press, 2005), pp. 31–50.

19. Muhammad Qasim Zaman, "The Scope and Limits of Islamic Cosmopolitanism and the Discursive Language of the 'Ulama,'" in Miriam Cooke and Bruce Lawrence, eds., *Muslim Networks from Hajj to Hip Hop* (Chapel Hill: University of North Carolina Press, 2005), pp. 84–104; see the terms of the debate with Marshall Hodgson and Albert Hourani on p. 103.

20. Archibold Lewis, "Maritime Skills in the Indian Ocean, 1368–1500," *JESHO*, 16/2–3, 1973: 238–239.

21. Abu-Lughod, *Before European Hegemony*, pp. 256–257.

22. G. F. Hourani, *Arab Seafaring in the Indian Ocean in Ancient and Early Medieval Times* (New York: Octagon, 1975), pp. 89, 100, 105.

23. Ibid., p. 65.

24. Ibid., p. 264.

25. For some other interesting texts in this vein, see Clifford Hawkins, *The Dhow: An Illustrated History of the Dhow and Its World* (Lymington, England: Hampshire Nautical Publishing, 1977); Allan Villier, *Sons of Sinbad* (New York: Scribners, 1969); Dionisius Agius, *In the Wake of the Dhow: The Arabian Gulf and Oman* (Reading, England: Ithaca, 2002); David King, *Mathematical Astronomy in Medieval Yemen: A Bibliographical Survey* (Cairo: American Research Center in Egypt, 1983).

26. Gen Miss: Van Outhoorn, Van Hoorn, Pijl, De Haas, Van Riebeeck, XXIII, November 23, 1699 (Kol. Arch. 1503, fol. 12–237), p. 88.

27. VOC, Gen Miss: Van Hoorn, Van Riebeeck, Van Swoll, De Wilde, Douglas, IX, November 30, 1705 (Kol. Arch. 1588, fol. 16–381A), p. 380; VOC, Gen Miss: Van Hoorn en Raden van Indie, XIII, March 31, 1706 (Kol. Arch. 1608, folio 516–570), p. 409; VOC, Gen Miss: Van Hoorn, Van Riebeeck, Van Swoll, De Wilde, Douglas, XVI, November 30, 1706 (Kol. Arch. 1608, fol. 23–488), p. 458.

28. VOC, Gen Miss: Van Hoorn, Van Riebeeck, Van Swoll, Douglas, De Vos, XXI, November 30, 1707 (Kol. Arch. 1627, fol. 406–729), p. 504. Such sea passes were common by this time; we have actually seen the Portuguese *cartaz* variant earlier in the chapter.

29. VOC, Gen Miss: Van Swoll, Castelijn, De Haan, Zwaardecroon, Timmerman, XV, November 30, 1717 (Kol. Arch. 1779, folio 14–600), p. 312; VOC, Gen Miss: Zwaardcroon, Castelijn, De Haan, Timmerman, Faes, VIII, November 30, 1720 (Kol. Arch. 1824, folio 472–954), p. 509; VOC, Gen Miss: Diderik Durven V, November 30, 1729 (Kol. Arch. 2005, VOC 2113, fol. 2521–3260), p. 60.

30. VOC, Gen Miss: Abraham Patras, IX, April 2, 1737 (Kol. Arch. 2257, VOC 2365, fol. 2030–2303), p. 815.

31. See the argument presented in Miriam Cooke and Bruce Lawrence, "Introduction," in Miriam Cooke and Bruce Lawrence, eds., *Muslim Networks from Hajj to Hip Hop* (Chapel Hill: University of North Carolina Press, 2005), p. 1.

32. David Parkin, "Inside and outside the Mosque: A Master Trope," in David Parkin and Stephen Headley, eds., *Islamic Prayer across the Indian Ocean: Inside and outside the Mosque* (London: Curzon, 2000), p. 2.

33. Edmund Burke, "Islamic History as World History," *IJMES*, 10/2, 1979: 246.

34. Mohamed El Amrousi, "Beyond Muslim Space: Jeddah, Muscat, Aden and Port Said," PhD Dissertation, University of California, Los Angeles, 2001, pp. 1–20, 55–98.

35. Cooke and Lawrence, "Introduction," p. 3.

36. Patricia Risso, "Muslim Identity in Maritime Trade: General Observations and Some Evidence from the Eighteenth Century Persian Gulf/Indian Ocean Region," *IJMES*, 21/3, 1989: 390.

37. Stephen Headley, "Afterword: The Mirror in the Mosque," in David Parkin and Stephen Headley, eds., *Islamic Prayer across the Indian Ocean: Inside and outside the Mosque* (London: Curzon, 2000), p. 226.

38. David Gilmartin perhaps captured this ethos best when he termed these relationships along the routes as being part of a "networked civilization," a term that has many uses in this context and describes accurately the flow of peoples and culture along broad, global spaces. David Gilmartin, "A Networked Civilization?" in Miriam Cooke and Bruce Lawrence, eds., *Muslim Networks from Hajj to Hip Hop* (Chapel Hill: University of North Carolina Press, 2005), p. 54.

39. William Clarence-Smith, "Hadhramaut and the Hadhrami Diaspora in the Modern Colonial Era: An Introductory Survey," in Ulrike Frietag and William Clarence-Smith, eds., *Hadhrami Traders, Scholars, and Statesmen in the Indian Ocean, 1750s–1960s* (Leiden: E. J. Brill, 1997), p. 18; Ulrike Freitag, *Indian Ocean Migrants and State Formation in Hadhramaut: Reforming the Homeland* (Leiden: Brill, 2003); Anne Bang, *Sufis and Scholars of the Sea: Family Networks in East Africa* (London: Routledge, 2003). See also Michael Feener, "Hybridity and the Hadhrami Diaspora in the Indian Ocean Muslim Networks," *Asian Journal of Social Science*, 32/3, 2004: 353–372.

40. Jon Swanson, "Histoire et Conséquences de l'émigration hors de la République Arabe du Yemen," in Paul Bonnenfant, ed., *La Péninsule Arabique D'Aujourd'hui* (Paris: CNRS, 1982), p. 108.

41. R. B. Sargeant, "The Hadhrami Network," in R. B. Sargeant, *Society and Trade in South Arabia* (Aldershot, England: Variorum, 1996), pp. 147–149.

42. Engseng Ho, "Hadhramis Abroad in Hadhramaut: The Muwalladin," in Ulrike Frietag and William Clarence-Smith, eds., *Hadhrami Traders, Scholars, and Statesmen in the Indian Ocean, 1750s–1960s* (Leiden: E. J. Brill, 1997), p. 131.

43. Ulrike Freitag, "Hadhramis in International Politics, 1750–1967," in Ulrike Frietag and William Clarence-Smith, eds., *Hadhrami Traders, Scholars, and Statesmen in the Indian Ocean, 1750s–1960s* (Leiden: E. J. Brill, 1997), p. 130.

44. See generally Huub de Jonge and Nico Kaptein, eds., *Transcending Borders: Arabs, Politics, Trade and Islam in Southeast Asia* (Leiden: KITLV, 2002); also specifically Omar Khalidi,

"The Hadhrami Role in the Politics and Society of Colonial India," in Ulrike Frietag and William Clarence-Smith, eds., *Hadhrami Traders, Scholars, and Statesmen in the Indian Ocean, 1750s–1960s* (Leiden: E. J. Brill, 1997), p. 67. Another excellent source is Michael Feener and Terenjit Sevea, eds., *Islamic Connections: Muslim Societies in South and Southeast Asia* (Singapore: ISEAS, 2009).

45. Christian Lekon, "The Impact of Remittances on the Economy of Hadhamaut, 1914–1967," in Ulrike Frietag and William Clarence-Smith, eds., *Hadhrami Traders, Scholars, and Statesmen in the Indian Ocean, 1750s–1960s* (Leiden: E. J. Brill, 1997), p. 265, passim.

46. Statements to the contrary are simply wrong; see Jon Swanson, *Emigration and Economic Development: The Case of the Yemen Arab Republic* (Boulder, CO: Westview, 1979), p. 51.

47. Peter Riddell, "Religious Links between Hadhramaut and the Malay-Indonesian World, 1850–1950," in Ulrike Frietag and William Clarence-Smith, eds., *Hadhrami Traders, Scholars, and Statesmen in the Indian Ocean, 1750s–1960s* (Leiden: E. J. Brill, 1997), p. 230.

48. Mohammad Othman, "Hadhramis in the Politics and Administration of the Malay States in the Late Eighteenth and Late Nineteenth Centuries," in Ulrike Frietag and William Clarence-Smith, eds., *Hadhrami Traders, Scholars, and Statesmen in the Indian Ocean, 1750s–1960s* (Leiden: E. J. Brill, 1997), pp. 85, 88.

49. William C. Gervaise-Smith, "Hadhrami Entrepeurs in the Malay World, 1750–1940," in Ulrike Frietag and William Clarence-Smith, eds., *Hadhrami Traders, Scholars, and Statesmen in the Indian Ocean, 1750s–1960s* (Leiden: E. J. Brill, 1997), p. 301. See also Michael Gilsenan, "Topics and Queries for a History of Arab Families in Inheritance in Southeast Asia: Some Preliminary Thoughts," in Eric Tagliacozzo, ed., *Southeast Asia and the Middle East: Islam, Movement, and the Longue Duree* (Palo Alto, CA: Stanford University Press, 2009), pp. 199–234; and Ulrike Freitag, "From Golden Youth in Arabia to Business Leaders in Singapore: Instructions of a Hadrami Patriarch," in Eric Tagliacozzo, ed., *Southeast Asia and the Middle East: Islam, Movement, and the Longue Duree* (Palo Alto, CA: Stanford University Press, 2009), pp. 235–249.

50. L. W. C van den Berg, *Le Hadhramout et les Colonies Arabes dans L'Archipel Indien* (Batavia: Imprimerie du Gouvernement, 1886).

51. Sumit Mandal, "Natural Leaders of Native Muslims: Arab Ethnicity and Politics in Java under Dutch Rule," in Ulrike Frietag and William Clarence-Smith, eds., *Hadhrami Traders, Scholars, and Statesmen in the Indian Ocean, 1750s–1960s* (Leiden: E. J. Brill, 1997), p. 186; and Huub de Jonge, "Dutch Colonial Policy Pertaining to Hadhrami Immigrants," in Ulrike Frietag, and William Clarence-Smith, eds., *Hadhrami Traders, Scholars, and Statesmen in the Indian Ocean, 1750s–1960s* (Leiden: E. J. Brill, 1997), p. 99. See also Mona Abaza, "M. Asad Shahab: A Portrait of an Indonesian Hadrami Who Bridged the Two Worlds," in Eric Tagliacozzo, *Southeast Asia and the Middle East: Islam, Movement, and the Longue Duree* (Palo Alto, CA: Stanford University Press, 2009), pp. 250–274.

52. Alain Rouaud, "Remarques sur Quelques Aspects de l'Emigration Hadrami en Insulinde," in *Migrations, Minorités et Échanges en Ocean Indien, XIX–XX Siecle* (Aix, France: Université de Provence, 1978), pp. 68–92; J. G. T. Shipman, "The Hadhramaut," *Asian Affairs*, 15, 1984: 154–162; Linda Boxberger, *On the Edge of Empire: Hadhramawt, Emigration, and the Indian Ocean, 1880s–1930s* (Albany: State University of New York Press, 2002); Ulrike Freitag, "Hadhrami Migration in the 19th and 20th Centuries," *British-Yemeni Society Journal*, 7, 1999: 25–32.

53. See in the British Library Manuscripts Collection both Add. 12358, F: ff. 21r.–27v.; and Add. 12365, C: ff. 10r–17r.

54. See in Cambridge University's Emmanuel College Library 3.2.10 Hikayat Muhammad Hanafiah; also in the British Library's India Office Collection Malay B. 6 (IO 2588); and back at Cambridge, in the Main Library Add. 3814 Hikayat Muhammad Hanafia.

55. Again in the British Library's India Office Collection, see Malay D. 12 Undang-Undang Aceh.

56. In the British Library, see Or. 8154, #39.

57. The Omani communities were always much smaller than the Hadrami and South Asian ones. I have met Arab-Indonesians claiming Omani descent in several places, including Banjarmasin and Palembang.
58. Michael Laffan, "Finding Java," footnote 128.
59. Peter Riddell, *Islam and the Malay-Indonesian World*, pp. 116–117, passim.
60. Many students and teachers primarily stayed with their own communities, but there was also clearly a certain amount of cross-cultural interaction in these journeys as well. For further details, see Azyumardi Azra, *The Origins of Islamic Reformism in Southeast Asia: Networks of Malay-Indonesian and Middle Eastern "Ulama" in the Seventeenth and Eighteenth Centuries* (Honolulu: University of Hawai'i Press, 2004).

2

Mecca's Tidal Pull

The Red Sea and Its Worlds

All this my captain at his return gave me an account of, and not only of this, but of the more renowned city of Mecca, which is the greatest and most frequented of all Mahometan mosques.... with two towers of extraordinary height and architecture.... On one side of this there is a fountain, whose water is salt and believed by the superstitious Mahometans to have the vertue of washing away their sins...
— *The Journal of William Daniel, 1700–1701*

Theorists of the Indian Ocean and its many histories have argued that this huge maritime space changed only slowly over the centuries—patterns of interaction generally took long periods of time to work themselves out, and this was all the more so when the processes under discussion were taking place on a large, pan-oceanic scale. This case has been made convincingly for the early modern history of the ocean, stealing the thunder from the once-normative narrative of violent and near-immediate European ascendancy after da Gama's entrance at the end of the fifteenth century.[1] A similar tempering function has been performed in studies of the transitional age between roughly 1700 and 1800, and more recently some of the tenets of this perspective have been brought into the nineteenth and even early twentieth centuries as well, showing how a *longue duree* vantage on cultural, economic, and political change can reach nearly into our own times.[2] Even ethnography can be connected to history in fleshing out these processes, as has been done clearly and cogently in recent work on the functioning of diasporas of the Indian Ocean, from historical time into the contemporary period.[3] It would not be an oversimplification to say that Indian Ocean studies as a field has helped in no small part to rewrite the interconnected history of the world in the past two to three decades. This has been especially so in the field's ability to connect large swaths of the Southern Hemisphere with the diverse and overlapping expansion histories of Europe, over what amounts to five hundred years of maritime contacts and convergences.

In this second chapter of the book, one particular place in this Indian Ocean world, the Red Sea and the adjacent coasts of southwestern Arabia, become the focal point of the story. This thin ribbon of water and coast was where all of Southeast Asia's pilgrims were heading for several hundred years. Yet they came not only with God in their thoughts but also with a culturally formed sense of this place as a region. Europeans journeying to the Red Sea not from the east but from farther west also came with certain tropes in their minds about this space. Both conceptions evolved through the increased contact being mediated through trade and the Hajj, especially from the sixteenth century forward. The first half of the chapter examines this median ground of the Red Sea through the lens of commodities in motion and asks how the passage of a range of goods—among them frankincense and myrrh (figure 2.1), as well as coffee and cloth, among many other commodities—helped fashion this world being described.[4] The second half of the chapter focuses on the "local histories of a translocal place," with the place in question corresponding to the Southern Arabian Peninsula, or what is today for the most part the country of Yemen.

The Ottomans, Portuguese, Dutch, British, and French all had a part in the unfolding of this entwined history, which acted to bring the Red Sea region very much

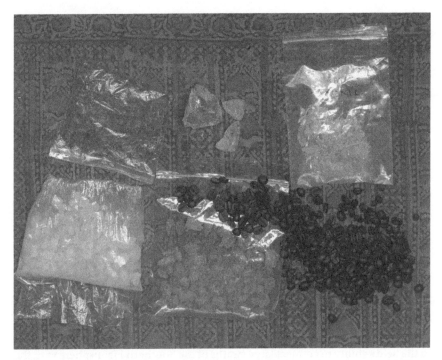

Figure 2.1 Luxurious Trades: Frankincense, Myrrh, Gum Copal, Raw Arsenic, Saffron, Coffee.
Credit: Author's Photo.

into the center of regional and even global events over a period of several hundred years. This is a history written in incense and coffee, as well as in the blood of commerce, rivalry, and political struggle. I argue here that trade routes and diplomatic maneuvering form part of the crucial backdrop for the religious history at the center of this book.[5] From VOC sources in archaic Dutch, Malay-language Islamic manuscripts, Italian-language scholarship on incense, and French-language scholarship on the birth of global coffee culture in the salons of the greater Mediterranean world, a glimpse of how the Indian Ocean changed the course of human history during the passing of the early modern era can be gained. Southeast Asia's pilgrims to Mecca were one of the communities involved in the construction of this evolving new world. Far from home, they help us to see the multiple channels of trade, religiosity, and movement spinning from the Hejaz in a number of different directions.

Commodities in Motion

Many people were in motion along the trade routes of the early modern Indian Ocean: Sufi mystics, spice merchants, and Hadrami wanderers in diaspora, among numerous other groups. Pilgrims made up only a subset of these earliest voyagers, but they were an important subset in terms of both numbers and the impact they had on these transregional connections. Noting the apparent waffling of the VOC on a policy involving Hajjis from their own Indies territories, the nineteenth-century British writer and administrator Sir Thomas Stamford Raffles famously said of the company that "their sole objects appear to have been the safety of their own power, and the tranquility of the country."[6] In fact, VOC policy on Hajjis and what to do with them was closely connected to the company's business interests. In the first half of the seventeenth century, the VOC actively tried to convert indigenes east of the Cape and also placed bans on Muslim proselytizing within their Asian dominions in 1642 and 1651.[7] By 1680, however, they seemed to realize that these religious proscriptions were bad for business, and thereafter, they were less energetic in pursuing attempted bans on local pilgrims. Instead, the Hajj was frowned upon if pilgrims did not have the money to pay their passage on Dutch ships. This was a pecuniary rationale much more in line with the *geist* of the company, even if it overrode certain instructions from the religious establishment back in the Netherlands.[8] Pilgrims were occasionally dissuaded from embarking for Mecca on political grounds, but more often than not, the VOC stated that Hajjis were welcome, partially because the sums of money they spent on such voyages helped out the company's exchequer in increasingly lean times.[9] The lure of cash made the Hajj a deeply paradoxical phenomenon for the Dutch: it was thought to potentially spread Islamic militancy, yet it also was a magnet for trade and profit.

This intertwining of economic and religious impulses seems to have been at the heart of the Hajj from very early times. People were constantly in motion in the Red Sea and the Hejaz generally, and often for religious reasons, but the trade in this region's commodities, and particularly in medicines and medicinal flora and fauna, went back to ancient times. Among the medically useful plants and minerals traveling Red Sea routes were the following products: lead sulfate, *Myristica fragrans Houttuyn*, *Eletteria cardamomum Maton*, *Cassia fistula*, *Piper retrofractum*, *Zingiber officinale Rosc.*, beeswax, *Acacia* sp. (a legume), dammar, *Piper nigrum*, *Rubia tinctorum*, sulfur, and *Cuminum cyminum*.[10] In fact, the Yemeni Red Sea coasts on the way to Jeddah, Mecca's port city, yielded a richer milieu of plant life than any other part of the Arabian Peninsula (figure 2.2).[11] The Tihama rises up dramatically from the water to a large escarpment, and then to a high plateau where many of western Yemen's cities and towns are located. Behind this is the *mashriq* (the eastern slope of the mountains) and finally the near-barren sands of one of the largest and hottest deserts on earth. The dramatic changes in topography and altitude conditioned this region for plant life perfectly, and many travelers passing through—including pilgrims—took advantage of this abundance to trade in these commodities.[12]

The items that were most sought after in places outside the local Arabian trade orbit were gum resins, such as frankincense and myrrh, which were used as incense and medicinally in a range of premodern Eurasian societies. They grew only on the coasts of southeastern Arabia and the adjoining East African coast, and nowhere else in the world. The environs of Mecca, Jeddah, and the Yemeni strand were mentioned in the Old Testament because of these products; the Queen of Sheba became a famous figure in antiquity, partially as the guardian of such treasures. Greek geographers such as Theophrastus, Eratosthenes, and Agatharchides wrote testaments on how to reach these Red Sea coasts, and their Roman descendants such as Pliny and Ptolemy safeguarded the same knowledge and eventually added their own compilations of sailors' accounts of winds and currents along the way.[13] The harvest of such items, climatic factors, uses of the monsoons to reach the trees, the prices of incense, and even estimations on the numbers of camels needed to transport exports were all entered into these geographies, simply because the items were so highly desired.[14]

These resins put this region on the economic map of the world and conditioned intellectual geographies for centuries to come. Italian-language scholarship has been among the best at chronicling these ancient connections, perhaps in part because the Romans left such glowing testaments to the powers of these commodities.[15] The archaic Italian aristocracy in central Italy had a major role in importing these incenses to Italy, and this was solidified later after the rise of Rome.[16] The incenses went not only to the classical Mediterranean but also as far away as China, linking these two poles of the ancient trade routes in a continent-

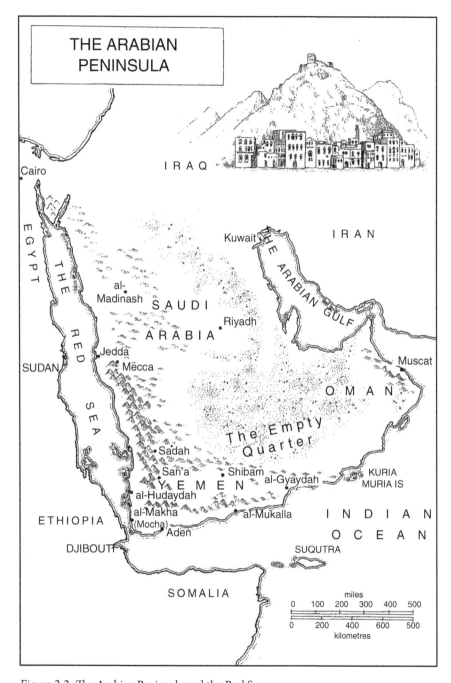

Figure 2.2 The Arabian Peninsula and the Red Sea.

Credit: Tim Mackintosh-Smith, *Yemen: The Unknown Arabia* (New York: Overlook, 2000).

long embrace.[17] Settlements grew along the Arabian Red Sea coasts partially in response to these long-distance trades, sparking caravan routes that crisscrossed the interior of the desert and the rise of small towns.[18] If people already existed in these spaces, as has been shown through pottery finds between Eastern Arabia and southern Mesopotamia, they were starting to agglomerate in larger and larger centers, with trade—and increasingly profitable long-distance trade—as a powerful inducement for collective settlement.[19] Commercial routes that abetted the conduct of the Hajj in later centuries were pioneered through these products, making the Red Sea a hot spot for cross-fertilization even before Muhammad himself was born.[20]

Other products also helped to make this region a well-known destination for seafarers who eventually would be transporting pilgrims as well. The trade in ceramics involved Chinese celadons and blue-and-white wares, as well as Vietnamese, Siamese, Indian, and Persian pieces.[21] Indigo, a dye used by royalty and the upper classes in a number of Levantine societies, was traded in large quantities in the seaports of the Red Sea.[22] Silver was an important trade item, as were certain stimulants, such as a range of valuable spices. Slaves were sent from the Horn of Africa to various Middle Eastern societies, where they were used as soldiers, laborers, and concubines in the courts.[23] Textiles, too, found a ready business in the markets of the Red Sea ports, transiting to Europe, east to the Indian Ocean, and eventually to Asia.[24] Although the products and many of the actors trading them over the centuries changed, the Red Sea remained an important avenue of commerce over a very long stretch of time.

However, during the early modern period, coffee became the undisputed prestige item of trade in the region of the holy cities. Natural, wild arabica coffee was first cultivated under tree cover in Ethiopia, but the deliberate, formal growing of the plant first occurred in Yemen in the fourteenth century, and it was exclusively cultivated there until the seventeenth century.[25] It was only after this movement of the crop from Harar to Mocha's environs across the Red Sea that Europeans got involved in its collection and sale.[26] Archaeologists have postulated that the drinking of coffee passed from mystics to everyone else fairly quickly; it became something that people did to "keep up their health."[27] In 1682, the Italian Pietro della Valle said that people used it to warm themselves in winter, and around the same time, the Frenchman Thevenot postulated that many Muslims drank coffee as a stimulant, which was not forbidden by Islamic texts as was alcohol.[28] Although Mocha (al-Mukha) became the most important coffee port in the Red Sea, most of the Tihama cities up to Jeddah sold the beans, too, and in all of its bewildering Yemeni varieties: Adeni, Adeni Bayat, Burai, Benan, Benan Bayat, Touffahai, Sawat, Dawairy, Shabraque, Dohairj, and Dohairi (table 2.1).[29] Coffee picked up where the Arabian incenses had left off in antiquity—enticing merchants to the region in search of fantastic profits.

Table 2.1 **Al-Mukha (Mocha) as a Center for the Coffee Trade**

The Shipping Radials of Yemeni Mocha in the First Half of the Seventeenth Century: Trading Destinations and Trading Partners in Various Parts of the Indian Ocean World

Yemen:

Kamran, Luhayya, Hudayda, Aden, Masdjid Bamsar (Khanfar), Burum, Mukalla, al-Shihr, Hayridj, Kishn, Sukutra

The Red Sea and the Gulf of Aden:

Suez, Jedda, Suwakin, Dahlak, Zayla, Durdureh, Bandar "Hessen"

East Africa:

Mogdishu, Pati, Malindi, Mayotte Island, Madagascar

The Persian Gulf and the Gulf of Oman:

Hormuz, Bandar Abbas, Muscat

India's Western Coast:

"Pragana," Sind, Kutch, "Gingut," Miani, Goga, Ahmadabad, Cambay, Baroda, Broach, Surat, Daman, Bassein, Chaul, Dabhol, Carpatan, Goa, Bocanore, "Carnati," Mangalore, Monte "Delii," Cannanore, Calicut, Ponnani, Cranganore, Cochin, Ceylon

India's Eastern Coast:

Pipli, Narsapur, Musalipatnam, Pulicat

Southeast Asia:

Achin, Priaman, Batavia

Source: Abstracted from C. G. Brouwer, *Al-Mukha: Profile of a Yemeni Seaport as Sketched by Servants of the Dutch East India Company, 1614–1640* (Amsterdam: D'Fluyte Rarob, 1997).

If Italian scholarship can help us understand the allure of the Red Sea ports for frankincense and myrrh, then French-language scholarship is equally as persuasive in helping us to ascertain how coffee repeated the feat many centuries later. Coffee growing and production quickly spread from the Red Sea region across the Indian Ocean: to Java, first, in the 1690s, and from there to Ceylon in 1700. It was being planted in Reunion by 1716, in Mozambique by 1757, and in Tanzania by 1861.[30] French and particularly Marseilles merchants were important in this process, but in the Indonesian Archipelago itself, where there was Dutch primacy, coffee cultivation moved from Java to Sulawesi in 1725, to Timor in the 1750s, to Bali in 1788, and to Minahassa in 1796.[31] Within a century, the

Dutch and all other Europeans were highly dependent on the Red Sea port markets for their supplies, and a complicated system was set up in Mocha, Jeddah, and other seaports to satisfy international demand. These ports flourished, according to period Western travelers of the time.[32] Arab merchants maximized their own profits at the same time. The world came to the door of the Hejaz, therefore, for the aroma and concentrated flavor of the demitasse, and they came in increasingly large numbers. Very good data exist on the number of ships, the tonnages and the drafts of these vessels, the temporal duration of voyages, the wind and current systems that allowed these trips to take place, and the culture of the coffee market and its workings all along the Red Sea coasts.[33] All of this was happening just as the Hajj started to pick up numerically in the early modern world, binding together the seemingly separate energies of trade and religion.

The VOC sources from this period are filled with references to Jeddah as it started to become more and more important, both as a trading center and as a religious destination for international pilgrimage. The first mention of the port in the *Generale Missiven* is in 1639; by the 1670s and 1680s, the Dutch were discussing the progress of economic negotiations in the port with local administrators, as well as the fate of individual trade ships, such as one Siamese ship that shipwrecked off Cambodia after coming back from a trade mission to Jeddah.[34] By the 1690s, the news (at least from the Dutch perspective) was even worse, with English pirates taking prizes in the Red Sea, including the commodity-heavy ship of one "Abdul Gaffar" (al-Ghaffar), a prominent trader whose vessel was en route to Southeast Asia at the time.[35] In the eighteenth century, VOC notices of Jeddah continued to be morose, with local textile traders there and in Mocha described as price gougers. Yet the Dutch seemed to realize that they had little choice but to give in to such demands if they wanted to maintain a presence at this freewheeling and increasingly important port.[36] Ominously, by 1728, the Gentleman Seventeen (the VOC directors) back in Amsterdam were advising frigates to be used in trade with the city, as it was feared that Dutch traders might be mishandled by Ottoman regents in ongoing trade and negotiations in the city.[37] This change in tone is noticeable and instructive—an age of partnership in Asian and European commerce was slowly starting to close, to be replaced in the coming decades by a new alignment of power and trade relationships. Yet the Red Sea was being viewed by *all* parties as an increasingly important locus for transactions, politics, and religiosity and as a vital channel between Asia and Europe.

Arabia Felix: Local Histories of a Translocal Place

From further east, the notion of Arabia was a topic of interest for Southeast Asians from a very early date as well.[38] This interest was not only contemporary

with the writing of manuscripts themselves but also goes back even to mytho-
logical times in the deserts of the Middle East. A Javanese text written in the
early nineteenth century, for example, begins with Adam himself ruling in Mecca,
and another manuscript (written in Arabic but with a partial Javanese translation extant in the text) discusses the early pilgrimage to Arabia and has drawings
of several of the holy sites in Medina.[39] A Malay folio from around the same time
period notes the visit to the archipelago of an honored guest from Mecca, who
told local Southeast Asians about many pressing events in the Hejaz, including
the desecration of important tombs in Mecca and Medina by Wahhabis.[40] A
copy of the *Hikayat Tamim ad-Dari* was also owned in this period by a local Javanese Hajji from Central Java named Abdul-kudus bin Hasan.[41] Even translations
of Muslim matrimonial law copied in Mecca by Patani (now southern Thai)
Muslims found their way to Southeast Asia during the early nineteenth century.
This last example shows that some of these connections linked the Middle East
with boundary areas of Islam in the archipelago, too, not just "central places"
such as Aceh, Java, or cosmopolitan trading sultanates such as Brunei.[42] The
point is that transmission and exchange was widespread and ongoing. The Hejaz
was a place of reference for Southeast Asians writing in their own tongues, who
were interested in Arabia's history and in its connections with their own local
Muslim domains.

This tradition was probably shared by many people in the Islamizing world
who saw the Hejaz as a fabulous and faraway land, where many desirable things—
rare commodities and powerful blessings among them—might be obtained.
Even in the time of Muhammad himself, Mecca had been a central oasis town
where caravan routes connected large parts of the Hejaz; by the medieval period,
it also was becoming famed by sea via Jeddah, where Indian merchants (for
example) wrote glowing letters about the betel nuts, dates, hides, and carpets
available to passing ships.[43] Trade started to become so important in the twelfth
and thirteenth centuries that body searches were instituted for merchants
coming into Ayyubid-period Aden (1173–1228 CE) to combat smuggling, and a
number of different kinds of taxes were levied on the same cargo to make money
for local states.[44] Rasulid-period customs lists (1228–1454 CE) show at least
three hundred different kinds of commodities passing through medieval Yemeni
ports such as Aden, and nautical archaeology has found evidence of significant
trade in tortoise shell, copper, and other local commodities, from the Red Sea
coasts of the Tihama, around the headland of Aden, and across the southern
Arabian coasts to Oman.[45] The ancient trades in frankincense, myrrh, and other
aromatics continued, in other words, well into the medieval period, without any
diminution in the Hejaz's importance on these long-distance routes.[46]

From work done in the Turkish archives primarily, we know how these Red
Sea patterns looked on the eve of Europeans making their entrance into these

systems in the age of the great East India companies. The Ottomans gradually became the main political player in this region after the 1453 conquest of Constantinople, but the seaports of the Yemen were, for a very long time, distant outposts of the empire and were never controlled as tightly as some other landscapes (namely, Anatolia proper) more directly vital to the sultanate's economic and political interests.[47] Taxes and trade in this theater were important to the Ottomans, but the Red Sea was far away from the grain-basket regions that fed the empire, so for a long time much of the economic activity in this region was given a long leash. The leash eventually was shortened when the Ottoman state became older and poorer after centuries of rule, and smuggling in the Hejaz ports eventually became a big problem for Istanbul, as large amounts of revenue on legitimate trade never found its way into official government coffers.[48] One of the reasons this happened was that everyday prices on goods and services went up and kept going up throughout the empire, so that customs collectors and toll officers had to find other ways to supplement their incomes to make ends meet.[49] For the purposes of the Hajj and transregional commerce, this is important, because it means freewheeling trade was part of the economic and political scene from the eighteenth century onward in the Red Sea ports where the Hajj was an annual phenomenon of great importance. This would be a fact that Europeans noted right away when their own ships first started coming to the Hajj ports of this region, after the Cape had been rounded at the end of the fifteenth century.[50]

The various empires of European trade intertwined their business with religion in the Hejaz from almost the beginning of their interactions with this arena, making the Hajj a phenomenon of both commercial and social interest to them as observers.[51] It is equally clear that Europeans were willing to muscle each other for the spoils of this trade, as were the Ottomans, who gradually transformed in European writings from an enemy very much deserving to be feared to a political weakling ripe to be exploited.[52] The Portuguese were among the first to appear in the region, and sources such as a fairly recently discovered 1525 document in Portuguese show that they had more than just commercial considerations in mind.[53] Eventually, the Portuguese would make efforts to gain a more permanent foothold in this area, especially at Kamaran Island just off the Yemeni coast, which in the nineteenth century would become the most important medical quarantine station dealing with the Hajj.[54] Yet just as the Portuguese noted their own observations about Arabs and Yemenis in the Red Sea Hajj ports, local historians did the same, with men such as Shanbal, al-Shihri, an unidentified Yemeni author whose writing now lies in Saiyun, and al-Sana' al-Bahir all weighing in on these new visitors to the Tihama coasts between 1498 and 1577.[55] Contact was a two-way process. Though the Hajj appears sporadically in these early writings on both sides, it is clear that it was one of the phenomena linking the two sets of actors together, as pilgrims started to pass through this increas-ingly congested waterway nearly five hundred years ago.

The Dutch also became interested in the Red Sea trade very quickly after their arrival in the Indian Ocean. Historians have linked the story of this trade to the larger tendrils of VOC commerce in Asia, but getting at the local histories of this translocal place has been a more difficult task.[56] The Yemeni coast was explored by passing Dutch ships between 1614 and 1620, before a factory was set up in 1620. Profits never lived up to VOC hopes, however, and in 1655 the station ultimately was abandoned. Cargo manifests from some of the Dutch ships calling in the Tihama ports, as well as the correspondence and interactions between various company servants and elites in Yemen itself in the early seventeenth century, paint a fascinating picture of a seasonally busy place, though.[57] In 1616 alone, according to Dutch records, close to fifty ships from many far-flung desti-nations in the Indian Ocean came to Mocha alone.[58] Letters addressed by the Ottomans to the VOC (box 2.1), which they saw both as a nuisance and as a potential ally against other forces they deemed more powerful, show Mocha to have been a port of some importance, a place where economic and political pos-sibilities fused, at least for a time.[59] Unraveling this kind of regional history helps us to see the eventual maintenance and growth of the Hajj as one early modern phenomenon among others, the confluence of which explains why so many dif-ferent powers took such a concerted interest in the region.

In addition to the Portuguese and the Dutch, the English also became involved in the Red Sea as a field of commercial and political interaction at a fairly early date. Though English ships passed through this waterway and participated in the trade of many local items (coffee and textiles among the more important cargoes), it was not until the eighteenth century, when British power was growing in India, that the East India Company became heavily involved in Tihama politics, mainly as a way of keeping travel channels open between Europe and its Indian colony.[60] After this, however, an interest in "piracy" in the greater Arabian theater, as well as the British adoption of Aden as an important strategic base along the trade routes in the nineteenth century, signaled a deepening of British intent in the area.[61] The pearl industry in the Persian Gulf had been a British con-cern for some time, but after Aden formally became an English-administered port, the locus of much British energy shifted to the south, and all the more so as pilgrim traffic increased over the course of that century, as we shall soon see.[62] Eventually, British intrigues in Qatar, Oman, and Bahrain; missionization in the region by British Christians; and attempts to curb a flourishing regional arms trade all contributed to a greater British presence in and around the Arabian peninsula than had been the case previously.[63] Only with the passage of the nineteenth century would British strategic thinking place the Red Sea at the heart of much of its planning in the Middle East, however. Here again the

Box 2.1 **Firman by Mohomet Bassa on Dutch Trade in Southern Arabia**

Copia van 't translaet van her firman, door Mahomet Bassa van Jemen vergundt.

In Gods name.

Mandaet van Grooten Coninck aen den Vicereij van Jemen, gebiedende die dit sien ofte horren lesen ende alle gouveneurs die leven onder 't gebiet van den Grooten Coninck, ende alle rechters ende schriftgeleerden, den capiteign van de Naderlanders, zijnde ter plaetse van Jemen, ongemollesteert in haer geloff te laten handelen ende vercoopen aen alle cooplienden ende andere natien. Daer het haer sal gelieven t evercoopen. Sonder van iemant beiet te worden: dat. De Nederlanders haer coopmanschappen ofte goederen sullen mogen vercoopen aen alle die se begeren te coopen; ende voorts den capietjn ofte ienmant van de sijnne te laten varen met hare goederen. Waer het haer sal gelieven. Sonder van lemandt belet te worden; ende at haer goederen onbeschadicht/c ende ongeopent aen landt door d'alfandigo sullen laten passeren. Mits batalende de maniere van de wage.

Den Bassa schrift aen sijnne gouverneurs ende bevelhabberen het mandate van den Grooten Coninck selve gelesen ende gekust te hebben. Waerover beveelt ende begeert 'tselve nagevolght

Transcript of the translation of the firman granted by Mahomet basa of Jemen.

In the name of God.

Mandate of the Great King to the Viceroy of Jemen, ordering those who see it or hear it being read. And all governors who are under the command of the Great King, and all judges and interpreters of Scripture. To allow the captain of the Dutch. Being located in Jemen. To trade and sell to all merchants and other nations to whom they may like to sell. Unmolested in their religion without their being obstructed by anyone: to permit the Dutch to sell their merchandise or commodities to all who may wish to buy them: and. Subsequently, to allow the captain or anyone of his people to sail with their commodities to any place they want to sail to, without their being obstructed by anyone: and to allow their commodities to be put ashore, having passed undamaged through the *alfrandigo*. On condition that they pay the weighage.

The Pacha writes to his governors and commanders to have personally read and kissed the mandate of the Great King. He orders and demands the same to be obeyed. He, furthermore. Grants his Firman to the Dutch, permitting them to trade, live, sail and depart throughout the entire domain of the Pacha. And he commands them to obey all that has been written below:

That they shall joyfully receive the Dutch since he himself is welcoming them heartily.

That everyone shall permit the Dutch to go freely and without restriction. Extending to them perfect friendship.

te worden. Voorts dit firman aen de Nederlanders vergundt, om te mogen handelen, woonen, verseijlen ende

Vertrecken in 't helle gebiet van den Bassa. Ende gebiet n ate volgen alles hieronder is geschreven:

Dat se de Nederlanders blidelicken sullent ontfangen. Also sij hemzelven seer willecome zijn.

FIRMAN BY MOHOMET BASSA [MUHAMMAD BASHA] AT [CENEN] {SANA'A} TO THIS GOVERNORS AND COMMANDERS, IN FAVOUR OF THE DUTCH TRADING IN SOUTHERN ARABIA, TRANSLATED INTO DUTCH.

[(after?) October 15, 1620].

(200A)

Credit: C. G. Brouwer, *Activities of the United East India Company (VOC) in South Arabian Waters* (Amsterdam: D'Fluyte, 1999), p. 193.

---

demographic, religious, and political importance of the Hajj became one of the main reasons for the increased involvement of London in regional and transregional affairs.

Finally, the French also became crucial in setting the stage for the pilgrimage to Mecca to become a vital issue of consequence in a globalizing, nineteenth-century world. Much of this had to do with Napoleon's occupation of Egypt: the French were not strong enough geopolitically in any part of Asia (until the last third of the nineteenth century with the erection of their Indochinese empire) to have real designs on the Red Sea until that time. When Egypt was "lost," the Red Sea and its pilgrim ports became a more peripheral issue, but the traffic in and through this waterway remained of interest and concern to Paris for the duration of the nineteenth century, even if the forward base of Egypt was now denied to them (table 2.2). The growth of French vision and participation in Red Sea politics can be chronicled from a truly breathtaking array of sources, including a number of scattered French repositories, such as the Archives Nationale in Paris, the Ministere de la Marine in Vincennes, the Service Historique Marine in Brest, and the Archives Section Outre-Mer in Aix en Provence.[64] Such an exercise also provides a window into how the French saw the great-power politics of the nineteenth century in the Red Sea region and acts as a careful counterweight to the much more voluminous English-language scholarship, which has overemphasized the establishment of British Aden as a watershed in the region.[65] The passage of Hajj traffic through the Red Sea became a critical issue to the French as well, as Paris became one of the most important seats for international sanitary control in the later nineteenth century. The Hajj become a cause célèbre in this latter discussion for many decades, even into the twentieth century, with the French leading the way in many respects as to how this debate on disease control was framed in international politics.

Table 2.2 **British and French Consuls in Jeddah over the Nineteenth Century**

French Consuls in Jeddah	
Fulgence Fresnel	1837–1850
Rochet d'Hericourt	1852–1854
Outry	1855
Beillard	1855
De Monbrun/Mombrey	1856–1857
Eveillard	1858
Rousseau	1859–1860
Pellissier	1864
Schnepp	1866
Debreuil	1868–1870
Buez	1876
Lucciani	1879
Mapertuy	1881
De Costalet	1886
Gues	1901
British Consuls in Jeddah	
Lake, E.I. Co. Agent	1834
Ogilvie	Early 1850s
Cole	1853–1857
Polat (acting consul)	1859
Stanley	1858–1862
Calvert	1864

Hollas	acting UK agent
Zohrab	1879–1881
Moncrieff	1883
Jago	1886–1887
Wood	1888–1892
Richards	1893–1894
Devey	1896, 1906
Alban	1896

Source: Abstracted from Sarah Searight, "Jiddah in the Nineteenth Century: The Role of European Consuls," in Janet Starkey, ed., *People of the Red Sea* (Oxford: British Archeological Reports Series, 2005), pp. 115.

The translocal histories of southern Arabia and the Red Sea corridor therefore became more and more complex from the sixteenth century onward. This part of the world had always been connected to other places. Yet a combination of fertile geography (for growing a number of highly sought-after plants), good ports (which helped in the collection and shipment of these commodities), and religious topography (for several sites, most notably Mecca itself) made the Red Sea a crucial choke point in the history of the Middle East from a very early date. A number of the products involved in these transactions changed over time, as different commodities either lost or gained value. The people buying, selling, and transporting these goods changed, too, as different groups waxed and waned in their influence in the area over time. Yet what remained constant was the sense that the Red Sea and its environs was a place with a particularly powerful valence, whether that valence was commercial or religious in nature. Most travelers to the region did not have to choose between the two. Since a large number of the actors plying the trades of the Tihama were Muslim themselves (from what we now call Turkey, Arabia, Yemen, Oman, and Iran, and even Africa, India, and Southeast Asia), many traders to the region simply combined religious callings and commercial ventures and made Hajj while they conducted their business in the region. They did so in the last month of the Muslim lunar calendar, the only time when the Hajj was allowed to take place. Then they attended to their business.[66] The growing numbers of Europeans getting involved with this arena began to change this dynamic, however, as the Hejaz began to take on more and more political importance as well. This was a third "valence" that can be added to commerce and religion but perhaps not separated from it, as the history of this windswept strip of water and sand clearly shows.

Conclusion

Few places in the world can boast as complex a history as the Red Sea and its coasts in the early modern era. We know that trade was integral to this part of the Hejaz from a very early time, and we can rely on archaeological discoveries to substantiate this assertion. By medieval times, Arabic texts flesh out this picture and sketch a world of commercial routes running in many different directions. The numbers of ships and men in motion at this early date must have been relatively small, but both were growing all the time, until by the seventeenth century a large number of languages could be heard in this narrow ribbon of water. After 1600 or so, the Red Sea took on global importance, as it became one of the evolving battlegrounds for trade, political influence, and power between rival European merchant companies, on the one hand, and on the other, a number of indigenous states that were also trying to secure riches and political maneuverability in a tightly congested arena.[67] The Ottomans, Portuguese, Dutch, English, and French all took turns in being in the ascendancy in these terms, but none was ultimately able to enforce any kind of lasting hegemony—political or mercantile—over the narrow shores of the Red Sea. Policing and regulation eventually did come to this crucial waterway, but it was mostly in the form of international agreements, and this was a development of the later nineteenth century.[68] Throughout this time and the centuries leading up to it, however, Hajjis continued to sail through the gates of the Bab al-Mandab and venture to "Mecca's door" (the port of Jeddah) to complete their pilgrimages to the holy cities of the Hejaz. In this they completed the fifth pillar of Islam in much the same way that other Muslims had done for many centuries already in the past.

A rising number of sojourners were making their way along the maritime routes of Asia in the early modern world. Many of these voyages were religious or educational in nature, but traders also made up a significant number of these travelers across the Indian Ocean. Jeddah's main function may have been as an embarkation port for Mecca, but it was also a significant center for commerce and representative of other cities along the Southern Arabian coasts like Mocha, Aden, and Mukalla. These ports prospered more and more as the centuries wore on because of rising numbers of pilgrims making blue-water voyages to the Red Sea, but they also flourished as trade increased concomitantly, via a number of highly desired items. Frankincense, myrrh, textiles, and coffee were the engines of this commerce at various points in time. All had in common a sirenlike call to outsiders, who saw the Tihama as a strange and distant landscape but one that held the promise of profit and potential riches. This combination of ecumenical and spiritual attractions helped power the early centuries of the Hajj as a transregional phenomenon of the Indian Ocean. In the next chapter, we will concentrate more fully on the arguments and debates of the economics of the early Hajj, and how commerce helped make this vast system run.

NOTES

1. For only one example, see Sanjay Subrahmanyman, *The Career and Legend of Vasco da Gama* (Cambridge: Cambridge University Press, 1997).

2. Michael Pearson, *The Indian Ocean* (London: Routledge, 2003); Sugata Bose, *A Hundred Horizons: The Indian Ocean in the Age of Global Empire* (Cambridge, MA: Harvard University Press, 2006).

3. Eng Seng Ho, *The Graves of Tarim* (Berkeley: University of California Press, 2006).

4. In this discussion, I am influenced by the ideas of Arjun Appadurai, Igor Kopytoff, and others, who have outlined how "the social lives of things" act to shape and influence human history. See both Arjun Appadurai's and Igor Kopytoff's contributions in Arjun Appadurai, ed., *The Social Life of Things* (New York: Cambridge University Press, 1986).

5. See, for example, Robert Aldrich, ed., *The Age of Empires* (London: Thames and Hudson, 2007).

6. Thomas Stamford Raffles, *The History of Java* (1817), Part II, p. 3.

7. Johan Eisenberger, "Indie en de Bedevaart naar Mekka," PhD Dissertation, Leiden University, 1928, p. 11.

8. Ibid., pp. 12, 13.

9. Ibid., pp. 14, 15.

10. Gisho Honda, Miki Wataru, and Mitsuko Saito, *Herb Drugs and Herbalists in Syria and North Yemen* (Tokyo: Institute for the Study of Languages and Cultures of Asia and Africa, 1990), p. 19.

11. A. G. Miller and T. A. Cope, *Flora of the Arabian Peninsula and Socotra*, Vol. 1 (Edinburgh: Edinburgh University Press, 1996), pp. 497–573.

12. J. R. Wood, *A Handbook of the Yemen Flora* (Kew, England: Royal Botanic Gardens, 1997), p. 8.

13. Nigel Groom, *Frankincense and Myrrh: A Study of the Arabian Incense Trade* (London: Longman, 1981), pp. 1–22, 38–54, 55–76, 77–95, 143–164.

14. Richard Harrington, "On the Frankincense Road in Yemen," *Canadian Geographic Journal*, 95/3, 1978: 14–21; and Nigel Groom, "The Northern Passes of Qataban," *Proceedings of the Seminar for Arabian Studies*, 6, 1976: 69–80.

15. Some of this scholarship goes back to Italian colonial times astride the Red Sea; see, for example, R. Pirotta, "Contribuzioni alla Conoscenza della Flora dell'Africa Orientale," *Annuario del. R. Istituto Botanico di Roma* 5, 1894, and 9, 1902; G. E. Mattei, "Studi sulla Flora della Colonie Italiane," *Bell. Soc. Africana d'Italia*, 1911: 131–173.

16. F. De Romanis, "Tus e Murra: Aromi Sudarabici nella Roma Arcaica," in Alessandra Avanzini, ed., *Profumi d'Arabia: Atti del Convegno* (Roma: L'Erma di Bretschneider, 1997), p. 230.

17. P. M. Costa, "Il Ruolo dell'Arabica nel Commercio delle Spezie e dell'incenso: da Elio Gallo a Vasco da Gama," in Alessandra Avanzini, ed., *Profumi d'Arabia: Atti del Convegno* (Roma: L'Erma di Bretschneider, 1997), p. 437.

18. M. Liverani, "Beyond Deserts, Beyond Oceans," in Alessandra Avanzini, ed., *Profumi d'Arabia: Atti del Convegno* (Roma: L'Erma di Bretschneider, 1997), p. 560.

19. S. Mazzoni, "Complex Society, Urbanization and Trade: The Case of Eastern and Western Arabia," in Alessandra Avanzini, ed., *Profumi d'Arabia: Atti del Convegno* (Roma: L'Erma di Bretschneider, 1997), p. 24.

20. See C. Rossetti, "Gomma Arabica," *Atti a Congr. Ital. all'Estero*, 1, 1911; U. Brizi, "Le Piante Utili delle Nostre Colonie," *Boll. Associaz. Ital. Puo Piante Medicinali*, 1919; F. Cortesi, "Le Piante da Profumo, da Aroma e da Essenza delle Nostre Colonie," *Riv. Coloniale*, 1919.

21. John Hansman, *Julfar, an Arabian Port: Its Settlement and Far Eastern Ceramic Trade from the Fourteenth to the Eighteenth Centuries* (London: RASGB and Ireland, 1985), pp. 25–65; R. B. Serjeant, "Pottery and Glass Fragments from the Aden Littoral, with Historical Notes," in R. B. Serjeant, *Studies in Arabian History and Civilisation* (London: Variorum, 1981), pp. 108–133; Axelle Rougeulle, "Coastal Settlements in Southern Yemen: The 1996–1997 Expeditions on the Hadhramawt and Mahra Coasts," *Proceedings of the Seminar for Arabian Studies*, 29, 1999: 123–136; Claire Hardy-Guilbert and Axelle Rougeulle, "Archaeological Research into the Islamic Period in Yemen: Preliminary Notes on the French Expedition," *Proceedings of the Seminar on Arabian Studies*, 25, 1995: 29–44.

22. Penny Balfour-Paul, "Indigo and South Arabia," *Journal of Weavers, Spinners, and Dyers*, 139, 1986: 12–29.

23. Christian Robin, "The Mine of ar-Radrad: Al-Hamdani and the Silver of Yemen," in Werner Daum, ed., *Yemen: 3000 Years of Art and Civilisation in Arabia Felix* (Innsbruk: Pinguin-Verlag, 1987), pp. 123–124; Husayn 'Abd Allah al-Amri, "Slaves and Markets in the History of Yemen," in Werner Daum, ed., *Yemen: 3000 Years of Art and Civilisation in Arabia Felix* (Innsbruk: Pinguin-Verlag, 1987), pp. 140–157.

24. John Baldry, *Textiles in Yemen: Historical References to Trade and Commerce in Textiles in Yemen from Antiquity to Modern Times* (London: British Museum Department of Ethnography, 1982), p. 41.

25. J. Brian Robinson, *Coffee in Yemen: A Practical Guide* (San'a: Ministry of Agriculture and Water Resources, 1993), pp. 1, 8.

26. Ho, *The Graves of Tarim*, pp. 87, 112.

27. Ralph Hattox, *Coffee and Coffehouses: The Origins of a Social Beverage in the Medieval Near East* (Seattle: University of Washington Press, 1985), p. 11; Edward Keall, "The Evolution of the First Coffee Cups in Yemen," in Michel Tuchscherer, ed., *Le Commerce du Café Avant l'ère des Plantations Coloniales* (Cairo: Institut Français d'Archéologie Orientale, 2001), pp. 35–50; C. G. Brouwer, "Al-Mukha as a Coffee Port in the Early Decades of the Seventeenth Century According to Dutch Sources," in Michel Tuchscherer, ed., *Le Commerce du Café Avant l'ère des Plantations Coloniales* (Cairo: Institut Français d'Archéologie Orientale, 2001), pp. 276, 289.

28. Surenda Gopal, "Coffee Traders of Western India in the Seventeenth Century," in Michel Tuchscherer, ed., *Le Commerce du Café Avant l'ère des Plantations Coloniales* (Cairo: Institut Français d'Archéologie Orientale, 2001), p. 299.

29. Robinson, *Coffee in Yemen*, p. 8; Brouwer, "Al-Mukha as a Coffee Port," p. 289.

30. Julien Berthaud, "L'origine et la Distribution des Caféiers dans le Monde," in Michel Tuchscherer, ed., *Le Commerce du Café Avant l'ère des Plantations Coloniales* (Cairo: Institut Français d'Archeéologie Orientale, 2001), pp. 364, 369.

31. Ernestine Carreira, "Les Français et le Commerce du Café dans l'Ocean Indien au XVIIIe Siecle," in Michel Tuchscherer, ed., *Le Commerce du Café Avant l'ère des Plantations Coloniales* (Cairo: Institut Français d'Archéologie Orientale, 2001), p. 334; William Gervase Clarence-Smith, "The Spread of Coffee Cultivation in Asia, from the Seventeenth to the Early Nineteenth Century," in Michel Tuchscherer, ed., *Le Commerce du Café Avant l'ere des Plantations Coloniales* (Cairo: Institut Français d'Archéologie Orientale, 2001), p. 382.

32. John Ovington, in William Foster, ed., *The Red Sea and Adjacent Countries at the Close of the Seventeenth Century* (London: Hakluyt, 1949), p. 173; see also Ovington's *A Voyage to Surat in the Year 1689* (London: Hakluyt, 1929), pp. 268–272.

33. Nancy Ajung Um, "A Red Sea Society in Yemen: Architecture, Urban Form and Cultural Dynamics in the Eighteenth-Century Port City of al-Mukha," PhD Dissertation, University of California, Los Angeles, 2001, pp. 103–108; C. G. Brouwer, *Al-Mukha: Profile of a Yemeni Seaport as Sketched by Servants of the Dutch East India Company, 1614–1640* (Amsterdam: D'Fluyte Rarob, 1997), p. 2833 and also chapters 10 and 12.

34. VOC, Gen Miss: Van Diemen, Caen, en Van der Lijn, VIII, December 18, 1639 (1039 fol. 1–129) p. 39; VOC, Gen Miss: Van Goens, Pit, Overwater, Van Hoorn en Paviljoen, II, February 15, 1678 (1212, fol. 386–387), p. 232; VOC, Gen Miss: Camphuys, Hurdt, Van Outhoorn, Pit, Van Quaelbergh, VII, March 18, 1685 (Kol. Arch. 1284, fol. 1053–1085), p. 787.

35. VOC, Gen Miss: Van Outhoorn, Van Hoorn, Pijl, De Saint-Martin, De Haas, II, March 24, 1692 (Kon. Arch. 1381, fol. 11–127), p. 501.

36. VOC, Gen Miss: De Haan, Huysman, Haselaar, Blom, Durven, XIV, March 31, 1727 (Kol. Arch. 1933, fol. 3222–3413), p. 111; VOC, Gen Miss: De Haan, Huysman, Haselaar, Blom, Durven, XIV, December 8, 1728 (Kol. Arch. 1975, fol. 517–1071), p. 209.

37. VOC, Gen Miss: De Haan, Huysman, Haselaar, Blom, Durven, XIV, December 8, 1728 (Kol. Arch. 1975, fol. 517–1071), p. 214.

38. In chapter 4, I discuss some of the earliest known Southeast Asian manuscripts that mention Mecca, some five hundred years ago.

39. For the former manuscript, see Add. 12328 in the British Library; for the latter, see Javanese #50 (IO 2613) in the India Office Library.

40. See Add. 12389 f. 56r., also in the British Library.

41. See Add. 3785 *Hikayat Tamim ad-Dari*, Cambridge University Library.

42. See Scott Lower Left 7 *Idah al-albab li-murid an-nikah bi's-sawab*, also in the Cambridge University Library.

43. Mahmood Ibrahim, "Social and Economic Conditions in Pre-Islamic Mecca," *IJMES*, 14/3, 1982: 343; Patricia Crone, *Meccan Trade and the Rise of Islam* (Princeton, NJ: Princeton University Press, 1986); W. Montgomery Watt, *Muhammad's Mecca: History and the Qur'an* (Edinburgh: Edinburgh University Press, 1988); Fred McGraw, "Mecca's Food Supplies and Muhammad's Boycott," *JESHO* 20/3, 1977: 249–250. For the Indian trade, see a rare translated Indian letter from the twelfth century, part of which reads as follows: "The letter of my lord, the most illustrious elder has arrived; I read and understood it, and I was happy to learn that you were well.... From what you have mentioned, my lord, I learned that you sent the two locks and the two thousand white and red betel nuts.... I have sent you a bundle of Berbera mats...a new, first-rate unbleached Dabiqi scarf...two sets of fine, large paper (and) two *raba'iyyat* of sugar and raisins." S. D. Goitein, "From Aden to India: Specimens of the Correspondence of India Traders of the Twelfth Century," *JESHO*, 23/1-2, 1980: 43–66.

44. G. Rex Smith, "Have You Anything to Declare? Maritime Trade and Commerce in Ayyubid Aden, Practices and Taxes," *Proceedings of the Seminar for Arabian Studies*, 25, 1995: 127–140; G. Rex Smith, "More on the Port Practices and Taxes of Medieval Yemen," in G. Rex Smith, *Studies in the Medieval History of the Yemen and South Arabia* (Aldershot, UK: Variorum, 1997), pp. 208–218.

45. J. Owen, "Do Anchors Mean Ships? Underwater Evidence for Maritime Trade along the Dhofar Coast, Southern Indian Ocean," in Alessandra Avanzini, ed., *Profumi d'Arabia: Atti del Convegno* (Roma: L'Erma di Bretschneider, 1997), p. 351. See also two very good articles in French (Radhi Daghfous, "Des Sources de l'Histoire Médiévale du Yemen," *Cahiers de Tunisie*, 28/113, 1980: 201–227; and Yussuf Abdallah, "Le Yemen: le Pays et le Commerce de l'Encens," in André Lemaire, ed., *Les Routes du Proche-Orient* (Paris: Desclée de Brouwer, 2000), pp. 87–92), as well as some of the many works of R. B. Sargeant, such as "Yemeni Merchants and Trade in Yemen, 13th–16th Centuries," in R. B. Sargeant, *Society and Trade in South Arabia* (Aldershot, UK: Variorum, 1996), pp. 61–82; "The Ports of Aden and Shihr (Medieval Period)," in R. B. Serjeant, *Studies in Arabian History and Civilisation* (London: Variorum, 1981), pp. 207–224; and "Early Islamic and Medieval Trade and Commerce in Yemen," in Werner Daum, ed., *Yemen: 3000 Years of Art and Civilisation in Arabia Felix* (Innsbruck: Pinguin-Verlag, 1987), pp. 163–166.

46. C. J. Robin, "Arabie Meridionale: L'État et les Aromates," in Alessandra Avanzini, ed., *Profumi d'Arabia: Atti del Convegno* (Roma: L'Erma di Bretschneider, 1997), p. 47; M. Morris, "The Harvesting of Frankincense in Dhofar, Oman," in Alessandra Avanzini, ed., *Profumi d'Arabia: Atti del Convegno* (Roma: L'Erma di Bretschneider, 1997), p. 232; G. W. Bowersock, "Perfumes and Power," in Alessandra Avanzini, ed., *Profumi d'Arabia: Atti del Convegno* (Roma: L'Erma di Bretschneider, 1997), pp. 249–250.

47. Gabor Agoston, "A Flexible Empire: Authority and Its Limits on the Ottoman Frontiers," in Kemal Karpat and Robert Zens, eds., *Ottoman Borderlands: Issues, Personalities, and Political*

Changes (Madison: University of Wisconsin Press, 2003), p. 15; Qutb al-Din al-Nahrawali al-Makki, *Lightning over Yemen: A History of the Ottoman Campaign, 1569–1571* (London: Tauris, 2002); Venetia Porter, "The Ports of Yemen and the Indian Ocean Trade during the Tahirid Period, 1454–1517," in J. F. Healey and V. Porter, *Studies on Arabia in Honour of Professor G. Rex Smith* (Oxford: Oxford University Press, 2002), pp. 171–190.

48. Isa Blumi, "Thwarting the Ottoman Empire: Smuggling through the Empire's New Frontiers in Yemen and Albania, 1878–1910," in Kemal Karpat and Robert Zens, eds., *Ottoman Borderlands: Issues, Personalities, and Political Changes* (Madison: University of Wisconsin Press, 2003), pp. 255, 267; Caesar Farah, "Smuggling and International Politics in the Red Sea in the Late Ottoman Period," in G. Rex Smith et al., eds., *New Arabian Studies* (Exeter: University of Exeter Press, 2000); Daniel Panzac, "International and Domestic Maritime Trade in the Ottoman Empire during the 18th Century," *IJMES* 24/2, 1992: 190.

49. Sevket Pamuk, "Prices in the Ottoman Empire," *IJMES*, 36, 2004: 451–467; Sevket Pamuk, *A Monetary History of the Ottoman Empire* (Cambridge: Cambridge University Press, 2000).

50. R. T. O. Wilson, "The Tihama from the Beginning of the Islamic Period to 1800," in Francine Stone, ed., *Studies on the Tihama* (Essex, England: Longman, 1985), pp. 31–35; John Baldry, "The History of the Tihama from 1800 to the Present," in Francine Stone, ed., *Studies on the Tihama* (Essex, England: Longman, 1985), pp. 45–50.

51. Juan Cole, "Rival Empires of Trade and Imami Shi'ism in Eastern Arabia, 1300–1800," *IJMES*, 19/2, 1987: 199.

52. Alastair Hamilton et al., eds., *Friends and Rivals in the East: Studies in Anglo-Dutch Relations in the Levant from the Seventeenth Century to the Early Nineteenth Century* (Leiden: Brill, 2000); Asli Cirakman, *From the "Terror of the World" to the "Sick Man of Europe": European Images of Ottoman Empire and Society from the Sixteenth Century to the Nineteenth* (New York: Peter Lang, 2002).

53. Michel Lesure, "Un Document Ottoman de 1525 sur L'Inde Portugaise et les Pays de la Mer Rouge," *Mare Luso-Indicum*, 3, 1976: 137–160.

54. John Baldry, "Foreign Interventions and Occupations of Kamaran Island," *Arabian Studies*, 4, 1978: 89–111.

55. R. B. Serjeant, *The Portuguese off the South Arabian Coast: Hadrami Chronicles, with Yemeni and European Accounts* (Beirut: Librairie du Liban, 1974); Henri Labrousse, "L'Arabie du Suud et L'Europa a l'aube des Temps Modernes," in Joseph Chelhod, ed., *L'Arabie du Suud: Histoire et Civilisation*, vol. 1 (Paris: G. P. Maisonneuve et Larose, 1984), pp. 91–109; see also the very useful juxtaposition of Arabic and Portuguese period sources lain side by side in Jean-Louis Bacque-Grammont and Anne Kroell, *Mamlouks, Ottomans et Portugais en Mer Rouge: L'Affaire de Djedda en 1517* (Paris: Le Caire, 1988).

56. Om Prakash, *Precious Metals and Commerce: The Dutch East India Company in the Indian Ocean Trade* (Aldershot, UK: Variorum, 1994); R. J. Barendse, *The Arabian Seas, 1640–1700* (Armonk, NY: M. E. Sharpe, 2002).

57. C. G. Brouwer, *Cauwa ende Comptanten: de VOC in Yemen* (Amsterdam: D'Fluyte Rarob, 1988); C. G. Brouwer, "Willem de Milde, Kani Shalabi en Fadli Basha, of: Een Dienaar van de VOC op Audientie bij de Beglerbegi van Jemen, 1622–1624," *De Gids*, 143, 1980: 713–742.

58. C. G. Brouwer, *Al-Mukha: Profile of a Yemeni Seaport as Sketched by Servants of the Dutch East India Company, 1614–1640* (Amsterdam: D'Fluyte Rarob, 1997), pp. 426–427.

59. C. G. Brouwer, "Le Voyage au Yemen de Pieter van den Broeke en 1620," in Ibrahim El-Sheikh et al., eds., *The Challenge of the Middle East: Middle Eastern Studies at the University of Amsterdam* (Amsterdam: University of Amsterdam, 1982), pp. 1–11; C. G. Brouwer, *Al-Mukha*, and C. G. Brouwer, "A Stockless Anchor and an Unsaddled Horse: Ottoman Letters Addressed to the Dutch in Yemen, First Quarter of the 17th Century," *Turcica*, 20, 1988: 173–242.

60. John Baldry, "The English East India Company's Settlement at al-Mukha, 1719–1739," *The Arab Gulf*, 13/2 (1981): 13–34.

61. See N. R. Dalziel, "British Maritime Contacts with the Persian Gulf and Gulf of Oman, 1850–1900," PhD Dissertation, University of Lancaster, 1989; R. J. Gavin, *Aden under British Rule,*

1839–1967 (New York: Harper and Row, 1975), especially pp. 62–90, 174–194, and 446–447.

62. Roy Facey, "The Development of the Port of Aden," *British-Yemeni Society Journal*, 6, 1998: 5–9; Cesar Farah, "Anglo-Ottoman Confrontation in the Persian Gulf in the Late Nineteenth and Early Twentieth Centuries," *Proceedings of the Seminar for Arabian Studies*, 33, 2003.

63. For Oman in particular, see Calvin Allen, "The State of Masqat in the Gulf and East Africa, 1785–1829," *IJMES*, 14/2, 1982: 117–127; Mark Speece, "Aspects of Economic Dualism in Oman, 1830–1930," *IJMES*, 21/4, 1989: 495–515; Fred Halliday, "Oman and Yemen: An Historic Re-Encounter," *British-Yemeni Society Journal*, 8,2000: 41–52; and Beatrice Nicolini, "Little Known Aspects of the History of Muscat and Zanzibar during the First Half of the Nineteenth Century," *Proceedings of the Seminar for Arabian Studies*, 27, 1997: 193–198.

64. Roger Daguenet, *Histoire de la Mer Rouge* (Paris: L'Harmattan, 1997).

65. Roger Daguenet, *Aux Origines de l'Implantation Française en Mer Rouge: Vie et Mort d' Henri Lambert Consul de France a Aden, 1859* (Paris: L'Harmattan, 1992).

66. If pilgrims came at the wrong time of the year, or even mid-cycle during the rites, they could not perform the Hajj. So balancing the trade and religious aspects of this huge voyage took careful consideration (and some luck).

67. Again, see Giancarlo Casale's *The Ottoman Age of Exploration* here.

68. A cogent summary of this process is put forward in Timothy Mitchell, *Colonising Egypt* (Cambridge: Cambridge University Press, 1988).

3

Financing Devotion

The Economics of the Premodern Hajj

> The poor people who come to pay a visit to the noble Ka'ba do not have
> a pre-determined spot [in which to spend the night]. Therefore they
> settle in a corner of the noble sanctuary.... Her Highness the late prin-
> cess purchased a piece of land close to the soup kitchen she had
> established, and suitable for the construction of a hostel for the afore-
> mentioned people.
>
> —Muhimme Defterleri, Ottoman Prime Minister's
> Archive, 1556, quoted in Farooqi

The Hajj is first and foremost a religious ritual. Yet devotion cannot be divorced
from the ways and means of performing it, namely, the financial wherewithal of
undertaking a pilgrimage that may be thousands of miles from one's home.
Significant economic resources had to be accumulated and earmarked for the
Southeast Asian Hajj before it could realistically be planned. The economics of
Hajj, thus, was serious business. The pilgrimage contributed both to regional
and transregional economies, and it also was vital to the financial planning of
millions of individuals and their families over the centuries. This chapter outlines the economics of the pilgrimage as part of the Indian Ocean system and
during the early modern and colonial periods, when it eventually became an
economic phenomenon controlled at least partially by nonindigenous hands.[1]
Taking an everyday, utilitarian point of view, it looks at how the pilgrimage was
possible not in people's minds or hearts, but rather through their bank accounts.
It therefore connects Southeast Asians' practical decisions and priorities about
the Hajj with larger concerns about a life well-lived.

The financing of Muslim devotion as seen through the Hajj was adapted from
a predominantly singular or family-clan endeavor to a phenomenon primarily
organized by the state. In the precolonial era, the ability and energy to perform
the pilgrimage to Mecca was incumbent upon the individual Hajji or Hajja. Sov-
ereigns could help these journeys along in a variety of ways, and often were

crucial in doing so, but premodern forms of organization, transport, and travel meant the onus of Hajj primarily rested upon the pilgrim, or a small group of his or her fellows. In the colonial period, the state began to take a more active role in these deliberations, directing pilgrim traffic across the Indian Ocean both in the interest of the welfare of colonial subjects and in the very real surveilling interests of imperial states themselves. The imposition of concerted colonial rule over large parts of Southeast Asia from the nineteenth century onward changed existing dynamics. Subjects of British Colonial Malaya and the Straits Settlements, as well as from the Dutch East Indies, had more of an opportunity to go on Hajj now than previously.[2] Colonial steamship lines and expanding financial services ensured a lower cost pilgrimage than had been possible in the past. These same European regimes in the colonies also worked to ameliorate debt bondage and some of the other egregious violations of pilgrims' rights, both in Southeast Asia and on the Arabian peninsula.

At the same time, colonial governments were reluctant to cede too much control to Hajjis themselves in arrangements to get pilgrims out to the Hejaz and then back again to Southeast Asia. As it became economically more realistic to perform one's Hajj during these decades on either side of the fin de siècle than it had been previously, it also became increasingly unrealistic to do this on one's own terms. Singapore and Batavia, especially, saw the pilgrimage as a potentially dangerous transmitter of militancy and radical ideas to their own subject populations. The financing of devotion, therefore, was made available to the indigenous populations of the archipelago but largely through channels that colonial governments themselves could check and approve on a regional basis. This desire for absolute or near-absolute control on the part of imperial regimes in their dealings with the Hajj was one important hallmark of the late colonial age. This chapter examines how these patterns evolved and changed over the centuries.

The Economic Connections of the Precolonial Hajj

There is considerable historiographical disagreement about how important the Hajj was to the economy of the early modern Indian Ocean. Some interpreters of commerce and society in the Indian Ocean basin during the fifteenth to eighteenth centuries have put forward the notion that the pilgrimage to Mecca was a primary mover for trade in these seas, thereby seeing the Hajj as a central axis for commerce around which much other trade functioned.[3] If weather and political conditions cooperated, merchants coming from as far away as Western India could expect to make gross profits of approximately 50 percent on their trade goods in Mecca, for example, a huge return on initial investments.[4] From this historiographical vantage, the Hajj was seen as an engine for trade, attracting vessels that would have stopped further down the Red Sea coasts to offload their cargoes of textiles in return for coffee and other local products that we have already examined. Such was the transregional dependence on Hajj traffic that a year of low pilgrimage numbers or even the expectation of one would create a serious depression, from Jeddah all the way to parts of Asia.[5] Other important scholarship on the Hajj and Indian Ocean commerce, however, sees this emphasis on the economic role of the Hajj as misguided. For this school, Jeddah (Mecca's feeder port) was just another harbor way station on the oceanic routes, and the Hajj a mere appurtenance to traffic that would have stopped there anyway. These scholars feel that Jeddah would have survived without the Hajj and that the pilgrimage actually linked what otherwise was a fairly insulated city (Mecca, at least, from a financial point of view) with trade routes that prospered very much on their own economic terms.[6]

It is still not clear which of these two views is substantially correct. Contemporary eyewitness descriptions of the Red Sea and its economic connections to the Indian Ocean call attention, however, to the relative importance of trade. An anonymous account dating from around 1580 reported that forty or fifty large ships were coming to Jeddah each year, laden with precious merchandise and sundries, and that these ships were paying large sums in customs duties to the local rulers in order to trade.[7] A few decades later, the itinerant traveler Saris recorded the actual size of these ships to impart a sense of scale. Vessels coming from India carried pilgrims but also significant quantities of commodities to fund their voyages, and these ships could be more than 150 feet long and 40 feet wide, with depth displacements into the water reaching around 30 feet.[8] These were large, blue-water vessels, in other words. Substantial numbers of these large ships were making the voyage to Jeddah from other ports in the Indian Ocean as well, including vessels in the 1,400- to 1,600-ton range, that were filled to bursting with pilgrims, apparently.[9] "The superstitious custom of pilgrimages to Mecca made by those who follow the infamous Koran" encouraged these trips, according to another seventeenth-century chronicler, "since the ships which sailed to Juda made excellent business profits."[10] The Hajj was fairly linked with regional and oceanic commerce, therefore; each seems to have depended on the other in a mutually enhancing relationship of religious and commercial profit.

In the late seventeenth century, the French traveler Tavernier detailed how intertwined the Hajj and regional business practices had become (figure 3.1). Tavernier sketched the mechanisms of these contacts as they related to trade, political patronage, and religious devotion between Mughal India and the holy city of Mecca:

> Every year the Great Mogul sends two large vessels there (to Surat), to carry pilgrims, who thus get a free passage. At the time when these

vessels are ready to depart, the *fakirs* come down from all parts of India in order to embark. The vessels are laden with good articles of trade which are disposed of at Mecca, and all the profit which is made is given in charity to the poor pilgrims. The principal only is retained and this serves for another year, and this principal is at least 600,000 rupees. It is considered a small matter when only 30 or 40 per cent is made on these goods....Added to which all of the principal persons of the Great Mogul's Harem, and other private persons, send considerable donations to Mecca.[11]

The scale of these voyages is again discernible from contemporary records. In 1662, a ship from Bijapur, India, arrived in Aden with pilgrims and merchandise on its way to Jeddah. The amount of merchandise was so great (four hundred bales of goods) that the cargo had to be brought into Aden via an alternative route as the city gates were too small. If the notice is correct, there were close to 1,500 pilgrims on this single ship, all of them en route to Mecca.[12] The goods were to be sold in various ports of the Red Sea to help finance the voyage, a common practice among many Hajj ships at the time. Other ships calling at Jeddah around the same time, mixed between cargoes and pilgrims, carried values of 200,000 pounds sterling, and still others weighed in at 250,000 rupees.[13]

Figure 3.1 Late Seventeenth-Century Mughal Hajj Ship (from Tavernier).
Credit: "Mughal Pilgrim Ship as Seen by Tavernier in 1686" (W. H. Coates, *The Old Country Trade of the East Indies* (London: Imray, Laurie, Nories and Wilson, 1911), p. 125).

Gifts, charity, merit making, and the reputations of Muslim rulers in their dealings with their subjects and with other Muslim potentates therefore all came
into play.

Sitting astride the sea routes, Yemen was vital in structuring the conditions
for these long-distance economies to function. Even in the time of the great
Portuguese explorer Alfonso De Albuquerque, who pulled his ship into Aden's
harbor on Easter Day of the year 1513, it was already making an impression as
the commercial choke point for the entire Red Sea economy. The city helped
connect the Mediterranean and Indian Ocean worlds. An engraving in the explorer's record of his travels shows a large, prosperous city of rectangular Yemeni
houses climbing up the steep hills of Aden's bay. De Albuquerque believed that
the traffic of ships through the Red Sea made the city one of the best positioned
ports in the world and a natural stopping place for vessels, despite the fact that
the metropolis had no source of running water.[14] The flourishing commerce with
other Muslim lands and Aden's strategic location combined to be stronger than
this impediment, however. Writing a century later, in 1609, another European
traveler, John Jourdain, also landed in Aden, though his curiosity about the
commercial possibilities of the place took him into the interior of Yemen as well.
Traveling by caravan to Taiz, Ibb, Saiyun, and Sana'a, he was one of the first Westerners to become aware of the internal economies that linked the thriving towns
of the hills to the littoral systems of exchange on the coasts. This transit was
already at this early date becoming partially predicated on the steady traffic of
Hajjis passing through the region.[15]

During the late sixteenth century, the lightning Ottoman campaign to subdue
Yemen between 1569 and 1571 would transform this region's economy.[16]
Although military and political conquests have traditionally been emphasized in
the literature of this same time period, the Ottomans left an economic legacy
that was probably more important in the *longue duree* history of the region.[17]
They fixed the roads and secured the long-distance caravan routes; they also
made sure that water was available on these same trade routes and that sentry
posts were stationed for many miles in every direction coming out of the country.
Ports were revamped all along the coasts.[18] Trade, in fact, prospered as never
before. The rise in the number of Hajjis coming to the Hejaz during this time was
partially dependent on these structural conditions, which made the end terminus
of the pilgrimage much safer and more reliable than it had been. We know, for
example, that the Ottomans invested large sums of money from their central
administrative budget on the holy cities and on pilgrim maintenance; 4.2 million *akce* (roughly 100,000 gold coins) in 1527–28, 7.1 million *akce* (140,000
gold coins) in 1653, 10.8 million *akce* (200,000 gold coins) in 1660–61, and
16.5 million *akce* (300,000 gold coins) in 1690–91.[19] Despite some period (and
later) images of the Ottoman Empire as the "sick man of Europe," these early

decades of rule and administration in the late sixteenth century were anything but anemic (box 3.1).[20] The Ottomans put Yemen back on the commercial map of transregional commerce in the Middle East, though it remained dependent on boom and bust cycles that followed prices and surplus and scarcity in the global commercial system as a whole.[21] The Hajj rode these changing economic structures to some degree, rising steadily as a diasporic phenomenon over the years, even if individual seasons could still be difficult.

Box 3.1 **The Phasing of Ottoman Power in European Eyes,
Late Sixteenth to Late Seventeenth Centuries**

English Request for Ottoman Help against Spain, 1587:
(English envoy William Harborne to Mehmed III)
"Do not let this moment pass unused, in order that God, who has created you a valiant man (the Ottoman Sultan) and the most powerful of all worldly princes for the destruction of idol-worshipers, may not turn his utmost wrath against you if you disregard his command, which my mistress, only a weak woman, courageously struggles to fulfill. The whole world, with justice, will accuse you of the greatest ingratitude if you desert in her danger your most trusting confederate, who in the confidence of friendship and promises of Your Highness, has placed her life and her kingdom in jeopardy that cannot be greater on this earth. For the Spaniard, since my mistress had declined to grant him peace, is determined to destroy her completely, relying on the maximum assistance of the pope and all idolatrous princes. And when, finally, there will not remain any other obstacle in Christendom, he will direct his invincible military forces toward your destruction and that of your empire and will become the sole ruler of the world."

English Appraisal of Grandeur and Decay in Constantinople, 1618–1622:
(English Envoy Sir Thomas Roe)
"If I should speak of the situation of this place…there is nothing in the world of that magnificence and delight. But if we then consider the people that possess it, and the uncleanly order and government in it, it is a sink of men and sluttishness.…This might empire hath passed the noon, and is declining apace, if not very near its dissolution."

English Appraisal of Authoritarianism among the Ottomans in 1666:
(English Envoy Paul Rycaut)
"The continual supply of slaves…fills Constantinople with such a strange race, mixture, and medley of different sorts of blood, that it is hard

to find many who that can derive a clear line from ingenuous parents; so that it is no wonder that amongst the Turks a disposition be found and disposed to servitude, and that it is better governed with a severe and tyrannical hand, then with sweetness, and lenity which is unknown to them and their forefathers."

Sources: Arthur Leon Horniker, "Anglo-French Rivarly in the Levant from 1583 to 1612," *Journal of Modern History*, 18/4, 1946: 289–305, here pp. 309–310; Michael Strachan, *The Life and Adventures of Sir Thomas Roe, 1581–1644: A Life* (London: Oxford University Press, 1962), p. 283; Paul Rycaut, *Present State of the Ottoman Empire* (1666) quoted in T. S. Hughes, *An Appeal on Behalf of the Greeks* (London, 1824), p. 17.

Southeast Asia and the Transoceanic Economies

There are reliable records of Southeast Asians performing the Hajj as far back as 1561, when an Acehnese ship laden with gold and a palanquin to be shipped to the Ottoman sultan made the voyage, the latter two items intended for trade and diplomacy. Even at that early date, commerce and the Hajj were intertwined, as the contents of this ship make clear.[22] From elsewhere in Southeast Asia, there were other Hajjis, including perhaps most famously the renowned Shaykh Yusuf of Makassar, who had collected enough money to undertake his pilgrimage in 1644 after being initiated into a Sufi order in Aceh on his voyage across the Indian Ocean.[23] The *Tuhfat al-Nafis* ("The Precious Gift"), the famous chronicle of the Bugis kings of Riau, mentions the financial dealings of the hero Raja Ahmad, who performed Hajj as part of his wanderings as well.[24] Raja Ahmad first had to travel to Java to raise cash for the journey; he ended up accumulating 14,000 Straits dollars for the trip and left on a pilgrim ship from Penang with twelve companions for the Holy Land. The *Tuhfat al-Nafis* spills almost as much ink on the economic aspects of this voyage as on the spiritual dimensions: while in the Hejaz, Ahmad bought land and houses for the use of archipelago pilgrims (other archipelago pilgrims did this, too) and gave money generally for religious purposes.[25] In the careers of men such as Raja Ahmad, one can see the financial and monetary necessities that went along with the devotional responsibilities of Hajj, even in the centuries well before the high colonial age.

Because the VOC was increasingly involved in the commercial orbits of both the Red Sea and Southeast Asia over the course of the seventeenth century, it seems natural that Dutch records provide examples of how the Indian Ocean economy started to have a more unitary character during this time period. A Dutch servant of the VOC named Pieter van den Broeke noted these connections in the 1620s, when he was charged with an expedition to the Red Sea.[26]

Van den Broeke, who already had experience in Yemeni waters by the time of this expedition, established a small trading post on the Tihama coasts and had at least one of his crewmen, Abraham Crabee, learn enough Arabic so that they could profitably deal with local actors. Among the products that he brought with him to sell were cloves, benzoin, and camphor, all from the VOC's new trading posts in Indonesia.[27] He noted in passing the presence of Malays on these same Yemeni coasts, some of them trading in commodities similar to his own. A number of these men, he surmised, were trading while on pilgrimage voyages to the Red Sea.

Yet the most detailed records on Hajj from the "lands beneath the winds" in this early period primarily come from Java. Javanese came on Hajj for religious purposes, but they also knew that the Hajj was invested with political and economic opportunities. The Sultanate of Banten in West Java is one of the earliest places we see this at work. One of Banten's rulers in the late seventeenth century called himself simply "Sultan Haji" (reigned, 1682–1687) as a mark of his voyage to the Holy Land. He performed the pilgrimage twice before ascending the throne in Banten and made sure this experience was memorialized in his title.[28] Undertaking the Hajj cost him money, of course, but he recouped those funds in increasing the number of followers available to him as a result of his raised status as a successful pilgrim. Other Javanese also knew the many different values of the Hajj. One of the Central Javanese sultans made vessels ready on the northern coast of the island to go on Hajj but then decided not to go himself, sending others on his behalf in 1700 and 1701. It is unclear what was at work in this decision, but it seems plausible that it may have even been dangerous to be away from Java during this period of early VOC aggression. Sending one's subjects therefore still conferred merit, and made economic and even political opportunities for others who could then be subsequently recruited, but it also left one's own *kraton* (or palace) defended in case of Dutch adventurism. When this adventurism did come a few decades later, the Surakarta Major *Babad* says that Hajjis were at the forefront of Javanese forces in fighting the Europeans, right alongside the ulama, who were also praised for their bravery.[29] By the middle of the eighteenth century, Sultan Mangkubumi was sending missions to repair his own houses in Mecca—an economic perquisite that he could provide to followers—so that they could be used by his subjects in their travels across the width of the Indian Ocean.[30] And on the eve of the comprehensive Dutch takeover of Java, Prince Diponegoro (figure 3.2) himself was having Hajjis appear to him in his dreams, as he planned and shortly afterward executed his five-year rebellion against all other standing authority in Java.[31]

The pilgrimage was certainly significant in a religious sense. Yet it was also important economically, as the Hajj provided a spiritual rationale for the agglom-

Figure 3.2 Prince Diponegoro.
Credit: Painted by J. W. Pieneman, Rijksmuseum, Amsterdam.

eration of peoples from many societies, all at the same time.[32] These pilgrims
from different lands met and mingled while upon Hajj, and they prayed side by
side in the great mosques of the Arabian Peninsula. Yet they also traded and
bought and sold while on the pilgrimage, linking the Indian Ocean orbit into a
system of financial exchange that was at least partly based on their movements as
religious wanderers. Carpets, brassware, gems, spices, and other valuable commodities traveled on these circuits. Southeast Asians brought some of these
items from home, but others they collected on their voyages. Spiritual travel,
therefore, was always linked with the more earthly advantages of travel, as pilgrims sold various kinds of merchandise from their own homelands to help pay
for their trips. This pattern seems to have been a long-standing phenomenon in
much of the Islamic world, but it was particularly important in the Indian Ocean

because the distances that needed to be crossed were often so immense. Financing devotion before the nineteenth century therefore took some concerted planning, and the numbers of devotees grew slowly as the mechanics of going on the pilgrimage gradually evolved. It would only be in the mature colonial period from the mid-nineteenth century forward, however, that more voluminous records of the economic importance of the Hajj would be revealed in existing period documents.

Colonial Southeast Asian Connections: The British Case

Performing the Hajj in the colonial dominions of British and Dutch Southeast Asia was a sacred duty that many indigenes accomplished, with or without the sanction of local imperial regimes. Financial concerns helped determine who could go on these journeys, how long they might last, and the chances of pilgrims returning home safely. In British Malaya, the average Hajji was usually male, in the middle decades of his life, and fairly well-off financially. He was also, more often than not, from the west coast or from the southern states of the Malay Peninsula.[33] Contrary to some expectations, pilgrims were not predominantly from the more Malay-dominated, poor, and religiously conservative Muslim east coast states like Kelantan and Trengganu. Having a substantial nest egg of cash was essential to be able to go. It cost roughly 300 Straits dollars to perform the Hajj in 1896, though larger sums had to be saved for the three-week trip across the Indian Ocean and subsequent months that might be spent in Arabia.[34] The cash earned from the pepper boom on the peninsula in the 1890s helped many Malays go to Mecca. In 1927, according to one scholar's statistics, 12,000 Malays went on Hajj, but five years later, during the nadir of the Great Depression, only eighty were able to make the journey in one year.[35] Peasants saved money for decades to perform the trip, often selling their possessions to acquire extra cash. The accumulation of vast quantities of money to perform the pilgrimage, even to the point of indigence afterward, was not uncommon. Dying in the Hejaz while on Hajj was seen as a ticket to special prestige, so few efforts were spared to round up the necessary funds, even if this meant the potential for serious financial hardship upon one's return.[36]

An important institution for financing the Hajj in British-controlled Southeast Asia was *waqf*, the Islamic endowment. *Waqf* were established in a number of different places in the region, especially Singapore, where there was already a great concentration of surplus funds in Muslim hands. Powerful Arab families in Singapore such as the al-Saqqaf and al-Kaf, both of which had strong connections with clan members still in the Hejaz, were particularly important in extending the benefits of *waqf* to ordinary Southeast Asian pilgrims who needed financial help.[37] *Waqf* endowments lent money, helped pay for steamship tickets, fronted cash or credit for housing in the holy cities, and put forth a network of contacts and handlers so that pilgrims from the Malay world could attempt this daunting journey. Operating under Islamic banking principles, *waqf* were supposed to insulate pilgrims to a degree from some of the more rapacious groups of capitalists in Singapore, both indigenous and foreign, who made huge sums of money every year off the Hajj trade.[38] The British colonial government kept a very close watch on the *waqf* endowments, both because they were suspected of illegal transactions and abuses of their charges and because they were considered to be anticolonial in nature on a number of occasions. Despite these concerns, many local Muslims felt safest organizing their pilgrimages through *waqf* endowments, though this did not prevent some of them from being cheated or bilked of funds by some of their less scrupulous coreligionists.[39]

Though Islamic teachings frowned upon commercial risk taking to undertake the Hajj, many Malays went into debt to fulfill this fifth pillar of the faith. Statistics from the fin de siècle show many Malays who had a difficult time maintaining themselves in the Hejaz, and also returning home.[40] In 1916 and then again in the years of World War II in Asia (1941–45), these numbers reached into the thousands (2,000 and 1,500 per annum, respectively), but destitution on this large a scale among Malay pilgrims was generally the exception to the rule. The shaykhs who controlled the pilgrim-brokerage and pilgrim-transport businesses were almost uniformly seen as sharks, men who preyed on their coreligionists in an attempt to earn fast money on unsuspecting souls. Pilgrims were constantly extorted at each step of the journey: they were made to wait for their passage and use up funds on housing until the proper steamers arrived, overcharged for tickets, given passage to only the next port, and frequently lied to about the overall costs involved.[41] For all of these reasons, the British finally assented to the appointment of a Malay pilgrimage officer in 1924, who went off with the first Malay ships of the Hajj season and who came back on the last one, tending his flock as a kind of officially sanctioned guardian.[42] Yet it was only after many decades of graft, including several high-profile court cases (such as one involving the famous al-Saqqaf family in 1881, who were accused of essentially keeping pilgrims in a position of slavery before and after the Hajj through debt bondage), that matters were ameliorated by the British.[43] Nevertheless, destitution among Malay pilgrims was still a matter of some concern to civil servants and statisticians chronicling the Hajj, as table 3.1 suggests.

The problem of indigence among archipelago pilgrims continued to be serious past the turn of the twentieth century. In the 1880s and 1890s, growing economic prosperity in Southeast Asia meant that Malay pilgrims were coming in the thousands, and sometimes in the tens of thousands, but after World War I the numbers shrank considerably for a time, and the rubber slump of the 1920s, the

Table 3.1 **Malay Pilgrim Costs, 1923–1939**

Year	# Pilgrims	Pilgrimage Cost	# Destitute	$ Expended
1923	5,576	680	—	1,329
1924	13,024	500	18	—
1925	5,500	n/a	71	—
1926	3,073	500	n/a	—
1927	12,184	500–600	22	1,000
1928	9,875	600	0	—
1929	4,646	900	n/a	—
1930	4,353	500–600	2	—
1931	1,334	500	n/a	1,000
1932	329	550–650	6	1,395
1933	320	550–600	40	1,600
1934	514	600	n/a	—
1935	712	480	12	500
1936	1,046	400	0	—
1937	2,882	500	0	—
1938	5,115	550	0	—
1939	2,059	625	2	—

Source: Abstracted from Mary Byrne McDonnell, "The Conduct of the Hajj From Malaysia and Its Socio-Economic Impact on Malay Society: A Descriptive and Analytical Study, 1860–1981" (PhD Dissertation, Columbia University, 1986), pp. 626, 639, 640.

Hejaz War of the later 1920s, and the global depression of the 1930s caused serious harm.[44] Poor Hajjis who could not pay to get back to Southeast Asia came from both the British and Dutch sides of the Straits, and there was often a stream of correspondence between the civil servants of both colonies trying to figure out how to get these pilgrims home at the lowest possible cost.[45] Calculated political surveillance sometimes met genuine colonial philanthropy (and paternalism) in a number of these cases. The unfortunates of both colonies, who could be stranded in the Hejaz for months, often with little or no means of supporting themselves and their families, sometimes even traveled back across the

Indian Ocean on the same ships, putting into British and then Dutch Indies ports in keeping with the sailing schedules of the main ocean passenger lines.[46] Yet not all pecuniary matters involved indigence when it came to the Hajj; a number of other prosaic matters made the entire system of transport and traffic run on an Asia-wide basis. Sometimes Malay elites applied for loans from the government to send family members to Mecca, like Dato Bandar of Sungei Ujong, who did just this in an attempt to get his wife to the Hejaz in 1905.[47] Even more common than this was a vast system of remittances that developed to keep archipelago pilgrims solvent while they were in Arabia, constantly supplied with funds from their family members and associates who were still back in Southeast Asia.[48] Banking facilities in the Hejaz were still rather underdeveloped even into the second decade of the twentieth century, necessitating all sorts of arrangements to ensure that capital could move over large oceanic distances and then be available to traveling Muslims.[49] Even certain Malay state governments (such as Kedah) used these systems, often to pay salaries to their own shaykhs and pilgrim agents during the months they were away from the peninsula.[50]

Colonial Southeast Asian Connections: The Dutch Case

In the Dutch East Indies, the Batavia administration tried to regulate the Hajj as much as possible, keeping detailed records on this subject throughout the nineteenth century. Local *controleurs* (mid-level civil servants, usually European but often assisted by indigenous helpers) were told by their superiors to record the details of the pilgrimage to Mecca from their residencies, and much of this reporting ended up being financial in nature. The reports from a single place, the residency of Banten in West Java for the year of 1860 alone, are illustrative in this sense. The reports were written by the local resident, who informed Batavia of the names of local people who had returned from Mecca that same year: villagers such as Mochamad Markoem, Inam, Hadjie Djamiel, and Hadji Daham. In addition to recording the names of many illiterate farmers and fishermen, the records show that 222 of these people came back to the residency that year from Mecca, a very high number considering the costs and difficulties of travel in 1860.[51] Since 1858, almost a quarter of a million guilders had left the residency on these trips, as pilgrims took whatever funds they could get their hands on to facilitate their voyages. This was a cause for some alarm to local officials, and the problem of "silver drain" became commented upon in every level of government reportage examining the mechanics of the Hajj.[52] Finally, these reports spelled out exactly how much money each pilgrim was bringing on his or her person for the trip. Kardja brought 150 Spanish dollars in 1860, Kaman brought 100, and Abdulah and Oesman, from Petier and Dragem villages, respectively, brought

200 dollars each.[53] The level of detail in the reporting is quite astonishing, and given the fact that this was happening all across the more settled districts of the Dutch Indies, a large cache of data exists to flesh out the conduct of the Indonesian Hajj, even at this early date.[54]

Fees were charged for the right to go on pilgrimage, and these escalated from 110 guilders at mid-century to 200 guilders in 1873 and then to 300 guilders in 1890. Shortly after this, the price was lowered to 100 guilders again, but a return ticket on a steamer was a condition of being let out of the Indies so that pilgrims would not be stranded in the Middle East.[55] An enormous system of brokers developed to take care of the ever-burgeoning Indies pilgrim traffic, most of which went through Singapore. In 1880, there were 180 shaykhs in charge of the Indies' flow alone, a number that grew to 400 by the eve of World War I and 600 to 700 in 1926, according to the chronicler Haji Abdul Majid, who made the trip himself that year.[56] Many of these Indies pilgrims were leaving the archipelago for the first time and had little idea of the vagaries of international commerce on the great shipping lanes stretching across the vast Indian Ocean. As a result, many of these Hajjis were charged quite a bit more than their Malay counterparts, despite the fact that they were ultimately leaving from the same Southeast Asian ports.[57] A steady stream of pilgrims found their way to the Hejaz via these intricate connections, leaving the Indies from a series of Dutch harbors and stopping over in the British dominions (usually Singapore or Penang), before making the big jump across the sea to the Arabian Peninsula (table 3.2).

Table 3.2 **The Financial Worth of the Netherlands East Indies Pilgrimages, 1872–78**

Year	# Pilgrims	# Passes Issued	Passes' Worth (Dutch guilders)	Avg/Person
1872	5,360	3,127	f 1,392,113	f 445
1873	3,833	2,639	f 1,317,093	f 499
1874	4,801	3,673	f 2,392,003	f 651
1875	5,655	4,331	f 2,100,944	f 485
1876	5,106	3,642	f 1,768,429	f 485
1877	6,093	5,294	f 2,524,896	f 476
1878	5,632	4,467	f 2,176,520	f 487

Source: Abstracted from Johan Eisenberger, "Indie en de Bedevaart naar Mekka" (PhD Dissertation, Leiden University, 1928), p. 32.

Yet just as with the Malay pilgrims, many Indies Hajjis suffered at the hands of middlemen who took advantage of their comparative naiveté and powerlessness as they tried to complete their Hajj.[58] An 1876 Dutch consular report suggested that approximately 30 percent of all Indies pilgrims eventually found themselves destitute in the Hejaz, a number and a percentage far higher than for Malay pilgrims.[59] Many of the archipelago Hajjis entered into contracts to raise cash for their journeys, agreeing to work in Singapore, Malaya, or even the Holy Land for years so that sufficient funds could be raised.[60] The rate of return on these menial jobs (usually on plantations) was so low that some pilgrims could find themselves in a perpetual cycle of debt from which they could never hope to escape.[61] Shaykhs who perpetuated this cycle of indebtedness were often Arabs resident in Southeast Asia, but after several decades, indigenous archipelago returnees also entered this very profitable business. When the Dutch gradually restricted the numbers of Indies pilgrims allowed to go on the pilgrimage for economic and security reasons, many started to go illegally by way of Singapore, putting themselves even more at the mercy of the shaykhs since they had little recourse to colonial laws meant to protect them. A report in the *Indische Gids* in 1897 catalogued some of the deceptions that were practiced on Indies pilgrims but offered little by way of practical solutions.[62] Even if the Dutch knew their subjects were being fleeced, often on a systemic basis, doing something about it seemed to be beyond the organizational powers of Batavia's administrators.

Conclusion

In the centuries before European hegemony in Southeast Asia, the pilgrimage to Mecca was performed by relatively few people from a total population standpoint. The Hajj was outside the economic reach of all but a few; sultans and nobles could hope to go if their devotion or their connections were particularly strong, but for the greater percentage of ordinary people, Mecca was simply too far way to be an attainable destination. Some archipelago rulers helped finance the pilgrimages of their subjects, and a few poorer Southeast Asians found their own way out to the Hejaz, sometimes staying there for months or even years as part of their initial Hajj. These communities in turn acted as gatekeepers for other people from the region who followed, helping them to perform their religious obligations and to acclimatize to the holy cities of the desert. Despite some scholarly assertions to the contrary, however, it seems that the Hajj was an important—but not always a crucial—linchpin to the economic orbit of the greater Indian Ocean. Pilgrims' funds helped invigorate a far-flung oceanic economy that transited across these maritime spaces, yet the available precolonial and early colonial sources suggest that the numbers of devotees were simply too small to have had an overwhelming effect on the early modern economy of the region, even if this effect was indeed financially important in all sorts of ways.

Undertaking the Hajj in the burgeoning world of colonial Southeast Asia certainly remained possible, despite European fears of pan-Islamic influences, and even despite global recessions that periodically swept the region. Yet it was always a difficult journey at best, filled with danger, deception, and disease, as well as the possibility of life spent in penury for the very best motives of fulfilling one's religious duties. Colonial states tried to ameliorate some of the practical financial problems facing their Asian subjects, but often these challenges were too great for regimes on the brink of administrative modernity. The numbers of Britons and Dutchmen in Southeast Asia were still small in the middle to late nineteenth century; the sustained surge of Europeans migrating to the colonies to find work would not take place until the turn of the twentieth century. Period documents also suggest that Western fears over the results of the Hajj, both spiritual and political, may have weakened imperial resolve to completely fix existing deficiencies. It is not clear how much of a role this anxiety may have played, but by the late nineteenth century, Southeast Asians were nonetheless able to go on pilgrimage in far larger numbers than they ever had in prior times. The attendant risks and difficulties were seen as part of the voyage, and the large sums of money that had to be raised were almost always viewed as resources well spent.

NOTES

1. The best overview of the Hajj generally as a historical and a contemporary phenomenon is still F. E. Peters, *The Hajj: The Muslim Pilgrimage to Mecca and the Holy Places* (Princeton, NJ: Princeton University Press, 1994); only a tiny fraction of this book touches on the role of Southeast Asians, however.
2. Pilgrims also started to come from some of the other colonies of Southeast Asia during this period, most notably the Spanish Philippines and French Indochina, but they were so small in overall number at this point that I have not treated this phenomenon here. For a summary, see chapter 10.
3. Ashin Das Gupta, "Indian Merchants and the Trade in the Indian Ocean," in *Cambridge Economic History of India*, vol. 1 (Cambridge: Cambridge University Press, 1982), p. 430.
4. Ashin Das Gupta, "Gujarati Merchants and the Red Sea Trade, 1700–1725," in B. B. Kling and M. N. Pearson, eds., *The Age of Partnership* (Honolulu: University of Hawai'i Press, 1979), p. 124.
5. Ashin Das Gupta, *Indian Merchants and the Decline of Surat, c. 1700–1750* (Wiesbaden: Harrasowitz Verlag, 1979), pp. 68–69. Das Gupta saw the Hajj as an engine primus-inter-pares among any other economic phenomena in the Indian Ocean. "The major consideration in any season at Surat was the market of the haj. A Major part of the city's shipping was engaged in the Red Sea run, and they took their textiles directly to the port of Mocha which was the principal trading center in the Red Sea at the time. Some of the ships would sail past Mocha and make for Jedda further up the coast, but this was probably because of the proximity of Jedda to Mecca.... The market at Mecca... functioned every year as pilgrims from all over the Ottoman empire and the Islamic world assembled at this city." Ibid, pp. 68–69.

6. M. N. Pearson, *Pious Passengers: The Hajj in Earlier Times* (Dhaka, Bangladesh: University Press Limited, 1994), p. 158; F. E. Peters, *Jerusalem and Mecca: The Typology of the Holy City in the Near East* (New York: New York University Studies in Near Eastern Civilization #11, 1986), pp. 70–71.

7. Anonymous, "A Description of the Yeerly Voyage or Pilgrimage of the Mahumitans, Turkes and Moores unto Mecca in Arabia," in Richard Hakluyt, *The Principal Navigations*, vol. 5 (Glasgow, 1903–5), pp. 340–365.

8. Saris quoted in Samuel Purchas, *Purchas, His Pilgrimes*, vol. 3 (Glasgow: Hakluyt, 1905–7), p. 396.

9. William Foster, *Early Travels in India* (Delhi: S. Chand, 1968), pp. 301–302.

10. Jeronimo Lobo, *The Itinerary of Jerinomo Lobo*, trans. Donald M. Lockhart (London: Hakluyt, 1984), pp. 89–90. Lobo further described Jeddah as a city "which has been made so famous in these times in all of the East by the great numbers of ships that go there and the rich trade the merchants find there.... Because of the great wealth of the universal market of people and merchandise carried out in that city, they (the ships) became so famous in India that when people wanted to indicate that something was very costly and valuable they would call it a ship from Mecca." Ibid, p. 89–90.

11. Tavernier quoted in W. H. Coates, *The Old Country Trade of the East Indies* (London: Imray, Laurie, Nurie, and Wilson, 1911), p. 124.

12. Suraiya Farooqhi, *Pilgrims and Sultans: The Hajj under the Ottomans, 1517–1683* (London: IB Tauris, 1994), pp. 159–160.

13. Foster, *Early Travels*, pp. 301–302; and Pearson, *Pious Passengers*, p. 157.

14. Walter de Grey Bird, *The Commentaries of the Great Alfonso Dalboquerque, 2nd Viceroy of India*, vol. 4 (London: Hakluyt Society, 1884); see especially Map #1 in his account.

15. William Foster, ed., *The Journal of John Jourdain, 1608–1617*, series 2, vol. 16 (London: Hakluyt Society, 1905); see especially Map #2 in his account.

16. Qutb al-Din al-Nahrawali al-Makki, trans. and ed. Clive Smith, *Lightning over Yemen: A History of the Ottoman Campaign, 1569–1571* (London: Tauris, 2002).

17. Colin Heywood, *Writing Ottoman History: Documents and Interpretations* (Aldershot, England: Ashgate, 2002).

18. Rifa'at 'Ali Abou-El-Haj, *Formation of the Modern State: The Ottoman Empire Sixteenth to Eighteenth Centuries* (Albany: State University of New York Press, 1991).

19. Farooqji, *Pilgrims and Sultans*, pp. 76, 78.

20. Asli Cirakman, *From the Terror of the World to the Sick Man of Europe: European Images of Ottoman Empire and Society from the Sixteenth Century to the Nineteenth* (New York: Peter Lang, 2002).

21. Farhad Nomani and Ali Rahnema, *Islamic Economic Systems* (London: Zed, 1994); and Sevket Pamuk, *A Monetary History of the Ottoman Empire* (Cambridge: Cambridge University Press, 2000).

22. M. N. Pearson, *Pious Passengers*, p. 164.

23. Martin van Bruinessen, *Tarekat Naqsyabandiyah di Indonesia: Survei Historis, Geografis dan Sosiologis* (Bandung, Indonesia: Penerbit Mizan, 1992), pp. 34–46; and Abu Hamid, *Syekh Yusuf Makassar: Seorang Ulama, Sufi dan Pejuang* (Jakarta: Yayasan Obor Indonesia, 1994).

24. For an overview, see Virginia Matheson and Barbara Watson Andaya, eds. and trans., *The Precious Gift, Tuhfat al-Nafis* (Kuala Lumpur: Oxford University Press, 1982).

25. Virginia Matheson and A. C. Milner, eds., *Perceptions of the Haj: Five Malay Texts* (Singapore: ISEAS, 1984), pp. 15, 20.

26. C. G. Brouwer, "Le Voyage au Yemen de Pieter van den Broecke (serviteur de la VOC) en 1620, d'apres son livre de resolutions," in F. E. Peters et al., eds., *The Challenge of the Middle East* (Amsterdam: Institute of Modern Near Eastern Studies, 1982), pp. 175–182.

27. C. G. Brouwer, "Pieter van den Broecke's Original Resulutieboeck Concerning Dutch Trade in Northwest India, Persia, and Southern Arabia, 1620–1625," in C. G. Brouwer, *Dutch-Yemeni Encounters: Activities of the United East India Company (VOC) in South Arabian Waters since 1614* (Amsterdam: D'Fluyte Rarob, 1999), pp. 77–102.

28. Merle Ricklefs, *A History of Modern Indonesia* (Stanford, CA: Stanford University Press, 1993), pp. 78–79.

29. Merle Ricklefs, *Mystic Synthesis in Java: A History of Islamization from the Fourteenth to the Early Nineteenth Centuries* (Norwalk, CT: Eastbridge, 2004), pp. 75–76, 94.

30. P. B. R. Carey, *Pangeran Dipanagara and the Making of the Java War* (PhD. Dissertation, Oxford University, 1975), vol. 1, p. 76.

31. Ibid., pp. 359–381.

32. See Michael Laffan, *Islamic Nationhood and Colonial Indonesia* (London: Routledge, 2003). Laffan has presented some useful material on the specifics of lodges, meeting houses, study committees, and the like, not just in Mecca but in Cairo as well.

33. Mary McDonnell, "The Conduct of the Hajj from Malaysia and Its Socio-Economic Impact on Malay Society" (PhD Dissertation, Columbia University, 1986), p. 74. Although contemporary Malaysians from all over the country go on Hajj, there is still a strong stereotype of the east coast peninsular states as being more "Muslim" than the heterogeneous west coast states. Part of this is demographic—the west coast states, with their histories of tin mines, rubber plantations, and cities, were the places that received the most overseas laborers, usually from China and India. Likewise, Sarawak and Sabah, in east Malaysia (Malaysian Borneo), have large indigenous populations of "Dayaks" who have not converted to Islam. Despite these historical patterns, and despite the overwhelming "Malay" nature of places such as Kelantan and Terengganu, historically and today Malaysian Hajjis hail from all over the country. Every Malay state, for example, has branch offices of the Tabung Haji, the modern governmental institution charged with overseeing the contemporary Hajj. These trends are examined later on in this book.

34. Ibid., p. 75.

35. William Roff, "The Conduct of the Hajj from Malaya and the First Malay Pilgrimage Officer," *Kuala Lumpur: Occasional Paper #1 of the Institute of Malay Language, Literature, and Culture, U.K.M,* 1975, p. 104. The numbers reported by Roff here do not entirely coincide with those reported by McDonnell, as reflected in table 3.1 of this chapter.

36. J. M. Gullick, *Indigenous Political Systems of Western Malaya* (London: Athlone, 1958), pp. 139–141.

37. Rajeswary Ampalavanar Brown, "Islamic Endowments and the Land Economy in Singapore: The Genesis of an Ethical Capitalism, 1830–2007," *South East Asia Research* 16/3, 2008: 343–403.

38. D. S. Powers, "The Islamic Endowment (Waqf)," *Vanderbilt Journal of Transnational Law*, 32, 1999: 4.

39. Stephanie Po Yin Chung, "Western Law in Asian Customs: Legal Disputes on Business Practices in India, British Malaya and Hong Kong, 1850s–1930s," *Asia Europe Journal*, 1, 1993: 527–529.

40. McDonnell, "The Conduct of the Hajj from Malaysia," p. 71, also p. 640.

41. Moshe Yegar, *Islam and Islamic Institutions in British Malaya: Policies and Implementation* (Jerusalem: Magnes, 1979), p. 228. For all of these reasons, the British colonial government took an active interest in policing the conduct of Hajj traffic as it moved across the Indian Ocean from Britain's Southeast Asian possessions. Though it took several decades for these efforts to really bear fruit, by the turn of the century there were already some inroads being made into the coordination and control of some of the worst abuses of the Hajj. See the *Straits Settlements Government Gazette*, Ordinances #12 (1901) and #3 and #17 (1906), for changes made to the laws on pilgrim ships and pilgrim brokers.

42. Haji Abdul Majid, "A Malay's Pilgrimage to Mecca," *Journal of the Malaysian Branch of the Royal Asiatic Society*, 14/2, 1926: 269–287. This happened earlier in British-controlled India in 1888.

43. See the *Straits Times Overland Journal*, July 28, 1881; and William Roff, *The Origins of Malay Nationalism* (Kuala Lumpur: Penerbit Universiti Malaya, 1974), p. 39. The al-Saqqaf family,

one of the two richest and best connected Arab clans in Singapore, made money off the pilgrim trade, though sometimes in ways deemed illegal by the colonial powers.

44. McDonnell, "Conduct of the Hajj from Malaysia," p. 629.
45. ARNEG, "List of British Javanese Pauper Pilgrims Repatriated by S.S. 'Sardar' dated the September 26th, 1916," in ARNEG, High Commission, Secretary of Police Bombay to Sec., Foreign and Political Dept, December 21, 1916, #491/1917.
46. ARNEG, High Commission, Dutch Consul, Singapore to Sec. for the High Commission, March 31, 1919, #402.
47. ARNEG, High Commission, 1905, #945.
48. See, for example, ARNEG, High Commission, 1918 #279 and 1918 #720.
49. ARNEG, High Commission, Sec. to the Comm. to Sec. of the Resident, Perak, March 20, 1918, #279/1918.
50. ARNEG, High Commission, Advisor to Kedah Gov't to High Comm, Sing, May 16, 1918, #1187/36.
51. ANRI, Residentie Bantam Algemeen Verslag, Appendix: Opgave van de Personen die ter Bedevaart naar Mekka zijn Teruggekeerd (1860).
52. ANRI, Residentie Bantam Algemeen Verslag (1860).
53. ANRI, Residentie Bantam Algemeen Verslag, Appendix: Opgave van de Personen die ter Bedevaart naar Mekka zijn Vertrokken (1860).
54. For an incredible example of the depth of this reportage, see the archive bundle titled "Rapporten Dari Perkara Hadji Hadja njang Minta Pas dan njang Baru Datang dari Mekka, 1860/61/62/63/64," in the Arsip Nasional Indonesia (Jakarta) Tegal archive (#196/5, "Laporan Pergi dan Pulang Haji"). This is only one of a number of 500-page bundles of local letters and reports on the Hajj in Tegal alone—just one small residency in Java. A small book could be written simply on the basis of this one archival bundle alone.
55. J. Eisenberger, *Indie en de Bedevaart Naar Mekka* (Leiden: M. Dubbeldeman, 1928), pp. 27, 175.
56. See generally Jacob Vredenbregt, "The Hadj: Some of Its Features and Functions in Indonesia," *Bijdragen tot de Taal-, Land-, en Volkenkunde*, 118, 1962: 91–154; and Haji Abdul Majid, "A Malay's Pilgrimage," p. 270. Keeping track of all of these shaykhs and the various dangers they represented to the colonial Dutch government was a small but very active group of diplomats scattered across several Indian Ocean ports. The Dutch had their own servants reporting on Hajj movements and patterns via salaried European consuls, and they also maintained a quiet network of indigenous Southeast Asian spies who reported on local movements for money. Dutch consuls and vice consuls charged with keeping an eye on the Hajj were stationed in Batavia, Singapore, Penang, and Jeddah, so that irregularities or potential rebellion or dissent traveling on the religious radials of pilgrimage could be watched.
57. McDonnell, "The Conduct of the Hajj from Malaysia," p. 76.
58. For a partial overview of some of the legislation against this, see Eisenberger, "Indie en de Bedevaart," pp. 31–37. Ann Kumar has suggested that despite widespread notices of indigence, pious (but poor) men could receive generous gifts of clothes, sustenance, and other presents from benefactors when they returned to Southeast Asia; see Mas Rahmat's experiences in Ann Kumar, *The Diary of a Javanese Muslim: Religion, Politics and the Pesantren, 1883–1886* (Canberra: Faculty of Asian Studies Monographs, 1985).
59. Marcel Witlox, "Met Gevaar voor Lijf en Goed: Mekkagangers uit Nederlands-Indie in de 19de Eeuw," in Willy Jansen and Huub de Jonge, eds., *Islamitische Pelgrimstochten* (Muiderberg, Netherlands: Coutinho, 1991), p. 30.
60. See Roff, *The Origins of Malay Nationalism*, pp. 38–39.
61. Jacob Vredenbregt, "The Hadj," pp. 113–115.
62. See the *Indische Gids* (1897), p. 390.

4

Sultanate and Crescent

Religion and Politics in the Indian Ocean

> The reason why this banner has been sent to you is that we in Mecca
> have heard that Your Highness, being a truly princely leader, is much
> feared in battle. Value it and make use of it, Please God, in extermi-
> nating your enemies and all unbelievers. Good wishes and greetings are
> conveyed to Your Highness on behalf of the old Godfearing people of
> Mecca and Medina.
>
> —Al-Palimbani in Mecca to Prince Mangkunagara
> in Java, early 1770s

In the preceding pages of this book, the forging of a series of tentative links bet-
ween Southeast Asia and the Middle East has been established. The Hajj in
Southeast Asia is deeply connected to the presence and historical growth of such
Muslim connections with the region.[1] Islam came through a number of channels
to Southeast Asia, including via Arab, Persian, Indian, and Chinese influences.[2]
Though there are brief glimpses of Muslim presences earlier, Muslim city-states
as such began to appear at the latest in the late thirteenth century. From Samudra-
Pasai in north Sumatra, other city-states gradually became Muslim as well:
Melaka, Aceh, Brunei, Patani, Banten, Cirebon, and others followed in turn.[3] By
the early seventeenth century, it was not at all out of place to speak of a clear
pattern of Islam and statecraft mixing along the littorals of parts of maritime
Southeast Asia.[4] Throughout this process, the Hajj played a vital role in fusing
religious and political power in the region.

Malay-language period texts offer a fascinating window into how knowledge
and interpretation of the Hajj changed in Muslim Southeast Asia over time.[5] The
earliest mentions date back to the 1370s, but there are particular concentrations
of notices from around the year 1600, from the seventeenth century as a whole,
and in the early nineteenth century. These texts illustrate how a number of
pilgrimage-related designations—such as *Hajj*, *Hajji*, and *Mecca*—entered into
the religio-political writing of the Malay chronicles and other period tracts. Such

documents then, in turn, offer a glimpse of the intellectual milieu and power dynamics of the evolving Malay courts. The manner in which the Hajj informed the marriage of statecraft and religion on the Malay Peninsula is analyzed in this chapter, before a parallel world taking shape in the Indonesian archipelago itself is examined. Though both of these regions were part of the larger "Malay World," they were essentially bifurcated by colonialism with important repercussions, so they are analyzed separately here. The chapter concludes with an analysis of three texts—one each from the seventeenth, eighteenth, and nineteenth centuries—to see what their contents can tell us about the evolution of Islam, the Hajj, and regional politics in Muslim Southeast Asia. Throughout these centuries, it is argued, the pilgrimage to Mecca played a vital role in fusing religious and political power, both in the local world of the lands beneath the winds and in the wider arena of the Indian Ocean *dar al-Islam*.

The Growth of Malay Writing on Politics and Islam

A number of the earliest surviving Malay-language texts show the convergences between religion and politics that were taking place in Southeast Asia almost seven hundred years ago (figure 4.1). The *Hikayat Bayan Budiman,* a collection of tales in Sanskrit that was eventually translated into Persian, was translated in 1371 by a Malay scribe known as Kadi Hassan. The terms for Malay royalty in this text do not follow the common usage of the times, but rather seem attributable to the cosmopolitan, maritime Malay ecumene that was then developing in Island Southeast Asia. The trading culture of the sea routes clearly was already starting to vie with the older political economies of the Malay courts at this early date, in other words.[6] By the 1380s, other Persian manuscripts were circulating on the coasts of Insular Southeast Asia and were also being translated into Malay. The *Hikayat Muhammad Hanafiyyah* was one of these, as was the *Hikayat Air Hamzah,* which was discovered in Pasai, North Sumatra, the traditionally attributed "birthplace" of political Islam in Southeast Asia and the home of the first known Muslim polity.[7] In 1390, the *Hikayat Raja Pasai,* or "History of the Kings of Pasai," was composed in that port, beginning a long line of Muslim political chronicling.[8] Surprisingly, Mecca is mentioned in all four of these very early texts, showing an awareness of the pilgrimage to the holy cities from the earliest written sources. The trip itself may have been beyond the realm of possibility for most Southeast Asians, but the religious rites of the Hajj and the great centers of the Hejaz were clearly already entering local politicial consciousness.

There is something of a gap after this in our records vis-à-vis such texts and the Hajj, but around the year 1600 or so, some of the Malay manuscripts began borrowing significant numbers of words from Arabic, showing a different

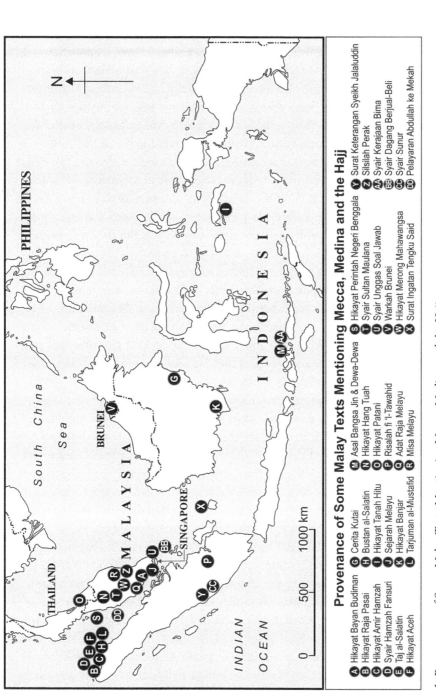

Figure 4.1 Provenances of Some Malay Texts Mentioning Mecca, Medina, and the Hajj.
Credit: Map drawn by Lee Li-kheng, Geography Department, National University of Singapore.

Provenance of Some Malay Texts Mentioning Mecca, Medina and the Hajj

Ⓐ Hikayat Bayan Budiman
Ⓑ Hikayat Raja Pasai
Ⓒ Hikayat Amir Hamzah
Ⓓ Syair Hamzah Fansuri
Ⓔ Taj al-Salatin
Ⓕ Hikayat Aceh
Ⓖ Cerita Kutai
Ⓗ Bustan al-Salatin
Ⓘ Hikayat Tanah Hitu
Ⓙ Sejarah Melayu
Ⓚ Hikayat Banjar
Ⓛ Tarjuman al-Mustafid
Ⓜ Asal Bangsa Jin & Dewa-Dewa
Ⓝ Hikayat Hang Tuah
Ⓞ Hikayat Patani
Ⓟ Risalah fi 'l-Tawahid
Ⓠ Adat Raja Melayu
Ⓡ Misa Melayu
Ⓢ Hikayat Perintah Negeri Benggala
Ⓣ Syair Sultan Maulana
Ⓤ Syair Unggas Soal Jawab
Ⓦ Warkah Brunei
Ⓧ Hikayat Merong Mahawangsa
Ⓧ Surat Ingatan Tengku Said
Ⓨ Surat Keterangan Syeikh Jalaluddin
Ⓩ Silsilah Perak
ⒶⒶ Syair Kerajaan Bima
ⒷⒷ Syair Dagang Berjual-Beli
ⒸⒸ Syair Sunur
ⒹⒹ Pelayaran Abdullah ke Mekah

relationship vis-à-vis the transmission process of both statecraft and religion. Using the original Arabic became important, and one of the first extant Malay texts to do this was the '*Aqa 'id of al-Nasafi*, tentatively dated to 1590.[9] The poems of the great Hamzah Fansuri were likely being produced even a bit earlier, and both of these texts refer to the Hajj and to Mecca, demonstrating that this religious obligation was already becoming a theme across genres in Malay writing of the time.[10] The latter poet's words are particularly effective on this theme: "Hamzah Fansuri in Makkah, searches for God in the House of the Ka'bah; from Barus to Kudus he wearily goes, at last he finds [Him] in his house."[11] The *Taj al-Salatin* from 1603 contains quotes from the Qur'an and the Hadiths, as well as other material from Persian and Arabic sources, all written in Arabic and woven into the larger Malay text.[12] Yet the crowning achievement of this period is undoubtably the *Hikayat Aceh*, likely penned circa 1625. Aceh was already an important political player in maritime Southeast Asia by this date, and the sultanate's power grew throughout the seventeenth century.[13] The vocabulary of this great history blends Acehnese, Persian, Arabic, and Malay into one amalgam of elegant text. Hajjis appear numerous times in the *Hikayat Aceh*, traveling back and forth across the sea-roads between Mecca and the polity that came to be known quite simply as the "verandah of Mecca" on the other side of the Indian Ocean, Aceh itself. Medina also starts to be mentioned at this time, not just Mecca, showing a wider knowledge of the places and centers of the Hejaz than had previously been available in Malay religious or political texts.[14]

Seventeenth-century texts stress the mechanics and dynamics of cross-culturalism in the region. The sea routes between Southeast Asia and the Middle East were becoming safer, which increased the pace of contact between Muslims on both sides of the Indian Ocean, not just between Muslim Southeast Asians and sojourning Europeans. Although the Christian-Muslim interface in Southeast Asia (between Western traders and local kingdoms) has received significant scholarly attention for this era, Malay texts of the period show that in the realms of politics and Islam, the dialogue with coreligionists across the sea was just as important to local sensibilities. The *Bustan al-Salatin*, for example (begun in 1638 and finished before 1643), composed by the great Muslim scholar Nur al-Din Muhammad bin 'Ali Hassanji Hamid al-Raniri, spanned seven volumes and comprised a kind of universal Muslim history of heaven and earth, the politics of prophets and kings, the geostrategic growth of Aceh, and the foundation tales of Adam and Abraham in Arabia, all for good measure.[15] The totality of the whole can be seen as one of the most eclectic works of commentary on political statecraft in seventeenth-century Islamic civilization, in Southeast Asia or anywhere else. Other Malay manuscripts abound during this period, too, many of them touching in some way—as did the *Bustin al-Salatin*—on the Hajj and its place in the larger Muslim world of Southeast Asia, as well as this world's connections to the Middle East. The *Cerita Kutai* (roughly 1625), the *Hikayat Tanah Hitu* (roughly 1650), the *Hikayat Ibrahim ibn Adham* (roughly 1650), the great opus known as the *Sejarah Melayu* (roughly 1650), the *Hikayat Banjar dan Kota Waringin* (1663), and the *Bab Takzir* (1680) all mention—in one place or another—the Prophet's Arabian cities and the pilgrimage, generally, as part of the fabric of their texts.[16] Taken as a group, these documents demonstrate that readers (likely literate elites) and listeners (almost anyone else) in the greater Malay world still highly valued the interconnection between politics and religion generated by trans–Indian Ocean ties during this period. Such a concern did not simply fade away in the face of European settlement and aggression in the region.

During parts of the eighteenth century, texts concerning the pilgrimage and its connections with Malay political and religious texts were less common, at least in volume. Two texts dated circa 1700 CE, the *Cerita Asal Bangsa Jin dan Segala Dewa-Dewa* and the great Malay epic, the *Hikayat Hang Tuah* from the Malay Peninsula, both mention the pilgrimage in the course of their narratives, but in the first of these manuscripts, there is only a single notice, whereas in the latter, the pilgrimage is mentioned more than a dozen times.[17] Not until three decades later, in the *Hikayat Patani* (c. 1730) did mention of the pilgrimage appear in another Malay text. Only in the middle decades of the century did the pilgrimage to Mecca or notice of the Middle East become noticeable again in these religio-political documents. In roughly 1750, the *Surat al-Anbiya* was composed, and it mentions the pilgrimage and Mecca more than any other Malay manuscript, the *Hikayat Hang Tuah* excepted, since the beginning of recorded Malay writing.[18] For the second half of the century, only a few texts seem to keep up this intellectual thread with any regularity, including the *Risalah fi 'l-Tawhid* (or *Kitab Mukhtasar*) (1760s), the *Adat Raja-Raja Melayu* (1779), and the *Misa Melayu* (roughly 1780), all of which mention the Hajj.[19] The first of these texts emphasizes the politico-religious connections between the Malay world and the Middle East, as it was concerned with stemming the perceived marginalization of *shari'a* because of the growth of mysticism in Southeast Asia.

Following more sporadic discussions in parts of the eighteenth century, religio-political texts bonding the Middle East and the Malay world began to be composed, annotated, and translated again at a furious pace in the early nineteenth century.[20] Some of this probably had to do with the ferocity of the Napoleonic Wars in Europe: with the Low Countries overrun and England occupied elsewhere, the transit and travel of Muslim texts and Muslim men across the Indian Ocean *dar al-Islam* became easier than before. There was certainly less surveillance and supervision than there had been previously, allowing religious and political tracts (and combinations of the two) to circulate more freely. Developments in shipping and navigation ensured that greater percentages of these cargoes (both paper and human) reached their destinations than was previously possible. Much of the outstretched Malay world was now awash with tracts, in fact, many of them moving between courts and influencing both religious practice and political discourse—both within the entwined framework of Islam—in equal measure. Among the most important texts of this time that referenced the pilgrimage or the Arabian Peninsula and intellectual trends emanating from both into the Malay world were the *Hikayat Perintah Negeri Benggala* (1811), the *Syair Sultan Maulana* (1815), the *Syair Unggas Soal Jawab* (before 1841), the *Warkah Brunei* (1819–22), the *Syair Siti Zubaidah Perang Cina* (c. 1800), the *Hikayat Merong Mahawangsa* (1821), the *Surat Ingatan Tengku Said* (1824), the *Surat Keterangan Syeikh Jalaluddin* (1821), and the *Silsilah Perak* (1826) (table 4.1).[21] All are important because they were moving in a time of relative freedom in the lands beneath the winds. They are also notable because their messages—varied and diffuse as they were, covering issues of doctrine, sectarianism, mysticism, and religious change—helped to frame the debate about how Islam and politics went hand in hand in this part of the world. They provided a menu of choices to local people on how to construct their intellectual, political, and moral worlds within Islamic idioms, ones that were both "known" and dynamically evolving at the same time.

The middle decades of the nineteenth century were the last period of any consequence before European dominion came to most of the Malay world. Some of the Malay-language texts being produced and circulating at this time connect more or less to these earlier traditions of writing. Religion and politics might be discussed in many of these tracts, with the different ways of seeing Islam being part of this conversation, but the continuity of tradition was clearly apparent. A number of texts, all of them discussing the pilgrimage and Arabia to some degree, would fall into this category: the *Syair Kerajaan Bima* (1830), the *Syair Dagang Berjual-Beli* (1831), the Malay-language letters organized by Cyril Skinner about the civil war in Kelantan in 1839, and the *Syair Sunur* (1850) are all good examples.[22] These texts continued previous religious and political discourses within the ambit of Islam and also managed to refract the concerns of the time, the last decades before autonomy was really lost to Europeans in the region. Yet these tracts also carved new ways of thinking and writing about politics and religion within this vast maritime world. The most expansive text in this sense is the various renderings of the so-called Voyages of Abdullah, where we see something of a new sensibility being born.[23] Thoughts, ruminations, and reflections such as Abdullah's also became available to the evolving religio-political order of the day and helped to sketch out new ways of conceptualizing the Muslim ecumene of the mid-nineteenth century, in ways that had not been tried before.[24] Autobiography, cognizance of the possibilities of travel, and the notion of the first-person religious quest were all part of this change in the fabric of writing. This notion (and Abdullah's

Table 4.1 **A Selection of Classical Malay Texts Mentioning the Hajj, Mecca, or Medina over Centuries (Mid-Fourteenth to Mid-Nineteenth)**

Text	Date	Text	Date
Hikayat Bayan Budiman	1371	*Risalah fi 'l-Tawahid*	1760
Hikayat Raja Pasai	1390	*Adat Raja Melayu*	1779
Hikayat Muhammad Hanafiah	1450	*Misa Melayu*	1780
Hikayat Amir Hamzah	1600	*Hikayat Perintah Negeri Benggala*	1811
Aqa id al-Nasafi	1590	*Syair Sultan Maulana*	1815
Syair Hamzah Fansuri	1590	*Syair Unggas Soal Jawab*	1841
Taj al-Salatin	1603	*Warkah Brunei*	1819
Hikayat Aceh	1625	*Syair Siti Zubaidah Perang Cina*	1800
Cerita Kutai	1625	*Hikayat Merong Mahawangsa*	1821
Bustan al-Salatin	1640	*Surat Ingatan Tengku Said*	1824
Hikayat Tanah Hitu	1650	*Surat Keterangan Syeikh Jalaluddin*	1821
Hikayat Ibrahim ibn Adam	1650	*Silsilah Perak*	1826
Sejarah Melayu	1650	*Syair Kerajaan Bima*	1830
Hikayat Banjar	1663	*Syair Dagang Berjual-Beli*	1831
Tarjuman al-Mustafid	1670	*Pelayaran Abdullah Ke Kelantan*	1838
Bab Takzir	1680	*Ceretera karangan Abdullah*	1843
Asal Bangsa Jin & Dewa-Dewa	1700	*Syair karangan Abdullah*	1848
Hikayat Hang Tuah	1700	*Syair Sunur*	1850s
Hikayat Patani	1730	*Hikayat Abdullah bin 'Abdul Kadir*	1842
Surat al-Anbiya'	1750	*Pelayaran Abdullah ke Mekah*	1854

Some dates are not in perfect sequence because the datable physical manuscript is later than the hypothesized provenance of the text.

text itself) is discussed in greater depth later in this chapter and then again in a subsequent chapter on pilgrimage memoirs later in the book. But for now, it is important to note that a new world of observation and interpretation of the pilgrimage in Southeast Asia was being born as the high colonial age dawned in the region in the mid-nineteenth century.

Malay Texts and Multiple Understandings
of the Middle East

Religion and politics were inextricably linked in the conduct of the Hajj in historical times. High-ranking pilgrims were given safe conduct to perform their Hajj in times of strife and war by the Ottoman state, for example. Gifts were also routinely exchanged between Muslim plenipotentiaries when one side of the Indian Ocean sent pilgrims to the Arabian Peninsula, and the Ottomans then received these delegations and sent them home after looking after them in the Hejaz.[25] Among the Mughals, such politics regarding the Hajj were very apparent, as deals often had to be cut with the Portuguese to get ships through the Arabian Sea and past blockades of Iberian squadrons stationed there for military, political, and economic reasons. The Mughal emperor Akbar eventually worked out a normative system whereby one of his ships a year was given a *cartaz* by the Portuguese, with the stated objective of this vessel being the performance of Hajj by the emperor's ladies and courtiers. Plenty of commerce seems to have accompanied this annual ship as well, since elite families worked all available political angles to get their commodities on this one protected vessel, which they knew would be safe from predation.[26] These were some of the parameters and wheels that needed to be greased in the Ottoman and South Asian spheres of the Indian Ocean. Yet how did religion and politics mix further east in the Malay courts of the same era? How can we get a sense of the importance of the Hajj to these equations by reading through period Malay texts?

One of the best places to start in an examination of the texts is with the word *Haj* or *Hajj* itself—the simple description of the actual pilgrimage to Mecca in the Malay chronicles (table 4.2). The appearance of the actual term is important, of course, because it shows knowledge at specific temporal and geographic junctures in the Malay world of this all-important conduit between Southeast Asia and the Middle East. The fact that Malay scribes were instructed to write the Hajj into the histories of the various Malay sultanates is evidence that this religious institution was deemed vital to record in political documents, probably as a signpost of Muslim legitimacy between the periphery and the center. A bond that crosses space and distance is therefore being showcased. The first notice of the Hajj being specifically mentioned in a Malay text is in the *Hikayat Muhammad Hanafiah*, which has been dated to roughly 1450; the next notices after this are not until the very late sixteenth century, when both the *'Aqa 'id al-Nasafi* (c. 1590) and the *Syair Hamzah Fansuri* both mention the pilgrimage as such.[27] Throughout the seventeenth, eighteenth, and nineteenth centuries after this, the Hajj appears again and again in the various Malay histories, sometimes only sparingly—such as in the *Hikayat Aceh* (c. 1625), the *Hikayat Tanah Hitu* (c. 1650), and the *Adat Raja Melayu* (1779), where it is mentioned only once in

Table 4.2 **Textual Fragments: The Hajj and Hajjis in the Malay Texts over Five Centuries**

Hikayat Bayan Budiman (1371 CE):

"...*lamanya maka baginda pun minta izin hendak pergi haji kepada anakanda baginda dan kepada segala wazir menteri. Maka....*"

"...for a long while already His Majesty had been requesting permission to go on Hajj to his son and to all the viziers and ministers...."

Aqa id al-Nasafi (c. 1590 CE):

"...*ketiga, memberi zakat; keempat, puasa; kelima, hajj. Didahulukan Nabi, salla Allahu 'alayhi wa sallam, sebut akan....*"

"...third, to pay out the tithe; fourth, to fast; and fifth, the Hajj. So said the Prophet of Allah, peace be upon Him...."

Hikayat Aceh (c. 1625 CE):

"...*kamu dua orang, di mana negeri kamu?" Maka sahut haji Ahmad: "Negeri kami hampir negeri Acéh Dar as-Salam dan datang....*"

"...You two, where do you two come from?" And Hajji Ahmad answered, "Our country is just near Aceh, the Abode of Peace...."

Hikayat Patani (1730 CE):

"...*Haji Abdul Rahman itu asalnya orang Jawa, turun dari haji ia beristeri di Patani ini. Adapun Fakih Abdul Manan itu orang....*"

"...Haji Abdul Rahman was a man who hailed from Java, but when he came back from Hajj he married in Pattani...."

Surat Keterangan Syeikh Jaluluddin (c. 1821 CE):

"...*Batu Tebal, sebab ada masa dahulu, sebalum ia pergi haji, adalah ia diam pada nagari itu, karena ia mengambil ilmu....*"

"...because previously, before he had undertaken his Hajj, he had been residing in that country, because he was accumulating knowledge...."

All translations by Eric Tagliacozzo from provided vernaculars.

Sources: R. O. Winstedt, ed., *Hikayat Bayan Budiman* (Kuala Lumpur: Oxford University Press, 1966), p. 244, line 9; Syed Muhammad Naquib Al-Attas, ed., *The Oldest Known Malay Manuscript: A 16th Century Translation of the `Aqâ´id of al-Nasafî* (Kuala Lumpur: University of Malaya, 1988), p. 3; Teuku Iskandar, ed., *De Hikajat Atjéh* ('s-Gravenhage: Nijhoff, 1958), p. 240, line 9; Siti Hawa Salleh, ed., *Hikayat Merong Mahawangsa* (Kuala Lumpur: Penerbit Universiti Malaya, 1991), p. 77, line 11; E. Ulrich Kratz and Adriyetti Amir, eds., *Surat Keterangan Syeikh Jalaluddin karangan Fakih Saghir* (Kuala Lumpur: Dewan Bahasa dan Pustaka, 2002), p. 6.

each text—but sometimes far more often, as when the term appears in other tracts more than a dozen times.[28] The descriptions can be anecdotal, as when mentioning the Hajj as part of a season or time of year, or the descriptions can be doctrinal, as when the Hajj is referenced as an important institution that all Muslims, at least once in their lives, must try to accomplish in a particular city-state. Either way, it is noticeable that mentions of Hajj become most frequent during the seventeenth century and then again in the early nineteenth century, in contrast to the eighteenth century, when such descriptions are rarer.

The term *Hajji* appears over a long period of time and over large geographies in the Malay texts of this period. The distinction with the term *Hajj*, of course, is personal—when Hajjis are being referenced, it is people, and often solitary individuals, who are being written into the record. The first record of a Hajji in the *Hikayat Bayan Budiman* (1371) significantly predates any record of the Hajj as an institution.[29] This implies that at least a few individuals were able to make the extremely long and dangerous sea voyage to Arabia at this time. Although there are references to the Hajj itself after this as a practice or institution, the next mention of individual Hajjis does not come until the early seventeenth century. The *Hikayat Aceh* (c. 1625) then mentions a number of different pilgrims (a Haji Ahmad and a Haji Abdullah, among others) as having made the pilgrimage across the Indian Ocean.[30] Aceh was in its period of florescence at this time, and its relative geographic proximity to Mecca explains why more pilgrims left from here than anywhere else in the region. In subsequent centuries after this, diverse Malay texts describe Hajjis traveling and preparing to travel, bringing messages and ideologies back and forth across the ocean, and even participating in court intrigues back in Southeast Asia. The diversity and breadth of these notices is rather remarkable, in fact. Taken together, these mentions demonstrate individuals weaving together religion and politics on a very personal basis during this time.

The mention of Mecca in these Malay texts is also noticeable and signified many things beyond the physical locality of a town. It has already been discussed how Mecca gradually became the tidal center of the Red Sea and, by extension, of a larger maritime space stretching west into the Mediterranean, south toward Africa, and east toward South and Southeast Asia over time. Mecca was the center of the vast maritime world of the *dar al-Islam*, despite the fact that the city was not even a port, but was rather removed to the hinterland of the coastal city of Jeddah. *Mecca* appears very early in the Malay records, and the term repeats itself in classical Malay texts more than *Hajj*, *Hajjis*, or any other appellation that has connections with the pilgrimage. Interestingly, it certainly appears far more often than Medina (table 4.3).[31] As was the case with the term *Hajji*, Mecca first appears in the late-fourteenth-century text the *Hikayat Bayan Budiman* and remained thereafter quite central to many of the most famous texts, and even

Table 4.3 **Textual Fragments: Mecca and Medina in the Malay Texts over Five Centuries**

Hikayat Humammad Hanafiah (c. 1450 CE):

"...*datang dari benua Syam juga, karena segala isi Makkah dan Madinah semuhanya kasihan. Maka diceriterakan oleh orang....*"

"...there were those who came from the land of Siam too, because all of those in Mecca and Medina felt compassion. So it is said by the people..."

Syair Hamzah Fansuri (c. 1590 CE):

"...*Hamzah Fansuri di dalam Makkah, mencari Tuhan di bayt al-Ka'bah, di Barus ke Qudus terlalu....*"

"...while in Mecca, Hamzah Fansuri was searching for God in the Ka'ba, from Barus to Jerusalem...."

Hikayat Sultan Ibrahim ibn Adam (c. 1650 CE):

"...*itu maka Muhammad Tahir itu pun sampailah ke Makkah, lalu masuk ke Mesjid al-haram. Adapun umurnya Muhammad Tahir....*"

"...and when Muhammad Tahir finally got to Mecca, he then entered the Prophet's mosque ('the forbidden mosque'). His age at that point...."

Hikayat Hang Tuah (c. 1700 CE):

"...*sampai tiga hari lamanya amir haji duduk di Mekah itu, lalu memakai emas dan perak itu masing-masing dengan surat....*"

"...for three days the Hajji sat in Mecca, and later he used both gold and silver in turn to write letters...."

Hikayat Perintah Negeri Benggala (1811 CE):

"...*ke benua Rum dan Mesir dan negeri benua Cina ke Mekah Medinah, sekalian orang negeri itu mari bernyaga dan berbegar....*"

"...from the Ottoman lands and Egypt, and (even) from China they come to Mecca and Medina, all of them come here for trade and circumambulation..."

All translations by Eric Tagliacozzo from provided vernaculars.

Sources: L. F. Brakel, ed., *The Hikayat Muhammad Hanafiyah* (The Hague: Martinus Nijhoff, 1975), p. 16, line 210; G. W. J. Drewes and L. F. Brakel, *The Poems of Hasmzah Fansuri* (Dordrecht: Foris, 1986), p. 21, line 14; Russell Jones, *Hikayat Sultan Ibrahim ibn Adam* (Berkeley: Center for South and Southeast Asia Studies, University of California, 1985), p. 144, line 16; Kassim Ahmad, ed., *Hikayat Hang Tuah* (Kuala Lumpur: Dewan Bahasa dan Pustaka, 1975), p. 477, line 23; Cyril Skinner, ed., *Ahmad Rijaluddin's Hikayat Perintah Negeri Benggala* (Leiden: Martinus Nijhoff, 1982), p. 28, line 18.

many obscure ones.[32] Mecca appears in the transmission of Muslim founding narratives and entered the Malay world in this way a number of times in the early modern period.[33] Yet it appears as a historical place as well, where Southeast Asians go on their travels and then return from, back to the lands beneath the winds.[34] Crucially, it is also referenced as a place that legitimates power in the archipelago, establishing and broadcasting connections between learned religious men in residence in the Hejaz and the various cosmopolitan city-states of the Malay world.[35] This cosmopolitanism is continually reinscribed with the mention of Mecca in the texts, each time being done so publicly by regional players in the political orbit of the region. Considering the efficacy and indeed the potency of this toponym for both political and religious reasons, it is therefore little wonder that the term *Mecca* appears so frequently in so many of the surviving texts.

Sufi brotherhoods, too, were crucial in the marriage of the religious and the political. These organizations became vitally important to the dissemination of Islam in various parts of the world.[36] Though some orders (like the Qadiriyya) became well-known in many places, in Southeast Asia members of a number of different brotherhoods traveled through the region, including men such as Hamzah al-Fansuri, Shams al-Din al-Sumatrani, and 'Abd al-Ra'uf al-Singkili.[37] From roughly the fifteenth century to the end of the eighteenth century, Sufism played an important role in conditioning the kinds of Islam that were practiced in the courts, as well as in the countryside among less literate populations. It has been said that Shams al-Din initiated Sultan Iskandar Muda of Aceh into the Naqshbandiyya order, for example, and 'Abd al-Ra'uf al-Singkili converted many in Southeast Asia to his particular branch of Sufi knowledge, the Shattariyya. The main orders ended up being diffuse in this corner of Asia, comprising the Qadiriyya, Shadhiliyya, Rifa'iyya, Naqshbandiyya, Shattariyya, and the Ahmadiyya, though all appeared in widely varying concentrations.[38] An established orthodoxy was not instilled until the late eighteenth and early nineteenth centuries, at least for the most part.[39] The Hajj allowed these kinds of disparate ideas to circulate rather freely, and for many streams of thought to wash up along the same set of shores. The pilgrimage therefore played an important part in the diffusion of Sufism and in the elaboration of Sufi ideas and ideologies into a number of different forms among the many political centers of the region.

Regional Differences and Three Archetypal Texts

Azyumardi Azra was among the first to trace the clear genealogies of religion and politics moving between Southeast Asia and the Middle East during the early modern era. Azra established the web of patronage connections—both intellectual and interpersonal—between various itinerant Sufi teachers in the Indian Ocean across the seventeenth and eighteenth centuries. He started these genealogies with the rather obscure figures of Sibghat Allah (d. 1606) and 'Ala' al-Din al-Babili (d. 1666) but also included better known religious travelers, such as Al-Raniri, al-Sankili, and al-Maqassari.[40] Many of these men were Hajjis. These travelers and their relationships were very important in forging a combination of religion and politics in the Malay courts. Some foundational scholars have argued that the Padri War in West Sumatra could be directly attributed to the return of three specific Hajjis to Padang in 1803, for example.[41] Newer work has now attributed the war's causes to an ongoing struggle for influence between different Sufi orders (specifically the Naqshbandis, who ultimately won, and the Shattaris, who eventually lost out on power).[42] This West Sumatran example is only the most famous one, yet it shows how the Hajj and larger circuits of religious travel impacted the region. Geographically, contests such as this one played out in numerous places across the archipelago, even in very old ports such as the Sultanate of Brunei in the mid-nineteenth century.[43]

The scattered geography of these frictions is interesting. The spatial diffusion of period Malay-language sources underscores how wide-ranging and long-standing debates were among sultanates over what sort of Islamic societies they wanted to be. On the Malay Peninsula, these contestations date back to the *Sejarah Melayu*, which has been given a seventeenth-century provenance but is certainly from much earlier times. Mecca is referenced on numerous occasions in this famous history, showing an early concern with ideas and discourse emanating from the distant city.[44] The *Hikayat Hang Tuah* (c. 1700, from Kedah) evinces some of these tensions as well and gives more weight to the Hajj's importance in its worldview than any previous Malay text.[45] One line from this *hikayat* gives us this sense of Mecca and its grandeur: "all of the people of Mecca assemble to go with the sharif, each with their thrones of honor, hundreds of standards and banners of silk, tapestry, velvet, and gold cloth all fluttering in the breeze like a floating fort, moving on the pilgrimage to the hill of Arafat."[46] In the early nineteenth century, the *Hikayat Merong Mahawangsa* (1821) also mentions events in Mecca, and the *Silsilah Perak* (1826) speaks of Hajjis just a few years later.[47] Similar references to Hajjis exist in Kelantanese texts of the late 1830s as well.[48] Fitting these pieces together—from Melaka, Kedah, Perak, Kelantan, and other sultanates on the peninsula—demonstrates that ideas about how to marry Islam and politics in everyday life were a constant preoccupation of Malay writers. Up and down the peninsula, Malay elites were continually integrating and reintegrating information, some of it doctrinal, some of it political, and some of it historical. They refashioned themselves and their courts in the process. The Hajj and news of the Arabian Peninsula appear to have been crucial to these ongoing processes, as the pilgrimage continually brought new ideas about religion and politics to the wider Malay world.

What was true in the courts of the Malay Peninsula also occurred across the Straits in the islands of the archipelago. The *Hikayat Raja Pasai*, one of the earliest of this genre of texts and traceable to 1390 in the northernmost part of Aceh,[49] mentioned Mecca in its pages, as did another late-fourteenth-century Malay-language tract, the *Hikayat Muhammad Hanafiyyah*.[50] Clearly, archipelago eyes were already on the Middle East at this time. By the seventeenth century, there were also outposts of Islam in Borneo, and texts such as the *Kutei Chronicle* (c. 1625) and the *Hikayat Banjar* (c. 1663) show that even courts outside the main archipelago population centers were beginning to combine Islam and politics in interesting ways.[51] These texts were local histories and elite genealogies, but they also portrayed the Islamic statecraft of emerging polities and their connections with the Middle East, both for internal and external audiences. A number of these manuscripts were copied, such as the *Syair Ken Tambuhan* (c. 1750) and various texts from Makassar, Palembang, Bengkulu, and Singapore.[52] By the nineteenth century, there are texts or documents from comparatively backwatered places, such as the *Warkah Brunei* (1819–22), and from emerging ones, such as the *Surat Ingatan Tengku Said al-Qadri* (1824) from Belitung. Both of these texts specifically mention the circulation of Hajjis as well. Cognizance of the pilgrimage to Mecca and the spiritual (and political) benefits of this journey was therefore spreading to even the most out-of-the-way places in the archipelago.[53]

The rest of this chapter deals with a closer examination of three representative Malay texts: one from the seventeenth, one from the eighteenth, and one from the nineteenth century. The *Bustan al-Salatin* was begun in 1638 and finished sometime over the next five years; it has been briefly shown already that this text references a number of disparate topics, including the heavens and earth, prophets and kings, the history and politics of Aceh, and the foundation stories of Adam and Abraham.[54] As was the case with the *Syair Ken Tambuhan*, the *Bustan al-Salatin* existed in multiple copies.[55] In addition to the subjects sketched out previously, it also deals with the nature of the sun, moon, and stars; with Nature as a totality; with the rivers and the seas; and with a great variety of other topics. It is an encyclopedic text. Within this encyclopedic corpus, though, are also references to Muslim pilgrims, some of them leaving the Malay world for Hajj, others on their way for Umrah, or the "lesser pilgrimage." The prices of pilgrimage are mentioned, as are the possibilities of performing the rites more than once.[56] Mecca (a place that would have still been difficult to get to in the middle decades of the seventeenth century) is also cited a number of times.[57] In sketching out a cosmology of the world, the Hajj and travel to Mecca take their place alongside natural phenomena, history, and myth. It is not hard to see why the

Hajj and connections to the Middle East could be part of this vision. These distant desert landscapes were not only actual places of religious and political power but also historical domains of potency and efficacy portrayed in the foundation stories of Islam itself. Religion informed politics, politics informed history, and history informed religion in an unending circle.

The *Hikayat Patani*, likely written in 1730, contains other useful clues as to how religion and politics mixed in these courts. Pattani (today in southern Thailand, a predominantly Buddhist country) was a vigorous Muslim polity in the eighteenth century, exerting influence far beyond its size and frontier geographic position. The *Hikayat Patani* tells the history of this important sultanate and of its rulers and elites, and it describes Hajjis in continual motion between the Middle East and the Southeast Asian realms. Hajjis from Java, Pasai (Aceh), and the Malay Peninsula are all referenced as being in transit.[58] Some of these same men reappear later in the 1700s. One Pattani scholar, Daud ibn Abd Allah al-Patani, journeyed to Mecca in the second half of the century and became the most important Southeast Asian Muslim living, writing, and teaching in the city during this time.[59] He probably studied in Arabia with another prominent Southeast Asian teacher who had preceded him, 'Abd al-Samad al-Palimbani, so it is clear that there were others among these Hajjis who had stayed.[60] Al-Patani trained other Malay world Muslims during the thirty-five years he was there, many of whom gained status because of their time in the Hejaz and who fanned out across the archipelago to teach their own students when they returned.[61] While he was there, he wrote at least fifty-seven works on an extremely broad range of topics.[62] Al-Patani's fatwas and decrees became part of the political, juridical, and religious worlds of Pattani over time, partially because a steady stream of sojourners across the Indian Ocean kept these connections fresh.

Finally, the *Pelayaran Abdullah ke Mekka*, or "The Voyage of Abdullah to Mecca," written in 1854, is notable in a number of respects, not least of which is the way that traditional politics are absent from the central concerns of the text.[63] This is an individual's journey, not an exegesis on how Islam's currents have been incorporated or rejected by any particular polity in the Malay world (box 4.1). The narrator performs a journey to the holy cities, but he does so as a single actor, not in the slipstream of religio-political transmission of the sort we have now seen for several centuries. He describes personal moments, such as a conversation with a ship captain, another pilgrim's actions and demeanor, and specific events he experienced while on the journey.[64] Yet that does not mean that no politics are incipient in this text. Abdullah also seems to offer commentary on certain aspects of the Muslim Malay world of the sultanates that he knew were under siege. Where did allegiances belong—to one's Malay sovereign (as Malays had been taught since time immemorial) or to the global *umma* of Muslims as a whole? Which center represented the true center of a Malay

---

Box 4.1 **Munshi Abdullah's Pelayaran Ka-Judah,**
"The Journey to Jeddah"

Munshi Abdullah was a Malay man who spent much of his existence in Melaka and Singapore in the mid nineteenth century. He journeyed to the Hejaz in 1854 and died in Jeddah that same year. Here is a section of his account, and also a poem he left, both about his journey to the heart of the Muslim faith.

"Maka ada-lah ku-lihat negeri Judah itu terlalu ramai-nya, oleh sebab itu-lah pangkalan segala kapal kapal dan berjenis-jenis orang yang datang daripada sagenap sagenap negeri. Maka saudagar pun terlalu banyak dan dagang pun tumpah ruah-lah di-situ. Maka orang pun berbagai-bagai bangsa boleh di-lihat di-situ. Maka kedai pun terlalu-lah banyak berjenis-jeis barang oleh sebab datang daripada tiap tiap negeri karena negeri itu-lah pangkalan beberapa negeri. Hatta, maka tinggal-lah beberapa hari di-Judah itu oleh sebab menantikan sheikh datang dari Mekah. Maka kemudian datang-lah Haji Adam. Sa-telah sudah bertemu lalu memberi salam, maka dudok-lah ia dua hari di-Judah, lalu menyewa unta serta bermuat barang barang. Lalu berjalan-lah naik ka-Mekah dari waktu asar itu; maka samalam-malaman itu berjalan. Maka pada esok-nya pagi pagi masok-lah ka-Mekah dari Kubbah Mahmud berjalan dengan Sheikh Haji Adam serta memakai ihram berkain puteh dan berselimut puteh."

"I saw that Jeddah is very busy. At the pier, ships and all sorts of people arrive from every country. There are many traders and merchandise is everywhere. People of many different races can be seen there. There are many ships with all kinds of goods brought from every country because Jeddah is the port for several countries. The stay at Jeddah was for several days because of the need to wait for the Sheikh to arrive from Mecca. Then Haji Adam came. After meeting and making our greetings, he stayed two days in Jeddah before hiring a camel and loading it with supplies. The departure for Mecca was after the afternoon prayer. We traveled all night and reached Mecca the following day, early in the morning. Accompanied by Sheikh Haji Adam we entered the Kubbah Mahmud (Mahmud's Arch), wearing the two white sheets of the *ihram* and a white covering."

"Serta masok-kah aku ka-dalam
   negeri yang mulia
Maka terlupa-lah aku akan
   Nicmat dan kesukaan dunia
Saperti mendapat shurga dengan

"I go within the noble city
I am oblivious of the joys
   and pleasures of this world.
As if already possessed of
   heaven and all it holds

Isi-nya sedia   I give thanks a thousand
Menguchap-lah aku sa-ribu.   times to the most noble God.
   Shukor akan Tuhan yang   I am oblivious of the troubles
   Mahamulia   and torments of the journey.
Terlupa-lah aku beberapa   The months and torments
   Kesusahan dan siksa di-jalan   brought about by the
Oleh sebab berahi dan rindu   passion, the longing, for
   Akan bait Allah beberapa bulan."   The house of Allah."

Sources: Virginia Matheson and A. C. Milner, eds., *Perceptions of the Haj: Five Malay Texts* (Singapore: ISEAS, 1984), pp. 22–23; Kassim Ahmad, ed., *Pelayaran ka-Judah* (Kuala Lumpur: Oxford University Press, 1964), pp. 155–156.

Muslim's life—his homeport and polity or the holy cities of the Prophet in a far-away desert? These religious and political concerns, very much intertwined, signal a new consciousness in Malay writing that was fairly avant-garde with Abdullah's text.[65] Abdullah's writings also show the beginnings of a new path, one where individuals—rather than the collective—had the right to make their own decisions about these questions. Situated as it was on the cusp of the colonial takeover of most of Southeast Asia, his text seems prescient and achingly modern in certain ways. Abdullah's account signaled the end, in some respects, of an era of the Malay Muslim world and the florescence of a new regional situation, where these concerns would soon become both widespread and common.

Conclusion

Examining period texts clearly shows that religion and politics in the historical period mixed in the Malay world in diverse and interesting ways. An enormous amount of translation of Malay texts occurred during these centuries, both of Middle Eastern materials into Southeast Asian languages and of the translation of concepts, mores, and doctrines into local idioms. Many manuscripts that came to the lands beneath the winds had little to do with politics: a number of them focused on historical figures, such as the *Hikayat Nur Muhammad* ("Story of the Mystic Light of Muhammad") or the *Hikayat Iskandar Zulkairnan* ("Story of Alexander the Great"). Other texts received Malay renderings as they traveled, such as the *Qisas al-Anbiya*, and still others dealt with the martial exploits of relatives of the classical Hassan and Hussein, the sons of the murdered Caliph 'Ali (The *Hikayat Muhamad Hanafiyyah*).[66] Yet by the early seventeenth century, there was enough of a milieu of scholarship, translation, and transmission taking place between the two sides of the Indian Ocean that it became clear that religious and political concepts were being fused in the courts of the Malay world. Aceh seems to have been at the vanguard of this process, as there were a number of known Acehnese Hajjis in the Ottoman Empire by 1600.[67] Scholars such as Hamzah Fansuri were traveling to the Hejaz just before this time, and these men were being initiated into some of the great Sufi brotherhoods, so it makes sense to see these fusions, too, as part of this quickening of contact. The Hajj became the single most important strand in this bundle of transmission possibilities that included religion, diplomacy, education, and trade, and it played a key role in the evolution of Southeast Asian sultanates during this time.

When Hang Tuah supposedly made his pilgrimage in the fifteenth century, the Hajj, it is reported, was mostly an afterthought; the great Malay traveler's main reason for being in the Middle East was political, but he performed the religious duties because he was already nearby.[68] A few centuries later, this nonchalance would have likely been unthinkable—any Muslim who managed to get across the vast spaces of the Indian Ocean would have undertaken Hajj as one of the main reasons for the voyage and would have proudly proclaimed this fact. We very much hear this in the *Tuhfat al-Nafis*, published in the 1860s in the islands just south of Singapore:

> (The Prince) went to Baqi, to the grave of the companions. He then traveled to Mount Uhud to the grave of the uncle of the prophet (may Allah bless him and grant him peace). Raja Ahmed made pilgrimages to all of the places people visit. After Raja Ahmed had been in Medina for about eleven days, he returned to Mecca the Exalted.... (He) was the first prince from Riau and Lingga to make the pilgrimage. No one before him had done so. It could be said that he opened the way for other Riau princes to make the pilgrimage to Mecca the Exalted.[69]

Despite its geographic marginality, Southeast Asia was an increasingly acknowledged part of this religio-political world. Archipelago scholars, not only Hamzah but also many others, such as Abd al-Ra'uf and Ali al-Jawi al-Fansuri al-Singkili, helped make this so by sending religious opinions back to their homelands and describing what a just Muslim polity should be through their fatwas and their rulings.[70] A number of these scholars, such as Shaykh Abdul Malik Abdullah of Trengganu, eventually stayed in the Hejaz for significant periods of their lives. Their disciples and various Hajjis carried their words on statecraft and the correct manner of a Muslim life well lived back to the Malay world.[71] The Hajj was therefore a vast enabler of this transoceanic system, merging religion and politics into one oceanwide embrace over the course of hundreds of years.

NOTES

1. Arab geographers clearly knew something of this part of the world by the time that the second millennium ce began, and by Marco Polo's voyage in the late thirteenth century, the first steps of Islamization as a combined religious and political process in Southeast Asia were already under way. See G. R. Smith, "Ibn al-Mujawir's 7th/13th Century Arabia—The Wondrous and the Humorous," in A. K. Irvine, R. B. Serjeant, and G. Rex Smith, eds., *Miscellany of Middle Eastern Articles in Memoriam Thomas Muir Johnstone 1924–83* (Harlow, England: Longman, 1988), pp. 111–124; Henri Yule and Henri Cordier, *The Book of Ser Marco Polo*, vol. 2 (Amsterdam: Philo, 1975), p. 284; G. R. Tibbetts, *A Study of the Arabic Texts Containing Material on South-East Asia* (Leiden: Brill, 1979), p. 114; and for a good overview, Michael Laffan, "Finding Java: Muslim Nomenclature of Insular Southeast Asia from Srivijaya to Snouck Hurgronje," in Eric Tagliacozzo, ed., *Southeast Asia and the Middle East: Islam, Movement, and the Longue Duree* (Palo Alto, CA: Stanford University Press, 2009), pp. 17–64.

2. Much ink has been spilled about the arrival of Islam in this region, and some of the foundational interpretations of both how and when this happened have been challenged recently by new scholarship pointing to potential holes in the early theories and also to the likely provenance of multiple wells of inspiration for Islamization as a social and religious process. Elizabeth Lambourne, "Tombstones, Texts, and Typologies: Seeing Sources for the Early History of Islam in Southeast Asia," *JESHO*, 51, 2008: 252–286; L. Kalus and C. Guillot, "Réinterprétation des plus anciennes stèles funéraires islamiques nousantariennes: I. Les deux inscriptions du 'Champa,'" *Archipel*, 64, 2003: 63–90; L. Kalus and C. Guillot, "Réinterprétation des plus anciennes stèles funéraires islamiques nousantariennes: II. La stèle de Leran (Java) datée de 475/1082 et les stèles associées," *Archipel*, 67, 2003: 17–36; G. W. J. Drewes, "New Light on the Coming of Islam to Indonesia?" *Bijdragen tot de Taal-, Land- en Volkenkunde*, 124 (1968): 433–459; Stuart Robson, "Java at the Crossroads," *Bijdragen tot de Taal-, Land- en Volkenkunde*, 137/2–3 (1981): 259–292; Elizabeth Lambourn, "From Cambay to Samudera-Pasai and Gresik: The Export of Gujerati Grave Memorials to Sumatra and Java in the Fifteenth Century C.E.," *Indonesia and the Malay World*, 31/90 (2003): 221–289.

3. See the useful description of this in Mohamed Taib Osman, "Introduction," in Mohamed Taib Osman, ed., *Islamic Civilization in the Malay World* (Kuala Lumpur: Dewan Bahasa dan Pustaka, 1997), pp. xxxxi, xlii.

4. Hussin Mutalib, "The Islamic Malay Polity in Southeast Asia," in Mohamed Taib Osman, ed., *Islamic Civilization in the Malay World* (Kuala Lumpur: Dewan Bahasa dan Pustaka, 1997), pp. 1–48, especially pp. 7–9.

5. On the ambit of texts and history and their intersections in the Malay world, see Hendrik Maier, *We Are Playing Relatives: A History of Malay Writing* (Leiden: KITLV, 2004). See also the newest encyclopedic contribution to debates on Malay literature, Vladimir Braginsky, *The Heritage of Traditional Malay Literature: A Survey of Genres, Writings, and Literary Views* (Leiden: KITLV, 2004).

6. See R. O. Winstedt, ed., *Hikayat Bayan Budiman* (Kuala Lumpur: Oxford University Press, 1966); see also Fritz Schulze, "Islamizing Malay Culture: The Evidence of Malay Court Chronicles," in Fritz Schulze and Holger Warnk, eds., *Insular Southeast Asia: Linguistic and Cultural Studies in Honour of Bernd Nothofer* (Wiesbaden: Harrassowitz Verlag, 2006), pp. 131–140.

7. The translation we now have of the *Hikayat Muhammad Hanafiyyah* was composed of some eight different versions of the manuscript. Marco Polo actually mentioned Perbak as the first Muslim polity. L. F. Brakel, ed., *The Hikayat Muhammad Hanafiyyah, a Medieval Muslim-Malay Romance* (The Hague: Martinus Nijhoff, 1975), Bibliotheca Indonesica of KITLV, 12; A. Samad Ahmad, ed., *Hikayat Amir Hamzah* (Kuala Lumpur: Dewan Bahasa dan Pustaka, 1987). The dates given are for the time periods that scholars think the texts themselves were written.

8. See Russell Jones, ed., *Hikayat Raja Pasai* (Kuala Lumpur: Fajar Bakti, 1987); also see A. H. Hill, "*Hikayat Raja-Raja Pasai*, a Revised Romanised Version," *JMBRAS*, 33/2, 1960; and Russell Jones, "The Texts of the *Hikayat Raja Pasai*, a Short Note," *JMBRAS*, 53/1 (1980).

9. Syed Muhammad Naquib al-Attas, ed., *The Oldest Known Malay Manuscript: A 16th Century Translation of the 'Aqā'id of al-Nasafī* (Kuala Lumpur: University of Malaya, 1988).

10. G. W. J. Drewes and L. F. Brakel, *The Poems of Hamzah Fansuri* (Dordrecht: Foris, 1986). In Hamzah alone, see pp. 9, 18, 19, 21, and 34.

11. Syed Muhammad Naquib al-attas, *The Mysticism of Hamzah Fansuri* (Kuala Lumpur: University of Malaya Press, 1970), p. 9.

12. See *Bukhari al-Jauhari, Taj al-Salatin*, ed. Khalid M. Hussain (Kuala Lumpur: Dewan Bahasa dan Pustaka, 1992). Also see the catalogue compiled by E. P. Weiringa, *Catalogue of Malay and Minangkabau Manuscripts in the Library of Leiden University and Other Collections in the Netherlands. Volume I, Comprising the Acquisitions of Malay Manuscripts in Leiden University up to the Year 1896*, ed. Joan de Lijster-Streef and Jan Just Witkam (Leiden: Legatum Warnerianum, 1998), p. 487.

13. For four excellent studies both of the past of Aceh and the past as seen in the present, see Denys Lombard, *Le Sultanat d'Atjeh au Temps d'Iskandar Muda, 1607–1636* (Paris: EFEO, 1967); Anthony Reid, *An Indonesian Frontier: Acehnese and Other Histories of Sumatra* (Singapore: Singapore University Press, 2005); James Siegel, *The Rope of God* (Berkeley: University of California Press, 1969); James Siegel, *Shadow and Sound: The Historical Thought of a Sumatran People* (Chicago: University of Chicago Press, 1979).

14. Teuku Iskandar, ed., *De Hikajat Atjéh* ('s-Gravenhage: Nijhoff, 1958), Verhandelingen van het Koninklijk Instituut voor Taal-, Land en Volkenkunde, deel 26. For Hajjis, see pp. 239, 240, 241, and 242, for example; for Medina, see pp. 197, 235, 239, 240, and 241. See also Vladimir Braginsky, *Structure, Date and Sources of the Hikayat Aceh Revisited, BKI*, 162/4, 2006: 441–467.

15. See Saya Shiraishi, "A Study of Bustanu's Salatin (The Garden of the Kings)," in Takashi Shiraishi et al., eds., *Reading Southeast Asia: Translations of Contemporary Scholarship on Southeast Asia* (Ithaca, NY: Cornell Southeast Asia Program, 1990), pp. 41–55.

16. See, for just a few examples, C. A. Mees, "De Kroniek van Kutai" (PhD Dissertation, Universiteit te Leiden, Santpoort, 1935), p. 240; Hans Straver, Chris van Fraassen, and Jan van der Putten, eds., *Ridjali: Historie van Hitu. Een Ambonse geschiedenis uit de zeventiende eeuw* (Utrecht: LSEM (Landelijk Steunpunt Educatie Molukkers), 2004), pp. 28 and 59; Russell Jones, *Hikayat Sultan Ibrahim ibn Adham: An Edition of an Anonymous Malay Text with Translation and Notes* (Berkeley: Center for South and Southeast Asia Studies, University of California, 1985), Monograph series no. 27, pp. 138, 142, 225, and 226; Hendrik Maier, "Sedjarah Melayu—Maleise Geschiedenissen," in *Oosterse Omzwervingen—Klassieke Teksten over Indonesia uit Oost en West* (Leiden: KITLV, 2000), pp.153–184; A. Samad Ahmad, ed., *Sulalatus Salatin* (Sejarah Melayu) (Kuala Lumpur: Dewan Bahasa dan Pustaka, 1979), pp. 52–54; J. J. Ras, *Hikajat Bandjar: A Study in Malay Historiography* (The Hague: Nijhoff (Koninklijk Insitituut voor Taal-, Land- en Volkenkunde), 1968), pp. 307, 309, 315, and 325; Peter Riddell, *Transferring a Tradition: 'Abd Al-Ra'ūf Al-Singkilī's Rendering into Malay of the Jalalāyn Commentary* (Berkeley: Centers for South and Southeast Asia Studies, University of California, 1990), Monograph no. 31 (see especially the "autobiographical codicil" in the appendix); and Mohamad Jajuli A. Rahman, *The Malay Law Text* (Kuala Lumpur: Dewan Bahasa dan Pustaka, 1995), p. 14.

17. Henri Chambert-Loir, ed., *Cerita Asal Bangsa Jin dan Segala Dewa-Dewa* (Bandung: Penerbit Angkasa and Ecole français d'Extrême Orient, 1985), p. 2; and Kassim Ahmad, ed., *Hikayat Hang Tuah* (Kuala Lumpur: Dewan Bahasa dan Pustaka, 1975), pp. 472, 477, and 517. See also Hendrik Maier, "Tales of Hang Tuah—In Search of Wisdom and Good Behavior," *BKI*, 155, 1999: 342–361.

18. Hamdan Hassan, ed., *Surat al-Anbiya'* (Kuala Lumpur: Dewan Bahasa dan Pustaka, 1992); this is my count, at least.

19. G. W. J. Drewes, *Directions for Travellers on the Mystic Path* (The Hague: Nijhoff, 1977), Verhandelingen van het Koninklijk Instituut voor Taal-, Land- en Volkenkunde, 81, pp. 25 and 66; Panuti H. M. Sudjiman, ed., *Adat Raja-Raja Melayu* (Jakarta: Penerbit Universitas

Indonesia, 1983), pp. 61, 80; and Raja Chulan bin Hamid, *Misa Melayu*, ed. R. O. Winstedt (Kuala Lumpur: Pustaka Antara, 1962), pp. 52, 53, 57, 74, and 92.

20. This relative temporal disconnect for much of the eighteenth century has been confirmed by Annabel Teh Gallop of the British Library, personal communication, June 29, 2011.

21. See Raja Chulan bin Hamid, *Misa Melayu*, ed. R. O. Winstedt (Kuala Lumpur: Pustaka Antara, 1962), p. 28; C. Skinner, ed., *The Battle for Junk Ceylon: The Syair Sultan Maulana, Text, Translation and Notes* (Dordrecht: Foris, for the Koninklijk Instituut voor Taal-, Land- en Volkenkunde, 1985), p. 189; Jumsari Jusuf, Tuti Munawar, Retnadi Geria, and Amin Fukri Hoesin, eds., *Antologi Syair Simbolik dalam Sastra Indonesia Lama*, part 4 (Jakarta: Proyek Pembangunan Media Kebudayaan, Departemen Pendidikan dan Kebudayaan, Republik Indonesia, 1978), pp. 26, 29–30; Annabel Teh Gallop, "Malay Sources for the History of the Sultanate of Brunei in the Early Nineteenth Century: Some Letters from the Reign of Sultan Muhammad Kanzul Alam," in Victor T. King and A. V. M. Horton, eds., *From Buckfast to Borneo: Essays Presented to Father Robert Nicholl on the 85th Anniversary of His Birth, 27 March 1995* (Hull, England: University of Hull, 1995), pp. 207–235; Abdul Rahman al-Ahmadi, *Syair Siti Zubaidah Perang China, Perspektif Sejarah* (Kuala Lumpur: Perpustakaan Negara Malaysia, 1994), pp. 281, 431, 535, 540, and 590; Liaw Yock Fang, *Sejarah Kesusasteraan Melayu Klasik* (Jakarta: Erlangga, 1993), pp. 234–236; G. L. Koster, "Making It New in 1884: Lie Kim Hock's *Syair Siti Akbari*," *BKI*, 154/1, 1998: 95–115; Siti Hawa Salleh, *Hikayat Merong Mahawangsa* (Kuala Lumpur: Penerbit Universiti Malaya, 1991), pp. 77–78, 100, 103, and 105; Anonymous, "Surat Ingatan Tengku Said Mahmud Zaini ibnu almarhum al Habib 'Abdurrahman al Qodri," in *Surat-Surat Perdjandjian antara Kesultanan Riau dengan Pemerintahan2 V.O.C dan Hindia-Belanda, 1784–1909* (Djakarta: Arsip Nasional Republik Indonesia, 1970), p. 346; E. Ulrich Kratz & Adriyetti Amir, eds., *Surat Keterangan Syeikh Jala-luddin karangan Fakih Saghir* (Kuala Lumpur: Dewan Bahasa dan Pustaka, 2002), multiple mentions.

22. Amelia Ceridwen, "The Silsilah Raja-Raja Perak I: An Historical and Literary Investigation into the Political Significance of a Malay Court Genealogy," *JMBRAS*, 74/2 (2001): 69; W. E. Maxwell, "Notes on Two Perak Manuscripts," *JSBRAS*, 2, 1871: 181–191; Henri Chambert-Loir, ed., *Syair Kerajaan Bima* (Jakarta: Ecole français d'Extrême Orient, 1982), Naskah dan dokumen Nusantara III, pp. 28, 37, 99, 143, and 145; Henri Chambert-Loir, "Les Sources Malaises de l'histoire de Bima," *Archipel*, 20, 1980: 269–280; Muhammad Haji Salleh, ed., *Syair Tantangan Singapura abad kesembilan Belas* (Kuala Lumpur: Dewan Bahasa dan Pustaka, 1994); Cyril Skinner, *The Civil War in Kelantan in 1839* (Kuala Lumpur: Monographs of the Malaysian Branch, Royal Asiatic Society, 1965), pp. 14, 18, 20, and 22; Suryadi, *Syair Sunur: Teks dan Konteks 'otobiografi' Seorang Ulama Minangkabau Abad ke-19* (Padang, Indonesia: YDIKM and Citra Budaya, 2004), several mentions.

23. Amin Sweeney, *Karya Lengkap Abdullah bin Abdul Kadir Munsyi, Jilid 1* (Jakarta: Kepustakaan Populer Gramedia/École française d'Extrême-Orient, 2005), pp. 105, 107, 109, 111, and 139.

24. For a useful discussion of the trans–Indian Ocean Islamic milieu at the end of the nineteenth century, see Nico Kaptein, *The Muhimmat al-Nafa'is: A Bilingual Meccan Fatwa Collection for Indonesian Muslims from the End of the Nineteenth Century* (Jakarta: INIS, 1997); and Nico Kaptein, "Meccan Fatwas from the End of the Nineteenth Century on Indonesian Affairs," *Studia Islamika*, 2/4, 1995: 141–159.

25. Suraya Faroqhi, *Pilgrims and Sultans: The Hajj under the Ottomans, 1517–1683* (London: I. B. Tauris, 1994), pp. 127–142, 147–148.

26. Michael Pearson, *Pious Passengers: The Hajj in Earlier Times* (Dhaka, Bangladesh: University Press, 1994), pp. 105–106. In 1572–73, Akbar conquered Gujarat; he could have overrun the Portuguese enclave of Daman there, too, but he wanted peace with the Portuguese. Akbar wished for his ships to be able to trade to the Red Sea, but more than this, he also wanted his mother and other elite women to be able to go on Hajj. So, peace was quickly restored after his conquest of the province. Following this, Akbar was given one *cartaz*-pass a year by the

Portuguese. This meant that for this one ship only, he did not have to pay any duties on commodities going back and forth to and from the Red Sea. Powerful and politically well-connected merchants in Gujarat seized on this agreement and loaded their most valuable goods on this one ship to Jeddah every year, thereby escaping tax. On their own ships, they sent back less pricey commodities. The Portuguese felt they had to accept this state of affairs because they could not risk alienating Akbar. Akbar, meanwhile, complained of the Portuguese and their harrying of his trade and pilgrims, but the complaints seem to have been mostly window dressing for other Muslims, to show him as a valiant defender of the faith. He took no effective action, though he clearly could have done so. Portuguese policy in and around the Red Sea was a nuisance, therefore, but didn't manage to end trade, or the Hajj; it just dented both. The Portuguese also wanted trade, and despite the efforts of their own zealous priests, they allowed both commerce and the pilgrimage through their ships to keep the existing balance of trade going.

27. Brakel, *Hikayat Muhammad Hanfafiyyah*, p. 16; al-Attas, *Oldest Known Malay Manuscript*, several mentions; Drewes and Brakel, *Poems*, pp. 9, 19.

28. Iskandar, *Hikajat Atjéh*, p. 239; Straver et al., *Ridjali*, p. 28; Sudjiman, *Adat Raja-Raja Melayu*, p. 80.

29. Winstedt, *Hikayat Bayan Budiman*, p. 244.

30. Iskandar, *Hikajat Atjéh*, pp. 239–242, with many citations here.

31. Brakel, *Hikayat Muhammad Hanafiyyah*, pp. 12, 13, 17, and 25; al-Attas, *Oldest Known Manuscript*; Iskandar, *Hikajat Atjéh*, pp. 197, 235, and 239–241; Riddell, *Transfering a Tradition*, multiple citations; Ahmad, *Hikayat Hang Tuah*, pp. 475–477, 501; Skinner, *Hikayat Perintah Negeri Benggala*, p. 28; Salleh, *Hikayat Merong Mahawangsa*, p. 103; and see also more generally Sweeney, *Karya Lengkap Abdullah bin Abdul Kadir Munsyi*; and Suryadi, *Syair Sunur*.

32. Winstedt, *Hikayat Bayan Budiman*, pp. 244–245.

33. Russell Jones, ed., *Nuru'd-din ar-Raniri, Bustan al-Salatin Bab IV Fasal I (A Critical Edition of the First Part of Fasal I, Which Deals with Ibrahim ibn Adam)* (Kuala Lumpur: Dewan Bahasa dan Pustaka, 1974).

34. This is the most common use of Mecca in the texts, to delineate journeys in real time and space. But the reason of these journeys almost always has a meaning; they are not just narrative devices.

35. For just a few examples of this geographic spread, spanning Pasia (Aceh), Melaka, Banjramasin, Kedah, and Kelantan, see Jones, *Hikayat Raja Pasai*, pp. 24–26, 28, and 33; Ahmad, *Sulalatus Salatin (Sejarah Melayu)*, pp. 52–54; Ras, *Hikayat Banjar*, p. 3925; Salleh, *Hikayat Merong Mahawangsa*, pp. 77–78, 100, 103, and 105; Sweeney, *Karya Lengkap Abdullah bin Abdul Kadir Munsyi*, p. 139.

36. W. Stoddardt, *Le Soufisme* (Lausanne: Trois Continentes, 1979), p. 43.

37. Peter Riddell, *Islam and the Malay-Indonesian World: Transmission and Responses* (Honolulu: University of Hawai'i Press, 2001), p. 168.

38. O. B. Bakar, "Sufism in the Malay-Indonesian World," in S. H. Nasr, ed., *Islamic Spirituality II: Manifestations* (London: SCM, 1991), pp. 259–289, especially 259 and 271. See also Martin van Bruinessen, *Tarekat Naqsyabandiyah di Indonesia: Survei Historis, Geografis, dan Sosiologis* (Bandung, Indonesia: Mizan, 1992).

39. A. Milner, "Islam in the Muslim State," in M. B. Hooker, ed., *Islam in South-East Asia* (Leiden: Brill, 1988), pp. 23–49, especially p. 46.

40. See the detailed diagrams provided in Azra, *Origins of Islamic Reformism*, on pp. 14 and 26; see also the itineraries of these three last-mentioned men, on pp. 61, 72, and 100.

41. See, for example, Anthony Reid, "Nineteenth Century Pan-Islam in Indonesia and Malaysia," *Journal of Asian Studies*, 2, 1967: 272.

42. Michael Laffan's work has been notable in this respect; see also the best new book on West Sumatra, Jeffrey Hadler, *Muslims and Matriarchs: Cultural Resilience in Indonesia through Jihad and Colonialism* (Ithaca, NY: Cornell University Press, 2008), for further details on these events.

43. Spencer St. John, *Life in the Forests of the Far East*, 2 vols. (Kuala Lumpur: Oxford in Asia Historical Reprints, Oxford University Press, 1974), 2:258–259.

44. See Ahmad, *Sulalatus Salatin*, pp. 52, 53, and 54; for an overview, see also R. Roolvink, "The Variant Versions of the Malay Annals," *BKI*, 123/3, 1967: 301–324; R. O. Winstedt, "The Malay Annals, or Sejarah Melayu," *JMBRAS*, 16/3, 1938; and T. D. Situmorang and A. Teeuw, *Sedjarah Melaju, Menurut Terbitan Abdullah bin Abdulkadir Munsji* (Jakarta/Amsterdam, 1952).

45. Ahmad, *Hikayat Hang Tuah*, see, for example, pp. 472, 474, 475, 476, 477, 501, and 517.

46. V. Matheson and A. C. Milner, "*Hikayat Hang Tuah*," in their *Perceptions of the Hajj: Five Malay Texts* (Singapore: ISEAS, 1984), p. 7.

47. Salleh, *Hikayat Merong Mahawangsa*, pp. 77–78, 100, 103, and 105; see also H. M. J. Maier, *In the Center of Authority: The Malay Hikayat Merong Mahawangsa* (Ithaca, NY: Cornell University Southeast Asia Program, 1988). Also see Amelia Cerdiwen, "The Silsilah Raja-Raja Perak I: An Historical and Literary Investigation into the Political Significance of a Malay Court Genealogy," *JMBRAS*, 74/2, 2001: 23–129, especially p. 69; and W. E. Maxwell, "Notes on Two Perak Manuscripts," *JMBRAS*, 2, 1871: 181–191.

48. Skinner, *Civil War in Kelantan*, pp. 14, 18, 20, and 22.

49. Jones, *Hikayat Raja Pasai*, pp. 24–26, 28, and 32–33.

50. Brakel, *Hikayat Muhammad Hanafiyyah*, pp. 12–13, 17, and 25.

51. See Mees, *Kroniek van Kutai*; and J. J. Ras, *Hikajat Bandjar*.

52. See A. Teeuw, ed., *Shair Ken Tambuhan* (Kuala Lumpur: University of Malay Press, 1966). These copies are now scattered around the world, at SOAS, the Royal Asiatic Society, Cambridge, Leiden, and Singapore.

53. Gallop, "Malay Sources," p. 16; Anonymous, "Surat Ingatan," p. 346; and Raja Ali Haji ibn Ahmad, *Precious Gift*, more generally. From the Warkah Brunei we can also see very mundane matters, in addition to a concern for the Hajj—such as a British request for orangutans, as well as the trade in rosewater and flowered cloth.

54. See Sallah, *Bustan al-Salatin*; Shiraishi, "A Study of Bustanu's Salatin"; Jelani Harun, ed., *Bustan al-Salatin (I and II)* (Kuala Lumpur: Dewan Bahasa dan Pustaka, 2004).

55. See Raffles Malay 42 in the Royal Asiatic Society, London; Ms. #41, University of Malaya Library, Kuala Lumpur; MI 286D, Perpustakaan Nasional Republik Indonesia, Jakarta; and Malayo-Polynesien 275, Bibliotheque Nationale, Paris.

56. For both prices and multiple pilgrimages in this text, see the Kuala Lumpur mss., 3/2: 429.

57. For this, see the London (Royal Asiatic Society) mss., 2/9: 164; 2/13: 236; 2/8: 139; 2/10: 187; and 2/1: 86.

58. See, for example, Salleh, *Hikayat Patani*, pp. 77: "Haji Abdul Rahman itu asalnya orang Jawa, turun dari haji ia beristeri di Patani ini. Adapun Fakih Abdul Manan itu orang..."; "dan Syekh Abdul Kadir itu asalnya orang Pasai dan Haji Abdul Rahman itu asalnya orang Jawa, turun dari haji ia beristeri..."; "cucu Rasulullah, Bait al-Muqaddis nama negerinya, dan Haji Yunus itu Jawi Patani asalnya dan Syekh Abdul Kadir itu asalnya...."

59. V. Matheson and M. B. Hooker, "Jawi Literature in Patani: The Maintenance of a Tradition," *JMBRAS*, 41/1, 1988: 6; see also Francis Bradley, "The New Social Dynamics of Islamic Revival in Southeast Asia: The Rise of the Patani School, 1785–1909" (PhD Dissertation, University of Wisconsin, Madison, 2010).

60. Matheson and Hooker, "Jawi Literature in Patani," p. 20.

61. Mohammad Rezuan Othman, "The Role of Makka-Educated Malays in the Development of Early Islamic Scholarship and Education in Malaysia," *Journal of Islamic Studies* 9/2, 1998: 147; see also the work of Francis Bradley.

62. H. Nasution et al., eds., *Ensiklopedi Islam Indonesia* (Jakarta: Jambatan, 1992), p. 203; Peter Riddell, *Islam and the Malay-Indonesian World: Transmission and Responses* (Honolulu: University of Hawai'i Press, 2001), p. 199.

63. Sweeney, *Karya Lengkap Abdullah bin Abdul Kadir Munsyi*.

64. Ibid.; see, for example, pp. 21, 24, and 6.

65. See H. A. Klinkert, "Verhaal eener Pelgrimsreis van Singapoera naar Mekah, door Abdoellah bin Abdil Kadir Moensji, gedaan in het jaar 1854," *BKI*, 1867: 384–410; also see Ahmad Kassim, ed., *Kisah Pelayaran Abdullah* (Kuala Lumpur: Oxford University Press, 1964).

66. Riddell, *Islam and the Malay-Indonesian World*, pp. 103–104.

67. Djajadiningrat, "Critisch Overzicht van de in Maleisch Werken Vervatte Gegevens over de Geschiedenis van het Soeltanaat van Atjeh," *BKI*, 65, 1911: 135–269, especially p. 178.

68. This is part of the tale of Hang Tuah, at any rate. See Bradley, "The New Social Dynamics of Islamic Revivalism in Southeast Asia," chapter 3.

69. V. Matheson and A.C. Milner, "Tuhfat al-Nafis," in their *Perceptions of the Hajj*, pp. 17–18.

70. Azyumardi Azra, *The Origins of Islamic Reformism in Southeast Asia* (Crows Nest, Australia: Allen and Unwin; Honolulu: University of Hawai'i, 2004), p. 42.

71. Mohammad Rezuan Othman, "The Role of Makka-Educated Malays in the Development of Early Islamic Scholarship and Education in Malaysia," *Journal of Islamic Studies*, 9/2, 1998: 147.

PART II

SAILOR, DOCTOR, STATESMAN, SPY

The Hajj through Four Colonial Windows

5

In Conrad's Wake

Lord Jim, the "Patna," and the Hajj

Indeed this affair, I may notice in passing, had an extraordinary power
of defying the shortness of memories and length of time: it seemed to
live, with a sort of uncanny vitality, in the minds of men, on the tips of
their tongues.

—Joseph Conrad, *Lord Jim* (p. 146).

Precisely at the turn of the twentieth century, the Polish novelist Joseph
Conrad—then living and writing in London, the capital of England's burgeoning Southeast Asian empire—published his book *Lord Jim*. The novel was almost
an instant success, and it catapulted Conrad into the first rank of authors writing
in English almost immediately after it appeared in print. Twenty years prior to
this, in 1880, a ship carrying Muslim pilgrims from Southeast Asia to Arabia met
with disaster en route in the Indian Ocean, and this incident became the basis
for much of Conrad's celebrated book. The novel, in many ways, brought the
realities of the Southeast Asian Hajj home to a globalizing reading public. It did
this through fiction, but Conrad's story holds enormous verisimilitude with the
mechanics of the pilgrimage from this part of the world. The author himself had
spent a significant amount of time on ships traveling in Southeast Asia, including
as an officer, and he had seen the Hajj functioning with his own eyes. *Lord Jim* is
therefore a unique social document in two ways. It became important historically in the year 1900 and thereafter in helping to shape perceptions of the Hajj,
as it was a literary sensation in its own time and read by a large number of people.
It also was important in retelling—in great detail—the history of the nineteenth-
century Southeast Asian pilgrimage through the real-life disaster of one particular
ship. In both of these senses, the book serves as a fascinating window onto the
Southeast Asian Hajj during the height of the colonial age.

This chapter argues that *Lord Jim* can and should be read as a historical product of its time, alongside other period historical sources. Before the case for New
Historicism was made more than thirty years ago, most critics saw historical

texts as rather featureless background for any individual piece of literature.[1] The work of literary art therefore appeared as a timeless, ahistorical creation, completely independent of its historical context. New Historicism made the case that no work of literature could or should be read in this way, and that texts and contexts (i.e., historical documents) were mutually constitutive of each other and fundamentally important to each other's creation, and to each other's reading. This approach has been utilized before to some extent in scholarship on Joseph Conrad, but that agenda is explicated here in dealing specifically with the Hajjis who appear in Lord Jim.[2] The appearance of Lord Jim in 1900 was not only a literary event but also important in placing Islam in general—and the Southeast Asian Hajj in particular—into public consciousness at a crucial time in the colonial moment. Publication and the great critical and commercial success of the book ensured that this happened on a wide scale, in Europe, North America, and among populations in Southeast Asia itself. In the first third of this chapter, Conrad's own words about the Hajjis of the Patna are examined, his pilgrim ship sailing from Southeast Asia to Arabia that meets with calamity in the wastes of the Indian Ocean. In the second third of the chapter, the factual, real-life Southeast Asian background of Conrad's discourse on these pilgrims is put forth, including the close resemblances of the Patna to the historical disaster of the Jeddah, the actual ship sailing the same pilgrim route that Conrad knew about prior to writing Lord Jim. The final third of the chapter looks at empire and the Hajj through the prism of Conrad's period novel, and at how critical visions of Conrad's work can shed more light on the place of Hajjis in colonial Asian worlds. In the "historical disarray of a region invaded by colonial powers," I attempt to situate the pilgrim ship episode not only in the larger oeuvre of Conrad's writing, but also in the larger context of the real-life colonial Hajj itself.[3]

Conrad on the Hajj and Islam in His Own Words

When Joseph Conrad started Lord Jim, he thought it was going to be a short story of roughly 20,000 words; it originally was to be paired with Heart of Darkness as stories in a single volume.[4] Yet by the time Conrad had finished with the tale, it had grown to more than 100,000 words, and it had taken on a life of its own.[5] Conrad had begun the book in May 1898, and nearly two years later he wrote in a letter that "I am old and sick and in debt…why is it that a weary heaven has not pulverized me with a…thunderbolt?"[6] Inspiration came only in fits and starts; he could not finish the novel, despite growing pressure from London that the book was expected and that his slowness was causing problems. Finally in July 1900, more than two years after he had begun the work, he wrote to John Galsworthy: "The end of LJ has been pulled off with a steady drag of

21 hours.... Cigarette ends growing into a mound similar to a cairn over a dead hero."[7] It is not clear whether Conrad was sure he had penned a classic upon the end of his writing; the book had been in serialization for many months, and the public had an inkling of the project already. *Lord Jim* did go on to become Joseph Conrad's most famous book, however, and it is still regularly lauded, critiqued, and read by an eager public, both cognoscenti and pleasure readers alike.

The entire first half of *Lord Jim* is taken up with "the pilgrim ship episode," as Conrad called it.[8] After this, the balance of his novel shifts to Southeast Asia itself, where Jim retreats after the action (and the consequences) of the first part of the work has unfolded. The particulars of the case and how they related to events occurring in Asia and the Indian Ocean at the time of Conrad's writing of the book are explored later in this chapter. For now, however, several of the passages related to Hajjis can be highlighted to see how Conrad described these passengers on the *Patna* in the novel, as well as in a number of his letters written around the same time. Both of these sources explicate something of how Southeast Asian pilgrims were seen at the fin de siècle in the eyes of the West. The Hajjis in question appear very early in the book, in fact; they are introduced quickly as the reason for the passage of Conrad's ship across the Indian Ocean, from Singapore to the Arabian Peninsula. Conrad's first glimpse of them proceeds in this way:

> The *Patna* was a local steamer as old as the hills, lean like a greyhound, and eaten up with rust worse than a condemned water-tank. She was owned by a Chinaman, chartered by an Arab, and commanded by a sort of renegade New South Wales German.... After she had been painted outside and whitewashed inside, eight hundred pilgrims (more or less) were driven on board of her as she lay with steam up alongside a wooden jetty.
>
> They streamed over three gangways, they streamed in urged by faith and the hope of paradise...without a word, a murmur, or a look back; (they) spread on all sides over the deck, flowed forward and aft, overflowed down the yawning hatchways, filled the inner recesses of the ship—like water filling a cistern, like water flowing into crevices and crannies, like water rising silently even with the rim....
>
> They came covered with dust, with sweat, with grime, with rags—the strong men at the head of family parties, the lean old men pressing forward without hope of return; young boys with fearless eyes glancing curiously, shy little girls with tumbled long hair; the timid women muffled up and clasping to their breasts, wrapped in loose ends of soiled head-cloths, their sleeping babies, the unconscious pilgrims of an exacting belief.
>
> "Look at dese cattle" said the German skipper to his new chief mate.[9]

If there is a democratic feel to the cramped conditions of the pilgrims aboard the *Patna*, then this is dispelled by the presence of a single figure, whom Conrad introduces right after the Hajjis themselves—an Arab traveler, who seems to be an authority figure among the passengers. He, too, is a pilgrim en route to Mecca, though a man of a different sort:

> An Arab, the leader of that pious voyage, came last. He walked slowly aboard, handsome and grave in his white gown and large turban. A string of servants followed, loaded with his luggage; the *Patna* cast off and backed away from the wharf.... The Arab, standing up aft, cried aloud the prayer of travelers by sea. He invoked the favour of the Most High upon that journey, implored His blessing on man's toil and on the secret purposes of their hearts; the steamer pounded in the dusk the calm water of the Strait; and far astern of the pilgrim ship a screw-pile lighthouse, planted by unbelievers on a treacherous shoal, seemed to wink at her its eye of flame, as if in derision of her errand of faith.[10]

Conrad's invocation of the "Most High" here is interesting—God and gods appear with some frequency in the author's work, though they are usually mentioned only in passing, almost as observers to the central events of mankind (the beings who truly interested Conrad). Yet Conrad also referenced higher spiritual authorities in his letters, even if always in a way that left his allegiance to them in doubt.[11] He may not have been a believer in the strict (Victorian, Christian) sense of the term, but Conrad had his uses for gods—and he could understand a journey such as the Hajj (figure 5.1).

In Conrad's narrative, the *Patna* then passed into the Straits of Malacca, laden down with its cargo of Hajjis—Arabia lay thousands of miles to the west in a long journey across the entire width of the Indian Ocean. The ship was nearly bursting to capacity: people were everywhere, occupying every inch of space available for this slow crawl across the surface of the sea. In his writing, one can almost feel the utter discomfort of the voyage; Conrad's pilgrims are ground one against another, with no hope of escape from this collective misery of travel for several weeks. They did not live without any hierarchy whatsoever, though:

> The five whites on board lived amidships, isolated from the human cargo. The awnings covered the deck with a white roof from stem to stern, and a faint hum, a low murmur of sad voices, alone revealed the presence of a crowd of people upon the great blaze of the ocean.
>
> Below the roof of awnings, surrendering to the wisdom of white man and to their courage, trusting the power of their unbelief and their iron

Figure 5.1 The Singapore Docks in the Late Nineteenth and Early Twentieth Centuries.
Credit: Singapore Harbor: The Starting Point of the SS Jeddah; "Meal Hour for Workers at Albert Dock, 1892" and "Tongkangs on the Singapore River, 1930s," both from the National Archives of Singapore.

shell of their fire-ship, the pilgrims of an exacting faith slept on mats, blankets, on bare planks, on every deck, in all the dark corners, wrapped in dyed cloths, muffled in soiled rags, with their heads resting on small bundles, with their faces pressed to bent forearms: the men, the women, the children; the old and the young, the decrepit with the lusty—all equal before sleep, death's brother.[12]

And then—crisis. Off the easternmost tip of Africa (Cape Guardafui, off Somalia and the coast of Yemen), the *Patna* strikes an object in the water in the middle of the night. The ship starts to take on water at an alarming rate; although the mass of nearly one thousand Hajjis are not aware of it, the ship is in grave peril. The crew has only a few moments before the Hajjis discover what has happened, and they madly try to see if the ship can be salvaged by removing the water the *Patna* has take on in the midst of the ocean. There is a chance they will sink.

> The two Malays had meantime remained holding the wheel. Just picture to yourselves the actors in that, thank God! unique, episode of the sea, four beside themselves with fierce and secret exertions, and three looking on in complete immobility, above the awnings covering the profound ignorance of hundreds of human beings, with their weariness, with their dreams, with their hopes, arrested, held by an invisible hand on the brink of annihilation.
>
> The chief was there, ready with a clutch at him to whisper close to his head, scathingly, as though he wanted to bite his ear—"You silly fool! Do you think you'll get the ghost of a show when that lot of brutes is in the water? They, they will batter your head for you from those boats."[13]

Conrad wanted to understand the mechanics of a ship in distress and possibly destined to sink; he wrote in one of his letters a query on how steamships worked, including in it a diagram (which he hand-drew) of how a boiler apparatus might come to break so that a ship might take on water very quickly.[14] Conrad had a vast experience of the sea from his travels, and he tried to be scrupulous in his details when writing his fiction. He was similar in this respect about minutiae having to do with Asia (not just the sea) and with the personalities of people he met on his travels. All of this "substrate" had to be correct for his novels.[15] This is one of the reasons that *Lord Jim* and, indeed, his other fiction had such resonance for the reading public of the time—it made sense. It had *veritas*.

In the confusion of events in the middle of the night, stranded out at sea and taking on water, Jim and the other Europeans make a fateful choice—they try to leave the ship in lifeboats before the hundreds of Hajjis become aware of their going. They have consigned the pilgrims to death—the Hajjis cannot be saved by the inadequate number of lifeboats available on the *Patna*. Jim jumps into one of the lowering boats, and when the Hajjis become aware of what is happening, they try to swamp the vessels, and one boat at least is lost with its occupants, swallowed by the sea. The rest of the Europeans and a small complement of indigenous crewmen escape, are eventually picked up the next day by a passing ship, and are brought to Aden in Yemen. There they tell the British authorities that the *Patna* has been lost at sea at great cost of human life. There is only one problem. The *Patna* survives the night, enough water is evicted from the hold to save the ship, and the next day the vessel is towed by another passing vessel to Aden as well, to the great horror of the surviving European crew. An inquest is ordered, and the tale becomes the calumny of the eastern seas. Jim eventually retreats further east in shame, and into the second half of Conrad's novel, where he meets his fate. And the Hajjis? What becomes of them? Joseph Conrad is not sure:

> What were the various ends their destiny provided for the pilgrims I am unable to say; but the immediate future brought, at about nine o'clock next morning, a French gunboat homeward bound from Reunion. The report of her commander was public property. He had swept a little out of his course to ascertain what was the matter with that steamer floating dangerously by the head upon a still and hazy sea. There was an ensign, union down, flying at her main gaff (the *serang* had the sense to make a signal of distress at daylight); but the cooks were preparing the food in the cooking-boxes forward as usual. The decks were packed as close as a sheep-pen: there were people perched all along the rails, jammed on the bridge in a solid mass; hundreds of eyes stared, and not a sound was heard when the gunboat ranged abreast, as if all that multitude of lips had been sealed by a spell. The Frenchman hailed, could get no intelligible reply, and after ascertaining through his binoculars that the crowd on deck did not look plague-stricken, decided to send a boat.[16]

We can assume that the pilgrims eventually did make their Hajj. They probably had more reason than most, however, to be thankful to God for the successful outcome of their journey across the endless ocean.

The Southeast Asian Dimension

What can an examination of Conrad's pilgrims circa 1900 tell us about the colonial Southeast Asian Hajj, and especially about the real-life pilgrim ship disaster from twenty years earlier that Conrad memorialized in his book? The Polish seaman Jozef Korzeniowski—later known as Joseph Conrad—first came to Southeast Asia in 1883. He had been second mate on the ship *Palestine*, which one day caught fire when it was heavily weighed down with coal; Conrad ended up ashore on the island of Bangka, astride the sea lanes between Singapore and Batavia in the southernmost reaches of the South China Sea. During this first sojourn in the region, he likely read a number of European authors on Southeast Asia, including Alfred Russel Wallace, Belcher, McNair, and Multatuli (the pen name of Eduard Douwes Dekker, the great critic of Dutch imperialism in the Indies). He also became fascinated with the figure of James Brooke, the "White Raja of Sarawak," who had carved out an independent kingdom for himself in western Borneo from the 1840s onward. Four years after his first sojourn to the archipelago, in 1887, he came back to the region as a British subject, and after injuring himself on one of his ships, he ended up spending a fair bit of time in the hospital in both Semarang and in Singapore. This was shortly after he had likely read Multatuli's masterpiece, *Max Havelaar*, and its scathing indictment of Dutch policy in the Indies seems to have greatly influenced his worldview. Singapore became Conrad's base in the region: it was from this port that he sailed to Borneo, Sulawesi, and other parts of the archipelago, especially on the ship SS *Vidar*.[17] In much of his fiction, Conrad went on at length about the crews of the ships he sailed on, but interestingly not in *Lord Jim*, where the crew of the *Patna* is practically faceless, an exception to the rule in his writings.[18] He was in Southeast Asia for this short time and then never returned to the region when he left, though he continued to write about this part of the world until right before his death in 1924.

A number of contemporary authors have endeavored to show how important history and lived experience were to Conrad's representations of Southeast Asia during this period. The earliest of these exercises go back to 1923, when Conrad was only just still alive, but these first attempts also spawned a number of competent successors, each of which has added further to our knowledge about Conrad's real-life historical inspirations in the region.[19] One modern scholar has noted that "Conrad repeatedly explained that he could not invent but had to rely on factual data. At the same time, he was concerned not with the literal accuracy of the facts but with literary creation that was faithful to them."[20] His fiction was fiction, in other words, but it nevertheless relied heavily on actual events and people that surrounded Conrad during his time in Southeast Asia. Some scholars have taken this "complected fiction" very seriously in teasing out Conrad's whereabouts and contacts in the Indies of the late nineteenth century, sketching out a world of trade in rare forest products and wooden vessels, where the profits were exceedingly high and the ships (usually) exceedingly small.[21] Others have attempted to pin down every fictional place in the novel with its actual counterpart in Asia, with one going so far as to even track down the historical source for a huge Bornean diamond of 361 carats that found its way into one of Conrad's narratives, based on a real stone reported in Banjarmasin in 1849.[22] Even the merchant and sailing activities of Conrad's *Vidar* have been committed down to carefully tabulated charts and tables, showing how this ship (among others) connected the commerce of out-of-the-way places in Borneo and Sulawesi with the wider world over a number of decades. This was done through cotton, opium, beeswax, and salt, as well as through beads, edible sea cucumbers, and the sale of munitions.[23]

Yet how close was Conrad's description of the pilgrim ship episode of the *Patna* to real-life precedents that occurred in the region around the same time? The author's novel helped to form a generation's perception of the Southeast Asian Hajj; before its appearance, it is safe to say that the average Westerner knew almost nothing about this phenomenon. It is clear that the *Patna* of *Lord Jim* is based very strongly in most ways on the foundering of the pilgrim ship *Jeddah* in 1880, an occurrence that Conrad must certainly have been aware of, given its notoriety in eastern seas at the time of his own journeys. In a Reuter's telegram of August 10, 1880, reprinted in the London *Times* two days later, the missive reported to the world that the steamer *Jeddah* with 953 pilgrims on board, en route from Singapore to Jeddah, had sunk off the east coast of Africa; a number of European survivors had made it to Aden, picked up by the passing steamer *Scindia*.[24] A second Reuters telegram the same day was then quickly published as well, informing the public that the ship had *not* foundered and that, in fact, it had just been towed to Aden by the steamship *Antenor*.[25] A Lloyd's telegram later in the day confirmed the new report and gave the further information that the *Jeddah* had been built in Dumbarton in 1872 and was owned by the Ocean Steamship Company in Singapore, a reputable outfit (figure 5.2).[26] Two weeks later, notice came up in the House of Commons in

Figure 5.2 The Rigging of the "Jeddah."
Credit: National Maritime Museum Greenwich, England; reproduced from Thomas Moser, *Joseph Conrad Lord Jim* (New York: Norton, 1996), p. 327.

London, asking if a wider inquiry would and could be made into the incident—it was clear that with the abandonment of the *Jeddah* by her British crew, something had gone very, very wrong.[27] The governor of the Straits Settlements in Singapore chimed in shortly after this that there was a near-universal sense of indignation against the captain and crew of the *Jeddah* in Singapore, its home port. If they had indeed abandoned their crew of nearly one thousand Hajjis to die in the Indian Ocean, then this was a scandal that could not be hidden.[28]

The story of the Jeddah incident was trumpeted as first-page news in the *Times* of London almost immediately, as such a huge potential loss of life in the pilgrim trade had never happened before (if it indeed had even happened now). The editors of the *Times* felt that it needed to explain to its readers what was at stake. There was still a sense of confusion as to what exactly had occurred:

> It would have been terrible that nine hundred helpless pilgrims should have perished at sea. But that they should have been abandoned by the officers of the ship to which they had entrusted themselves, and saved by the accidental services rendered them by another vessel, is scarcely credible.
>
> The number of pilgrims on board the vessel seems enormous, but will not be incredible to anyone who has traveled in the East.... Islam has one faith, with one learned language as its medium of communication, from Sierra Leone to Shanghai, and from the Siberian Steppes to the Cape Colony; and as a rule wherever the Mahomedan faith exists, the duties it prescribes are observed with the most scrupulous attention. In the present day, the particular duty of pilgrimage has been facilitated by the same means as those which have stimulated traveling generally. To make the pilgrimage to Mecca was a short time ago an arduous and dangerous undertaking. But steamers now convey Mahomedans with security and rapidity from all parts of the world to their sacred shrines.
>
> The Mahomedan, however poor, is ardent in his devout wish to visit Mecca, and he shrinks from no hardship in the process. The pilgrims crowd, with the barest necessities, not in the hold, but on the decks of vessels like the *Jeddah*. It is hard to distinguish between their clothing and their bedding; and they are packed like sheep in the open air, exposed to all of the heat and hardships of the climate.... These pilgrimages will continue and will increase. It is very possible that Mahomedan enthusiasm may be still further augmented; and it will consequently be a duty to make the most stringent inquiry into the circumstances of this alleged disaster, and into the conduct of those who were in charge of the vessel.[29]

The judicial machinery of the British Empire went into action shortly after the crew of the *Jeddah* had been caught in their lie that their ship had foundered with all hands in the middle of the ocean. A "Report of Inquiry Held at Aden to Investigate the Abandonment of the Steamship *Jeddah*" was the first to lay out the facts and make an official, public pronouncement on the case. The ship had left Penang on July 17, 1880, after taking on more pilgrims after its initial run from Singapore; there were 600 tons of cargo on board, consisting mostly of sugar, wood, and other general merchandise. Of the ship's crew of fifty, only five were Europeans, and these included the captain, his wife, the first and second mates, and the third engineer. Upon arrival in Aden, the Europeans had said the ship had foundered and that two of their number had been murdered by the Hajjis. When some of the Europeans had gotten into lifeboats, the pilgrims had told them to come out, fearing that they were trying to save their skins and abandon them. When they refused, the lines of the boats were cut and at least one fell into the sea bow first, with its occupants presumed dead. The court then rendered its opinion, placing blame on most of the European crew, but with its harshest words reserved for Augustine Williams, who served as the likely basis for Conrad's Lord Jim:

> The court considers that the actions of the pilgrims tends to prove that they never intended to harm the master and his officers had they remained in the *Jeddah*; that their demeanor is accounted for by the evidence that they had made up their minds that they would not be deserted by the only persons capable of protecting and helping them … and consequently they would prevent to the utmost the master or his officers leaving the ship … the master was misled in regard to the real intentions of the pilgrims, but he has himself to blame for not making more certain of these intentions … (finally) the captain entirely forgot his first duty as a shipmaster, and proceeded to be one of the first instead of the last to leave his disabled vessel to her fate. This last act roused the pilgrims to violence in attempting to swamp his boat, and such the court consider might naturally have been expected from any body of human beings, even Europeans, situated as the pilgrims were.
>
> G. R. Goodfellow, Resident and Sessions Judge, Aden, 20 August 1880[30]

The assessor's report compiled by W. K. Thyne, also at Aden and also delivered to the public on August 20, concurred with the report of inquiry.[31] When the damages were discussed in court and the salvage award delivered for the services rendered by the steamship *Antenor*, the court opined that "taking into consideration the number of lives thus rescued from the probability of impending death, this is,

I believe, a case of life-salvage of a totally unprecedented character.... The principal feature in this case is undoubtedly the life salvage...the value of the property salved is (also) large."[32]

If it was quintessentially Victorian to pronounce on the value of (Asian) life and (British) property in one long exclamation in this case, then the initial reaction to the tale of the *Jeddah* in the media of the English-speaking world also ran true to form. Racialized discourse from some, perhaps best exemplified by the letter to the editor in the *Times* by a Captain Carter, himself formerly in the pilgrim-ship trade, epitomized some of this body of opinion:

> No one who has not witnessed the pilgrims actually en route can form the slightest conception of the unromantic and unpicturesque appearance of these wretched fanatics.... There are horrors on board such a ship which no Christian has ever dreamt of...wickedness worse, by far, than was ever found on board a slaver.... Of course, if these wretched beings die en route to Mecca, their eternal happiness is assured, so that they generally seem glad to give up the ghost and fly to the realms of joy. I wish you could have seen some of our little scenes of excitement. You must understand that my "batch" consisted of Turcomans, Arabo-Persians, and Bedouins. They all came on board armed to the teeth, but of course, I had all their weapons taken charge of by my officers and locked up in safety. I mean all the weapons we saw.[33]

Captain Carter was backed by an anonymous writer named "F.R.G" in a subsequent letter (box 5.1), who described pilgrims as "filthy" and the voyages as horrific, but one other letter also cautioned that standards on these ships were much higher from British Singapore than elsewhere, and that Captain Carter's comments should not apply to the *Jeddah*.[34] Yet many other letter writers to the main newspapers of the day had only sympathy for the pilgrims and approbation for the Englishmen they felt had deserted them in the middle of the ocean, to the latter's enduring shame. A missive to the *Daily Times* said: "As a rule, the pilgrims make quiet and contented passengers. When roused, however, by injustice or ill-treatment, they have been known to give a great deal of trouble."[35] The *Straits Overland Journal* was firmer: "Words would fail any right minded man to express his indignation of the wretched cowardice displayed by this contemptible clique of would-be sailors, who are a disgrace to their country, and a disgrace to their cloth.... It is well-known that the poor Hadjis are often subjected to gross injustice, and it is a sin and shame that the religious prejudices which dictate their pilgrimages to the tomb of their prophet are taken advantage of to impose penalties upon them which would never bear the calm investigation of an English court of law."[36] The Straits Settlements Legislative Council, the highest ruling

Box 5.1 To the Editor of *The Times* from "F.R.G.," August 17, 1880, p. 8

Sir,—Having read in the *The Times* of to-day the extract from Captain Carter's letter, I am in hopes that public attention will now be called to the frightful manner in which the pilgrim traffic is carried on and some steps be taken to put a stop to its flagrant evils.

My brother went out to Bombay as chief officer of the *King Arthur*, under Captain Carter's command, and at Bombay exchanged into a larger steamer engaged in the same trade. In his letters he has repeatedly described the state of affairs on board, and these descriptions quite bear out the facts as stated in Captain Carter's letter.

The following is an extract from a letter written at Calcutta last January:

"We arrived at Calcutta on the 2nd of January after a weary passage of 27 days. I told you in Aden we had smallpox on board; they took out ten people and put them in the hospital. After two days' delay we proceeded for Calcutta. On our way small pox again broke out worse than ever. Then we ran short of coals and began to pull to pieces the woodwork of the ship in order to fire up, and, after great delay, succeeded in getting into Colombo. There they immediately put us into quarantine, but took out of the ship all the smallpox patients, 15 in numbers. We remained Christmas Day and the next day, so you may guess what a pleasant Christmas we spent, all diseases around us and hundreds of pilgrims starving. They have to bring their food with them, but many of them are destitute. Forty-six of them died during the passage, some from disease and some from starvation. After we left Colombo smallpox again broke out, and as soon as we arrived in Calcutta we were again put in quarantine, but we were glad to get rid of the 1,200 pilgrims. One baby was born, but it died before morning for want of attendance; we carry no medical man. The brutes will not help one another and we have nothing to do with them. However, as the mother was a deck passenger and was dying, we put her in an empty cabin, gave her good food, and pulled her through. Seven hundred of the pilgrims live between decks; the other 500 live on deck in the open air, rain or no rain."

The steamers engaged in the pilgrim trade are all, or nearly all, owned by native firms, although they sail under the British flag and carry British officers. These native owners make large profits out of the traffic, and the intervention of the law is the only chance of any attention being paid to the claims of humanity.

I am, Sir, yours faithfully,

F. R. G.

August 14, 1880.

body in British Southeast Asia, essentially concurred with this view in its published deliberations of September 20, 1880, taking a public stance on the disgrace of the crew and the hope that Singapore's reputation for honest dealings and fairness would not be tarnished before the court of world opinion.[37]

Empire, the Hajj, and Colonial Vision

When *Lord Jim* finally appeared in print en to to in 1900, it caused quite a stir; the public knew that something special had happened in literature, and also knew that Conrad's story bore the imprimatur of real events in the fiber of its telling. The incident involving the *Jeddah* some twenty years previously had not been forgotten, and those who may have forgotten it were treated to retellings of the story alongside the critical reception for the historical novel. Whether agnostic or elegiac in tone, reviewers quickly felt the correspondence between the story and "real life" in the eastern seas. The *New York Daily Tribune* printed: "The ship leaves port carrying eight hundred native pilgrims.... It is all a record of little truths; it is a mosaic, formed with zealous solicitude for justice, of the thousand and one facts.... It is as accurate as a legal document."[38] An unsigned review in *Public Opinion* was less fulsome in its praise but nevertheless recognized Conrad's attempts at veracity as well: "the aggravating part is that Mr. Conrad can write admirably...nothing could be better than the description of the *Patna* voyaging up the Arabian Gulf.... We feel the author knows the sea and these Eastern colonies as we know our own native streets."[39] The *Spectator* correctly noted that Conrad's sympathies often rested with the indigenes in his novels and that he "he identified himself with the standpoint of the natives," while the *Daily Chronicle* admired his fortitude in writing from his own rough travels, so that "the story itself takes you far away from the trivialities of literary coteries, and the mean little streets of cities. You get out into the greater world ...the wind blows in your face."[40] This was indeed correct: Conrad may have been in high authorial circles already, corresponding regularly (as his letters show) with the likes of H. G. Wells, Ford Maddox Ford, Stephen Crane, and Henry James, but he had certainly put in his years before the mast (table 5.1).[41] His presentation of the pilgrim-ship episode of Southeast Asia bore all the hallmarks of truth. The *Pall Mall Gazette* summarized what many may have been thinking when it said that "the main impression left upon the reader's mind will be, we think, a phantasmagoria, a changing scene of life in Eastern seas."[42]

This idea that Conrad had painted "a changing scene of life in Eastern seas" is an important one. Conrad was, of course, only one of a number of writers who were describing Southeast Asia to the Western world and the "colonial situation" there generally at this time. Much of this evolving discussion, as has already been seen in

Table 5.1 **Joseph Conrad's Trading Milieu in Southeast Asia, Late Nineteenth Century**

Voyages of the Historical Captain Lingard, Later "Lord Jim"

In Conrad's Novels

Ship:	Master:	Departs Sing. For:	Arrives back Sing. From:
Trade from Singapore to Java, East Borneo, and Sulawesi, 1864–1883			
Coeran	Lingard		Makassar, 11/1864
Coeran	Lingard	Borneo, 12/1864	
Coeran	Lingard		Surabaya, 7/1865
Coeran	Lingard	Borneo, 8/1865	Borneo, 10/1865
Coeran	Lingard	Surabaya, 7/1866	Borneo, 11/1866
Coeran	Lingard		Berau, 6/1868
Coeran	Lingard	Surabaya, 6/1868	
Coeran	Lingard	Bulungan, 7/1869	
Coeran	Lingard		Borneo, 3/1870
Coeran	Lingard	Borneo, 4/1870	Berau, 8/1870
Coeran	Lingard	Borneo, 9/1870	
Coeran	Lingard		Borneo, 3/1871
Coeran	Lingard	Borneo, 4/1871	
W. Indian	Lingard		Makassar, 12/1871
W. Indian	Lingard		Berau, 8/1872
W. Indian	Lingard	Berau, 9/1872	
W. Indian	Lingard		Borneo, 2/1874
W. Indian	Lingard	Borneo, 8/1875	Bulungan, 12/1875
W. Indian	Lingard	Semarang, 1/1876	Makassar, 7/1876
W. Indian	Lingard		Berau, 12/1876
W. Indian	Lingard		Berau, 12/1876
W. Indian	Lingard	Berau, 5/1877	Borneo, 8/1877
W. Indian	Lingard	Borneo, 10/1877	Berau, 1/1878

(continued)

Ship:	Master:	Departs Sing. For:	Arrives back Sing. From:
W. Indian	Lingard	Makassar, 1/1878	Borneo, 7/1878
W. Indian	Lingard	E. coast, 9/1878	
W. Indian	Lingard		Kutai, 12/1878
Rajah Laut	Lingard		Borneo, 11/1879
Paknam	Lingard	Gorantolo, 2/1883	Gorantalo, 2/1883
Paknam	Lingard	Berau, 3/1883	Bulungan, 7/1883

Source: Abstracted from James Warren, "Joseph Conrad's Fiction as Southeast Asian History," in James Warren, ed., *At the Edge of Southeast Asian History* (Quezon City, Philippines: New Day, 1987), pp. 15–20.

intimation, was written from a vantage of presumed superiority. Frederick McNair, one of the authors Conrad had read before heading out to the region, encapsulated much of this stance when he wrote in 1878: "The effects of such a mild form of policy will not only be vastly advantageous to ourselves, in bringing a large mass of people into a more civilized state, and opening up to our commerce the mineral and other wealth of this country; but we shall be able to take to ourselves the satisfaction of having at least done our duty in bringing no inconsiderable portion of the earth's surface under the benign influence of British rule, and within the reach of that Christian truth."[43] Rudyard Kipling, who became infinitely more famous than McNair, shared many of these viewpoints, extolling the "white man's burden," even if, in at least some of his earlier writing, he was slightly more ambivalent on imperialism as an endless adventure for his native Britain.[44] Ambivalence swung in the other direction as well decades earlier: James Brooke was actually quite damning in much of what he wrote about Europeans coming to the Malay archipelago, though this did not stop him from carving out his own swath of territory in Western Borneo in the 1840s when the opportunity to do so presented itself.[45] Alfred Russel Wallace, the great naturalist and traveler in these waters, was less equivocal in 1869: "I have lived with communities of savages...in the East, who have no laws or law courts but the public opinion of the village freely expressed. Each man scrupulously respects the rights of his fellow, and any infraction of those rights rarely or never takes place. In such a community, all are nearly equal. There are none of these wide distinctions, of education and ignorance, wealth and poverty, master and servant, which are the product of our civilization."[46] By the time of Queen Victoria's Diamond Jubilee, this sense of self-critique and self-doubt, even at the height of British power when *Lord Jim* was being written, was as palpable a feeling as the pride most Britons felt in the fact of their clearly ruling the world.[47]

Conrad was not British but Polish, though he became a naturalized British subject in between his two voyages to Southeast Asia. Yet it is clear that this dualism in British self-perception about the nature of the empire was shared by Conrad, though in a slightly different way, perhaps, than it was for most Britons of the time. Conrad's youth as a Pole in the Russian-controlled Ukraine gave him a profound distaste for colonialism—he hated the Russian occupation and wrote in venomous terms about it until the end of his life. His novels tended to cut away the imperial adventure's claims—any imperialism's—toward being anything more than a rapacious outing for loot, which Conrad saw at the bottom of nearly all colonial projects, in Southeast Asia and elsewhere. Yet because Conrad was Polish and also an Anglophile, he felt that British imperialism was preferable to certain other variations on the theme, and that there were certainly places where Englishmen were held in high regard by indigenous communities as men of honor or good intent, or as a combination of both. Conrad had seen this himself on his wide travels by sea throughout the empire, and this was certainly the opinion of many Muslim Malays, at least, who dealt with the British as colonial intermediaries on their way to Arabia for the Hajj.[48] One critic may be right, therefore, in saying that "the discourse in *Lord Jim* produces a critique of imperialism's official ethos; all the same there are compelling reasons for reading it as a novel that manifestly has not cut the umbilical cord connecting it with the dominant ideology."[49] Conrad was a critic of imperialism but also was a realist, in other words. He lived in an imperial age, and if one must by force be ruled by another power, he thought, British civilization had the most to offer mankind, at least in terms of its high-sounding rhetoric. London, after all, did not forbid the pilgrimage, but rather facilitated its conduct for its Southeast Asian subjects, even if the religion of the colonized was often mistrusted and not the colonizer's own.

As with colonialism, "race" was a fraught category and tool of human subjugation as well, something that Conrad struggled to make sense of in his fiction, especially with groups such as the Southeast Asians in *Lord Jim*. He knew he was presenting his experiences of contact with these peoples to the world, and he wanted to do so accurately. Postcolonial readings about race tend to see darker-skinned peoples demoted to minor characters in the larger story of the eighteenth, nineteenth, and early twentieth centuries; they become bit-part players in what is essentially a narrative of the West "discovering" and then taking control of the rest of the world. Yet in Conrad's novels, written right at the very height of the colonial era, Asians trade as voraciously as Westerners, but they don't hide this commercialism with high-sounding rhetoric. This is "preferable to the sleek hypocrisy, to the polite disguises, to the virtuous pretenses of white people," as Conrad put it in his own words.[50] In this, Conrad was certainly ahead of his time, as he had been in his thinking on colonialism generally. If Kipling had portrayed the brown-skinned peoples of the planet as "lesser breeds without the law,"[51] then Conrad's introduction of characters in his fiction such as Almayer, Willems, and Kurtz—not to mention Lord Jim himself as the paragon example of this idea—soon destroyed the neat binary between the virtuous Westerner and the barbarous native in previous genres of English fiction. There was to be no such line in Conrad's work, no clean and tidy distinction based solely on race. The Muslim pilgrims in his story were seen for the most part as victims and presented as such to an inquisitive reading public at the turn of the twentieth century. In his book, the boundaries of race in a place like Southeast Asia blurred, even if certain stereotypes and racialized conceptions were kept as tropes through a number of his fictional works.[52] He presented complexity to the audience of his time, therefore, in all of its multihued varieties.

Finally, in terms of Islam, it is clear that the *Jeddah* scandal of 1880 was part and parcel of a larger opening of European imagination and knowledge to the religion at this time. The *Jeddah* affair hit the newspapers only eleven years after the opening of the Suez Canal in 1869, which was global news of the first import, and it also happened two years before the British occupation of Egypt in 1882 and right before the death of the British General Gordon fighting "Islamic fanatics" in the Sudan at Khartoum. Conrad clearly knew of all of these events, and his novel was published at a time when Islam was simultaneously seen as a weak and degraded religion and as a gathering threat to colonial dominion and the European export of "progress" to the world. There is good evidence to show that the single most important source for Conrad's writings on Islam (other than his own travels and alongside a number of other books) was Sir Richard Burton's *Personal Narrative of a Pilgrimage to El-Medinah and Meccah*, which was published in 1855/1856.[53] Through close literary analysis of a number of superimposed passages from both authors' works, it has been proven that Conrad not only used Burton's account but also knew parts of it from memory (that is to say, he wrote passages of his own works at times when he likely had no physical access to Burton's book).[54] It is crucial to note that a large portion of Conrad's interest and knowledge about Islam, therefore, came from a Western account of the pilgrimage to Mecca. The Hajj colored Conrad's thinking about Islam and found its way into his narratives, which he passed on to the reading public at large. It served as a backdrop and as substrate for his musings on the religion's place in the world and on how Islam and Western values were colliding in a new, uncertain present of which Conrad himself was a part at the fin de siècle.

In 1880, when the *Jeddah* incident occurred, there were already three English translations of the Qur'an in print, alongside many other books in English that pronounced on or purported to explain the religion to Europeans, either in "objective" or sometimes in quite deprecatory frames of voice.

Both of these worldviews can be found in Conrad's fiction when it pertains to Muslims, either in Southeast Asia or in other parts of the world. Muslims are often portrayed as violent, as hateful toward nonbelievers, and as exclusionary when it comes to whom they keep company with on a daily basis. They also continually refer to nonbelievers as the offspring of Satan, as infidels, and as people hidden from the truth of the Qur'an, and therefore as beings worthy of being despised or at best shunned for their ignorance.[55] Yet if Conrad portrayed many Muslim characters in his work as bigoted and ignorant, they were almost never more so than the Christian counterparts they were meeting in the sea-lanes of Africa, the Indian Ocean, and Asia in his novels. One Conrad scholar has opined that "Islam is used in the early works not only to give an exaggerated reflection of Christian failings, but also to act as . . . a way of presenting the faults of religion without incurring the wrath of Christian Victorians."[56] In this way, Conrad was able to use popular conceptions of Muslims as crass, violent, and difficult while equating such behavior with Caucasians out in the world as well. He escaped condemnation from Victorian and Edwardian Britain in this way, while also being able to state his innermost belief that religion generally was far more problematic than just Islam, in and of itself. It is difficult to find a single work of Conrad where Muslims as a whole are painted in any less flattering a light than the European Christians they are meeting, and this is certainly the case in *Lord Jim*. The Hajjis of the *Patna* are painted as the victims of European hypocrisy and failures, and not the other way around.

Conclusion

Lord Jim was Conrad's third full-length novel, and one critic has called it his most serious attempt to write a bildungsroman, a "novel of education tracing a youthful protagonist's confrontation with and painful initiation into the moral and social demands of adulthood."[57] But it was more than this, and it was much more than just a novel about the title character's coming of age. The Southeast Asian pilgrims whose fate was at the center of a large part of the book helped to make the author famous and introduced the concept of the Hajj to a burgeoning reading public who knew little about this massive annual event. It seems quite incredible that Conrad did not speak English until he was twenty and that his first novel was not published until he was close to forty, but he became a household name in educated circles almost directly after *Lord Jim* came into public view.[58] As such, he was a public interpreter of sorts for the Hajj, particularly the Asian variants of the journey that were so tightly bound up with European colonial projects of domination and control. Although

Conrad became a naturalized British subject, he still felt himself to be part of a colonized tradition because of his Polish birth and upbringing, and this shows in his book, even though he was an acknowledged Anglophile and an admirer of what Britain might possibly bring to mankind. When he wrote to a British friend that it was different being Polish than English, and that "you forget that we have been used to going to battle without any illusions. It's you Britishers who go to win only,"[59] he was perhaps keeping his distance from his adopted culture, even though he found much to admire in it. In this, Conrad was both a part and apart from Britain at the fin de siècle, especially when it came to explaining the colonial moment, and the plight of his famous Hajjis who were based on real pilgrims who traveled in a similar ship to his own some twenty years before. He saw the empire both as an intellectual and as a traveler at its best and worst, and his novels reflect that disjunction—perhaps none of them more so than *Lord Jim*.

A generally negative view of Islam was held by many late-nineteenth-century Europeans, and attitudes toward Hajjis can certainly be grouped within this larger framework.[60] Conrad himself seems to have been of two minds about such Muslim pilgrims, and his descriptions for the most part reflect this admiration and his embeddedness within a wider tradition of European self-perceived superiority at the same time. Yet Conrad was remarkably even-handed in doling out human frailty and fragility to all people in his novels, regardless of their race or creed. One critic has pointed this out in Jim, as someone whose "ideal aspirations are courageous and whose real conduct in a crisis is ignoble."[61] But it is Jim's refusal to run away from the *Patna* inquiry and the shame that will undoubtedly be his as a result of its findings that marks him as a man of moral superiority when compared with the narrator of *Lord Jim*, the ever-present Marlow, and far more so than the German captain of that same ship. When the German captain says, "Look at deze beasts" in pointing out the Hajjis, it speaks volumes that Jim does not answer him.[62] Jim—and by extension, likely Conrad himself—saw the hapless pilgrims, dirty and crowded and poor, as spiritual travelers, however humble in origin. He saw the captain—representative of imperialism and to some extent of European civilization as a whole—as repugnant and describes him in that way. In this, Conrad used the pilgrim-ship episode as emblematic of larger concerns that he and a number of other Europeans had about the nature of the colonial project in general, and about European control over indigenous subjects in rituals such as the Hajj in particular. As one critic has argued in a well-crafted book, Conrad saw the events of the foundering pilgrim ship as "colouring the whole sentiment of existence"—a lens by which humanity, race, religion, and power could all be judged.[63]

NOTES

1. This case was made initially and most forcefully by Stephen Greenblatt; a good summation of his ideas and the directions they took after their initial exposition can be found in Catherine Gallagher and Stephen Greenblatt, *Practicing New Historicism* (Chicago: University of Chicago Press, 2000). *Lord Jim* and Conrad's work generally have been critiqued from a number of different angles in modern scholarly criticism. Bakhtinian approaches have been attempted, which usually emphasize the freedom of language and the idea of polyphony, but in the case of *Lord Jim* have focused instead on language as a coercive instrument of power as used in the novel. Deconstructivist modes have also been utilized, most notably by J. Hillis Miller, in trying to disentangle what Miller has called the "warring forces of signification" in Conrad's narrative. Marxist approaches have found favor, and even psychoanalytic approaches have been tried, which have shown the fears and conflicts buried in the subconscious of the author, yet still remain manifested in the text. All of these literary lines of reasoning have in common the assumption that the text is very much more than the sum of its parts, and that many other things were at work in the life arc of the central character—Lord Jim—than appear at first glance. It may not be an exaggeration at all to state that *Lord Jim* has emerged as something of a test case for modern literary criticism: how a historical novel can be picked apart to reveal fundamentally social science issues at its core. See Aaron Fogel, *Coercion to Speak: Conrad's Poetics of Dialogue* (Cambridge, MA: Harvard University Press, 1985); J. Hillis Miller's essay "Heart of Darkness Revisited" in Ross Murfin, ed., *Joseph Conrad, Heart of Darkness: A Case Study in Contemporary Criticism* (New York: St. Martin's Press, 1989); and Terry Collits, "Imperialism, Marxism, Conrad: A Political Reading of Victory," *Textual Practice*, 3, 1989: 313–322.

2. For an example of this approach to the work of Conrad, see Brook Thomas, "Preserving and Keeping Order by Killing Time in Heart of Darkness," in Ross Murfin, ed., *Joseph Conrad, Heart of Darkness: A Case Study in Contemporary Criticism* (New York: St. Martin's Press, 1989), p. 239, passim.

3. The phrase is Lloyd Fernando's; see his "Conrad's Eastern Expatriates: A New Version of His Outcasts," *Proceedings of the Modern Language Association*, 91/1, 1976: 79–90. See also P. M. Henderson, *The Transformation of Fact into Fiction in the Historical Novels of Joseph Conrad and Upton Sinclair, and the Relation of These Novels to the Genre of Reportage* (Zurich: Zentralstelle der Studentenschaft, 1992).

4. In Yale's Beinecke Rare Book Library is a manuscript in Conrad's own hand where he states this very clearly: "But seriously, the truth of the matter is that my first thought was of a short story, concerned only with my pilgrim ship episode, nothing more.... It was only then that I perceived that the pilgrim ship episode was a good starting point for a free and wandering tale; that it was an event too which could conceivably color the whole 'sentiment of existence' in a simple and sensitive character" ("Author's Note: Autograph Manuscript of the Preface to Lord Jim," first appearing in the 1917 London edition published by J. M. Dent & Sons, Conrad Manuscripts Box 1, 1857–1924). I have also made use of a number of other handwritten letters from the period 1898–1902 when he was writing *Lord Jim* and right after its publication to gauge something of Conrad's mind-set and influences during this time. These letters are to be found in boxes 1–6 of the Beinecke's collection and are principally from the following: Box 1 ("Authors; Note," as here), Box 4 ("Telegrams and Letters to Ford Maddox Ford, 1898–1904"), Box 6 ("Letters to Edward Lancelot Sanderson and His Wife, 1896–1922") and Box 6 ("13 Letters to Charles Zagorski and His Wife, 1890–1899").

5. Joseph Conrad to Edward Garnett, May 28, 1898; Joseph Conrad to William Blackwood, February 14, 1899, both in Thomas Moser, ed., *Joseph Conrad Lord Jim: Authoritative Text, Backgrounds, Sources, Criticism* (New York: Norton, 1996), pp. 291–292.

6. Joseph Conrad to Edward Garnett, March 26, 1900, in Edward Garnett, *Letters from Joseph Conrad* (Indianapolis, IN: Bobbs-Merrill, 1928), pp. 168–169.

7. Joseph Conrad to John Galsworthy, July 20, 1900, in Thomas Moser, *Joseph Conrad*, p. 306.

8. Constant promises to his publisher that the "end was in sight" went unfulfilled, and he seems to have been carried along by the plot of the book almost as if he were a skiff in tow behind a much larger ship. At times the entire process was painful, as he wrote to Edward Garnett, his publisher, on November 13, 1899. He said then that "*Jim* is dragging his slow length along," yet at other times he found the entire creative process to be excruciating, as when he described to Garnett his second installment of the book as being "too wretched for words." Joseph Conrad to Edward Garnett, November 13, 1899; Joseph Conrad to Edward Garnett, November 19, 1899, in Frederick Karl and Laurence Davies, eds., *The Collected Letters of Joseph Conrad*, vol. 2 (Cambridge: Cambridge University Press, 1986), pp. 220–221.

9. Joseph Conrad, *Lord Jim*, ed. Cedric Watts (Peterborough, Ontario: Broadview Literary Texts, 2001), pp. 46–47.

10. Ibid., p. 47.

11. See, for example, Joseph Conrad to Edward Garnett, September 16, 1899, in Thomas Moser, *Joseph Conrad*, p. 296; Joseph Conrad to Edward Garnett, September 16, 1899, and Joseph Conrad to Edward Garnett, January 20, 1900, both in Edward Garnett, *Letters from Joseph Conrad* (1928), pp. 154, 163.

12. Joseph Conrad, *Lord Jim*, p. 48.

13. Ibid., p. 114.

14. Joseph Conrad to R. B. Cunninghame Graham, January 7, 1898, in C. T. Watts, ed., *Joseph Conrad's Letters to R. B. Cunninghame Graham* (Cambridge: Cambridge University Press, 1969), p. 59.

15. Joseph Conrad to Hugh Clifford, December 13, 1899, in C. T. Watts, *Joseph Conrad's Letters*, p. 226; Joseph Conrad to Hugh Clifford, December 13, 1899, in Thomas Moser, *Joseph Conrad*, p. 299.

16. Joseph Conrad, *Lord Jim*, pp. 145–146.

17. G. J. Resink, "The Eastern Archipelago under Joseph Conrad's Western Eyes," in G. J. Resink, *Indonesia's History's between the Myths* (The Hague: van Hoeve, 1968), pp. 307–308.

18. Gene Moore, "Joseph Conrad in Indonesia," in Gene Moore, ed., *A Joseph Conrad Archive: The Letters and Papers of Hans van Marle, Conradian*, 30/2, 2005: 11.

19. Richard Curle, "Conrad in the East," *Yale Review*, 12, 1923: 497–508.

20. J. N. F. M. a Campo, "A Profound Debt to the Eastern Seas: Documentary History and Literary Representation of Berau's Maritime Trade in Conrad's Malay Novels," *International Journal of Maritime History*, 12/2, 2000: 86–87.

21. Gene Moore, "The Missing Crew of the Patna," *The Conradian* 25/1, 2000: 83.

22. Hans van Marle and Pierre Lefranc, "Ashore and Afloat: New Perspectives on Topography and Geography in Lord Jim," *Conradiana*, 20, 1988: 109–135; Hans Lippe, "Reconsidering the Patna Inquiry in Lord Jim," *The Conradian*, 15, 1, 1990: 59–69; Hans Lippe, "Lord Jim: Some Geographic Observations" *The Conradian*, 10/2, 1985: 135–138; J. H. Stape and Gene Moore, "The Stone of the Sultan of Succadana: Another Source for Lord Jim," *The Conradian*, 27/1, 2002: 44–50.

23. J. F. Warren, "Joseph Conrad's Fiction as Southeast Asian History: Trade and Politics in East Borneo in the Late Nineteenth Century," in James Warren, ed., *At the Edge of Southeast Asian History* (Quezon City, Philippines: New Day, 1987), pp. 15–19.

24. Reuters Telegram, August 10, 1880, in *The Times of London*, August 12, 1880, p. 5.

25. Reuters Telegram, August 11, 1880, in *The Times of London*, August 12, 1880, p. 5.

26. Lloyd's Telegram, August 11, 1880, in *The Times of London*, August 12, 1880, p. 5.

27. "Notice before House of Commons, August 23, 1880," in CO 273/111.

28. Gov. SS (Weld) to Sec. of State, Straits Settlements Dispatches, September 20, 1880, Ministry of Trade 4/300 #2777 (1881).

29. *The London Times*, August 12, 1880, p. 9.

30. "Report of a Court of Inquiry held at Aden to investigate the Abandonment of the steamship Jeddah," in Norman Sherry, *Conrad's Eastern World* (Cambridge: Cambridge University Press, 1966), pp. 299–309.

31. "Assessor's Report on the Abandonment of the Steamship Jeddah," in Ibid., p. 309.

32. *Cases Heard and Determined in Her Majesty's Supreme Court of the Straits Settlements,* 1808–1884, 4 vols., ed. J. W. N. Kyshe (Singapore: Singapore and Straits Printing Office, 1885–90), 2:42–44.

33. Letter from Captain Carter to the *Times of London,* August 14, 1880, p. 5.

34. "To the Editor of the Times from F.R.G. " *Times of London,* August 17, 1880, p. 8.

35. "The S.S. Jeddah," in the *Daily Times,* September 10, 1880.

36. "Summary of the Week," *Straits Times Overland Journal,* September 13, 1880, pp. 1–4.

37. SSLCP, January 14, 1880, as reported in the *Straits Times Overland Journal,* September 20, 1880, pp. 2–3.

38. "Unsigned Review," *New York Daily Tribune,* November 3, 1900, p. 10.

39. "Unsigned Review," *Public Opinion,* 78 (November 23, 1900), pp. 656–658.

40. "Unsigned Review," the *Spectator,* 85 (November 24, 1900), p. 753; "Unsigned Review," the *Daily Chronicle,* October 29, 1900, p. 3.

41. See, for example, Joseph Conrad to Edward Garnett, November 9, 1999; Joseph Conrad to Edward Garnett, January 15, 1900; and Joseph Conrad to Edward Garnett, November 12, 1900 (pp. 158, 163, 172), all in Edward Garnett, *Letters from Joseph Conrad;* also Joseph Conrad to Stephen Crane, September 10, 1899, in Frederick Karl and Laurence Davies, ed., *The Collected Letters of Joseph Conrad,* vol. 2 (Cambridge: Cambridge University Press, 1986), p. 197.

42. "Unsigned Review," the *Pall Mall Gazette,* 71 (December 5, 1900), p. 4.

43. Frederick McNair, *Perak and the Malays* (London: Tinsley Brothers, 1878), pp. 448–451.

44. Rudyard Kipling, "Recessional," *London Times,* July 17, 1897, p. 13. Kipling's poem "Recessional" warns against imperialist arrogance; all empires, we are told, fold and die, and eventually suffer the same fate as Nineveh and Tyre. The poem proceeds in part: "Far-called our navies melt away— / On dune and headland sinks the fire— / Lo, all our pomp of yesterday / Is one with Nineveh and Tyre! / Judge of the Nations, spare us yet, / Lest we forget—lest we forget!"

45. "Lastly, I must mention the effect of European domination in the Archipelago. The first voyages from the West found the natives rich and powerful, with strong established governments, and a thriving trade with all parts of the world. The rapacious European has reduced them to their present condition." See Rodney Mundy, *Narrative of Events in Borneo and Celebes, Down to the Occupation of Labuan: From the Journals of James Brooke, Esq., Rajah of Sarawak,* 2 vols. (London: Murray, 1848), 1:68–71.

46. Alfred Russel Wallace, *The Malay Archipelago,* vol. 2 (London: Macmillan, 1869), pp. 459–463.

47. See Henry Norman, "The Globe and the Island," *Cosmopolis,* 7/19, 1897: 79–92. Norman's article says in part: "In a word the Jubilee has evoked and expressed alike profound loyalty and profound national self-confidence. This is what made it unique as a British festival. I felt while watching it that if I could remember to tell truthfully to my son, he will start with a large equipment of the ideas and ideals which make the good citizen and the good Englishman."

48. See Owen Knowles and Gene Moore, eds., *Oxford Reader's Companion to Conrad* (Oxford: Oxford University Press, 2000), pp. 77–80.

49. Benita Parry, *Conrad and Imperialism: Ideological Boundaries and Visionary Frontiers* (London: Macmillan, 1983), p. 86.

50. Ibid., p. 337.

51. Rudyard Kipling, "Recessional," *London Times,* July 17, 1897, p. 13.

52. Knowles and Moore, *Oxford Reader's Companion to Conrad,* p. 338.

53. Ibid., 203–204.

54. Hans van Marle, "Conrad and Richard Burton on Islam," *Conradiana,* 17, 1985: 139.

55. John Lester, *Conrad and Religion* (London: Macmillan, 1988), p. 43.

56. Ibid., p. 58.

57. J. H. Stape, "Lord Jim," in *The Cambridge Companion to Joseph Conrad* (Cambridge: Cambridge University Press, 1996), p. 63.

58. Robert Kuehn, "Introduction," in Robert Kuehn, *Twentieth Century Interpretations of Lord Jim: A Collection of Critical Essays* (Englewood Cliffs, NJ: Prentice Hall, 1969), p. 1.

59. Quoted in Edward Said, *Joseph Conrad and the Fiction of Autobiography* (Cambridge, MA: Harvard University Press, 1966), p. 63.

60. See Syed Muhammad Khairudin Aljunid, "Edward Said and Southeast Asian Islam: Western Impressions of Meccan Pilgrims (Hajjis) in the Dutch East Indies, 1800–1900," *Journal of Commonwealth and Postcolonial Studies*, 11/1–2, 2004: 159–175.

61. Tony Tanner, *Lord Jim* (London: Edward Arnold, 1963), p. 6; Gail Fraser, *Interweaving Patterns in the Works of Joseph Conrad* (Ann Arbor, MI: UMI Research Press, 1988), p. 30.

62. Jan Verleun, *Patna and Patusan Perspectives: A Study of the Function of the Minor Characters in Joseph Conrad's* Lord Jim (Groningen, Netherlands: Bert Hagen Castricum, 1979), p. 9.

63. Richard Ambrosini, *Conrad's Fiction as Critical Discourse* (Cambridge: Cambridge University Press, 1991), pp. 116–117.

6

A Medical Mountain

Health Maintenance and Disease Control on the Hajj

> Why should the ghastly spectre of cholera, said to have been imported
> from India, lie hidden somewhere amongst the pilgrims, like the woes
> of the human race in Pandora's box?
>
> —Dr. Abdur Razzaq, Assistant Surgeon and
> British Vice-Consul in Jeddah (1882)

Disease was an important yardstick in how Europeans conceptualized the rest of the world during the past several hundred years.[1] This was particularly so as the industrial age wore on, and definite links started to be established between sanitation and public health in the metropolitan capitals of the West.[2] Yet the industrialization of steamshipping, increased transoceanic travel, and global commerce all went hand in hand, and in fact facilitated the spread of pathogens on a heretofore unparalleled scale.[3] The non-West may have been seen as filthy, diseased, and dangerous by Europeans, therefore, but in the very act of conquering the rest of the world with state-of-the-art technologies, the West also laid down some of the preconditions necessary for a number of diseases to spiral out of control. This was true in the German Pacific, where the colonial presence both fought and spread disease in a number of isolated island chains, such as the Carolines, the Marianas, and the Marshalls.[4] This was also true in the Philippines, where the Americans attempted to establish a new sanitary order (mostly against the spread of cholera), with only mixed success after the turn of the twentieth century.[5] In Central Africa, sleeping sickness killed more than a quarter of a million Africans in British Uganda alone between 1900 and 1905, while in the nearby Belgian Congo—and even British India, the "jewel in the crown" of England's global empire—cholera spun out of control on a number of occasions throughout the nineteenth century.[6] The French dealt with the spread of smallpox, cholera, typhus, and plague almost as broadly as the British, lending employment to generations of Gallic medical professionals from Algeria all the way to Indochina.[7]

In this chapter, the nexus between the Hajj and health is examined, particularly through the lens of cholera and other diseases that traveled on the steamships that made the pilgrimage to Mecca possible from places like Southeast Asia. This was truly a medical mountain to climb—millions of Hajjis made these journeys by ship during the entirety of the colonial period, and the prospect of contagion traveling in the wake of the Hajj became one of the great health issues of the late nineteenth and early twentieth centuries. This state of affairs is foregrounded here with a brief section of background to both cholera and the structures that were put into place to try to control it, before the field of vision is narrowed down to the Red Sea region. How was a regime enacted to deal with this disease as it spread every year on the myriad pilgrim ships that pulled into Jeddah? The Middle Eastern theater of disease control was mirrored in Dutch and British Southeast Asia, with varying degrees of success. The fight against cholera on the Hajj became a global phenomenon, with the center of action focused on the Red Sea and important tendrils of prophylaxis stretching all the way to small villages in distant Muslim lands, such as parts of India and Southeast Asia. This fight became a European crusade as well, though, as the disease was terrifying in its outcomes and acknowledged as all too dangerous to Western societies. I argue that aggressive and increasingly assertive European powers therefore sought to manage the Hajj on the grounds of global epidemiological survival.

Cholera and the Road to Ruin

There are, perhaps, few worse ways to die than through contracting cholera.[8] Cholera moves with astonishing swiftness: someone healthy can contract this disease and be dead less than a day later. Essentially, it kills by removing the body's fluids: extreme diarrhea is accompanied by small achromic particles floating in the victim's stool; these particles are actually parts of the intestinal lining literally peeling off the afflicted body. Once the diarrhea starts, vomiting is never far behind, and the subject starts to lose at an alarming rate the 90 percent fluidity that makes up the substance of all human beings. The body begins to painfully cramp from the loss of water; eventually, patients turn blue and sallow, their eyes sinking farther and farther into the skull. The body itself quickly shrinks. Descriptions of people with cholera are horrific. Left untreated, close to half of cholera's victims die of the disease. Contracted by drinking the bacterium *Vibrio cholerae* in unclean water, the disease is almost always a result of feces appearing in a common, public water supply. A long sea voyage with passengers in close proximity, as was the case with pilgrims coming from Southeast Asia by sea to Jeddah, was almost tailor-made for cholera to thrive and then spread. The disease found in the nineteenth-century Hajj the perfect vehicle to survive and imprint its misery on millions of human beings, all of them in perilous close contact in the holds of slow-moving ships.[9]

In 1821, cholera was found in Arabia for the first time, and it is likely that it came to the peninsula from India via the Persian Gulf. Ten years later, it was in the Hejaz, and thereafter it became a mainstay on the pilgrimage routes. The 1831 epidemic in the Hejaz killed 20,000 people, and subsequent epidemics came to the region of the holy cities in 1841, 1847, 1851, 1856–57, and 1859. Cholera had entered Europe during the middle decades of the nineteenth century, too, from Russia, and eventually it spread into Germany. However, the 1865 epidemic was so powerful in the Hejaz and did such damage not only in Europe but all the way to the United States that the Hajj became a matter of international concern and scrutiny. Fumigant devices, new disinfection techniques, and the distillation of water on a mass scale were experimented with on a very short time frame to try to combat the disease.[10] Yet cholera continued to plague the pilgrimage routes to Mecca, and there were further outbreaks of the disease in 1883, 1889, 1891, and 1893. The last of these epidemics was simply catastrophic in scale. After this time, European powers set aside their bickering and mistrust to try to combat the disease.[11] Smallpox, malaria, dengue fever, and amebic dysentery were also in grim evidence during the annual months of the Hajj, ensuring that the pilgrimage and disease were equated in the Western consciousness of the time.[12]

To check the spread of infection and misery, quarantine stations were established at several points in and around the Red Sea and the holy cities. Several of these stations were erected for land caravans, but the more important ones (from a numerical point of view of the steady stream of pilgrims passing through them) were on either side of the Red Sea waterway. The single most important station was on the barren, tiny island of Kamaran (figure 6.1), just off the Yemeni coast through which almost all pilgrims from Southeast Asia passed.[13] The bare spit of land had an embarkation jetty, a disinfection station, buildings for administration services, a bacteriological laboratory, campsites for pilgrims to stay in their thousands while they awaited "cleansing," a hospital, and a few small fishing villages where residents scraped together a living by smuggling, pearling, or fishing in the blazing heat of the Tihama.[14] Pilgrims had to stay in Kamaran for between ten and fifteen days, while the colonial or Ottoman authorities hoped to isolate anyone sick with one of the more serious communicable diseases. Kamaran had no banking facilities, and all pilgrims had to pay "dues" for the sanitary processes that were enforced on the island, so the entire procedure was cumbersome and rather inefficient.[15] In addition, there was constant wrangling between the various powers and Muslim interests in the Red Sea region as to who was to control Kamaran, its operations, and its revenues.[16] This was the

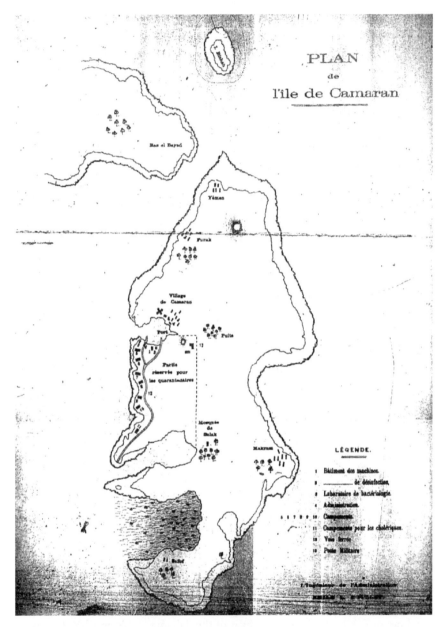

Figure 6.1 The Island of Kamaran in a French Map, 1896.
Credit: Map from Rapport de la Commission des Lazarets Présenté Au Conseil Supérieur de Santé le 23/24 Août 1896, Plan Général des Lazarets de Camaran et Abou-Saad (Mer-Rouge) avec Planches, following page 15, in National Archief, Den Haag (Netherlands), Djeddah Archives (2.05.53) 1.2.4 Medische Aangelegenheden, Fiche # 155.

reality of the Hajj: pilgrimage, politics, disease, and revenue all were part of the same sprawling system.

Kamaran and the other quarantine stations in the Red Sea were set up as part of the sanitary conventions, a series of large-scale international meetings held primarily to deal with the threat of cholera but also other contagious diseases. The first of these meetings was held at Constantinople in 1866, and subsequent meetings were held every few years in Dresden (in 1883), in Venice (in 1892), and in Paris (in 1894). The Paris meeting came about so soon after the Italian symposium because of the devastations wrought by cholera during the 1893 Hajj, as previously mentioned.[17] Contemporary observers were extremely frustrated by the spread of cholera, with a blend of hard-won facts about the disease and enduring superstitions existing side by side in an uneasy, anxious mix.[18] A British surgeon commented that in the last great epidemic of the disease prior to his writing (in the mid-1880s), some 88 percent of cholera victims had died—and these were British soldiers in India, who were "placed under the best possible conditions—conditions it would be impossible to equal in any civil community."[19] Yet despite the international character of these meetings, the epicenter of scholarship, debate, and eventual collective action on the emerging sanitary regime became Paris, where most of the most detailed reports were written and assembled. For this reason, the list of important period studies on cholera, containment, and the operation of the sanitary system in the Hejaz is preserved in the Biliotheque Nationale in Paris, which became an unofficial archive of sorts of how late-nineteenth-century humans were going to try to deal with this truly frightening disease.[20]

The mechanics of policy and the enforcement of the sanitary regimes were both highly political in an era of rapidly expanding and aggressive imperial states (figure 6.2). Some of this political maneuvering was between Europeans themselves, who saw the Middle East (and the Red Sea waterway in particular, especially after Suez opened in 1869) as part of the great game of international politics. Therefore, the British exacted close scrutiny upon German designs in the region, for example, in and around the World War I period, and London did all it could to support King Hussein, whom they saw as a valuable ally in the region.[21] This kind of international politicking around the Hajj was also exercised during World War II, when the British competed with the Japanese in Southeast Asia to assure the millions of local Muslims in the region that the Hajj would be allowed under their respective jurisdictions. Japanese news broadcasts on this subject are particularly interesting in their form and content and were translated by Europeans.[22] Shipping stations' statistics recorded how many pilgrimage vessels were coming to the Hejaz from each European colony, with the British, French, and Dutch all tabulating the numbers to keep an eye on their neighbors' movements.[23] Yet there was also a sense of playing the politics of the

IL HEDJAZ, IL PELLEGRINAGGIO E IL CHOLERA.

NOTE

del Dott. Comm. **Elia Rossi** Bey.

Scopo del Legislatore deve esser quello di sopprimere il morbo alla sua sorgente od almeno, quando tanto non fosse possibile, quello di circoscriverlo. Ciò premesso, siccome è una verità di fatto che il pellegrinaggio islamico è causa di dispersione di gravissima malattia, ne viene di necessità che sieno sciolti i seguenti quesiti, l'importanza dei quali sarà da ognuno agevolmente apprezzata.

1.° Il cholera è desso un resultato delle condizioni geo-climatiche dello Hedjaz?

2.° È desso una conseguenza dei disagi di un lungo, penoso e pericoloso viaggio, dell'agglomeramento di tante migliaia di persone, oppure delle cerimonie religiose che lo accompagnano?

3.° E se non dipende nè dall'una nè dalle altre cause suaccennate, dove se ne dovrà cercare la vera sorgente?

Donde, prima d'ogni altra cosa, il bisogno di farsi un'idea chiara ed esatta tanto delle condizioni geo-climatiche del Hedjaz, che del modo con cui viene effettuato il pellegrinaggio del quale in Europa si ha idea o incompleta o alterata.

Un soggiorno di due anni e nove mesi in quella contrada, e l'averla percorsa in tutti i sensi, mi permettono di parlarne con qualche cognizione di causa, come pure di dare del pellegrinaggio un rapporto sufficientemente dettagliato.

Nel 1866, quando l'Europa smagata dalla recente invasione cholerica mosse la crociata contro il fanatismo islamico — che tale essa qualificava questo convegno devoto — e si radunava a Congresso allo scopo d'intendersi sulle misure da adottarsi per prevenire nuove invasioni, io alzava la voce per mezzo d'un periodico locale onde ottenere una giustizia distributiva e dare ad ognuno il suo. Ma essa non trovò eco, e si presero al solito delle mezze misure che giustamente il Machiavelli qualificava ruine di Stato. Ora, in questa nuova occasione, non credo ozioso di ritor-

	MORTS de choléra.
Minah et la Mecque, du 29 juillet au 22 août . .	2,531
Djeddah, du 1er août au 9 septembre	1,347
Médine, du 18 août au 9 septembre	572
Yambo-sur-Mer, du 28 août au 17 septembre .	53
Lith (au sud du Hedjaz), du 8 au 14 août . . .	50
Confoudah (port de l'Assir), du 26 au 30 août.	8
Total des décès	4,561

Mais ces chiffres approximatifs donnés comme officiels sont loin d'être complets. Ainsi, par exemple, ne figurent pas dans ce tableau les décès cholériques qui ont eu lieu au Taïf, dans le district de Gamid, à Yambo de terre ou Yambo-des-Dattes, dans les

Figure 6.2 Italian and French Cholera Notices.

Credit: E. Rossi, "Il Hedjaz, il Pellegrinaggio e il cholera," *Gior. D. Soc. Ital,* ig., 4, 1882: 549; and A. Proust, "Le cholera de la Mer Rouge en 1890," *Bulletin Acad. de Med.,* 3S, 25, 1891: 426.

Hajj vis-à-vis the Muslim world as well. European powers tried to show Muslim populations, who were increasingly "restive," both in the Middle East and in Southeast Asia, that the West had their best interests at heart. The emplacement of Muslim pilgrimage officers (who sometimes doubled as medical personnel) for each of the European powers in Jeddah in the 1920s was part of this trend.[24] Politics was never far away from the medical situation of the Hajj in the Hejaz, throughout the colonial period and into the early twentieth century.

Medical professionals stationed in the Middle East (or who visited as members of epidemiological study tours, often under the patronage of the sanitary conventions) left important eyewitness accounts of the medical management of the Hajj.[25] The author of the *Relation Medical d'un Voyage au Hedjaz*, Dr. M. Carbonell, published a memoir of his experiences as a doctor in the Hejaz in the first decade of the twentieth century, containing horrendous descriptions of the overcrowding, dirt, disease, and suffering of the ethnically mixed choleric populations of Arabia during that time.[26] The disease was on the road to really being mapped and understood as a plague to humanity at this juncture. But the abilities of both the local Muslim governments and the European powers were not yet developed enough at the moment of his writing to fully eradicate cholera as a ghostly presence hovering over the global pilgrimage. Carbonell's account does stand out as a scientific and moral document in a landscape of lower-class despair and rapidly shifting politics during the fin de siècle period, however. One gets a sense through its pages that a corner was being turned in epidemiological efforts against the disease but that ignorance and superstition of cholera had not yet disappeared as a danger to the Hajj. In these decades on either side of 1900, there was still plenty of misconception about the best way to tackle a plague such as this.[27] But there was a growing sense that the problem could be examined, both in the laboratory and out in the field "among the believers," and that the disease could be halted. This would not happen quickly, but by the mid-twentieth century, cholera was a far less threatening problem than it had been a century earlier.

The Dutch Connection: The Indies to the Desert

Large numbers of the pilgrims who sailed into the Red Sea came from the Dutch East Indies, so knowledge and cognizance of the health situation in the Hejaz was a matter of keen concern in distant Indonesia. The *Koloniaal Verslag* (or *Colonial Report*), published annually in the Indies, makes careful mention that chiefs of residencies were responsible for letting indigenes within their administrative orbits know the state of cholera in Mecca. This information included the charges for sanitary control in the Red Sea, as well as the possibility in certain years that Indies pilgrims would not be allowed in the Hejaz at all.[28] In 1875 in Japara (Java), for example, cholera statistics were kept on each village, and local Javanese there made decisions on whether to go on Hajj partially based on the rumors they were hearing about health conditions in Arabia.[29] A few years later in Besoeki, the numbers of pilgrims dropped off, apparently because of the fear of cholera then prevalent in the Hejaz, the resident said.[30] The local legal edifice in the Indies for dealing with this cycle of disease and transport eventually enacted laws requiring all Hajj aspirants to be inoculated against cholera and typhus before they left the Indies.[31] These rules were often ignored, however, and enforcement was not uniform. Yet even by the late 1930s, there was a steady transport of medical officers from the Indies to the Red Sea, including one Javanese named Manjoedin, a civil servant first-class at the Batavia Central Laboratory, who was sent to Kamaran to look after Dutch interests there. By this time, the British and Dutch were consolidating their operations on the island in an effort to save costs in the event a war broke out.[32]

What happened in the Indies was one thing; regulating health on the long voyages across the Indian Ocean was quite another. This was the incubation chamber for the worst of the infections to spread, so strict care was paid to those factors that might affect the health of travelers. Doctors on board were required to have certain qualifications and experience by Indies law.[33] The decks of the steamships were to be made of wood, iron, or steel, and the upper decks had to be covered to protect pilgrims from sun exposure.[34] Adequate provisions had to be brought on board for the whole voyage, not only the roughly three weeks for one ocean crossing but also the ten days to two weeks earmarked for quarantine. Canned foods such as sardines and salmon were favored, as were dry goods such as biscuits that did not go off in the heat of the Red Sea.[35] Rice, sugar, and meat were also reckoned into these calculations by weight per person.[36] Medicines down to individual dosages and chemical minutiae of prophylaxis, as well as drug treatments, were also legislated (table 6.1), so that outbreaks of infection could be dealt with quickly and efficiently by trained medical personnel on board.[37] Finally, a system was instituted so that any ship approaching port (or other vessels) flying a yellow flag immediately signaled that cholera or some other contagious disease was on board, and that everyone should maintain a strict distance.[38]

When the Dutch ships finally docked into Kamaran, most of the pilgrims were exhausted from weeks at sea living in very close quarters. Although every care was taken to try to protect the passengers against epidemic, quite often a number of sick people were on board. The Dutch consul at Jeddah would spend time at Kamaran during the pilgrimage seasons, collecting information about the ships coming in. One representative report from January 1938 recorded data from multiple pilgrim ships that year. The *Clytoneus*, which arrived from

Table 6.1 **Dutch Medical Supplies Required for Pilgrim Ships from the Indies to Jeddah, 1923 (Credit: *Staatsblad van Nederlandsch-Indie*, 1923, #597).**

Ampullae hydrochlor morphinet scopolamine

(1 cc. 0.01 gram hydrochlor morphine. ¼ milligram hydrobrom. Scopolamine)

[*morphine ampullae*]

Neosalvarsan

(Tube van 0.45 gram)

(de aan boord aanwezige voorraad van dit geneesmiddel moet bij of na den aanvang van het pelgrimsseizoen vernieuwd zijn)

[neosalvaran tube; "the medical provisions present on board must upon the departure of pilgrims be replenished"]

• *"Verbrandstoffen"*

["flammable items"]

Hospitallinnen

Verbandkatoen

Verband rottan voor Inlanders

(op elk schip 1 voor het geheele aantal passagiers)

["hospital linens; binding cottons; binding rattan for natives"; "on every ship one for the entire complement of passengers"]

• *"Instrumenten en Utensilien"*

Doozen Petri

Koortsthermomenters

["Petri dishes and fever thermometers"]

• *"Microscoop"*

Alcohollamp (2 stuks)

Lakmoespapier rood (boekje); blauw (bookje)

Ampullae hydrochlorat emitini (0.030 cc.)

["alcohol lamps; litmus paper red and blue small books; hydrochloric ampullae"]

Source: Staatsblad van Nederlandsch-Indie #597, 1923.
Translation by E. Tagliacozzo.

Singapore, carried 680 passengers, subdivided by gender and age, and the data included the number of sick on board, as well as the nature and outcomes of the sicknesses. The *El Amin*, a much smaller ship, arrived the next day from Aden, and the *Buitenzorg* arrived on January 4 from Batavia, with several deaths reported.[39] Like colonial armed forces elsewhere in the world at this time, the Dutch took a keen interest in finding out the routes of contagion across the seaways.[40] The entire system of Kamaran and its health procedures for Southeast Asian and other pilgrims became public knowledge. Another Dutch report, also from the 1930s, gives us a sense of the size of the numbers of the afflicted: 223 new patients and 322 repeat patients for one month of December alone.[41] A variety of authors (writing in Dutch, French, and English, primarily) debated this vast medical apparatus that stretched its radials of surveillance, maintenance, and care across the oceans.[42] At the same time, some of the actual travelers, such as the regent of Bandung, Raden Adipati Aria Wiranata Koesoma, wrote autobiographies that provide a more human sense of the scope of Kamaran and its operations (box 6.1). He finished his narrative of travels through Kamaran with the notice of two Indies children who died en route to Mecca, and who were buried in Jeddah only a few miles from the destination they had traveled so far to see.[43]

For Dutch Indies pilgrims, Jeddah became a crucial way station from a medical point of view. Because of this, the Dutch spent a fair bit of time trying to decide who would be their medical representatives in the city. In the early 1930s, for example, a Dr. Hartmann was put forward, but some civil servants who debated

---

Box 6.1 **"In Quarantine": The Journal of the Regent of Bandung, Raden Adipati Aria Wiranatakoesoema (1924)**

"Schumig gekleede verpleegsters van Arabische en Neger-afkomst lipene rond. Het lijk van een Sumatraansche vrouw lag op den grond uitgestrekt dichtbij den dokter. Zij was bezweken, nadat zij stuiptrekkende aan wal was gegaan ze ward op een brancard weggevoerd, warrna de dokter den dood constateerde.

"Alle pilgrims werden ontkleed, gebaad en daarna mochten zij naar de quarantaineloodsen. Voor het bad (in Lysol) kreeg ieder een roodkatoenen sarong en ik was benieuwd of mij hetzelfde zou overkomen.

"Een krankzinnige Makassar sloop naar mij toe, die mij—evenals aan boord—weer om hulp kwam vragen tegen denkbeeldige menschen, die hem wilden vermoorden. Ik trachtte hem gerust te stellen en na een licht verzet, ondergigng ook hij de Lysol-behandeling.

"Later op den dag mocht ik mij in een volkomen leege kamer afscheiden, slechts met een stallantaren en mign veldbed bewoonbaar gemaakt. De krankzinnige Makassar bleef al seen kind in mijn burrt....

"Ook den volgenden morgen was de man er nog. Zijn vrouw en kind waren al geisoleerd in een andere loods.

"Het ontsmetten ging intusschen voort, Kinderen huilden en een oude man werd bewusteloos weggedragen. Nadat ik den oude had bijgestaan, begaf ik mij met Oenoes naar de leege kamer, waar nu ook een stole was geplaatst. Ik mocht mijn klleren aanhouden, na vrijgesteld te zijn van de Lysol-behandeling en had gelegenheid een blik om mij heen te slaan."

"Shabbily-clad care-givers of Arab and African origin walked around. It appeared that a Sumatran woman lay outstretched on the ground near the doctor. She was convulsing, and after her trembling was finished she was carried away on a stretcher-plank, after the doctor had made sure she was dead.

"All of the pilgrims were disrobed, bathed, and after that they could go to the quarantine hangar. For the bath (in Lysol) all of them got a red cotton sarong to use, and I was curious if I myself was going to die from this.

"A crazy Makassarese slouched toward me who—even as he had when we were on board ship—again wanted to ask my help against imaginary foes, who wanted to murder him. I tried to calm him down, and after a light was lit, he also received the Lysol treatment.

"Late in the day I found myself in a completely empty room, made habitable only with a stall and by my field-bed. The crazy Makassarese man appeared as a child in my vicinity....

"The following morning the man was still there. His wife and child were isolated in another hangar.

"Meanwhile the disinfection went forward. Children cried and an old man who became senseless was dragged away. After I had stayed there, I went with Oenoes to the empty room, where now a stool had been placed. I had to hold onto my clothes after exemption for the Lysol-procedures and I had the opportunity to glance at myself."

Translation by E. Tagliacozzo

Source: Raden Adipati Aria Wiranatakoesoema, *Mijn Reis naar Mekka* (G. A. Bovene, 1924), pp. 27–28.

candidates for the post felt that he did not have enough experience for the task, despite several years of shipboard medical service on the SS *Tapanoeli* and the SS *Niewkerk*.[44] To give a sense of scale, during the month of Ramadan in 1933, more than five hundred patients passed through the Dutch clinic in the city, many of them suffering from debilitating diseases.[45] Yet the Dutch medical facility was only one among four; there was also a local Arab station, a Russian station, and an English one, the latter staffed with a British-Indian (Muslim) doctor.[46] The Dutch establishment in the city had between sixty and one hundred beds, but care was very limited, as the patients' families needed to provide for their loved one (the

Dutch gave the afflicted only small quantities of bread and milk).[47] The Dutch clinic did have a drug dispensary, however, which gave out medicines not only to Dutch subjects but also to a number of poor Arabs as well.

From Jeddah, the Indies pilgrims would finally trek into the desert and toward Mecca, Medina, and the other holy sites that made up the religious stations of the Hajj. The Dutch consul in Jeddah in the 1930s knew that, realistically, his facility was the last one where they could expect to receive substantial care, as the medical stations in the interior were far less modern. These latter facilities were staffed by Muslim doctors as a rule because of religious prohibitions; the dispensary in Medina had an Egyptian doctor, the one in Yambo was staffed by an Ottoman Turk, and the three in Mecca were all run by Syrian doctors.[48] In a report from November 1936, the Dutch consul told the minister for foreign affairs in The Hague the kinds of diseases he was treating as the Hajj season progressed. He had just seen more than one hundred patients with a variety of ailments ranging across the spectrum of pathologies (malaria, influenza, amebic dysentery, gonorrhea, rheumatic disease, lymph disease, laryngitis, acute bronchitis, bronchiopneumonia, bronchial asthma, dental disorders, diarrhea, menstrual problems, and abscesses).[49] He pointed out to his superiors that a number of Hajjis were starting to use automobiles to cover the large distances across the desert to places like Medina, though the majority who still went by foot were in greater need of his help. He tried to provide for their immediate needs, he explained, but he also gave them things that they were likely to require for the journey (such as stomach medicine, prophylaxes, and skin-protecting balms) once they were out of his reach.[50] This treatment demonstrates the confluence of philanthropy and epidemiological self-interest of the Western regimes now firmly ensconced in the Hejaz. They continually attempted to regulate the massive flood of pilgrims upon whose health so much had come to depend.

The British Connection: The Malay Peninsula to the Holy Cities

In terms of health maintenance, the British Hajj from Southeast Asia largely mirrored the Dutch regime, although there were places in which the two projects diverged. The British in Southeast Asia, particularly in Singapore, prioritized disease control and the erection of a "sanitary port," putting them ahead of the Dutch, who had a far larger and more unruly colony to administer in the region.[51] By the 1870s and 1880s, bills of health were being issued to pilgrim ships sailing from Singapore's harbor, clearly instituted in response to the plague reports from Mecca.[52] Singapore was expressly tasked to ensure its ships were cholera free.[53]

In an exasperated letter to his administrative superiors in Asia, the British consul at Jeddah singled out shipping companies in Singapore for their negligence in allowing too many pilgrims on board in that port.[54] In fact, within local colonial circles the entire exercise of the Hajj was often considered much more trouble than it was worth, both from political and public health points of view.[55] The High Commission in Malaya after the turn of the century seems to have shared this perspective, considering the health of pilgrims a millstone of sorts around the colonial government's neck.[56] Yet the death statistics didn't lie; Malay pilgrims died in large numbers while performing the Hajj. In 1865, some three thousand perished, or 30 percent; in 1881, 4,292 died, or 42 percent. By 1891, the numbers were around the 3,000 mark and 30 percent again, but these were still alarming figures.[57]

Once the Hajj boats left British Southeast Asia, they faced many of the same challenges as the Dutch ships. Overcrowding was the serial killer of the vessels. A letter from the Dutch consul in Jeddah to the Foreign Office in London described how captains turned a blind eye to extra pilgrims to make more money; only 100 extra Hajjis would easily pay off any fine if the captain was caught overcrowding his ships, but many more than this could be crowded onto vessels.[58] The British colonial administration in Singapore fought a long battle with the steamship companies, particularly the Alfred Holt line, to ensure that qualified doctors were on board every ship, though the doctors' salaries and any enforcement against overcrowding cut into the companies' profits.[59] Legislation annually tightened ships' requirements for pilgrim traffic, as a series of acts published in the *Straits Settlements Government Gazettes* makes clear. The number of passengers, the amount of space each was to have, provisions for food and water, search procedures, and fines were all laid out in meticulous detail.[60] The regulations also spelled out how female passengers were to be searched, since many women were hidden away from the public by the older male members of their families.[61] Yet the imperfect understanding of how cholera and other infectious diseases spread still made the regulations (and their enforcement) quite difficult, even as a fuller cognizance of containment regimes developed and was instituted in various ports.[62]

Many of the ships at Kamaran were from British Southeast Asia, which was reflected in the fact that signs posted on the island often had Javanese or Malay inscribed upon them (many Indies pilgrims chose to make their journeys via Penang or Singapore in British-owned bottoms) (table 6.2).[63] The report of the civil administrator of Kamaran in 1939 even specified diseases that were particularly common among the "Malay races" coming to the island: paralysis, furunculosis, bronchopneumonia, and gangrene, in addition to the more common epidemic sicknesses.[64] Occasionally vessels from British Southeast Asia were put into detention there for longer than usual periods of time, if

Table 6.2 **Statement Showing the Arrival at and Departure from Kamaran of Pilgrim Ships during Part of the Pilgrimage Season of 1891**

No.	Arrival Date	Ship Name	Flag	Arriving from
1	March 9	Deccan	British	Bombay
2	March 15	Voorwartz	Dutch	Batavia
3	March 18	Sculptor	British	Bombay
4	March 19	Port Fairy	British	Singapore/Penang
5	March 27	Noord Bealand	Dutch	Batavia
6	March 31	Hooseince	British	Bombay
7	April 2	Sultan	British	Calcutta
8	April 4	Jason	British	Surabaya
9	April 10	Tanjore	British	Bombay
10	April 14	Cheang Chew	British	Singapore/Penang
11	April 16	Gelderland	Dutch	Batavia
12	April 17	Akbar	British	Singapore
13	April 20	Cornocopia	British	Basra
14	April 21	Khiva	British	Calcutta
15	April 25	Deccan	British	Bombay
16	May 2	Sculptor	British	Bombay
17	May 6	Hampshire	British	Singapore
18	May 18	Taif	British	Bombay
19	May 22	Atjeh	Dutch	Batavia
20	May 25	King Arthur	British	Bombay
21	June 3	Mobile	British	Bombay
22	June 5	Somali	Portuguese	Zanzibar
23	June 8	Akhbar	British	Bombay
24	June 10	Hooseince	British	Bombay
25	June 13	Tanjore	British	Bombay

26	June 19	Deccan	British	Bombay
27	June 21	Sculptor	British	Bombay
28	June 28	Michigan	British	Bombay
29	July 2	Avoca	Zanzibar	Zanzibar/Muscat
30	July 4	Cheang Chew	British	Singapore
31	July 5	Propontis	British	Singapore
32	July 6	Somali	Portuguese	Aden

Source: Abstracted from "Report on the Quarantine Stations at Camaran for the Year 1891" in Foreign Office 195/1730, Appx. "A," PRO, London.

suspected pathogens were on board that might endanger the Hajj.[65] The flow of ships from the Straits Settlements and the Malay Peninsula remained fairly constant, allowing the sanitary board on Kamaran to make large sums of money from their taxes.[66] Fewer and fewer stones were being left unturned by the colonial authorities, in other words. In the years before the outbreak of the World War II, the payment of dues at Kamaran by Malayan pilgrims produced a very large amount of money, sums that seem all the greater considering from how far away these Straits dollars had come. There were few other parts of the Muslim world, in fact, that could rival this Southeast Asian combination of cash and religiosity.[67]

In Jeddah, as was the case with Hajjis coming from the Dutch sphere of Southeast Asia, British officials in Singapore and Malaya kept a close eye on disease vis-à-vis the health of their own pilgrims. Straits correspondence is full of letters between colonial civil servants discussing the health situation in that port (box 6.2). In years of plague or cholera, news of local epidemics and their progress traveled to Southeast Asia very quickly, both through official and unofficial channels.[68] The British in the tropics monitored the hospital situation for their charges from afar, noting how many Hajjis were in formal medical care in Jeddah's facilities and what ailments they suffered.[69] Those Malay pilgrims who died in Jeddah had to be buried and their final affairs arranged. Not infrequently, family members wanted to get refunds on the Hajjis' return tickets, as many poor Malays often considered this a lot of money. Only in the 1920s were procedures set up to allow the unused part of the ticket to be repatriated as a bank draft to the deceased's family.[70] The confluence of health and financial concerns grew in importance, especially during wartime, when the imperial powers—and particularly Britain—attempted to

Box 6.2 **Sickness in the Hejaz According to a British Traveler,** *1920*

Pilgrimage day was the 24th August and the Id on the 25th, 26th and 27th. Unfortunately for the ten preceding days there was a continuous heat wave, which the local inhabitants say was the hottest they remember for forty years. The effect on the pilgrims was very bad. The last Indian boats arrived on the 15th, 16th, and 17th August; there was a great shortage of camels and Shouk-doufs, so that many died from sunstroke and heat exhaustion. At Bahra, the main halting place between Jeddah and Mecca, about 250 pilgrims are buried, and many died along the road, and were lying incompletely buried or unburied, the prey of scavenging dogs. The mite Government made no plans for the succour of these pilgrims. They did not, as in previous years, open an aid post at Bahra, and did nothing to arrange to transport fresh water for those who fell out by the way.

The hot weather ceased in Jeddah on the 24th August but it remained hot at Arafat, and the mortality there was very high.

The total number of pilgrims at Arafat has been estimated differently by different authorities, but the number probably did not exceed 80,000. The total pilgrimage death rate also is variously estimated, but if we compare the numbers who arrived by sea and the number who departed, the death rate must have been very high, and about 10,000 pilgrims remain unaccounted for.

The pilgrims began to return to Jeddah early in September and came down in large numbers. The ships were rapidly filled but after the "Koweit" left on the 8th of September there was a long delay, the next Indian boat "Nairung" leaving on the 20th of September. During these twelve days conditions in Jeddah were as bad as they could be. Pilgrims were camped in the streets, and all round the quarantine buildings, Beledia, and customs sheds there was a pilgrim camp. The majority of the pilgrims were old, emaciated and unable to fend for themselves. Many suffered from diarrhea and dysentery. Many were dying absolutely untended and almost naked, and excreta and filth were not removed. The open space behind the quarantine was an open latrine. We organized stretcher parties from the Indian hospital and collected all the worst cases there. Many cases were also taken to the civil Arab hospital, but they were left in the corridors and outhouses, men and women together, and their condition were terrible.

Source: Report by Major W. E. Marshall on the Pilgrimage, 1920, in F.O 371/5094B, PRO, London.

win the hearts and minds of Southeast Asian pilgrims through programs such as these.[71] Jeddah became the clearing port, therefore, both for epidemiological matters and for attendant administrative issues, which frequently needed to be dealt with together. The coffin industry and the gravestone makers each had a part in this story, as did the many levels of bureaucrats who ensured that the remains of Hajjis—bodily and pecuniary—were properly returned and handled.

The last step in the medical journey was the holy cities, and here, too, the authorities in British Southeast Asia were vigilant about goings-on, despite the fact that non-Muslims were not allowed into Mecca and Medina. Singapore knew very clearly when there was cholera in Mecca, not just in Jeddah or Kamaran, as reports circulated back and forth with the Foreign Office in London.[72] Right after the end of hostilities in World War I, the British began to prepare detailed reports on individual diseases circulating in the holy sites, with separate folders on cholera (and the application of quarantine measures), plague (including the progress made on the destruction of sources of infection), typhus (again on the eradication of sources, which included lice and vermin on people, in dwellings, and even on railways for this particular disease), and influenza, which had become a new pandemic in 1918.[73] Similarly, when World War II ended, new reports were commissioned on Mecca and Medina concerning disease by land-quarantine, air-quarantine, and quarantine at Jeddah, from the older and more populous route by sea.[74] The British high commissioner in Kuala Lumpur engaged in discussions in the early 1950s with the British consul in Jeddah as to how to reduce the amount of time that Malay pilgrims spent in the Hejaz, partially for political reasons but also as an epidemiological precaution after a particularly grim death toll in the Hajj of 1951.[75] The confluence of health and the Hajj continued to stretch into the age of decolonization, therefore. It became an old issue facing a new world of independent Muslim states, whose policies had been decided for them for decades by the imperial powers.

Conclusion

Diseases have often been ascribed to individual countries or races as a kind of national disgrace—the "English sweat"; the "Danish disease" (scurvy); the *morbus Hungaricus*; the *plica polonica*.[76] To name a malady together with a people was to derogate the latter by implication with the former, the disease itself. One of the reasons that cholera is so interesting and why it was also so exceedingly dangerous in the eyes of late-nineteenth- and early-twentieth-century humans was that it was not identifiable with any particular group. It killed indiscriminately.

Cholera may have had its origins in India, but the pilgrimage routes to and from Mecca were one of the main arteries that spread the disease. Though Western and Muslim societies had rather different concepts of what contagion might actually be at this time, it became clear that the most important task at hand was stopping cholera before it literally spiraled out of control and massacred entire civilizations.[77] Theories of how infection worked gradually progressed in Europe during the middle decades of the nineteenth century and helped with this program. By the second half of the 1800s, cholera itself was being used as a tool for social and economic analysis, propagating a number of reasonably accurate theories about how close physical proximities of people and a lack of cleanliness helped contribute to illness.[78] The medical pluralities that existed in the contemporary Ottoman world made it difficult to enforce sanitary regimes, however, and increasingly European governments took it upon themselves to guarantee the overall health of the Hajj on a large, systemwide basis.[79] This was accomplished as part of only a very slow process, however, with very real difficulties of politics, nascent epidemiology, and enforcement militating against saving thousands of lives. Many people (both Muslim and Western) were fatalistic about this outcome of the pilgrimage, and as a result, the graves of members of both communities still litter the Hejaz.

The transmission of cholera along the transoceanic pilgrimage routes in the late nineteenth and early twentieth centuries effectively rendered the Hajj a dangerous institution and often a fatal one, not only to the community of believers practicing its rites (the *umma*) but also to Westerners in general. Because of this, the maintenance of public health measures as part of the global pilgrimage became a matter of pressing concern to the expanding imperial powers, and never more so than after years of particularly serious epidemics, such as 1831, 1865, and 1893. These three dates, roughly thirty years apart, reminded all parties involved in the Hajj how serious the consequences of inaction were, and attempts were increasingly made to ameliorate the situation. Legislation was passed in the various colonial empires to try to rationalize shipping and to maintain clean and adequate water supplies, as well as a modicum of space for individual pilgrims. Sanitary conventions produced extensive public documents on epidemiological plans of action, as well as points of view. Finally, land itself was commandeered for the purpose of quarantine stations, set up at semiregular intervals wherever caravans or ships might pass into the Red Sea region carrying pilgrims bound for the religious cities of the Hejaz. Stations like Kamaran became emblematic of the possibilities of the modern age: bacteriological laboratories, docking complexes, and limed-in grave sites all appeared within a few hundred meters of one another. The living, the sick, and the dead all passed through on their way in and out of the cities of the Prophet.

NOTES

1. David Arnold, "Disease, Medicine and Empire," in David Arnold, ed., *Imperial Medicine and Indigenous Societies* (Manchester, England: Manchester University Press, 1988), p. 7.
2. Jean-Pierre Goubert, *The Conquest of Water: The Advent of Health in the Industrial Age* (Princeton, NJ: Princeton University Press, 1989), pp. 58–67.
3. Myron Echenberg, *Plague Ports: The Global Bubonic Plague of 1906* (New York: New York University Press, 2007). For a review that puts this book into context with the rest of the Indian Ocean world, see Eric Tagliacozzo, "Underneath the Indian Ocean: A Review Essay," *Journal of Asian Studies*, 67/3, 2008: 1–8.
4. Wolfgang Eckart, "Medicine and German Colonial Expansion in the Pacific: The Caroline, Mariana and Marshall Islands," in Roy Macleod and Milton Lewis, eds., *Disease, Medicine, and Empire* (London: Routledge, 1988), pp. 81, 89, 91.
5. Reynaldo Ileto, "Cholera and the Origins of the American Sanitary Order in the Philippines," in David Arnold, ed., *Imperial Medicine and Indigenous Societies* (Manchester, England: Manchester University Press, 1988), p. 131.
6. Maryinez Lyons, "Sleeping Sickness, Colonial Medicine and Imperialism: Some Connections in the Belgian Congo," in Roy Macleod and Milton Lewis, eds., *Disease, Medicine, and Empire* (London: Routledge, 1988), p. 247; I. J. Catanach, "Plague and the Tensions of Empire: India, 1896–1918," in David Arnold, ed., *Imperial Medicine and Indigenous Societies* (Manchester, England: Manchester University Press, 1988), p. 149.
7. Anne Marcovich, "French Colonial Medicine and Colonial Rule: Algeria and Indochina," in Roy Macleod and Milton Lewis, eds., *Disease, Medicine, and Empire* (London: Routledge, 1988), pp. 105, 109.
8. I have made extensive use of the Academy of Medical Sciences Library in writing this chapter, but the Wellcome Institute's Collection (London) is particularly important for getting a sense of the genealogy of cholera in nineteenth-century science; the materials here in terms of correspondence are second to none. Anyone desiring to see how conceptions of cholera grew and changed during this period must stop through London to peruse these papers. A few highlights, only, here: an 1854–55 chart showing hospital equipment in the possession of different British regiments abroad, which is important because it shows how a number of different measures were used to try to lower the chances of cholera spreading among the troops (blankets, bell tents, chamber pots, spitting cups, mops, surgical kits, etc., are all mentioned in this respect); see RAMC/397/F/RR/6 O/S #22 Sanitary Concerns (1854–1855). Nearly forty years later, see Sir David Bruce's Notebook re Cholera Literature, compiled when he was assistant professor of pathology at the Army Medical Station in 1893. This notebook is fascinating because it is a handwritten treatise comparing and combining many observations about cholera; each page of the notebook is on a different topic, as he tried to triangulate and understand what he was up against. Rubrics include "stool," "presence in mucus membranes," "presence in blood and organs," "presence in vomit," "morphology," "vitality in artificial culture media," and "inoculation experiments." This item is located at RAMC/600 Box 129 (1893) Cholera Literature. Nearly forty years on again, in the 1930s, see "Disposal of Waste Products in Peace and War: Epidemiology and Infectious Diseases" (a typed notebook for use of British civil servants in the 1930s). Under "Cholera" is written: "Essentially a disease of defective sanitation, no community under good sanitary control, including a pure water supply, need fear cholera. The disease is water-borne; vibrios can multiply and retain virulence in water for many days. Disposal of waste and unclean sources is vital. Soldiers to be inoculated with anti-cholera injection. Water sources must be kept sterile." This notebook is found at RAMC/755/1/4 Box 154 Disposal of Waste Products in Peace and War (1930s) of the collection. The change in tone and anxiety in these accounts, spread over the decades, comes across very forcefully; so, too, does the confidence of the medical pronouncements.
9. Period journal articles preserved in the New York Academy of Medicine's library are very useful in getting a sense of how cholera was appraised at the high point of the epidemic period.

Some of the more important articles include: S. W. Johnson, "Cholera and the Meccan Pilgrimage," *British Medical Journal*, 1, pp. 1218–1219; A. Proust, "Le choléra de la Mer Rouge en 1890," *Bulletin Acad. de Med.*, 3S/25, 1891: 421–445; Anonymous, "Cholera on Pilgrim Steamers at Camaran," *Lancet*, 2, 1912: 913; Anonymous, "Small-pox and Cholera in the Pilgrimage," *Lancet*, 1, 1910: 1792; Anonymous, "Cholera at Jiddah and Mecca," *US Public Health Report*, 23/1, 1908: 289; E. Rossi, "Il Hedjaz, il Pellegrinaggio e il cholera," *Gior. D. Soc. Ital*, ig., 4, 1882: 549–578; R. Bowman, "Cholera in Turkish Arabia," *British Medical Journal*, 1, 1890: 1031–1032; and Anonymous, "Cholera, the Haj and the Hadjaz Railway," *Lancet*, 2, 1908: 1377. This is by no means an exhaustive list; there are dozens upon dozens of period sources available here.

10. C. Izzedine, *Le Choléra el l'hygiène à la Mecque* (Paris, 1909), pp. 30–36.

11. D. Oslchanjetzki, "Souvenirs de l'epidemie de choléra au Hedjaz en 1893," in F. Daguet, ed., *Le pelerinage de la Mecque* (Paris, 1932), p. 297.

12. Izzedine, *Le Choléra*, pp. 9–11.

13. For an interesting history of this station, see Nigel Groom, "The Island of Two Moons: Kamaran 1954," *British-Yemeni Society Journal*, 10, 2002: 29–37. Also see S. Kuneralp, "Pilgrimage and Cholera in Ottoman Hedjaz," *Turkish-Arab Relations*, 4, 1989: 69–81.

14. ARA, Djeddah Archives, 1.2.4 Medische Aangelegenheden, Fiche #155: *Rapport de la Commission des Lazarets Présenté Au Conseil Superieur de Santé le 23/24 Août 1896, Plan Général des Lazarets de Camaran et Abou-Saad (Mer-Rouge) avec Planches*, following page 15.

15. See Col. Sec., Singapore to Gov't of India Dept. of Education, Health and Lands, January 26, 1928, #1202, in IOR/L/E/7/1513/File 4070.

16. Inter-Departmental Pilgrimage Quarantine Committee, July 25, 1922, E7501/113/91 in IOR/L/E/7/1908/File 7376.

17. For the details on these conferences, see William Roff, "Sanitation and Security: The Imperial Powers and the Haj in the Nineteenth Century," *Arabian Studies*, 6, 1982: 143–160; see also Valeska Huber, "The Unification of the Globe by Disease? The International Sanitary Conferences on Cholera, 1851–1894," *Historical Journal*, 49, 2, 2006: 453–476.

18. Wellcome, Sir William Gull to Sir Joseph Fayrer, n.d., 1885, in RAMC/571/Box 126, Letter from Sir William Gull to Sir Joseph Fayrer on the Causes of Cholera (1885).

19. Wellcome, Surgeon-Major Hamilton, *Cholera: Its Endemic Area and Epidemic Progression* (Dublin: John Falconer, 1885), p. 20, in RAMC/474/47 Box 87: Parkes Pamphlet Collection. For more on the Indian Hajj situation vis-à-vis health, see I. J. Catanach, "South Asian Muslims and the Plague, 1896–1914," in Asim Roy, ed., *Islam in History and Politics: Perspectives from South Asia* (Oxford: Oxford University Press, 2008, pp. 97–120).

20. The list on useful period studies to be found in the Paris collections of the National Library is very long. I list just a few of the more important sources here: H. E. Mahmoud, "Communications sur le Choléra. Le Choléra et le Haddj," *Union Medical*, 2/28 1865: 260–264 (but especially p. 261 on descriptions of cholera entering epidemic phases); E. A. Buez, "Le Pélerinage de la Mecque," *Gaz. Hebd. De Med.*, 2/10, 1873: 633–634 (on shipping between the Hejaz and Penang and Batavia); A. Fauvel, "Note sur l'épidémic de Choléra Observée Parmi les Pélerins à leur Retour de la Meque," *Recueil des Travaux du Comité Consultatif d'Hygiène Publique de France et des Actes Officiels de L'Administration Sanitaire* 7 (Paris, 1878), pp. 1–9 (on sanitary cordons on both sides of the Red Sea waterway); M. le Catelan, "Choléra au Hedjaz en 1890: Prophylaxie Sanitaire dans la Mer Rouge," *Recueil des Travaux du Comité Consultatif d'Hygiène Publique de France et des Actes Officiels de L'Administration Sanitaire*, 21 (1891): 830–842 (especially p. 839, which shows the spread of cholera on the Asian sea routes, including Formosa, the Philippines, Tonkin, Annam, Cochinchina, Java, Sumatra, Siam, and Burma).

21. See, for example, all in the PRO: Minutes of a Conference on the Pilgrimage, FO, March 18, 1919; Cypher Telegram, FO to General Allenby, Cairo, May 18, 1919, #616 Very Urgent; Telegram, FO to General Allenby, Cairo, June 6, 1919, #710; "Note on the Present Situation with Regards to Kameran" by S. Buchanan, Medical Officer and Ministry of Health, Chairman Hedjaz Quarantine Committee, June 8, 1919, all in "Peace Conference" (1919) (FO 608/101/17).

22. See PRO, Netherlands Embassy to M. E. Dening, FO, May 27, 1943, #1710, in "Hajj of Muslims from Japanese-Controlled Lands (1943)," FO 371/35929. The translated Japanese proclamation reads: "Tokyo reports in English to the world, April 7, Singapore: Assurance by the Chief of the Military Administration that efforts are being made for resumption of the pilgrimages by Mohammedans to Mecca has evoked an expression of loyalty to Japan from the Mohammedan Religious Conference which closed yesterday. The Conference represented 10,000,000 followers of Islam. Mohammedans all over the world are said by observers to have hailed the assurance of provision of ships for the Mecca pilgrimages despite pressure of war on shipping space. This further evidence of Japan's solicitude for the millions of Mohammedans under its protection has smashed malicious Anglo-United States propaganda that Japan is intolerant of religion."

23. See, for example, the shipping statistic documents (from FO 195/2320, and FO 195/2350, both from 1907–1910 period) reproduced in *Records of the Hajj*, pp. 341–369.

24. See IOL, Gov't of India, Foreign and Political Dept, to UK Consul, Jedda, January 25, 1926, #482E, in "Kamaran: Establishment of Pilgrimage Officer" (1926) (IOR/R/20/A/4121).

25. A list of just a few of the studies that I have found helpful in this respect are as follows: Dr. B. Schnepp, *Le Pélerinage de La Mecque* (Paris, 1865); Dr. P. Remlinger, *Police Sanitaire: Les Conditions Sanitaires du Pélerinage Musulman* (Paris, 1908); Dr. F. Duguet, *Le Pélerinage de La Mecque au Point de Vue Religieux, Social et Sanitaire* (Paris, 1932); L. Couvy, *Le Choléra et le Pélerinage Musulman au Hedjaz* (Paris, 1934).

26. See Marcelin Carbonell, *Relation Médicale d'un Voyage de Transport de Pelerins Musulmans au Hedjaz 1907–1908* (Aix-en-Provence: Publications de l'Université de Provence (reprint), 2001).

27. See, for example, Anonymous, "Travaux Originaux: Epidémiologie," *Gazette Hebdomadaire de Medecine et de Chirurgie*, September 19, 1873, #38, p. 604; also Anonymous, "Sociétés Savantes: Académie des Sciences," *Gazette Hebdomadaire de Médecine et de Chirurgie*, November 14, 1873, #46, p. 734.

28. *Koloniaal Verslagen* for 1872, p. 98, and 1875, p. 122.

29. See ANRI, Japara #59: in K. 18 Japara, #59. Tahun 1875. Aankomende brieven (Vendu kantoor; Bedevaart; ziekte rapport; politiezaken), January–April 1875 (blz. 30).

30. See ANRI, Algemeen Verslag over het Jaar 1883, Residentie Besoeki, in K. 23 Besuki, #78 (Nomor lama 9/14) (1883). B.b. Uitbreiding van het Mohamedanisme toe–en afname van het aantal bedevaartgangers.

31. *Bijblad*, #44114 (1885), P. 376–377; *Bijblad* #10236 (1922), p. 387–388; *Bijblad* #11780 (1928), p. 605.

32. ARA, Djeddah Archives, 1.2.4 Medische Aangelegenheden, Fiche #164: Chief of Health, Kamaran to Batavia Central Laboratory, October 31, 1937; and "Uitreksel van het Register der Besluiten van het Hoefd van den Dienst der Volksgezondheid, Batavia, July 26, 1939, #24724."

33. Bijblad #11018 (1926), p. 362.

34. Staatsblad #557 (1912), p. 3; Staatsblad #507 (1937), p. 3.

35. ARA, Djeddah Archives, 1.2.4 Medische Aangelegenheden, Fiche #156: Inspector for NEI to Captains of Pilgrimships of the Rotterdamsche Lloyd, January 30, 1922.

36. ARA, Djeddah Archives, 1.2.4 Medische Aangelegenheden, Fiche #156: "Regeling Betreffende Extra Voeding Pelgrims" (enclosed in above).

37. Staatsblad #597 (1923), pp. 4–5.

38. Staatsblad #208 (1911), pp. 1–2.

39. ARA, Djeddah Archives, 1.2.4 Medische Aangelegenheden, Fiche #157: Maandrapport, Dutch Consul in Jeddah (Kamaran, January–February 1938).

40. P. Adriani, "De Bedevaart naar Arabie en de Verspreiding der Epidemische Ziekten," *Nederlandse Militair Geneeskundig Archief*, 23, 1899: 7, 156, 245, passim.

41. ARA, Djeddah Archives 1.2.4 Medische Aangelegenheden, Fiche #158, Medical Services, December 31, 1933, #5.

42. J. Eisenberger, "Indie en de Bedevaart naar Mekka" (1928), pp. 103–111.

43. G. A. van Bovene, ed., *Mijn Reis Naar Mekka: Naar het Dagboek van het Regent van Bandoeg Raden Adipati Aria Wiranata Koesoma* (1924), p. 38.

44. ARA, Djeddah Archives, 1.2.4 Medische Aangelegenheden, Fiche #161: Dutch Consul, Jeddah to Directors, NHM (Amsterdam), September 16, 1932, and Dutch Consul, Jeddah, to MvBZ, January 20, 1933, #84.

45. ARA, Djeddah Archives, 1.2.4 Medische Aangelegenheden, Fiche #158: Medical Service of the Dutch Consulate, Mecca, to Dutch Consulate, Jeddah, December 31, 1933, #5.

46. ARA, Djeddah Archives, 1.2.4 Medische Aangelegenheden, Fiche #158: Medical Service of the Dutch Consulate, Mecca, to Dutch Consulate, Jeddhah, December 15, 1933.

47. ARA, Djeddah Archives, 1.2.4 Medische Aangelegenheden, Fiche #163: Dutch Consul to MvBZ, January 5, 1934, #33.

48. Ibid.

49. ARA, Djeddah Archives, 1.2.4 Medische Aangelegenheden, Fiche #159: Vice-Consul, Dutch Consulate, Jeddah, to MvBZ, November 11, 1936, #896.

50. ARA, Djeddah Archives, 1.2.4 Medische Aangelegenheden, Fiche #159: Vice-Consul, Dutch Consulate, Jeddah, to MvBZ, February 2, 1936, #93.

51. Brenda Yeoh, *Contesting Space in Colonial Singapore: Power Relations and the Urban Built Environment* (Oxford: Oxford University Press, 1996), especially pp. 85–93, 119–135.

52. Because the volume of correspondence is so large in this series and would take up far too much space here, in this subsection of the chapter I provide only rubrics for the CO/273 series, which can then easily be consulted by subsequent researchers. For this cite, see CO 273, 142/12072 (January 8, 1886).

53. See the correspondence in CO 273, 53/11250 (October 14, 1871).

54. UK Consul, Jeddah, to Sec. of Gov't, Bombay, April 30, 1875 (FO 78/2418) in *Records of the Hajj*, 3.07.

55. William Roff, "Sanitation and Security," before table 1.

56. ARNEG, High Commission, #1305/1928.

57. Mary McDonnell, "Conduct of the Hajj," p. 641.

58. UK Consul, Jeddah, to FO, London, August 20, 1875 (FO 78/2418) in *Records of the Hajj*, 3.07.

59. See CO 273/396/28656 (July 22, 1913); CO 273/402/26309 (July 30, 1913); CO 273/408/35816 (September 19, 1914); CO 273/418/34307 (September 9, 1914); and CO 273/418/38345 (October 5, 1914).

60. *SSGG* 1867 (#31); *SSGG* 1868 (#12); *SSGG* 1890 (#7).

61. *SSGG* 1897 (#16), see clause 34, "Medical inspection of women"—the inspection of women was, as far as possible, to be carried out by women officers.

62. See Wellcome, Clippings of Revisions to "Notations on Diseases, Manual of Medicine" in MS 1495/5: Box 32. For cholera on the seaways, see Wellcome, Extract from Law #3 Dated February 9, 1918, Issued by the Minister of the Interior and Published in the *Journal Officiel* #12, dated February 11, 1918, in RAMC/1756/5/1 Box 354: Rules for Containment of Cholera, Port Said (1923).

63. PRO, Note from Col. E. Wilkinson to the Committee, December 15, 1919, in FO 608/275/1: "Peace Conference (1919)."

64. PRO, Report of the Civil Administrator and Director, Kamaran Quarantine Station (1939), in CO 323/1699/14, "Health and Sanitary (1939–40)."

65. See, for example, CO 273/355/18927 (June 5, 1909).

66. See CO 273/256/11913 (March 24, 1900); CO 273/264/4246 (February 7, 1900); CO 273/264/13611 (May 2, 1900), for some of the details.

67. ARNEG, High Commission, #187/1936.

68. See CO 273/232/12204 (July 8, 1897); CO 273/232/12416 (July 9, 1897); CO 273/232/13471 (July 21, 1897); CO 273/232/13559 (July 23, 1897).

69. See CO 273/501/50389 (September 16, 1920); CO 273/505/37352 (July 27, 1920).

70. IOL, "Report on the Pilgrimage of 1923," Eastern Confidential E 25/11/91 in (IOR/R/20/A/4347), File 44/1.

71. PRO, Confidential Memo from W. H. Lee-Warner, c/o UK Consul Batavia, October 11, 1918, #6115 (Prop. 21/18), in Sanitary and Destitute Pilgrims, 1920–23, T161/1086.

72. See CO 273/209/11948 (July 9, 1895) and CO 273/491/21684 (April 5, 1919) as only two examples.

73. PRO, "Report by the Delegate of Great Britain on the Autumn Session of the Committee of the Office International d'Hygiene Publique, Paris 1919," in Peace Conference 1919 (FO 608/275/1).

74. PRO, "Report of Dr. N. I. Corkill on the Jeddah Quarantine and Certain Related Matters as Seen during the 1948 Mecca Pilgrimage, November 25, 1948," in Anti-Cholera Certificate: Report and Correspondence, 1937–55 (MH 55/1888).

75. PRO, UK Embassy, Jeddah, to High Commissioner, Federation of Malay, January 17, 1952, #1784/3/52, in Arrangements of Pilgrimages to Mecca from Southeast Asia (1952–53) CO 1022/409.

76. Vivian Nutton, "The Contact between Civilizations," in Mario Gomes Marques and John Cule, eds., *The Great Maritime Discoveries and World Health* (Lisbon: Escola Nacional Saude Publica Ordem dos Medicos, 1991), p. 77.

77. Saul Jarcho, *The Concept of Contagion in Medicine, Literature, and Religion* (Malabar, FL: Krieger, 2000), pp. 1–20, 21–26, for the Greco-Roman and classical Muslim worldviews, respectively, as bases for later thought.

78. See J. K. Crellin, "The Dawn of Germ Theory: Particles, Infection and Biology," in F. N. L. Poynter, *Medicine and Science in the 1860s* (London: Wellcome Institute, 1968), pp. 61–66 for the period 1830s to the 1870s; see also Charles Rosenberg, *Explaining Epidemics and Other Studies in the History of Medicine* (Cambridge: Cambridge University Press, 1992), p. 109.

79. See Yaron Perry and Efraim Lev, *Modern Medicine in the Holy Land: Pioneering British Medical Services in Late Ottoman Palestine* (London: Tauris Academic Studies, 2007); and Bridie Andrews and Mary Sutphen, "Introduction," in Mary Sutphen and Bridie Andrews, *Medicine and Colonial Identity* (London: Routledge, 2003), p. 5.

7

The Skeptic's Eye

Snouck Hurgronje and the Politics of Pilgrimage

> (No one) can accept the opinion of many officials who see in all Hajjis fanatical enemies of the government.... (Yet) the interests of the Hajjis are usually contrary to those of the government, whilst many have brought from Mekka pan-Islamic tendencies which can easily develop into fanaticism.
>
> —C. Snouck Hurgronje, *Mekka in the Latter part of the 19th Century* (Leiden, KITLV, 2007), pp. 89, 288.

One person was more responsible for interpreting the colonial-era Southeast Asian Hajj from a scholarly point of view, and implementing it from a policy point of view, than any other. This man was C. Snouck Hurgronje, professor of Arabic at Leiden University and political advisor to the Dutch Indies government for several decades. Snouck filled this dual role as a scholar of Islam and as a willing servant of a repressive and increasingly anxiety-filled Indies colonial state. In the late nineteenth and early twentieth centuries, he oiled the Netherlands' apparatus of domination and control and seemed (on occasion) unsure and unhappy with this role at the same time. Thousands of indigenous inhabitants from the Indies made the trip to Arabia each year, and Snouck was charged with surveilling their passage, both as an occupation and as matter of his own intellectual interest. He wrote copiously about the pilgrimage to Mecca in books, articles, and correspondence.[1] An analysis of Snouck's writings reveals the Hajj as a transmission vehicle of religion and also of militancy, the latter greatly feared by the Dutch colonial state. Yet it is especially through his private letters that we see how his politics, intellect, and own moral convictions merged in the issue of the Hajj, forming a window into colonial mentalities about Islam and movement at the turn of the twentieth century.

This chapter focuses on how Snouck's work on the Hajj can help discern important patterns of politics, classification, and religion in the functioning of a high colonial state. Snouck had in-depth experience on the ground in Arabia that colored his writings on the Hajj to a great degree. He entered Mecca in

February 1885 and stayed there for six months studying Islam and the Southeast Asian (or "Jawa") community in particular.[2] While he was in residence in the holy city, he was able to meet and interact with prominent personalities from the archipelago, including members of the Acehnese war party who still were engaged in a vigorous project of resistance against their Dutch colonial overlords.[3] The time he spent in the Hejaz became an important part of his personality, shaping his views on Islam and also adding to his self-belief that he had put in the time and energy to understand cultural and religious patterns in this part of the world better than almost all of his contemporaries.[4] Snouck also converted to Islam (although the sincerity of this conversion has been hotly debated by many), and he married two Indies women, the first from Aceh and the second from Prianger, West Java, fathering five children in all between his two wives.[5] It was this combination of personal, family, and intellectual experience with both the Middle East and Southeast Asia that gave Snouck great influence in Dutch colonial policy-making circles. Indeed, as many contemporary scholars (most of them Dutch) have shown, it was from this foundation that Snouck went on to become arguably the Netherlands' greatest Orientalist and interpreter of Islam, a moniker Snouck might have agreed with himself (figure 7.1).[6]

The respect and borderline adulation that Snouck received from many Dutchmen has not been reciprocated in the last half-century by Indonesians themselves. One Indonesian historian has traced what he calls Snouck's campaign against Indonesians of Arab descent.[7] Another has tried to show how the burgeoning nationalism of the early-twentieth-century Indies was actually a front erected by Snouck and other prominent Dutch planners, all in an effort to distract archipelago natives away from the callings of Islam in the Indies.[8] Exclamations of his rabid objections to anything he saw as "pan-Islamic" have also been registered in contemporary Indonesian historiography.[9] It is difficult to square these often angry accusations with the alternate image of Snouck as scholar, chronicler, and traveler to the Middle East, let alone to his professed conversion to Islam and his extended Muslim family. Yet it is true that a map he commissioned by one of his Gayo servants ended up being sent to the Dutch military to help in their pacification of the Gayo lands in North Sumatra.[10] It is also true that Snouck wrote prolifically on Aceh, and that these writings often were used to help the European effort to win the long guerrilla war there that dragged on for decades around the turn of the twentieth century.[11] The Acehnese apparently have a special term for him that roughly translates to a "dead, rotting dog" that is left in the street.[12] These kinds of designations—"learned Orientalist" and "rotting dog"—give an indication of the paradoxes of Snouck's life and of his legacy. This chapter examines some of this duality through the lens of Snouck Hurgronje and his views on the Southeast Asian Hajj.

CHRISTIAAN SNOUCK HURGRONJE
8 februari 1857 - 26 juni 1936

Figure 7.1 C. Snouck Hurgronje.

Credit: E. Gobee and C. Adriaanse, *Ambtelijke Adviezen van C. Snouck Hurgronje* (The Hague: Martinus Nojhoff, 1957), p. xvi.

Policy and the Making of the Netherlands Indies Hajj

From fairly early on in his life as a scholar, Snouck was against most forms of Dutch interference in the pilgrimage, and he was constantly advising his countrymen not to meddle in affairs that were better left alone. At the very end of the nineteenth century, he was called upon by Batavia to explain why so many archipelago pilgrims, once registered as aspirant Hajjis in the Indies, were not coming home to Southeast Asia after they had completed their religious obligations. This matter was of some concern to Dutch officials in various parts of the Indies. Snouck answered that the issue of nonreturn should not be used as a political tool to interfere with the pilgrimage, as a certain number of Hajjis were indeed dying on the voyage, and some even went with this ultimate goal in mind.[13] Later, after the turn of the twentieth century, Snouck also criticized the dreaded enforcement of return-passage tickets for Hajjis, warning that many archipelago pilgrims would do anything to avoid the stipulations. Their reason was a lack of funds: many Hajjis could not hope to raise enough money at one time for both legs of the voyage to and from Arabia and intended to work in the Hejaz or elsewhere to earn enough money for the return passage home. From a practical standpoint, however, this meant that Indies Hajjis were sailing outside Dutch surveillance channels, including from Singapore to places like the tiny Red Sea principality of Djibouti.[14] Snouck felt that passes were indeed necessary for Dutch maintenance of the Hajj as an institution, but that this was as far as colonial supervision should go on what was ultimately a journey of faith and religious conviction.[15]

If Snouck was against making the Hajj more difficult for Netherlands Indies subjects as a matter of principle, he was even more against it in the day-to-day manifestations of attempted colonial controls. He argued against the proposal of the Dutch Indies state that it should regulate the kinds of clothing its subjects wore on returning from Hajj. Some in high policy-making circles believed that sartorial distinctions based on the Hajj should be reduced as a matter of governance, so that returnees would not have so much visible power and influence. Snouck advised the director of education, religion, and industry in the Indies that this would be extremely difficult to enforce, likely purposeless, and ultimately dangerous to attempt.[16] Archipelago Hajjis had enjoyed the distinctions of their pilgrimage—sartorial and otherwise—for hundreds of years, and it would be folly, Snouck thought, to try to change this. He related a story to his superiors that a Pontianak Hajji had smiled and told the Dutch consul in Jeddah that "your government is afraid of our turbans," a kind of scorn the colonial authorities could do without, Snouck felt.[17] Nevertheless, he advocated continuing some coercive forms of Dutch governance such as fingerprinting, despite pilgrims' protests against it, because colonial authorities could glean useful information from this practice.[18]

In the face of Dutch policy makers who continued to agitate for ever-tighter controls on the Hajj, Snouck found himself in the position of defending the continuance of the pilgrimage as a religious act of devotion. Some of these complaints had to do with security. In the mid-1890s, for example, the consuls of France, Britain, Russia, and Portugal were attacked by Bedouins in Jeddah, causing fear for the safety of European legations in the doorway city to Mecca. Snouck pointed out that the grand sharif of Mecca and the governor of the Hejaz were both well aware of the situation, that they knew exactly who the culprits were, and that they were being brought to justice.[19] Other causes of complaints included the spread of disease though water in the holy cities. Snouck had brought a sample of holy Zamzam water from Mecca back to Holland for chemical analysis a decade earlier than this to demonstrate that it was not the original wellspring of water that was spreading disease, but simply the overwhelming numbers of pilgrims all congregating in one place and at one time.[20] He also pointed out that disease was often spread by the mismanagement of Europeans, as in the case of the *Gelderland*, a ship carrying seven hundred Hajjis en route from Jeddah to Batavia in 1890 that reported cholera along the voyage but carried no doctor on board to help treat it. British ship crews in the Red Sea threatened to strike if any of the afflicted Hajjis were allowed to disembark and join up with their own fleet.[21] Snouck was constantly trying to correct what he saw as misrepresentations in the colonial apparatus that he felt would negatively affect Dutch policy.

Snouck blamed much of this situation on the colonial system of governance in Asia itself. In a memo to the Netherlands Indies administration in 1890, he pointedly told his superiors that there were official statistics on the Hajj, as well as real numbers—and that these were not necessarily the same thing.[22] Part of the problem, according to Snouck, was that Dutch officials both in the Hejaz and in Southeast Asia were often unprepared for the kinds of reporting duties expected of them. Very few spoke or read Arabic, which was a drawback not only in Jeddah and in the holy cities but also in the Straits Settlements and in the Dutch Indies ports.[23] Snouck felt that language—or a lack of appropriate languages—was only part of the problem, however. In addition to the language barrier, Dutch civil servants in the Hejaz had little notion of the history and culture of the region, which could be acquired only with years of experience. It was precisely this long experience that was lacking in Netherlands officialdom in Arabia, Snouck said.[24] Officials' naiveté led to exaggerations of dangers and misinterpretations of real problems, both of which retarded the Dutch cause in trying to understand and manage a yearly event of such enormous proportions as the Hajj.

If policy problems could not be solved in the Hejaz, many Dutch planners felt that it would be wise to issue warnings to the Indies pilgrims about the dangers they might face there. Snouck was resolutely opposed to this idea. He told the minister for the colonies in 1922 that he had held his position for over thirty years and that he was convinced that such warnings would do more harm than good. Part of the Indies population and many in the Middle East would see this as colonial Christian attempts to stem the tide of pilgrimage. Snouck adamantly insisted that "pilgrims can only with difficulty be protected against their own ignorance" and that they were at risk of attack on the roads between Mecca and Medina whether they were warned or not.[25] In a much earlier missive to the Indies government, Snouck had stressed that warning the pilgrims had absolutely no effect and might indeed be counterproductive. Archipelago sojourners had been warned in 1890 after troubles the previous year in the Hejaz; nonetheless, the number of Hajjis from the Indies that year outstripped that of the previous eight seasons.[26]

Dealing with adverse perceptions in the Middle East of Batavia's organization of the Hajj on behalf of its own Asian subjects took up much of Snouck's time (table 7.1). The Dutch, like other European colonial powers, felt they had to be seen as protectors of their respective colonial pilgrimages, rather than as custodians or religious police. Especially with a thirty-year guerrilla war raging against the Acehnese, who hoisted the banner of Islam as high as they could, this was important. Nonetheless, the pan-Islamic press, he complained, constantly beat the drum of "religious brothers" having to perform one of their five sacred duties under the yoke of repressive (and Christian) powers.[27] Snouck identified the inflammatory writings as coming from both Arabic and Turkish semiofficial newspapers, despite some efforts to quell them by the Ottoman government.[28] By the onset of World War I, Snouck was finally overruled by his compatriots, and official warnings were issued to Indies pilgrims in 1915, provoking immediate protest from the government in Istanbul.[29] Snouck and indeed many other European policy makers were united in not wanting to see the Ottomans emerging as the "official voice" of Muslims worldwide.[30] Many European disagreements could be smoothed over, in fact, when it came to this one very basic premise of pancolonial accord concerning the Hajj.

The instability and chaos of World War I caused a hardening of many Dutch policies toward the conduct of the pilgrimage and toward movement between Southeast Asia and the Middle East generally. Beacons and lights along the Red Sea routes were washed away and not maintained, and navigation became dangerous in much of the Middle East because of a lack of personnel to care for the maritime channels. Many of the big shipping companies did not give over vessels for the Hajj in the early days of the war, and the price of travel rose.[31] The Dutch issued a warning, against Snouck's wishes, as we have seen, and temporarily banned the Hajj in 1915.[32] Many archipelago travelers were stranded in the Hejaz, regardless of whether they were there to perform their pilgrimage. Snouck knew from his own experiences in Mecca that many Indies subjects were studying or working in Arabia, and these people were affected by the draconian enforcement of the Dutch ban as well.[33] In 1914–15, there seem to have been roughly 5,600 Jawa in Mecca alone, a very large number overall, with some six hundred of these people hailing from Batam, four hundred from East Kalimantan, an equal number from the Priangan districts, and hundreds spread out from other parts of the archipelago.[34] He tried to make policy makers in The Hague see that a ban on the Hajj was causing problems for a broad spectrum of Dutch subjects, but his pleas fell on deaf ears. Snouck finally sent a forlorn letter to the minister for the colonies in 1916, pleading that Indies Hajjis must be told as soon as possible that their pilgrimage would not be interfered with again once all had returned to normal. Not to do so, Snouck sighed, would only fuel moves toward an angry pan-Islam.[35]

Table 7.1 **Policy Advice of C. Snouck Hurgronje on the Indies Hajj: Rubrics and Range of Advice**

Hajjis as priests upon return to the Indies	Examination of Hajjis
Costs of the Indies Hajj	The Hajj from specific Indies places
Government hindering of the Hajj	Protection of Hajjis against fraud
Pilgrim clothing	Caravan safety
Thievery against Hajjis	The worth of the title Hajji
Government taxes on Hajj	The erection of "help funds" for Hajjis
The consulate and Hajjis	Transport of Hajjis
Trade in pilgrims	Free choice of guides among Hajjis
Temporary bans on Hajj	Repatriation of Dutch Hajji subjects
Legislation on Hajj debts	Travel routes of Hajjis
Exploitation of Hajjis by Grand Sheriff	Work contracts of Hajjis
The al-Sagoff firm in Singapore and Hajj	International oversight of Hajj
Hajj transit of Indies pilgrims in Batavia	Turkey, World War I, and the Hajj
International congresses on the Hajj	Economic effect of the Hajj

Source: E. Gobee and C. Adriaanse, eds., *Ambtelijke Adviezen van C. Snouck Hurgronje* (The Hague: Martinus Nijhoff, 1965), multivolume.

Snouck Hurgronje and the Problems of the Pilgrimage

In addition to his policy work, Snouck was keenly interested in the problems archipelago pilgrims faced in the Hejaz. He wrote copiously in his correspondence about the trials and tribulations ordinary pilgrims encountered in the holy cities (box 7.1). The majority of Indies Hajjis, he believed, had little idea of what they would experience in Arabia, and they should be prepared for hardships, he argued.[36] It was well-known, Snouck told the governor-general of the Indies, that archipelago pilgrims were attacked more frequently than other Hajjis, partially because many people on the ground knew that by necessity these pilgrims had to carry large sums of cash to make their long journeys. Snouck argued that Indies subjects should be reminded before they left home that the Hajj was compulsory only for adults who could perform it without burdening their families, a warning that he hoped might stem at least some enthusiasm for this journey that was so important—yet also so dangerous—to many.[37]

Box 7.1 **Snouck Hurgronje on the Hajj, in His Own Words (1889)**

If we wish to accompany the average Jawah on all paths, there now remain to us (apart from the real pilgrimage ceremonies and the daily circuits around the Kaabah and ritual prayers in the mosque, made as numerous as possible) about three worthy of mention. Whereas the measures described are taken by nearly all Hajjis, only those have time for the occupations now to be described who either enter Mekka shortly before or shortly after Ramadhan, or who remain some weeks in Mekka after the Hajj. We will first speak of those Jawah who settle for a longer period.

Some, who weeks before the Hajj dwell in Mekka under guidance of a pious sheikh of pilgrims are instructed by the sheikh himself (particularly if the pilgrims are his country folk), or by a competent compatriot under his orders, in the rules of the Sacred Law regarding the pilgrimage. For that purpose a manasik-book, written in Malay or other language according to the individual, is used. We must not forget that by far the greater number of pilgrims to the Holy Land come without any idea as to the ceremonies which comprise the Great and Little Pilgrimages. Many in fact return home, as Hajjis, as wise as before. In fairly large throngs they are urged day after day through the town, from one holy place to another, the ceremonies are very carefully rehearsed to them; the repetition of the prayer formulae is less conscientious, as the strangers in any case understand almost nothing of them. Who could have time to explain the meaning of the various arrangements, even in a fleeting manner, to an individual in those restless weeks? Whence shall the Jawah learn that the visits to innumerable cupolas and memorial houses, the entry into the Kaabah, the sprinkling with Zemzem-water etc. do not at all belong to the obligatory pilgrimage? In any case his guide will not tell him this, for then there would be less participation in the wearisome walks, and the takings by the guide's friends and also those of the guide himself would sustain damage. Many a pilgrim retains from the day's exertions but a very confused memory in which horrible crowds, crushing and shouting, heat and thirst play a considerable part. He takes the word of his sheikh for it that everything done is in order but demands from him no detailed description. For this reason, Hajji examinations, such as were formerly held in the Dutch-Indies by Government officials are quite useless. Those sheikhs are very conscientious who beforehand enable their pilgrims to comprehend the ceremonies to be passed through, as parts of a ritualistic whole. To such Jawah, who have already arrived long before the Ramadhan their instructed countryfolk, settled in Mekka, give instructions in the Law of the Fast.

The second spiritual gain for which many Jawah use a short stay in Mekka, is the improvement of the Qur'an-recitation, for Malay lips the recitation according to the rules of the art is extraordinarily difficult—to which must be added that in many Jawah lands there is a lack of qualified teachers. In the course of a few weeks one cannot of course make such progress, but one can learn at least how to recite the fathah (1st Surah)—repeated in every ritual prayer several times—fairly well under leadership. Teachers are paid for instruction in the qirayah (recitation) all over the Moslim world. The authorities on the Law say expressly that one may teach the Qur'an or recite it (i.e. on solemn occasions) for money and such an occupation is much to be commended. For that reason Qur'an-teachers take no holiday so long as there is anything to be earned and some faqihs in Mekka are really specialists in the training if the Jawah pilgrims who remain some time before or after the Hajj.

Those who have much time or specially favorable opportunities learn either an entire *juz'* (1/30th of the Qur'an) or at least many short Surahs; otherwise they devote about an hour every morning to learning the fat'hah, until they can recite this to the satisfaction of their Arab teacher. Among these teachers Ahmed Faqih, the Imam mentioned above, enjoys the greatest reputation. For him it is very advantageous when as sometimes happens older pupils give up after the first Surah, as he thus gains time to chant to new pupils, and most presents are given in the beginning of the teaching period.

C. Snouck Hurgronje, *Mekka* (Leiden: Brill, 1970), pp. 239–240.

There was a certain amount of resignation in Snouck's dealing with the dangers of the Hajj, a kind of recognition of his limited powers to change long-existing dynamics. He acknowledged that plundering the Mecca-Medina caravans was a way of life in the desert.[38] He also acknowledged that demands for compensation in the wake of these attacks were likely to continue well into the future, until local governments and foreign consuls in the Hejaz could guarantee some kind of safety for the camel trains that crossed the Arabian wastes.[39] But he did not think that this state of affairs would be changing anytime soon. Late in his career, he wrote that such plundering of pilgrim caravans had been a part of his experience for forty years in the Hejaz and that it likely had been part of the "pilgrim experience for one thousand years before this."[40] There were limitations as to what the foreign governments could do, in other words. Mecca and Medina were open to Muslims only, he intoned to the governor-general in Batavia, and the open spaces of the desert were lawless for everyone. Any attempt for Europeans to travel there was an invitation to "purchase death."[41]

Snouck devoted even more attention to the role of health and sanitation in the experience of archipelago pilgrims than to the safety of the Indies caravans. He felt that cholera was more or less endemic to the holy cities.[42] The situation was helped along, Snouck wrote to the governor-general in Batavia, by Indies pilgrims sailing both across the Indian Ocean and locally in Red Sea waters secretly, outside the surveillance (sanitary and otherwise) of the European powers.[43] The quarantine station at Kamaran was not really fully equipped in its early years to stop an epidemic of cholera, should the disease break out during the time of the Hajj, however.[44] Snouck pointed out that archipelago pilgrims both drank and bathed in the limited supplies of water available in the Hejaz, making real sanitary control extremely difficult. Certain basic behavioral practices would have to change, he said, before anything approaching an integrated system of health management could be expected while thousands upon thousands of pilgrims were on Hajj.[45]

If Snouck saw problems with the behavioral practices of pilgrims, he also found fault with those charged with keeping them safe and healthy while they performed their religious duties in 1908. He termed the international sanitary office in the Red Sea region "a comedy and a means toward making money," an accusation that may not have been far from the truth.[46] A suggestion by the Dutch consul in Jeddah five years prior to this to appoint a health inspector for the region, however, did not sit well with Snouck. He had little faith, he confided in the minister for the colonies, that this would help matters because the system, and the administrator, would eventually be co-opted by the Ottoman government.[47] In the Turks, he saw no real friendship or caring for the flood of Hajjis; their main concern was making money from the health regulations, he stated bitterly in a missive to the minister for the colonies.[48] If relief was going to come, it would have to be from somewhere other than the guardians of the holy cities.

Although Snouck demonstrated a keen eye for identifying problems, he offered little by way of solutions for helping the Hajjis, whom he held in a mild contempt common to many Europeans of that age, and also close to his heart. Snouck correctly identified the graft of low-level officials in the Red Sea sanitation controls as the main impediment to progress. These men merely lined their pockets under the existing system, he wrote, fleecing pilgrims out of their savings while offering little in return.[49] He told the minister for the colonies that so long as the Turkish government continued to appoint the inspectors, doctors, and officials populating the system, the current rates of disease and mortality could be expected to continue.[50] Graft, he said, was simply endemic to the system as it was presently conducted.[51] Snouck had vitriol for everyone in terms of the problems facing Hajjis (including pilgrims themselves), but for the most part, he had little to put forward to ease their often difficult lot.

Snouck Hurgronje and the Everyday Life of the Hajj

A keen observer of everyday life on the Hajj, Snouck spilled much ink on the everyday comings and goings of the Indies pilgrims. From these observations, a sense can be obtained of how the Southeast Asian Hajj looked during colonial times in all of its complexity, both negative and positive (table 7.2). Snouck commented voluminously on the problematic work contracts that many Hajjis signed to finance their passage to the Holy Land, for example.[52] Certain high-profile facilitators of the Hajj in Southeast Asia, such as the al-Sakoff family in Singapore, dragged pilgrims into debt by overcharging them for their passages.[53] Yet curiously, Snouck was skeptical—and probably wrong to be so skeptical—about reports of slavery in the Hejaz involving archipelago pilgrims, even going so far as to say that that because this was so forbidden by Islam, it could not be happening on a wide scale as a part of the Hajj.[54] Snouck may have taken the canonical dictates of Islam—which he knew better than

Table 7.2 **Items Found on Various Archipelago Pilgrims Returning to the Indies from the Hejaz**

1. A small green bamboo model of a sword, and a paper on which the name of Allah was written, the first and the last prophets (Adam and Muhammad), the first four caliphs.

2. A mystical figure, upon which the names of Allah and Muhammad were written several times.

3. Formulas against sickness (mostly pox) but also formulas to induce erections in men.

4. Local medicines of various kinds, many of them unknown.

5. Mystical formulas in Arabic and Javanese (and smaller amounts in Sudanese).

6. Formulas for finding auspicious days, for finding lost articles, etc.

7. Items of Islamic law written in Arabic; same for Malay.

8. Several very small Qur'an pages, loose.

9. Pieces of metal, pieces of bamboo.

10. A list of spirits and secret beings who live in various parts of Java.

11. Drawings of the mosque in Mecca.

12. Fragments of orthodox Muslim law written on scraps of paper.

Source: Abstracted from C. Snouck Hurgronje to Resident of Batavia, January 27, 1894, in E. Gobee and C. Adriaanse, eds., *Ambtelijke Adviezen van C. Snouck Hurgronje* (The Hague: Martinus Nijhoff, 1965), multivolume.

almost anyone else at this time—more seriously than the lived realities of many pilgrims, who found their travels choked with difficulties that also were a part of this longest of journeys.

Snouck also invested much of his time in learning the ins and outs of how pilgrim guides (or shaykhs) worked in the conduct of the Hajj. Crucial to the entire system, shaykhs ferried hopeful Hajjis to and from their own countries, took care of them in the Arabian Peninsula, and generally were responsible for their welfare. Hajjis had stamps on their passports explicating clearly which shaykhs they "belonged to," and these same shaykhs (especially the ones from Southeast Asia) paid very large sums to obtain their licenses.[55] Because the business was so profitable, many Dutch policy planners wondered if the number of these men wasn't mushrooming, though Snouck supplied figures showing their numbers were more or less constant at least toward the end of the nineteenth century.[56] He described some of these shaykhs in a letter to the General Secretariat in Batavia in 1896, focusing on one in particular who was well-known in Mecca for supplying pilgrims from the wealthy region of Banyu-wangi in Java. These Hajjis were much desired in the holy cities because they were considered to be rich, and they brought considerable quantities of cash to spend on goods while they were in the Hejaz.[57] But Snouck also focused on the role of shipping companies in this process, which by the 1890s were even hiring men to work for them to find pilgrims to fill all available berths. Such men were paid two and a half guilders per head if they were able to convince potential Hajjis to buy a ticket, and five guilders per head for those who bought tickets directly from them as agents.[58]

The pilgrim guides, for Snouck, were abusive and basically parasitic on the Hajji community. In another long letter to the General Secretariat in 1893, Snouck explained that pilgrims could do almost nothing without the help of their shaykhs: every step they made in the Holy Land, all of their purchases, and all matters concerning both spiritual and worldly concerns were to be taken up by their shaykhs as official intercessors for the Hajjis (figure 7.2).[59] This was a shame, he stated, because many shaykhs were completely crooked, men who barely looked after their charges and who were not above stealing the worldly possessions of any of their pilgrims who died in the Hejaz.[60] It was well-known that the shaykhs were often as predatory on the Jawa communities of sojourners as many of the Bedouins and Arabs of the desert.[61] Foremost among these, Snouck told the governor general, was the grand sharif himself, the hereditary emir of Mecca. The shaykhs were only next in line after the emir, yet they had even more influence than he did on pilgrims' day-to-day lives in Arabia. Hajjis were, however, reluctant to complain about the vile treatment they received, because they thought to do so would tarnish the memory of their spiritual quest in the Hejaz.[62]

Chief of Mutawwifs for Jawah pilgrims.   Jāwah (Banten) woman pilgrim.

Figure 7.2 Shaykh and Female Indies Pilgrim.
Credit: C. Snouck Hurgronje, *Mekka* (Leiden: Brill, 1970), pp. 79 and 268.

Though Snouck was extremely critical of the shaykhs as exploiters of Hajjis, he held a nuanced opinion about many religious men who wanted to return to the Indies, sometimes even as shaykhs, to recruit new Hajjis. One man in particular, a famed religious teacher in Mecca originally from Lampung, in South Sumatra, excited Snouck's attention in 1894. Ahmad Lampung wanted to return to the Indies that year to ferry new pilgrims back to the Hejaz. Snouck was worried that he would not be given permission to reenter the Dutch possessions in Southeast Asia because of Batavia's heightened conservatism toward *Vreemde Oosterlingen* ("Foreign Orientals"). There was a good chance his plea for repatriation would not be accepted. Snouck pointed out that the man was a famed teacher who wanted to return under totally peaceful and acceptable terms to his homeland after a lifetime of learning in the holy cities.[63] The plight of a second man, a religious teacher from Madura named Ahmad Sarkawi, prompted Snouck to write to his superiors six years later. Like Ahmad Lampung, Ahmad Sarkawi wanted to return to Madura, partially to lecture at the mosques on his home island, partially to see family, and partially to encourage new pilgrims to go to Arabia. By 1914, at least fifty-seven Jawa were teaching in the mosques and religious institutions of Mecca; these men's names, ages, provenances in the Indies, and even how long they had been in the Hejaz were all known.[64] Snouck argued strongly that these movements should be allowed.[65] This intensity of feeling was

sometimes directed against shaykhs, or generally against many Hajjis as "ignorant" and "troublesome," though sometimes it was even channeled against his
own government.

Snouck was also keenly interested in the mechanics of pilgrim transport. This
subject was under massive internal debate in Dutch administrative circles in the
late nineteenth century, concerning the best procedures to use for passes, tickets,
and compulsory practices to enforce a smooth (and from the Dutch standpoint,
obedient) Hajj.[66] Snouck correctly pointed out to his superiors in 1895 that
many current and former government practices vis-à-vis pilgrim transport awak-
ened hatred and distrust of Europeans in the hearts and minds of Hajjis.[67] By the
early twentieth century, almost all of the pilgrim traffic from the Indies was in
the hands of three large companies, and prices had risen to the highest levels that
ever had been recorded for the trip across the Indian Ocean.[68] Snouck cautioned
the minister for the colonies that somehow the situation would have to be stabi-
lized or there would be dire consequences, and he made a plea for some kind of
"honorable understanding" between shipping companies, agents, and the Hajjis
themselves.[69]

Such an honorable understanding was not on the horizon, however. Many
Hajjis in the Hejaz waited years to be able to return to the Indies after their initial
sojourns. These were many of the *blijvers* ("those who stayed"), archipelago subjects
who had completed their Hajj but decided to stay on in the Arabian Peninsula to
work or further their religious study. The shipping companies had few provisions for these people because they had not purchased the round-trip tickets the
companies desired, and they were sometimes classified by the Dutch colonial
state as *Vreemde Oosterlingen* (regardless of their ethnicity) if they had stayed
away from the Indies for too long.[70] Other complications were caused by passengers on outbound ships who were found to be destitute or in debt to agents or
the shipping companies, and even those whose belongings (and savings) had
been plundered in the Hejaz and had no way home.[71] The problems, sighed
Snouck, led inexorably back to the shaykhs—everyone had to depend on them
(caravan drivers, shipping companies, lodgers, and victualizers) to get the Hajjis
back and forth between the Indies and Arabia. Yet these men could frequently
not be trusted.[72]

If Snouck was hard on the shaykhs and their role in the transport regime
across the Indian Ocean, he was equally critical of the European shipping companies for being complicit in the miseries of many pilgrims. He saw the existing
international accords as useless, ultimately a collection of rules and regulations
put in place to further line the pockets of many who made money on the voluminous paperwork. This portion of his scorn was reserved for officialdom.[73] The
majority of his bile was reserved for the shipping companies themselves, however, which he accused of agitating for forty years to enforce the system of return

tickets, first "in the interests of the Hajjis," then "in the interests of the government," but really only in their own self-interest.[74] The compulsory return passage did not help most Hajjis because it put the initial cost of the journey outside the realm of possibility for many and limited their freedom to stay in the Hejaz as long as they wished.[75] When the aforementioned three giant shipping companies won the legal right to enforce round-trip passages as a condition of applying for Hajj in 1922–23, Snouck saw this as a personal defeat.[76] In this, as in many other matters, Snouck showed the complexity of his position as both warden and advocate for the average Southeast Asian pilgrim.

Conclusion

Snouck was a man of his times, and as such, he generally saw colonialism as helpful and potentially salutary for the peoples he helped rule. Nevertheless, there is something distinctly modern about Snouck as well, an almost ethnographic desire to get close to his subject, understand it, and then take his information and tales home for the benefit of his audience (and, of course, for himself). Much of his perspective on the Hajj was as an administrator responsible for a huge and unwieldy transregional phenomenon. Yet he was also interested in the problems faced by archipelago pilgrims as they wound their way across the Indian Ocean and into the deserts of the Hejaz to perform their religious duties. Snouck found solutions for few of the dangers and annoyances they faced, and there is a tone of resignation in much of his writings about the Hajj, as he realized that it was too large an event for any one man to fully master or control. Nonetheless, he left through his fastidiousness a detailed record of the passage of many thousands of people from the tropics to the desert over four decades of sojourning.

Snouck loved the Islamic world, and he was particularly fascinated by the connections between the Hejaz and "his own" Netherlands Indies, where he got his start as an administrator, civil servant, and scholar. He was capable of writing about these connections in very lucid, and sometimes very moving, terms. He knew that archipelago pilgrims dearly wanted to "kiss the black stone, drink from the Holy well at Zemzem, … and throw stones in the dale of Mina."[77] He saw in the great radials of the pilgrimage the seeds of fraternity, knowledge, and equality, as when he said that "in the mosques of Mecca men can see during seminars students and professors of all shades and colors: coal-black, green (which is what Arabs call those of a lighter complexion), brown, yellow, and white, all brothers, and the same differences are seen in the denizens of the Holy City, even sometimes in the members of a single Meccan family."[78] This was perhaps a form of paradise to Snouck: a place where learning and scholarship came before all other worldly pursuits and divisions. Indeed, he took it as part of his intellectual program to explain that which he loved and found so fascinating to a wider public.[79]

Yet his role was much more complex than as a mere interpreter of Islam for the uninitiated in the Western world. He was captivated by the Hajj and moved by it, but he also saw the seeds of danger in the passage of so many men and ideas across the vast spaces of the Indian Ocean separating the Hejaz and the Netherlands' "own Indies." Snouck reported regularly on Hadramis passing back and forth between Arabia and Southeast Asia, and his notations were duly catalogued (and his recommendations for surveillance acted upon) by an anxious Batavia regime.[80] Snouck also made sure to weave a tight but ever-expanding web of informants and information gatherers while he was in Mecca, men he could count on to supply him with intelligence—scholarly, religious, and other— while he sat in the mosques and pursued his studies.[81] He was also completely immersed in the ongoing conflict in Aceh, so it is extremely difficult to see where his ethnographic and scholastic interests ended and his role as a conduit for useful information to the colonial government began.[82] Snouck's individuality, life experiences, and penchant for self-belief (accompanied often by a denigration of other scholars' and officials' opinions) led him to have enormous influence in Dutch policy circles. Yet it is perhaps through his writings on the Hajj that these paradoxical aspects of his personality and of his lived experience are seen best, as they reveal him for what he was—sagacious, competent, and politically implicated in morally complex ways—all at once. In some senses, he was a paragon of the model scholar-official who became prevalent in colonial projects worldwide in the first half of the twentieth century, though this might be accounted to be an ambiguous legacy at best.

NOTES

1. His two most famous published works in this vein were *Het Mekkaansche Feest*, his 1880 doctoral dissertation from Leiden, and his masterpiece, *Mekka in the Latter Part of the 19th Century: Daily Life, Customs and Learning, the Moslims of the East-Indian-Archipelago* (Leyden: E. J. Brill, 1931).

2. P. Sj. Van Koningsveld, "Orientalistik sebagai Ilmu-Bantu Kolonial: 'Masuk' Islamnya Snouck Hurgronje," in P. Sj. Van Koningsveld, *Snouck Hurgronje dan Islam: delapan karangan tentang hidup dan karya seorang orientalis zaman kolonial* (Jakarta: Girimukti Pusaka, 1989), p. 95. Snouck was one of several colonial-era men from the West who eventually made it to Mecca, though doing so as a non-Muslim was explicitly forbidden. He was an eccentric and one of a fair number of Europeans at the time who experimented with "different modes of living" away from Western norms. This group included theosophists and others; Indonesia seems to have held a particular fascination for some of these travelers.

3. See Jan Just Witkam's introduction and translation in Christian Snouck Hurgronje, *Mecca in de Tweede Heift van de Negentiends Eevw: Schetse vit het Dagelijks Leven* (Amsterdam: Atlas, 2007); P. Sj. Van Koningsveld, "Izharu 'l-Islam Snouck Hurgronje: Segi Sejarah Kolonial yang Diabaikan," in P. Sj. Van Koningsveld, *Snouck Hurgronje dan Islam: delapan karangan tentang hidup dan karya seorang orientalis zaman kolonial* (Jakarta: Girimukti Pusaka, 1989), p. 172.

4. A. J. P. Moereels, *Chr. Snouck Hurgronje* (Rijswijk, Netherlands: V. A. Kramers, 1938).
5. P. Sj. Van Koningsveld, "Raden Jusuf di Bandung Mengakhiri Kebungkamannya sekitar Pernikahan-Pernikahan Islam Ayahnya, Christian Snouck Hurgronje," in P. Sj. Van Koningsveld, *Snouck Hurgronje dan Islam: delapan karangan tentang hidup dan karya seorang orientalis zaman kolonial* (Jakarta: Girimukti Pusaka, 1989), pp. 164–165; and Snouck Hurgronje to Th. Noldeke, April 28, 1924, in P. Sj. Van Koningsveld, *Orientalism and Islam: The Letters of C. Snouck Hurgronje to Th. Noldeke from the Tubingen University Library* (hereafter OI) (Leiden: Leiden University Press, 1985), p. 324.
6. Snouck always had his critics as well, in his own time as in the present; see Harry Benda, "Christiaan Snouck Hurgronje and the Foundations of Dutch Islamic Policy in Indonesia," in Ahmad Ibrahim et al., eds., *Readings on Islam in Southeast Asia* (Singapore: ISEAS, 1985), pp. 61–69; P. Sj. Van Koningsveld, "Snouck Hurgronje Zoals Hij Was," *De Gids*, 9/10, 1980: 763–784; F. Schroeder, "Orientalistische Retoriek: Van Konongsveld over de Vuile Handen van Snouck Hurgronje," *De Gids*, 9/10, 1980: 785–806; L. I. Graf, "Christiaan Snouck Hurgronje en Zijn Critici," *De Gids*, 9/10, 1980: 807–830; and Fred Lanzing, "Snouck Hurgornje, Schrijver," *Indische Letteren*, 16/4, 2001: 154–169; and Peter van der Veer, "De Orientalist en de Dominee," in Peter van der Veer, ed., *Modern Orientalisme* (Amsterdam: Meulenhoff, 1995), pp. 167–202. The Benda article is particularly important; in it, Benda stressed that, unlike most of his Dutch contemporaries, Snouck saw the Hajj through the prism of its existence as part of a belief system and less for its political implications.
7. Hamid Algadri, "Snouck Hurgronje Menentang Asimilasi Keturunan Arab," in Hamid Algadri, *C. Snouck Hurgronje, Politik Belanda terhadap Islam dan Keturunan Arab* (Jakarta: Penerbit Sinar Harapan, 1984), pp. 85–94.
8. Tengku Hasan M. de Tiro, "Indonesian Nationalism: A Western Invention to Contain Islam in the Dutch East Indies," in M. Ghayasuddin, ed., *The Impact of Nationalism on the Muslim Word* (London: Muslim Institute, 1986), pp. 61–73.
9. Hamid Algadri, "Prof. Snouck Hurgronje Menentang Gerakan Pan-Islam," in Hamid Algadri, *C. Snouck Hurgronje, Politik Belanda terhadap Islam dan Keturunan Arab* (Jakarta: Penerbit Sinar Harapan, 1984), pp. 117–152.
10. P. Sj. Van Koningsveld, "Penulisan Sejarah Suatu Perang Ekspansi Kolonial. Lima Puluh Tahun Setelah Kematian Snouck Hurgronje," in P. Sj. Van Koningsveld, *Snouck Hurgronje dan Islam: delapan karangan tentang hidup dan karya seorang orientalis zaman kolonial* (Jakarta: Girimukti Pusaka, 1989), p. 261.
11. Snouck Hurgronje, *Het Gajoland en Zijne Bewoners* (Batavia: Landsdrukkerij, 1903), pp. 314–315; K. van der Maaten, *Snouck Hurgronje en de Atjeh Ooorlog*, vol. 1 (Rotterdam: Oostersch Instituut te Leiden, 1948), pp. 38–41.
12. Interview with "Achmed" (not his real name), Universitas Islam Antarabangsa, Gombak (Kuala Lumpur), June 18, 2004.
13. Snouck Hurgronje to the Director of Education, Religion, and Industry, September 28, 1897, in E. Gobee and C. Adriaanse, eds., *Ambtelijke Adviezen van C. Snouck Hurgronje* (The Hague: Martinus Nijhoff, 1959) [multivolume, hereafter AASH], 2, 32: 1324. Many Hajjis did indeed die on the voyage or while in the Hejaz, but this was not considered to be a "problem" by many pilgrims, who saw the added blessings of such a death if a Hajji passed away while performing the fifth pillar of the faith.
14. Snouck Hurgronje to Governor General, NEI, May 19, 1904, in AASH, 2, 32: 1330.
15. Snouck Hurgronje to Governor General, NEI, September 7, 1900, in AASH, 2, 32: 1326. See also Snouck Hurgronje, "Hadji Politiek?" *Java-Bode*, March 6–8, 1899: 353–368.
16. Snouck Hurgronje to Director of Education and Industry, December 25, 1900, in AASH, 2, 32: 1326.
17. Snouck Hurgronje to the General Secretariat, March 26, 1890, in AASH, 2, 32: 1322.
18. Snouck Hurgronje to Minister for the Colonies, September 5, 1910, in AASH, 2, 32: 1506. See also Snouck Hurgronje, "De Hadji-Politiek der Indische Regeering," *Onze Eeuw*, 1909: 331–360.

19. Snouck Hurgronje to Government Secretary, December 3, 1895, in AASH, 2, 32: 1346.

20. Snouck Hurgronje to Director of Education, Religion, and Industry, January 8, 1901, in AASH, 2, 32: 1338.

21. Snouck Hurgronje to Director of Education, Religion, and Industry, January 12, 1891, in AASH, 2, 32: 1335.

22. Consideratieen en advies naar aanleiding van het verslag van den Consul te Djeddah over te gevaren, waaraan de hadji's van het volgend jaar zullen zijn blootgesteld, November 21, 1890, in AASH, 2, 32: 1332.

23. Snouck Hurgronje to Director of Education, Religion, and Industry, May 25, 1889, in AASH, 2, 32: 1466.

24. Snouck Hurgronje to the First Government Secretary, October 26, 1895, in AASH, 2, 32: 1343.

25. Snouck Hurgronje to Minister for the Colonies, April 20, 1922, and Snouck Hurgronje to Minister for the Colonies, December 9, 1923, both in AASH, 2, 32: 1348–1349.

26. Snouck Hurgronje to Director of Education, Religion, and Industry, May 30, 1891, in AASH, 2, 32: 1336.

27. Snouck Hurgronje to Minister for the Colonies, September 25, 1915, in AASH, 2, 32: 1353. See also G. S. van Krieken, *Snouck Hurgronje en het Panislamisme* (Leiden: Brill, 1985); and Snouck Hurgronje to Th. Noldeke, August 15, 1912, in OI, p. 169.

28. Snouck Hurgronje to Minister for the Colonies, October 2, 1915, in AASH, 2, 32: 1355.

29. Minister for the Colonies to Advisor for Indies and Arabian Matters, September 28, 1915, enclosed in Snouck Hurgronje to Minister for the Colonies, October 2, 1915, in AASH, 2, 32: 1356.

30. Snouck Hurgronje to Minister for the Colonies, 26 Augustus 1916, in AASH, 2, 32: 1364.

31. "Waarschuwing van de Algemeene Secretaris" (1915), enclosed in Snouck Hurgronje to Minister for the Colonies, October 2, 1915, in AASH, 2, 32: 1357.

32. Snouck Hurgronje to Minister for the Colonies, October 23, 1915, in AASH, 2, 32: 1359. See also Snouck Hurgronje, "De Mekkagangers en de Oorlog," *Nieuwe Rotterdamsche Courant*, November 24–5, 1915: 299–310.

33. Snouck Hurgronje to Minister for the Colonies, August 24, 1916, in AASH, 2, 32: 1361.

34. See Shaleh Putuhena, *Historiografi Haji Indonesia* (Yogyakarta: LKIS, 2007), p. 415.

35. Snouck Hurgronje to Minister for the Colonies, September 10, 1916, in AASH, 2, 32: 1366.

36. Snouck Hurgronje to Minister for the Colonies, January 8, 1910, in AASH, 2, 32: 1313.

37. Snouck Hurgronje to Governor General, NEI, June 20, 1889, and Snouck Hurgronje to Governor General, January 30, 1906, both in AASH, 2, 32: 1307 and 1310.

38. Snouck Hurgronje to Minister for the Colonies, September 18, 1922, in AASH, 2, 32: 1316.

39. Snouck Hurgronje to Governor General, NEI, January 30, 1906, in AASH, 2, 32: 1311.

40. Snouck Hurgronje to Minister for the Colonies, June 13, 1923, in AASH, 2, 32: 1317.

41. Snouck Hurgronje to the General Secretariat, December 30, 1893, in AASH, 2, 32: 1472.

42. Snouck Hurgronje to Governor General, NEI, June 6, 1903, in AASH, 2, 32: 1455.

43. Snouck Hurgronje to Governor General, NEI, May 23, 1905, in AASH, 2, 32: 1455.

44. Snouck Hurgronje to Minister for the Colonies, December 1931, in AASH, 2, 32: 1463.

45. Snouck Hurgronje to the Resident of Batavia, December 23, 1905, and Snouck Hurgronje to Governor General, NEI, both in AASH, 2, 32: 1462 and 1474.

46. Snouck Hurgronje to Minister for the Colonies, December 23, 1908, in AASH, 2, 32: 1458.

47. Snouck Hurgronje to Governor General, NEI, April 24, 1903, in AASH, 2, 32: 1453–1454.

48. Snouck Hurgronje to Minister for the Colonies, December 14, 1908, in AASH, 2, 32: 1457.

49. Snouck Hurgronje to Director of Education and Industry, May 30, 1894, in AASH, 2, 32: 1451.

50. Snouck Hurgronje to Minister for the Colonies, April 2, 1909, in AASH, 2, 32: 1460.

51. Snouck Hurgronje to Minister for the Colonies, July 2, 1910, in AASH, 2, 32: 1461.

52. Snouck Hurgronje to Director of Education and Industry, January 3, 1891, in AASH, 2, 32: 1440. See also Georg Stauth, "Slave Trade, Multiculturalism and Islam in Colonial Singapore:

A Sociological Note on Christian Snouck Hurgronje's 1891 Article on Slave Trade in Singapore," *Southeast Asian Journal of Social Science*, 20/1, 1992: 67–79.

53. Snouck Hurgronje to Director of Education, Religion, and Industry, October 15, 1895, in AASH, 2, 32: 1443.

54. Snouck Hurgronje to Governor General, NEI, August 16, 1898, and Snouck Hurgronje to Director of Education, Religionl, and Industry, October 15, 1895, both in AASH, 2, 32: 1449 and 1444.

55. Snouck Hurgronje to Director of Education, Religion, and Industry, July 19, 1892, in AASH, 2, 32: 1377.

56. Snouck Hurgronje to Director of Education, Religion, and Industry, July 4, 1898, in AASH, 2, 32: 1379. Hurgronje stated that in 1884, there were 180 Indies shaykhs in Mecca, while in 1898, according to the Dutch consul in Jeddah, there were 186. The numbers, however, were certainly increasing generally from the late nineteenth into the early twentieth centuries.

57. Snouck Hurgronje to General Secretariat, September 24, 1896, in AASH, 2, 32: 1391.

58. Snouck Hurgronje to Director of Justice, March 17, 1893, in AASH, 2, 32: 1381.

59. Snouck Hurgronje to General Secretariat, October 7, 1893, in AASH, 2, 32: 1383.

60. Snouck Hurgronje to Director of Education, Religion, and Industry, March 10, 1891, in AASH, 2, 32: 1371.

61. Snouck Hurgronje to Governor General, January 20, 1905, and Snouck Hurgronje to Governor General, January 13, 1905, both in AASH, 2, 32: 1400 and 1396.

62. Snouck Hurgronje to Governor General, October 22, 1904, in AASH, 2, 32: 1478.

63. Snouck Hurgronje to Resident, Lampung Districts, September 24, 1894, in AASH, 2, 32: 1386.

64. See Putuhena, "Historiografi Haji," pp. 417–418.

65. Snouck Hurgronje to Governor General, March 1, 1900, in AASH, 2, 32: 1387. See also Snouck Hurgronje, *De Islam in Nederlandsch-Indie* (Baarn, Netherlands: Hollandia, 1913), p. 24.

66. Snouck Hurgronje to Director of Education and Industry, August 23, 1893, in AASH, 2, 32: 1402. For more on this issue, see P. Sj. Van Koningsveld, "Snouck Hurgronje alias Abdul-Ghaffar. Beberapa Catatan-Pinggir Kritik Sejarah," in P. Sj. Van Koningsveld, *Snouck Hurgronje dan Islam: delapan karangan tentang hidup dan karya seorang orientalis zaman kolonial* (Jakarta: Girimukti Pusaka, 1989); P. Sj. Van Koningsveld, "Sisa-sisa Kolonial dalam Kebijaksanaan Negeri Belanda Dewasa ini mengenai Islam," in P. Sj. Van Koningsveld, *Snouck Hurgronje dan Islam: delapan karangan tentang hidup dan karya seorang orientalis zaman kolonial* (Jakarta: Girimukti Pusaka, 1989), p. 275; and Jan Willem Naarding, *Het conflict Snouck Hurgronje-van Heutsz-van Daalen: een onderzoek naar de verantwoordelijkheid* (Utrecht: A. Oosthoek, 1938), pp. 1–116.

67. Snouck Hurgronje to Director of Education, Religion, and Industry, July 19, 1895, in AASH, 2, 32: 1405.

68. Snouck Hurgronje to Governor General, October 16, 1903, in AASH, 2, 32: 1421.

69. Snouck Hurgronje to Minister for the Colonies, March 4, 1910, in AASH, 2, 32: 1427.

70. Snouck Hurgronje to Minister for the Colonies, July 21, 1907, in AASH, 2, 32: 1426.

71. Snouck Hurgronje to Minister for the Colonies, July 29, 1906, in AASH, 2, 32: 1436.

72. Snouck Hurgronje to Governor General, NEI, October 22, 1904, in AASH, 2, 32: 1478.

73. Snouck Hurgronje to Minister for the Colonies, August 16, 1923, in AASH, 2, 32: 1429.

74. Snouck Hurgronje to Minister for the Colonies, March 23, 1923, in AASH, 2, 32: 1428.

75. Snouck Hurgronje to Director of Education, Religion, and Industry, May 2, 1900, in AASH, 2, 32: 1419.

76. Snouck Hurgronje to Minister for the Colonies, June 5, 1932, in AASH, 2, 32: 1439.

77. Snouck Hurgronje, *De beteekenis van den Islam voor zijne belijders in Ost-Indië* (Leiden: E. J. Brill, 1883), p. 14.

78. Snouck Hurgronje, *De Islam en het Rassenprobleem* (Leiden: E. J. Brill, 1922), pp. 19–20.

79. For just a sampling of these writings, see Snouck Hurgronje, "De Islam," *De Gids*, II: 239–273; 454–498; III: 90–134; "Nieuwe Bijdragen tot de Kennis van de Islam," *BTLV*, 4/6, 1882:

357–421; "Le Droit Musulman," *Revue de l'Histoire des Religions,* 19/37, 1898: 1–22, 174–203; "De Beteekenis van den Islam voor jijne Belijders in Oost-Indie," in *Wetenschappelijke Voordrachten Gehouden te Amsterdam in 1883, ter Gelegenheid der Koloniale Tentoonstelling* (Leiden: E. J. Brill, 1894), pp. 93–122; "Het Mohammedanisme," in H. Colijn, ed., *Neerlands Indie* (Amsterdam: 1911), 1:243–265; "Politique Musulmane de la Hollande," in *Collection de la Revue du Monde Musulman* #14 (Paris, 1911); "Notes sur le Mouvement du Pélerinage de la Mecque aux Indies Néerlandaises," in *Collection de la Revue du Monde Musulman* #15 (Paris, 1911), pp. 397–413; "De Islam in Nederlandsch-Indie," in *Groote Godsdiensten* (Baarn, Netherlands: Hollandia-Drukkerij, 1913), II, #9; "Vergeten Jubile's," *De Gids,* 87/7, 1923: 61–81. In one of Snouck's most important tracks, he specifically reminded his civil servant audience that performing the Hajj did not necessarily make any Indies pilgrim a revolutionary; see Snouck Hurgronje, *Nederland en de Islam* (Leiden, 1915).

80. See Huub de Jonge, "Contradictory and against the Grain: Snouck Hurgronje on the Hadramis in the Dutch East Indies, 1889–1936," in Huub de Jonge and Nico Kaptein, eds., *Transcending Borders: Arabs, Politics, Trade, and Islam in Southeast Asia* (Leiden: KITLV, 2002), pp. 219–234.

81. See Michael Laffan, "Raden Aboe Bakar: An Introductory Note Concerning Snouck Hurgronje's Informant in Jeddah, 1884–1912," *BKI,* 155/4, 1999: 517–542.

82. W. F. Wertheim, "Counter-Insurgency Research at the Turn of the Century—Snouck Hurgronje and the Aceh War," in W. F. Wertheim, *Dawning of an Asian Dream: Selected Articles on Modernization and Emancipation* (Amsterdam: University of Amsterdam Press, 1973), pp. 136–148, and Snouck Hurgronje to Th. Noldeke, June 25, 1898, in OI, p. 65.

8

The Jeddah Consulates

Colonial Espionage in the Hejaz

Watchfulness and care is to be taken against any attempts to waken
fanaticism among our native population.... Governor General of the
Netherlands Indies, 1881

It has been argued that modern, state-sponsored surveillance involves two
principal activities: the accumulation of coded caches of information and the
exercise of direct supervision over subject populations.[1] One of the signal aspects
of the colonial pilgrimage to Mecca was the attempt—and ultimate success—of
a range of European colonial powers to surveil and control the passage of Muslim
bodies to the holiest sites of global Islam. At first, this was done on a piecemeal,
ad hoc basis. Yet by the middle decades of the twentieth century, structures were
in place to make this process as scientific and as rigorous as colonial states could
possibly make it. If the connection between power and the sovereign was crucial
to ruling in early modern times, then by the turn of the twentieth century, the
ties between efforts at domination and various forms of "high modernist"
government were the driving force of colonial governments.[2] Indeed, the art of
state-sponsored surveillance, it might be argued, is one of the best ways to see
the evolution of the modern state in all of its terrifying power. In the surveillance
and criminalization of parts of the Hajj, European regimes found a vast transnational vehicle to test their advancing abilities of control. This chapter examines
this dialectic through three discrete windows, each of which sheds light on these
processes.

The Red Sea region was a test arena of sorts for various colonial projects and
their surveillance systems from the mid-nineteenth century to the middle
decades of the twentieth (figure 8.1). The first part of this chapter examines the
outlines of the three projects situated on the northern and eastern rim of the Red
Sea (French, British, and Dutch), before touching on the most important colonial apparatus of knowledge and control on the southern and western side of the

waterway—the emerging project of colonial Italy in the horn of Africa. Southeast Asian Hajj ships had to pass the gauntlet of all four of these powers en route to Jeddah and were watched by each in turn. The second third of the chapter then concentrates more fully on the Dutch architecture of vision and control in the later decades of the nineteenth century, and the connections between the Red Sea region and the Netherlands' most important global colony, the Dutch East Indies. The final third of the chapter then proceeds to the British surveillance project, as London's optic vis-à-vis the pilgrimage became the most important of all of these systems, particularly after the turn of the century. By the middle decades of the twentieth century a huge and ever-expanding apparatus of colonial control was in place, and all of these colonial partners (and sometimes-rivals) depended on the information that this project was able to acquire. With the advent of international socialism and nascent third world nationalisms after 1900, the stakes were not solely those of international pan-Islam and the specters associated with this term. I argue that control over the Hajj became seen as fundamental to ensuring the bedrock of European rule, a state of affairs that lasted until after the Second World War.

Surveilling the Red Sea Region: The Breadth of European Projects

French scholarship, as has been previously noted, was vital in decoding and codifying the threat of cholera and other diseases on pilgrim ships in the late nineteenth and early twentieth centuries. Not only were the French one of the principal European presences in the Hejaz in both diplomacy and trade but also Gallic vision of the political aspect of the Hajj was important and commented on regularly in French-language publications. Nineteenth-century French tracts on this topic tended to focus mainly on the connections between the Hajj and Paris's interests in the Arab world, which included parts of the Middle East and stretches of the North African Maghreb.[3] Other French publications of this period were written by Francophone Muslims, who saw an opportunity to explicate—and in some cases demystify—the Hajj for larger French-speaking audiences, including in Paris.[4] As the nineteenth century bled into the twentieth, more and more Francophone authors weighed in on these topics.[5] The pilgrimage went from being a relative cipher to increasingly passing through fields of French vision on the Middle East, mostly via ever-larger numbers of pilgrims from French-dominated lands.[6] Paris kept a close eye on all of this emerging literature—and carefully archived it—for their own geopolitical interests.

The British in the Red Sea region also constructed an intelligence edifice in the area, which was ultimately bent at least partially toward carefully monitoring

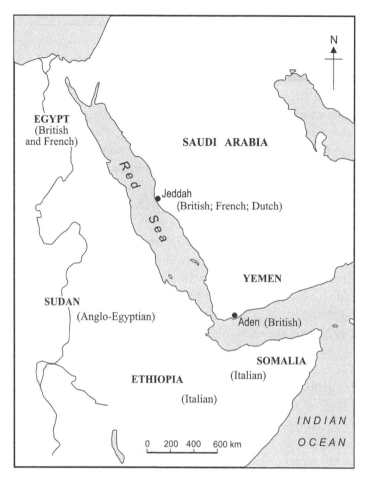

Figure 8.1 Map of the Greater Red Sea Region, and the Imperial European Presence.
Credit: Map drawn by Lee Li-kheng, Geography Department, National University of
Singapore.

and tabulating the Hajj, including its Southeast Asian varieties. Their intelligence
narrative began with the occupation of Egypt and then continued on through
the Saudi restoration, Faisal's first reign, the renewed occupation of the region,
and Faisal's second reign, as well as through the rise of 'Abd Allah and the house
of Saud.[7] The British capture of Aden in 1839 was crucial in this story, as were
the geostrategic dealings with Abyssinia on the other side of the Red Sea
waterway in the 1840s and 1850s, and finally intrigues with the Ottoman court
for many decades after this. England slowly realized—concomitant with the
growth of its own power in the world—that London would be embroiled in
politics in this maritime choke point for many years to come.[8] The bedrock of
London's covert empire in the region, however, despite these precedents, was

really laid during the late nineteenth and early twentieth centuries. At that time, the worlds of Edwardian agents and great power politics collided with the discovery of oil in the region, alongside the perceived emergence of the Hajj as a feared transmission vehicle of "militancy and subversion" for colonial powers generally.[9] This British story is picked up in earnest later in this chapter to show how the trends identified in thumbnail fashion here relate to the passage of Southeast Asian Muslims on Hajj in particular.

The Dutch were also vital players in the Red Sea espionage game of the international Hajj. Perhaps no one exemplified this complicated history more than Daniel van der Meulen, who was Dutch consul in Jeddah for two stints both before and after the Second World War. Van der Meulen's diaries kept a close eye on the Southeast Asian pilgrimage to Mecca. The consul's scribbles take in the travels, customs, and predilections of the Jawa community, much as Snouck Hurgronje had done before him in Snouck's own capacity as a scholar and official resident in the Hejaz for six months. The difference is that van der Meulen was in Arabia far longer, and his travel diaries show his cognizance and watchfulness of Southeast Asians as he moved around the vast desert peninsula between the mid-1920s and the early 1950s, a period of nearly thirty years. Van der Meulen wrote on Muslim brotherhoods, murders of Southeast Asian pilgrims, and protonationalist "conspiracies," and his observations were eagerly sought by the Dutch political apparatus in Jeddah and in The Hague.[10] Yet he also published a number of his reflections in missionary journals, newspapers (such as *De Telegraaf*, the *Deli Courant*, and the *Palembanger*, all with large circulations), and other periodicals like *The Moslem World*, the last for an English-speaking audience. His topics of interest, in addition to the diary notations mentioned previously, included what happened upon the return of pilgrims to the Indies and the contours of Muslim revival movements.[11] His reflections were only the tip of the spear, though, when it came to Dutch reportage on this huge phenomenon, as materials later in this chapter will show.

On the southern and western side of the Red Sea waterway, the Italian project of colonialism was also increasingly coming into contact with pilgrim ships. Surveillance was also important here, as Rome attempted to grow its empire in the Horn of Africa over a period of several decades on either side of the fin de siècle period. Geography was in many ways at the heart of this endeavor: Italian militarists and civil servants of the burgeoning colonial bureaucracy tried to map out the terrain of the envisioned Italian sphere in increasingly broad sweeps. Much of this, at least in the cartographic realm, had to do with drawing accurate hydrographic charts of the Red Sea, which Italian ships had to traverse on their way to Rome's colonial settlements in Eritrea and Somalia.[12] This brought Italian scientists into contact with the pilgrim traffic up and down this waterway on a regular basis. Italian knowledge and expertise on the African coasts of the Red

Sea was well-known to be accurate and was eventually utilized by the other great powers in their own mapmaking and charting of the arena as a whole. Italian expertise also was reflected in an active geographical publishing industry that circulated information about the parameters of the Red Sea coasts of Africa in increasingly minute detail after the turn of the twentieth century.[13] The letters of Italian explorers and missionaries back to the Fascist fatherland also contained important information in this regard, which was kept on file in Rome as Mussolini's Italy grew into a regional power of note.[14]

Yet the Italian knowledge project went beyond this one branch of science. Because the coastal parts of the Horn where Italy began its colonies were largely Muslim, Rome's planners became interested in the study of Islamic societies in the 1920s and 1930s. By the early 1900s, Italian authors had already been writing serious journal articles about Muslim interaction in places such as Yemen and Eritrea.[15] The pace on publication of these contributions picked up in subsequent decades.[16] The birth and development of anthropology as a field of study throughout Europe also aided the production of knowledge; eventually, Rome had ethnographers in the arid landscapes of the Horn talking to a vast range of people and trying to understand their lifeways.[17] Produced under the Fascist regime, the studies were rarely critical of Italian colonialism and usually presented the "light of Rome" coming to the "dark continent" as only a good thing. The private letters written from the field by Italian ethnographers to their home institutes, and by Italian missionaries to their own superiors, echo these conclusions.[18] Yet their contributions supported larger European opinions on Islam in general and the pilgrimage in particular, as a translocal phenomenon with long roots and deep importance in the region. Alongside similar kinds of French, British, and Dutch reportage, Italian surveillance encircled the Red Sea as a geographic entity. The sea flowed in and out of this waterway, both through Suez and at the Bab-al-mandeb, and pilgrims flowed with the currents in both directions. Muslims brought into this space were, in fact, constantly being studied and entered into the ledgers of an expanding colonial machinery, on either side of this international channel.

The Early Designs of the Dutch Surveillance Project

Though the Dutch East Indies were technically the Muslim-majority location farthest away from Mecca on the planet, from a relatively early date, these islands were supplying large numbers of pilgrims to the holy cities. By the eve of the First World War, these numbers were 24,025 in 1911, 26,321 in 1912, and 28,427 in 1913, but the more telling statistic is that these were roughly one-quarter of the global total of pilgrims for these years.[19] In the eyes of the Dutch, this paradoxical fact necessitated the beginnings of a surveillance network on these subjects. From the mid-nineteenth century in Java, especially, voluminous documents were produced to keep track of the Hajj, with much of the information centering on the community level. From Besoeki in the 1850s came notations on whether the pilgrimage was deemed a threat by local administrators at this time, for example.[20] Semarang, around the same time, produced reams of sea passes that noted the date, the pilgrim's name, the ship's name, and the shipping company's.[21] From Tegal come records of the routes that some of these ships took, often jumping from the Java coasts to places such as Pontianak, Riau, and Singapore, human collection depots along the maritime routes within the archipelago.[22] The Tegal pilgrims were away for two years at a time in the 1850s, according to these statistics; others were gone for three and occasionally six years or more.[23] One document bundle from this residency in the early 1860s, "*Rapporten Dari Perkara Hadji Hadja njang Minta Pas dan njang Baru Datang dari Mekka, 1860–64,*" chronicles in Rumi (Romanized Malay) and Dutch the comings and goings to Mecca from this single regency in more than five hundred pages. It gives little away about the feelings or details of individuals, but as a source for data compilation, it is an astonishing record of movement from a very small place.[24]

Documents of a more personal nature from this period also exist. Writing primarily in Rumi, local indigenous officials supplied information about individual pilgrims who were leaving the Java coasts for Mecca in large numbers. Other documents in Dutch record the names of those leaving in short, patterned detail:

> Wordt bij deze verlof aan den Javaan Peto, behoorende tot de desa Wanatawang district Lebaksioe Regentschap Bribes Residentie Tagal, om verkeer naar Mekka ter vertrekken. Tagal, 22 Augusuts 1855, De Resident.
>
> By this document is permission granted to the Javanese "Peto," who is from the village Wanatawang, district Lebaksioe, Bribes Regency, in the residency of Tegal, to go to Mecca, August 22, 1855, signed, "the Resident."[25]

A number of pilgrims decided to change their names after coming back from their Hajj, a personal act that was sometimes committed at the conclusion of a successful trip to Mecca. A man named Fasilan, the Dutch censors in Semarang in the 1850s noted, became Abdullah; Fasidjan wanted to be known as Abdulmajid, and Arscah turned into Abdusjamad.[26] This kind of very personal, individual attention to Hajjis and Hajjas even in small villages started early in the Indonesian records but eventually became more detailed as surveillance and record gathering became more important to the Dutch later in the 1800s. By the early twentieth century, Batavia was using this Hajj-reportage apparatus to look for connections between the pilgrimage and Sarekat Islam membership on a local level, and then, using the information for political ends, and eventually for repression.[27]

If the Jakarta archives provide a view into local surveillance, in nineteenth-century Java other repositories demonstrate how Dutch oversight over the Hajj was becoming more and more transoceanic in nature. The archives of the *Ministrie van Buitenlandse Zaken,* or Foreign Affairs Ministry in The Hague, is one such place: here surveillance material was gathered from the other side of the Indian Ocean when dealing with the Dutch-administered Hajj. As such, a certain amount of the information reflects Middle Eastern reporting. The Dutch consulate in Jeddah stockpiled boiled water, oil, spirits, and petroleum in 1878 to throw down at potential Bedouin attackers, for example. The building was designated as the city's pan-European gathering point because of its large size and its defensibility; this status shows how much the Dutch valued their toehold in the Hejaz as a means of surveilling their transoceanic subjects.[28] At other moments, an active Dutch spy network was activated, as in 1881 when The Hague was informed that a man purporting to be the "second coming of Muhummad" had stepped forward ("his name is Imam Imhabil, 38 years of age, born in Mecca"). The Dutch minister for foreign affairs was warned that the Ottoman sultan had already sent letters to Muslim lands to prepare for a jihad in two years as a result of Imhabil's birth, and the Dutch consul in Singapore performed a similar version of this preparation by writing to Batavia, as the rumors were "quite enough to justify precautions" locally.[29] That same year, dip-lomatic correspondence warned of the arrival of three Meccan shaykhs—Syed Hussein Alkoods, Shaykh Abdul Hamid Murdad, and Shaykh Ahmed Salawi—in Singapore, which put the Dutch Hajj-surveillance network on high alert. All three men "occupy so important a role in the Mahomedan world that their movements seldom fail to have a political object," the governor-general of the Indies was told.[30] They needed to be watched, particularly if they were planning on moving into the Indies to preach hate against Europeans. In this, they were seen as part of a long line of "rabble-rousers and demagogues."[31]

For an even more nuanced feel for how transnational Hajj surveillance had become in Dutch circles in the fin de siècle period, other sources from the nineteenth and early twentieth centuries can be examined, all of which com-ment on this enormous oceanic undertaking. Some of this material was public and put into the realm of public discourse by officials writing in their capacity as officials, but also as experts who could translate the "threat" of the Hajj for a public eager and willing to know about this phenomenon's huge global contours. Journals such as the *Indische Gids* fall into this public press category (table 8.1).[32]

Table 8.1 **Pilgrimage from the Dutch East Indies in 1909/1910: Statistics on Netherlands East Indies Pilgrims, and Provenances**

Java and Madura			*Outer Islands*		
Place	1326/ 1909	1327/ 1910	Place	1326/ 1909	1327/ 1910
Bantam	497	749	Padang Lowlands	208	379
Batavia	396	542	Padang Uplands	229	352
Preanger	1,857	2,044	Tapanoeli	44	55
Cheribon	434	494	Benkoelen	68	65
Pekalongan	396	439	Lampong	95	102
Semarang	375	380	Palembnag	310	514
Rembang	284	191	Djambi	77	93
Soerabaja	492	618	Sumatra East Coast	137	205
Madoera	380	342	Aceh and Environs	30	76
Pasoeroean	334	340	Riouw and Environs	14	78
Besoeki	344	257	Banka	121	44
Banjoemas	143	55	Billiton	22	18
Kedoe	546	256	Borneo, West	119	237
Djokjakarta	36	32	Borneo, SE	668	518
Soerakarta	54	59	Menado	51	51
Madioen	91	110	Celebes	265	536
Kediri	255	164	Amboina	83	66
			Ternate and Environs	52	52
			Timor and Environs	10	129
			Bali and Lombok	227	232
Total	6,914	7,972	Total	2,830	3,802

Source: Anonymous, "De Bedevaart naar Mekka, 1909/1910," *Indische Gids*, 2, 1910: 1637.

The *Koloniaal Verslag*, a dense report of many hundreds of pages published in the Indies, also put out yearly composites of information on the Indies Hajj, showing the public the trends and directions of the pilgrimage. All of this information was important in setting a tone and also in preserving information and a record of such carefully gleaned data.[33] Yet the majority of the material in question was private and intended only for the use of civil servants to keep tabs on a phenomenon that was thought to be potentially dangerous to the stability of the Dutch overseas empire. Dutch consular reports from places such as Penang and Singapore were crucial in this respect. They provided a yearly template for policy planners in The Hague to know what the Hajj looked like in ports just outside Dutch jurisdiction but very much on the doorstep of the Indies. Religious "demagogues" were thought to use these places as bases to agitate in the Indies, for example.[34] The massive run of Colonial Office records known as *mailrapporten* (or mail reports) were also crucial in this regard, as they provide an unbroken record of many decades connecting Dutch authority in the Indies, the Hejaz, and Europe on the question of the Hajj. Dutch officials could follow the *mailrapporten* through various colonial record offices, giving them a long-term view as they contemplated changes in policy.[35]

Ultimately, the root of Dutch uncertainty, anxiety, and fear in controlling the Hajj was the Indies, however, as the Dutch maintained only a tiny coterie of officials and traders in the face of a huge subject population of Muslim human beings. The Hajj might be a peaceful, unthreatening phenomenon that the Dutch were "required" to manage at the best of times, but if "extremists" did succeed in poisoning the relationship between masters and subjects in the Indies, as many Dutchmen feared in the decades leading up to the period of burgeoning nationalism in the early twentieth century, it would be the Dutch in the Indies who would pay the price. For this reason, Batavia tried to learn all it could about Islam and its permutations in every corner of the archipelago, wherever such knowledge was possible. Almost every general report, administrative report, and political report in every residency in the Indies had space for civil servants to comment on the nature of Islam in their particular area.[36] Specialized political reports were also commissioned for the so-called *Buitenbezittingen* (or residencies outside Java and Madura, the latter being the heartland of Dutch rule), so that Islam in the extremities of the colony could be examined with special rigor. Some of these districts, such as Aceh, had long histories of resistance against occupation by a foreign power.[37] Finally, in the documents known as *Memories van Overgaven*, Dutch provincial officials were asked to comment about the *geest* or "spirit" of Islam in their particular residency, when they finished their tours in a particular place and were about to hand over their landscape to another official. They noted at great length the details and trends in the Hajj in a vast array of Indies locales across the archipelago. All of these documents show changes over time as events unfolded in the Indies.[38]

Acting on the knowledge claimed by all of this surveillance was the province of the law. The Indies legal edifice set up to deal with the pilgrimage to Mecca required large numbers of codes, laws, and statutes to manage its sheer size and volume (table 8.2). From the *Staatsbladen* and *Bijbladen*, vast legal and policy compendia, it is evident that acquiring knowledge about the pilgrims themselves was deemed important by Batavia. This was so both before they set out from the Indies and once they reached the Hejaz, especially for Hajjis who wanted to stay longer in the Middle East.[39] Other laws stipulated that pilgrims were required to pay 100-guilder fines if they flouted the Netherlands East Indies pass laws, and dictated pilgrims' responsibilities to check in with Dutch port officials in the Indies cities of their departure, then again in Jeddah with the Dutch consul, and finally back in Indies ports again upon their return to Asia.[40] Because the majority of the journey was maritime, Dutch naval authorities got involved in adjudication as well. They determined rules regarding the requisition of ships for the express purpose of the Hajj (safety matters, such as the provisioning of an adequate number of lifeboats and safety vests) and the amounts of cubic space allowed to each individual passenger to try to stave off the dangers of epidemic disease.[41] It was also legislated that the Dutch were not legally obligated to financially help pilgrims in the Middle East, which was only partially effective at preempting cost savings to protect them against shaykhs.[42] These legal protections and enforcements were eventually extended to a large number of Indies ports serving as Hajj depots, including Batavia, Surabaya, Makassar, Palembang, Jambi, Belawan/Deli, Padang, Sabang, Banjarmasin, and Pontianak by 1930.[43]

Table 8.2 **Translations of Pilgrimage Surveillance Regulations from the Hajj Surveillance Regulations and Laws found in the Bijbladen and Staatsbladen van Nederlandsch-Indie**

Bijblad #5741 (1902) p. 5740, passim:

Pilgrims' Travel Passes. We must get the most reliable information possible on the pilgrims before we give them the actual passes.

Bijblad #7130 (1909) p. 319, passim:

Pilgrims' Travel Passes. Passes must be given in to the harbor master of the departing port by pilgrims. They must also be shown to the Dutch consul in Jeddah, and exchanged for a residence pass. They must be returned to the first official upon arrival back in the Indies. Pilgrims should also be classified on these passes.

Bijblad #7469 (1911) p. 444, passim:

Pilgrimage to Mecca. Pilgrims often ask for help, but they must be told firmly before they leave the Indies that they cannot expect to receive help in the Hejaz. We are indeed helpful but we cannot be expected to be so all of the time, and in every case.

Bijblad #11689 (1928) p. 381, passim:

Pilgrims' Travel Passes. There shall be a 100 guilder fine on those who flaunt the pass laws. This applies to those who travel though Singapore, Penang, Bombay, and Jeddah.

Staatsblad #236 (1906) p. 1, passim:

Shipping and Pilgrims. The Commander of the Navy and Chief of the Department of Marine can be involved with pilgrim traffic too, and lend ships for Hajjis if he feels such ships are available for use.

Staatsblad #531 (1912), p. 1, passim:

Shipping and Pilgrims. Surveillance on pilgrims during their voyages must be exercised in their own interest, too—including the insurance that there are enough life-boats on board steamers; that there are enough flotation devices; and that each pilgrim has a certain number of cubic meters space to stay in on deck during the voyage.

Staatsblad #15 (1923), p. 1, passim:

Shipping and Pilgrims. If an Indies pilgrim wants to stay in the Hejaz longer than his or her pilgrimage, then this must be reported to the proper Dutch authorities.

Staatsblad #44 (1931), p. 1, passim.

Travel Passes and Pilgrims. The number of Indies harbors now supporting Hajj traffic has grown; these now include Makassar, Surabaya, Tanjong Priok (Batavia), Palembang, Jambi, Belawan (Deli), Padang, Sabang (Aceh), Banjarmasin and Pontianak.

Staatsblad #554 (1932) p. 1, passim:

Shipping, Pilgrims: There must be real regulation in how the *mutawifs* (shaykhs) work.

Translations by E. Tagliacozzo.

By the middle third of the twentieth century, the Dutch consular office in Jeddah had acquired a primary status as a body surveilling the Indies Hajj. Some of this oversight was actually in the interest of protecting pilgrims themselves. Reports from Jeddah on the murder of Javanese pilgrims in the Hejaz and on the continuance of the slave trade alongside the Hajj both bear this Dutch imprint of responsibility and philanthropy.[44] Shaykhs who took charge of the Jawa community were also listed, tabulated, and tracked—there were 241 of them in 1928, and all of their names are still known—by a wary colonial state.[45] Yet far more of the reportage is concerned with politics than protection by this time. Some of this writing concerns great power maneuvering, such as Russian movements and oil shipments in conjunction with the Russian Hajj and the dissemination of German propaganda (in Turkish) to local Hejazi populations in an attempt to stir up hate against the Allies in the years leading up to the Second World War.[46] More of it has to do with ideas of Muslim linkages and potential subversion traveling alongside the Hajj, especially vis-à-vis a number of brotherhoods and reformist sects who were shuttling between the holy cities and places such as the al-Azhar in Cairo.[47] The largest single set of documents after the turn of the twentieth century focuses on Dutch espionage on Indies communities in the Hejaz. These provided translations of "subversive" Rumi-language letters found in Arabia and identified new organizations (such as the Committee for the Defense of Islam in Indonesia and Malaya, or Comite Pembela Islam Indonesia-Malaya) that were being set up in an attempt to speed along the independence of an Indonesian nation.[48] Recruitment of the Jawa community was said to be high in the Hejaz during this period, and the Dutch kept careful tabs on their subjects there as a result of these suspicions.[49] Ultimately, some of these people and parties did play a part in the decolonization of the Indies, though the onset of the Second World War disrupted many of these forces.

The Later Designs of British Surveillance

If the golden age of Dutch surveillance over the Hajj began in the second half of the nineteenth century, then the British became the most important players in this transnational enterprise in the twentieth century. British reportage on the parameters of the pilgrimage was active well before then; a succession of travelers beginning in the 1800s and stretching into the 1900s saw to this with a steady stream of writing, some of which became part of the fiber of British public consciousness of the Hajj. Burton, Palgrave, Doughty, and even Philby are all in this category.[50] Other early-twentieth-century Englishmen can give us an idea of the huge range of topics that interested the British as often allied subjects to the pilgrimage, all part and parcel of reportage on Arabia at this time. These topics ranged from meteorology, health, geology, pearl and mother-of-pearl production, and date farming to missionization, telegrams, and the slave trade, to name just a few.[51] All were viewed as part of a bundle of issues that made the Arabian Peninsula worth knowing, alongside the vast stream of Muslim bodies that made the holy cities centers of transnational movement. But extant accounts always stressed this proverbial stream of humanity somewhere, as if acknowledging that this was the lifeblood of the region. In his detailed descriptions of the Malay Hajj in the first third of the twentieth century, the British traveler Eldon Rutter observed dryly that "Malays die quickly if they are over-crowded," as if talking about so many hamsters put into a terrarium.[52] The origins of British surveillance of the Hajj contain much of this sort of writing, both in the Hejaz among authors and officials of Rutter's ilk and in Southeast Asia itself, where colonial ports such as Singapore and Penang became vast feeder-centers for Malay pilgrims.

Many British considerations on the viability of the Hajj had to do with very practical considerations, such as the effect of the pilgrimage on the morale of England's subject populations in Asia, an issue especially important during and around the First World War. Just before the war, Malays were coming in record numbers to perform the pilgrimage, with this community rising to 10 to 15 percent of all pilgrims present in the Hejaz at the outbreak of hostilities.[53] The British consul in Batavia, for example, wrote to his superiors just after the conflict ended that one of the best ways of countering German influence among the Arab community in the Indies would be to resume the Hajj in 1918. He even suggested combining religious and economic concerns by allowing British Muslim Southeast Asian subjects to carry sugar on their ships to Port Said, which could then be transshipped to Britain, with the pilgrim ships afterward returning to Asia with other goods on board.[54] The head of the army in Singapore was in some agreement, but cautioned:

> I personally would much like to see an opportunity given to Muhammadans in the Malay Peninsula to participate in any pilgrimage from the NEI if it were possible. Local Muhammadan feeling, while sound in most places, needs a slight fillip in some localities where the shadow of suppressed disaffection due to ignorance still lurks ... the great majority of Muhammadans of all races in the Malay peninsula are thoroughly loyal, and any efforts to obtain special facilities for the resumption of pilgrimage which might be made on their behalf would, I feel sure, be appreciated and regarded as a recognition for loyalty.... But it is wholly out of the question to use a British ship for this purpose.[55]

A subsequent memorandum on this topic asked policy planners what they hoped to get out of this scheme from both political and pecuniary points of view.[56] Yet it was clear that the British had an eye on the big picture of the Hajj and that reimposing an official presence in the Hejaz was important as the war drew to a close. This was certainly in part to keep an eye on Britain's political rivals. The British consul in Cairo wrote to London that the French, Italians, and Dutch were all in the process of reappointing consuls and legates to Jeddah, in some cases under false pretenses. The new Dutch envoy claimed that he was in

Jeddah because of his health, "in which connection it may be stated with certainty that he is the first European who has found a health resort in the notoriously bad climate of Jeddah. It is clear, now that the pilgrims have all left, that he is being kept at Jeddah by his government for other purposes other than pilgrimage questions, and in order that he may act as Dutch representative, and report on the political situation."[57]

In the interwar years, the British continued to surveil the Southeast Asian Hajj in the Hejaz through a number of different indices. One of the most important was financial: London wanted to know exactly how much the Hajj cost for different Muslim communities globally and what this meant for how many people could afford to actually make the trip. Copies of Meccan newspapers such as the daily *Umm al-Qura* were therefore circulated between different branches of British government when issues contained data of this kind; a clipping preserved in the India Office Library of one issue from November 1926 includes a small section earmarked specifically for Javanese pilgrims.[58] Translations were also made from the Arabic for the official Hejazi tariffs on the pilgrimage for any given year. Quarantine dues, inspection committee fees, portage rates, house rental prices, municipality dues, gratuities for the mutawwifs, water charges, camel hire, and tent costs all were listed, so the British had a clear idea of how much pilgrims were expected to pay and at what points along their journeys.[59] London also kept very accurate statistics not only on its own Southeast Asian Hajj shipping from Singapore, Penang, and outlying ports but also from the rest of the region and the entire Muslim world.[60] These statistics passed from the British envoy in Jeddah to his superiors in London, and templates were also drawn up to organize annual additions to longitudinal data. This involved writings on prices and shipping, customs, religious policies, and shaykhs, as well as pilgrim data on every imaginable group and subgroup of people, including annual runs of Hajjis from such seemingly innocuous and out-of-the-way places as Sarawak in British Borneo.[61] One scholar has calculated that even though Malays were going in smaller and smaller absolute numbers than Indonesians or Indians, as a percentage of available Muslim travelers inside the colony, they were actually performing Hajj in very high proportions, so the collection of all of this data was deemed crucial by the colonial state.[62]

Not all places and themes were equal in the official British mind-set of pilgrimage surveillance, however. Because London had a global political presence, certain political issues were treated as more potentially dangerous than others. The growth of Communism as an ideology on the world stage was one of these, as it bled into Hajj surveillance. Tsarist Russia and, after 1917, the Soviet Union were seen as hotbeds of such ideological contagion, so much so that when Soviet pilgrimage parties came to the Hejaz, such as one cohort of nearly ten thousand pilgrims who came from Odessa in 1927, they were closely watched.[63] The reasons for surveillance here were clear, according to the acting British consul in Jeddah in his report to London:

> The advantages of Mecca and the Hejaz generally as a headquarters for anti-European agitation in the Near and Far East need hardly be dwelt upon.... In Mecca malcontents from Morocco can meet refugees from Syria, and agitators from India can compare grievances with their sympathizers from Java and Sumatra.... The atmosphere of the Hejaz is different from that of ordinary countries. The air does not blow freely here. There are no free newspapers, no easy means of communication with the outer world; the Hejaz is an enclosed space in which prejudice (reigns).... The climate of the Hejaz fosters men on whose sharpened nerves the suggestion of Islam in danger from the West would produce jarring chords with immeasurable reverberations.... There is, then, excellent ground here for suggestive propaganda. The question is what use the present Soviet Agency have made of it.[64]

These links between Communism and Islam were not wholly imagined. In 1920, the PKI (or Communist Party of Indonesia) was formed, and it was quickly criminalized by an anxious Dutch colonial state in Batavia. This did not escape the notice of the British in the Hejaz, who exchanged secret letters with their own consul in Java as to the nature of the links between local Communist cells there and pilgrim ships arriving in Jeddah (box 8.1). Several of these letters survive, and they paint an entrancing picture of surveillance in action—missives shuttling back and forth across the length and breadth of the Indian Ocean, tracking the confluence of a decades-old ideology and a thousand-year-old religion, entwined as one as a threat to European rule.[65]

Confluence—real or imagined—was one thing, but being able to act on this union was quite another. Ships were vital to this calculation in the Southeast Asian case, because pilgrims relied on European vessels and would always be at the mercy of Western surveillance. In 1938, however, it came to the attention of the British security apparatus in the Hejaz that pro-independence groups in the Dutch Indies were trying to fund and build their own large-scale shipping lines, the express purpose of which was to shuttle Indies Hajjis on indigenous-owned ships. The vernacular press in the Indies announced that this was being done under the auspices of the Muslim political party Muhammadiyah, with the object of bringing the pilgrim traffic to Arabia wholly into native hands. While the British and the Dutch ran the numbers on capital accumulation and profit ratios, other Malay-language newspapers in the Indies added more details to the story.[66] The *Pewarta Deli* in Sumatra, for example, stressed that the prime movers behind the idea were receiving help from Germans, who were trying to get the

Box 8.1 **1927 Letter, Sarekat Islam and Communism (British Consul
Batavia to FO, July 25, 1927, #100 Secret, PRO, London)**

Secret

No. 100.   British Consulate-General,

Batavia.

July 25th, 1927.

Sir,

I have the honour to enclose herewith a translation of a letter, copy
of which has been kindly furnished to me, under the pledge of secrecy, by
the Chief of the Political Intelligence Service of the Dutch East Indian
Government.

1. Though it is not so stated, the letter is evidently from the Dutch
Consul at Jeddah, and is no less evidently addressed to the Governor-General
of the Netherlands East Indies. It reports the activities of two communist
organizations recently formed at Mecca for the purpose of conducting propaganda among the pilgrims arriving there from this country. As you will
observe, six of the leading members of these organizations were arrested by
King Ibn Saud. They have since been dispatched to Dutch India, where they
have been taken into custody by the authorities.

2. In my confidential dispatch No. 66 of May 17th last, I had the honour
to report the departure from Java for Mecca of Haji Agoes Salim, one of
the leaders of the local Mahomedan association known as Sarikat Islam.
I have received from the Chief of the Political Intelligence Service here a
note (translation enclosed), stating that this man is reported to have been
in contact with the Soviet representatives in the Hedjaz. His return to Java
is expected before the month of October next. The Chief of the Intelligence
Service will be grateful for any information which we ourselves be able to
supply to him regarding the doings of H. A. Salim in Arabia. I am communicating this request to His Majesty's Consul at Jeddah, to whom also I am
forwarding a copy of the present dispatch.

I have the honor to be,

With the highest respect,

Sir,

Your most obedient,

Humble Servant,

Copies to:

His Majesty's High Commissioner in Egypt.

His Excellency The Governor of the Straits Settlements, Singapore.

> The Secretary to the Government of India in the Foreign and Political
>   Department, Simla.
> His Majesty's Minster at the Hague.
> His Majesty's Consul at Jeddah.
> The Director of the Political Intelligence Bureau, Singapore.

initial scheme off the ground using a chartered German vessel. Another newspaper said that there was a growing Indonesian tendency to regard Italy as the
protector of Islam—with Italian colonial stations stretched along the Red Sea's
southern littoral, this idea was taken very seriously—and that negotiations had
begun with Japanese interests as well.[67] This entire story eventually came to
naught because of a combination of European suppression and the onset of the
instabilities of the Second World War. Yet it is not hard to see where the fears of
this endeavor potentially succeeding were leading or which bedfellows London
and The Hague imagined Muhammadiyah would wake up with in their attempt
to make the Indies Hajj "indigenous." The fact that German, Italian, or Japanese
ships were no more indigenous than British or Dutch ones meant little in the
end. What was at stake was control over the movement of human beings, and
what these humans had access to over the course of their long voyages to the
Hejaz, both from materialist and intellectual points of view.

The Second World War signaled the beginning of the end to the colonial
supervision of the pilgrimage to Mecca, though this took longer than the six
years of the war itself. A new order of the Hajj did not appear until well after the
hostilities were over in 1945. When the war began, the number of Southeast
Asian Hajjis who actually made it to Mecca or back to Southeast Asia from the
holy cities dropped precipitously. The 1940 British pilgrimage report suggests
that only fifty-four Hajjis made it to Mecca from Southeast Asia that year, though
these were mixed between Malay pilgrims from the peninsula; Javanese, Sumatrans,
and Indies Arabs from the Dutch territories; and a few itinerant Jawa who made
the trek from Aden or Cairo, having already been in the Middle East when the
war began.[68] Once the hostilities started, the real battle in terms of colonialism
and surveillance was propaganda, as both the Allies and the Axis tried to "sell" to
Muslims under their control the belief that their own brand of rule would be best
for Muslim interests. For the British, this involved accommodating the Saudi
government in the Hejaz far more than had previously been the case, including
the matter of information control, which had been a hallmark of British action in
the Red Sea for many decades. They did so through film censorship but also bro-
chures, such as one document that laid out all of the stations of the Hajj in a large
pictographic image, replete with Muslim travelers' sketches and descriptions of

Figure 8.2 Mecca in a British Propaganda Map.
Credit: Fragment of a Large Map in CO/732/87/18; PRO, Kew, London

Hajj rites from the ages, all in flowing Arabic script (figure 8.2).[69] The brochure was presented to those who were identified as "notable Hajjis" as a gift of the British government, in a good-will gesture aimed at showing London's continuing tolerance of the pilgrimage as a vital institution of the Muslim faith.[70] When it came down to requisitioning ships to carry Asian pilgrims who wanted to get to the Hejaz in the closing months of the war, however, London remained firm. The Admiralty expressed understanding of his majesty's Asian subjects' desire to perform the Hajj, but no ships were to be made available for these purposes until after the fighting was over.[71] War was war, after all, and commerce was commerce—but religion and its exigencies were another matter entirely.

Conclusion

Maritime surveillance across the vast spaces of the Indian Ocean world was one of the many ways in which the West kept tabs on Islam as a knowable global phenomenon in the late nineteenth and early twentieth centuries. Few aspects of surveillance were deemed as important as the collective European vision that was cast on the radials of the Hajj at this time. Though much of the annual pilgrimage to Mecca was seen as relatively harmless, the political implications of a growing pan-Islamic movement lent a dangerous tinge to some of these proceedings. Paris, London, and The Hague—among other European capitals—equated the Hajj with a potential of dangerous rebelliousness against the status quo, alongside a raft of other negative conceptions that became stock Western images of this huge transnational flow of human beings.[72] In this, the Hajj was part and parcel of a larger civilizational discourse that was being constructed, one that took in places of Islamic learning such as the al-Azhar in Cairo, Mecca, and Medina as nodes of potential subversion, as well as sites of religious authority and dissemination.[73] In this worldview, prevalent among policy makers and much of the European general public, the sacred and the profane mixed in the Hajj, and necessitated close supervision of this annual religious exercise by the secular regimes of the Western world.

The surveillance extended over the pilgrimage to Mecca was part of larger structures of European vision that were being enacted on large parts of the world at this time. Much of this process ultimately had to do with the mechanics of criminalization, as "acceptable" forms of behavior were legislated in colonial cities for much of the planet's population. In Asia, this took on many forms, from sanitary surveillance in British colonial Singapore to the birth of policing regimes in Dutch, American, and French Southeast Asia, or what is now Indonesia, the Philippines, and Cambodia and Vietnam.[74] In China, split between a variety of Western powers, the forms of criminalization and surveillance could be diffuse, often adjoining and abutting different forms of European authority, all within the confines of a single city, such as cosmopolitan Shanghai.[75] In India, where only one foreign power was master by the mid-nineteenth century, regimes of control were more uniform, encompassing the acts and behaviors of dacoits (bandits), *thugi* (thugs), and so-called "dangerous castes," all into one system of supervision ultimately ruled from London.[76] What all of these modes of criminalization had in common was the aim of knowledge, legality, and coercion working hand in hand toward more complete systems of European control. The global Hajj became part of this larger paradigm in the late nineteenth and early twentieth centuries. Pilgrim traffic from Southeast Asia—almost exclusively confined to ships and passing along Western-dominated sea-lanes—was subsumed into these structures of long-distance surveillance and carefully channeled movement. The pilgrimage to Mecca became part of this disciplinary whole.

NOTES

1. See Christopher Dandeker, *Surveillance, Power and Modernity: Bureaucracy and Discipline from 1700 to the Present Day* (New York: St. Martin's Press, 1990), p. 32; his treatment of this topic is an elaboration and reinvigoration of Anthony Giddens's classic critique of paternalistic regimes.

2. Barry Hindess, *Discourses of Power: From Hobbes to Foucault* (London: Blackwell, 1996).

3. See, for example, M. Saddik, "Voyage à La Mecque," *Bulletin de la Société Khediviale de Géographie du Caire*, 1, 1881: 5–40; S. Soubhy, "Pélerinage à La Mecque et à Medine," *Bulletin de la Société Khediviale de Géographie du Caire*, 4, 1894: 45–88, 105–144.

4. Muhamed Bel Khodja, *Le Pélerinage de la Mecque* (Tunis, 1906); Zadeh H. Kazem, "Relation d'un Pélerinage à La Mecque," *Revue du Monde Musulman*, 19, 1912: 144–227.

5. See A. d'Avril, *L'Arabie Contemporaine, avec la Description du Pélerinage à La Mecque* (Paris, 1868); G. Cordier, "Un Voyage à La Mecque," *Revue du Monde Musulman*, 14, 1911: 510–513; E. Dinet and S. Baamer, *Le Pélerinage à la Maison Sacrée d'Allah* (Paris, 1930); M. Gaudefroy-Demombynes, "Notes sur la Mekke at Medine," *Revue de l'Histoire des Religions*, 77, 1918: 316–344; D. Kimon, *La Pathologie de l'Islam et les Moyens de le Detruire. Étude Psychologique* (Paris, 1897); B. Schnepp, *Le Pélerinage de La Mecque* (Paris, 1865).

6. From the inscriptions in the front covers of some of these books still kept in the Bibliotheque National, for example, or in the Bibliothèque de SciencesPo in Paris, we can see the linkages between a number of these people (such as one book given to the French ambassador to Syria by a Muslim Lebanese doctor, who had written on what he termed the "psychology of the Hajj"). Modern French scholars such as Laurence Husson have categorized and explicated some of these trends, including how French scholars imagined the Southeast Asian Hajj over time. Laurence Husson, "Les Indonésiens en Arabie Saoudite pour la foi et le travail," *Revue Européene des Migrations Internationales*, 13/1, 1997: 125–147.

7. R. Bayly Winder, *Saudi Arabia in the Nineteenth Century* (New York: St. Martins Press, 1965).

8. Thomas Marston, *Britain's Imperial Role in the Red Sea Area, 1800–1878* (Hamden, CT: Shoe String, 1961), p. 64, passim.

9. Priya Satia, *Spies in Arabia: The Great War and the Cultural Foundations of Britain's Covert Empire in the Middle East* (Oxford: Oxford University Press, 2008), p. 23, passim; p. 59, passim; p. 165, passim.

10. For the relevant diary entries, see KIT, Daniel van der Meulen Dairies, Dagboek, January 11, 1926, to June 13, 1927 (pp. 38–39); Dagboek, Tweede Z. W. Arabie Exploratie, February 2 to May 21, 1939 (p. 1); Dagboek, Makassar to Jeddah, January 4 to May 7, 1941 (pp. 1–6); Dagboek, Jeddah, January 11, 1942 to February 4, 1942 (p. 15); Dagboek, Saudi Arabia, December 15, 1944 to February 14, 1945 (p. 1); Dagboek, Arabia Reis met Bram Drewes, January 1 to March 31, 1952 (p. 2).

11. For van der Meulen's relevant publications on the Hajj, see "De Bedevaart naar Mekka en haar beteekenis voor Nederlands-Indie," *Zendingstijdschrift De Opwekker*, 86/1, 1942: 474–486; "The Mecca Pilgrimage and Its Importance to the Netherlands Indies," *Moslem World*, 31, 1941: 48–60; "The Revival of the Pilgrimage to Mecca," *Niewsblad voor de Residentien Palembang, Djambi, en Banka*, September 14, 1937; "The Revival of the Pilgrimage to Mecca," *De Telegraaf*, October 2, 1937; "The Return of the Mecca Pilgrims to the Dutch East Indies," *Deli Courant*, March 25, 1938; "The Pilgrimage to Mecca," *Palembanger*, June 18, 1938; "The Mecca Pilgrimage," *Palembanger*, 1938 (n.d., clipping).

12. The Italian archive at the Istituto Italiano per l'Africa e l'Oriente in Rome is a great center for this kind of period scholarship written in Italian. See several period maps produced in 1885 and 1911, respectively; see F. Garbolino, "Carta del Mar Rosso e Teatro di Guerra in Africa" (Firenze: Benelli e. Co, 1885); Istituto Geografico Militare, "Mar Rosso e Costa Orientale dell'Africa (foglio C2)" (Firenze, IGM: 1885); Istituo Geografico de Agostini, "Mar Rosso e Possedimenti Italiani in Africa" (Novara: De Agostini, 1911). For textual sources, see G. B. Licata, "L'Italia nel Mar Rosso" *Boll. Sez. Fiorentina della Soc. Africana d'Italia*, March 1885, p. 5; A. Mori, "Le Nostre Colonie del Mar Rosso Giudicate dalla Stanley," *Boll. Sez. Fiorentina della Soc. Africana d'Italia*, May 1886, p. 84.

13. G. Mangano, "Relazione Riassuntiva di un Viaggio di Studi nell'A.O., India, Ceylon, Malacca, e Giava," *L'Agricoltura Coloniale*, 4/5, 1909: 272, 313; A. Mori, "Il Problema Coloniale nei suoi Rapporti con le Scienze Geografiche e l'Attivita dell'Istituto Coloniale Italiano nei Primi Quattro Anni di Vita," *Congresso Geografico Italiano Palermo 1910* (Palermo, 1911), p. 478; R. Almagia, "Relazione due'Esplorazione Geografica delle Nostre Colonie in Rapporto allo Sfruttamento delle Loro Risorse Economiche," *Atti Convegno Nazionale per il Dopoguerra delle Nostre Colonie* (Roma, 1919), pp. 350–364; F. Santagata, "La Colonia Eritrea nel Mar Rosso Davanti all'Abissinia," in *Libreria Internazionale Treves di Leo Lupi* (Napoli, 1935), p. 229; V. Zoppi, "Civiltà Fascista," in *Il Mar Rosso*, 1935, p. 321; A. Pirzio Biroli, "Il Mar Rosso e l'A. O. I.," in *Rivista delle Colonie Italiane*, 1936, p. 1426.

14. See, for example, the letters of G. Bianchi to M. Camperio (6-6/1879); G. Rohlfs to M. Camperio (3–30/1880); G. Casati to M. Camperio (8–30/1883 and 9-5/1883); and M. Camperio to G. Casati (4–15/1889), all reproduced in Cesira Filesi, *L'Archivio del Museo Africano in Roma: Presentazione e Inventario del Documento* (Roma: Istituto Italiano per l'Africa e'Oriente, 2001).

15. D. Odirizzi, "Studio Storico della Provincia Arabica dello Jemen e Sulle Relazioni Etniche con l'Eritrea e l'Etiopia," *Atti Congresso Coloniale Italiano di Asmara* (Asmara, 1905), p. 323.

16. D. Odirizzo, *Note Storiche sulla Religione Mussulmana e Sulle Divisioni dell'Islam in Eritrea* (Asmara: Tip. Fioretti, 1916); E. Cerulli, "Note sul Movimento Musulmano in Somalia," *Riv. Di Studi Orientali* 10/1, 1923: 1; E. Massara, "Islamismo e Confraternite in Eritrea: I Morgani," *L'Ilustraz. Colon.* 8, 1921: 306.; R. Cantalupo, *L'Italia Musulmana* (Roma: Casa Editrice Italiana d'Oltremare, 1929).

17. N. Puccioni, "L'esplorazione Antropologica delle Colonie Italiane," *Atti I Congr. Studi Colon.*, vol. 3 (Firenze, 1931), p. 309; R. Corso, "Per l'Etnografica delle Nostre Colonie," in *La Rivista d'Orientale*, 1934, p. 73.

18. Again, see P. Vigoni to G. Casati (8-2/1891); U. Ferrandi to P. Vigoni (3–24/1894); P. Vigoni to G. Casati (2-1/1895); G. Carerj to G. Casati (3–21/1895); and E. Bencetti to G. Casati (6-1/1895), all reproduced in Cesira Filesi, *L'Archivio del Museo Africano in Roma: Presentazione e Inventario del Documento* (Roma: Istituto Italiano per l'Africa e'Oriente, 2001).

19. See Shaleh Putuhena, *Historiografi Haji Indonesia* (Yogyakarta: LKIS, 2007), p. 413.

20. ANRI, Resident Besoeki to Gov Gen NEI, February 23, 1856, #541, in K23. Daftar Arsip Besuki (1819–1913). This and all of the following ANRI cites are from the Gewestilijke Stukken Archive.

21. ANRI, #4369 Semarang: Sea Passes enclosed in #4362–4370 "Stukken Inzake de Bedevaart naar Mekka" in K10. Semarang (1816–1880).

22. ANRI, Regent Tegal to Resident, Tegal, June 5, 1857, #571 in K8. Tegal (1790–1872).

23. ANRI, Resident Tegal, Opgave der Uitgereiktepassen voor de Bedevaart naar Mekka voor 1856, January 2, 1857, in K8 Tegal (1790–1872).

24. ANRI, "*Rapporten Dari Perkara Hadji Hadja njang Minta Pas dan njang Baru Datang dari Mekka,* 1860/61/62/63/64" in same.

25. ANRI, "Rapport, Residentie Tagal, #27" in "Laporan Pergi dan Pulang Haji," #196/5, in K8. Tegal (1790–1872).

26. ANRI, Regent of Tegal to Resident of Tegal, June 5, 1857, #571 in K8. Tegal (1790–1872).

27. ANRI, May 18, 1914, Resident Batavia to Assistant Resident Tangerrang, in "Stukken Betreffende Mohammedanaansche Zaken, o.a. Mekkagangers, 1913–1914" in K2. Tangerrang.

28. See the documents around this newspaper clipping in ARA, "Arabie: Onlusten te Djeddah," *Handelsblad*, December 31, 1878, in "A" Dossiers, #74, "Correspondentie over woelingen, slavenhandel en slavernij in de Hedjaz 1872–1936."

29. ARA, W. H. Read, Dutch consul, to Count de Bylandt, Dutch Minister, March 19, 1881, in same.

30. ARA, UK Gov. Weld, Singapore, to Gov Gen NEI, May 13, 1881, Confidential, in same. See Michael Laffan, "A Watchful Eye: The Meccan Plot of 1881 and Changing Dutch Perceptions of Islam in Indonesia," *Archipel* 63, 2002: 79–108.

31. See Eric Tagliacozzo, *Secret Trades, Porous Borders: Smuggling and States along a Southeast Asian Frontier,* 1865–1915 (New Haven, CT: Yale University Press, 2005), pp. 149–151, 171–175.

32. See "De Bedevaart naar Mekka, 1919/10," *Indische Gids*, 1910, 2, pp. 1637–1638. For a larger view on Islam, danger, and the pilgrimage at this time, see Michael Low, "Empire and the Hajj: Pilgrims, Plagues, and Pan-Islam under British Surveillance, 1965–1908," *International Journal of Middle Eastern Studies*, 40, 2008: 269–290.

33. See *Koloniaal Verslag* 1878, pp. 120–121; 1881, pp. 104–105; 1884, pp. 102–103.

34. *Consulaat-General der Nederlanden te Singapore, Verslag,* 1872 (p. 354); 1874 (p. 544); 1875 (p. 490). See also *Consulaat-General der Nederlanden te Penang, Jaarlijksh Verslag,* 1904 (p. 971).

35. The *mailrapporten* dealing with the Hajj and "dissident Islam" and surveillance are too numerous to list in full here, but the most important files include MR 1872, #820 +; MR 1878, #474; MR 1879, #668 +; MR 1881, #259 +, #563 +, #709 +, #839 +, #860, #1107, #1139 +; MR 1883, #252 +, #1075 +, #1173; MR 1885, #638 +.

36. See ANRI, Residentie Bangka, Politiek Verslag 1872, and Algemeen Verslag, 1890; Residentie Billiton, Algemeen Verslagen 1874, 1880, 1885, and 1890; Residentie Lampong, Politiek Verslagen 1864, 1867, 1886, 1887, 1888, and 1890; Residentie Ternate, Diverse Stukken 1892; Residentie Riouw, Administratief Verslagen 1867–1874; and Residentie West Borneo, Algemeen Verslagen, 1875, 1886 and 1891 for details. Residentie Borneo Zuidoost, Algemeen Verslag 1889/1890, has a particularly good table on local Hajjis en route to Mecca for the entire decade of the 1880s from southeastern Borneo.

37. The political reports from the Outer Islands (*Politieke Verslagen van de Butengewesten*) give us a huge arc of reporting on Dutch visions of Islam across the outer edges of the Indies archipelago in the late nineteenth and early twentieth centuries. For the northern half of Sumatra, we have reporting on the ongoing insurgency from Aceh, armed "Muslim gangs" in Tapanuli, the spillage of Muslim violence into the plantation districts of East Sumatra, and "troublemaking" of Muslim chiefs such as Djandi Radja, whose attacks solicited the response that "our prestige demands that we make an end to this matter." See Gov. Atjeh G. Van Daalen to Buitenzorg, June 4, 1907, Telegram #608; "Extract uit het dagboek van het Controleur van Toba, June 10, 1906"; Resident, Sumatra OK to Buitenzorg, December 3, 1904, Telegram #117; and Resident Tapanoeli to Gov Sumatra WK, November 9, 1901, #7502. In the southern half of Sumatra, the reporting is often similar: the necessitated redrawing of political contracts with the sultan of Riau, the need to strengthen the colonial military apparatus in Jambi and Palembang because of a Muslim rebellion in the highlands, and attacks and general hatred against the Dutch by the local population in Lampung, reported as "*slechte geest onder de bevolking van afdeeling.Depoetih, en tegenwerking van het bestuur.*" See "Verslag van den aan den Sultan van Lingga, Riouw, en Onderhoorigheden Verleende Audentie, 9 Mei 1903"; Gov Gen NEI to Min Kol, February 16, 1901, #327/3; "Kort verslag omtrent den stand van zaken en het personeel in de residentie Palembang over de maand Januari 1915, #2194/23"; and "Residentie Lampongsche Districten, Mailrapport 1906/7." For Borneo and Eastern Indonesia, there is reporting on murders in the vicinity of Sambas in West Borneo; more murder upstream from the Dutch controleur in Berau, East Borneo; attempts by the Boni Sultanate in Sulawesi to exercise sway over non-Muslim upland populations; and cross-border troubles (including more murders) between Ternate and its maritime Muslim neighbor of Mindanao in the southern Philippines. See "Kort verslag der Residentie Westerafdeling van Borneo over de maand November 1899"; Resident ZO Borneo to Gov Gen NEI, May 26, 1899, #5278/1; "Kortverslag van het Gouvernement Celebes en Onderhoorigheden over de maand Juni 1898"; and "Extract out de rapporten van den Commt. Van H.M. vaartuig 'Edi', August 15 to September 28, 1898."

38. *Memories van Overgaven* from West, Central, and East Java tell us of the context of Muslim "fanatacism" as revealed in Banten; of the situation of Indies Arabs in urban places like Semarang, Pekalongan, and Tegal; and the growth of Sarekat Islam alongside the nascent nationalist parties, among other things. See West-Java, MMK 1, Hardeman, J. A. (resident) *Memorie van Overgave* (1906); Midden-Java, MMK 40, Gulik, P. J. van (Gouverneur) *Memorie van Overgave* (1931); Oost-Java, MMK 83, Hardeman, W. Ch. (Gouverneur) *Memorie van Overgave* (1931). In Sumatra, we can glean information on the ostensible connections between Islamic disturbances against the state and Communist uprisings in places such as Idi on the east coast of Aceh, on the weaponry of jihadists on the west coast of Sumatra, and on the large differences in Muslim "dissent" between the Jambi uplands and the adjacent lowlands. For these subjects, see Sumatra (Atjeh), MMK 158, Goehart, O. M. (Gouverneur) *Memorie van Overgave* (1929), p. 2; Sumatra Westkust, MMK 163, Heckler, F. A. (Gouverneur) *Memorie van Overgave* (1910, p. 6); and Sumatra, Jambi, MMK 216, Helfrich, O. L. (Resident) *Memorie van Overgave* (1908), pp. 7–8. In Western Borneo, residents reported on the conversion practices of Dayaks to Islam, and in Southeastern Borneo on how many indigenes can actually

speak and use Arabic, as well as the importation (again) of Sarekat Islam after 1911; see Borneo West, MMK 261, Vogel, H. de (Resident) *Memorie van Overgave* (1918), pp. 18–19; and Borneo Zuidoost, MMK 271; Rickmans, L. J. F (Resident) *Memorie van Overgave* (1916), p. 58. In Eastern Indonesia, material can be gleaned on Islamization in the highlands of Sulawesi and on the nature of violence—Muslim and otherwise—in outstretched residencies like Ternate. See Celebes, MMK 281, Swart, H. N. A. (Gouverneur) *Memorie van Overgave* (1908), p. 21; and Ternate, MMK 329, Sandick, L. W. H. (Gouverneur) *Memorie van Overgave* (1926), p. 9.

39. *Bijblad*, August 19, 1902, #5741; *Staatsblad*, January 17, 1923, #15.
40. *Bijblad*, June 15, 1928, #11689; *Bijblad*, July 27, 1909, #7130.
41. *Staatsblad*, April 29, 1906, #236; *Staatsblad*, October 25, 1912, #531.
42. *Bijblad*, May 16, 1911, #7469; *Staatsblad*, November 18, 1932, #554.
43. *Staatsblad*, January 26, 1931, #44.
44. ARA, Djeddah Archives, 1.2.6 Politieke Aangelegenheden, Fiche #175: Dutch Vice Consul (Widjodjoatmodjo) to MvBZ, August 22, 1933, #1183 Secret; Fiche #193: Minister of Foreign Affairs, Mecca, to Dutch Consul, Jeddah, February 15, 1938; Fiche #192: Dutch Consul to GGNEI, May 10, 1940, #619/B-10. For a good overview of the consuls, see Sarah Searight, "Jiddah in the Nineteenth Century: The Role of European Consuls," in Janet Starkey, ed., *People of the Red Sea* (Oxford: British Archeological Reports Series, 2005), pp. 109–116.
45. See Putuhena, "Historiografi Haji," pp. 419–422.
46. ARA, Djeddah Archives, 1.2.6 Politieke Aangelegenheden, Fiche #182: Dutch Consul to MvBZ, February 18, 1932, #10/P42; Fiche #197: Dutch Consul, Jeddah, to MvBZ, January 7, 1941, #9/P-8.
47. ARA, Djeddah Archives, 1.2.6 Politieke Aangelegenheden, Fiche #188: Dutch Consul to MvBZ, June 8, 1937, #497/P-105; Fiche #200: Dutch Consul, Jeddah to MvBZ, April 27, 1929, #695/98.
48. ARA, Djeddah Archives, 1.2.6 Politieke Aangelegenheden, Fiche #199: Dutch Consul, Jeddah to GGNEI, April 26, 1931, #511/H; Fiche #201: Adviser for Internal Affairs, NEI, to GGNEI, August 14, 1939, #1048/K-1.
49. ARA, Djeddah Archives, 1.2.6 Politieke Aangelegenheden, Fiche #202: Dutch Consul, Bombay to Dutch Consul, Jeddah, November 22, 1944, #2754; Fiche #203: "Memorandum on Terms of Employment." For context, see Tom van den Berge, "Indonesiers en het door hen Gevolgde Onderwijs in Mekka, 1926–1940," *Jambatan*, 7/1, 1989: 5–22.
50. Robin Bidwell, *Travellers in Arabia* (London: Hamlyn, 1976).
51. J. G. Lorimer, *Gazeteer of the Persian Gulf, Oman, and Central Arabia* (Calcutta: Government Printers, 1915).
52. See Eldon Rutter, *The Holy Cities of Arabia*, vol. 1 (London: G. P. Putnam's Sons, 1928), p. 14.
53. Mary McDonnell, "Conduct of the Hajj from Malaysia and Its Socio-Economic Impact on Malay Society: A Descriptive and Analytical Study, 1860–1981" (PhD Dissertation, Columbia University, 1986), pp. 626–628.
54. UK Consul, Batavia to Gov't Secretary, India, May 15, 1918, #79, in IOL/L/PS/11/137 P 3174.
55. IOL, Gen. Commanding Troops, Singapore, to UK Consul, Batavia, July 2, 1918, #12920 in IOL/L/PS/11/137 P 3174.
56. Memorandum of Observations on Batavia Despatch #79, in IOL/L/PS/11/137 P 3174.
57. PRO, UK Consul, Cairo, to Arthur James Balfour, London, January 28, 1917, #18, in FO 141/668/1/.
58. IOR, Extract of *Ummal-Qura*, #100, November 12, 1926, #100, preserved in Gov't Secretary India to Gov't of India Dept. of Education, Health and Lands, December 30, 1926, #1840, in IOR/R/15/2/1439.
59. IOR, "Translation of the Official Tariff Published by the Hejazi Government: Dues and Transport Charges Imposed on Pilgrims for the Pilgrimage Season of AH 1351 (1933)," in IOR/L/PJ/8/783/Coll 125/7B.

60. IOR, UK Consul, Jeddah, to FO, August 16, 1938, #1800/402/203 in IOR/L/PJ/7/789.

61. IOR, UK Consul, Jeddah, to FO, August 9, 1937, #E4922/201/25.

62. See McDonnell, "Conduct of the Hajj," pp. 631–635. McDonnell postulates that in the first half of the twentieth century, Malays made up some 7 percent of total Hajjis, as compared with 15 percent from the Dutch Indies and 20 percent from British India. But as a percentage of available Muslims to go, she says that Malays actually were leaving in ten times the numbers of the other two groups.

63. FO, UK Consul-General Batavia to FO, March 29, 1927, E 1793/323/91 Secret in FO 371/12248, "Records of the Hajj."

64. FO, Acting British Agent to FO, March 18, 1927 in FO 371/12248, "Records of the Hajj."

65. See, for example, the two fascinating letters enclosed in British Consul, Batavia, to FO, July 25, 1927, #100 Secret, in "Records of the Hajj."

66. IOR, UK Consul, Batavia, to FO, March 14, 1938, #75E in IOR/R/20/B/1454.

67. IOR, UK Consul, Batavia, to FO, September 21, 1938, #260E, in IOR/R/20/B/1454.

68. IOR, Pilgrimage Report for 1940 in UK Consul, Jeddah, to FO, September 28, 1940, #71 Confidential, in IOR/L/PJ/8/755 Coll. 125/1A.

69. IOR, Under-Secretary of India to UK Consul, Cairo, January 22, 1941, #F.9 (34)-G/40; FO to R. T. Peel, Esq., September 3, 1936, P/3041/128/150 Confidential; British Board of Film Censors to India Office, July 9, 1936, all in IOR/L/PJ/8/127/Pt. Vi.

70. PRO, Ministry of Information, London to CO, April 10, 1943, #FP 39/12 in CO 732/87/18.

71. PRO, Head of Military Branch I, Minute Sheet Comments, August 3, 1944, P.O. 21240 in Admiralty 1/12119.

72. Syed Muhammad Khairudin Aljunied, "Western Images of Meccan Pilgrims in the Dutch East Indies, 1800–1900," *Sari*, 23 (2005): 105–122.

73. Holger Warnk, "Some Notes on the Malay Speaking Community in Cairo at the Turn of the Nineteenth Century," in Fritz Schulze and Holger Warnk, eds., *Insular Southeast Asia: Linguistic and Cultural Studies in Honour of Bernd Nothofer* (Wiesbaden: Harrassowitz Verlag, 2006), pp. 141–152.

74. See Brenda Yeoh, *Municipal Sanitary Surveillance, Asian Resistance and the Control of the Urban Environment in Colonial Singapore* (Oxford Geography Research paper #47, 1991); and for colonial Indonesia, the Philippines, and Indochina, see the relevant chapters in Vincente Rafael, ed., *Figures of Criminality in Indonesia, the Philippines and Colonial Vietnam* (Ithaca, NY: Southeast Asia Program Publications, 1999).

75. The best extant source for this is Frederic Wakeman, *Policing Shanghai, 1927–1937* (Berkeley: University of California Press, 1995).

76. See, for example, Anand Yang, ed., *Crime and Criminality in British India* (Tucson: University of Arizona Press, 1985); for Bengal in particular, see Ranjan Chakrabarti, *Authority and Violence in Colonial Bengal: 1800–1860* (Calcutta: Bookland Private, 1997), and Arun Mukherjee, *Crime and Public Disorder in Colonial Bengal, 1861–1912* (Calcutta: K. P. Bagchi, 1995).

PART III

MAKING THE HAJJ "MODERN"

Pilgrims, States, and Memory

9

Regulating the Flood

The Hajj and the Independent Nation-State

Hajj Guideline Objectives: 1. Increased knowledge and understanding of the Hajj, Umrah, and Visiting. 2. To increase awareness of and concerning the actual situation in the Holy Land. 3. Assist in creating pious Muslims who understand their function after returning from the pilgrimage.
—Malaysian *Tabung Haji* Web site, accessed October 11, 2010

The Southeast Asian Hajj in the premodern and colonial periods had certain definitive features that are easy to identify. Starting from a small, irregular stream of pilgrims who wound their way across the Indian Ocean at the mercy of tides, monsoons, and irregular patterns of shipping, by the late nineteenth century complex systems were in place to regulate an increasing annual flow of human beings. The colonial edifice of politics, administration, and transoceanic steamshipping brought Hajjis across this sea in both directions. As Southeast Asia decolonized in the 1940s, 1950s, and 1960s, these patterns of control were first disrupted and then regrafted onto nonstate spaces, until the amalgam of ships, aircraft, and pilgrims reached numbers that had never previously been imagined. State structures were erected by newly independent Southeast Asian nations to cope with these flows, and to facilitate arrangements that were almost wholly dictated by the desires of a trans–Indian Ocean *ummah* of Muslims themselves, both in Southeast Asia and in Arabia. This was done for utilitarian reasons and for the sake of surveillance on both ends.[1] A pilgrim management edifice established in Malaysia in the 1960s became a blueprint for Muslim nations elsewhere in the world, and the Tabung Haji still often fulfills that function today.[2] This institution not only explains the Hajj to the country's citizens but also instructs them on everything having to do with the journey, from the form and content of prayer, to issues of translation and logistics, to the customs of "Muslim cousins" on the other side of a shared sea.[3] In Indonesia, the other principal exporter of pilgrims from the region, similar institutions exist. Although the activities of these bureaus are analogous to their Malaysian counterparts, the challenges faced in organizing the Indonesian Hajj are considerably greater, given its size. The yearly embarkation of some 200,000 Indonesians to Mecca must surely count as one of the great logistical management achievements in the modern world.[4] Yet all of these voyages, whether Malaysian, Indonesian, or from other parts of the lands beneath the winds, share a common historical heritage that binds these pilgrims into a single web. As members of the community called by Arabs the Jawa, Southeast Asians make up one of the most important of the world's subsets of Muslim pilgrims to the Middle East. They also travel under their own auspices, as free citizens of states where Southeast Asians now hold the levers of government and control.

This chapter begins by looking at some of the ways that Southeast Asia's transition to independence was achieved from the 1940s through the 1960s and how the Hajj was part of this often painful process. It then explores the modern Hajj practices of two different Southeast Asian states, Indonesia and Singapore, which represent opposite approaches to pilgrimage management. This is at least partially based on the dictates of population size and national wealth, which are so disparate between these two countries. It next focuses on the modern history and functioning of the Tabung Haji, Malaysia's Hajj-management bureau, often seen as a paragon for Hajj administration and control by third world Muslim nations that are on the track of infrastructural development and growth. Finally, the chapter looks at how the Hajj is managed and controlled from Southeast Asia—and crucially from Arabia—in current times. How did the Southeast Asian Hajj transition from a colonial to a postcolonial phenomenon? What were the parameters of this experience? Which patterns fell by the wayside of history, and which continued into the present? This chapter seeks to answer these interrelated questions across the width and breadth of the Muslim arc in the region, one that connects a fraternity of coreligionists astride a vast ribbon of land and sea.

The Transition to Independence

The years right before the onset of World War II were halcyon ones for the Hajj—pilgrims were coming in huge numbers to the Hejaz, attracting the attention of many in the international arena. The United States, an emerging power at this time, was no exception: Washington and its officers abroad kept a close eye on the pilgrimage and what it meant for stability in the Middle East. The American legate in Cairo in 1938 informed his superiors that Southeast Asian devotees were particularly numerous, numbering in the tens of thousands, and were edging out the number of pilgrims even from India that year.[5] Yet these

American period documents also show that events in Europe were clearly going to take a toll on the overall health of the Hajj. By 1940, the number of pilgrims had dropped from 59,627 two years previously to just 32,288—a substantial loss of income to the Saudi kingdom.[6] They would drop further after this date. As a result, Saudi Arabia's finances were precarious for long portions of the year, as the king relied on pilgrimage revenues to keep his country afloat before oil was discovered in much larger than expected quantities after the war.[7] There were also internal politics to watch: one American official informed Washington that "(King Saud) is pro-British and extremely pro-American, but...members of his council (are) very pro-German and others are anti-British...the Axis are doing effective political work."[8] An alliance was eventually signed with the Germans, though not over military matters. The Allies were cognizant of the difficulties the king faced, particularly in the months when the Hajj revenues dwindled. King Saud needed to keep his retainers happy for stability's sake, and, as one analyst commented, "good will comes at a higher price during wartime."[9] At the height of the war, the king himself acknowledged his difficulties in a major policy speech, decrying the fact that conflict was "depriving us from meeting our Moslem brethren in North Africa, India and Java."[10] Utilitarian leanings by the Saudis toward both the Allied and Axis powers were necessary for the times.

By the closing months of the war, many of the Southeast Asian pilgrims who had left for the Hejaz were stranded there without funds to return. The British government dealt with this by distributing cash to their Southeast Asian subjects, but the Dutch allowed less leeway in this respect, handing out rice instead to Indies pilgrims in an effort to keep them from starving.[11] This worked only partially. Indonesian-language petitions show that many Indonesians were still in dire straits:

> Telah diketahoei Pemerintah kita, beberapa banjak bilangan orang sakit sebab kekoerangan zat makanan jang perloe....Patoet sekali Pemerintah Belanda memperbaiki nasib moekimin jang ada sekarang di Tanah soetji Mekka.[12]
>
> It is already known by our government that many of us are sick because we have insufficient amounts of food to eat....It would be appropriate that the Dutch government can improve the lot of the Muslim pilgrims here in the Holy Land of Mecca.

The Netherlands stood by their position; the Dutch consul in Jeddah allowed only a very small rise in payments to pilgrims, though rice handouts were still continued on a widespread scale. The consul's research into the situation had discovered 251 elderly and 90 unattended women among their Southeast Asian Hajjis, so these two groups were specially targeted for aid.[13] Yet in a bow to the changing political realities of the Hajj and moves toward decolonization right as the war ended, the Dutch also decided to appoint an indigenous consul to Jeddah rather than a Dutchman, as had been the case for many decades. The present consul, Mr. Dingemans, was leaving to take up a professorship in Batavia, and an indigenous successor was thought proper to placate nationalist feelings back in the Indies.[14]

After the war, there was a period of difficulty while shipping and organizational structures got back to normal, and the Indonesian revolution, too, adversely affected the Hajj from 1945 to 1949. Only after this time did Indonesian pilgrims begin to travel in much larger numbers again, as conditions improved and safety and stability returned to this part of the world. It was during this period that George Kahin, then a young professor at Cornell University, started to make detailed surveys of Islam in the country. Kahin explained in a letter to the secretary general of Indonesia's new Department of Religion what he was after; his new "Cornell Modern Indonesia Project" was seeking to understand the beginnings of the country's independence period, and a serious look at how Islam functioned in Indonesia was part of this program.[15] Kahin was given almost unparalleled access during the mid-1950s to surveying and census data, and he was able to compare the statistics from the 1930 census and the 1955 one in a large series of accurate charts, graphs, and tables.[16] This data helped to flesh out where Hajjis were coming from inside the country, with the numbers on what the Dutch had earlier termed "provinces, residencies, and regencies" stretching down to smaller and smaller units.[17]

The Kahin papers offer something of a summary on the Hajj in Indonesia during the 1950s; they show the incredible complexity of religiosity, region, and distributed wealth, all acting in moving human beings toward Mecca under the watchful eyes of the state. These pages are particularly useful in showing the regional roots of piety and eventual transit to Mecca from places such as Eastern Borneo, Southwest Sulawesi, and parts of Java. Kahin did not stop there; his surveyors also tried to map the local-level Hajj alongside mosque and madrasa numbers in the same *kabupaten* (districts) as the pilgrims of his research.[18] The result was a statistical compendium of what the Indonesian Hajj actually looked like during the earliest years of independence, when the new country was starting to send pilgrims on its own terms (and not by Dutch dictates) to the center of organized Islam. When coupled with period newsletter reportage from the *Berita PHI*, the Indonesian Hajj Bureau of the time, these sources provide a strong sense of how enormous a project it was to connect Indonesia to the Hejaz on Jakarta's own terms, rather than having this done for Indonesians by a Dutch colonial government that owned most or all of the shipping.[19] It is also clear why certain parts of Borneo, Sulawesi, Sumatra, and Java still send more pilgrims to Mecca than others, based on a historical continuum of piety, wealth, and transport access that still, to some extent, continues to this day.

In British Malaya after the war, there was also a short pause before conditions returned to normal, but by 1949 Malay pilgrims were starting to arrive again in the Hejaz in what appear to be large numbers (box 9.1). In that year, for example, at least five large ships made the voyage from the Malay Peninsula to Jeddah: the SS *Melampus* carried 693 pilgrims, the SS *Prometheus* arrived with 987, the SS *Rhesus* with 251, the SS *Atreus* with 430, and the MV *Autolycus* with 565. These pilgrim aspirants came from across the entire colony: Malacca, Pahang, Perak, Kedah, Trengganu, Johore, Negri Sembilan, Selangor, Penang, Perlis, Kelantan, Sarawak, and Brunei, with Selangor sending the most Hajjis and the Bornean territories sending the fewest.[20] The British kept careful tabs on the monies their subjects would need to spend while they were in the Middle East: 30 riyals for water, 8 riyals for charcoal, 140 riyals for food (excluding rice brought from Malaya itself), 15 riyals for cigarettes, and 5 riyals to give as charity at the mosques and at the well of Zamzam.[21] The British also instituted new procedures in concert with the Saudi government to deal with the deaths of Malay Hajjis while they were in Arabia, since this happened so frequently. The process was normalized so that the authorities had more say in divvying up the pilgrim's belongings, rather than just entrusting this to the shaykhs, who were still judged to be rapacious.[22] Finally, the British reined in the often freewheeling sale of pilgrim passes, so that it became much harder to forge or otherwise work the system back in Malaya, by carefully cross-tabulating the numbers of passes sold and received with printer's copies, numbered sets, and accounting along the length of the pilgrims' journey.[23] All of these steps were implemented in the postwar period in an effort to control and rationalize the Hajj.[24] The Saudi government was only too glad to assist with such measures, as it was actively trying to rationalize, organize, and oversee the Hajj for its own ends, too.

By 1955, as in the Indonesian case, there was strong pressure on the British to give more representation to ethnic Malays in running the yearly journey across the ocean to the Middle East. The British noted in internal correspondence in that year that Nigerian Muslims in Mecca had asked that officials among their countrymen be allowed to come to Mecca to look after their interests; British civil servants, who were Christians and thus not allowed to enter the holy cities, could not do so. A similar call went up from the Malay community in Mecca that same year.[25] A short time later, it was agreed that a delegation of prominent Malays—including Enche Mustapha Albakri bin Haji Hassan (the minister for industrial and social relations), Dr. Kamil Mohamed Ariff, and Tungku Syed Abdullah bin Tungku Syed Omar (of the Malayan Civil Service)—would be sent for this purpose.[26] The transit of ethnic Malays to help along the Malay Hajj became routinized after this, with doctors, nurses, hospital attendants, and welfare officers all being sent regularly, and these Malays, too, hailed from all over Malaya (including Selangor, Negri Sembilan, Penang, Trengganu, Kedah,

Box 9.1 **The Malay Pilgrimage Season in *1949–50* in British Eyes**

Johore Bahru, February 5, 1950
No. 4 in SSJ. 170/50
To the Honourable, the Chief Secretary,
Federation of Malaya, Kuala Lumpur
Sir,

With reference to your letter F.S. 12064/50/2 dated January 21st, 1950, forwarding a copy of the report of the 1949 Mecca Pilgrimage Season compiled by the Malayan Pilgrimage Commissioner, I am directed to append hereunder the following comments:

1. Page 3, early return home after pilgrimage. Every effort should be made with the shipping co. to effect return of pilgrims as early as possible after the pilgrimage is over. Delay is disastrous to the pilgrims.
2. Page 4, amendment of pilgrim-pass to include 3 names of accompanying relatives or friends. Agreed—this is very essential.
3. Page 5, leave certificates to gov't servants. This should be put into use.
4. Page 6, preventive methods to safeguard the interests of pilgrims. Publicity of improper dealings or approach by mutawifs is necessary. Pilgrims would then know the adverse effect of such touting. If it is at all possible Mutawifs from Mecca should not travel in pilgrim boats along with pilgrims. They may return by any other boat they prefer. If we can stop mutawifs coming from Mecca altogether so much the better.
5. Page 6 of Appendix A. Government should take steps through the British Embassy to iron this out. Payment to Mutawifs by the Saudi Government should be prompt as it is the pilgrims' money. Pilgrims must not suffer on this account.
6. Page 8 of Appendix A. Orthodox belief on the merit of "Fadhilah." This is again a question of publicity. The Malayan Pilgrimage Commissioner should obtain the views of Alims Ulama and publish such views in his advice to pilgrims. However if shipping is limited and we decide to limit stay up to 3 months only, this argument does not arise.

I am, Sir, your obedient servant,
The State Secretary of Johore

State Secretary of Johor to Chief Secretary, Federation of Malaya, Kuala Lumpur, February 5, 1950, #4 in SSJ, 170/50; from Arkib Negara, Malaysia.

Malacca, and Johore).[27] By 1957, more issues arose, including the Saudi government's consternation that contraband of all sorts was being brought into Mecca against the wishes of the regime. This contraband included arms, explosives, liquor, narcotics, unauthorized medical preparations, pornography, and even cinema projectors and films.[28] At the same time, the Hajj became more standardized in an era of peace and prosperity in Southeast Asia. Between the late 1950s and the early 1970s, Malay pilgrims always made up roughly 2 percent of the global totals, with four to six thousand arriving annually.[29] The pilgrimage became something that people did from the nearby city, from the next village, and even from one's own hometown. An article from the *Times of London* in 1957 described a British surgeon's sea pilgrimage from Malaya to Jeddah to its substantial readership:

> Some five thousand pilgrims go by sea from Malaya to Mecca each year. They are prepared to stay in Saudi Arabia for up to three months while awaiting their return passage....After we had entered the calm of the Red Sea and left behind the rough monsoon weather a children's party was held. Forty children attended in a great variety of dress....Musical chairs, the egg and spoon race, pinning the tail on the donkey, but—the donkey became a camel.[30]

Indonesia and Singapore: Two Varieties of the Modern Hajj

The economic instability of the transition to independent nation-states, replete with depressions and changing currencies, policies, and personnel, meant that performing the pilgrimage was still difficult, despite the improving international infrastructure of the Hajj. In 1952, for example, British consular reports said that "the Indonesian pilgrimage reflects fairly closely the economic situation of the archipelago, and we expect that if the present deterioration continues, the numbers next year will decline."[31] Nevertheless, only two years later, some ten thousand pilgrims, scattered from locales across the islands, were making the voyage from Indonesia. The finances of the Hajj were transferred from the failing Bank Rakjat Indonesia to a committee of religious officials, who were explicitly tasked with cutting corruption in the mechanisms of allocating who was allowed to perform the Hajj from a vast number of willing pilgrims.[32] There were still problems in this respect many years after independence, but it was an achievement that after four years of world war and another four years of revolution, Indonesian Hajjis were paying for and making the pilgrimage again in the early 1950s.

In the decades that followed, LIPI (the Indonesian Government Research Bureau), in conjunction with the Hajj Research Center in Mecca, undertook some highly detailed studies of Indonesians who were able to perform the Hajj. Their results were both surprising and enlightening. A 1982 report suggested that fully one-third of Indonesian pilgrims were from the lowest classes; a further third were labeled as "middle-class" by GDP/family; and a final third were labeled as "upper-class." Not only were a third of Indonesian Hajjis classified as poor but still performing the Hajj despite its ever-rising costs but also almost 40 percent were classified as farmers, an extremely high number compared with many other societies.[33] These percentages suggest that the Hajj maintained its prestige, even in an era of rapid development and change in this quickly modernizing country. From the early 1970s to the early 1980s, the cost of a ticket to Mecca more than doubled, making these LIPI tabulations even more surprising.[34] Sea travel across the Indian Ocean from Indonesia also began to be phased out, as air travel became a much more viable alternative. A journey that once took weeks by steam or even months by sail could now be done in ten hours, directly from Jakarta to Jeddah. Garuda Airways, Indonesia's national airline, was quick to profit during this transitional period, as table 9.1 makes clear.

A newer phenomenon in the Indonesian Hajj, as well as elsewhere in the region, has been the rise of Hajj-plus, the luxury Hajj package. Most Indonesian Hajjis still buy basic tours, which find them a place to stay, get them on an airplane, and take care of their itineraries while they are in the Holy Land for sev-

Table 9.1 **The Indonesian Pilgrimage by Air and Sea, 1974–82**

Year	# Pilgrims (Air)	Garuda Earnings (US$)	Cost/Ticket (US$)	# Pilgrims (Sea)
1974	53,752	38,432,680	715	15,396
1975	45,140	37,014,800	820	9,719
1976	17,904	15,039,360	840	7,351
1977	27,660	23,234,400	840	6,578
1978	73,030	61,345,200	840	—
1979	41,838	43,678,872	1,044	—
1980	75,998	99,253,388	1,306	—
1981	67,141	101,411,128	1,570	—
1982	55,264	91,296,128	1,652	—

Source: Adapted from Zamakhsyari Dhofier, "Dampak Ekonomi Ibadah Haji di Indonesia," *Prisma*, 12/4, 1984: 53; and Zamakhsyari Dhofier, "The Economic Effect of the Indonesian Hajj," *Prisma*, 36, 1985: 65.

eral weeks. It is also possible to perform the Hajj in much more comfortable circumstances, however. Accommodations can be upgraded to five-star hotels, of which there are now several in Mecca, some just outside the central mosque containing the Ka'ba. Instead of traveling through Indonesian government-leased planes, Hajj-plus pilgrims can take regular commercial airlines, which generally have far fewer delays and are subject to regular competition for service and meals on board. Many basic-package Hajjis do their own cooking in Saudi Arabia or depend on the many small food stalls that litter the streets of Mecca, especially during Hajj season. Hajj-plus packages often come with their own cook, so that pilgrims can taste a bit of local food if they desire, but they also know they can eat their own dishes, which will be hygienically prepared and cooked to their own tastes. Doctors also come on these tours, and buses can be arranged with air-conditioning and professional drivers.[35] One Indonesian pilgrim I spoke with remembered living frugally for several years to go on one of these latter packages, both to improve her experience and to help her concentrate on her religious duties rather than being constantly uncomfortable.[36] The director-general of the Indonesian Hajj, Dr. H. Taufiq Kamil, told me that of course the percentages of Indonesians able to perform journeys like these were very small, though the numbers do seem to be increasing.[37]

If Indonesia is able to put together Hajj-plus packages along these lines, Singapore—much smaller and with a far higher GDP—has not surprisingly also improved the economic efficiency of the Hajj. The Singaporean government has set up a body of laws that regulate the economic transactions of the Hajj to a minute degree, ensuring the smooth flow of pilgrims from the island nation and the maintenance of good credit. The Administration of Muslim Law (Haj) Rules (1999) is one of the cornerstones of this legislation, setting out approval of travel agents, advertising, accounts, and welfare in carefully stipulated rules.[38] Perhaps as a result of this efficiency, almost all Singaporean Hajjis I interviewed praised the handling of their country's Hajj. One woman was able to lay out the exact costs of her recent pilgrimage from memory, telling me that it was all made so clear by the government-regulated agents that she was able to plan almost the exact amount of money that she would spend on the entire trip.[39] Another Hajja told me that she had sold her apartment at a profit and invested the surplus in the pilgrimage.[40] By 2004, Singaporean Hajj packages were selling from approximately $4,500 to $9,500 Singaporean dollars exclusive of airfare, depending on the extras desired in the tour (table 9.2).[41] The startling efficiency and financial sureties of the modern Singaporean Hajj package are a far cry from the Southeast Asian Hajj even fifty years ago, when such matters could never be taken for granted.

In some sense, Indonesia and Singapore present two extremes of the modern pilgrimage experience in Southeast Asia. This was certainly true in the decades

Table 9.2 **Singapore Hajj Packages, Pilgrim Numbers and Prices (Singapore $),
1990–2004**

Year	# Pilgrims	Lowest Package $	Highest Package $
1990	3,532	5,200	6,450
1991	2,854	5,149	6,599
1992	5,216	5,700	6,699
1993	4,464	6,250	6,950
1994	4,019	6,500	6,999
1995	4,117	6,700	7,348
1996	4,872	6,299	7,599
1997	4,085	7,091	7,957
1998	4,068	6,140	8,450
1999	4,004	6,750	8,890
2000	3,963	3,840	6,500
2001	3,963	3,750	6,650
2002	3,929	4,790	6,650
2003	3,332	4,940	6,680
2004	2,709	4,689	7,085

Source: Majlis Ugama Islam Singapura (MUIS), 2004 data (prices do not include airfare).

from independence to the turn of the twenty-first century. Indonesia, a much larger but also a much poorer nation, sent Hajjis in vast numbers to Mecca over the course of the past sixty years, usually on passenger steamships and later by air. These pilgrims made up a sizable number of the devout in the holy places during Hajj season, though they were often far worse off materially than other Southeast Asians. Singaporeans, by contrast, came in much smaller numbers, under the auspices of a highly coordinated state apparatus that took care of their every need. This was the case for decades, and this state of affairs still holds true for the Singaporean Hajj today. The differences between the top end of the Indonesian pilgrim market and the normative Singaporean pilgrimage have now narrowed, however. Global capitalism has ensured that the wealthy of any society can enjoy the same privileges, even on a religious quest such as the Hajj, which tries to level the economic differences between human beings. It is no accident that many merchants and businessmen in Arabia learn to speak at least some Indonesian, as they know the sheer volume of this country's pilgrims promise a chance at good profits, even if the average Indonesian pilgrim still goes on Hajj in generally poorer circumstances than a Singaporean one. This legacy of the colonial age and the first few decades of independence will in all likelihood continue into the near and medium-term future.

The Case of Malaysia: The Tabung Haji at Work

An interesting contrast between the vast size of the Indonesian Hajj and the controlled efficiency of the much smaller Singaporean pilgrimage is the case of Malaysia. Since 1969, the Malaysian Hajj has been controlled through the Tabung Haji, the government office located in downtown Kuala Lumpur, but with offices all throughout the country, that manages and oversees almost all citizens leaving for the Hejaz.[42] By the mid-1970s, the Tabung Haji already counted more than 250,000 Malaysians as its depositors, everyday citizens who were using its auspices to save for their eventual journeys to Mecca. New depositors were growing at the rate of five thousand per month, and by 1976 the total amount of money invested in the Tabung Haji was close to 200 million ringgit, some $65 million. The Tabung Haji invested this money in various enterprises to try to grow the funds and provide ever-increasing sums for its depositors. Oil palm estates, real estate in both Malaysia and Saudi Arabia, and financial agreements with international airlines were all part of these investments, diversifying the funding sources for hundreds of thousands of ordinary Malaysians who sought to perform their religious obligations.[43] The organization is run as a wide-ranging and sophisticated modern business, yet also along Islamic banking principles. Even the building of the Tabung Haji has become emblematic of the new nation-state modernity of the Hajj, with the Kuala Lumpur headquarters rising effortlessly above the city's traffic, curved and sinuous in an elegant Islamic-themed architectural design.

Today, the Tabung Haji has more than 4.5 million subscribers, and the organization manages a fund of over 10 billion ringgit.[44] Though some of the depositors are wealthy citizens who made their money in the new economy of cyber-Malaysia, the majority are ordinary people who simply save over many years to be able to fulfill the fifth and final pillar of Islam. Literature that the Tabung Haji distributes free of charge to potential pilgrims highlights the sacrifices people have made to go on Hajj. One story tells contemporary pilgrims of the hardships former Malay Hajjis and Hajjas had to endure on their travels to the holy places.[45] Another focuses on the frugality of Pak Omar, who sold street cakes in the night markets of Bangsar (a fashionable Kuala Lumpur neighborhood) to be able to make the trip.[46] A third speaks of the savings practices of a shrimp seller from

Perak province, and a fourth highlights the struggles of a vegetable farmer from Perlis in the far north of the country.[47] This last gentleman was seventy-three years old at the time of his interview with the Tabung Haji and had just returned from Mecca.[48] All of these articles serve the didactic purpose of encouraging prospective pilgrims to assiduously follow the Tabung Haji's long-term savings and investment programs.

Malaysian pilgrims are not absolutely compelled to go the holy places through the Tabung Hajji. For the lesser pilgrimage, or Umrah, many do indeed choose to use private tour groups, of which there are no shortage of options. Some of the competitive rates for an Umrah package to Mecca and Medina are given in table 9.3.

Yet many do indeed choose to perform their entire experience in Saudi Arabia through the national organization's auspices. In partnership with many other businesses, the Tabung Haji has perfected the notion of taking care of its customers in all aspects of life while pilgrims are in the holy places. These services include mobile phone plans that Hajjis can use to call their loved ones and a monthly skimming of an entire family's wages so that the required sums for Hajj are reached as quickly and responsibly as possible.[49] Banking facilities and comprehensive packages that also deal with *zakat* (the tithe) and other Islamic financial matters are also available.[50] The Tabung Haji has become a symbol of the modern government-chaperoned Hajj looking after its citizens in all possible ways, for the latter's convenience and protection, as well as for the stability and order of Malaysia's national pilgrimage.

Malaysians generally seem to be very satisfied with the financial planning and services rendered by the Tabung Haji. In conversations all around the country,

Table 9.3 **Malay Umrah Options (Malaysian Ringgit) from Three Companies, 2004**

Sri Sutra Travel Co.		Sakinah Travel Co.		Tabung Haji Travel Co.	
Package	*Price*	*Package*	*Price*	*Package*	*Price*
9 days	3,455	6/22–7/6	4,290	9 days/econ	3,690
11 days	3,620	6/23–7/7	3,990	9 days/basic	4,190
12 days	3,705	7/7–7/18	3,760	9 days/special	7,890
13 days	3,790	7/21–8/5	3,990	11 days/econ	3,880
14 days	3,870	8/4–8/15	4,390	11 days/basic	4,380
16 days	4,050	9/1–9/14	4,050	11 days/special	9,690

Source: 2004 promotional literature from Sri Sutra, Sakinah, and Tabung Haji Travel.

I was told repeatedly about Indonesia and its history of economic and organizational problems with the Hajj, usually with a sigh of sympathetic relief. Most Malaysians seem to appreciate the efficiency in their country, even if they give a nod to the much larger numbers (and generally much poorer people) Indonesia directs toward Mecca. A Hajj tour operator told me that most Malaysian Hajj packages average close to 10,000 ringgit per trip now, though this could climb significantly higher, depending on the amenities involved.[51] To raise this sum, Malaysian pilgrims generally save over many years, though others secure various forms of sponsorship from wealthy individuals or organizations, and still others receive some compensation toward Hajj or Umrah from their employers as part of doing a good job.[52] One Hajja told me that she knew of a Malaysian Indian man who sold his land at rock-bottom prices in order to go on Hajj, to the great consternation of his son, who had advised him to wait so that the land could appreciate in value and eventually be handed down through the family's sons. The elderly Indian gentleman demurred, however: the imperative for going on Hajj before he died was too strong, and he felt he needed to go soon to finish the last pillar of his faith.[53]

This story seems to sum up the continuity in the history of the Southeast Asian Hajj very neatly. Performing the pilgrimage has never been and still isn't a matter only of money. It is about a kind of devotion and a kind of experience upon which a price cannot be levied, even if the Hajj requires the earthly transit of currency and value to make this wish of a lifetime come true. The experience of the Hajj in Southeast Asia suggests that even people very much in the stream of global modernity still make the decision to undertake the pilgrimage, even if it will set them back huge sums of money. This is done by new urban elites and more traditional rural people alike, and for many of the same reasons. The Hajj is a religious duty and is to be performed once in every Muslim's lifetime, if the person has the means to do so. But it is also a social and a class phenomenon of both traditional and modern life in Southeast Asia, an experience that confers status and value on the pilgrim, regardless of his station in society. The vast sums of money and savings spent on the pilgrimage over the years, therefore, can be seen as an investment not only in one's religion and ethics but also in one's place in the global-local community.

The Southeast Asian Hajj in the Modern Era

Today, Southeast Asians are only a part of the global stream of Muslims who make the journey to Mecca from nearly every corner of the planet. Scholars have become interested in chronicling and measuring these sojourns, usually through the lens of the nation-state.[54] There are good studies now of the Hajj from

Nigeria, for example, particularly from the perspective of its impact on that na-tion's economy.[55] There are also studies of the Turkish Hajj, as well as the pil-grimage from places like Pakistan, three highly populated countries that are ful-crum states for their particular geographies, whether these lie in West Africa, the Middle East, or the frontier districts between South and Central Asia.[56] There are even now starting to be studies that lay out a comparative framework across nation-states for the contemporary Hajj.[57] For Southeast Asia, there has been generally less writing, despite the fact that the numbers of Hajjis coming from this region have been historically important and continue to be important to this day. Studies on the Malaysian and Indonesian Hajj have been more common than those on any other countries in Southeast Asia, yet these are still relatively few in number. The infrastructure of the Hajj from Southeast Asia alone merits further study (figure 9.1). In the late 1970s, relations between Indonesia and countries like Sri Lanka were partially predicated on these arrangements; aircraft could not then make the entire journey from Jakarta to Jeddah directly and required stopovers for refueling.[58] Delegations traveled between the two coun-tries to try to make these arrangements, which were deemed beneficial to both states.[59] The infrastructural challenges were not just international but profoundly national as well, as internal correspondence in Indonesia, the largest pilgrimage state, makes clear. In 1979, a new Hajj terminal was mooted for Medan's airport to serve as the depot for pilgrims coming from Aceh, North Sumatra, West Sumatra, Riau, and Jambi combined. In 1977–78, some 18 million rupiah were spent on the project, but by 1980 the expenditures were up to 85.5 million rupiah, almost 300 pilgrims could be passed through the structure at one time, and the complex stretched over thirty square kilometers.[60] Surviving architec-tural planning drawings of the complex show how ambitious the project was in its inception stages, with even a small-scale recasting of the Ka'ba placed close to Medan's airfield.[61] By 1980, the regional government of Southern Kalimantan had planned its own Hajj air terminal, showing that these development schemes related to the pilgrimage were watched carefully by provincial-level civil servants throughout the archipelago.[62] In 1981, Western Kalimantan also began to gen-erate increasing paperwork on its own Hajji population, as the trend spread to other locales.[63] It is clear that the pilgrimage became a growth industry, not just at the national level but at smaller, regional levels as well.

This shift was mirrored on the other side of the Indian Ocean in Saudi Arabia itself. The Hajj has been for many years an enormous organizational under-taking, with a huge array of state-sanctioned offices, institutions, and policies in place to make it run smoothly. The cost of Hajj services has increased markedly over the years, but the basic government charges for undertaking one's pil-grimage have remained the same for the past quarter of a century due to funding from Saudi Arabian oil.[64] The Islamic Development Bank helps the *ummah* with

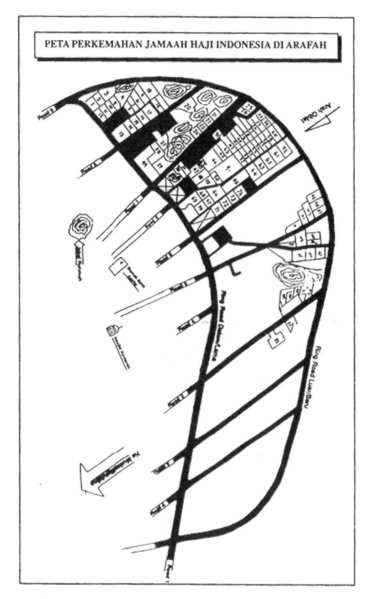

Figure 9.1 Sketch Map of Indonesian Hajj Camp at the Plain of Arafat.
Credit: From Anonymous Informant.

interest-free loans, equity participation, and the cost of animal sacrifices; this last program alone is now used to help the poor of twenty-eight countries (including many Southeast Asians), with almost 6,000 camels and 75,000 sheep purchased every year and distributed to pilgrims free of charge.[65] Jeddah has become a city of Hajj-satellite cities within a city, with three now in existence: Madinat Al-Hujjaj Al-Bahar ("Pilgrim City for Those Arriving by Sea"), Madinat Al-Hujjaj Al-Matar

Qadeem (by air), and Madinat Al-Hujjaj Al-Afrikein (for Africans). Rent is nominal as these are nonprofit facilities; the Air City is mainly used by Malaysian and Indonesian pilgrims.[66] The pilgrim tents erected in a giant array in Mina (nicknamed "tent city") for the flood of annual Hajjis have become something close to permanent structures and are made of high-tech, fire-resistant materials that can withstand the desert's searing temperatures.[67] The contemporary Hajj exudes an air of modernity, in other words. The experience of the historical Hajj and its hardships—though still borne by many Hajjis even today, in certain ways—is more often remembered than lived these days. In their narratives, pilgrims consign privations to the past, even if they continue to experience some today.[68]

The Hajj has also become friendlier to women and children in its most modern incarnation. In a perusal of modern Malay-language Hajj literature, this becomes immediately evident, with countless publications discussing gender issues. Many of these books are indeed sponsored by the state, and the media in general—not only the book-publishing industry but also television, radio, and film—convey a society-wide image of what the Hajj should be for the region. One publication, for example, lays out the rules for women performing the pilgrimage alone or with their husbands and also explains what needs to be done if one's husband should happen to die on the journey.[69] Another lays out the Islamic legal opinions about whether a woman who is menstruating can perform all aspects of the Hajj (Shafi'i and Hanafi sects say slightly different things on this).[70] Some books discuss whether one can wear perfume on the journey, and others are more narrative in nature, and relate (among other things) what happened when one woman's father disappeared from her group while on Hajj.[71] Any of these things might happen to a Southeast Asian woman while on her journey, and these publications try to provide information for any eventuality. Partial segregation at specific moments in the Hejaz is a part of the conduct of the Hajj, so women need to know how to do certain things by themselves. Children are now covered in these kinds of books, too: one specifically tells an underage audience why the aspirant is doing what he or she is doing, and for what reasons.

> "Kadang-kadang, kita tidak percaya mendengarnya, tetapi memang benar terjadi. Engkau ingin tahu apa sebabnya?" Tanya Pakcik Ibrahim. "Ya ayah! Ayah ceritakanlah!" jawab Idris. "Di tanah suci, kita dapat melihat atau merasakan kebesaran dan kekuasaan Allah...."[72]
>
>   "Sometimes we don't believe what we hear, but these things really are true. Do you want to know what happens, why that is?" asked Pakcik Ibrahim. "Yes father!" answered Idris. "Please tell me! In the Holy Land, we can see or feel the greatness and power of God...."

It makes sense that one activity of the modern Southeast Asian nation-state has been to encourage such books. More and more pilgrims from these countries are now women, and children are currently brought in growing numbers as well. The pilgrimage in its most modern manifestation, with jet travel, mass media, and government oversight, opens the explanatory space of the Hajj to ever wider populations.[73]

Indeed, the how-to book of Hajj has become an increasingly powerful tool in shaping this institution across the breadth of Southeast Asian societies. These kinds of books—written in both Malay and Indonesian, primarily—are also sold in adjacent Malay-speaking areas in other countries, including Brunei, Singapore, and southern Thailand. They lay out the voyage and its contents in an easily digested format with rules, expectations, dangers, and annoyances all catalogued and presented by those who have already accomplished the journey. These guides explain how to perform the steps of the Hajj correctly, as well as how to pray accurately (figure 9.2) and when, where, and how to use certain invocations for a variety of desired ends (entering Mecca and Medina, important hadith on the Hajj, prayers to be said at the well of Zamzam, what to utter if performing the Hajj for someone else).[74] The tracts also convey much more utilitarian information to the Southeast Asian pilgrim: the phone numbers and addresses of Malay consulates and embassies in Mecca, Jeddah, and Riyadh; airline timetables from Borneo to the Hejaz; and the current prices of goats and camels for the necessary sacrifices in the desert.[75] Indonesian publications are no different than their Malay counterparts in this respect: vast varieties of how-to guides across the Melaka Strait serve a very large reading public. Books sold in airports, malls, and even on pushcarts on the street deal with a great range of issues, from the Ka'ba and its histories to desert site distances and particular events of the Indonesian Hajj in every year of the 1990s.[76] The sheer volume of books from the Sukarno period up to the present day is astounding. They are published in many places across the archipelago, from Jakarta and Bandung to Semarang and Malang, but also outside Java in places like Medan.[77] These guides are crucial in preparing the pilgrim for his or her Hajj, but they also impart a particularly Southeast Asian sensibility to proceedings and often "other" the Saudis generally as guardians of the holy places.

A salient part of the modern Southeast Asian Hajj is also government record keeping, manifested in many kilometers' worth of official reports.[78] The official reports of both the Tabung Haji and the Department Agama/Kantor Urusan Hajji in Kuala Lumpur and Jakarta, respectively, chronicle in exhaustive detail how the Hajj works from both Malaysia and Indonesia. Thumbing through the publications of the Tabung Haji, for example, one can see how streamlined (and, at the same time, diverse) the record keeping of their Hajj operation has become: large compendia narrate in microscopic detail the age, gender, provenance, and

I. DO'A MEMASUKI KOTA MAKKAH

اَللَّهُمَّ هَذَا حَرَمُكَ وَأَمْنُكَ فَحَرِّمْ لَحْمِي وَدَمِي
وَشَعْرِي وَبَشَرِي عَلَى النَّارِ وَامِنِّي مِنْ عَذَابِكَ
يَوْمَ تَبْعَثُ عِبَادَكَ وَاجْعَلْنِي مِنْ أَوْلِيَائِكَ
وَأَهْلِ طَاعَتِكَ .

Allāhumma hāzā haramuka wa amnuka faharrim lahmī wa dāmī wasya'arī
wabasyarī 'alannāri wa āminnī min 'azābika yauma tab'asu 'ibādaka waj'alnī
min auliyā ika wa ahli tā'atika.

Artinya :
*"Ya Allah, kota ini adalah Tanah Haram-Mu dan tempat yang aman-Mu,
maka hindarkanlah daging, darah, rambut dan kulitku dari neraka. Dan
selamatkanlah diriku dari siksa-Mu pada hari Engkau membangkitkan
kembali hambaMu, dan jadikanlah aku termasuk orang-orang yang selalu
dekat dan taat kepada-Mu.*

J. DO'A MASUK MASJIDIL HARAM

اَللَّهُمَّ أَنْتَ السَّلَامُ وَمِنْكَ السَّلَامُ وَإِلَيْكَ
يَعُوْدُ السَّلَامُ فَحَيِّنَا رَبَّنَا بِالسَّلَامِ وَأَدْخِلْنَا
الْجَنَّةَ دَارَ السَّلَامِ تَبَارَكْتَ رَبَّنَا وَتَعَالَيْتَ
يَا ذَا الْجَلَالِ وَالْإِكْرَامِ . اَللَّهُمَّ افْتَحْ لِي
أَبْوَابَ رَحْمَتِكَ ، بِسْمِ اللهِ وَالْحَمْدُ لِلّٰهِ
وَالصَّلَاةُ وَالسَّلَامُ عَلَى رَسُوْلِ اللهِ .

Allāhumma antassalām wa minkassalām wailaika ya'ūdussalam fahayyinā rabbanā
bissalam wa adkhilnaljannata dārassalām tabārakta rabbana wata 'ālaita yazal
jalāli wal ikrāmi. Allāhummaftahlī abwāba rahmatika bismillāhi walhamdulillāhi
wassalātu wassalāmu'alā rasulillāh.

Artinya :
*"Ya Allah, Engkau sumber keselamatan dan dari pada-Mulah datangnya
keselamatan dan kepada-Mu kembalinya keselamatan. Maka hidupkanlah
kami wahai Tuhan, dengan selamat sejahtera dan masukkanlah ke dalam
surga negeri keselamatan. Maha banyak anugrah-Mu dan Maha Tinggi
Engkau. Wahai Tuhan yang memiliki keagungan dan kehormatan. ya Allah,
bukalah untukku pintu rahmat-Mu. (Aku masuk Masjid ini) dengan nama
Allah disertai dengan segala puji bagi Allah serta salawat dan salam untuk
Rasulullah."*

Figure 9.2 Prayer Translation Page: Arabic to Romanized Arabic to Indonesian.
Credit: Prayer Fragment Page, Given to Author by Pilgrim.

financial resources of hundreds of thousands of ordinary citizens, offering a kind of snapshot of Malay life in miniature.[79] These publications also make available for the Malay public knowledge of the ways in which a proper Hajj should be completed.[80] In Indonesia, the apparatus of such record keeping is even more elaborate and complex, covering the evolution of Hajj permission forms, local statistics and reportage on the pilgrimage from discrete portions of the archipelago (such as East Java and South Sulawesi), and maps, charts, and diagrams of the route of the country's pilgrims from station to station in various parts of the Arabian desert.[81] The material on the medical aspects of the modern Indonesian Hajj alone—pages upon pages of chemical lists, medical accoutrements, and sanitation precautions to be taken by pilgrims—is extraordinary and reveals public health concerns.[82] Some of this information is about Saudi quarantine regulations, especially in the age of swine flu, SARS, and AIDS, but much of it is of a more prosaic nature. Indeed, the raft of statistics and official reportage has now spawned an allied industry of academic theses on the modern Southeast Asian Hajj.[83] Foucault would have instantly recognized this relationship. The dialectic between power and knowledge in making the Hajj "modern" in this part of the world has become well developed and cyclical, with each component rationalizing the existence of the other and contributing to the success of both. The Southeast Asian pilgrimage is not perfectly run, but it would be no exaggeration to say that it is now better managed and better understood in all of its complexities than at any other point in its many centuries of existence. This is no small feat.

Conclusion

Born out of a period of many years of global conflict, and many centuries of colonial annexation prior to this, the story of the modern pilgrimage in Southeast Asia is filled with contradictions. The decade or so after World War II saw pilgrimage increase from most parts of the globe, yet the instabilities and poverty caused by the conflagration meant that many arrangements had to be made from scratch, as the colonial empires buckled and then eventually fell after another sustained period of conflict in the region. The Hajj continued throughout this era, as different independent regimes gradually shook off foreign rule and started to send their own pilgrims to the Middle East. Yet even after this, many Southeast Asians found that the old enemies—corruption, inefficiency, and venality—continued to accompany the journey. Southeast Asian states gradually became better at managing this journey, yet the nuts and bolts have taken quite some time to master. There are signs that the mechanics of controlling the pilgrimage for the benefit of average Hajjis are starting to become more practical, as oversight committees, task forces, and regulatory commissions bring their expertise to bear on existing problems, both in Southeast Asia and in the Arabian Peninsula. Yet the transfer of millions of bodies annually from one part of the globe to another will, perhaps, always be rife with difficulties. Ultimately, it is amazing how well the whole system functions, given the extremely complicated undertakings in managing human movement on a massive, global scale.

Modern, independent governments in the region still try to control the pilgrimage to Mecca down to tiny details of everyday living. Economically, most Hajjis' entire trips are paid for even before they leave their respective countries. One Singaporean Hajja told me that she did not have to bring along any money at all, only funds for gifts for her friends and family (dates, carpets, water from the well at Zamzam), though this is not entirely the case for all pilgrims coming from the region.[84] Yet the impetus to monitor, regulate, and control this massive movement of people across such large global spaces has become an administrative imperative. The Saudi government insists on this oversight, and Southeast Asian administrations, by and large, have lived up to these cooperative regulatory requirements, too, but with different degrees of energy, willpower, and success.[85] Performing the Hajj has become a possibility for most segments of Southeast Asia's populations, with many gradations in how this religious obligation can be experienced on the ground. Future Southeast Asian governments will no doubt try to rationalize and streamline these organizational procedures even further than the forms in which they now exist. If this is accomplished, it should allow all of the region's citizens who desire to act on their Islamic devotion to do so in the years to come.

NOTES

1. The best single repository of information about the modern Hajj in the world—including the Southeast Asian pilgrimage—is a legacy of the laying of these structures, the Hajj Research Center in Mecca.

2. Anonymous, *Le Voyage Aux Lieux Saints de L'Islam* (Kuala Lumpur: Tabung Haji, 1986), p. 9.

3. For instructions and information on all of these issues, see Haji Ali Haji Hasbullah, *Soal-Jawab Haji dan Umrah* (Kuala Lumpur: Penerbitan Pustaka Antara Malaysia, 1993), pp. 12–13; Haji Mohamad Daud bin Che' Ngah, *Panduan Haji dan Umrah* (Kuala Lumpur: Pustaka Al-Mizan, 1989), pp. 113–114; Dato' HJ Mohamad Saleh Bin Haji Awang, *Teman Anda ke Tanah Suci* (Singapore: Times Books, 1992), pp. 37 and 79; T. M. Hasbi Ash Shiddieqy, *Pedoman Haji* (Johore Bahru, Malaysia: P. T. Bulan Bintang, 1986), pp. 20–23 and 26–27; Haji Joharai Haji Alias, *Panduan Ibadah Haji, 'Umrah dan Ziarah* (Kuala Lumpur: Darul Nu'man, 1994), pp. 205–237; Haji Usman Muqim Hasan, *Bimbingan Ibadat Haji, Umrah dan Ziarah* (Selangor, Malaysia: Pustaka ILMI, 1994), pp. 17–18; Muhammad Taufiq Jauhari, *Rahsia Ka'bah dan Masjid Nabawi* (Kuala Lumpur: Jasmine Enterprise, 2004), pp. 4–7; 18; 30, passim; 46, passim; 189, passim.

4. For aspects of this organization, see K. H. A. Wahid Hasjim, *Menudju Perbaikan Perdjalanan Hadji* (Jakarta: Departemen Agama, n.d); A. Hamid, *Petundjuk Petundjuk Tjara Menunaikan*

Ibadah Hadji (Jakarta: Departemen Agama, 1962); Anonymous, *Himpunan Risalah Rapat Kerja Urusan Haji Seluruh Indonesia* (Jakarta: Departemen Agama, 1982); Anonymous, *Pedoman dan Petunjuk Pelaksanaan Bimbingan Calon Jamaah Haji di Asrama Embarkasi* (Jakarta: Departmen Agama, 1982); H. Abdurrahman Sjihab, *Penuntun Hadji Tjara Mengerdjakan Hadji Dengan Praktis* (Medan, Indonesia: Forma Islamyah, 1963); H. Junus Mahmud, *Manasik Hadji* (Bandung, Indonesia: P. T. Alma'arif, 1967); Amir Hamzah Hayat, *Petundjuk Djalan ke Tanah Sutji* (Bandung, Indonesia: Penerbit Tarate, 1962?); Prawiranegara H. Sjafruddin, *Djangan Mempersulit Ibadah Hadji* (Jakarta: D. P. P. Husmai, 1970).

5. Despatch, US Embassy, Cairo, to Sec. State, Washington DC, February 25, 1938, #1215, in Ibrahim al-Rashid, ed., *Saudi Arabia Enters the Modern World* (Salisbury, NC: Documentary Publications, 1980).

6. US Embassy, Cairo to Sec of State, Washington, November 11, 1940, #2, in ibid.

7. US Consul, Cairo, to Sec of State, Washington, March 9, 1940, #2019 Confidential, in ibid.

8. K. S. Twitchell to Dept. of Near Eastern Studies, Washington, May 14, 1941, in ibid.

9. Memorandum of Conversation between Mr. Raymond Hare and Mr. FHW Stoenhewer-Bird, UK Minister in Saudi Arabia, September 8, 1941, Strictly Confidential, in ibid.

10. Translation of a Speech of King Saud, December 19, 1942, Mecca, Omul Qura #938, in ibid.

11. ANRI, Dutch Consul, Jeddah, to MvBZ, London and Dutch Consul, Cairo, April 14, 1945, #188, in Algemeene Secretarie, #1044.

12. ANRI, Motie: Openbare Vergadering Moekimin Indonesia di Mekka, April 27, 1945 (written by Mohd. Koerni Barak, Ketoea: Djamhir Djalal), in Algemeene Secretarie, #1044.

13. ANRI, Dutch Consul, Jeddah, to MvBZ, London and Dutch Consul, Cairo, May 2, 1945, #237, and ANRI, Dutch Consul, Jeddah, to MvBZ, London and Dutch Consul, Cairo, July 13, 1945, #388, both in Algemeene Secretarie, #1044. It is not entirely clear that most of those women came to the Hejaz unattended, or perhaps were widowed when they were there, but women lacking male protection in Arabia were particularly vulnerable to abuses and dangers, including molestation.

14. ANRI, Lt. Gov Gen NEI to Minister, Overseas Territories, Hague, May 6, 1946, #6440, and ANRI, Minister for Overseas Territories to Lt. Gov Gen NEI, March 29, 1946, #25/09, both in Algemeene Secretarie, #1052.

15. George Kahin to R. Mohammad Kafrawi, March 3, 1956, in Kahin Papers, Cornell University.

16. "Rates per 100,000 Population: Mesdjid, Langgar; Applicants for the Hadj; Students in Madrasah, 1930 and 1955," in Kahin Papers, Cornell University.

17. "Statistiek Djemaah Hadji, 1950–1954," in Kahin Papers, Cornell University.

18. "Number of Medsdjid/Langgar per 100,000 of 1955 Population." In Kahin Papers, Cornell University.

19. See the very useful volumes of the *Berita PHI* newsletters for 1953, 1954, and 1957.

20. Arsip Negara, Malaysia: "Report of the Pilgrims to Mecca from Malaya during the 1949 (1368 A.H.) Season," enclosed in State Secretary's Office, Johore, to Chief Secretary, Kuala Lumpur, February 5, 1950, #4.

21. Arsip Negara, Malaysia: "Extract of a Letter from the MPC, 12-3-49 to Mr. Kidner of the Federal Secretariat" (Appendix A of previous document).

22. Arsip Negara, Malaysia: "Procedure to be Adopted by the Saudi Authorities When a Malay Pilgrim Does [*sic*] in the Hejaz" (Enclosure A in previous document).

23. See the many examples reproduced in Arsip Negara, Malaysia: "Mecca Pilgrimage 1950," #53 in Krian 835/49.

24. Federal Secretariat Files, Kuala Lumpur: #14047/1949; #14050/1949; #12064/1950; #12456/1950.

25. R. L. Baxter, Colonial Office, to L. S. Ross, May 6, 1955, #FED 206/4/2, in *Records of the Hajj*, 8.24.

26. L. S. Ross, to Foreign Office, May 16, 1955, #ES 1781/8 Restricted, in *Records of the Hajj*, 8.24.

27. Outward Telegram from Commonwealth Relations Office to UK High Commissioner, Pakistan, March 28, 1957, #78, Restricted, in *Records of the Hajj*, 9.26.

28. Inward Telegram to Commonwealth Relations Office from High Commissioner in Pakistan on Malayan Pilgrimage Mission to Mecca, #57 Restricted; and "Article 95 Extract: Prohibited Goods," both in *Records of the Hajj*, 8.36.

29. Mary McDonnell, "The Conduct of the Hajj from Malaysia and Its Socio-Economic Impact on Malay Society: A Descriptive and Analytical Study, 1860–1981" (PhD Dissertation, Columbia University, 1986), pp. 626–628.

30. "Pilgrimage Surgeon: Scenes of a Ship Taking Muslims from Singapore to Jeddah," *Times* (of London), n.d., 1957. Five thousand pilgrims per year was a fairly high percentage of the population in 1957, given that Malaya was still almost entirely agricultural at this time.

31. British Embassy, Jakarta, to F.O., October 23, 1952, #A.1782/10/52.

32. British Embassy, Jakarta, to F.O., March 19, 1954, #782/3/54 Restricted.

33. Zamakhsyari Dhofier, "The Economic Effect of the Indonesian Hajj," *Prisma*, 36, 1985: 62. Dhofier has synthesized much of the data and has come up with some extremely interesting economic patterns not only on the composition of Indonesian pilgrims but also on how they acquire their Hajj funds. For instance, according to his calculations, only 24.9 percent, or roughly one-fourth of all income gathered by Indonesian Hajjis to pay for their pilgrimage comes from savings. Fully 60 percent of these funds actually come from selling off possessions, a strikingly high number as it implies literally parting with material possessions to undertake the journey. This kind of economic behavior would be highly unusual in the Western world, no doubt. Other sources of funding, such as loans or assistance from family living either in Indonesia or outside of it, and even remittances from working while in Saudi Arabia, are negligible in the overall financial accumulation patterns. Dhofier has also calculated how much Indonesian Hajjis were spending on different goods and services while performing their pilgrimages in the late 1970s. Some 44 to 47 percent of their total costs were spent on the airfare required to get them to and from the Hejaz, from 18 to 21 percent of their funds were spent on local housing, and 14 to 17 percent of their costs were food while in Saudi Arabia. Other costs, such as special Hajj garments (*ihram*), taxes, inflation, and various kinds of services, were significantly lower percentages of Indonesians' total pilgrimage costs. See tables 4 and 7 in this article.

34. Zamakhsyari Dhofier, "Dampak Ekonomi Ibadah Haji di Indonesia," *Prisma*, 12/4, 1984: 52–53.

35. Moeslim Abdurrahman, "Ritual Divided: Hajj Tours in Capitalist Era Indonesia," in Mark Woodward, ed., *Toward a New Paradigm: Recent Developments in Indonesian Islamic Thought* (Tempe: Arizona State University Program in Southeast Asian Studies, 1996), pp. 122–123.

36. Interview with Upik Djalins, August 29, 2003.

37. Interview with Dr. H. Taufiq Kamil and his staff, Kantor Urusan Haji, Jakarta, August 13, 2004.

38. "Administration of Muslim Law (Haj) Rules," *Singapore Government Gazette*, September 24, 1999, S406/66, pp. 1838–1849.

39. Interview with Zuraidah Ibrahim, May 1, 2004.

40. Interview with Nazreen bte. Mohammad Osman, May 5, 2004. This pattern of using real estate sales as a vehicle for helping to fund the Hajj is also a fairly common phenomenon in parts of Indonesia, especially in some of the surrounding neighborhoods of the greater Jakarta area. Orang Betawi (native Jakartans) have been known to sit on land that has appreciated in value greatly over the past few decades. Often these lands were far away from downtown Jakarta, but with the enormous physical growth of the city and the absorption of satellite towns into Jakarta as a whole, the land has skyrocketed in value in just a few years. Some Orang Betawi wait to sell these lands until right before they intend to go on Hajj and finance a large part of their journeys through the profits made on such deals. Often the land is sold to developers, who can pay cash readily, so that the time between transaction and pilgrimage is not very long. See Dhofier, "The Economic Effects," p. 63.

41. Interview with Kesty Pringgoharjono, May 3, 2004.

42. "Lembaga Tabung Haji": VCD produced by the Tabung Haji, Kuala Lumpur, available in several languages, including Malay, English, Arabic, and French. The best substantive account produced on the history of the Tabung Haji is one of their own publications: Anonymous, *Sejarah Perkembangan Tabung Haji Malaysia* (Kuala Lumpur: Tabung Haji, 1993). For the wider context of Islam in contemporary Malaysia, see Michael Peletz, *Islamic Modern: Religious Courts and Cultural Politics in Malaysia* (Princeton, NJ: Princeton University Press, 2002).

43. Awang Had Salleh, "Modern Concept of Hajj Management," in Z. Sardar and M. A. Zaki Badawi, eds., *Hajj Studies*, vol. 1 (London: Croom Helm, 1979), pp. 73–86. Although interest is forbidden under Islamic banking, making sound investments is not; if the money accrued from such investments increases, it can certainly be used for the pilgrimage to Mecca.

44. *Tabung Haji: Hasten toward Prosperity* (Kuala Lumpur: Tabung Haji, 2004), p. 3.

45. Wan Hasnan Hasan, "Ajal dan Bertemu Jodoh di Atas Kapal," *Tabung Haji*, December 27, 2003, pp. 15–17.

46. Helmi Mohamad Foad, "Apam Balik: Jejakkan Kaki Pak Omar ke Mekah," *Tabung Haji*, December 27, 2003, pp. 28–29.

47. Zaini Hassan and Helmi Mohamad Foad, "Menjala Udang: Tampung Simpanan ke Mekah," *Tabung Haji*, December 27, 2003, pp. 29–30.

48. Ahmad Syahir Kassim, "Lapan Kali: Pak Mad Sayur ke Tanah Suci," *Tabung Haji*, December 27, 2003, p. 31.

49. See the pamphlets *Salam: Pelan Panggilan Pertama Bercirikan Islam* (Celcom, 2004), and *Skim Potongan Gaji Diri dan Keluarga* (Kuala Lumpur: Tabung Haji, 2004).

50. For these services, see *Perkhidmatan Simpanan Tabung Haji Melalui Agen Kutipan Simpanan* (Kuala Lumpur: Tabung Haji, 2004) and *Manfaatnya Bukan Sekadar ke Makkah* (Kuala Lumpur: Tabung Hajji, 2004)

51. Interview with Lt. Col. Haji Ramli Kinta, June 4, 2004. Colonel Ramli was an interesting informant about the economics of Hajj, as he had performed the pilgrimage himself (twice) and now was on the other side of the equation, ferrying Hajjis across the Indian Ocean so that they could fulfill their own duties. He pointed out (correctly) that long-term savings used to be by far the most common option for Malaysians going on Hajj. Yet the burgeoning new national economy, based on high-tech and service businesses and not just the traditional staple trades of Malaysia (palm oil, rubber, fishing, etc.) ensured that many more people could now perform the pilgrimage, and often at a younger age as well. This was seen as a good thing in terms of Muslims meeting their religious duties. But Colonel Ramli also commented that it might potentially mean less if you had to save for a short while for the eventual "result" of Hajj, rather than having to accrue over a much longer time of patience, frugality, and hard work. These latter aspects of saving for the Hajj were now becoming less and less common, as the journey—fueled by modern air travel, business competition, and changing ways of making money—has now become more readily available to more and more people.

52. Interview with Che Adenan Mohammad, June 15, 2004; interview with Sharifah Ismail, June 11, 2004.

53. Interview with Moomala Othman, June 11, 2004.

54. The great critique of nationalism, of course, which includes a cogent discussion of the Hajj in the evolution of the concept, is Benedict Anderson, *Imagined Communities: Reflections on the Origin and Spread of Nationalism* (London: Verso, 1983).

55. See O. E. Tangban, "The Hajj and the Nigerian Economy, 1960–1981," *Journal of Religion in Africa*, 21/3, 1991: 141–167.

56. For the modern Turkish experience, see Mehmed Erkal, "The Pilgrimage Organization in Turkey," in Zafarul-Islam Khan and Yaqub Zaki, eds., *Hajj in Focus* (London: Open Press, 1986), pp. 137–150; for Pakistan, see Robert Bianchi, *Guests of God: Pilgrimage and Politics in the Islamic Word* (New York: Oxford University Press, 2004), pp. 77–112.

57. I agree with much of Bianchi's vision on how the modern Hajj is run in Malaysia and Indone-sia, but I have deepened the picture here; Bianchi does not use Malay and Indonesian lan-guage materials.

58. ANRI, Secretary, Office of the President to Director of Hajj Affairs, November 16, 1978, #B-875, in RA26. Sekretariat Wapres Adam Malik Tahun 1978–1982, #823.

59. ANRI, "Pemberitahuan" ("Proclamation"), November 16, 1978, in RA26. Sekretariat Wapres Adam Malik Tahun 1978–1982, #823.

60. ANRI, "Pokok Penjelasan Pimpinan Bagian Proyek Pada Bapak Wakil Presiden RI (from H. Said Muhammad, Project Director)," December 2, 1979, and ANRI, Amir Rusly Thaib, Project Manager, to Financial Dept, September 7, 1979, both in RA26. Sekretariat Wapres Adam Malik Tahun 1978–1982, #835.

61. ANRI, Asrama Haji di Gedong Johor Medan (arsitek: S. P. Wijaya), (n.d)., in RA26. Sekretar-iat Wapres Adam Malik Tahun 1978–1982, #835.

62. ANRI, Governor, Kalimantan Selatan to President, RI, November 4, 1980, #400, in RA26. Sekretariat Wapres Adam Malik Tahun 1978–1982, #846.

63. ANRI, Secretary of the President, RI to Minister of Religion, Jakarta, May 26, 1981, #485/V/81, in RA26. Sekretariat Wapres Adam Malik Tahun 1978–1982, #856.

64. Anonymous, "Haj Charges," Haj and Umra, 57/6, 2002: 12.

65. Habib Shaikh, "IDB's Haj Services," Haj and Umra, 57/6, 2002: 28–29.

66. See Ghazy Abdul Wahed Makky, Mecca: The Pilgrimage City: A Study of Pilgrim Accommodation (London: Croom Helm, 1978); also Syed Afsar, "Haj Cities in Jeddah," Haj and Umra, 57/4, 2002: 18.

67. Nazar Asri, "Total Tranquility," Haj and Umra, 58/1, 2003: 35.

68. Sameen Khan, "Carrying One's Own Food and Water on Haj," Haj and Umra, 57/4, 2002: 14–15. The author of this article met an older Hajji, Aslam Khan, who had lived in Dammam for the past twenty-five years and who recounted to him what it was like to perform the Hajj in the 1970s. He told Khan that "performing Hajj was tough, and I lost five kilos. But there was immense enthusiasm and a spirit which came from your soul." It took six hours at that time to travel from Jeddah to Mecca. Zamzam water was drawn up out of the earth by a pulley, not by modern electronics, and there was no running water.

69. Anonymous, Soal-Jawab Ibadah Haji/Umrah (Kuala Lumpur: Tabung Haji, 1987), p. 10.

70. Haji Abu Mazaya Al-Hafiz, A Guideline to Umrah and Ziarah, Complete with the Supplications and Performing Procedures (Kuala Lumpur: Al-Hidayah, 2003), p. 141.

71. Muhammad 'Attiyah Khamis, Fiqh Wanita Haji (Kuala Lumpur: Penerbit Hizbi, 1987), pp. 36–40; and Suratman Markasan, Perempuan Kerudang Hitam (Kuala Lumpur: Dewan Bahasa dan Pustaka Kementerian Pendidikan Malaysia, 1991).

72. Anonymous, Haji ke Baitullah (Kuala Lumpur: Penerbitan 'Asa, 1985).

73. It is no longer primarily for the elderly as a "summation" of one's life; it is also now a credential, a signifier for those hoping to deploy a meaning for other things. I'm grateful to Jeffrey Hadler for suggesting this notion to me.

74. See in that order Al-Ustaz Haji Hassan Salleh, Konsep Ibadat Haji Dalam Islam (Kuala Lumpur: Dewan Ulama PAS Wilayah Persektuan, 1988), and H. A. Fuad Said, Adab Manasik Haji dan Umrah (Kuala Lumpur: Penerbitan Kintan, 1994), pp. 119, 127, 196–208; Abdul Wahab Haji Hamid, Panduan Sistematik Haji dan Umrah (Kuala Lumpur: K Publishing, 1990), p. 75, and Muhammad Nashiruddin al Albani, Haji dan Umrah Mengikut Sunnah Rasullah S.A.W. (Kuala Lumpur: Perniagaan Jahabersa, 1995), pp. 48–51; and Abu Asyraf al-Hamidi, Perjalanan Men-cari Haji Mabrur (Kuala Lumpur: Era Ilmu, 1995), p. 202, and Suhaimee Yassin, Panduan Haji (Kuala Lumpur: Bahagian Hal Ehwal Islam Jabatan Perdana Menteri, 1995), pp. 308–311.

75. Anonymous, Risalah Penerangan Pakej Haji Bagi Jemaah Haji Malaysia, 1409H—1989M (Kuala Lumpur: Tabung Haji, 1989), pp. 66–67; Anonymous, Risalah Penerangan Kepada Jemaah Haji Malaysia 1409 Hijrah (Kuala Lumpur: Tabung Haji, 1989), pp. 7, 10–15; and Anonymous, Risalah Soal Jawab Ibadat Haji dan Umrah (Kuala Lumpur: Tabung Haji, 1984), p. 43.

76. H. Aboebakar, *Sedjarah Ka'bah dan Manasik Hadji* (Jakarta: Bulan Bintang, 1963); Anonymous, *Tuntunan: Manasik Hadji* (Bogor: Tjiawi, 1973); and S. Satya Dharma, *Haji Kita: Fakta dan Problema Penyelenggaraan Haji di Indonesia 1990–2000* (Jakarta: AWAM, 2000).

77. Fahmi Amhar and Arum Harjanti, *Buku Pintar Calon Haji* (Jakarta: Penerbit Buku Andalan, 1996); Al-Ghazali, *Rahasia Haji dan Umroh* (Bandung: Penerbit Karisma, 1993); Amat Iskandar, *Ketika Haji Kami Kerjakan* (Semarang: Dahara Prize, 1994); M. Julius, *Kenangan Rohani Perjalana Haji* (Malang: Rumah Sakit Islam Aisyiyah, 1994; T. A. Lathief Rousydiy, *Manasik Haji dan 'Umrah Rasulullah S.A.W.* (Medan: Penerbit Firma Rainbow, 1989).

78. Robert Bianchi, *Guests of God*, especially p. 1–6; 70–75.

79. Anonymous, *Laporan Kajian Mengenai Jemaah Haji Menunaikan Haji Lebih Daripada Sekali* (Kuala Lumpur: Tabung Haji, 1989).

80. Anonymous, *Buku Panduan Ibadat Haji, Umrah dan Ziarah* (Kuala Lumpur: Tabung Haji, 1983), especially pp. 20–25; 32; 110; and 139.

81. Anonymous, *Himpunan Risalah Rapat Kerja Urusan Haji Seluruh Indonesia Ke-XV* (Jakarta: Departemen Agama, 1983); Anonymous, *Laporan Hasil Kunjungan Kerja* (Studi Perbandingan) Penyelenggaraan Urusan Haji di Propinsi Jawa Timur & Sulawesi Selatan (Jakarta: Kantor Urusan Haji, 1987); Anonymous, *Laporan: Penyelenggaraan Urusan Haji* (Jakarta: Kantor Urusan Haji, 1986). Two reports which are very worth reading and which give an idea of the width and breadth of the Indonesian Hajj in just the past few years are: Anonymous, *Data dan Profil Jemaah Haji Indonesia Tahun 1996 s.d. 2002* (Jakarta: Departemen Agama, 2002), and Anonymous, *Gambaran Umum tentang Penyelenggaraan Haji Indonesia* (Jakarta: Departemen Agama, 2004).

82. H. Sumarmo Ma'sum, *Kesehatan Haji* (Jakarta: Badan Koordinasi Ikatan Persaudraan Haji Indonesia, 1991); Anonymous, *Loka-Karya Peningkatan Pelayanan Haji Indonesia* (Jakarta: Direktorat Jendral Urusan Haji, 1975); Anonymous, *Pedoman Kerja Bagi Anggauta Majelis Pimpinan Haji Indonesia* (Jakarta; Direktorat Jendral Urusan Haji, n.d.).

83. See, for example, A. Yunus, *Pengaruh Optimalisasi Koordinasi dan Komunikasi terhadap Efektivitas Pelayanan Ibadah Haji di Kebupaten Sumedang* (M.Si Thesis, Univeristas Satyyagama, Jakarta, 1999); Nursi Arsyirawati, *Pengembangan Strategi dan Kebijakan Peningkatan Manajemen Kualitas Pelayanan Haji Indonesia* (M.Si Thesis, Universitas Indonesia, 1999); Subandi, *Pengaruh Pelatihan terhadap Produktivitas Kerja Suatu Studi Terhadap Tim Pembimbang Haji Indonesia Non Kelompok Terbang* (M.Si, Thesis, Universitas Indonesia, 1995); and Cuk Hudoro Ridhwan, *Haji Mandiri: Kasus Lima Keluarga Asy Syifa* (M.Si, Thesis, Universitas Indonesia, 1998).

84. Interview with Aisha bte. Mohamad Osman, Singapore, May 5, 2004.

85. Several contemporary analysts of the Hajj have noted the active participation of the Saudi government in trying to constantly better the "Hajj experience"; see Awang Had Salleh, "Modern Concept of Hajj Management," p. 262–267, and Moeslim Abdurrahman, "Ritual Divided: Hajj Tours in Capitalist Era Indonesia," p. 117–132.

10

On the Margins of Islam

Hajjis from Outside Southeast Asia's "Islamic Arc"

Allah, please free us from oppression, free us from suppression, free us
from dictatorship.
—Anonymous Burmese Hajji, Mandalay, January 2007

Although most Southeast Asian Hajjis have come from the Muslim arc of landscapes stretching from southern Thailand to Malaysia and Indonesia, and then
up again through Brunei and the southern Philippines, Muslim voyagers have
also come, and still come, from parts of Southeast Asia where they are distinct
minorities, and sometimes persecuted minorities. Some of the earliest extant
records of Southeast Asian Islam, in fact, are not found in Muslim-dominated
parts of the region. Chinese references to communities of Muslims show that the
kingdom of Champa, visited by Muslim seafarers on their way to southern China
from the Middle East, played at least some role in the transmission of the religion to the region. By 1310, Muslim gravestones started to appear in Sulu in the
southern Philippines, right around the same time that Islam was coming to Pasai
in North Sumatra on the other end of the archipelagic world.[1] This chapter
examines the Hajj from places outside Southeast Asia's Islamic arc, and asks how
patterns of movement and religious travel have remained constant or differed
when Islam has not been the dominant faith of a pilgrim's place of origin.

The records for this sort of investigation are often more problematic than for
the Muslim-dominated parts of Southeast Asia. For the second half of the twentieth century, Saudi sources, when utilized alongside a range of Southeast Asian
materials, give a good sense of the numbers and experiences of pilgrims from various countries in Southeast Asia that are outside the Muslim arc.[2] The first part of
this chapter lays out a brief outline of this "marginal history," showing how outlying areas of Southeast Asian Islam came to be Muslim and also came to be
incorporated into the larger flow of the pilgrimage routes to the Middle East
over time. The second part of the chapter looks at some of the contemporary

manifestations of Islam generally, and the Hajj specifically, in these same places, stretching in a broad ribbon of territory across the northern half of Southeast Asia (Burma to northern Thailand to Laos, Cambodia, and Vietnam, before ending up in Luzon in the Philippines). The final part of the chapter is based on oral history interviews with Hajjis in these same nonmajority landscapes I carried out inter- mittently over the course of five years, between 2004 and 2009. By speaking to Hajjis and Hajjas in their homes, markets, and schools in places like Thandwe (Burma), Kampong Cham (Cambodia), and Quezon City (the Philippines), I gained a sense of what the pilgrimage means to Muslims when most people around them are not members of their own faith. In Muslim-dominated commu- nities of Southeast Asia, the Hajj may mean one thing, I argue, yet the institution of this longest of journeys often means something else in lands outside the Muslim arc of the region.

The Hajj and History "Outside" the Arc

One place well suited to examining the history of the Hajj from outside the core areas of Islam in the region is Burma, the physically closest Southeast Asian landscape to the Middle East. Arab ships touched down in Burma as early as the eighth century CE, though we do not know how much Islamization followed these voyages.[3] In the Mongol conquests of Asia, Muslims were among the con- quering Yuan troops that overran Burmese Bagan in the late thirteenth century, including the Yunnan governor and general Sai-Tien-Chi'ih Shan-sau-ting Wu- ma-erh (Sayyid Ajal Shams al-Din Umar) and his son Nasruddin (Nasir al-Din).[4] Eventually Panthays (Chinese Muslims from Yunnan) became very important to the economic life of Upper Burma, connecting caravan routes that stretched from the provinces of southwest China to Vietnam, Laos, Siam, Burma, Tibet, and eastern India, across the hills of this vast inland region.[5] The British became aware of these caravans quite early and, by the nineteenth century, saw that Islam was pivotal on the frontier between Burma and China, the latter a primary economic target for the expanding British empire.[6] By this time, there were sev- eral Muslim communities in Burma, not just the Chinese Muslims of the north and the Muslims of Arakan on the western coast. Muslims of Indian origin had also come to Burma, as had much smaller numbers of Burmese Muslims claiming Persian origin known as "Zerbadee" in the British census of 1891.[7] King Mindon tried to facilitate the Hajj for this mixed Muslim population by sponsoring a waqf house in Arabia to service Burmese Muslim needs while his subjects were on pilgrimage.[8] After British rule ended in the mid-twentieth century, the independent Burmese state sent some four to five hundred Muslims per year on Hajj, assisting them in obtaining passports, foreign currency, and other documents for their journeys. With the coup of 1962, however, Burmese Muslims were regarded with the utmost suspicion by the ruling authorities and were subject to discriminatory practices.[9]

The history of the Hajj—and Islam generally—in Thailand has certain affinities with the Burmese case. Anne Maxwell Hill has pointed out that the Panthays of Burma and the Haw of northern Thailand have similar roots in the historical communities of Yunnanese Muslims who have been trading down to mainland Southeast Asia for centuries, with a particularly important event in this history being the failed Muslim rebellion in Yunnan (1855–1873) against the Ch'ing state, which drove many Chinese Muslims south to Southeast Asia.[10] Several recent researchers have shown a continuity between these communities and present-day Muslim Chinese in the northern parts of Thailand, one predicated on travel and merchant activity that has been a part of this landscape for at least two centuries.[11] Just as in the Burmese case, there has also been a strong coastal dimension in attracting Islam to Thai landscapes and in keeping it connected with the Muslim Middle East via the wings of the Hajj and religious education, as elsewhere in Southeast Asia. The Pattani Sultanate has been preeminent in this regard in the Thai south, dispensing religious students and scholars to Cairo and Mecca, as well as disseminating new Muslim learning to the rest of the Malay Peninsula over the course of several centuries.[12] In the nineteenth century, the British had long deliberations about what to do with the Muslim polities of the Thai south; these areas were situated dangerously close to Britain's growing dominion on the lower Malay Peninsula.[13] Siamese aristocrats and, indeed, the Siamese court held similar deliberations at the same time.[14] Yet just as in the Burmese case, the heterogeneity of Siamese Muslims—Chinese Muslims in the north, Malay-Siamese subject-citizens in the south, and a Persian-Indian Muslim minority scattered elsewhere in the kingdom—made for a diffuse experience of "being Muslim" in Siam and later (after the 1930s) in Thailand. The Hajj acted as a vehicle to unite Thai Muslims not only with the rest of the Muslim *ummah* but also with each other, as often these communities had a greater chance of meeting in Mecca than in Southeast Asia itself.

Farther east, there has also been a significant Muslim minority in Indochina— what we know today as Vietnam, Cambodia, and, to a much lesser extent, Laos— from as early as the eighth century CE. French scholars noticed that Arab geographers of the thirteenth and fourteenth centuries knew of Champa as a place famed for eaglewood on these mercantile routes, as well as the presence of Shi'ite communities, a mix of economic and social information that would have been highly valued by Arab sailors.[15] The Shi'ite connection is particularly interesting: many Vietnamese Chams today describe themselves as "Bani Cham," a highly localized version of the religion that nevertheless has certain attributes in common with Shi'ite doctrines.[16] There has even been supposition that Javanese contacts between

Java and Champa helped to solidify Islam in both places in the early centuries of the second millennium CE, with linguistics and archaeology suggesting close ties between the two places around one thousand years ago. A few centuries later, Malacca may have also been important in moving Islam between Java and the lower Mekong region. As the port city became a magnet for traders all over the region in the fifteenth century, it increasingly connected Islamizing places through trade and seasonal contact.[17] Not coincidentally, Southeast Asians began going on Hajj to the Hejaz around this time, as Malacca became a great hub both for trans–Southeast Asian travel and transoceanic journeys outside the region to distant shores, such as China, India, and the Middle East.

French academics became increasingly interested in the Chams as an important minority group in Cambodia and Vietnam and have struggled to explain the connection between the Chams and the wider Muslim world over time.[18] French colonial scholars tried to work out what precisely was Muslim about the Chams in Indochina, how much the Cham variants of Islam had to do with other religions (mainstream, local, and translocal), and how far into the past these legacies extended.[19] One seminal scholar teased out the cultural nuances and differences of the various Cham communities from Tonkin to Annam to Cochin China and Cambodia, explaining demographics, economic life, religious worldview, and ritual praxis.[20] As part of the Gallic *mission civilitrice*," Cham Muslims from Indochina were allowed to take a ship to Jeddah to perform their Hajj, though relatively few ever had the economic means to do so. The development of the French steamboat line Maritime Messagiers helped this passage along, but many Chams made alternative arrangements for their Hajj through their contacts in the rest of the Muslim Southeast Asian world. In this sense, ties to the Malay Peninsula and other places afforded opportunities for travel with kin, who often were coming from Muslim-majority areas in the region under colonial domination (figure 10.1).[21]

The Philippines, like Vietnam, had very early contact with Islam via the Sulu Archipelago in the far south. The pathbreaking work on interpreting the arrival of Islam to the southern part of the Philippine Archipelago, one of the farthest outposts of the religion in the world, was done in the 1990s, just as a Muslim consciousness was beginning to reassert itself in that part of the archipelago. One scholar phrased the dynamics of this process thus:

> The phrase "coming of Islam" is indeed capable of various meanings. It could mean the coming of Muslim traders or the arrival of Muslim missionaries, or even the advent of Muslim chiefs or adventurers with the intention of founding a principality. Clearly, none of these alternatives necessarily imply the Islamization of a people. Muslim traders, or even settlers, might decide to return to their places of origin while

Figure 10.1 Cambodian River Mosque.
Credit: Cambodian River Mosque: Authors' Photo.

missionaries might fail in their endeavors. Muslim adventurers might succeed in carving out principalities for themselves but might fail in inducing their subjects to embrace the Faith; some might have had no such intent or interest.... When Legazpi arrived in Philippine waters in 1565, the process of Islamization was already manifested in varying degrees, in both extent and kind in the various parts of the country. For a while it can be asserted that Islam had acquired a firm hold among the rulers and held sway in Sulu and Maguindanao, it still held a tenuous sway on other islands. For example, in Manila, where the ruling family was identified as Muslim, there is not much evidence of widespread Islamic practices among the inhabitants.[22]

This formulation of a patchwork advance of Islam in the Philippines fits with later interpretations of how chiefly power worked in the archipelago. Subsequent research has shown how political structure and social stratification combined to make Islam an attractive alternative for some Philippine chiefdoms.[23] The Tausug, for example, were expressly Muslim in their "public orientation" but bent some Muslim orthodoxies (such as the bans on the slavery of fellow Muslims, for example) to local norms when it suited them.[24] The fact that Islam came early to the Philippines and remained an almost entirely maritime phenomenon throughout the long centuries of colonial contact, rarely penetrating far inland, helps to explain how, even on the eve of World War II, Muslim Filipinos mostly went on Hajj via the south, eschewing Manila and the regular transoceanic steamship lines that called there. At that time it still took over a year to complete the journey to Arabia and back from the Philippines. Yet this southern cadence toward the Muslim-dominated island world of Southeast Asia was still seen as preferable to making Hajj under the aegis of what was seen as a repressive, Christian-dominated colonial state.[25]

A single episode from 1950 suggests why this may have been the case. At this time, the Philippines was independent, albeit run by Catholic Filipinos, considered to be little better than Western colonizers by many Filipino Muslims.[26] Two Philippine pilgrim ships left for Jeddah that year, the *Chung Hsing* and the *Cristobel*. The first ship arrived with some two thousand pilgrims on board; many of the Hajjis evaded customs on arrival in the Hejaz and never paid their fares. The second ship was pushed through home clearances by a local Philippine senator, despite irregularities: 1,816 pilgrims managed to get on board, even though only 1,283 were on the passenger list. It was suggested by the British that the Philippine senator had oiled the wheels of the boarding and departure procedures because he was up for reelection, and he wanted to be seen in his Mindanao constituency as a "friend of Islam" by getting as many pilgrims onto the ships as he could. A large number of the pilgrims on both ships ended up having little or no money for their stay in the Hejaz, or for their return trip, as per global regulations on the Hajj by this time. Two hundred more died in the Hejaz because of lax health measures taken by the Philippine officials, and a further two hundred died either on the way home or shortly after returning to their country, all of disease, principally beriberi. The British official writing up the report intoned that "the story of the Filipinos is in so many respects an example of how not to handle the pilgrimage that it merits separate treatment. The Philippine government appeared to have taken no interest in its conduct or organization."[27] The thoughts of this one official seem to have been applicable to a number of cases involving Southeast Asian pilgrims coming from non-Muslim-majority areas in the region. What was already a difficult journey could become a brutal one because of mismanagement and neglect. This state of affairs would continue into the era of postindependence states.

The Contemporary Situation

How does the Hajj look now in these lands outside the Muslim arc of the region? The picture is a complex one, with the pilgrimage easy or very difficult, depending on the landscape under scrutiny. In Burma, Muslims of the various heritages officially make up some 4 percent of the population but may, in fact, represent a larger segment of Burmese society, potentially triple this amount.[28] Although most of Burma's Muslims are poor and are represented as such in the global media (and indeed in Myanmar itself), exceptions to this rule go back to the independence era to Tun Razak, a revolutionary hero who was murdered alongside Aung San in 1947.[29] Regardless of wealth, it has been quite difficult for Burmese Muslims to get permission to go on Hajj, as the act of procuring a passport is forbidden to most members of Burmese society. The numbers of Hajjis have gone up recently to three or four hundred per year, despite Muslims being targeted as a "problem community" by the ruling junta since the 1962 coup.[30] In 2007, for example, the regime expressly warned pilgrims not to get involved in politics in the Hejaz, and by this, Burmese politics were meant (protests, exchanging information about the plight of local Muslims under Yangon's rule, etc.), not the politics of the Middle East.[31] The seminal issue has been the displacement of Muslims in Arakan province, where tens of thousands of dirt-poor Muslim refugees have streamed into Bangladesh by the land border and also, more recently, into Thailand in the west via boats.[32] A number of parties have been formed to represent the interests of Arakan Muslims, stretching from the Northern Arakan Muslim League (founded in 1946) to the Arakan Rohingya National Organization, founded more than forty years later. Yet they have had very little success in moving the Yangon regime to help Burmese Muslims who wish to complete the Hajj.

In Thailand, the issues are not entirely different when it comes to the state and its Muslim populations. The data on indigenous Muslims living in contemporary Thailand are far better than for Burma; quite accurate reporting is available for the demographics of this community, as well as for its participation in the Hajj.[33] A number of scholars have pointed to the Hajj as a salient force in forging community between southern Thai Muslims, in particular, and the larger Muslim community of the world outside the nation. This has been especially important in the south, with its decades-long history of sporadic armed insurrection, poverty, situational repression by the Buddhist majority, and unrest in local relations with the Thai state as a whole.[34] In the years after World War II, some two thousand Thai Muslims were going on Hajj per year, and Bangkok facilitated their movement through a government-sponsored travel agency, medical teams, and the like.[35] In 1982, only ten Thai companies specialized in this kind of travel, but less than a decade later, there were nearly four times as many, giving an indication of some of the scale at hand.[36] Yet because these Thai Muslim communities are primarily agriculturalists and miners, they have often been at the mercy of world prices for the commodities they either grow or excavate, and pilgrimage numbers reflect these boom and bust periods (box 10.1). The stream of Thai Muslims to Mecca and Medina therefore very much follows these cycles, and this is not necessarily the case in other parts of Southeast Asia.[37] In nearby Laos, which has only a very small Muslim minority, a tiny Lao Muslim delegation goes

---

Box 10.1 **The *Bangkok Post* on Thai Pilgrims, May 22, 1954**

Because following decline in the tin and rubber trade individual incomes have fallen, only a relatively few Thai Muslims of South Thailand will be making the pilgrimage to Mecca this year, according to Nai Praphanna Pattalung, Governor of Yala, in Bangkok on official business.

Nai Praphan said that despite efforts by southern National Assemblymen to stir up interest in the pilgrimage, less than 100 Muslims have indicated desire to go to Mecca this year. (Assemblymen and others who obtain passengers for pilgrim ships are given a commission.)

The Governor said Pattani may send more pilgrims than the other provinces. Last year 1,200 Thai Muslims made the pilgrimage.

Meanwhile, it was learned from Nai Rangsarit Chavapasiri, representative of the Chularajmonti (Muslim Adviser to the Cabinet) on the Interior Ministry's board for assistance to pilgrims, a new agreement has to be drafted with the pilgrim carriers.

Because of the number of pilgrims is expected to be much reduced this year, the three companies—Ngow Hock, Thepviwat and Siam Rice Company—which have been granted permission to carry pilgrims are planning a merger to organize the journey to Mecca.

The proposed amalgamated company is to be known as Thai Pilgrims Company.

Nai Rangsarit reported that the company is now asking for an increase in the pilgrim fare (including return trip as well as guarantee money in Saudi Arabia) from 4,800 to 5,000 baht per head. The Ministry of Interior will consider this request Monday.

---

many years to the Middle East, too, but in this case the community is mostly urban, living in a few satellite towns around Vientiane. Lao Muslims are not affected so much by commodity prices, as their livelihoods and incomes are mostly drawn from urban occupations.[38]

The case of Muslims in the Philippines has often been compared with the southern Thai case. In both countries, Muslims form a poor but still sizable minority population in the south, and violence and Muslim secession have been an integral part of the modern story of the nation. The breadth of the Philippine Muslim community is quite astonishing: the Islamic sultanates of the historical Philippine Archipelago have metamorphosed into a broad array of peoples living in today's Philippine south, scattered across a very sizable geography.[39] The Muslim "attributes" of these communities have been studied across a number of markers, from the arrival of Islam to contemporary lived practices, from clothing and sartorial matters to everyday ceremonial life.[40] The quest for a separate Muslim homeland has been ongoing, and the Hajj has certainly been implicated in this narrative.[41] When relations between Manila and the various Muslim groups in the south started to thaw ever so slightly in 1967, the only issue that the government was willing to compromise on was the Hajj, and Manila stepped up its regulation of the yearly voyages west from the archipelago after that. Between 1978 and 1980, nearly five thousand self-identified Moros performed the pilgrimage, a very large number considering the distance and the widespread, abject poverty of the Philippines during this period.[42] At this time, the Philippine Pilgrimage Authority was erected, and only a few years later, a self-standing ministry was founded to deal with the Hajj and other issues, such as banking, scholarships, and mosques, all of interest to the community.[43] Although peace treaties now exist between Manila and the main secessionist Muslim organizations in the south, the realities of the Philippine Hajj are still quite difficult on a day-to-day basis, as the country's continuing cycle of poverty and violence still renders the Hajj out of reach for most Muslim Filipinos.[44]

One place where violence, the Hajj, and Islam have rarely been linked is Singapore, a Muslim-minority nation by virtue of the history of the city-state since 1819. Despite the fact that Singapore is roughly three-quarters Chinese in its population, it holds an important place in the history and functioning of the Southeast Asian Hajj, simply because for many years Singapore was the most modern shipping (and later, flight-centered) depot in the region. Southeast Asian pilgrimages often originated from Singapore, so Singapore's place in the modern Hajj has always been an anomalous one. Singapore also has its own Muslim community, and the government has been at pains to ensure that its citizens can perform the pilgrimage every year. The fact that this tiny city-state exists between two much larger Muslim-dominant neighbors probably helped this sentiment also for Singapore leaders. The organization Majlis Ugama Islam Singapura (MUIS) was created in 1968 to serve the needs of the nation's Muslim community, and one of its primary tasks from the very beginning was to look after the country's pilgrims, both before they set out on their journey and once they were actually in the Hejaz.[45] The medical services, financial planning, logistics, and technological help provided by MUIS are all first-rate and belie the fact that Muslims are a small minority on the island. Singapore's prosperity has been responsible for some of this, but an accommodationist stance by the People's Action Party (PAP), so often maligned in the West as ultra-authoritarian, has also made things run smoothly. From training courses to cash grants, from work improvement teams to "product differentiation" in the kinds of Hajj sought by its citizens, MUIS has been a real success story in the modern management of the Hajj.[46] The organization reflects the wealth of Singapore in what it can do for its Muslim clients; it reflects the modernity of the island nation in doing things professionally, and this is particularly true when it comes to the Hajj.

The situation in Cambodia is almost the polar opposite of Singapore. The Cambodian Muslim community is extremely complex in its makeup, varying between Cham, Chvea, and Jahed variants of ethnicity and religion, all of them "Cambodian" but with different roots and histories making up these subcommunities.[47] Yet the richness of this tapestry was nearly destroyed in the Khmer Rouge years between 1975 and 1979. Although there is still some debate over whether the Khmer Rouge actively targeted Cham Muslims everywhere because of their religion, there can be no doubt that the death toll among Cham Muslims was shockingly high and disproportionate to other groups in the country.[48] The numbers stretch from 90,000 deaths in one study to many times this in others, but the testimonies of Cham Muslims who survived the horror make it clear that this community was decimated by the regime and was hunted by their agents.[49] The revival of Islam in Cambodia has been a part of the awakening of the nation after the Khmer Rouge period.[50] In terms of the Hajj, the single most important impetus in getting Cham Muslims to the Hejaz has been overseas aid, usually coming from Malaysia but also from Saudi Arabia and Kuwait (table 10.1). These latter two countries have provided assistance in the form of grants in aid, but they have also been active in building schools and mosques in Muslim areas of Cambodia, as well as in missionization. This, in turn, has led to renewed scrutiny by the West for Al-Qaeda and Jemaah Islamiyah links to the country, as in

Table 10.1 **Southeast Asian Pilgrims from Outside the Muslim Arc, 1979–1984**

	1979	1980	1981	1982	1983	1984
Burma	10	74	156	167	148	201
Cambodia	—	3	55	—	—	—
Philippines	1,699	1,836	1,851	1,955	2,630	2,526
Singapore	1,838	2,490	3,103	2,328	2,998	2,947
Thailand	1,906	2,978	2,753	1,888	2,273	2,610
Vietnam	1	—	—	-	—	—
Totals	5,454	7,381	7,918	6,338	8,049	8,284

Source: Adapted from Saudi Ministry of Interior, the Directorate General of Passports, Pilgrim Statistics for A.H. 1403–1983 AC, pp. 4–5, 28–29; and Pilgrim Statistics for A.H. 1404–1984 AC, pp. 10, 13, 26, in James Piscatori, "Asian Islam: International Linkages and Their Impact on International Relations," in John Esposito, ed., Islam in Asia: Religion, Politics, and Society (New York: Oxford University Press, 1987), p. 251.

one instance in 2003 when two Thais, an Egyptian, and a Cambodian were all thrown into prison on suspicion of terror links to the Middle East.[51] Yet even while Saudis help finance the Cambodian Hajj because most Khmer are too poor to go on their own, there are indeed a few better-off Cambodian Muslims who have helped finance trips to Mecca for their countrymen, such as two figures who took several dozen Khmer pilgrims to the holy cities in 2007 at a subsidized cost of roughly $2,000 per person.[52]

Finally, the Hajj from contemporary Vietnam is also important in the wider scope of the region's pilgrimage routes. Two of the principal areas in Vietnam in this respect have been Ho Chi Minh City and its environs and the city of Chau Doc, on the Cambodian frontier. Chau Doc's history shows how translocal Cham Muslim culture is and (nearly always) has been, even though the river city is in the interior of a rice and jungle landscape that is "remote" in most senses of the term. Cham Muslims in Chau Doc have connections not only to the larger Cham Muslim *ummah* in metropolitan Ho Chi Minh City but also across the frontier in Cambodia and farther afield to Malaysia, India, and the Middle East through the wanderings of Muslim students and teachers.[53] The Hajj is important in this world, too; Vietnam controls its citizens' pilgrimage to Mecca with some care, as Muslim Cham in the country have often been seen as an outsider group that needs to be watched. The forms of Islam practiced by Cham in Vietnam seem to be especially syncretic in many cases, with vestiges of older beliefs—often shorthanded as "Bani Islam Cham"—in evidence among many of the religion's local practitioners. An active debate still rages in the literature on how Muslim this community is, given these accretions and also these vestigial elements of belief from an earlier time before Islam may have come to Vietnam.[54] There is also starting to be some careful, on-the-ground research of the Vietnamese Hajj, especially among the Bawean community of Ho Chi Minh City. This particular subgroup of Vietnamese Muslims claims ancestry from a small island in the Java Sea, at a time when Muslim voyagers from the island and mainland worlds of Southeast Asia were just starting to intermarry and mix along the maritime trade routes. It is interesting that this community has proven to be one of the best studied subgroups of Muslims in the country, especially vis-à-vis their connections with their Hajj, as these movements seem to continue an earlier history of journeying that is now over one thousand years old in the region.[55]

Oral Histories beyond the Muslim Arc

To understand the importance of the Hajj in Muslims' lives, I visited many places outside the Muslim-dominated lands of Southeast Asia to ask questions about pilgrimage and its role in the lives of Muslim minorities in the region. The interviews took place in five broad areas: in western Arakan state and Yangon in Burma, among Rohingyas and Indian Muslims; in Sagaing and Mandalay in north-central Burma among Chinese (Panthay) Muslims, as well as in Chiang Mai, northern Thailand; in Cambodia among Muslim Chams; in Vietnam, again among Chams; and in Luzon, the northern Philippines, among Filipino Muslims living far away from the Muslim-dominated south. In western Burma and in Yangon, these interviews were mostly conducted in English; in northern Burma and Thailand, the interviews were mostly done in (Mandarin) Chinese; among Chams in Cambodia and Vietnam, the interviews were predominantly in Malay; and in Luzon, the conversations were in English. In Burma, Cambodia, and Vietnam, I have changed respondents' names in the notes to protect their identities, as Muslims are still persecuted in some of these places, though certainly less in Vietnam and especially in Cambodia than in Burma. A map shows the locations of the interviews and the broad subethnic groups being spoken to in each place.

Conversations with Muslims in Arakan Province, a site designated by the Burmese government as "recalcitrant" and even sometimes as "rebellious," were difficult. I spoke to people only indoors, as ordinary Muslims were justifiably afraid to be seen with a foreigner, though several indicated to me through intermediaries when I made discreet inquiries that they did want to speak. A man in Thandwe told me that he had been on Hajj in 2004; he had been allowed to go with his wife, and they stayed three married couples to a room to be able to make

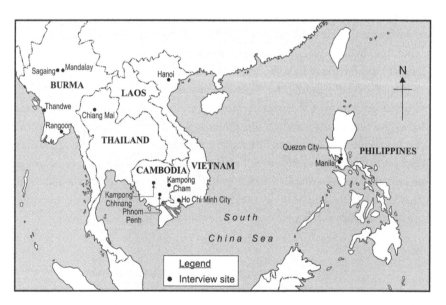

Figure 10.2 Author's Interviewing Sites in Southeast Asia Outside the Muslim Arc. *Credit*: Map drawn by Lee Li-kheng, Geography Department, National University of Singapore.

do financially. It was very difficult for him to get a passport to go, and he had to stay in Yangon and then in Bangkok for nearly three weeks before all of the necessary permissions came through. His son now lives in Yangon, but he was not allowed to visit him, as all Muslims in Arakan were forbidden at the time of my interviews to travel more than two miles outside their domicile by order of the government. Given that Rohingyas like him have been in Burma for hundreds of years, he was outraged to be treated this way in their own country.[56] An Indian Muslim man in Yangon echoed some of these sentiments: it was easier for him to go than for Muslims in Arakan, but this did not mean that it was easy. He, too, had to wait in a long queue to be able to make the trip, and eventually he traveled through Bangkok, with more than two thousand other Burmese Muslims who were able to go the same year. He traveled on Qatar Air, and the Rohingya man traveled via Bahrain. Both underscored how important the largess of the Gulf States has been in recently getting more Burmese Muslims to the Hejaz.[57] A third pilgrim I spoke with in Yangon, a woman whose mother and sister had both recently been on Hajj, too, described the Burmese lottery system for the pilgrimage as very difficult: it could be manipulated by the government to reward or punish the behavior of specific Muslim citizens, she said, or for Muslims as a group in years of particular strife.[58]

Chinese Muslims I spoke with in Mandalay, Sagaing, and across the border in Chiang Mai echoed many of these sentiments, though they had different perspectives as well. Panthay Muslims, whom I spoke with mostly in Chinese, are not considered to be as "troublesome" or rebellious as Rohingyas by the state; this part of Burma is also more prosperous, as trade links with China have been booming, and Panthay Burmese with language abilities and often kin ties across the border have been able to help these commercial contacts. One person in Mandalay showed me a confidential government report (in Burmese and English) of how many Muslims actually live in these north-central districts of Burma, and the numbers are substantial: in the year 2000, Sagaing had nearly 60,000 Muslims and Mandalay more than 200,000 Muslims, with more than 100 and 200 mosques in each place, respectively.[59] Another Panthay man told me that when he finally made it to Mecca on his Hajj, one of the principal things he prayed for was deliverance from the Burmese government: "free us from oppression; free us from suppression; free us from dictatorship" were his exact words.[60] Two men I met, one in front of the "Bo Ho" (or Central Mosque) and one in front of the Joon Mosque, both in Mandalay, were working-class people, as opposed to my earlier interviews with intellectuals. Although only the former had been on Hajj, both told me that it was getting easier to go from this part of Burma than elsewhere.[61] Yet in the temple city of Sagaing, a Hajji I spoke with at his mosque said that performing the pilgrimage from a place like Burma was never easy. He and his wife were able to afford public transport for the first week that they were in the holy cities, but then they had to walk many, many miles to the holy sites. In the first week, they ate curry, but when their money started to dwindle, they ate anything they could get their hands on for the remainder of their journey.[62] Chinese-Thai Muslims I spoke with in Chiang Mai were better off but also felt rather marooned in the Hejaz. They were very conscious that they came from lands where they were minorities and that this showed in the arrangements made for them, as opposed to Muslim-majority populations who were better cared for by the relevant authorities (table 10.2).[63]

Table 10.2 **Some Important Dates in Relation to Modern Southeast Asian Islam Outside the Muslim Arc**

1946	Burma	Northern Arakan Muslim League founded
1948	Thailand	Narathiwat uprising kills 400 Thai-Malay Muslims
1948	Burma	Rohingya insurgency in Arakan state (April)
1959	Thailand	Barisan Nasional Pembebasan Patani (BNPP, National Liberation Front of Patani) formed
1962	Burma	Military rule begins; range of discriminatory measures implemented against Muslims
1963	Thailand	Barisan Revolusi National (BRN, National Revolutionary Front) established
1968	Thailand	Pertubuhan Pembebaan Patani Bersatu (PULO Patani United Liberation Organization) formed
1968	Philippines	Corregidor incident in which group of Christian soldiers murder between 28 and 68 Muslim soldiers (18 March); outcry from Muslim groups
1969	Philippines	Nur Misuari forms Moro National Liberation Front (MNLF)
1972	Philippines	Outbreak of MNLF rebellion in Mindanao
1975–1979	Cambodia	Cham Muslims persecuted under Khmer Rouge, resulting in an estimated 90,000 deaths
1978	Burma	200,000 Rohingyas flee across the border into Bangladesh to escape persecution in Arakan under regime's Naga Min Operation
1978	Philippines	Split in MNLF sees Salamat Hashim form the Moro Islamic Liberation Front (MILF) (February)

1982	Burma	Rohingya Solidarity Organization (RSO) formed
1987	Burma	Arakan Rohingya Islamic Front (ARIF) established as a breakaway from RSO
1989	Philippines	Central government agrees to establish an Autonomous Region in Muslim Mindanao (ARMM) (August); referendum held in November
1991	Philippines	Abu Sayyaf Group established
1992	Burma	Exodus of 300,000 Rohingyas into Bangladesh after regime crackdown
1996	Philippines	Government agrees to Nur Misuari as governor of ARMM (June); peace treaty with MNLF signed in September
1998	Burma	Arakan Rohingya National Organization (ARNA) formed

Source: Abstracted from Greg Fealy and Virginia Hooker, *Voices of Islam in Southeast Asia: A Contemporary Sourcebook* (Singapore: ISEAS, 2006), xxi–xxix.

In Cambodia, as stated previously, the Muslims are Cham, an ancient ethnic group that first migrated to the mainland many centuries ago. Many of Cambodia's Cham now adhere to what might be called Muslim orthodoxy—they pray five times a day and try to live without what has been described as accretions of "superstition" in their lives. In my interviews with experts on this topic in Cambodia, a real sense was imparted to me how divisive this split is between Cham who still adhere to the older, more local ways and those who have either of their own accord or through missionization adopted models closer to Sunni international norms.[64] A Muslim community activist in Phnom Penh told me that this division has been a source of conflict not only within the Cambodian Cham community but also between Chams on both sides of the Cambodia-Vietnam frontier. The Hajj, when Cambodian Chams get to perform it, tends to move local Muslims more toward the Sunni ideal than to an adherence to local traditions of syncretism, which have comparatively less religious (and perhaps also less social) prestige.[65] Indeed, signs of Cambodia's rapidly increasing connections with the outside Muslim world—particularly the Gulf States and Malaysia—are everywhere. This was especially so in the dozen or so mosques I counted while sailing up the Mekong River to Kampong Cham, and some very large, august mosques on the Tonle Sap River.[66] In the central marketplace of Kampong Cham, I interviewed two food-selling Cham women, who told me that

Hajjis and Hajjas were now a dime a dozen in Kampong Cham; the connections have become that routinized. Some wealthy Cambodian Chams help pave these connections through their own philanthropy, but most of the money is from the Gulf, where countries like Cambodia are seen as fertile fields for conversion to "true paths" and an expansion of the global *ummah*.[67] The presence of Cambodian Muslim agencies in Phnom Penh is now quite substantial, and though the West has looked for evidence of Al-Qaeda and other extremism in Cambodia, the largest part of people of different faiths here really do seem to get along.[68]

Many of these same dynamics can be applied to the other center of Cham heritage and population in Southeast Asia, in Vietnam. I interviewed the secretary of a mosque not far from Cholon, Saigon's Chinatown, a man who had been on Hajj twice, in 1973 and 2003. Because he was part of the official hierarchy of Islam in the country, he had gone to western Asia as part of Vietnamese Muslim delegations, once as the guest of the president of Iran and once as the guest of the king of Saudi Arabia. He felt that the Vietnamese Hajj was split almost equally between those local Cham who managed to get permits and pay for the journey themselves and those who went through some sort of benefactors in the Middle East, again usually via the Gulf. He was unashamed to admit that Muslim Cham in Vietnam courted this kind of patronage because the realities of currency and distance made it very difficult for local Cham to make pilgrimage otherwise. He also said that this was a way to see the world and to bring money back to his own mosque through ties with wealthier Muslims in other places. This gentleman had clearly figured out how to work the system and was proud that he had done so.[69] In other Saigon locales, I spoke to other Muslims, such as in front of the Indian Jamia Muslim mosque downtown, which also hosts the Noorul Imaan Arabic School and the Haji J. M. M. Ismael Library. The whole complex was built in 1935 during the French colonial period and still has an air of its Indian Muslim roots, derived from Asian laborers who also traveled with the French to these new lands.[70] A Vietnamese Hajja told me that the Hajj was now a real possibility for some Vietnamese Muslims, whether they were Cham or Indian in origin, because the socialist regime wanted to show minorities that it championed their individual causes. This, plus the availability of Gulf oil money, meant that many more Vietnamese could find their way to Mecca than had ever previously been the case.[71]

The last place I journeyed to in order to speak with Hajjis from outside Southeast Asia's Muslim arc was Luzon, the main northern island of the Philippines, very much outside the Muslim zone of Mindanao and Sulu in the south. A considerable community of Muslims in and around Manila live and work in discrete communities scattered in a few areas of the capital. Muslims I spoke with in greater Manila and Quezon City ranged from highly placed academics in some of the country's best universities to Muslim staffers of the Philippine Muslim

Affairs Bureau, one of whom had fought years in the jungle for Muslim autonomy. Another one of these Muslims, a Hajja who had made pilgrimage in 1993, told me that Filipinos were noticeably worse off than most other Southeast Asians in their Hajj contingents, though conditions were not abominable on the whole. She reminded me that Saudi Arabia institutionalizes much of the pilgrimage now for Muslims coming from all nations, though she did say that the doctors and medical supplies coming with the Philippine contingent were clearly fewer in number, and inferior in quantity and quality, than those available to most other Southeast Asians.[72] Another Filipino who went as part of an official Philippine delegation told me that his Hajj was run "perfectly" but that he understood his conditions were far better than the average Filipino's because the auspices under which he came were much more controlled and monitored.[73] The fact that the Filipino Hajj cost some US$1,850 dollars in 2004 put it out of the reach of most Filipinos.[74] Finally, a staff officer at the Bureau of Philippine Pilgrimage and Endowment, a man originally from Basilan, listened quietly while I interviewed his superior in July 2004. But at one point in our interview, he interjected; he lifted his trouser leg and showed me a huge purple scar on his leg, where fully half of his calf muscle had been shot away by government forces when he was with the MNLF fighting in the bush in the mid-1970s. This was also part of being a Muslim in the Philippines, he told me.[75]

Conclusion

Paradoxically, the story of Islam in Southeast Asia—home to the world's largest Muslim nation—is one that has some of its earliest roots in a number of countries where the Prophet's faith is no longer felt much at all. Certainly, one of the early landfalls of Islam in Southeast Asia was on the Cham coasts sometime in the eleventh century, though there is good indirect evidence that Muslim seafarers may have touched these coasts even sooner on their way to the mosques and markets of T'ang Canton. Several centuries later, the Mongol interregnum in China brought Muslim-inflected armies to the door of Southeast Asia again, as the Yuan troops who sacked Bagan were headed and staffed by at least some Muslim soldiers. Roughly around this time, too, Islam was cropping up in the southern Philippines. The religion was seeping slowly into Southeast Asia from Burma west to the Philippines, from the borderlands of South Asia all the way to the maritime frontiers of Oceania. Islam gradually came to these places via fleets of trading ships, but it also came overland in the mule caravans of Yunnanese Muslims, whose trade routes from southwestern China brought them to the highlands of Burma, Siam, Laos, and Vietnam. The descendants of these early sojourners, both maritime and land based, still live in the region, although as minority populations in the Buddhist and Catholic states of contemporary Southeast Asia. Some of these communities can, in fact, trace their lineages back many dozens of generations, literally to the time when the religion was first passing through parts of the region.

The present-day portrait of Islam generally and the Hajj in particular in these places is a mixed one. Poverty is a real issue facing the Muslim minorities of nearly all the countries outside Southeast Asia's Muslim arc. The majority of Muslims in these places live fairly close to the internationally defined poverty line, making a ritual like the Hajj—which normally requires expenditures of thousands of U.S. dollars—out of the reach of all except for the chosen few. Muslims from these places do, indeed, go on Hajj every year, but a significant proportion of these people can only do so via the good offices of aid programs from the Middle East, usually Saudi Arabia and the Gulf states. Yet at the same time, the presence of active secessionist movements in a number of these places has made regional governments wary of allowing too much contact between local Muslims and the Middle East. The Rohingya flag in Burma has Arabic calligraphy in a circle on green background, and the Patani flag in Thailand sports the Muslim crescent and moon, after all. The paradigm of global terror, which posits these regions as potential "breeding grounds" and sometimes even as training terrain for militants linked to Al-Qaeda or Jemmah Islamiyah (or other terrorist organizations, such as Abu Sayyaf in the Philippines), discourages certain Southeast Asian regimes from allowing their populations to participate too fully in the Hajj. As a result of this cycle of systemic poverty and occasional violence, the numbers of Hajjis from Muslim-minority Southeast Asia has been relatively few over the years. Yet the numbers have been rising slowly over time, due to the easing of travel arrangements, the expansion of aircraft travel, and the growth of grants in aid. It will be interesting to see if this trend—only a few decades old at this point—continues into the future, given the diametrically opposed nature of such forces on the functioning of Muslim pilgrimage across global spaces.

NOTES

1. Greg Fealy and Virginia Hooker, eds., *Voices of Islam in Southeast Asia: A Contemporary Sourcebook* (Singapore: ISEAS, 2006), p. xxi.
2. James Piscatori, "Asian Islam: International Linkages and Their Impact on International Relations," in John Esposito, ed., *Islam in Asia: Religion, Politics, and Society* (New York: Oxford University Press, 1987), p. 251.
3. J. A. Berlie, *The Burmanization of Myanmar's Muslims* (Bangkok: White Lotus, 2008), p. xvii.
4. Ba Shin, "The Coming of Islam to Myanma down to 1700 AD," in *Asian History Congress* (New Delhi: Azad Bhavan, 1961), p. 2.
5. Maung Maung Lay, "The Emergence of the Panthay Community at Mandalay," in *Studies in Myanma History* (Yangon: Thein Htike Yadana, 1999), p. 93. This landscape has recently been

christened as "Zomia" by Willem van Schendel, James Scott, and others who have taken a broad, comparative interest in this high-altitude terrain.

6. Public Records Office, Foreign Office/Confidential Print (hereafter, PRO/FO/CP): Gov. Gen India to Marquis of Salisbury, May 11, 1876; reprinted in Kenneth Bourne et al., eds., *British Documents on Foreign Affairs: Reports and Papers from the Foreign Office Confidential Print*, vol. 26, part 1, series E (Washington, DC: University Publications of America, 1995), p. 122.

7. Berlie, *Burmanization*, p. 7.

8. I am grateful to William Clarence Gervaise Smith of SOAS/London for alerting me to this information, which I have since reconfirmed; personal communication, March 12, 2007.

9. Moshe Yegar, *The Muslims of Burma: A Study of a Minority Group* (Wiesbaden: Harrassowitz Verlag, 1972), p. 91.

10. Ann Maxwell Hill, *Merchants and Migrants: Ethnicity and Trade among Yunnanese Chinese in Southeast Asia* (New Haven, CT: Yale Southeast Asia Studies, 1998), pp. 13, 15.

11. Suthep Soonthornpasuch, "Islamic Identity in Chiengmai City: A Historical and Structural Comparison of Two Communities" (PhD Thesis, University of California, Berkeley, 1977), p. 15; Andrew Forbes and David Henley, *The Haw: Traders of the Golden Triangle* (New Zealand: Asia Film House Editions, 1997). See also David Atwill, *The Chinese Sultanate: Islam, Ethnicity, and the Pan-Thai Rebellion in Southern China, 1856–1873* (Palo Alto, CA: Stanford University Press, 2006).

12. For background on this, see Francis Bradley, "Moral Order in a Time of Damnation: The Hikayat Patani in Historical Context," *JSEAS*, 40/2, 2009: 267–294.

13. Public Records Office, Foreign Office/Confidential Print, PRO/FO/CP: "Affairs of China, Corea, Japan, and Siam: In Continuation of Memorandum of January 1, 1899, Confidential Paper #7197," reprinted in Kenneth Bourne et al., eds., *British Documents on Foreign Affairs: Reports and Papers from the Foreign Office Confidential Print*, vol. 26, part 1, series E (Washington, DC: University Publications of America, 1995), p. 268.

14. See especially Tamara Loos, *Subject Siam* (Ithaca, NY: Cornell University, 2006), chapter 3.

15. Pierre Yves Manguin, "Etudes Cam II: L'Introduction de l'Islam au Campa," *Bulletin de l'Ecole Francaise d'Extreme-Orient*, 66 (1979): 255–287.

16. Yasuko Yoshimoto, "Is Cham Bani Indigenized Islamic Cham? A Study on Islamization and Religious Syncretism," unpublished paper. I am grateful to the anthropologist Edyta Roszko of the Max Planck Institute in Germany for supplying me with a copy of this fascinating paper.

17. A recent contribution is a good example: Mathieu Guerin's wonderfully encompassing article, "Cambodge—Les Cham et leur 'veranda sur la Mecque'—l'influence des Malais de Patani et du Kelantan su l'islam des Cham du Cambodge," has been one of the more important recent additions to this literature, and takes the idea of regional "connective histories" very seriously in its pages. Yet Guerin's approach is merely the latest incarnation of this kind of writing. See Georges Maspero, *Le Royaume de Champa* (Paris: Van Oest, 1928); and Georges Coedes, *The Indianized States of Southeast Asia* (Honolulu: University of Hawai'i Press, 1968), pp. 238–239.

18. Mathieu Guerin, "Cambodge—Les Cham et leur 'veranda sur la Mecque'—l'influence des Malais de Patani et du Kelantan su l'islam des Cham du Cambodge," *Aseanie*, December 2004: 29–67.

19. M. E. Aymonier, *Les Tchames Leurs Religions* (Paris: Ernest Leroux, 1891), esp. p. 98.

20. Marcel Ner, "Les Musulmans de l'indochine francaise," *Bulletin de l'ecole Francaise d'extreme orient*, 2, 1941: 151–202.

21. Several other French-language contributions have been useful to me in writing up this synopsis; see R. P. Durand, "Les Chams Bani," *BEFEO*, 3/1, 1903: 54–62; A. Labussiere, "Rapport sur les Chams et les Malais de L'Arrondissment de Chaudoc," *Excursions et Reconnaissance*, 6, 1880: 373–380; Pierre-Bernard Lafont, "Contribution a l'Etude des Structures Sociales des Cham du Vietnam," *BEFEO*, 52, 1964: 157–171; and Denys Lombard, "Le Campa vu du Sud," *BEFEO*, 76, 1987: 311–317.

22. Cesar Majul, *Muslims in the Philippines* (Quezon City: University of the Philippines Press, 1973), p. 36.

23. Laura Junker, *Raiding, Trading, and Feasting: The Political Economy of Philippine Chiefdoms* (Honolulu: University of Hawai'i Press, 1999), especially chapters 3 and 5.

24. James Francis Warren, *The Sulu Zone* (Singapore: University of Singapore Press, 1981), p. 216.

25. Thomas Kiefer, *The Tausug: Violence and Law in a Philippine Moslem Society* (Prospect Heights, IL: Waveland, 1986), p. 119; see also Midori Kawashima, "The Islamic Reform Movement at Lanao in the Philippines during the 1930s: The Founding of the Kamilol Islam Society," *Journal of Sophia Asian Studies*, 27, 2009: 141–154.

26. I was told this by the late Professor Cesar Majul in 1992 after a talk he gave at the University of California, Berkeley's South and Southeast Asian Studies Program. Majul was at that time, arguably, the most respected Muslim intellectual in the Philippines.

27. The entire case can be found in England's Public Record Office in Kew, Surrey, PRO/FO/371/82698 (1950).

28. Harry Priestly, "The Outsiders," *The Irrawaddy*, January 2006: 18.

29. Yeni, "Burma's Muslim Hero," *The Irrawaddy*, January 2006: 19.

30. J. A. Berlie, *Burmanization*, pp. 31, 90, 107.

31. "Myanmar Warns Hajj Pilgrims to Steer Clear of Politics in Mecca," www.monstersandcritics.com (December 10, 2007).

32. Curtis Lambrecht, "Burma (Myanmar)," in Greg Fealy and Virginia Hooker, eds., *Voices of Islam in Southeast Asia: A Contemporary Sourcebook* (Singapore: ISEAS, 2006), pp. 22–29; "Rohingya Solidarity Organisation," in Greg Fealy and Virginia Hooker, eds., *Voices of Islam in Southeast Asia: A Contemporary Sourcebook* (Singapore: ISEAS, 2006), pp. 266–271; Yeni, "Stateless in Arakan," *The Irrawaddy*, January 2006: 22–23.

33. John Funston, "Thailand," in Greg Fealy and Virginia Hooker, eds., *Voices of Islam in Southeast Asia: A Contemporary Sourcebook* (Singapore: ISEAS, 2006), pp. 77–88; Edward Zehner, "Muslims in Thailand: The State of the Field," unpublished paper presented to the Comparative Muslim Societies Program, Cornell University, February 2009.

34. Peter Gowing, "Moros and Khaek: The Position of Muslim Minorities in the Philippines and Thailand," in Ahmad Ibrahim et al., eds., *Readings on Islam in Southeast Asia* (Singapore: ISEAS, 1990), pp. 180–192. See also Duncan McCargo, *Tearing Apart the Land: Islam and Legitimacy in Southern Thailand* (Ithaca, NY: Cornell University Press, 2008).

35. Moshe Yegar, *Between Integration and Secession: The Muslim Communities of the Southern Philippines, Southern Thailand, and Western Burma/Myanmar* (Lanham, MD: Lexington, 2002), p. 137.

36. See Chaiwat Satha-Anand, "Spiritualising Real Estate, Commoditising Pilgrimage: The Muslim Minority in Thailand," in Joseph Camilleri and Chandra Muzzafar, eds., *Globalisation: The Perspectives and Experiences of the Religious Traditions of Asia Pacific* (Selangor, Malaysia: International Movement for a Just World, 1998), pp. 135–146. Also see for the larger context Michel Gilquin, "Musulmans et Malais de Thailande," in Michel Gilquin, ed., *Atlas des Minorites Musulmanes en Asia Meridionale et Orientale* (Paris: CNRS Editions, 2010), pp. 159–182.

37. Anonymous, "Incomes Down, Fewer Pilgrims," *Bangkok Post*, May 22, 1954, p. 10.

38. Andrew Forbes, "The Crescent in Laos," *Saudi Aramco World*, 48/3 1997: 36–39.

39. Shinzo Hayase, *Mindanao Ethnohistory beyond Nations: Maguindanao, Sangir, and Bagobo Societies in East Maritime Southeast Asia* (Quezon City, Philippines: Ateneo de Manila, 2007), pp. 16–38, 39–79. See also Solomon Kane, "Les Musulmans des Philippines," in Michel Gilquin, ed., *Atlas des Minorites Musulmanes en Asia Meridionale et Orientale* (Paris: CNRS Editions, 2010), pp. 243–262.

40. See Peter Gowing, *Muslim Filipinos: Heritage and Horizon* (Quezon City, Philippines: New Day, 1979), especially pp. 17, 60–61, 85, and 93.

41. See, for example, Kristina Gaerlan et al., eds., *Rebels, Warlord and Ulama: A Reader on Muslim Separatism and the War in the Southern Philippines* (Manila: Institute for Popular Democracy,

2000), p. 21, passim; Rosalita Tolibas-Nunez, *Muslims, Christian and the Mindanao Struggle* (Makati City, Philippines: Asian Institute of Management, 1997), p. 83; Patricio Abinales, *Making Mindanao: Cotabato and Davao in the Formation of the Philippine Nation-State* (Quezon City, Philippines: Ateneo de Manila, 2000); Samuel Tan, *Internationalization of the Bangsomoro Struggle* (Quezon City: University of the Philippines, 1995), p. 93.

42. Moshe Yegar, *Between Integration and Secession: The Muslim Communities of the Southern Philippines, Southern Thailand, and Western Burma/Myanmar* (Lanham, MD: Lexington, 2002), pp. 279, 137.

43. Nagasure Madale, "The Resurgence of Islam and Nationalism in the Philippines," in Taufik Abdullah and Sharon Siddique, eds., *Islam and Society in Southeast Asia* (Singapore: ISEAS, 1986), pp. 289, 307–310.

44. Kit Collier, "The Philippines," in Greg Fealy and Virginia Hooker, eds., *Voices of Islam in Southeast Asia: A Contemporary Sourcebook* (Singapore: ISEAS, 2006), pp. 63–70; for a primary source on this, see "Salamat Hashim" in "The Philippines," in Greg Fealy and Virginia Hooker, eds., *Voices of Islam in Southeast Asia: A Contemporary Sourcebook* (Singapore: ISEAS, 2006), pp. 264–266.

45. See Anthony Green, *Our Journey: Thirty Years of Haj Services in Singapore* (Singapore: MUIS, 2006), especially pp. 42–49, 61, 73–81, 107–108, 112–119, and 127.

46. For some of the details on programs available through MUIS, see *Majlis Ugama Islam Singapura* (MUIS) Annual Reports, 1982–1986; also useful is Laurent Metzger, "Politiques d'Integration de la Minorite Musulman de Singapour," in Michel Gilquin, ed., *Atlas des Minorites Musulmanes en Asia Meridionale et Orientale* (Paris: CNRS Editions, 2010), pp. 217–242.

47. William Collins, *The Chams of Cambodia* (Phnom Penh: Interdisciplinary Research on Ethnic Groups in Cambodia, Center for Advanced Study, 1996), p. 62, passim; see also Ben Kiernan,"Chams," *Encyclopedia of Islam*, pp. 173–180; and Emiko Stock, "Les Communautes Musulmanes du Cambodge: Un Apercu," in Michel Gilquin, ed., *Atlas des Minorites Musulmanes en Asia Meridionale et Orientale* (Paris: CNRS Editions, 2010), pp. 183–216.

48. Ben Kiernan, *How Pol Pot Came to Power* (London: Zed, 1985), pp. 382, 387–388.

49. Greg Fealy and Virginia Hooker, eds., *Voices of Islam in Southeast Asia: A Contemporary Sourcebook* (Singapore: ISEAS, 2006), p. xxvi; Anonymous, *Islam in Kampuchea* (Phnom Penh: National Council of the United Front of Kampuchea, 1987), p. 11.

50. Mohamad Zain Bin Musa, "Dynamics of Faith: Imam Musa in the Revival of Islamic Teaching in Cambodia," in Omar Farouk and Hiroyuki Yamamoto, eds., *Islam at the Margins: The Muslims of Indochina* (Kyoto: CIAS, 2008), pp. 59–69; Omar Farouk, "The Re-Organization of Islam in Cambodia and Laos," in Omar Farouk and Hiroyuki Yamamoto, eds., *Islam at the Margins: The Muslims of Indochina* (Kyoto: CIAS, 2008), pp. 70–85.

51. "Asia/Pacific—Cambodia/Laos—Islam," WorldWide Religious News (WWRN), www.wwrn.org.

52. Personal communication with Dr. Emiko Stock, April 25, 2007.

53. Philip Taylor, *Cham Muslims of the Mekong Delta: Place and Mobility in the Cosmopolitan Periphery* (Singapore: NUS Press, 2007), esp. chapters 2, 4, and 5.

54. Rie Nakamura, "Cham in Vietnam: Dynamics of Ethnicity" (PhD Thesis, Anthropology Department, University of Washington, Seattle, 1999); Trung Phu, "Bani Islam Cham in Vietnam," in Omar Farouk and Hiroyuki Yamamoto, eds., *Islam at the Margins: The Muslims of Indochina* (Kyoto: CIAS, 2008), pp. 24–33.

55. See Malte Stokhof, "The Baweans of Ho Chi Minh City," in Omar Farouk and Hiroyuki Yamamoto, eds., *Islam at the Margins: The Muslims of Indochina* (Kyoto: CIAS, 2008), pp. 34–58; Taylor, *Cham Muslims*, pp. 120–127.

56. Anonymous Hajji, Thandwe town, January 13, 2007.

57. Anonymous Hajji, Yangon, January 6, 2006.

58. Anonymous Hajja, Yangon, January 6, 2006.

59. Anonymous Hajji, Mandalay, January 6, 2007.

60. Anonymous Hajji, Mandalay, January 7, 2007.

61. Anonymous Hajji, Mandalay, January 7, 2007; Anonymous Hajji, Mandalay, January 7, 2007.

62. Anonymous Hajji, Sagaing, January 8, 2007.

63. Anonymous Hajji, Chiang Mai, January 10, 2007. This conversation was representative of several other interviews I did in Chiang Mai with Chinese Muslims.

64. Interview with Emiko Stock, Phnom Penh, October 26, 2009.

65. Interview with Anonymous Community Activist, also in Phnom Penh, October 27, 2009. Ironically, the restaurant where we met was known to everyone I spoke with as a Halal eatery, which had been set up by a successful Cham entrepreneur who had made his money in Germany.

66. The mosque pictured in the photograph here (on the Tonle Sap River on the way from Phnom Penh up to Kampong Chhnang) is the largest and most stately mosque I saw, but I counted quite a number of mosques of varying sizes, shapes, and architectures on this river and on the Mekong heading up to Kampong Cham. Clearly, there is a large and active Cham Muslim population centered on both of these rivers, despite the best efforts of the Khmer Rouge to wipe out these communities entirely in the horrors of the late 1970s.

67. Anonymous Muslim woman and her daughter in Kampong Central Market, Kampong Cham, October 27, 2009.

68. I am grateful to Emiko Stock for supplying me with this information; Alberto Perreira also was very helpful in setting up contacts and providing background knowledge. Some of these Muslim organizations in Phnom Penh include the Cambodia Muslim Development Foundation, the Cambodia Islamic Women's Development Association, the Cambodia Muslim Students Association, the Islamic Medical Association of Cambodia, and the Cham Khmer Islam Minority Human Rights and Development Association. This is by no mean an exhaustive list.

69. Anonymous Hajji, Saigon, October 24, 2009.

70. Fieldwork notes, "Mosquee Musulmane," Saigon, October 27, 2009.

71. Interview with Anonymous Hajja, Saigon, October 26, 2009. This was even true in Hanoi, where I also was able to visit the one mosque I saw in the north (a far less Muslim part of Vietnam), the Thanh Duong Jamiul Islamiyah.

72. Dr. Carmen Abubakar, professor and head of the Islamic Institute, UP-Diliman, interviewed July 28, 2004.

73. Julkipli Wadi, professor UP Diliman Islamic Center, interviewed July 28, 2004.

74. Anonymous, *Philippine Haj, 1424 [2003–2004], Basic Information*, pamphlet prepared by the Philippine Bureau of Pilgrimage and Endowment, 2004.

75. Anonymous Hajji, Manila, July 28, 2004.

11

I Was the Guest of Allah

Hajj Memoirs from Southeast Asia

I climbed further to the place where it is said the Prophet Abraham
stood before God, here too crowds of people were praying. . . . Indeed,
it was a beautiful view over the plain of Arafat, which was completely
covered by tents. I sat for a long time on the top of the hill and the
voices of men unceasingly chanted . . . .
—Harun Aminurrashid, *Chatetan ka-Tanah Suchi* (1961)

One of the more important ways that accounts of the Hajj have been transmitted is through memoirs. Few experiences have been deemed more worthy
of a written account than those activities involving a spiritual quest of one sort
or another.[1] Yet the memoir as artifact is not a record of actual events, preserved
in complete veracity with "what happened," but is, rather, a constructed narrative, with "truth passing toward art," in the words of one prominent critic.[2]
Distortion, whether intended or unconscious, is always a part of this process,
and is part and parcel of translating one's lived experiences into a format ready
to be read by other people.[3] As such, memoirs must be dissected to reveal how
such stories are generated and what their very inscription means.[4] One scholar
has noted that memoirs have their own rhythms and patterns as a genre, often
following certain themes in their quest to lay out and explain lived experience.[5]
These critical dimensions of gauging the worth of memoirs are useful and
instructive in thinking through the value of such accounts, especially in the
telling of a journey as large and as diverse as the Hajj, which allows millions
of people to undertake a voyage in many of the same ways.

This chapter discusses how Hajj memoirs can be set out, discussed, and
problematized. These memoirs nearly all come from a half-century or so (the
postindependence period in Southeast Asia), and nearly all of them were written
in Indonesian or Malay. The chapter begins by looking at Hajj memoirs crafted
earlier than this period to provide something of a limited genealogy to these
accounts. After these accounts have been examined, the notion of place (topos)

in the pilgrimage is studied, as Southeast Asian pilgrims narrate their experiences in a variety of important locales in the Hejaz. Jeddah (the disembarkation point in Arabia), Mecca, the plain of Arafat, Mina, and Medina are all briefly examined. The second half of the chapter looks at the Hajj and the self, that is to say, where the Hajji or Hajja fits into his or her conception of the Hajj based on their own provenance, whether this is geographic, occupational, or gender specific. These sorts of considerations play a large part in the narration of Hajj memoirs as well. The chapter ends with a look at the notion of introspection in the memoir, as well as the idea of the return to Southeast Asia after a successful pilgrimage has been undertaken. Throughout the chapter, there is a focus on the published memoirs of a wide variety of regional Muslims, whose autobiographical accounts constitute an impressive and understudied body of literature.

The Faded Text: Hajj Memoirs from the Preindependence Period

As has been previously shown, small numbers of Southeast Asians were making the Hajj from a very early date, and these numbers increased over the course of the centuries, until in the nineteenth century, the numbers started to reach into the thousands year after year. Yet for the premodern era before this time, the number of accounts available to be studied is even smaller than the trickle of Hajjis who were actually able to ply back and forth across the Indian Ocean on these distant maritime routes. One of the first memoirs written by an early Hajji, if it can indeed be called such, is the *Hikayat Hang Tuah*, "Tale of Hang Tuah."[6] Hang Tuah was ostensibly a subject of the Malay sultan of Melaka, and this account refers to events in the fifteenth and sixteenth centuries, though it was probably written later, in the mid-seventeenth century. Hang Tuah's construction of a pilgrimage to Mecca is mentioned in this account but only as an aside to his journey; his real destination was Rum, or what might now be called Ottoman Turkey. He undertook this long, dangerous voyage to make political contact with the Ottoman court, and to bring cannon back to the lands beneath the winds to help his sultanate fight off local military challenges, including those of the first European invaders.[7] While en route to his diplomatic mission in Rum, Hang Tuah sees Jeddah and is persuaded to drop anchor and perform Hajj. Though Hang Tuah's description of the Hajj processionals stretching from Jeddah to Mecca is opulent, his language in general on the Hajj is curt and rather muted.[8] One scholar has suggested that this was because a Malay's allegiance at the time was to be solely to his sultan, and any superfluous descriptions of other powers and allegiances—especially spiritual ones—were to be carefully avoided on shrewd political grounds.[9]

By the mid- to later eighteenth century, other Southeast Asian authors were leaving occasional memoirs touching on their activities in the Middle East while performing the Hajj. Abd al-Samad of Palembang was one of these men. A prolific Sufi author who wrote both in Arabic and in Malay, he penned a number of important tracts in Mecca in the 1780s, including a narrative of his time while on pilgrimage.[10] In the early nineteenth century, men like Syaikh Daud of Sanur were also appearing in Mecca, and they, too, left notices of their time on Hajj. Syaikh Daud implored other archipelago Muslims to come to the Hejaz to increase their religious understanding, so that their knowledge would become "sharp as a straight thorn."[11] It is clear from collections on both the Malaysian and Indonesian sides of the Straits that the art of letter writing became very important around this time as well. Formal, highly stylized letters were being sent back and forth across the Indian Ocean, often with news on a particular archipelago eminence's time while on Hajj.[12] In all of these ways, and through these various kinds of media, memoirs of the pilgrimage trickled into the consciousness of Southeast Asian Muslims, shaping perceptions of the possibilities of a journey to Arabia.

By the second half of the nineteenth century, much more rounded and fuller accounts of the Hajj as memoirs had started to appear, even if they were still comparatively few in number. The *Tuhfat al-Nafis* (or "Precious Gift") was written at this time (the 1860s, in Penyengat, Riau), and though it described earlier events, in its pages something of the sensibility of the age can be discerned. This text has been examined briefly before in chapter 3, vis-à-vis financial matters, but it bears remembering that in its pages Raja Ahmad, the son of the Bugis hero Raja Haji, performs the Hajj after voyaging to several places in Southeast Asia to raise funds for the voyage. The main thrust of his memoir, however, is less about his Hajj and more on the houses and land he buys in the Hejaz for the use of archipelago pilgrims, as well as other acts of charity he performs and then notes in his text.[13] Munshi Abdullah, writing as a Malay from the peninsula around the same time that the *Tuhfat* was penned, actually died in Mecca while completing his Hajj. His memoir, written in temporal proximity to the *Tuhfat*, bears a different *geist* altogether in its qualities as a memoir. Munshi Abdullah uses the first-person "I" in narrating his journey, one of the first to do so in all of traditional Malay literature. There is something novel and modern about his text: his allegiance is no longer unequivocally to his Malay sovereign, but rather to Allah as Supreme Being and Creator. He is now a member of the global *ummah* and less a subject of a Malay *kerajaan*, or kingdom.[14] Other Malay-language memoirs of this period start to show evidence of this change in perspective among writers, too. Around this time, the Hajj began to be seen as something that all Muslims might share, regardless of their political affiliations within the Malay world. The breakdown in the tension between a local political life and a larger, even global religious life seems to have been a hallmark of this late colonial age, at least among the memoirists from Southeast Asia's seas.[15]

This notion of "modernity" coming to Hajj memoirs as a genre is an interesting one that is given further weight as a literary phenomenon by published accounts of the 1920s. In 1925, the regent of Bandung, Raden Adipati Aria Wiranata Koe-soema, had a memoir of his pilgrimage published in the *Algemeen Dagblad de Pre-angerbode*, but there was enough interest in it that it was eventually reissued as a small book. The regent talked about his spiritual journey while on Hajj but also made careful notes about the trip by sea and about his fellow passengers; the colonial quarantine station at Kamaran; the architecture of a number of religious buildings, palaces, and libraries; and his journey through the rugged mountain interior of Yemen. Effectively a modern travel narrative, it would not be out of place in a contemporary bookstore.[16] A year later, Haji Abdul Majid, a Malay Muslim from the peninsula, published his own account of his Hajj in the *Journal of the Malay Branch of the Royal Asiatic Society* (box 11.1).[17] Majid's narrative was remarkably similar in many ways to the Javanese regent's, except that Majid came from British-controlled Malaya rather than Dutch-controlled Java. He also described his approach and entrance by sea to Jeddah, which appeared "very pretty to look at from the sea and from a distance," but which he found to be squalid and disorganized upon his disembarkation. Majid was full of admiration for his fellow pilgrims, realizing the sacrifices that many of them had made to get to the Hejaz, and he pointed out that 15 percent of his fellow Malay Hajjis died while he was there, a number in keeping with the statistics of mortality rates for the Malayan pilgrimage as a whole.[18] The Hajj as a social, religious, medical, political, and economic phenomenon was starting to be fleshed out at this time, in other words, by archipelago pilgrims who were coming from an increasing variety of places, and in ever-larger numbers. This modern idiom of reportage in the religious memoir would continue after independence.

Topos: Seeing Sacred Sites

One of the ways that modern Hajj memoirs are often organized is through the lens of visiting sites, or "place"; this emphasis on *topos* (geography) is a common organizational focus for these accounts and is repeatedly used in modern Southeast Asian narratives of a voyage to the Hejaz. Almost invariably, the first place mentioned is Jeddah, the traditional feeder port for the holy cities, histori-cally by sea but now by air. Pilgrims writing letters home in the 1970s told of long, segmented journeys from the archipelago to Jeddah, often stopping in sev-eral cities such as Medan and Colombo (Sri Lanka), before the aircraft touched down in Jeddah.[19] By the 1990s, communication was just as likely by cell phone

---

Box 11.1 **Haji Abdul Majid's "A Malay's Pilgrimage to Mecca,"** *Journal of the Malay Branch of the Royal Asiatic Society,* **4/2, 1926: 269–270, 287.**

A Malay's Pilgrimage to Mecca
By Haji Abdul Majid

As a rule, a Malay does not go on any journey, much less a perilous one like going to Mecca, in which he has to cross the seas (*melangkab laut*), without first consulting the horoscope to find out an auspicious day on which to start from his home, so as not to encounter "dangers and foes" on the way. Then he gives a feast (*kbenduri*) which, apart from prayers said thereat for his *bon voyage* and safe return, serves him also as a means to meet his friends and relatives before going away. After this, he has to get provisions ready for voyage from Singapore to Penang to Jeddah, the port of Mecca, a voyage which lasts from 13 to 17 days. He books his passage at either of the two above-mentioned Malayan ports, and this is done through the pilgrim-brokers who receive the pilgrim at the railway station on arrival, provide him with lodging all the time he is waiting for the pilgrim shop and send him with his luggage to the ship when his turn comes to sail.

The town of Jeddah is very pretty to look at from the sea at a distance, the tall buildings rising like square boxes placed on top of one another and varying in size and height in fantastic disorder. The flat roofed buildings nestle together like a lot of pigeon-lofts leaning against each other, the whole with the blue sea as a foreground and the sky with the parched Arabian desert as a background. But inside the town! The streets are dusty, dirty and narrow. None of them are straight, except one or two main ones. They are not named, nor are the houses numbered, and as they all look almost exactly alike to the newcomer, the chances are that he will lose his way if he does not take a guide when he ventures far from his lodging-house. Another thing that one can hardly fail to notice in Jeddah is the flies; they can be seen in thousands everywhere; they swarm over everything and everybody in the houses and in the shops. At night time the mosquitoes come out in their thousands! Between the flies and the mosquitoes, the tired and weary pilgrim is harassed for twenty hours during the twenty four.

---

or e-mail rather than by mail, and the flights were more likely direct and not in a trunk line.[20] Jeddah fascinated many pilgrims and continues to do so, with Hajjis and Hajjas writing in astonishment of the numbers of planes coming from all over the world, emblazoned with the logos of many countries, particularly the rich Gulf states (box 11.2).[21] One pilgrim remembered that, even in the midst of all of these impressive aircraft descending into Jeddah's airport, chaos was the

Box 11.2 **A Malay Memoir from Sarawak (Haja Maimunah Haji Daud,**
"The Haj—A Personal Experience," *Sarawak Gazette*, 119/1521, 1992: 22)

The Haj—A Personal Experience
By Hajah Maimunah Haji Daud

"...Pilgrimage thereto is a duty Men owe to God,—Those who can
afford the journey; but if any deny faith, God stands not. In need of any of
His creatures."

(Surah Al Imran: 97)

They came on beasts of burden, by dugout canoes, by boats, by ships,
cars, lorries, buses, aeroplanes and other means of conveyance, even on
foot to the Holy City of Makkah in Saudi Arabia, with one purpose—to
perform the Haj. Performing the Haj is the last of the five basic principles of
Islam (Rukun Islam yang kelima). All adult Muslims are enjoined to
perform the Haj at least once in their lifetime, on condition they are
berkuasa—financially, physically and spiritually able.

And with one voice the pilgrims cried, *Labbaika Allah umma labbaika
Lasyarika laka labbaika*...meaning "Here I am O Allah here am I in
Thy presence, there is no associate with Thee, here am I...."

On June 2, 1992, my husband and I joined other Malaysian pilgrims to
travel to the Holy Land to perform the Haj. Together we embarked the
plane from Kuala Lumpur and flew to Jeddah, the port of entry to the Holy
Land. The aircraft, a D.C. 10, carrying a full load of 380 passengers touched
down at the Jeddah International Airport on the morning of June 3.

As we disembarked, aircraft of other countries also began to empty
their passengers and we all moved to the arrival hall. Planes with logos
representing various countries particularly from the Gulf States landed and
took off at few-minute intervals, heralding the height of the Haj season.

Jeddah Airport

The airport itself was an enormous structure, a modern building, the last
word in elegance and symmetry. The roof was built like a series of tents, and
despite the multitude of people, and the high temperature at 46 degrees
Celsius the building was pleasantly airy, for one could feel the breeze
coming from the desert.

rule: large numbers of pilgrims could not read the Latin alphabet, so the arrival
and departure procedures in the King Abdulaziz airport could take a very long
time.[22] Others noted that Jeddah was not just an embarkation and disembarkation point, but interesting in its own right as well, with a number of important

historical mosques dotting the city's skyline (such as the Masjid Madinatul Juji-jaj, the Masjid bin Mahfudh, and the Masjid Shwafiyya). The fact that the city was outside the haram zone (forbidden area) meant that its cosmopolitan character was further enriched by crowds of non-Muslims who lived and worked there or otherwise made the city function through commerce or through the service industries, often in conjunction with the Hajj.[23]

Although Jeddah is the near-universal arrival point for pilgrims, Mecca is the place all of these global religious travelers are hoping to reach. In most memoirs, Mecca looms as the main geographical goal of the Hajj. The chaos of the city is palpable in these narratives, as a huge ribbon of humanity winds its way from Jeddah on the coast into the furnace interior of the Arabian Desert. Mecca finally appears almost as a mirage. The very old religious buildings, mixed in with newer buildings (mostly constructed of the same sand color to maintain a kind of archi-tectural uniformity), give Mecca a very different flavor from its littoral cousin on the Red Sea shore.[24] The crowd conditions are intense, not just at the religious sites but also in the markets and the streets. People constantly call out to the pil-grims "Hajji!" "Hajji!" and try to sell small amounts of fruit, cooked meat, or merchandise, often through a mixture of sign language, gestures, and phrases of Arabic and Malay.[25] These congested conditions also make Mecca somewhat dangerous for fire hazards, as has been commented upon regularly by a number of memoirists.[26] The accounts also tell of finding tiny places of silence in the city to pray, whether in the great mosques or elsewhere, and of the helping hands of strangers leading one slowly to the correct places for this, when so many people are all trying to get to required stations to perform their religious duties all at the same time.[27] The phrase "I was swimming in an ocean of humanity" in Mecca is used again and again to describe the shock of so many pilgrims entering the city during the Hajj season. Yet it seems this designation is not entirely a negative attribute, at least to many of the people who cross huge expanses of the globe to get to the Hejaz to perform their pilgrimages.[28]

From Mecca, the pilgrims eventually make their way out onto the plain of Arafat. Arafat is laced with memory for the pilgrim in his or her writing: this is where Abraham and Hagar and Isma'il walked; this is where the tears, trials, and tribulations of the ancients can still be felt.[29] The plain of Arafat has been described in some of these memoirs as a city without buildings. Rather, it is a city of tents, all of them white, looking like so many sails of stationary dhows beached in neat rows in the desert.[30] On Arafat, it can reach 130 degrees Fahrenheit in the height of the day in direct sunlight, which is simply too hot for humans to withstand for more than a few minutes at a time.[31] With pilgrims overnighting in Muzdalifah nearby, moving between this kind of heat and real cold in the middle of the night can be a serious health risk.[32] The Hajjis and Hajjas are in *ihram*, clad only in a simple white cloth garment, which the dictates of the pilgrimage require to ensure a state of nondistinction before God. The white cloth is of little use on Arafat against the blazing sun or against the evening cold. Yet it is precisely because of this isolation in the desert, coupled with the chaos of the exact opposite of this "aloneness," with millions of coreligionists all experiencing the same things together on that plain of hardscrabble rock, that the intensity of Arafat is written about so prominently in these memoirs. "My thoughts were only on Allah," writes one pilgrim, "there was a direct connection between us."[33] Authors of such narratives say again and again that it is very difficult to feel this way anywhere else, a kind of spiritual charge that is apparent on Arafat alone.

Arafat leads to Mina. There, the stone pillars are set, which every pilgrim must stone with small rocks to symbolize the casting out of the devil. This act is described somewhat matter-of-factly in a number of memoirs, yet video footage of the Hajj shows that this *topos* is actually fraught with an intense energy, as large crowds of pilgrims try to get close enough to the pillars to throw their stones while other pilgrims are simultaneously trying to leave.[34] Though Arafat and Mina are mostly flat and have been described as being part and parcel of a large plain with a number of very broad and well-constructed roads (the Nazca lines in Peru are evoked in some of these descriptions, interestingly enough), the bottleneck conditions of this station of the Hajj have caused serious problems in the past.[35] Best known, perhaps, was the immense crush of bodies and the ensuing panic and stampede that occurred in 1990, when 1,426 pilgrims lost their lives at Mina. In a number of memoirs, these events have been described in painstaking detail, including by eyewitnesses who saw breathing space just adjacent to the fenced avenues, had pilgrims been able to climb the barriers.[36] Other memoirs mention the tragedy as a rumor that whipped through the assembling crowds, though abjuring pilgrims were witness to pockets of weeping Hajjis and Hajjas who had just heard the news.[37] The Saudi state intervened soon after this and rebuilt sections of the Mina site, all in an effort to ensure that such a tragedy would never occur again. Yet the events had already entered into memory, and memoirs of pilgrims who were there are one of the best ways to get at the actual particularities on the ground of what actually happened. This was especially so as state explanations of how the disaster happened were rarely convincing, and a number of officials tried to dissociate themselves and their respective bureaus from responsibility for what had occurred.

The last important *topos* of the pilgrimage is Medina, the Prophet's city, which is situated at some distance from most of the other holy sites that together collectively make up the stations of the Hajj. Many Southeast Asian memoirists talk about the candescent stretch of desert that must be crossed to get to Medina— the desert here is not necessarily hotter than what has already been traversed, but the distances are longer, and pilgrims are tired from their journeys. One writer spoke of this terrain as being "true" desert and completely barren; "it is not beautiful like our own environment in the archipelago—no green, trees, or rivers, there is only blasted earth. But you feel very small here against nature; you have a sense of your place in the universe."[38] Many cars and buses, in fact, break down on the road to Medina, so that there is a kind of topography of failed vehicles on the roads leading into the city.[39] Once inside, the sense of chaos and confusion reigning there is apparent, as many narrators stress in their accounts. Things seem noticeably less coordinated than in Mecca; it is almost as if the pilgrimage officials and even the state itself are exhausted from having to deal with so many millions of Hajjis.[40] Street culture rules the city. Most buying and selling, and, indeed, almost all transactions generally, take place between cart vendors and pedestrians, a steady stream of humanity coming toward the end of their travels.[41] There are still mosques to be visited and still prayers to be intoned, but the chaos of everyday life begins to course through the crowds again. Medina in these narratives almost exudes a sense of relief: it is not the end of the journey, but the horizon line toward return is visible from here. Mecca will be entered again by most pilgrims and Jeddah almost certainly, but in Medina the sense of the spiritual *topos* being visited for the first time begins to come to an end. Medina, at least as far as Southeast Asian Hajj memoirs are concerned, feels like the tower on the hill that one must ascend before returning to one's own individual life.

The Hajj and the Self

These places figure prominently in Southeast Asian memoirs of the pilgrimage, but the Hajj is an inner journey, too, irrespective of which sites are being visited by an individual traveler. It is a noticeable feature of these memoirs that identity is given a prominent place in discussing one's pilgrimage, whether this is identity defined in terms of gender, occupation, or other self-representations.[42] One of the most common and important of these signifiers is geographical provenance—the pilgrim from X on Hajj. Many of these accounts seem to intentionally play up the provenance of the author Hajji, probably as an attempt to connect him or her to an audience of fellow pilgrims who either have already made Hajj or are likely to in the future. In lines somewhat akin to Benedict Anderson's "print capitalism" rationale, there may be an economic rationale, too, in that the publishing industry seems to have wagered that potential Hajjis are often likely to buy accounts of other pilgrims they see as locals, that is to say, "much like me or us."[43] Thus we get pilgrims such as Haji Danarto discussing the Hajj "from the perspective of a Javanese," as the author says in his foreword. Other Indonesians know immediately that Javanese are supposed to be inclined toward mysticism, so this self-identification means something in terms of the kind of Hajj one is expecting.[44] By contrast, a Sundanese account (West Javanese, as opposed to Central or Eastern Javanese) is cartoonish by comparison: on the cover of M. S. Maman's memoir, the author is sketched in lampooned lines but acting as a tour guide, with his hands raised and an overwide smile on his face (figure 11.1).[45] A Batak account (North Sumatra) is different again; Batak are stereotyped as *kasar* ("coarse") and blunt, and the jacket copy even tells the reader to expect a different approach to Hajj here: "What happens when a Batak goes on Hajj? This is different from a Javanese, with the emphasis there on esoteric and mystical experience."[46] These are only Indonesian examples. One can read through the literature on these memoirs and notice variances from Singapore to Brunei to Sarawak, each author claiming a different brand of religious experience based on his own geographic roots.[47]

Another important construct of the Hajj and the self concerns occupation, with one's job helping to define what kind of pilgrimage the traveler will have as a truth seeker in the Holy Land. As with geographic provenances, much is made in the memoir literature about one's occupation in life affecting very much the kind of Hajj one will have in the Hejaz. Some of these accounts are fairly prosaic, for example, by doctors paying special attention to medical matters in their pilgrimage narratives, such as the physical well-being of pilgrims and sanitary

Figure 11.1 Sundanese and Batak Pilgrimage Memoirs.
Credit: M. S. Maman, *Orang Sunda Munggah Haji* (Bandung, Indonesia: Penerbit Kiblat, 2004); and Baharuddin Aritonang, *Orang Batak Naik Haji* (Jakarta: Gramedia, 1997).

conditions.[48] Other such accounts are anything but prosaic, however. Rock stars, film actors, imams of prestigious (and sometimes very unpretentious) madrasas or mosques, artists, novelists, government officials, and even football coaches and players have all published accounts.[49] They describe the Hajj from their point of view, often mentioning special aspects of their journeys that touch on their experiences as specialists.

Politicians and royalty are no different: the Sultan of Brunei, one of the world's richest men, had a glossy memoir book made up out of his visit to the holy cities, replete with numerous photographs of him both in repose and having his hands shaken (and sniffed, in Southeast Asian custom) by a bevy of well-wishers.[50] The former dictator of Indonesia, Suharto, did the same, though his memoir book (befitting his Javanese roots, perhaps) was careful to depict him as pious and quiet while on his Hajj, as befitting an elected president.[51] The extensive coverage of Suharto's Hajj indicated that he was consciously trying to use his pilgrimage to show his religiosity to various wings of organized Islam in his country (figure 11.2). Famous politicians (and those aspiring to be famous) have followed suit, such as Amien Rais.[52] The media are a playground for Hajjis, conspicuously showing piety for those who wish to get this message across and occasionally deriding the piety of other Hajjis who are seen to be "convenient pilgrims." Even housewives have a subrubric of this well-established market, with a number of titles on "A Housewife Makes the Hajj" available both in libraries and in local bookstores in the region.[53] This last subcategory of memoirs is especially important because women from Southeast Asia are increasingly making the pilgrimage, and there is a huge and ever-expanding market on how to cater to their needs while on Hajj, as well as how to prepare them for the journey.

Gender—and not just in the form of "housewives on Hajj"—makes a strong appearance in many Southeast Asian memoirs (figure 11.3). This is true from places like Malaysia, where women can often be integrated into the tales pilgrims tell about their time in Arabia, but it is particularly true in Indonesia, where women have a higher social standing than in many other places in the Muslim world.[54] Women's concerns make up a small but growing percentage of this literature. Some women—even wealthy ones, such as the TV and film star Ida Leman—have talked about the initial conversations that took place to convince their husbands that a pilgrimage to faraway Arabia should be undertaken.[55] Other women have talked at length about very prosaic matters, such as bringing panty liners to the Hejaz to cope with menstruation and praying for the health of loved ones, particularly those in distress, as part of their journeys.[56] A number of accounts even talk about babies being born in the holy cities to pilgrims, a great blessing if it happens, but an enormous matter to arrange so far from home, and likely in a foreign language.[57] There is often a didactic tone in many of these gendered memoirs as well, as women tell other women what to expect, what to do,

Figure 11.2 The Hajj Memoir of President Suharto.
Credit: Anonymous, *Perjalanan Ibadah Haji Pak Harto* (Jakarta: Departemen Agama, 1993), cover photo.

and what not to do (for example, with regard to the correct wearing of *ihram* or prohibitions against perfume, anointing hair or cutting nails, and talk of sexual activities).[58] A number of accounts by women also deal with the emotional issues of the Hajj, and in this, they are little different than male-authored accounts, except that "heroines of Islam" (such as Hagar) have a more prominent place in female narratives than in male ones.[59] Statements by the well-known female singer Camelia Malik about her breaking into tears upon arrival in the Hejaz

Umrah Keluarga Bersama NooR & Ratih Sang

Paket dikemas khusus untuk pembaca NooR yang Yakin Cerdas & Bergaya, didampingi oleh Ratih Sanggarwati. Insya Allah selain ibadah di kedua Masjid Suci ada ziarah ke tempat yang menarik, siraman rohani oleh ustadz dari Madinah & Makkah serta silaturahim dengan para jama'ah dari negara lain.

HOTEL	
Madinah	Anwar Al Madinah Movenpick
Makkah	Sofitel Makkah Hotel
Jeddah	Jeddah Ka'ki Hotel

TRANSPORTASI		BIAYA	
Jakarta - Madinah	Pesawat SV Ekonomi Class	Double	USD. 1.350
		Triple	USD. 1.300
Madinah - Makkah	Bus Ac	Quadr	USD. 1.250

Harga Belum Termasuk Handling Fee, Fiskal, Airport Tax, Rp. 1. 450.000 / orang

NO	HARI	MASEHI 2005	HIJRIAH 1425 H	PROGRAM	KETERANGAN
1	Senin	04 Juli	27 Jumadil Awal	Jakarta - Madinah	Saudia/Garuda
2	Selasa	05 Juli	28 Jumadil Awal	Madinah	Ziarah Islami & Taushiah
3	Rabu	06 Juli	29 Jumadil Awal	Madinah	Ziarah Wisata & Taushiah
4	Kamis	07 Juli	30 Jumadil Awal	Madinah - Makkah	Ziarah Wada' -Bus AC- Umrah
5	Jum'at	08 Juli	01 Jumadil Akhir	Makkah	Sholat Jum'at di Masjidil Haram
6	Sabtu	09 Juli	02 Jumadil Akhir	Makkah	Ziarah dilanjutkan Umrah Kedua
7	Minggu	10 Juli	03 Jumadil Akhir	Makkah - Jeddah	Thawaf Wada' & Wisata Jeddah
8	Senin	11 Juli	04 Jumadil Akhir	Jeddah - Jakarta	Saudia/Garuda
9	Selasa	12 Juli	05 Jumadil Akhir	Jakarta	Tiba di Bandara Soekarno Hatta

Islami Menyajikan

Raihlah kesempatan 1 (Satu) Umroh Gratis setiap 6 bulan sekali, bagi Anda yang berlangganan selama 1 (Satu) tahun.

Cukup dengan Rp 62.400,00 (Jabotabek), Rp 102.400,00 (Luar Jabotabek), dan Rp 111.500,00 (Luar Jawa). Anda sudah bisa berlangganan Tabloid HAJI Indonesia selama 1 tahun (12 Edisi Reguler + 1 Edisi Khusus).

Informasi Haji, Umroh dan Gaya Hidup Islami
Hadir tiap bulan.

Berlangganan:
Bintaro River Park GH-3 No. 9 Bintaro Sektor 8, Jakarta, Telp (021) 745-6318, Fax (021) 7456343.

Pemasangan Iklan:
Gd. IBA Lt. 5, Jl. Raya Pasar Minggu No. 2 B-C, Pancoran, Jakarta 12780 Telp (021) 797-2581, Fax (021) 797-2317

NOOR Februari, 2005 ▓ 112

Figure 11.3 The Gendered Hajj in Modern Indonesia, February–May 2005.
Credit: Majalah Noor, May and February 2005, pp. 99, 112.

could just as easily have been penned by a man, given the circumstances and the context of the narrative.[60]

This element of introspection forms a crucial component of the memoir; it is the kernel in some ways of the connection between the Hajj and the self. The pilgrimage is a time for gaining inner knowledge—though provenance, occupation, and gender are all important in crafting these narratives, at the height of the spiritual awakening of the Hajj, one is alone with God and with one's own self in battling one's ego and inner demons.[61] The authors of Hajj memoirs deal with this "silence within" rather differently. The dreamlike state of the Hajj is constantly evoked in many memoirs, for example.[62] Narrating the journey as a dream allows it to be reachable again at other points in one's life, since sleep is always with us, and memory comes to us in sleep on a regular basis, usually in the form of dreams. Yet another and somewhat altered method of dealing with this vast silence of the time for introspection during the time of the Hajj has been to weave one's life with death—the great space before and after one's time on earth. Death is ever present in Southeast Asian Hajj memoirs: it appears with an uncanny regularity in scores upon scores of published accounts. Central here is the question that Yusuf Hasyim, an "average" Hajji, asked himself in his own memoir: "Is this the end of my life?"[63] Or as H. Ismail Saleh said in his own account, "Is there a reply after death?"[64] Modern lives are so cluttered and frantic and busy that having the time to merely sit and think in silence for several weeks (even with millions of our coreligionists surrounding us) is beyond life or death. It is precious. It is introspection of the sort that we may only hope to achieve once in our adult lives. And the Hajj gives this gift.

Then there is the return. By the time most Hajjis are ready to depart the Hejaz to come back to Southeast Asia, these moments of introspection (penned so emotionally and often so beautifully in memoirs) are long over. This is palpable in the majority of these accounts. The holy cities have been left behind; Southeast Asia and home beckon over the horizon, with all of the complications of a return to day-to-day life this implies. The airport in Jeddah is the last reality of this journey. Memoirists often talk about the difficult conditions of embarkation from the Hejaz: the wait for planes that always seem to be hours late, made longer still by waiting behind other late-arriving aircraft.[65] Ferocious lines are de rigueur, many of which are constantly being cut and recut by pilgrims who got in the wrong line to begin with, hearing Indonesian being spoken in one queue, though that plane was en route to Surabaya, say, and not Jakarta.[66] There are inevitably problems with luggage and with visas, as well as with the immigration authorities more generally: a huge phalanx of officialdom that must be negotiated, whether it is the pilgrim or his or her belongings that are being scrutinized before being let out of Saudi Arabia's desert kingdom.[67] It is not all bad. In what may perhaps be a backhanded compliment, one pilgrim described the conditions that enfold all of this chaos: "I felt like I was in a dream when I was leaving from the King Abdul Aziz Airport in Jeddah: luxury goods everywhere, and spotless clean; clean, crisp air-conditioning—it felt like Changi Airport in Singapore."[68] Yet it is clear that by this time the pilgrim's thoughts seem to be on other things.

The moment has passed, though it lingers in the consciousness; for the memoir, though, departure is a time for "coming back to this world," not remaining in the special one that the pilgrim has been inhabiting for the past few weeks. Only one modern memoir I read dwelled philosophically on this moment, holding onto a kind of lassitude: Emo Kastama described a "romantic return to *tanah air*" ("our land and water," that is, the archipelago). As the Red Sea fell beneath his airplane, he mused that this body of water astride the desert was "strange and mysterious, and full of secrets."[69]

Conclusion

Memoirs—of the Hajj or any other time or experience of one's life—are important social documents that narrate many things, some of them intended and some not. They are discourses in the fullest sense of the term: dialogues between the self and an intended audience, with all of the friction that such a meeting of viewpoints potentially implies.[70] One scholar has argued that memoirs allow the self to be put forward as a metaphor for other things, essentially for processes that concern the individual, but that are seen through the individual's lived experience as a human being on a journey in this life.[71] Although all memoirs may have this underlying characteristic in common, the many forms and formats of this genre allow the self to be conveyed in a number of different ways.[72] What is one person's value in telling the story of one's own life? How are memoirists set apart, or made special? When are they just part of a larger crowd's concerns, as when millions of people perform a journey such as the Hajj all at the same time, year after year after year?[73] The presentation of the self in such circumstances tells us much about the pilgrim as an individual human being, but in viewing larger patterns in the vast corpus of such memoirs, the role of culture and social norms also becomes clear in the genre.[74] The passage of time and memory itself both change in memoirs, but they both can be used, constructed, and played with in well-worn channels of written exegesis, too.[75]

The Southeast Asian Hajj memoirs discussed here reveal these processes in interesting ways. Narratives of the pilgrimage from this part of the world stretch back hundreds of years. Rare Jawi and Rumi texts began to give way to printed accounts in the mid-nineteenth century, but only after independence in the mid-twentieth century do large numbers of these narratives begin to appear. Print capitalism and the condensation of regional languages into discrete markets ensured that there were such accounts, both as pieces of emotional literature and as valuable how-to guides for subsequent pilgrims. The holy sites of the Hejaz were laid open to inspection by those yet to make the trip, and successful Hajjis and Hajjas were able to keep a record of the fulfillment of their religious duties as Muslims. Yet the self is always evident in these accounts as well, not just the narrative of a particular time (the pilgrimage season) and a particular place (the Arabian Peninsula). Pilgrims undertook this journey as doctors, housewives, imams, and heads of state; they also undertook it as denizens of Brunei, West Java, the Batak districts of Sumatra, and Singapore.[76] They traveled as Chinese converts and as Bumiputras, as women and as men. In their collectivity, these memoirs show something of the Hajj as an individual quest, but also certain lines of culture that seem to pervade their writing as a corporate enterprise of coreligionists. It is this complexity that makes them so fascinating to study as artifacts of Muslim life.

NOTES

1. Richard Hutch, *The Meaning of Lives: Biography, Autobiography and the Spiritual Quest* (London: Cassell, 1997). In Southeast Asia specifically, see William Roff, *Autobiography and Biography in Malay Historical Studies* (Singapore: ISEAS, 1972); for a discussion of the "uses of history" in this part of the world, see Jeffrey Hadler, "A Historiography of Violence and the Secular State in Indonesia: Tuanku Imam Bondjol and the Uses of History," *JAS*, 67/3, 2008: 971–1010. See also Franz Rosenthal, *History and Muslim Historiography* (Leiden: Brill, 1968).

2. Judith Barrington, *Writing the Memoir from Truth to Art* (Portland, OR: Eighth Mountain, 1997).

3. Jill Conway,*When Memory Speaks: Reflections on Autobiography* (New York: Knopf, 1998).

4. Francis Hart, "Notes for an Anatomy of Modern Autobiography," *New Literary History*, 1/3 (1970): 485–511.

5. Ian Fletcher, "Rhythm and Pattern in Autobiographies," in *An Honored Guest: New Essays on W. B. Yeats*, ed. by Denis Donoghue and J. R. Mulryne (New York: St. Martins Press, 1966).

6. See Kassim Ahmad, *Hikayat Hang Tuah* (Kuala Lumpur: Yayasan Karyawan dan Dewan Bahasa dan Pustaka, 1997).

7. Vladimir Braginsky, *The Heritage of Traditional Malay Literature* (Leiden: KITLV, 2004), pp. 284, 467.

8. Indeed, Henri Chambert-Loir has expressed surprise at how little is mentioned; see his "L'espere politique dans le Hikayat Hang Tuah," in D. Lombard and R. Ptak, eds., *Asia Maritima Images et Realites, 1200–1800* (Wiesbaden: Harrassowitz Verlag, 1994), pp. 41–61.

9. Shelly Errington, "A Study of Genre: Meaning and Form in the Malay Hikayat Hang Tuah" (PhD Thesis, Cornell University, 1975), p. 159.

10. Braginsky, *Heritage of Traditional Malay Literature*, p. 653. See also G. W. J. Drewes (ed., trans.), *Directions for Travelers on the Mystic Path* (The Hague: Martinus and Nijhoff, 1977), pp. 222–224.

11. Drewes, *Directions*, p. 229.

12. Annabel Teh Gallop, *Golden Letters: Writing Traditions of Indonesia* (London: British Library, 1993); and Annabel Teh Gallop, *The Legacy of the Malay Letter* (London: British Library, 1994).

13. See Virginia Matheson and Barbara Watson Andaya, eds., *The Precious Gift (Tuhfat al-Nafis)* (Kuala Lumpur: Oxford University Press, 1982).

14. V. Matheson and A. C. Milner, *Perceptions of the Haj: Five Malay Texts* (Singapore: ISEAS, 1984), pp. 21–23; also A. H. Hill, *Hikayat Abdullah: An Annotated Translation* (Kuala Lumpur: Oxford University Press, 1970); and Raimy Che Ross, "Munshi Abdullah's Voyage to Mecca: A Preliminary Introduction and Annotated Translation," *Indonesia and the Malay World*, 28/81, 2000: 173–212.

15. See, for example, *Syair Mekah Madinah* (Singapore: Tuan Syaikh Haji Muhammad Ali b. Haji Mustafa bala(d) Berbalingga Makam Cahaya, Lorong Masjid, Kampung Gelam, 1869); *Syair Mekah Madinah; Syair Mekah Syair Madinah* (Singapore: Tuan Haji Muhammad Nuh b. Haji Ismail ahl al-Jawi bil(d) Juwana namanya tempat Dusun Kajian, 1873); *Syair Mekah Madinah Jiddah Araafat dan Sekalian Tanah Arab dan Menyatakan Peri Hal Ihwal Orang yang Pergi Haj dan Keelokan* (Singapore: Ofis Cap Haji Sirat, 1885); *Syair Makkah al-Musyarrafah Madinah al-Munawwarat* (Singapore: Publisher Ibrahim, Kampung Gelam, 1886); *Syair Negeri Makkah al-Musyarrafah dan Madinah al-Munawwarat; Syair Macam Baru peri menyatakan Orang yang Pergi Haj dari Negeri Bawah Angin sampai kepada Negeri Atas Angin seperti Jiddah dan Mekah dan Madinah dan seperti lain-lainnya* (Singapore: Tuan Haji Muhammad Taib, 1888); and *Syair Negeri Makkah al-Musyarrafah dan Madinah al-Munawwarat* (Singapore: Haji Muhammad Sidik, 1889).

16. G. A. van Bovene, *Mijne Reis Naar Mekka: Naar het Dagboek van den Regent van Bandoeng Raden Adipati Aria Wirantakoesoema* (self-published? 1925). This may at least partially be the result of his writing this memoir in Dutch and thus trying to adhere to established genres.

17. The readership for both of these journals on either side of the Straits would have been almost entirely colonial in European nature.

18. Haji Abdul Majid, "A Malay's Pilgrimage to Mecca," *JMBRAS*, 4/2, 1926: 269–270, 287.

19. A. Hasjmy, *Surat Surat dari Tanah Suci* (Jakarta: Penerbit Bulan Bintang, 1979), p. 9.

20. R. M. H. Subanindyo Hadiluwih, *Ibadah Haji: Perjalanan Spiritual 40 Hari* (Medan, Indonesia: Penerbit Dhian-Doddy, 1990), p. 9.

21. Haja Maimunah Haji Daud, "The Haj—A Personal Experience," *Sarawak Gazette*, 119/1521, 1992: 22.

22. Fuad Hassan, *Pengdaman Seorang Haji* (Perlawatan ke Haramain) (Jakarta: Bulan Bintang, 1975), p. 41.

23. A. Roham, *Abujamin, Aku Pergi Haji* (Jakarta: Media Da'wah, 1992), p. 63.

24. A. A. Navis, *Surat dan Kenangan Haji* (Jakarta: Penerbit PT Gramedia Pustaka Utama, 1994), p. 62.

25. Hadiluwih, *Ibadah Haji*, p. 40.

26. H. Azkarmin Zaini, *Pengalaman Haji di Tanah Suci: Sebuah Reportase Lengkap tentang Menunaikan Ibadah Haji* (Jakarta: P. T. Gramedia, 1975), pp. 75, 81.

27. Mohamad Sobary, *Tamu Allah* (Jakarta: Pustaka Firdaus, 1996), p. 39; H. A. Gozali Katianda, "Tiba-tiba Tangan Saya Ada yang Membimbing," in E. Syarief Nurdin and E. Kosasih, *100 Keajaiban di Tanah Suci Pengalaman Unik Jamaah Haji* (Bandung, Indonesia: Pustaka Hidayah, 1996), pp. 67–68.

28. K. H. A. Mustofa Bisri, "Saya Merasa Diwelehke Tuhan," in Anonymous, *Haji Sebuah Perjalanan Air Mata* (Yogyakarta, Indonesia: Bentang, 1993), p. 135.

29. Navis, *Surat dan Kenangan Haji*, pp. 132–135.

30. Hasjmy, *Surat Surat Dari Tanah Suci*, p. 185.

31. Ismail Saleh, *Pengalaman Sebagai Amirul Haji* (Jakarta: Pustaka Kartini, 1990), p. 92.

32. Ir. H. Avicenia Darwis, *40 Hari Mencari Cinta: Kisah Nyata Berhaji di Tanah Suci* (Bogor, Indonesia: Ar-Rahmah, 2005), p. 151.

33. Drg. H. Ircham Machfudz, "Saya Menangis, Nikmat Sekali," in Anonymous, *Haji Sebuah Perjalanan Air Mata* (Yogyakarta, Indonesia: Bentang, 1993), p. 105.

34. Roham, *Abujamin, Aku Pergi Haji*, pp. 141–145.

35. Saleh, *Pengalaman Sebagai Amirul Hajj*, pp. 140–141.

36. Hadiluwih, *Ibadah Haji*, pp. 59–89.

37. Hj. Sri. Sumarni, "Bayangan Putih di Balik Tragedi Mina," in E. Syarief Nurdin and E. Kosasih, *100 Keajaiban di Tanah Suci Pengalaman Unik Jamaah Haji* (Bandung, Indonesia: Pustaka Hidayah, 1996), pp. 189–190.

38. Hassan, *Genglalaman Seorang Haji*, p. 41.

39. H. Sukarsono, *Liku-Liku Perjalanan ke Tanah Suci* (Jakarta: P. T. Pranadaya, 1975), p. 207.

40. Dra. Hj. Tuty Aliwiyah, "Saya Ketemu Yasser Arafat," in Anonymous, *Haji, Sebuah Perjalanan Air Mata* (Yogyakarta, Indonesia: Bentang, 1993), pp. 214–219.

41. Hendra Esmara, *Aku Datang Memenuhi Panggilanmu Ya, Allah* (Jakarta: Penerbit PT Gramdeia, 1993), p. 61.

42. On this notion, see also C. W. Watson, *Of Self and Nation: Autobiography and the Representation of Modern Indonesia* (Honolulu: University of Hawai'i Press, 2000).

43. Benedict Anderson, *Imagined Communities: Reflections on the Origin and Spread of Nationalism* (London: Verso, 1983).

44. Danarto, *Catatan Perjalanan Haji Danarto, Orang Jawa Naik Haji* (Pengantar Taufiq Ismail) (Jakarta: Penerbit PT Grafiti, 1984), p. v.

45. M. S. Maman, *Orang Sunda Munggah Haji* (Bandung, Indonesia: Penerbit Kiblat, 2004).

46. Baharuddin Aritonang, *Orang Batak Naik Haji* (Jakarta: Gramedia, 1997).

47. Anthony Green, *Our Journey: Thirty Years of Haj Services in Singapore* (Singapore: Majlis Ugama Islam Singapura, 2006); Anonymous, *Al-Mu'min Menjadi Tetamu Allah* (Bandar Seri Begawan, Brunei: Jabatan Pusat Sejarah Kementerian Kebudayaan, 1995); Haja Maimunah Haji Daud, "The Haj," pp. 22–29. For an interesting variation on this theme, see H. M. Jusuf Hamka, *Engkoh Bun Naik Haji* (Jakarta: Penerbit Pustaka Panjimas, 1985). In this case, the Hajj narrative is written by a Chinese convert to Islam from Indonesia. Engkoh Bun (as the pilgrim is called) is shown riding a camel on the cover of this book, clad in *ihram*, but distinctly Chinese, nonetheless, in his appearance. By picturing him on the cover of the book in this way, the publishers seem to be saying that anyone can enter the *ummah* if they take the dictates of the religion seriously—and they can even go on Hajj, the most strenuous of the five pillars of Islam.

48. Ahmad Ramali, *Perdjalanan Hadji: Naik Hadji dan Hubungan sebagai Dokter Djemaah Hadji* (Jakarta: Tintomas, 1969); H. Karkono Kamajaya, "Tidak Awur-awuran Atau Asal Haji-hajian," in Anonymous, *Haji Sebuah Perjalanan Air Mata* (Yogyakarta, Indonesia: Bentang, 1993), pp. 111–117.

49. See, for example, Didi Petet, "Allah Sekana Mengundang Saya ke Makah Setiap Tahun," in Anonymous, *Haji Sebuah Perjalanan Air Mata* (Yogyakarta, Indonesia: Bentang, 1993), pp. 87–93; H. S. Benyamin, "Kepasrahan," in E. Syarief Nurdin and E. Kosasih, *100 Keajaiban di Tanah Suci Pengalaman Unik Jamaah Haji* (Bandung, Indonesia: Pustaka Hidayah, 1996), pp. 34–35; K. H. A. Latif Muchtar, "Haji, Bukan Ibadah Puncak," in Anonymous, *Haji Sebuah Perjalanan Air Mata* (Yogyakarta, Indonesia: Bentang, 1993), pp. 130–133; H. Widayat, "Saya Bertemu Malaikat," in Anonymous, *Haji Sebuah Perjalanan Air Mata* (Yogyakarta, Indonesia: Bentang, 1993), pp. 225–231; H. Gazali Dunia, "Hanya GB pounds 60," in E. Syarief Nurdin and E. Kosasih, *100 Keajaiban di Tanah Suci Pengalaman Unik Jamaah Haji* (Bandung, Indonesia: Pustaka Hidayah, 1996), pp. 183–184; H. Johnny Wong, "Ingin Seperti Presiden," in E. Syarief Nurdin and E. Kosasih, *100 Keajaiban di Tanah Suci Pengalaman Unik Jamaah Haji* (Bandung, Indonesia: Pustaka Hidayah, 1996), pp. 45–46.

50. Anonymous, *As Guest of Allah: With Members of the Brunei Royal Family, a Memoir* (Bandar Seri Begawan: Brunei History Centre, 1999).

51. Anonymous, *Perjalanan Ibadah Haji Pak Harto* (Jakarta: Departemen Agama, 1993).

52. Amien Rais, "Saya Mina Keturunan, Dikabulkan Allah," in Anonymous, *Haji Sebuah Perjalanan Air Mata* (Yogyakarta, Indonesia: Bentang, 1993), pp. 30–37; H. Ismail Saleh, "Balasan Setelah Mati," in E. Syarief Nurdin and E. Kosasih, *100 Keajaiban di Tanah Suci Pengalaman Unik Jamaah Haji* (Bandung, Indonesia: Pustaka Hidayah, 1996), pp. 114–115; Mayjen (Purn.) H. Basofi Sudirman, "Semuanya Merupakan Paket," in Anonymous, *Haji Sebuah Perjalanan Air Mata* (Yogyakarta, Indonesia: Bentang, 1993), pp. 64–72.

53. Hajja Saida Cholifah, *Ibu Rumah Tangga Naik Haji* (Yogyakarta, Indonesia: Pustaka Marwa, 2006), p. 25.

54. Haji Mazlan Nasron, *Air Mata: Di Pintu Baitullah* (Kuala Lumpur: Progressive, 2002), pp. 83, 116.

55. Ida Leman, "Allah Mengundang Hajiku dengan Tiba-tiba," in Anonymous, *Haji Sebuah Perjalanan Air Mata* (Yogyakarta, Indonesia: Bentang, 1993), pp. 94–95.

56. Cholifah, *Ibu Rumah Tangga*, p. 25; H. Arifin C. Noer, "Tuhan Menidurkan Saya," in E. Syarief Nurdin and E. Kosasih, *100 Keajaiban di Tanah Suci Pengalaman Unik Jamaah Haji* (Bandung, Indonesia: Pustaka Hidayah, 1996), pp. 63–64.

57. H. A. Jutin, *712 Mudjahid Gambela Jang Menggemparkan* (Malang, Indonesia: Penerbit UB Milan, n.d.).

58. Haja Maimunah Haji Daud, "The Haj," pp. 22–29.

59. Hajja Eva Arnaz, "Tangan Besar yang Menyelamatkan Jiwaku," in E. Syarief Nurdin and E. Kosasih, *100 Keajaiban di Tanah Suci Pengalaman Unik Jamaah Haji* (Bandung, Indonesia: Pustaka Hidayah, 1996), pp. 35–36.

60. Camelia Malik, "Ada yang Menakut-nakuti Saya," in Anonymous, *Haji Sebuah Perjalanan Air Mata* (Yogyakarta, Indonesia: Bentang, 1993), p. 83.

61. H. A. A. Navis, "Penampilan Ego yang Tak Bertuah," in E. Syarief Nurdin and E. Kosasih, *100 Keajaiban di Tanah Suci Pengalaman Unik Jamaah Haji* (Bandung, Indonesia: Pustaka Hidayah, 1996, pp. 92–93.

62. H. Arifin C. Noer, "Tuhan Menidurkan Saya," in E. Syarief Nurdin and E. Kosasih, *100 Keajaiban di Tanah Suci Pengalaman Unik Jamaah Haji* (Bandung, Indonesia: Pustaka Hidayah, 1996), pp. 185–186.

63. K. H. Yusuf Hasyim, "Inikah Akhir Hidup Saya?" in Anonymous, *Haji, Sebuah Perjalanan Air Mata* (Yogyakarta, Indonesia: Bentang, 1993), pp. 233.

64. Saleh, "Balasan Setelah Mati," p. 114.

65. Sukarsono, *Liku-Liku Perjalanan ke Tanah Suci*, p. 231.

66. Zaini, *Pengalaman Haji di Tanah Suci*, p. 163.

67. Darwis, *40 Hari Mencari Cinta*, pp. 243–258.

68. Hendra Esmara, *Aku Datang Memenuhi Panggilanmu Ya, Allah* (Jakarta: Penerbit PT Gramedia, 1993), p. 143.

69. Emo Kastama, *Catatan Harian Seorang Jemaah Haji* (Jakarta: Cita Putra Bangsa, 1997), pp. 318–319.

70. Laura Marcus, *Auto/biographical Discourses: Theory, Criticism, Practice* (Manchester, UK: Manchester, University Press, 1994). For the Southeast Asian side of things, see the very interesting article by Henri Chambert-Loir, "L'extase en plus: Recits Indonesiens du Pelerinage a la Mecque, 1970–1994," in Claudine Salmon, ed., *Récits de Voyages Asiatiques* (Paris: EFEO, 1996), pp. 297–318.

71. James Olney, *Metaphors of Self: The Meaning of Autobiography* (Princeton, NJ: Princeton University Press, 1972).

72. William Spengermann, *The Forms of Autobiography: Episodes in the History of a Literary Genre* (New Haven, CT: Yale University Press, 1980).

73. Karl Weintraub, *The Value of the Individual: Self and Circumstance in Autobiography* (Chicago: University of Chicago Press, 1978).

74. Robert Folkenflik, ed., *The Culture of Autobiography: Constructions and Self-Representation* (Stanford, CA: Stanford University Press, 1993).

75. Sven Birkets, *The Art of Time in Memoir: Then, Again* (St. Paul, MN: Graywolf, 2008).

76. It was shown earlier that farmers still make up a solid percentage of pilgrims making the Hajj from Southeast Asia (often 30 percent, in Indonesia), but obviously most pilgrim memoirs do not come from this class of citizens.

12

Remembering Devotion

Oral History and the Pilgrimage

> I was finally standing there, in the crowds around the Ka'ba, and there
> were a thousand twinkling lights. I said out loud, "I am calling you
> Allah—here I come!
>
> —Hajja "X," Zamboanga, Mindanao (Southern Philippines)
> Interviewed by the author, July 2004

The eminent African historian Jan Vansina has commented that "without oral
traditions we would know very little about the past of large parts of the world,
and we would not know them from the inside."[1] This is certainly true—the histories of some places and some events require the intervention of living memory,
otherwise large parts of the human story would forever be lost. Vansina was
among the first to try to practice what he preached in this regard, but the tech-
nique quickly spread to other parts of the world as well, often with fascinating
results for the rewriting of established historical narratives.[2] In Southeast Asia,
the outlines for this kind of reinterpretation were called for in the early 1960s,
but not until the late 1970s and early 1980s did historians and anthropologists
start to use oral history as crucial source material in "fixing" the past of particular
places and peoples.[3] This was done for research among highland people of the
Philippines and Vietnam, but it was also a strategy eventually utilized in telling
urban histories, such as those of Japanese prostitutes who lived and worked in
the region's colonial ports.[4] The pendulum has swung so heavily toward acknowl-
edgment of the importance of this kind of research that there are now entire
manuals devoted to the writing of oral history in Southeast Asia, mainly penned
by Southeast Asian authors themselves.[5]

    This last chapter of the book showcases the extraordinary information
available for an oral history of the Hajj. The pilgrimage to Mecca is the central
religious event in the lives of millions of Southeast Asian Muslims. Although
colonial-era records on the Hajj could keep a scholar busy for an entire career, as
Vansina has cautioned, this is not the same as knowing the lived history of the

pilgrimage "from the inside." This is especially the case because the holy cities of Mecca and Medina are forbidden to non-Muslims. Since the spring of 2004, therefore, I have been traveling all over Islamic Southeast Asia for several months each year to speak to scores of Muslims about the nature of their pilgrimages to Mecca. I have performed these interviews in mosques, at bus stops, on docks, and in people's homes, among many other places. The language of almost all of the interviews was Indonesian (or Malay), though English was spoken in the southern Philippines and in Singapore. Men and women were questioned, old and young people, the rich and the poor, Muslims living in towns and cities of various sizes, as well as in rural areas. The journeys took me to the Muslim provinces of southern Thailand, all over Malaysia (Penang, Melaka, Kuala Lumpur, Kuala Terengganu, Kota Kinabalu), to the Sultanate of Brunei, to Mindanao and metro-Manila in the Philippines, to the high-rise flats of Singapore, and through several islands and river ports and seaports in Indonesia (Palembang and Medan, both in Sumatra; Banjarmasin, South Borneo; Makassar, Sulawesi; Mataram, Lombok; and Jakarta). Several weeks spent at the Universitas Islam Antarabangsa (International Islamic University) in Kuala Lumpur allowed me to speak to many more Muslims who had been on the Hajj from various other parts of Southeast Asia that I was not able to visit myself on these trips. In all, I was able to interview more than one hundred Hajjis and Hajjas, who had performed their pilgrimages to the Hejaz from a week prior to our discussion to some half a century ago.

What do pilgrims remember about their Hajj? What aspects of this incredible journey, which used to take months by sea but now takes hours by air, are worth remembering, and what is forgotten? How do Southeast Asians organize their experiences in their memories? What is considered crucial to a Muslim life well lived, and what is incidental? Are material circumstances remembered as vividly as spiritual obligations, and what do various pilgrims' memories have in common? Perhaps most important, how do Southeast Asian Muslims explain the Hajj to others and to themselves as they narrate their experiences? Is this process different from writing a memoir of the pilgrimage, which many Hajjis have done as an act of devotion? The pages that follow examine these questions first from the standpoint of several decades-old Hajj memories held in the Oral History repositories in the National Archives of Singapore, followed by recent recollections of pilgrims about the physical circumstances of their journeys, spanning travel, health, residence, and living in the Hejaz. A third section of the chapter explores the spiritual dimensions of the pilgrimage, as religion itself comes to the fore in the lived experience of devotion. The conclusion looks at how useful oral history may be in narrating the journey to Mecca, as a source of information and also as a vestige of what is often described as the most charged spiritual moment in any Muslim's lifetime.

Fossilized Oral History: Hajj Memories in a Vault

The National Archives in Singapore preserve some of the oldest oral history tapes of interviews with Southeast Asian Hajjis as part of the archives' collection of the "Malay experience," more broadly (table 12.1). Within these tapes are the self-narrations—with all of the complexity this implies—of many Muslims from Singapore's past, only some of whom were actually "Malay," or local to Singapore. The "Malay" category is a catchall cache for Muslims who were not of Indian origin, but whose families hailed from different parts of the archipelago. Therefore, alongside Malay memories from many decades in Singapore are those of Southeast Asian Muslims whose families came through the port throughout the twentieth century, though their ancestral homes were in modern-day Malaysia, Brunei, or Indonesia. The audiotapes have not been edited or redacted in any way and are remarkable for the amount of information they convey about Muslim life in general. Yet they offer particularly interesting descriptions of the pilgrimage to Mecca. The slow drone of the voices recount life in the 1920s, before the Great Depression; in the 1940s, during the height of wartime with Japan; and through the 1950s, 1960s, and 1970s, when Singapore moved from British colonial capital to part of the Malaysian merger to independent nation-state. The Hajj memories make up only a small part of the hundreds of hours of tapes, but they provide a fascinating window into the customs and concerns of pilgrims in a bygone age.

One Hajji, a man named Ali bin Sanat, remembered that the Hajj brought significant Middle Eastern influence to Singapore in 1912 by way of the pilgrims who returned to the colony. This came in the form of songs and other entertainment that were new to Southeast Asian Muslims, but there were also Middle Eastern Muslims who traveled, such as Persians who had business interests in Singapore.[6] Singapore's centrality as a Hajj shipping depot attracted people from all over the region who acted as shaykhs and brokers in this trade. Bugis from Southwest Sulawesi in Indonesia were very prominent—an anonymous account remembered wealthy Bugis shaykhs—but Singapore was also the transit point for pilgrims coming from Palembang (South Sumatra), Sarawak (British Borneo), and Pontianak and Sambas (Dutch West Borneo).[7] Many Malays also came down from Muar or Batu Pahat on the western Malay coast or even from as far away as Java or the Philippines, transiting through Singapore as their last stop on their way to Mecca.[8] The huge and bustling port facilities in the colony made it the rendezvous point for most Hajjis departing from Southeast Asia, as ships congregated in Singapore before undertaking the long steam voyage through the central latitudes of the Indian Ocean.

Table 12.1 **Oral History Interviews from the Audio Tape Collection, Oral History Centre, National Archive of Singapore**

Respondent	Date of Birth	Interview Length (h/m)	Language of Interview	Job Listed
Ali Bin Sanat (Haji)	1904	3 hr. 17 m.	Malay	Undertaker
Anonymous Malay #4	1911	9 hr. 58 m.	Malay	Fisherman
Haji Buang Bin Siraj	1917	5 hr. 3 m.	English	Clerk
Hamzah Haji Hussein	1917	4 hr. 28 m.	Malay	Self-employed
Hasnah Bte Sahlan	1919	2 hr. 1 m.	Malay	Housewife
Mohamed Sidek Bin Siraj	1912	2 hr. 59 m.	English	Officer
Mohd Yusof Bin Lana	1928	9 hr. 53 m.	Malay	Officer
Salamah Bte Tamby	1922	2 hr. 21 m.	Malay	Housewife
Abu Bakar b. Haji Abdul Halim	1921	9 hr. 0 m.	Malay	Unknown
Abdul Latiff Bin Ahmad	1916	4 hr. 40 m.	Malay	Fisherman
Yuharis Bte Haji Yusoff	1931	1 hr. 48 m.	Malay	Housewife

A pilgrim named Haji Buang Bin Siraj remembered his journey by sea in this manner in 1952, just a few years after the instability wrought by the Second World War had finally subsided. The background noise in his tape crackled, and he said slowly and in a quiet voice:

> In 1952, there was no air transportation, we traveled for 14 days by ship. The ship was called *Tindelrias*. The journey was hectic. There was no segregation of the passengers, which meant that everyone was treated equally. Each person is given a space of about 3 feet, basically just enough for one to sleep. . . . The duration of the Hajj is about 14 days but the journey alone could be between 18–20 days. I just had a calling to go to Mecca. Employees of the law firm I worked for were given $1200 and two months of leave to travel anywhere they liked after working in the company for 10 years. Many of the employees traveled to Hong Kong and Australia. When my turn came, I thought that I would be wasting money if I traveled to these places as I did not know anybody (there), so I decided to perform the Hajj. When I told my parents that I wanted to go for Hajj, they were shocked as they always considered me a nominal Muslim.[9]

It was not uncommon at this time for companies to offer the chance of performing Hajj as an incentive to long-term employees; indeed, the British government held out this possibility to many Malays who served the state. Government work was seen as desirable by many Malays precisely because of fringe benefits such as this, which would obviate the need for saving huge sums of money and guarantee the ability to perform one's religious duties at the end of one's term of service.

Other Muslims remembered the industries that sprang up alongside the Hajj brokerage businesses to support a huge number of people moving westward along the steam routes. Many shaykhs, or pilgrim brokers, doubled as tailors, for example, sewing Hajj skullcaps for pilgrims who would proudly wear them upon their return to Southeast Asia, an outward sign of an inner transformation. These men also sewed *jubbas* and turbans.[10] When the pilgrims were about to leave, Abdul Latiff bin Ahmad recalled, many friends and relatives would come to wish them well, and it was the practice for the eventual Hajji to throw a feast to thank his community for their caring and support.[11] Another Hajji, Abu Bakar Bin Haji Abdul Halim, remembered:

> When a person goes for Hajj, one would clean coins with tamarind water and they will throw the coin and *beras kunyit* (glutinous rice) towards the future Hajji/Hajjah before they leave the house. This tradition is called *semah-semah* which is Malay culture rather than an Islamic

ritual. I saw this happening at one of my neighbors' houses. . . . People board the ship at Gate 5, and spent a whole day at the harbor. They will recite the *azan* and wave the pilgrims off until the ship could no longer be seen.[12]

A mixture of indigenous Malay culture with Middle Eastern influence on music, songs, and dance was typical of the syncretism of the Hajj in colonial Singapore. People came to the port from a variety of places throughout the region, and the norms and customs of pilgrimage reflected these heterogeneous circumstances. The pilgrimage was very likely one of the most important factors in culture transmission among the various Muslims of Southeast Asia. Performing the Hajj brought local Muslims into the global *ummah* of culture, custom, and belief and allowed Islam to circulate to the farthest reaches of the archipelago via Singapore as a radiating center.

Memories of the Material World

The reflections preserved in the Singapore oral history archives are echoed in many observations of the living. As I traveled around Muslim Southeast Asia, I heard many similar stories of the impact of the Hajj on local people's lives. This kind of oral history gathering allowed me to hear the opinions of quite a wide range of people, geographically, ethnically, and nationally, as well as in terms of gender, class, and age (figure 12.1). The pilgrimage is the central event of many Muslims' religious experience on this earth: more capital, both financial and spiritual, is spent in performing the Hajj than in most other activities of one's religious life. The Hajj therefore becomes symbolic of one's connection with Islam and how important the religion will be in carrying out one's journey on earth.

Pilgrims spoke to me in interviews ranging from half an hour to whole afternoons or evenings, depending on the time they had available, the feeling of trust shared between us, and the intensity of the memories and conversation. The fact that I am American by citizenship came up in almost every interview; in a post 9/11 world, this information was important to divulge (in the interest of honesty) at the start of each session. I explained that I was an academic, that I was writing a history of the Hajj, and that I was not researching or even particularly interested in the connections—real or sensationalized—between Islam, violence, and/or secession that almost daily appeared in the news. I think this was believed in most cases, though it may have taken the entirety of the interview to demonstrate that my questions were indeed only on the topic of Hajj. It is certainly possible that I was *not* believed on occasion, too. A few interviews were

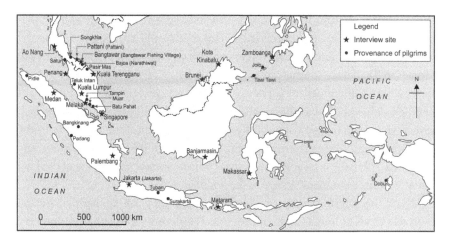

Figure 12.1 Author's Interviewing Sites in Southeast Asia's Muslim Arc.
Map drawn by Lee Li-kheng, Geography Department, National University of Singapore.

difficult or uneasy, and sometimes even unsatisfying; most, however, were fascinating and substantive and held both informant and questioner in deep conversation for hours at a time. I came with a list of questions I wanted to ask and tried to follow it to get a similar spectrum of opinions that I thought were important. But I also let the conversations naturally flow in many of the interviews, if someone had something particularly interesting to say. As a result, I heard about issues that seemed crucial to me as a researcher but also ended up hearing about things that I had not thought were important to ask or had never thought of in the first place.

One of the most important initial memories of the material world of the Hajj that I heard about involved the dynamics and mechanics of the long trip out to Mecca itself. Most flights from Southeast Asia to the Hejaz are now undertaken by a carefully managed system of national air carriers working together with the Saudi authorities. Flights are sometimes chartered, but they usually fly directly from various Southeast Asian cities directly to Jeddah, carrying a load of passengers who are partly or wholly composed of pilgrims. All of this is fairly recent, however. An elderly Malaysian Hajja with whom I spoke remembered performing her first Hajj at age ten by steamer in the 1950s. Her entire family left via Penang's docks in 1951. Halfway across the Indian Ocean, two elderly passengers died, and the captain summoned all of the pilgrims on deck to pay their respects before the two bodies, covered in canvas, were lowered by ropes into the deep.[13] Pilgrims who have made the journey in more recent years also told of new arrangements. A Pattani Hajji informed me that for over a century, Thai pilgrims have usually made their way down to Malaya or Malaysia to attach themselves to the much larger numbers of Muslims going on Hajj from that country. But recently,

he said, Malay pilgrims were coming north across the border, some of them illegally, to go with the Thai contingent so that they would not have to wait in the
Tabung Haji's long lines.[14] These flights now leave directly from Haatyai or even
Phuket in Thailand's southern provinces.[15] A hereditary princess from Sulu in
the southern Philippines told of new gendered arrangements as well: because of
her high status, she led a contingent of two thousand Filipino Muslims on Hajj
several years ago, the only woman heading a delegation from anywhere in the
world that year.[16] It is extremely rare for a woman to be given this honor, she
explained. All of these arrangements show how the actual journeying of the Hajj
mutates as circumstances change in the wider world.

When the pilgrims arrive in the holy cities, they are confronted by the
spectacle of all of humanity's cultures and colors thrown together in one very
crowded place. Many if not most Southeast Asian Hajjis have never come across
people from so many different countries before and are absolutely fascinated by
what they see. A Filipina Hajja spoke of coming into contact with a young
Chinese man who had hiked from the arid provinces of western China all the
way to Pakistan; the journey took him three months, and from there he was able
to join a Pakistani pilgrim group. When he arrived in Mecca, however, he was
illegal and not allowed to join the Chinese delegation, so the Filipina woman
and her companions took him in and fed him, as he had not eaten for several
days.[17] A Hajji from Palembang, South Sumatra, told me that he almost got into
very serious trouble while performing his Hajj as a nineteen-year-old: the lure of
seeing so many new and strange people nearly landed him in jail. He had never
seen Indians before, and some of the women who were en route to Mecca from
Jeddah were not yet covered in their *ihram* garments, but rather had their mid-
riffs exposed in their saris. A Saudi policeman noticed him ogling the women
and yelled at him to back away or he would be hauled off to prison.[18] The same
older Malay Hajja who witnessed the funerals on her steamer crossing also
remembered seeing Africans for the first time on that pilgrimage. She had never
seen groove scars on people's cheeks before and was fascinated by these marks of
West African beauty, as well as by the incredibly colorful clothes of the women
from Niger.[19] All of these descriptions of "first contact" are also part of the
experience of the Hajj, and the memories are often recounted by pilgrims in a
mixture of joy and awe.

I wondered if this incredible mingling of humanity—white, black, brown,
and many shades in between—ever gave way to racism or ethnocentrism, as the
sheer numbers of pilgrims, it seemed to me, had to engender difficulties of many
kinds. When I asked this question, I was almost always met with a similar
response: the feeling of goodwill and fraternity in the holy cities during the Hajj
season overcomes this.[20] But when I pressed, and tried to ask pilgrims to
remember their actual experiences while performing the seven proscribed

circumambulations of the Ka'ba, for example, I did eventually end up hearing different stories. Several Southeast Asian women: urban, cosmopolitan, and living lives where they mingled with many different kinds of people all the time, told me that Southeast Asians were simply physically smaller than Hajjis from many other nations, and thus they often were shoved to the side and trampled in the eagerness of pilgrims to perform the required rituals in heavy pedestrian traffic. Several said that West Africans and Afghanis were the most serious perpetrators of this kind of behavior, but then they hastened to add that such *kasar* ("coarse") actions were only seen as such by Southeast Asians and that perhaps this was normal in African or Afghani cultures. A female Javanese pilgrim was less understanding of such cultural differences, however, and expressed her disapproval of how Arab men treated their accompanying women while upon Hajj. "We do better in Southeast Asia," she told me, "and no man should ever be allowed to treat his wives or sisters in that way—he should be shamed."[21] Another pilgrim, a Muslim from Manila, told of meeting a young Afghan with a long beard while he was in Mecca: the man was smiling at him, and they embraced as brothers and spoke in halting English together about the seriousness of the war there.[22] These kinds of cross-cultural conversations are a big part of undertaking the Hajj, and the disparate friendships made on pilgrimage can sometimes last lifetimes. This mirrors the accounts of colonial-era pilgrimages a century ago, as news, fraternity, and friendship were exchanged in the holy cities, traveling back to distant Muslim lands and affecting local societies.

The question of communication seemed among the most important issues to understand in studying the Hajj: how do all of these people speak to one another, when they come from not only eleven different Southeast Asian societies but also scores of global nationalities? Is Arabic the most common lingua franca, or English, or Malay, or some combination of the three? Pilgrims had different answers to this question, depending on their own experiences. Thai Hajjis, for example, expressed some real difficulty in navigating Saudi society satisfactorily while they were on Hajj. Most Thai Muslims can speak some Malay, but their Malay is a regional dialect and not so close to standard Malay that it can automatically be understood. They certainly do not speak English or French, two other numerically important languages of the pilgrimage. But there are actually many Thai Muslims resident in Saudi Arabia, where they work as cooks and drivers and attend religious schools, and there is a built-in community of diasporic Thais to help the pilgrims with everyday needs.[23] An Indonesian student pointed out that since Indonesia has the largest global delegation each year to Mecca, numbering some 200,000 souls, it is in the interest of shopkeepers and businesspeople in the Hejaz—regardless of their own ethnicity—to learn some Indonesian to sell their goods (figure 12.2). Even if they cannot speak eloquently, many Saudis and Muslims working in the kingdom can speak enough of this

Figure 12.2 Mosques in Banjarmasin and Palembang, Borneo and Sumatra.

Southeast Asian lingua franca to help pilgrims get around.[24] Yet it was the comment of a blind Malay Hajji, a Chinese man from Johor who had converted to Islam some years ago, whose answer made the most sense to me. Deprived of his eyesight, he was completely dependent on his ears when he performed his Hajj as a young man, walking stick in hand. This man mentioned that he heard an array of languages constantly overlapping in the holy cities, pressed against one another in subtle gradations of distance from his ears.[25] Malay, Urdu, English, French, and Arabic, alongside many other languages, all coexist in the Hejaz, therefore, though people often have to use sign language to get their thoughts across when they meet each other in the street.

A further aspect of pilgrims' memories of the material world of the Hajj has to do with housing and health. Hajjis from Southeast Asia stay in a broad range of housing in the Hejaz, from five-star hotels right outside the main mosques in Mecca and Medina to shabby rented apartment blocks, located miles from the center of each city. These options represent the differences in wealth that are characteristic of the Southeast Asian pilgrimage: Singaporean and Brunei Hajjis, for example, mostly stay in extremely comfortable surroundings, while the pilgrims from the region's poorer nations (usually Thailand, the Philippines, and Indonesia, not to mention the small numbers who come from Cambodia, Vietnam, or Burma) stay in considerably less august domiciles. These differences in abode then also translate, to some extent, into differences in health while in the Hejaz. A Cham Cambodian Hajji, for example, told me that there was a large amount of airborne disease in his group, because forty-five of them were bunking together on the floor of an apartment bloc located at some distance from the main mosques.[26] An Acehnese confirmed this, stating that flu went around the compounds regularly and that the Hajj rituals themselves are demanding and very tiring, so that extra miles to walk and extra people sleeping on one's floor only meant a greater chance that the pilgrim would find himself sick at some point of the journey.[27] Yet Singaporean Hajjis described the rooms at the Hilton and the Swissotel in Mecca and Medina as exceedingly comfortable and managed according to international standards by very accommodating staffs. The Singaporean and Brunei governments oversee these arrangements, and Hajjis from both of these countries are virtually assured of plenty of rest and more than adequate food and health measures when they are out on the road performing their religious obligations.[28] These differences in experience show that the Hajj, though meant as an egalitarian experience for human beings no matter what their earthly power or station before God, may not always be so. Spiritually, this may indeed be the case, but there are discernible differences in the material circumstances of pilgrims that are readily available for all to see.[29]

Memories of the Spiritual World

The memories of Hajjis as they pertain to the spiritual world of the pilgrimage are no less varied than these experiences of material circumstances during the great journey. One of the first questions I asked many pilgrims was, having already performed the Hajj, would they try to do it again (figure 12.3). Was this

Figure 12.3 Interviewing near Pattani, South Thailand, and in Zamboanga, Southern Philippines.

important to them, and were they ready to invest huge sums of money and endure what could often be substantial privation to be able to make the voyage a second (or third or fourth) time? I usually heard a very quick yes to this question, and the reasons for this affirmation were profoundly spiritual. A Brunei Hajji told me of a calmness in his heart (*"tenang di dalam hati saya"*) that descended upon him when he was in the holy cities; it was impossible to reproduce this quiescence in any other place on Earth but in the heartland of Islam, he said.[30] Other pilgrims wanted to return to perform the Hajj for relatives of theirs who had died or who were unable to go on their own account. It is possible in Islam to perform the Hajj on someone's else's behalf, and this was stated as a reason for a return by several people, so that the blessings of Hajj could be showered upon those who, for one reason or another (death, age, disease), could not make the journey themselves.[31] Yet the ability to return to the Hejaz was not only predicated on wealth and material circumstances; there had to be a resolute inner will to go. One Filipina Hajja told me that it was remarkable that many poor Muslims managed to get back to Mecca several times for Hajj, despite their poverty, yet many wealthy Muslims, despite having the resources to go, did not manage to get back, even though it would be far easier for them to do so.[32] Although Islam states that performing the Hajj is incumbent upon every Muslim only once in their lives, so long as their monetary resources permit it, Muslims usually saw a return to Mecca as an inner decision, rather than a voyage that was dictated by one's material circumstances on earth.

The spiritual highlight of pilgrims' voyages to Arabia was different in the case of each pilgrim. One Hajja told me that the Prophet's mosque in Medina was particularly special to women performing the pilgrimage. She and her companions (all female) formed a cordon around each "sister" when they arrived in the mosque, so that each woman could take a turn praying in this highly charged physical space without being jostled by the crowds.[33] Many other pilgrims spoke of the Prophet's grave as a place with a special aura of power; they went to his resting place (also in Medina) and felt recharged by the knowledge that the founder of their faith had been in close proximity to them once in their lives. The plain of Arafat was also described as a place of great holiness and contemplation, as pilgrims walked the familiar paths of Muhammad's life, echoing his footsteps as the word of Allah was delivered to him and he brought this word to the clans that lived in the barren lands of this dusty plain. But the spiritual center of Islam is undoubtedly Mecca, and the spiritual center of Mecca is undoubtedly the Ka'ba. Pilgrims were constantly moved to tears in telling me about their first experiences in circumambulating the Ka'ba on their initial sojourns to Mecca. "I felt clean (*bersih*)," one man told me, "for the first time in my life."[34] "I was crying, most people were crying," another woman told me, "and if they weren't crying, I knew they were crying on the inside."[35] Even today, people who had performed their Hajj many years ago, and sometimes even decades ago, halted in their telling of this extraordinarily important act of devotion. The Ka'ba is the center of Islam, and as such, it became the center of meaning of many of these Muslims' experiences when they were in the Hejaz.

It was in Mecca, in fact, that many Hajjis experienced something they did not expect. "Signs and wonders" might be a phrase for this, but even this would not be adequate for what can only really be termed as a confrontation with the supernatural, in many different forms. Several Hajjis told me that in the crush of circumambulation around the Ka'ba, they saw faces of long-dead friends or relatives also performing the ritual, though at a distance and unreachable through the density of the crowd. I heard this over and over again—children who had died relatively recently, neighbors who had died some time ago, grandparents who had died decades ago, all were represented in Mecca. More eerily, one Hajji told me that several other pilgrims' faces turned into the visages of cats; he remembered stoning a cat when he was younger, and he was horrified when the face of that same cat appeared on Hajjis winding around the Black Stone with him in the center of Mecca. Another pilgrim's face—almost unbelievably, given the context—turned into a pig.[36] Hajjis told me of strange, chimeric cloud formations lingering over the holy city, which they could not explain: the swirls and incandescence of the cumulus suggested vague shapes and forms, but these had never been seen before in each pilgrim's lifetime, and they were afraid. Other Hajjis told me of medical miracles that happened while upon the pilgrimage—a brain tumor in one man's son that was diagnosed as inoperable in the best hospitals in Brunei and Singapore was somehow cured in the Hejaz. The water from the sacred well at Zamzam was implicated in this case, and upon the man's return to Southeast Asia, the doctors just scratched their heads in amazement at his cure, which was deemed medically impossible.[37] It is easy to attribute these kinds of stories to the exhaustion, stress, and spiritual ecstasy that often accompany a pilgrim's sojourn to the holy cities, but they crop up again and again, in different forms and tellings by different Hajjis. I had never thought to ask a question about these kinds of experiences, but the memories were volunteered at the end of several interviews in a row, and always in hushed tones, so I began to ask about such experiences toward the end of all of my remaining interviews.

I wanted to know if pilgrims felt closer to Islam as a direct result of their Hajj, and I expected quite a clear answer to this—of course, Muslims would feel this way, I reasoned; they had spent years saving up for this journey, so how could they feel any different? Early respondents did not disappoint me in this supposition: one Hajji looked at me incredulously when I asked and told me that it was inevitable that this would happen, unless the pilgrim was wasting his time in the Hejaz and doing (and thinking) all kinds of things that were forbidden by Islam (*haram*) on the journey (box 12.1). A Kelantanese Hajji told me that he felt closer to Islam because of the desolation of Arafat. He understood what Muhammad had gone through only after he walked in his footsteps on Arafat, and this brought him closer to the religion in an appreciation of the Prophet's suffering.[38] An Indonesian pilgrim expressed this differently, stressing that he learned the

Box 12.1 **The Emotion of Pilgrimage: the Hajj in Pilgrims' Own Words**

Abang A. Marohomsalic, Assistant Director of Hajj, Manila (Philippines): You feel everything that happened in the time of the Prophet—everything he observed, because of the landmarks around you.

Haji Gusti Ardianzar, Coal Business, Banjarmasin (Indonesia): It is true that you can see the long-departed in Mecca, too—mothers, fathers, grandparents. I have seen this with my own eyes.

M. Chairuddin, Hotel Manager, Palembang (Indonesia): I felt like I was doing my duty—not crying, not emotional—but I felt very content. We will all be judged on Arafat when we die—so when you go to Arafat to pray there, your mind and actions must be correct. The Hajj is preparation for Judgment Day.

Zenaida Lim, Businesswoman, Zamboanga (Philippines): I am more patient with what happens in life because of my Hajj. I remember that all is in Allah's plan, and all is His will. I just live, I don't plan.

Noryati Bte. Mohin, Travel Agent, Bandar Seri Begawan (Brunei): In Mecca, when I saw the Ka'ba, for the first time, I was crying—I finally knew who I was as a person. I feel comfortable in my own body now as a result of my Hajj.

Abu Talib bin Haji Yussof, Security Guard, Kuala Terengganu (Malaysia): We should be open to outsiders—this is important—not closed, as we can learn from everyone. The Hajj is good in this respect because Muslims from all nations, cultures, and communities all go. The Hajj shows you how to be patient, to wait, and to accept what comes. We are all dust, and going back into dust. We are acting out a play, you as a professor, me as a security guard, all of us playing parts in a play.

Hajja Waemah, Preschool Helper, Bangtawar Village, Pattani (Thailand): It was so hard to leave a place like that and come back; I was full of tears on my departure. There is such peace there—it is different than the real world.

Nazreen bte. Mohd. Osman, Hospital Technician (Singapore): I felt very lonely while on Hajj sometimes, even though I was with my husband. Women usually go on the roof of the great mosque to circumambulate the Ka'ba—there are so many birds there. One day I was in the hotel and I felt lonely; my husband was in the mosque praying. There was a sudden rush outside my window and then there were many birds there, all coming to rest on my windowsill. Even though I opened the window, they did not fly away. I prayed then in my loneliness. The moment I finished my prayers they all flew away.

very Islamic virtues of patience from his Hajj and from one experience in particular. His Hajj group landed in Jeddah alongside groups from many other countries, and there was a mad dash in the airport to get to the buses to take them to Mecca, as there didn't seem to be enough vehicles to take all of these incoming pilgrims. People were tired and a little exasperated from their long journeys. They wanted to get to Mecca as quickly as possible, and the resulting stampede was very unbecoming of the kinds of behavior expected on the Hajj. Nasrulla's group let the others stampede and resigned themselves to a very long wait to get to the holy city. But by waiting, they missed the massive traffic jam that snarled between Jeddah's airport and Mecca, and they passed the impatient Hajjis on their own bus (on a parallel service road to the highway) despite boarding their vehicles several hours later.[39] A Malay Hajja said that the pilgrimage should impart these kinds of lessons in bringing one closer to one's faith: "God, give me inspiration—how do I deal with myself?"[40] It is through these kinds of experiences in the Hejaz that pilgrims pull themselves closer to the core teachings of Islam and then live them more regularly as a part of their post-Hajj experiences when they return to their own countries.

It was this last thought—did performing the pilgrimage make you a better Muslim?—that always served as my last interview question. Was it all worth it, the pain and suffering and privation and ill health, the discomfort of the journey and the years of scrimping to put pennies away, all for a monthlong journey that would quickly fade in one's thoughts as the pilgrim got older, because memories always fade, even memories of the Divine? I was hesitant to ask this question: it seemed so deeply personal, and why should anyone give me an answer? But the pilgrims did answer, sometimes in very unexpected ways. Most, as might be expected, did surmise that they were now better Muslims—at least outwardly, because there were considerable social pressures that encouraged them to be so.[41] An Acehnese man told me that you cannot come back unchanged because your peers in your hometown will always remind you: you cannot act that way because now you are a Hajji, or so-and-so should be entrusted with this, because his pilgrimage means he should know how to deal with such things.[42] These pressures, symbolized by the wearing of the white *peci* (or *songkok*) hat in men or by the adoption of an honorific to one's name (Hajji or Hajja), encouraged pilgrims to remember their transformation. Indeed, many Muslims did point out that they were now more pious than ever before, praying five times daily with religious precision; handing out the *zakat* tithe, though before they had not done so regularly; and just generally trying to act in a way befitting a Hajji, someone who has seen God in his earthly palaces, the mosques and desert hills of the Arabian peninsula, a world far away from Southeast Asia. But one Hajja looked at me quietly for a moment and chose her words carefully. "I think proximity to God comes at low and high ebbs," she said, "and the Hajj does not necessarily affect that union. It's a little worse for me right now, unfortunately, though I have indeed been to the holy cities. So the answer to your question about whether I am now a better Muslim is 'not necessarily.' What is important, though, is finishing that fifth pillar. I still have a lot of homework to do to get closer to God."[43]

Conclusion

The place of oral history in helping to shape contemporary notions of the past has become accepted and de rigueur in modern scholarship. Many chroniclers of past events still caution that oral history must be used carefully, however, because of a variety of pitfalls and problems that are unique to the medium. Some scholars, for example, have noted that the reliability of memories is suspect and that they must be checked and counterchecked vigorously alongside other sources to ensure their veracity.[44] Other practitioners have talked about the format of oral materials and how they can be utilized, depending on what guise they come down to modern people, via stories, songs, or cautionary tales or in a variety of other avatars that potentially impact transmission and accuracy.[45] Still other scholars have spoken of the "unintended consequences" of memory and the ways memories of past events often prove to be malleable to fit present-day realities, especially shifting constellations of power that inevitably mark the telling of the past.[46] This "labyrinth of memory," in two authors' elegant phrasing, begs careful unraveling, lest the true flow of past events is "tainted" by contemporary realities that always threaten to obscure the actual progression of long-finished deeds.[47]

In Southeast Asia, these methodological concerns have entered the literature on regional histories in important and substantive ways. In Borneo, discussions on the accuracy and validity of oral history in specific circumstances have been heated and occasionally downright hostile. There is a sense that getting the story right, both from the standpoint of the indigenous actors interviewed and from the standpoint of "what actually happened," is difficult and sometimes maybe even impossible.[48] If this is true among shifting cultivators and seminomadic peoples in the Bornean rainforest, where written sources are scarce, then it need be no less true among urban elites from Singapore, Thailand, or the Malay upper class. Memories are contentious, even when there is corroborating evidence in other forms that proves or disproves notions of how the past unfolded in specific times and places.[49] What is important in both of these milieus is that the Southeast Asian present clearly affects the telling of the Southeast Asian past on matters of religion, economy, politics, and social interaction. This may be doubly true in the case of something as spiritually charged and religiously important as the Hajj, whose very nature as an act of devotion lends itself to many meanings and even shifting meanings from a single source over time. The good and the bad are remembered alongside one another but are often sifted for meanings vis-à-vis contemporary life, depending on what the raconteur wants to get across, either to an audience or to one's self.

Compiling an oral history of the Hajj allows entrance into one of the world's earliest and most sacred religiously exclusive spaces. Because non-Muslims are denied entry into the holy cities, oral transmission of experience there is extremely important for global knowledge, as there are few ways for non-Muslim researchers to check existing Hajj narratives without violating the precepts of Islam. Though there are many written sources to study the history of the pilgrimage, the narration of one's own journey to the spiritual center of Islam becomes an invaluable resource for understanding the importance of the Hajj in Southeast Asian life. Each experience of moving from the tropics to the Arabian Peninsula is different, and pilgrims have inevitably put forward contrasting memories of what was important to them in undertaking their voyages. No two pilgrimages are exactly alike, despite canonical signposting that aims for a certain uniformity in the execution of ritual. Yet there are also certain similarities that come out of these tellings, and these are just as instructive in painting a portrait of the importance of this rite to the millions of people who make enormous sacrifices to fulfill this religious obligation each year. From the material conditions of the Hajj to its deeper spiritual meanings, oral historical accounts of the pilgrimage flesh out the written codas of the centuries and put the experience of the Hajj into pilgrims' own words. These words help us understand what it means to fully give one's self over to devotion on a journey that lasts a few weeks or even several months but that resonates for a lifetime.

NOTES

1. Jan Vansina, *Oral Tradition as History* (Madison: University of Wisconsin Press, 1985), p. 198.
2. See, for example, Philip Curtin, "Field Techniques for Collecting and Processing Oral Data," *Journal of African History*, 9/3, 1968: 367–385; Jack Goody, *The Interface between the Written and the Oral* (Cambridge: Cambridge University Press, 1987); Sidney Mintz, "The Anthropological Interview and the Life History," *Oral History Review*, 7, 1979: 18–26, in this case, for the Caribbean; and Bernard Cohn, "History and Anthropology: The State of Play," in Bernard Cohn, *An Anthropologist among the Historians* (New Delhi: Oxford University Press, 1990), where most of his work was in India.
3. The critical intervention here was the seminal article of John Smail, "On the Possibility of an Autonomous History of Southeast Asia," *Journal of Southeast Asian History*, 2/2, 1961. I mean "fixing" here in two senses: both fixing something that is (or was) broken and fixing something in time and/or space.
4. Renato Rosaldo, *Ilongot Headhunting 1883–1974: A Study in Society and History* (Stanford, CA: Stanford University Press, 1980); Georges Condominas, *We Have Eaten the Forest: The Story of*

a Montagnard Village in the Central Highlands of Vietnam (New York: Hill and Wang, 1977); Gerald Hickey, *Sons of the Mountains: Ethnohistory of the Vietnamese Central Highlands to* 1954 (New Haven, CT: Yale University Press, 1982); and Tomoko Yamazaki, *Sandakan Brothel #8: An Episode in the History of Lower-Class Japanese Women* (Armonk, NY: Sharpe, 1999). More recently, see the work of Anton Lucas, Rudolf Mrazek, Ann Stoler, and Karen Strassler, all of them Indonesianists and all of whom have worked in this vein.

5. See, in this respect, Kwa Chong Guan, "The Value of Oral Testimony: Text and Orality in the Reconstruction of the Past," in P. Lim Pui Huen, James Morrison, and Kwa Chong Guan, eds., *Oral History in Southeast Asia: Theory and Method* (Singapore: National Archives of Singapore and the Institute of Southeast Asian Studies, 1998), pp. 19–32; Mohamad Taib Osman, *Manual for Collecting Oral Tradition with Special Reference to South East Asia* (Kuala Lumpur: Dewan Bahasa dan Pustaka, 1982); Hong Lysa, "Ideology and Oral History Institutions in Southeast Asia," in P. Lim Pui Huen, James Morrison, and Kwa Chong Guan, eds., *Oral History in Southeast Asia: Theory and Method* (Singapore: National Archives of Singapore and the Institute of Southeast Asian Studies, 1998), pp. 33–46; *Workshop to Prepare a Training Programme on Oral Tradition* (Bangkok: Office of the National Committee on Culture, Ministry of Education, 1980); and Daniel Chew, "Oral History Methodology: The Life History Approach," in P. Lim Pui Huen, James Morrison, and Kwa Chong Guan, eds., *Oral History in Southeast Asia: Theory and Method* (Singapore: National Archives of Singapore and the Institute of Southeast Asian Studies, 1998), pp. 47–54.

6. Oral History Tape A001036/07, Reel 7, Interview with Haji Ali bin Sanat, Undertaker.

7. Oral History Tape A000598/21, Reel 12, Interview with Anonymous Fisherman.

8. Oral History Tape A000560/04, Reel 2, Interview with Hajah Hasnah bte Sahlan, Housewife; Oral History Tape A000459/04, Reel 2, Interview with Hajah Yuhanis bte Haji Yusof, Housewife. The diversity of locales sending pilgrims on Hajj in late colonial Southeast Asia was nothing short of astounding. In Indonesia alone (the Dutch East Indies), there are records of Hajjis making their way from all over the archipelago as early as the 1870s. For some period notices of these trips preserved in the Indonesian archives, outlining locales in Sumatra, the Dutch-controlled South China Sea Islands, and Dutch Borneo, see Arsip Nasional Republik Indonesia (hereafter, ANRI), Algemeen Administratieve Verslag der Residentie Palembang 1874 (Palembang #64/17); ANRI, Algemeen Verslag der Residentie Banka 1875 (Banka #66); ANRI, Politiek Verslag der Residentie Borneo West 1870 (Borneo West #2/8); and ANRI, Algemeen Verslag der Residentie Borneo Zuid-Oost 1871 (Borneo Z.O. #9/2).

9. Oral History Tape A000715/11, Reel 3, Interview with Haji Buang bin Haji Siraj, Conveyance Clerk. Overcrowding on pilgrim ships was a very common problem; see, in addition to the oral history tapes, Governor, Straits to Secretary of State for the Colonies, 12-18-1873, #396, Colonial Office/273. On pilgrim ships leaving Singapore between 1870 and 1872, for example, the *Venus* had 582 people in excess of its registry by the time it landed in the Middle East, the *Fusiyama* was 267 over, the *Sun Foo* was 388 over, the *Ada* was 268 over, the *Rangoon* 265 over, and the *Jedda* was 338 over.

10. Oral History Tape A001255/06, Reel 3, Interview with Haji Mohamed Sidek bin Siraj, Executive Officer; Oral History Tape A000634/05, Reel 1, Interview with Hajah Salamah bte Tamby, Housewife; Oral History Tape A000608/07, Reel 1, Interview with Haji Taha bin Haji Abdullah, Policeman.

11. Oral History Tape 000902/10, Reel 5, Interview with Haji Abdul Latiff bin Ahmad, Fisherman.

12. Oral History Tape A000625/18, Reel 9, Interview with Haji Abu Bakar bin Haji Abdul Halim.

13. Interview with Dr. Badriyah bte Haji Salleh, Director of Museums (Melaka, Malaysia), November 20, 2003.

14. Interview with Dr. Hasan Madmarn, Yala Islamic College (Provenance: Songkla, S. Thailand), Pattani, South Thailand, July 1, 2004.

15. Logistics on Thai pilgrim itineraries and mechanics were supplied by three interviewees in Ao Nang, Southern Thailand: Rita Subaida (provenance: Satun), Pranee Peungla (provinance: Narathiwat), and "Het" (provenance: Ao Nang).

16. Interview with Princess Putli Amil-bangsa, Princess of Sulu (Provenance: Tawi-Tawi, Sulu) Zamboanga, August 1, 2004. I was told that the gendered component of this arrangement was very unusual; the fact that this particular person led the delegation shows a link with the past, however, too, as her lineage and status came from her family's provenance.

17. Interview with Surul-Ain Hedjazi, Retired Teacher (Zamboanga, SW Mindanao, Southern Philippines), August 1, 2004. Expressions of wonder at the diversity of global pilgrims gathered in the Hejaz during Hajj season have not been made by Hajjis and Hajjas alone. In the late nineteenth century, Western observers of the pilgrimage also commented on the tremendous variety of human beings gathering in Mecca. One of them, Wilfred Blunt, marveled that "Indians, Persians, Moors, Negroes from Niger, Malays from Java, Tartars from the Khanates, Arabs from the French Sahara, ... and even Mussulmans from the interior of China" all descended on Islam's holy cities. See his rather ethnocentric account, *The Future of Islam* (London: Kegan Paul Trench, 1882), pp. 1–2.

18. Interview with M. Chairuddin, Hotel Manager (Palembang, South Sumatra, Indonesia), August 5, 2004.

19. Interview with Dr. Badriyah bte Haji Salleh, Director of Museums (Melaka, Malaysia), November 20, 2003.

20. A former pilgrim I met in Banjarmasin, Southeast Borneo, utilized the term that many Malay and Indonesian speakers used to get this notion across to me—*persaudaraan*, or "brotherhood." Haji Gusti Ardianzar, August 8, 2004 (provenance: Banjarmasin).

21. Interview with Kesty Pringgoharjono, Museum Assistant and Translator (Provenance: Padang, West Sumatra, Indonesia [but Javanese]), Singapore, May 3, 2004. Crowd chaos, pushing, and overcrowding were to blame for the 2004 trampling of a large number of pilgrims—a considerable number of whom were Indonesian. The Saudi government came under attack by numerous parties after this happened (including Southeast Asian governments), and coordination of the Hajj was then streamlined.

22. Interview with Dr. Julkipli Wadi, Professor of Islamic Studies (Provenance: Jolo, Sulu, Southern Philippines), Manila, July 28, 2004.

23. Interview with Hajja Waemah, Preschool Helper (Bangtawar Fishing Village, Pattani, South Thailand), July 2, 2004. This thought was echoed by many Thai respondents, most of whom came from small fishing villages on the coast and who also had difficulty speaking standard Malay.

24. Interview with Nasrullah, Lawyer (Provenance: Bangkinang, Riau, Indonesia), Kuala Lumpur, Malaysia, June 11, 2004. This was confirmed by Haji Aziz, interviewed in Mataram, Lombok (May 27, 2006), whose provenance was the same city.

25. Interview with Abdul Rahman Tang, PhD Student (Provenance: Muar, Johor, Malaysia), Kuala Lumpur, Malaysia, June 14, 2004.

26. Interview with Dr. Fauzi bin Ahmad, Professor (Provenance: Phnom Penh, Cambodia), Kuala Lumpur, Malaysia, June 14, 2004. Surveillance of the Hajj by individual governments (colonial or postcolonial) has long been a part of the pilgrimage as well, either on a security rationale or a rationale of protecting Hajjis from dangers, or both. For a nineteenth-century variant on this, see accounts in the Dutch archives such as Algemeen Rijksarchief, den Haag, 1872, Mailrapport, MR #820 (Ministerie van Kolonien).

27. Interview with Buchari Yusuf, Student (Provenance: Pidie, Aceh, North Sumatra, Indonesia), Kuala Lumpur, Malaysia, June 11, 2004.

28. Many respondents told me this again and again, but for just two interviews along these lines, one for each country, see Tengku Mohamad Fouzy Jumat, Travel Agency Owner (Singapore), May 10, 2004; and Hajjah Noryati bte Mohin, Travel Agency Operator (Brunei), July 26, 2004.

29. Having disposable income to undertake the Hajj has been crucial over the centuries, even if Zenaida Lim was right in pointing out that many poor people manage to perform the Hajj while their wealthier neighbors decide not to go. As early as the nineteenth century, colonial administrators were discussing that there were obvious correlations between agricultural bumper crop years in parts of the archipelago (like Palembang), where cash crops were grown, and the numbers of people going on Hajj. See ANRI, Algemeen Verslag der Residentie Palembang, 1886 (Palembang #65/6).

30. Interview with Sahrin bin Haji Ismail, Hajj Officer (Brunei), July 26, 2004.

31. Interview with Dr. Hasan Madmarn, Yala Islamic College (Provenance: Songkla, S. Thailand), Pattani, South Thailand, July 1, 2004. I have been told by Michael Gilsenan that this is a Shaf'i practice. Personal communication.

32. Interview with Zenaida Lim, Businesswoman (Provenance: Jolo, Sulu, Southern Philippines), Zamboanga, Southern Philippines, July 31, 2004. Zenaida Lim was one of the most extraordinary Hajjas I met on my travels. To me, she epitomized the generous spirit of most of the pilgrims with whom I spoke. Her openness, honesty, and accommodating spirit, and the way that she and her family not only allowed me into their home but also went out of their way to help me speak to other Hajjis they knew in Zamboanga, was one of the highlights of my fieldwork in Southeast Asia.

33. Interview with Mbak Siapa, student [not this person's true name] (Provenance: Jakarta, Indonesia), Ithaca, New York, August 29, 2003.

34. Interview with Haji Sahrin bin Haji Ismail, Hajj Officer, Brunei, July 26, 2004.

35. Interview with Noryati bte Mohin, Hajj Tour Operator, Brunei, July 26, 2004.

36. Interview with Dr. Julkipli Wadi, Professor, Manila, July 28, 2004.

37. One of the most extraordinary sessions in this respect was with Haji Abdul Latif bin Muhammad, Government Worker and Hotel Owner, Brunei, July 26, 2004. This gentleman talked to me for many hours over the course of a long day; he even sketched maps for me of the holy places to better show me the layout of the miraculous events he was describing. Haji Abdul Latif had been a journalist for many years before going into government service; he had served on the staff of a newspaper in Australia when he was young, and he had also traveled widely in Europe and America. He wanted to know how it was possible that the well at Zamzam, which provided holy water for literally millions of global Muslims coming to Arabia on Hajj (most of whom would bring at least some back as gifts to their countrymen, not to mention using the well while they were in the Hejaz), never dried up. I had no answer to this question at the time, nor do I now. Discourses about holy water at sanctified sites are not unique to Islam and can be found about Lourdes, Fatima, and other places, but Haji Abdul was not the only pilgrim to tell me about the incredible properties of this water; Nadia and Lily Suripto, both of whom I interviewed outside Medan and who both came from that place, mentioned this, too (January 10 and 11, 2009).

38. Interview with Che Adenan, Islamic Insurance Agent (Provenance: Pasir Mas, Kelantan), Kuala Lumpur, June 15, 2004.

39. Interview with Nasrullah, Lawyer (Provenance: Bangkinang, Riau, Sumatra), Kuala Lumpur, June 11, 2004.

40. Interview with Dr. Badriyah bte Haji Salleh, Director of Museums (Melaka, Malaysia), November 20, 2003. This was echoed by three other Malay pilgrims I met in other cities around the country: Cikgu Muhamed Yahser in Penang, from that same city (interviewed July 5, 2004); Abu Talib bin Haji Yussof, in and from Kuala Terngganu (interviewed July 10, 2004); and Haji Muhammad Khairi bin Ismail, in and from Kota Kinabalu (interviewed July 22, 2004). The first of these men was a mosque keeper, the second a security guard, and the third a professor.

41. This is not only true in contemporary Muslim Southeast Asia; it has been true for a very, very long time in this region, almost definitely throughout the dar-al-Islam globally. Dutch colonial writers, for example, understood very clearly that there was a strong connection between making

the Hajj and one's status (and the resultant expectations of one's behavior) on return from the Hejaz. See P. J. Veth, *Java: Geographisch, Ethnologisch, Historisch*, vol. 4 (Haarlem, Netherlands: De Erven F. Bohn, 1907), pp. 128–167. It is very clear that while the Hajj is an inward journey, it is an outward one as well. The doing of the Hajj and one's changing status afterward in the community is as much a part of the pilgrimage as one's interior voyage toward Allah.

42. Interview with Buchari Yusuf, Student (Provenance: Pidie, Aceh, North Sumatra, Indonesia), Kuala Lumpur, Malaysia, June 11, 2004.

43. Interview with Mbak Siapa, student [not this person's true name] (Provenance: Jakarta, Indonesia), Ithaca, New York, August 29, 2003.

44. William Lang and Laurie Mercier, "Getting It Down Right: Oral History's Reliability in Local History Research," *Oral History Review*, 12, 1984: 81–99.

45. Alessandro Portelli, *The Death of Luigi Trastulli and Other Stories: Form and Meaning in Oral History* (Albany: State University of New York Press, 1991).

46. Iwao Ishino, "Memories and Their Unintended Consequences," in Marea Teski and Jacob Climo, eds., *The Labyrinth of Memory: Ethnographic Journeys* (Westport, CT: Bergin & Garvey, 1995), pp. 185–201.

47. Marea Teski and Jacob Climo, eds., *The Labyrinth of Memory: Ethnographic Journeys* (Westport, CT: Bergin & Garvey, 1995).

48. See, for example, G. N. Appell, "Guide to the Varieties of Oral Literature in Borneo," *Borneo Research Bulletin*, 22, 1990: 98–113; Carol Rubenstein, "Oral Literature Research and Review," *Borneo Research Bulletin*, 21/2, 1989: 83–94; Jerome Rousseau, "Response to Rubenstein," *Borneo Research Bulletin*, 21/2, 1989: 95–96; and Allen Maxwell, "Recording Oral Traditions and Language," *Borneo Research Bulletin*, 21/2, 1989: 97–142.

49. Lim How Seng, "Interviewing the Business and Political Elite of Singapore: Methods and Problems," in P. Lim Pui Huen, James Morrison, and Kwa Chong Guan, eds., *Oral History in Southeast Asia: Theory and Method* (Singapore: National Archives of Singapore and the Institute of Southeast Asian Studies, 1998), pp. 55–65; Yos Santasombat, "Oral History and Self-Portraits: Interviewing the Thai Elite," in P. Lim Pui Huen, James Morrison, and Kwa Chong Guan, eds., *Oral History in Southeast Asia: Theory and Method* (Singapore: National Archives of Singapore and the Institute of Southeast Asian Studies, 1998), pp. 66–85; and Azixah Mokhzani, "The Writing of the Biography of Tan Sri Fatimah Hashim," in P. Lim Pui Huen, James Morrison, and Kwa Chong Guan, eds., *Oral History in Southeast Asia: Theory and Method* (Singapore: National Archives of Singapore and the Institute of Southeast Asian Studies, 1998), pp. 140–152.

Conclusion

The Longest Journey

The Boeing 747 jumbo jet is perched high above the cumulus at 35,000 feet; the plane is moving almost silently, despite the lightning flashes in the mass of dark clouds below. It is twilight, but at this altitude the light is always sharp and clear, no matter what the time—the boiling monsoon clouds below simply don't affect an aircraft this high. The horizon is pink and a hazy blue, turning to violet at the place the sun has already gone down, where the sea and sky meet far, far away. The nearly four hundred Southeast Asian passengers on board the flight are all tired and still because their journeys over the past two days have already been long, shepherding them to Jakarta from all over the archipelago, the lands beneath the winds. There they gathered speaking a multitude of local languages—Javanese, Sundanese, Bugis, and Mingangkabau among them—though also communicating easily with each other in Indonesian, the tongue that binds across island chains in this diffuse, scattered part of the world. They finally boarded their plane in the specially designated pilgrimage hangar in the Jakarta airport. Now, quietly asleep and dreaming as their aircraft hurtles toward Mecca at subsonic speeds, they face few of the dangers and inconveniences of their forefathers who undertook these journeys. Their grandparents had made this same sojourn in the hulls of steamships, packed like sardines to get as many bodies to the Hejaz as possible for the purposes of colonial profit. And their grandparents, in turn, had made the trip on the decks of sailing ships, literally wandering across the face of an ocean for months to get to the same destination. The huge engines in the Boeing hum; there is no memory of those times in the steady, muted din of these machines. One of the pilgrims looks outside and sees the top of the Western Ghats, a craggy mountain chain in southern India, poking through the clouds. There are no ship beacons now; the journey is made through radar and azimuths, vectors and course speeds punched into a blinking computer. The pilgrim closes his eyes. Soon he will be in the Hejaz, and soon after that, it will be dawn. Every ounce of concentration will be needed for the prayers to be uttered while on Hajj. God is waiting in the west to embrace the faithful who have come from so far away.[1]

The Longest Journey documents the pilgrimage to Mecca from a distant, archipelagic part of the world, incorporating the stories of literally millions of people over the past five hundred plus years. The flow of pilgrims started out as a trickle, usually involving men of means who for religious and sometimes also for political reasons journeyed to the other side of the ocean's shores. These earliest voyagers were intrepid, as there were many dangers along the routes to Arabia and many ways to die in making this trip. By the high colonial era, the dynamics of the Hajj had started to change; European powers strove to control the main lines of the pilgrimage, so as to be able to manage the flows of people for their own purposes (table C.1). Some of these rationales involved politics and some involved money, but the result was a strengthening of the pathways in allowing the Hajj to function. More and more Southeast Asians took advantage of these evolving conditions, though a certain number of them also resented the fact that a central tenet of their religious lives was controlled by non-Muslim powers. By the middle decades of the twentieth century, there was another shift. The state maintained its preeminence in coordinating the mechanics of the Hajj, but individuals began to once again be able to choose many of the circumstances of their voyages. The idea of a singular pilgrimage began to be replaced by a more diffuse concept of the Hajj and "Hajj-plus"; one's pilgrimage could be accomplished in a multitude of manners. States and the differences in states helped to decide some of these differences—for example, tiny, ultramodern Singapore and enormous, chaotic Indonesia—but individual pilgrims themselves could also travel in ways according to their own choosing. The Hajj became more complex and varied yet again. Ironically, the age of postcolonial independence in Southeast Asia ushered in these changes across the board, as there are now rich pilgrims from poor countries and poor pilgrims from rich ones, alongside pilgrims representing myriad shades of socioeconomic gray, all side by side in the streets of Mecca.

Serious thinking about the nature of pilgrimage in the religious experience goes back at least to the time of Max Weber, if not even earlier. Weber wrote penetrating studies not only of the so-called Protestant ethic but also of Confucianism and Daoism in China and Hinduism in India; he also studied Buddhism and ancient Judaism, too. He had planned to write more about Islam as well but died in 1920 before he could realize his ambitions. Weber asserted that the religious and the economic have almost always been intertwined and that social stratification was important in how religion has been practiced. Both of these ideas jibe well with the realities of Hajj in this book.[2] Norbert Elias developed a notion from European history that a *habitus* is constructed among agglomerations of human beings, and that such codes of behavior develop over time and become

Table C.1 **Malay and Indonesian Pilgrim Numbers to Mecca: 1880s, 1930s, and 1980s**

	1884	1885	1886	1887	1888	1889
Malaya	3,176	3,685	2,889	2,524	2,659	2,361
NE Indies	4,540	4,692	2,523	2,426	4,328	3,146
	1934	**1935**	**1936**	**1937**	**1938**	**1939**
Malaya	514	712	1,046	2,882	5,115	2,059
NE Indies	2,854	3,693	4,012	5,402	10,327	10,884
	1979	**1980**	**1981**	**1982**	**1983**	**1984**
Malaysia	9,511	14,846	22,704	25,277	25,013	24,749
Indonesia	43,723	74,741	69,002	57,478	54,904	40,928

Sources: Adapted from Shalah Putuhena, *Historiografi Haji Indonesia* (Yogyakarta: LKIS (2007), 411–414; Mary Byrne McDonnell, "The Conduct of the Hajj From Malaysia and Its Socio-Economic Impact on Malay Society: A Descriptive and Analytical Study, 1860–1981" (PhD Dissertation, Columbia University, 1986), 626–627; and James Piscatori, "Asian Islam: International Linkages and Their Impact on International Relations," in John Esposito, ed., *Islam in Asia: Religion, Politics, and Society* (New York: Oxford University Press, 1987), 251.

Note: The 1930s data reflect the influence of the Great Depression.

equated with groups of people as part of their ways of living intact with one another. His ideas help, too, in conceptualizing the importance of a phenomenon such as the Hajj among very large composites of Muslims from all over Southeast Asia.[3] The pilgrimage to Mecca is a religious duty, but it is also an aesthetic, of sorts—something common to all of the so-called world religions—but something that at the same time is particular and singular to the values of Islam and its spiritual exegesis, as well as its human history.[4] If we are to attempt an archaeology of the Hajj as a religious and social project over the centuries, it is therefore important to ground our inquiry in these concepts. We must ask how and why the pilgrimage was performed, not only as an act of travel but also as a journey of the mind and heart, as scores of pilgrims have described it in the later chapters in this book.[5]

Contemporary theorists of pilgrimage can help with these questions. Some distinguish between types of pilgrimages, such as devotional ones, obligatory ones, and initiation-based pilgrimages, alongside a category of other forms that might be best described as simply "wandering" as the purpose of pilgrimage itself.[6] Other thinkers have spoken of peregrinology as part of a circuit of change and the desired memory of change, a required course of action before one can return to one's "normal life," but as an altered person as a result of the experience.[7] Another subset of scholars describe still other possibilities, with pilgrimages categorized under different sets of rubrics, including redeeming pilgrimages, therapeutic ones, and mystical pilgrimages, all as a set of broad archetypes.[8] One can certainly see aspects of nearly all of these ideas in the pilgrimage to Mecca, perhaps with the exception of the idea of wandering as the purpose of pilgrimage itself, which seems to be foreign to notions of the Hajj. Yet as one analyst points out unequivocally, "Islam is the one religion which actually *commands* its followers to undertake a pilgrimage."[9] The Qur'an itself states this, because the Ka'ba—built by Abraham himself—was later used for idol worship, before being cleansed by Muhammad in the seventh century CE. Pilgrims must therefore go to this site to see and be a part of this turning away from falsehood and to embrace God as the true force for good in the world. The fact that in Islam the Hajj is required only once, and that this is so regardless of how far the Muslim lives from the Hejaz, also seems important. It has not been lost on some theorists of religion that there seems to be a correlation between the distance and frequency of pilgrimage and the institution's power, both in religious efficacy and in the very real human attributes (social, political, economic) the pilgrimage imparts to those who perform it.[10] It is little wonder that we hear about miraculous cures, apparitions, and the trials and travails of performing the pilgrimage from Hajjis on a regular basis because this journey is *the* journey of a lifetime—a moment when all bounds of normalcy disappear. The Hajj is when human beings come face to face with larger forces in the universe.[11]

Temporal and Geographic Passages of the Longest of Journeys

The earliest records of Southeast Asians voyaging to Mecca indicate certain things about the fluid landscapes of the Hajj many centuries ago. Travelers were already moving on these routes in medieval times, with occasional sojourners (such as Ibn Battuta) able to conduct enormous journeys across the face of the known world. The Moroccan jurist was only one man amid this trickle of early figures, but his peregrinations show that the possibilities of travel—and especially travel for a Muslim with credentials and contacts—was certainly possible in this developing ecumene. The arrival of Europeans into the Indian Ocean around 1500 CE did not change these conditions immediately, though Europeans clearly started to write down notices of Hajjis moving across these vast oceanic spaces and to form opinions about these voyages. Commodities in motion— first rare and hard-to-find incenses, and later a range of other goods, especially coffee—made the Red Sea a vital corridor in global trade. Mocha and Jeddah became important ports, known from Rome all the way to China, and the ships of many countries pulled into the roads of these cities by the sea. From European scholarship written in a number of scholarly languages, it is now known that commerce helped along the Hajj on the wings of trade, encouraging people to venture from farther and farther afield to come to the Hejaz for a mix of religious and economic reasons. By the beginning of Ottoman times if not even slightly earlier than this, the ecumene was being set into place—a world of connection stretching from tiny islands off New Guinea to the Iberian Peninsula. Southeast Asians began to play an increasingly important role in the evolution of this world, as spices, Sufis, and ships scuttled back and forth across the sea-lanes, with the first Hajjis as part and parcel of these processes.

The role of economics in these formative centuries of the Hajj was crucial. Debates on the centrality of the Hajj to these economic systems have raged for years, with arguments presented both affirming and denying this notion. The Dutch were simultaneously facilitators and inhibitors of the Southeast Asian Hajj, depending on the (then contemporary) thinking within VOC administration. Profits and potential dangers of the Hajj were weighed very carefully by empire-building Europeans at this time. What was true of the Dutch was also true of the English, who were beginning to construct their own imperium in Southeast Asia during the eighteenth and nineteenth centuries as well. A steady stream of Malay and Indies pilgrims began to make the journey across the Indian Ocean, with a certain percentage of these Hajjis stuck every year in the Hejaz because of the crushing weight of their debts. Yet politics and religion were also crucial to the evolving system of pilgrimage as seen and interpreted in the Malay courts of Southeast Asia. Where previously European-language source materials were paramount, here indigenous chronicles, letters, and histories come to the forefront. *Hikayats, babads,* and *sejarahs* (the various Malay histories) can be explored to see what they can tell us about the growing importance of Hajj in Southeast Asian worldviews. It is argued here that the pilgrimage and the channel of human beings and ideas that it facilitated changed the nature of the Malay courts in terms of both statecraft and religious worldview over time. Itinerant Sufis played a particularly important role in this process, but the journeys of ordinary Hajjis also contributed to these changes. From the Malay texts, we can see how the Hajj increasingly became a vital part of political and religious reality in the lands beneath the winds, though this process took literally centuries to happen and did not affect all areas of the region with the same strength, or at the same time.

The colonial experience in Southeast Asia, and how this impacted the Hajj, is also of great relevance to our story. This time period is examined through four different windows here, centering on literary history and shipping, epidemiology and health, politics and governance, and espionage and great game maneuvering from the late nineteenth century to the middle decades of the twentieth. An examination of the furor that developed over the abandonment of a Southeast Asian pilgrim ship by British officers in 1880, and the subsequent retelling of the episode by Conrad some twenty years later, is one way to examine this period. Conrad was a famous critic of colonialism but was also sympathetic to the lofty ideas of the British Empire; the tensions between these two (at least partially) incompatible stances play out with great resonance in his masterpiece, *Lord Jim*. The novel is not only a fascinating window into the everyday facts and conduct of the Southeast Asian Hajj during the fin de siècle period but is also—crucially—a period artifact itself. Criticism and public opinion about the book helped lay some of the foundations of Western sensibilities about Islam, and certainly about the pilgrimage to Mecca at the turn of the twentieth century. Yet we can also move the narrative away from literature and criticism and into the altogether more frightening realm of disease control, specifically the passage of cholera on pilgrim ships from Southeast Asia. Cholera as transmitted by the Hajj became one of the first issues of global public health in the late nineteenth century; the disease frightened Europeans so much that a series of sanitary conventions were convened, especially after several outbreaks of cholera each killed tens of thousands of people. A tiny island in the Red Sea named Kamaran was eventually earmarked as a Hajj quarantine station, which hundreds of thousands of pilgrims passed through on their way to the holy cities during this time. Thousands of Hajjis died while performing their pilgrimages during these decades, and the medical reports on these disasters make up a salient part of this story. These reports are also a grim testament to the role of science and progress in the history of the Hajj, as the same steamships that brought Southeast Asian pilgrims to the Hejaz in unprecedented numbers also eventually became floating tombs. Overcrowding and poor sanitation killed devotees in droves.

Beyond literary representation and medical concerns, politics was also at the core of the Hajj. The career of one statesman within the machinery of Dutch Hajj governance—C. Snouck Hurgronje, one of the late nineteenth and early twentieth centuries' greatest Orientalists, regardless of nationality—was central here. Snouck was a scholar of Islam but also was important and influential within Dutch policy-making circles; he helped to coordinate much of the Netherlands' policy toward Islam in Indonesia and, by extension, rules and regulations about the mechanics of the Indies Hajj. In these respects, Snouck was an agent of colonial coercion, and his attitudes in his writings—as seen from his letters, which were not published while he was alive—bear this out. Yet Snouck also converted to Islam, married two Indies women (both Muslims), and lived in the Hejaz for a time, so his attitudes ended up being very complex on questions having to do with matters such as the Hajj. His stance on the Indies pilgrimage, both public and privately uttered, is under review here. Yet we can also enlarge this picture to a much broader frame and ask how the growth and development of European consulates in Jeddah, the feeder city for the Hajj, led to a vast system of espio-nage and control over the pilgrimage by various Western powers. Thousands of microfiches from the former Dutch consulate in Jeddah allow us to do this as source base, but these records are supplemented by available English-, French-, and Italian-language materials from the colonial repositories of all of these coun-tries. Together, these sources provide an encircling view into the evolution of European mastery of the Red Sea as a strategic corridor, one that became of vital importance to Great Power politics in the decades on either side of 1900. Commercial and military shipping was one of the crucial issues at stake with this waterway, but the Hajj as a conduit of thousands upon thousands of human beings was another pressing concern. These scattered documents from a number of different countries make this abundantly clear.

The modern experience of the Southeast Asian Hajj, in the age of independent nation-states, brings this story up to date. The Hajj was taken over after the end of World War II by the aspiring new countries of the region, who were once again able to organize the pilgrimage as they saw fit after the colonial inter-regnum. The transition to self-rule was not easy, and new variants of organiza-tional models were required, spanning the Hajj from Singapore, Malaysia, and Indonesia. Modern transport, government record keeping, and the Saudi Hajj Bureau all have important places in this narrative. The modern Southeast Asian pilgrimage is significantly more multivalent and multifaceted now than ever before, with gender, wealth, and the state playing different roles in different societies. Yet the Hajj functions from outside Southeast Asia's Muslim arc, too (the ring of landscapes running from Pattani down through Malaysia and up through Indonesia and Brunei to Mindanao). The ability of Muslims to go on the pilgrimage from places such as Burma, Thailand, Cambodia, Vietnam, and the Philippines is varied; at certain junctures and in certain regional and subre-gional landscapes, these non-Muslim majority states have made the journey entirely possible. At other junctures and in other parts of these countries, performing the Hajj has been exceedingly difficult, as poverty, war, and systemic prejudice have made it nigh impossible for Muslims to even think about such a voyage. This has been a historical process, but it is also a contemporary issue for area Muslims in this respect, as prospects are tied to flashpoint issues that concern the Association of Southeast Asian Nations member states. Fieldwork in many of these landscapes, stretching from Arakan in western Burma to Zamboanga in the southern Philippines, supplements written documentation of the official (and unofficial) kind in sketching out this evolving state of affairs.

Yet it has been important to end with the words of modern Southeast Asian pilgrims themselves, as they put their own thoughts about their pilgrimages into the record, both through memoirs and through the hundred-plus interviews I was able to conduct in the region. Hajj memoirs stretch back to an initial historical period of the late nineteenth and early twentieth centuries but have appeared much more voluminously during the past several decades. These memoirs are almost entirely written in Malay and Indonesian and have become a huge publishing industry now in these two countries (as well as to a lesser extent in Singapore, Brunei, and other places). Writing a memoir, it is argued, implies wanting to get across a point of view; it also implies the erection of an image of what one did (and did not do) during a particular period of time. Memoirs of the pilgrimage to Mecca are fascinating in this respect because they show the hopes, concerns, and predilections of Hajjis as they leave their thoughts on their pilgrimages to be judged by posterity. This book closes with an account of Hajj memories as told to me by pilgrims from all across Southeast Asia, during many scattered months of interviewing in the region over the past seven years. It felt important to end the book in this way, to make sure that pilgrims got to have the last word in this history through their own quiet conversations. The kinds of things one says in an oral interview can be very different from utterances put into a written memoir, and this proved to be entirely the case in researching the Hajj. The oral history conversations that end this book show this dialectic in action, as a range of topics not usually discussed in such depth in memoirs—from gendered concerns to the appearance of what (for a lack of a better term) can only be termed *ghosts* and *miracles*—all made regular appearances. To me, these conversations were the most important result of the study, as they are the "sources" most fully owned by the pilgrims themselves. I hope that these recorded thoughts of a huge range of people—women and men, old and young, rich and poor, rural and urban—will find resonance with any Hajjis and Hajjas from the region who end up reading this volume. In the end this is their story, though one that can be told in group-form by the conventions and structures of a modern, academic book.

Traveling the Ocean's Circuit

It has been said by one prominent scholar that we should try to "make sense of Muslim history and society," a tall order if there ever was one.[12] The history of Islam is so broad and so varied that making sense of it seems the project of a lifetime or the project of many lifetimes of many people. My aims have been much more circumscribed in this book. I wanted to understand the life arc of one ritual of Islam and from only one part of the world, though this was already shaping up to be an enormous task.[13] A number of scholars have predicted that describing the trajectories of Islam in spaces not always associated with the centrality of the religion might bear sweet fruit, which I hope has at least partially happened here.[14] An analysis of the *longue duree* contours of the pilgrimage to Mecca from Southeast Asia gives not only a sense of the evolution of a religious phenomenon, but also insights into the politics, economics, and social histories of a variety of places. In economic terms alone—the vantage that is likely least identified with such a massive religious ritual– the pilgrimage is of enormous consequence, so one can imagine the political and especially the spiritual dimensions as being that much deeper.[15] When one tries to measure and describe these attributes not only at one moment but also through a continuum of time and space, the stakes become even larger.[16] How important has the Hajj been to Islamic history? How has this changed over time? Where and in what circumstances did the pilgrimage change Muslim societies, and what are the signs that this has happened? In short, what is the lineage and genealogy of the Hajj across the ocean's circuit, in the centuries when the Indian Ocean became, for all intents and purposes a vast Islamic lake?

The Ottomans certainly have a part in any story along these lines. Though the Hajj from Southeast Asia to Mecca probably existed in some small sense before the rise of the Ottomans, for most of recorded history, this journey from monsoon Asia to the Middle East was an Ottoman trip because there was little way around the Ottomans if one wanted to make a pilgrimage to the Hejaz.[17] The crucial period in this sense was the early modern era, when the Ottomans started to extend their rule over the Red Sea and made Yemen and other parts of the Tihama part of their outstretched empire, even if their dominion was very tenuous at times.[18] By the sixteenth and seventeenth centuries, this littoral already had a very complex history, with a vast range of actors pulling into the ports on the northern rim of the Red Sea channel. Many of these people were pilgrims, but others were not on their way to the holy cities. Yet their presence—especially from political and economic vantages—significantly complicated these histories.[19] By the nineteenth century, territorial imperatives were also becoming significant, as foreign powers began to impact the working of the Hajj not only from the sea but also by land, as the European presence became stronger on the ground.[20] British, French, Dutch, and other Western states all vied for a presence in the region. Even the Russians and Italians attempted to pursue gains there. Southeast Asian pilgrims passed through this channel of competing interests every year, watched by many eyes on both sides of the Red Sea as they passed through the Bab al-Mandeb. Even the middle decades of the twentieth century saw these rivalries continuing to influence the conduct of the Hajj, from Southeast Asia all the way to northwest Africa, a ribbon of Muslim land and sea thousands of miles wide.[21]

That latter story is a transcontinental one, but the one being told here rests squarely in Asia. At the heart of this narrative is the Indian Ocean. Different scholars have approached this space in different ways, but all have shown underlying themes of unity in how the Indian Ocean acted to transit human beings and ideas across Asia for many centuries. Some of these approaches have focused on religion and prayer, that is to say, intellectual tacks that have been primarily eschatological in nature.[22] Others have looked more carefully at merchants and the trade diasporas that these merchant networks created in pursuit of the vast, scattered wealth of this region.[23] Still others have concentrated more on capital and the beginnings of new, complex systems as the early modern age slowly bled into the colonial era.[24] There is even a newer branch of scholarship, taking this research one step further, that examines the Indian Ocean as a system when it was thought to be moving into a kind of languorous, nineteenth-century decline.[25] What all of these scholarly endeavors have in common is a sense that the sea itself remains central—the waves in between Aden and Singapore were far from neutral and unchanging in the histories of this enormous track of pilgrimage. Rather, the ocean is an actor in the narrative of religious devotion as well. Storms, monsoons, Sufis, commerce, and transoceanic politics were all part of the same ever-changing tableaux of movement connecting the two sides of the Indian Ocean in a centuries-long embrace.

The Hajj was undoubtedly one of the main ingredients in making this system work for as long as it has. Writers on the pilgrimage to Mecca have pointed out the cohesive power of the Hajj in the modern world; the ritual possesses a kind of tensile strength in welding Muslim societies together, even when many of these societies do not have a common lingua franca or culture.[26] If this is true now, it was certainly true in much of historical time, when places such as the Indonesian archipelago and the wider Malay world generally had a much harder time maintaining links with the spiritual center of Islam because of the hardships of long-distance travel.[27] Muslims in various parts of the world kept a close watch on events and trends in places like the Hejaz, and even comparatively remote agglomerations of Muslims in places such as Southeast Asia could, in fact, stay abreast of changes, though it often took longer for news to travel to this corner of the Islamic world.[28] The Hajj was one of the main vehicles—if not *the* main vehicle—of doing this. Scholars and statesmen were aware of this fact, and many did their utmost to encourage the pilgrimage so that these links could be maintained. In many cases, links were nourished and strengthened by regular transits of ulama and other knowledgeable Muslims moving between the two poles of the Indian Ocean world. Yet this was also, of course, a populist story. It was not only elites who traveled but also the poor and destitute, the marginalized and the powerless—even Muslims from places where being a Muslim was potentially dangerous. These people, too, made the trip. The Hajj allowed a kind of communion between civilizations, one of them desert based and predominantly tribal and the other coastal and often cosmopolitan, across much of the known world. It is through this lens that we should judge the importance of the pilgrimage as a conduit, one that made all sorts of contact possible over the *longue duree*.[29]

It is worth remembering that Islam became one of the greatest connective strands not only between Southeast Asia and the Middle East but also between various Southeast Asian polities. The largest part of this story concerns Indonesia, the world's largest Muslim country in terms of population, which at the same time is also a physical behemoth, stretching thousands of miles along the equator in the heart of Southeast Asia. This is true now, but it was also true as "Indonesia" was itself coming into being, from its earlier topographical shape as a colony of the Dutch in the region.[30] The energies of Islam from what is now Malaysia were also important in seeding this kind of Muslim regionalism, as the religion spread in these precolonial, colonial, and postcolonial lands.[31] Local pilgrimages to the tombs of saints across putative national boundaries further encouraged this sense of a regional Islam. Smaller places, such as Singapore and Brunei, have also played parts in this story, especially in the importance of their ports and the shipping that moved people throughout the lands beneath the winds.[32] The faith eventually came to many shores in Southeast Asia and eventually traveled back to the Middle East—often via the Hajj, though also through education and increasingly now through tourism—to other parts of this huge area where Islam was, in fact, far older.[33] The pilgrimage to Mecca has therefore been not only an Indian Ocean narrative but also a Southeast Asian one. It has been part and parcel of historical circulations across expansive, maritime geographies, but it has also been quiet, intimate, and local in its own way.[34] The Hajj achieves both of these things concurrently. The history of this longest of journeys expresses this duality over the ages and reminds us why Southeast Asians continue to make such great sacrifices to perform this pilgrimage before they leave this world.

NOTES

1. Though these words are my own, the gist of this description was given to me of a pilgrimage by jet by an Indonesian Hajji. His was one of the most lyrical recountings of this experience that I heard in my several years of research about the Hajj.

2. Editions of Weber's work are easy to come by, but for a good explanation of his thought that puts his ideas into context, see Reinhard Bendix, *Max Weber: An Intellectual Portrait* (Berkeley: University of California Press, 1977). See also Bryan Turner, *For Weber: Essays on the Sociology of Fate* (London: Sage, 1996).

3. Norbert Elias, *The Civilizing Process: Sociogenetic and Psychogenetic Investigations* (Oxford: Blackwell, 1994).

4. On the notion of religion as an aesthetic, see S. Brent Plate, *Walter Benjamin, Religion and Aesthetics* (London: Routledge, 2004).

5. Michel Foucault, *The Archaeology of Knowledge*, trans. A. M. Sheridan Smith (London: Routledge, 2002). Foucault's notion of searching for the building blocks of knowledge and, in this case, self-knowledge seems important here.

6. Alan Morinis, "Introduction," in Alan Morinis, ed., *Sacred Journeys: The Anthropology of Pilgrimage* (Westport, CT: Greenwood, 1992), pp. 10–13.

7. R. P. B. Singh, "Time and Hindu Rituals in Varanasi: A Study of Sacrality and Cycles," in S. M. Bhardwaj, G. Rinschede, and A. Sievers, eds., *Pilgrimage in the Old and New World* (Berlin: Dietrich Reimer Verlag, 1994).

8. Anne Osterrieth, "Pilgrimage, Travel and Existential Quest," in Robert Stoddard and Alan Morinis, eds., *Sacred Places, Sacred Spaces: The Geography of Pilgrimages* (Baton Rouge, LA: Geoscience, 1997), p. 27.

9. Richard Barber, *Pilgrimages* (Woodbridge, England: Boydell and Brewer, 1991), p. 30.

10. Robert Stoddard, "Pilgrimage along Sacred Paths," in R. L. Singh, and Rana Singh, eds., *Trends in the Geography of Pilgrimages* (Varanasi, India: National Geographic Society of India, 1987), p. 96.

11. James Preston, "Spiritual Magnetism: An Organizing Principle for the Study of Pilgrimage," in Alan Morinis, ed., *Sacred Journeys: The Anthropology of Pilgrimage* (Westport, CT: Greenwood, 1992), pp. 33–35.

12. Ahmed Akbar, *Discovering Islam: Making Sense of Muslim History and Society* (London: Routledge, 1988).

13. "Do you know how enormous?" William Roff asked me in a cautionary manner when I had just started to conceptualize this project. I think I can report that I now have some sense of "how enormous" this project could be.

14. Richard Bulliet, *Islam: The View from the Edge* (New York: Columbia University Press, 1994).

15. On the economic angle, see, for example, Farhad Nomani and Ali Rahnema, *Islamic Economic Systems* (London: Zed, 1994).

16. Aziz Al-Azmeh, *Islams and Modernities* (London: Verso, 1993). See also Michael Gilsenan's erudite contribution, Michael Gilsenan, *Recognizing Islam: Religion and Society in the Modern Middle East* (London: Tauris, 2005).

17. Clive Heywood, *Writing Ottoman History: Documents and Interpretations* (Aldershot, England: Variorum, 2002).

18. Rifa'at 'Ali Abou-El-Haj, *Formation of the Modern State: The Ottoman Empire Sixteenth to Eighteenth Centuries* (Albany: State University of New York Press, 1991).

19. Husayn 'Abd Allah al-Amri, *The Yemen in the Eighteenth and Nineteenth Centuries: A Political and Intellectual History* (London: Durham Middle East Monographs #1, 1985).

20. Caesar Farah, *The Sultan's Yemen: Nineteenth-Century Challenges to Ottoman Rule* (London: Tauris, 2002).

21. Abdulrahman Al-Shamlan, "The Evolution of National Boundaries in the Southeastern Arabian Peninsula, 1934–1955" (PhD Dissertation, University of Michigan, 1987).

22. David Parkin and Stephen Headley, eds., *Islamic Prayer across the Indian Ocean* (London: Curzon, 2000).

23. K. N. Chaudhuri, *Trade and Civilisation in the Indian Ocean: An Economic History from the Rise of Islam to 1750* (Cambridge: Cambridge University Press, 1985); Sanjay Subrahmanyam, *Improvising Empire: Portuguese Trade and Settlement in the Bay of Bengal* (Delhi: Oxford University Press, 1990).

24. Eric Tagliacozzo, "Underneath the Indian Ocean: A Review Essay," *Journal of Asian Studies*, 67/3, 2008: 1–8.

25. Sugata Bose, *A Hundred Horizons: The Indian Ocean in the Age of Global Empire* (Cambridge, MA: Harvard University Press, 2006); Michael Miller, "Pilgrims' Progress: The Business of the Hajj," *Past and Present*, 191, 2006: 189–228.

26. Robert Bianchi, *Guests of God: Pilgrimage and Politics in the Islamic World* (Oxford: Oxford University Press, 2004).

27. M. Dien Majid, "Berhaji Tempo Dulu Dengan Kapal Laut," in Edi Sedyawati and Susanto Zuhdi, eds., *Arung Samudra: Persembahan Memperingati Sembilan Windu A. B. Lapian* (Depok, Indonesia: Pusat Penetitian dan Budaya Lembaga Penetitian UI, 2001); Huub de Jonge, "Heiligen, Middelen en Doel: Ontwikkeling en Betekenis van Twee Islamitische Bedevaartsoordelen op Java," in Willy Jansen and Huub de Jonge, eds., *Islamitische Pelgrimstochten* (Muiderberg, Netherlands: Coutinho, 1991); Henri Chambert-Loir and Claude Guillot, *Le Culte des Saints dans le Monde Musulman* (Paris: EFEO, 1995), pp. 81–100; Marcel Witlox, "Met Gevaar voor Lijf en Goed:

Mekkagangers uit Nederlands-Indie in de 19de Eeuw," in Willy Jansen and Huub de Jonge, eds., *Islamitische Pelgrimstochten* (Muiderberg, Netherlands: Coutinho, 1991), pp. 24–26.

28. Marianne van Leeuwen, "Politieke Geweld in Mekka," in Willy Jansen and Huub de Jonge, eds., *Islamitische Pelgrimstochten* (Muiderberg, Netherlands: Coutinho, 1991), pp. 57–68; Geert Jan van Gelder, "Pelgrims, Passie en Poezie," In Willy Jansen and Huub de Jonge, eds., *Islamitische Pelgrimstochten* (Muiderberg, Netherlands: Coutinho, 1991), pp. 69–73.

29. David Long, *The Hajj Today: A Survey of the Contemporary Mekkah Pilgrimage* (Albany: State University of New York Press, 1979).

30. Karel Steenbrink, *Dutch Colonialism and Indonesian Islam: Contacts and Conflicts, 1596–1950* (Amsterdam: Radopi, 1993); H. Aqib Suminto, *Politik Islam Hindia Belanda: Het Kantoor voor Inslandsche Zaken* (Jakarta: Lembaga Penelitian Pendidikan dan Penerangan Ekonomi dan Sosial, 1985); G. F. Pijper, *Studien over de Geschiedenis van de Islam in Indonesia, 1900–1950* (Leiden: E. J. Brill, 1977). See also Martin van Bruinessen, Muhammad Khalid Masud, and Armando Salvatore, eds., *Islam and Modernity: Key Issues and Debates* (Edinburgh: Edinburgh University Press, 2009).

31. Syed Muhammad Naguib al-Attas, *Islam dalam Sejarah dan Kebudayaan Melayu* (Kuala Lumpur: Penerbit Universiti Kebangsaan Malaysia, 1972); Moshe Yegar, *Islam and Islamic Institutions in British Malaya: Policies and Implementation* (Jerusalem: Magnes, 1979).

32. Anonymous, *Muslims in Singapore: A Shared Vision* (Singapore: Majlis Ugama Islam Singapura, 1994); Anonymous, *Islam di Brunei* (Bandar Seri Begawan, Brunei: Kementerian Kebudayaan, 1992).

33. Peter Gowing, *Muslim Filipinos: Heritage and Horizon* (Quezon City, Philippines: New Day, 1979); Moshe Yegar, *Between Integration and Succession: The Muslim Communities of the Southern Philippines, Southern Thailand, and Western Burma/Myanmar* (Lanham, MD: Lexington, 2002).

34. Again, Robert Bianchi's *Guests of God* is useful here; he shows very convincingly the power of local associations in Malaysia and Indonesia (and, by extension, elsewhere) to organize and control the Hajj so that this is very much a local as well as a translocal story. See pp. 13–21.

ARCHIVAL LISTINGS

I. Middle East

YEMEN

- *Centre Français des Etudes Yemenites, Sana'a*
French- and Italian-language sources on the Red Sea were consulted here.

- *American Institute for Yemeni Studies, Sana'a*
A variety of mostly Dutch- and English-language sources were consulted here.

- *National Library of Yemen, Aden*
A variety of English-language sources were consulted here.

OMAN

- *Bait Zubair Museum, Muscat*
The collection on historical Omani trade was utilized here.

QATAR

- *Museum of Islamic Art, Doha*
Manuscript collection was consulted here.

II. Southeast Asia

INDONESIA

- *Perpustakaan Negara Indonesia, Jakarta (National Library of Indonesia)*
A variety of Hajj memoirs were read here, mainly twentieth century in origin.

- *Arsip Nasional Republik Indonesia, Jakarta (National Archives of Indonesia)*
Gewestelijke Stukken Collection

- *K1. Banten (1674–1891)*
  #115. 1860, terdapat daftar orang pergi haji.

- *K2. Tangerrang*
  #137/3. Diversen onderwerpen, incl. "naik Haji," 1856–1905.
  #164/3. Stukken betreffende Mohammedaansche zaken, o.a. Mekkagangers, moske, 1913–1914.

- *K4. Krawang (1803–1891)*
  #29–35 (p. 4). Algemeen verslag der ass. Res. Krawang 1865–1871. Sebanyak 7 band a.1: Algemeen bestuur, "naik haji."

- *K7. Cirebon*
  #3/4. Opgave van Mekka-Grassen, 1845.

- *K8. Tegal (1790–1872)*
  #194a/4. Brieven mengenai naik Haji, 1857.
  #196/5. "Laporan pergi dan pulang haji."

- *K10. Semarang (1816–ca. 1880)*
  #4362–4370. Stukken inzake de bedevaart naar Mekka.

- *K13. Banjoemas*
  Various documents.

- *K18. Japara (1674–1891)*
  #59. Tahun 1875. Aankomende brieven (Vendu kantoor; Bedevaart; ziekte rapport; politiezaken), jan–apr. 1875.
  #74. Tahun 1856 1857. Aankomende brieven: bedevaart.

- *K23. Arsip Besuki (1819–1913)*
  #49. (nomor lama 6/5): Algemeen verslag van de Residentie Besoeki over het jaar 1855. Laporan umum dari keresidenan Besoeki tahun 1855. Isi: Opgave van de personen die van Mekka zijn teruggekeerd. Tentang kembalinya orang-orang dari Mekkah (naik haji).
  #78 (Nomor lama 9/14) (1883). B.b. Uitbreiding van het Mohamedanisme toe–en afname van het aantal bedevaartgangers.

- *K32. Bangka (1803–1890)*
  Politiek Verslag 1872, *Algemeen Verslag* 1890

- *K33. Billiton (1795–1890)*
  Algemeen Verslag 1874, 1880, 1885, 1890

- *K36. Lampong (1739–1890)*
  Politiek Verslag 1864, 1867, 1886, 1887, 1888, 1890

- *K44. Ternate*
  #335. Agenda Eeredienst en Nijverheid, 1892.
  #338. Diverse stukken met Agenda Eeredienst en Nijverheid, 1892.

- *K63. Riouw*
  Administratief Verslag 1867–1874

- *Arsip West-Borneo*
  Algemeene Verslagen 1875, 1886, 1891

Algemene Secretarie Collection (deel I, 1945–1950)
  #753–754. Mekka 1945–1948.
  #755–760. Correspondentie Mekka, Hadj, Mekkagangers, pilgrims, etc. (1947–1949).
  #1044. Stukken betreffende het verlenen van financiele steun aan de groep Moekimers te Mekka. 1945–1946.
  #1552. Stukken betreffende Raden Tarbidin Soeriawinata, consul te Mekka; met verslagen van een bedevaart en van een orientatiereis door Indonesie (1944–1949).

Sekretariat Wapres Adam Malik Tahun 1978–1982.
  #823. Seswapres kepada Mensesneg, cs: surat, tanggal 16 Nopember 1978 tentang musibah pesawat haji, dengan lampiran.
  #835. Kakanwil Departemen Agama, Medan: surat, tanggal 2 Desember 1979 tentang perkembangan asrama haji Medan, dengan lampiran. Asli.

#839. Setwapres: surat-surat, tanggal 26 Mei 1980–24 Agustus 1982 tentang permohonan dana untuk ongkos naik haji.

#846. DPRD Tk. I Propinsi Kalimantan Selatan: surat, tanggal 4 Nopember 1980 tentang usul Pelud Syamsudin Noor untuk ditetapkan menjadi pelabuhan haji udara, dengan lampiran. Asli.

#856. Seswapres kepada Menteri Agama: surat, tanggal 26 Mei 1981 tentang permohonan Kosasih Husin, Pontianak untuk menunaikan Ibadah Haji dan berkunjung ke Lembaga Amnesti International, dengan lampiran.

Arsip Departemen Agama II 1976–2000.
  Various correspondence.

MALAYSIA

• *Perpustakaan Negara Malaysia, Kuala Lumpur (National Library of Malaysia)*
  A variety of Malay-language sources were consulted here.

• *Universitas Islam Antarabangsa Library, Gombak*
  A variety of Malay-language sources were consulted here.

• *Arkib Negara Malaysia, Kuala Lumpur (National Archives of Malaysia)*
High Commissioner's Office
  1913/#1292: 1770, 1868, and 1889: Pilgrimage to Mecca by Sultan of Trengganu.
  1916/#332: Letter from Majlis Ugama re: conditions of Kelantan natives in Mecca.
  1917/#491: Expenditure on Repatriation of destitute Malay Pilgrims.
  1917/#1386: More on this 690/1920 Quarantine Fees on Pilgrims to the Hedjaz.
  1918/#279: Regulations re: Remittance of Money from Malay States to Mecca.
  1918/#720: Remittances to Mecca.
  1918/#2008: Cost of Repatriation to Netherlands India of Malay Pilgrims from Mecca.
  1928/#1305: Quarantine of Pilgrims from Malaya.
  1931/#310: Pilgrimage Tariff for 1931.
  1935/#1084: Passports for Kelantan Malays for Mecca Pilgrimage.
  1938/#654: Annual Report on the Malayan Pilgrimage for the Season 1937–1938.
  1938/#902: Issue of Passports by British Legation at Jeddah to Malay Pilgrims.
Federal Secretariat files
  1949/#14047: Mecca Pilgrimage: Pilgrim Dues.
  1949/#14050: Taking over SS *Tyndareous* for Mecca Pilgrim Trade.
  1949–1950/#12064: Report on 1949 Mecca Pilgrimage Season.
  1949–1950/#12456: List of Names and Addresses of Pilgrims Going to Mecca.

SINGAPORE

• *Singapore National History Archives, Singapore (Oral History Centre)*
  Recorded Interviews with Ali Bin Sanat (born 1904), Anonymous Malay #4 (b. 1911), Haji Buang Bin Siraj (b. 1917), Hamzah Haji Hussein (b. 1917), Hasnah Bte Sahlan (b. 1919), Mohamed Sidek Bin Siraj (b. 1912), Mohd Yusof Bin Lana (b. 1928), Salamah Bte Tamby (b. 1922), Abu Bakar b. Haji Abdul Halim (b. 1921), Abdul Latiff Bin Ahmad (b. 1916), Yuhanis Bte Haji Yusoff (b. 1931).

• *National University of Singapore Library, Singapore*
  Most of the Colonial Office correspondence (CO/273, Straits Settlements), as well as other CO series, were read here on microfilm.

III. Europe

FRANCE

• *Bibliothèque Nationale, Paris (National Library of France)*
  Most of the French-language period scholarly literature and reports were read here.

- *Bibliothèque SciencesPo, Paris (Library of the University of SciencePo)*
  Some modern and also period French-language material was read here.

ITALY

- *Istituto Italiano per l'Africa e l'Oriente, Roma (Italian Institute of Africa and Asia)*
  Most of the Italian-language period scholarly literature and letters were read here.

NETHERLANDS

- *Koninklijke Instituut voor de Tropen, Amsterdam (Royal Institute of the Tropics)*

Hard Copies of the Daniel van der Meulen Diaries:
- Dagboek, January 11, 1926, to June 13, 1927, "A"
- Dagboek, Tweede Z. W. Arabie Exploratie, February 2, 1939, to May 21, 1939, "B"
- Dagboek, Makassar to Jeddah, January 4, 1941, to May 7, 1941, "C"
- Dagboek, Jeddah, February 4, 1942, to January 11, 1942, "D"
- Dagboek, Saudi Arabia, December 15, 1944, to February 14, 1945, "E"
- Dagboek, Arabia Reis met Bram Drewes, January 1, 1952, to March 31, 1952, "F"

Daniel van der Meulen Article Collection:
- Meulen, D. van der, "De Bedevaart naar Mekka en haar beteekenis voor Nederlands-Indie," *Zendingstijdschrift De Opwekker*, 86/1, 1942: 474–486.
- Meulen, D. van der, "The Mecca Pilgrimage and Its Importance to the Netherlands Indies," *The Moslem World*, 31, 1941: 48–60.
- Meulen, D. van der, "The Revival of the Pilgrimage to Mecca," *Niewsblad voor de Residentien Palembang, Djambi, en Banka*, September 14, 1937.
- Meulen, D. van der, "The Revival of the Pilgrimage to Mecca," *De Telegraaf*, October 2, 1937.
- Meulen, D. van der, "The Return of the Mecca Pilgrims to the Dutch East Indies," *Deli Courant*, March 25, 1938.
- Meulen, D. van der, "The Pilgrimage to Mecca," *Palembanger*, June 18, 1938.
- Meulen, D. van der, "The Mecca Pilgrimage," *Palembanger*, 1938 (n.d., clipping).

- *Koninklijke Instituut voor Taal-, Land-en Volkenkunde, Leiden (KITLV)*
  Much of the period Dutch-language scholarly literature was consulted here.

- *Koninklijke Bibliotheek, Den Haag (Royal Library, The Hague)*
  Some period Dutch-language scholarly literature was consulted here.

- *Nationaal Archief, Den Haag (National Archives, Netherlands)*

Ministerie van Kolonien (Ministry for the Colonies)
Politieke Verslagen Buitenbezittingen (2.10.52)
- Atjeh (1905–1907), fiche #7
- Tapanoeli (1906–1940), fiche #108
- Sumatra OK (1898–1940), fiche #156
- Sumatra WK (1901–1940), fiche #224
- Riouw (1899–1940), fiche #295
- Djambi (1900–1940), fiche #324
- Palembang (1913–1935), fiche #368
- Lampongsche Districten (1906–1940), fiche #386
- Borneo West (1898–1940), fiche #393

- Borneo ZO (1898–1940), fiche #444
- Celebes (1898–1940), fiche #527
- Ternate (1898–1940), fiche #723

Mailrapporten (2.10.02 and 2.10.36)

- MR 1872, #820 +; MR 1878, #474; MR 1879, #668 +; MR 1881, #259 +; #563 +, 709 +, #839 +; #860; #1107; #1139 +; MR 1883, #252 +; #1075 +; #1173; MR 1885, #638 +.

Memorie van Overgaven (2.10.39)

MMK COLLECTION:

A. West Java (Bantam)
MMK 1   Hardeman, J. A. (resident) Memorie van Overgave (1906) 51 pp.
B. Midden Java (Provincie)
MMK 40   Gulik, P. J. van (Gouverneur) Memorie van Overgave (1931) 31 pp.
C. Oost-Java (Provincie)
MMK 83   Hardeman, W. Ch. (Gouverneur) Memorie van Overgave (1931) 114 pp.
D. Sumatra (Atjeh)
MMK 158   Goehart, O. M. (Gouverneur) Memorie van Overgave (1929) 27 pp.
E. Sumatra (Weskust)
MMK 163   Heckler, F. A. (Gouverneur) Memorie van Overgave (1910) 30 pp.
F. Sumatra (Jambi)
MMK 216   Helfrich, O. L. (Resident) Memorie van Overgave (1908) 78 pp.
G. Borneo West
MMK 261   Vogel, H. de (Resident) Memorie van Overgave (1918) 108 pp.
H. Borneo Zuid Oost (Z.O.)
MMK 271   Rickmans, L. J. F (Resident) Memorie van Overgave (1916) 76 pp.
I. Celebes
MMK 281   Swart, H. N. A. (Gouverneur) Memorie van Overgave (1908) 46 pp.
J. Ternate
MMK 329   Sandick, L. W. H. can (Gouverneur) Memorie van Overgave (1926) 600 pp.

Ministerie van Buitenlandse Zaken (2.05.38)

- "A" Dossiers, #74 "Correspondentie over woelingen, slavenhandel en slavernij in de Hedjaz 1872–1936," Correspondence in box #148.

- "B" Dossiers, #187 "Mekkagangers: Pelgrimaangelegenheden in de Hedjaz, 1871–1917," Correspondence in boxes #1804, #1816, #1829.

Koloniaal Verslagen

- Reports from years 1872, 1875, 1887, 1890, 1894, 1897, and 1903.

Djeddah Archives (2.05.53)

1.2.4   *Medische aangelegenheden*
155   Stukken betreffende adviezen van de internationale gezondheidsraad te Constantinopel inzake het inrichten van lazaretten voor pelgrims op de eilanden bij Djeddah. 1881–1907 18 microfiches.
Stukken betreffende de op 10 mei 1926 te Parijs gehouden conferentie.
tot herziening van de Sanitaire Conventie van 1912 alsmede de quarantaine op Kamaran en het vestigen van een internationaal quarantaine station op de Hidjazkust. 1920–1949.
156   1920–1926 30 microfiches.
157   1927–1949 50 microfiches.
Ingekomen medische rapporten van de legatiearts inzake de
gezondheidstoestand van Indonesische bedevaartgangers in Mekka. 1928–1949.
158   1927–1934 49 microfiches.
159   1935–1949 39 microfiches.

160 Stukken betreffende de medische behandeling van Straits- en Malakka-pelgrims in Mekka. 1931–1939 6 microfiches.

161 Stukken betreffende de vestiging van dr. A.G. Hartman als arts te Djeddah. 1932–1933 2 microfiches.

162 Stukken betreffende de bacteriologen dr. Ph. van de Hoog en dr. H. Vervoort inzake de organisatie van de gezondheids- en quarantainedienst in de Hidjaz. 1932–1939 1 microfiche.

163 Stukken betreffende de medische dienst in de Hidjaz. 1934 3 microfiches.

165 Stukken betreffende de samenwerking tussen Nederland en Groot-Brittannië inzake de medische verzorging van Moekimers en Brits-Maleisiërs. 1943–1947 7 microfiches.

166 Stukken betreffende het zenden van een medische missie naar de bedevaart te Mekka. 1949 4 microfiches.

1.2.6 *Politieke aangelegenheden*

175 Stukken betreffende de slavernij in de Hidjaz. 1924–1933 4 microfiches.

182 Rapporten van het gezantschap aan het ministerie van Buitenlandse Zaken inzake een Sovjet-vertegenwoordiging in de Hidjaz, afschriften. 1931–1932 1 microfiche.

188 Stukken betreffende het verdrag van het Arabische broeder- en bondgenootschap. 1935–1937 3 microfiches.

192 Stukken betreffende de dubbele nationaliteit van pelgrimssjeiks. 1937–1941 3 microfiches.

193 Stukken betreffende de moord op 13 Djawa-pelgrims te Mekka door Djawi-hadji Tamin bin Safar. 1938 2 microfiches.

197 Stukken betreffende Japanse en Duitse propaganda in Saoedi-Arabië. 1940–1941 3 microfiches.

1.2.6.2 *Indonesiërs in Mekka*

199 Stukken betreffende het verenigingsleven van Indonesiërs in Mekka. 1929–1932 13 microfiches.

200 Stukken betreffende de Djawa-kolonie te Mekka. 1929–1938 9 microfiches.

201 Stukken betreffende acties van in Saoedi-Arabië verblijvende Indonesiërs tegen de intrekking van de bijzondere toelatingsvoorwaarden van de Indische regering ten opzichte van christelijke zendingsorganisaties. 1939 2 microfiches.

202 Stukken betreffende de werving van Indonesiërs uit Mekka voor infiltratie en liaison werk ter herovering van Nederlands-Indië. 1942–1945 10 microfiches.

203 Naamlijsten van Indische vrijwilligers die deelnemen aan de bevrijding van Nederlands-Indië. 1943–1944 10 microfiches.

UNITED KINGDOM

- *Cambridge University Library, Cambridge*
Many nineteenth- and twentieth-century English-language materials were read here.

- *India Office, British Library (IOL), London*

- Mecca Pilgrimage of 1961 (1961–1962) (IOR/R/20/B/3437 File 8370/8)

- Kamaran: Establishment of Pilgrimage Officer (1926) (IOR/R/20/A/4121)

- Collection of Pilgrimage Dues (1948–1949) (IOR/L/PJ/8/765)

- Pilgrimage: Formation of a Native Shipping Co. in Java (1938) (IOR/ R/ 20/B/1454)

- Payment in Cash or Certified Bills of Kamaran Quarantine Dues (1927–1929) (IOR/ L/E/7/1513 File4070)

- Hejaz Pilgrimage (1947) (IOR/R/15/2/1440)

- Haj Pilgrimage Reports (1929–38) (IOR/L/PJ/7/789)

- Dutch East Indies: Arabs and the Mecca Hajj (1918) (IOR/L/PS/11/137 P3174)

- Mecca Pilgrimage (1961) IOR/R/20/B/2765 File 8370/8
- Hajj: Rules and Regulations, Pilgrim Traffic (1927–1947) (IOR/R/ 15/ 2/ 1439)
- Annual Reports for British Legation, Jeddah on Pilgrimage (1939–1944) (IOR/L/PJ/8/755) (Coll 125/1A)
- Mecca during Pilgrimage (1936–1941) (IOR/L/PJ/8/127/Pt. VI)
- Proposed Provision of Medical Treatment for Malay Pilgrims at Mecca (1928–1931) (IOR/ L/E/7/1547)
- Inter-Departmental Quarantine Committee: Minutes (1917–1922) (IOR/L/E/7/1908, File 7376)
- Jeddah Pilgrimage Report (1924–1939) (IOR/R/20/A/4347) File 44/1
- Pilgrimage, Statistics, Medical Requirements (1926–1950) (IOR/R/ 15/2/1057 File 2/5)
- Pilgrimage Tariff (1931–1940), IOR/L/PJ/8/783 Coll 125/7B

- *Public Records Office (PRO), Kew, Surrey*
- Peace Conference (1919) (FO 608/101/17)
- Peace Conference (1919) (FO 608/275/1)
- Dominions Office (1958): Pilgrimage by Tunku to Mecca (DO 35/9755)
- Arrangements for Hajj (1954) FO 371/110130
- Hajj Transport Problems, Sanitation and Illegal Entry (1953) FO 371/104884
- Chartering of Ships for Hajj (1950) FO 371/82698
- Hajj of Muslims from Japanese-Controlled Lands (1943) FO 371/35929
- Pilgrimage to Mecca: Transport (1927) CO 732/24/2
- Sanitary and Destitute Pilgrims (1920–1923), T161/1086
- Health and Sanitary (1939–1940) CO 323/1699/14
- Propaganda during War: Moslem Pilgrimage (1943) CO 732/87/18
- Sanitation Reports (1929) CO 732/39/10
- Quarantine Regulations (1898–1905) MH 19/279
- Financial Arrangement for a Pilgrimage (1944–1945) T 236/296 (Treasury)
- Control of Mutawwifs (1934) FO 905/9
- Dutch Representation in the Hejaz, Emile Gobee (1917–1925) FO 141/668/1
- Mecca Pilgrimage Medical (1937) CO 323/1461/14
- Mecca Pilgrims and Quarantine: Dr Abdur Razzaq (1882) FO 881/4762
- Quarantine Regulations (1906/1907) MH 19/280
- Desirability of Resuming Hajj Traffic to Mecca (1944) Admiralty 1/17119
- Anti-Cholera Certificate: Report and Correspondence (1937–1955) MH 55/1888
- Death of Pilgrims While on Hajj (1960–1961) CO 1015/2499
- Arrangements of Pilgrimages to Mecca from Southeast Asia (1952–1953) CO 1022/409

- *Wellcome Institute of Medicine, London*
- MS 1495/5 Box 32, Contributions to the Manual of Medicine, 1900
- RAMC/1756/5/1 Box 354, Rules for Containment of Cholera, Port Said (1923)
- RAMC/755/1/4 Box 154, Disposal of Waste Products in Peace and War (1930s)
- RAMC/600 Box 129, Cholera Literature (1893)
- RAMC/397/F/RR/6 O/S #22 Sanitary Concerns (1854–1855)

- RAMC/571/Box 126, Letter from Sir William Gull to Sir Joseph Fayrer on the Causes of Cholera (1885)
- RAMC/474/47 Box 87, Parkes Pamphlet Collection

IV. United States

- *Cornell University, Ithaca, New York.*
- A large amount of period material by C. Snouk Hurgronje was read here.

George Kahin Papers on Islam and the Pilgrimage to Mecca from Indonesia (1950s–1960s)
Cornell University Library Rare Books and Manuscripts Collection

- A large amount of correspondence and data on the Indonesian Hajj and Islam in the 1950s and 1960s period as collected by George Kahin and the Cornell Modern Indonesia Project was read here.

- *New York Academy of Medicine, New York City*
   Much of the medical period literature in English (and some articles in French and Italian) was read here.

- *National Archives, Washington D.C.*
   Some period and also some modern literature on the Middle East was read here.

- *Yale University, New Haven, Connecticut*

Beinecke Rare Book Library, Joseph Conrad Collection
Box 1: "Author's Note: Autograph Manuscript of the Preface to *Lord Jim* (Gift of Chauncy B. Tinker, 1952), handwritten with corrections."
Box 4: "Telegrams and Letters to Ford Maddox Ford, 1898–1904."
Box 6: "Letters to Edward Lancelot Sanderson and his wife, 1896–1922."
Box 6: "13 Letters to Charles Zagorski and his wife, 1890–1899."

BIBLIOGRAPHY

Abaza, Mona. "M. Asad Shahab: A Portrait of an Indonesian Hadrami Who Bridged the Two Worlds," in Eric Tagliacozzo, *Southeast Asia and the Middle East: Islam, Movement, and the Longue Duree* (Palo Alto, CA: Stanford University Press, 2009), pp. 250–274.

Abdallah, Yussuf. "Le Yemen: le Pays et le Commerce de l'Encens," in André Lemaire, ed., *Les Routes du Proche-Orient* (Paris: Desclée de Brouwer, 2000), pp. 87–92.

Abdurrahman, Moeslim. "Ritual Divided: Hajj Tours in Capitalist Era Indonesia," in Mark Woodward, ed., *Toward a New Paradigm: Recent Developments in Indonesian Islamic Thought* (Tempe: Arizona State University Program in Southeast Asian Studies, 1996).

Abinales, Patricio. *Making Mindanao: Cotabato and Davao in the Formation of the Philippine Nation-State* (Quezon City,Philippines: Ateneo de Manila, 2000).

Aboebakar, H. *Sedjarah Ka'bah dan Manasik Hadji* (Jakarta: Bulan Bintang, 1963).

Abou-El-Haj, Rifa'at 'Ali. *Formation of the Modern State: The Ottoman Empire Sixteenth to Eighteenth Centuries* (Albany: State University of New York Press, 1991).

Abu-Lughod, Janet. *Before European Hegemony: The World System, 1250–1350* (New York: Oxford University Press, 1989).

Abushouk, Ahmed, et al., eds. *The Hadhrami Diaspora in Southeast Asia: Identity Maintenance or Assimilation?* (Leiden: Brill, 2009).

Adriani, P. "De Bedevaart naar Arabie en de Verspreiding der Epidemische Ziekten," *Nederlandse Militair Geneeskundige Archief*, 23, 1899: 7–245, passim.

Afasar, Syed. "Haj Cities in Jeddah," *Haj and Umra*, 57/4, 2002: 18.

Agius, Dionisius. *In the Wake of the Dhow: The Arabian Gulf and Oman* (Reading, UK: Ithaca, 2002).

Agoston, Gabor. "A Flexible Empire: Authority and Its Limits on the Ottoman Frontiers," in Kemal Karpat and Robert Zens, eds., *Ottoman Borderlands: Issues, Personalities, and Political Changes* (Madison: University of Wisconsin Press, 2003).

Ahmad, A. Samad, ed. *Sulalatus Salatin* (Sejarah Melayu) (Kuala Lumpur: Dewan Bahasa dan Pustaka, 1979).

Ahmad, A. Samad, ed. *Hikayat Amir Hamzah* (Kuala Lumpur: Dewan Bahasa dan Pustaka, 1987).

Ahmad, Kassim, ed. *Hikayat Hang Tuah* (Kuala Lumpur: Dewan Bahasa dan Pustaka, 1975).

Akbar, Ahmed. *Discovering Islam: Making Sense of Muslim History and Society* (London: Routledge, 1988).

Al-Ahmadi, Abdul Rahman. *Syair Siti Zubaidah Perang China, Perspektif Sejarah* (Kuala Lumpur: Perpustakaan Negara Malaysia, 1994).

Al-Albani, Muhammad Nashiruddin. *Haji dan Umrah Mengikut Sunnah Rasullah S.A.W.* (Kuala Lumpur: Perniagaan Jahabersa, 1995).

Al-Amri, Husayn 'Abd Allah. *The Yemen in the Eighteenth and Nineteenth Centuries: A Political and Intellectual History* (London: Durham Middle East Monographs #1, 1985).

Al-Amri, Husayn 'Abd Allah. "Slaves and Markets in the History of Yemen," in Werner Daum, ed., *Yemen: 3000 Years of Art and Civilisation in Arabia Felix* (Innsbruk: Pinguin-Verlag, 1987), pp. 140–157.

Al-Attas, Syed Muhammad Naguib. *The Mysticism of Hamzah Fansuri* (Kuala Lumpur: University of Malaya Press, 1970).

Al-Attas, Syed Muhammad Naguib. *Islam dalam Sejarah dan Kebudayaan Melayu* (Kuala Lumpur: Penerbit Universiti Kebangsaan Malaysia, 1972).

Al-Attas, Syed Muhammad Naquib, ed. *The Oldest Known Malay Manuscript: A 16th Century Translation of the `Aqâ'id of al-Nasafî* (Kuala Lumpur: University of Malaya, 1988).

Al-Azmeh, Aziz. *Islams and Modernities* (London: Verso, 1993).

Aldrich, Robert, ed. *The Age of Empires* (London: Thames and Hudson, 2007).

Algadri, Hamid. "Prof. Snouck Hurgronje Menentang Gerakan Pan-Islam," in Hamid Algadri, *C. Snouck Hurgronje, Politik Belanda terhadap Islam dan Keturunan Arab* (Jakarta: Penerbit Sinar Harapan, 1984), pp. 117–152.

Algadri, Hamid. "Snouck Hurgronje Menentang Asimilasi Keturunan Arab," in Hamid Algadri, *C. Snouck Hurgronje, Politik Belanda terhadap Islam dan Keturunan Arab* (Jakarta: Penerbit Sinar Harapan, 1984), pp. 85–94.

Al-Ghazali, abu Hamid Muhammad. *Rahasia Haji dan Umroh* (Bandung: Penerbit Karisma, 1993).

Al-Hafiz, Haji Abu Mazaya. *A Guideline to Umrah and Ziarah, Complete with the Supplications and Performing Procedures* (Kuala Lumpur: Al-Hidayah, 2003).

Al-Hamidi, Abu Asyraf. *Perjalanan Mencari Haji Mabrur* (Kuala Lumpur: Era Ilmu, 1995).

Alias, Haji Joharai Haji. *Panduan Ibadah Haji, 'Umrah dan Ziarah* (Kuala Lumpur: Darul Nu'man, 1994).

Aliwiyah, Dra. Hj. Tuty. "Saya Ketemu Yasser Arafat," in Anonymous, *Haji, Sebuah Perjalanan Air Mata* (Yogyakarta, Indonesia: Bentang, 1993), pp. 214–219.

Aljunied, Syed Muhammad Khairudin. "Edward Said and Southeast Asian Islam: Western Impressions of Meccan Pilgrims (Hajjis) in the Dutch East Indies, 1800–1900," *Journal of Commonwealth and Postcolonial Studies,* 11/1–2, 2004: 159–175.

Aljunied, Syed Muhammad Khairudin. "Western Images of Meccan Pilgrims in the Dutch East Indies, 1800–1900," *Sari,* 23 (2005): 105–122.

Allen, Calvin. "The State of Masqat in the Gulf and East Africa, 1785–1829," *IJMES,* 14/2, 1982: 117–127.

Almagia, R. "Relazione dell'Esplorazione Geografica delle Nostre Colonie in Rapporto allo Sfruttamento delle Loro Risorse Economiche," *Atti Convegno Nazionale per il Dopoguerra delle Nostre Colonie* (Roma, 1919): 350–364.

Al-Makki, Qutb al-Din al-Nahrawali. *Lightning over Yemen: A History of the Ottoman Campaign, 1569–1571* (translated and edited by Clive Smith) (London: Tauris, 2002).

Al-Rashid, Ibrahim. ed. *Saudi Arabia Enters the Modern World* (Salisbury, NC: Documentary, 1980).

Al-Shamlan, Abdulrahman. "The Evolution of National Boundaries in the Southeastern Arabian Peninsula, 1934–1955." PhD Dissertation, University of Michigan, 1987.

Ambrosini, Richard. *Conrad's Fiction as Critical Discourse* (Cambridge: Cambridge University Press, 1991).

Amhar, Fahmi, and Arum Harjanti. *Buku Pintar Calon Haji* (Jakarta: Penerbit Buku Andalan, 1996).

Andaya, Barbara Watson. *The Flaming Womb: Repositioning Women in Early Modern Southeast Asian History* (Honolulu: University of Hawai'i Press, 2006).

Anderson, Benedict. *Imagined Communities: Reflections on the Origin and Spread of Nationalism* (London: Verso, 1983).

Andrews, Bridie, and Mary Sutphen. "Introduction," in Mary Sutphen and Bridie Andrews, eds., *Medicine and Colonial Identity* (London: Routledge, 2003).

Anonymous. "Travaux Originaux: Epidémiollogie," *Gazette Hebdomadaire de Medecine et de Chirurgie*, September 19, 1873, #38, p. 604.

Anonymous. "Sociétés Savantes: Académie des Sciences," *Gazette Hebdomadaire de Médecine et de Chirurgie*, November 14, 1873, #46, p. 734.

Anonymous. "De Indische Bedevaartgangers," *TNI*, 1, 1874: 55–67.

Anonymous. "Mar Rosso e Costa Orientale dell'Africa" (Firenze: Istituto Geografico Militare, 1885).

Anonymous. "A Description of the Yeerly Voyage or Pilgrimage of the Mahumitans, Turkes and Moores unto Mecca in Arabia," in Richard Hakluyt, *The Principal Navigations*, vol. 5 (Glasgow: James MacLehose and Sons, 1903–1905), pp. 340–365.

Anonymous. "Cholera, the Haj and the Hadjaz Railway," *Lancet*, 2, 1908: 1377.

Anonymous. "Cholera at Jiddah and Mecca," *US Public Health Report*, 23/1, 1908: 289.

Anonymous. "De Bedevaart naar Mekka, 1909/1910," *IG*, 2 (1910): 1638.

Anonymous. "Small-Pox and Cholera in the Pilgrimage," *Lancet*, 1, 1910: 1792.

Anonymous. *Mar Rosson e Possedimenti Italiani in Africa* (Novarra: Istituo Geografico de Agostini, 1911).

Anonymous. "Cholera on Pilgrim Steamers at Camaran," *Lancet*, 2, 1912: 913.

Anonymous. "Surat Ingatan Tengku Said Mahmud Zaini ibnu almarhum al Habib ʾAbdurrahman al Qodri," in *Surat-Surat Perdjandjian antara Kesultanan Riau dengan Pemerintahan2 V.O.C dan Hindia-Belanda, 1784–1909* (Djakarta: Arsip Nasional Republik Indonesia, 1970), p. 346.

Anonymous. *Tuntunan: Manasik Hadji* (Bogor, Indonesia: Tjiawi, 1973).

Anonymous. *Loka-Karya Peningkatan Pelayanan Haji Indonesia* (Jakarta: Direktorat Jendral Urusan Haji, 1975).

Anonymous. *Workshop to Prepare a Training Programme on Oral Tradition* (Bangkok: Office of the National Committee on Culture, Ministry of Education, 1980).

Anonymous. *Himpunan Risalah Rapat Kerja Urusan Haji Seluruh Indonesia* (Jakarta: Departemen Agama, 1982).

Anonymous. *Pedoman dan Petunjuk Pelaksanaan Bimbingan Calon Jamaah Haji di Asrama Embarkasi* (Jakarta: Departmen Agama, 1982).

Anonymous. *Majlis Ugama Islam Singapura* (MUIS) Annual Reports, 1982–1986.

Anonymous. *Buku Panduan Ibadat Haji, Umrah dan Ziarah* (Kuala Lumpur: Tabung Haji, 1983).

Anonymous. *Himpunan Risalah Rapat Kerja Urusan Haji Seluruh Indonesia Ke-XV* (Jakarta: Departemen Agama, 1983).

Anonymous. *Risalah Soal Jawab Ibadat Haji dan Umrah* (Kuala Lumpur: Tabung Haji, 1984).

Anonymous. *Haji ke Baitullah* (Kuala Lumpur: Penerbitan 'Asa, 1985).

Anonymous. *Laporan: Penyelenggaraan Urusan Haji* (Jakarta: Kantor Urusan Haji, 1986).

Anonymous. *Le Voyage Aux Lieux Saints de L'Islam* (Kuala Lumpur: Tabung Haji, 1986).

Anonymous. *Islam in Kampuchea* (Phnom Penh: National Council of the United Front of Kampuchea, 1987).

Anonymous. *Laporan Hasil Kunjungan Kerja (Studi Perbandingan) Penyelenggaraan Urusan Haji di Propinsi Jawa Timur & Sulawesi Selatan* (Jakarta: Kantor Urusan Haji, 1987).

Anonymous. *Soal-Jawab Ibadah Haji/Umrah* (Kuala Lumpur: Tabung Haji, 1987).

Anonymous. *Laporan Kajian Mengenai Jemaah Haji Menunaikan Haji Lebih Daripada Sekali* (Kuala Lumpur: Tabung Haji, 1989).

Anonymous. *Risalah Penerangan Kepada Jemaah Haji Malaysia 1409 Hijrah* (Kuala Lumpur: Tabung Haji, 1989).

Anonymous. *Risalah Penerangan Pakej Haji Bagi Jemaah Haji Malaysia, 1409H–1989M* (Kuala Lumpur: Tabung Haji, 1989).

Anonymous. *Islam di Brunei* (Bandar Seri Begawan, Brunei: Kementerian Kebudayaan, 1992).

Anonymous. *Perjalanan Ibadah Haji Pak Harto* (Jakarta: Departemen Agama, 1993).

Anonymous. *Records of the Hajj: A Documentary History of the Pilgrimage to Mecca* (Chippenham, UK: Archive Editions, 1993).

Anonymous. *Sejarah Perkembangan Tabung Haji Malaysia* (Kuala Lumpur: Tabung Haji, 1993).

Anonymous. *Muslims in Singapore: A Shared Vision* (Singapore: Majlis Ugama Islam Singapura, 1994).

Anonymous. *Al-Mu'min Menjadi Tetamu Allah* (Bandar Seri Begawan, Brunei: Jabatan Pusat Sejarah Kementerian Kebudayaan, 1995).

Anonymous. *As Guest of Allah: With Members of the Brunei Royal Family, a Memoir* (Bandar Seri Begawan: Brunei History Centre, 1999).

Anonymous. *Data dan Profil Jemaah Haji Indonesia Tahun 1996 s.d. 2002* (Jakarta: Departemen Agama, 2002).

Anonymous. "Haj Charges," *Haj and Umra*, 57/6, 2002: 12.

Anonymous. *Gambaran Umum tentang Penyelenggaraan Haji Indonesia* (Jakarta: Departemen Agami, 2004).

Anonymous. *Manfaatnya Bukan Sekadar ke Makkah* (Kuala Lumpur: Tabung Haji, 2004).

Anonymous. *Perkhidmatan Simpanan Tabung Haji Melalui Agen Kutipan Simpanan* (Kuala Lumpur: Tabung Haji, 2004).

Anonymous. *Salam: Pelan Panggilan Pertama Bercirikan Islam* (Jakarta: Celcom, 2004).

Anonymous. *Skim Potongan Gaji Diri dan Keluarga* (Kuala Lumpur: Tabung Haji, 2004).

Anonymous. *Tabung Haji: Hasten toward Prosperity* (Kuala Lumpur: Tabung Haji, 2004).

Anonymous. "Rohingya Solidarity Organisation," in Greg Fealy and Virginia Hooker, eds., *Voices of Islam in Southeast Asia: A Contemporary Sourcebook* (Singapore: ISEAS, 2006), pp. 266–271.

Anonymous. *Pedoman Kerja Bagi Anggauta Majelis Pimpinan Haji Indonesia* (Jakarta: Direktorat Jendral Urusan Haji, n.d.).

Appadurai, Arjun, ed. *The Social Life of Things* (New York: Cambridge University Press, 1986).

Appell, G. N. "Guide to the Varieties of Oral Literature in Borneo," *Borneo Research Bulletin* 22 (1990): 98–113.

Aritonang, Baharuddin. *Orang Batak Naik Haji* (Jakarta: Gramedia, 1997).

Arnaz, Hajja Eva. "Tangan Besar yang Menyelamatkan Jiwaku," in E. Syarief Nurdin and E. Kosasih, *100 Keajaiban di Tanah Suci Pengalaman Unik Jamaah Haji* (Bandung: Pustaka Hidayah, 1996), pp. 35–36.

Arnold, David. "Disease, Medicine and Empire," in David Arnold, ed., *Imperial Medicine and Indigenous Societies* (Manchester, England: Manchester University Press, 1988), p. 7.

Arsyirawati, Nursi. "Pengembangan Strategi dan Kebijakan Peningkatan Manajemen Kualitas Pelayanan Haji Indonesia" (MS Thesis, Universitas Indonesia, 1999).

Asri, Nazar. "Total Tranquility," *Haj and Umra*, 58/1, 2003: 35.

Atwill, David. *The Chinese Sultanate: Islam, Ethnicity, and the Pan-Thai Rebellion in Southern China, 1856–1873* (Palo Alto, CA: Stanford University Press, 2006).

Awang, Dato' HJ Mohamad Saleh Bin Haji. *Teman Anda ke Tanah Suci* (Singapore: Times Books, 1992).

Aymonier, M. E. *Les Tchames Leurs Religions* (Paris: Ernest Leroux, 1891).

Azra, Azyumardi, ed. *Perspektif Islam di Asia Tenggara* (Jakarta: Yayasan Obor Indonesia, 1989).

Azra, Azyumardi. "A Hadhrami Religious Scholar in Indonesia: Sayyid 'Uthman,'" in Ulrike Frietag and William Clarence-Smith, eds., *Hadhrami Traders, Scholars, and Statesmen in the Indian Ocean, 1750s–1960s* (Leiden: E. J. Brill, 1997), pp. 249–263.

Azra, Azyumardi. *The Origins of Islamic Reformism in Southeast Asia: Networks of Malay-Indonesian and Middle Eastern "Ulama" in the Seventeenth and Eighteenth Centuries* (Crows Nest, Australia: Allen & Unwin; Honolulu: University of Hawai'i, 2004).

Azra, Azyumardi. *Islam in the Indonesian World: An Account of Institutional Formation* (Bandung: Mizan, 2006).

Bacque-Grammont, Jean-Louis, and Anne Kroell. *Mamlouks, Ottomans et Portugais en Mer Rouge: L'Affaire de Djedda en 1517* (Paris: Le Caire, 1988).

Bakar, O. B. "Sufism in the Malay-Indonesian World," in S. H. Nasr, ed., *Islamic Spirituality II: Manifestations* (London: SCM, 1991), pp. 259–289.

Bakhtin, M. M. "The Bildungsroman and Its Significance in the History of Realism," in Caryl Emerson and Michael Holquist, eds., *Speech Genres and Other Late Essays* (Austin: University of Texas Press, 1986), p. 19.

Baldry, John. "Foreign Interventions and Occupations of Kamarin Island," *Arabian Studies*, 4, 1978: 89–111.

Baldry, John. *Textiles in Yemen: Historical References to Trade and Commerce in Textiles in Yemen from Antiquity to Modern Times* (London: British Museum Department of Ethnography, 1982).

Baldry, John. "The History of the Tihama from 1800 to the Present," in Francine Stone, ed., *Studies on the Tihama* (Essex, England: Longman, 1985), pp. 45–50.

Baldry, John. "The English East India Company's Settlement at al-Mukha, 1719–1739," *The Arab Gulf*, 13/2, 1981: 13–34.

Balfour-Paul, Penny. "Indigo and South Arabia," *Journal of Weavers, Spinners, and Dyers*, 139, 1986: 12–29.

Bang, Anne. *Sufis and Scholars of the Sea: Family Networks in East Africa* (London: Routledge, 2003).

Barber, Richard. *Pilgrimages* (Woodbridge, England: Boydell and Brewer, 1991).

Barendse, R. J. *The Arabian Seas, 1640–1700* (Armonk, NY: M. E. Sharpe, 2002).

Barrington, Judith. *Writing the Memoir from Truth to Art* (Portland, OR: Eighth Mountain, 1997).

Battuta, Ibn. *The Travels of Ibn Battuta*, AD *1325–1354* (London: Hakluyt, 2000).

Bel Khodja, Muhamed. *Le Pélerinage de la Mecque* (Tunis, 1906).

Benda, Harry. "Christiaan Snouck Hurgronje and the Foundations of Dutch Islamic Policy in Indonesia," in Ahmad Ibrahim et al., eds., *Readings on Islam in Southeast Asia* (Singapore: ISEAS, 1985), pp. 61–69.

Bendix, Reinhard. *Max Weber: An Intellectual Portrait* (Berkeley: University of California Press, 1977).

Benyamin, H. S. "Kepasrahan," in E. Syarief Nurdin and E. Kosasih, *100 Keajaiban di Tanah Suci Pengalaman Unik Jamaah Haji* (Bandung: Pustaka Hidayah, 1996), pp. 34–35.

Berg, L. W. C van den. *Le Hadhramout et les Colonies Arabes dans L'Archipel Indien* (Batavia, Indonesia: Imprimerie du Gouvernement, 1886).

Berge, Tom van den. "Indonesiers en het door hen Gevolgde Onderwijs in Mekka, 1926–1940," *Jambatan*, 7/1, 1989: 5–22.

Berlie, J. A. *The Burmanization of Myanmar's Muslims* (Bangkok: White Lotus, 2008).

Berthaud, Julien. "L'origine et la Distribution des Caféiers dans le Monde," in Michel Tuchscherer, ed., *Le Commerce du Café Avant l'ère des Plantations Coloniales* (Cairo: Institut Français d'Archéologie Orientale, 2001), pp. 364–369.

Bhardwaj, Surinder. "Geography and Pilgrimage: A Review," in Robert Stoddard and Alan Morinis, eds., *Sacred Places, Sacred Spaces: The Geography of Pilgrimages* (Baton Rouge, LA: Geoscience, 1997), pp. 1–24.

Bianchi, Robert. *Guests of God: Pilgrimage and Politics in the Islamic World* (Oxford: Oxford University Press, 2004).

Bidwell, Robin. *Travellers in Arabia* (London: Hamlyn, 1976).

Bird, Walter de Grey. *The Commentaries of the Great Alfonso Dalboquerque, 2nd Viceroy of India* (London: Hakluyt Society, 1884).

Birkets, Sven. *The Art of Time in Memoir: Then, Again* (St. Paul, MN: Graywolf, 2008).

Bisri, K. H. A. Mustofa. "Saya Merasa Diwelehke Tuhan," in Anonymous, *Haji Sebuah Perjalanan Air Mata* (Yogyakarta, Indonesia: Bentang, 1993), p. 135.

Bloom, Harold. "Introduction," in Harold Bloom, ed., *Joseph Conrad's Lord Jim* (New York: Chelsea House, 1987).

Blumi, Isa. "Thwarting the Ottoman Empire: Smuggling through the Empire's New Frontiers in Yemen and Albania, 1878–1910," in Kemal Karpat and Robert Zens, eds., *Ottoman Borderlands: Issues, Personalities, and Political Changes* (Madison: University of Wisconsin Press, 2003), pp. 255–267.

Blunt, Wilfred. *The Future of Islam* (London: Kegan Paul Trench, 1882).

Bose, Sugata. *A Hundred Horizons: The Indian Ocean in the Age of Global Empire* (Cambridge, MA: Harvard University Press, 2006).

Bourne, Kenneth, et al., eds. *British Documents on Foreign Affairs: Reports and Papers from the Foreign Office Confidential Print*, vol. 26, part I, series E (Washington, DC: University Publications of America, 1995).

Bovene, G. A. van. *Mijne Reis Naar Mekka: Naar het Dagboek van den Regent van Bandoeng Raden Adipati Aria Wirantakoesoema* (self-published? 1925).

Bowersock, G. W. "Perfumes and Power," in Alessandra Avanzini, ed., *Profumi d'Arabia: Atti del Convegno* (Roma: L'Erma di Bretschneider, 1997), pp. 249–250.

Bowman, R. "Cholera in Turkish Arabia," *British Medical Journal*, 1, 1890: 1031–1032.

Boxberger, Linda. *On the Edge of Empire: Hadhramawt, Emigration, and the Indian Ocean, 1880s–1930s* (Albany: State University of New York Press, 2002).

Bradley, Francis. "Moral Order in a Time of Damnation: The Hikayat Patani in Historical Context," *JSEAS*, 40/2, 2009: 267–294.

Bradley, Francis. "The New Social Dynamics of Islamic Revivalism in Southeast Asia: The Rise of the Patani School, 1785–1909" (PhD Dissertation, University of Wisconsin, Madison, 2010).

Braginsky, Vladimir. *The Heritage of Traditional Malay Literature* (Leiden: KITLV, 2004).

Braginsky, Vladimir. "Structure, Date and Sources of the Hikayat Aceh Revisited," *BKI*, 162/4, 2006: 441–467.

Brakel, L. F., ed. *The Hikayat Muhammad Hanafiyyah, a Medieval Muslim-Malay Romance* Bibliotheca Indonesica of KITLV, 12 (The Hague: Martinus Nijhoff, 1975).

Brizi, U. "Le Piante Utili delle Nostre Colonie," *Boll. Associaz. Ital. Puo Piante Medicinali* 1919.

Brouwer, C. G. "Willem de Milde, Kani Shalabi en Fadli Basha, of: Een Dienaar van de VOC op Audientie bij de Beglerbegi van Jemen, 1622–1624," *De Gids*, 143, 1980: 713–742.

Brouwer, C. G. "Le Voyage au Yemen de Pieter van den Broecke (serviteur de la VOC) en 1620, d'apres son livre de resolutions," in F. E. Peters et al., eds., *The Challenge of the Middle East* (Amsterdam: Institute of Modern Near East Studies, 1982), pp. 175–182.

Brouwer, C. G. "A Stockless Anchor and an Unsaddled Horse: Ottoman Letters Addressed to the Dutch in Yemen, First Quarter of the 17th Century," *Turcica*, 20, 1988: 173–242.

Brouwer, C. G. *Cauwa ende Comptanten: de VOC in Yemen* (Amsterdam: D'Fluyte Rarob, 1988).

Brouwer, C. G. *Al-Mukha: Profile of a Yemeni Seaport as Sketched by Servants of the Dutch East India Company, 1614–1640* (Amsterdam: D'Fluyte Rarob, 1997).

Brouwer, C. G. "Pieter van den Broecke's Original Resulutieboeck Concerning Dutch Trade in Northwest India, Persia, and Southern Arabia, 1620–1625," in C. G. Brouwer, *Dutch-Yemeni Encounters: Activities of the United East India Company (VOC) in South Arabian Waters since 1614* (Amsterdam: D'Fluyte Rarob, 1999), pp. 77–102.

Brouwer, C. G. "Al-Mukha as a Coffee Port in the Early Decades of the Seventeenth Century According to Dutch Sources," in Michel Tuchscherer, ed., *Le Commerce du Café Avant l'ère des Plantations Coloniales* (Cairo: Institut Français d'Archéologie Orientale, 2001), pp. 276–289.

Brown, Rajeswary Ampalavanar. "Islamic Endowments and the Land Economy in Singapore: The Genesis of an Ethical Capitalism, 1830–2007," *South East Asia Research*, 16/3, 2008: 343–403.

Bruinessen, Martin van. *Tarekat Naqsyabandiyah di Indonesia: Survei Historis, Geografis dan Sosiologis* (Bandung: Penerbit Mizan, 1992).

Bruinessen, Martin van. *Kitab Kuning, Pesantren dan Tarekat: Tradisis-tradisi Islam di Indonesia* (Bandung: Mizan, 1995).

Bruinessen, Martin van, Muhammad Khalid Masud, and Armando Salvatore, eds., *Islam and Modernity: Key Issues and Debates* (Edinburgh: Edinburgh University Press, 2009).

Buez, E. A. "Le Pélerinage de la Mecque," *Gaz. Hebd. De Med.*, 2/10, 1873: 633–634.

Bulliet, Richard. *Islam: The View from the Edge* (New York: Columbia University Press, 1994).

Burke, Edmund. "Islamic History as World History," *IJMES*, 10/2, 1979: 246.

Campo, J. N. F. M. a. "A Profound Debt to the Eastern Seas: Documentary History and Literary Representation of Berau's Maritime Trade in Conrad's Malay Novels," *International Journal of Maritime History*, 12/2, 2000: 86–87.

Cantalupo, R. *L'Italia Musulmana* (Roma: Casa Editrice Italiana d'Oltremare, 1929).

Carbonell, Marcelin. *Relation Médicale d'un Voyage de Transport de Pelerins Musulmans au Hedjaz 1907–1908* (Aix-en-Provence, France: Publications de l'Université de Provence (reprint), 2001).

Carey, P. R. B. "Pangeran Dipanagara and the Making of the Java War" (PhD Dissertation, Oxford University, 1975).

Carreira, Ernestine. "Les Français et le Commerce du Café dans l'Ocean Indien au XVIIIe Siecle," in Michel Tuchscherer, ed., *Le Commerce du Café Avant l'ère des Plantations Coloniales* (Cairo: Institut Français d'Archéologie Orientale, 2001).

Casale, Giancarlo. *The Ottoman Age of Exploration* (New York: Oxford University Press, 2010).

Cases Heard and Determined in Her Majesty's Supreme Court of the Straits Settlements, 1808–1884, 4 vols., ed. J. W. N. Kyshe (Singapore: Singapore and Straits Printing Office, 1885–1890), vol. 2.

Catanach, I. J. "Plague and the Tensions of Empire: India, 1896–1918," in David Arnold, ed., *Imperial Medicine and Indigenous Societies* (Manchester, England: Manchester University Press, 1988), p. 149.

Catanach, I. J. "South Asian Muslims and the Plague, 1896–1914," in Asim Roy, ed., *Islam in History and Politics: Perspectives from South Asia* (Oxford: Oxford University Press, 2008), pp. 97–120.

Catelan, M. le. "Choléra au Hedjaz en 1890: Prophylaxie Sanitaire dans la Mer Rouge," *Reviel des Travaux du Comité Consultatif d'Hygiène Publique de France et des Actes Officiels de L'Administration Sanitaire*, 21 (1891): 830–842.

Cerdiwen, Amelia. "The Silsilah Raja-Raja Perak I: An Historical and Literary Investigation into the Political Significance of a Malay Court Genealogy," *JMBRAS*, 74/2 (2001): 23–129.

Cerulli, E. "Note sul Movimento Musulmano in Somalia," *Riv. Di Studi Orientali*, 10:1, 1923: 1.

Chakrabarti, Ranjan. *Authority and Violence in Colonial Bengal: 1800–1860* (Calcutta: Bookland Private, 1997).

Chambert-Loir, Henri. "L'extase en plus: Recits Indonesiens du Pelerinage a la Mecque, 1970–1994," in C. Salmon, éd., *Récits de Voyages Asiatiques* (Paris: EFEO, 1996), pp. 297–318.

Chambert-Loir, Henri. "L'espere politique dans le Hikayat Hang Tuah," in D. Lombard and R. Ptak, eds., *Asia Maritima Images et Realites, 1200–1800* (Wiesbaden: Harrassowitz Verlag, 1994), pp. 41–61.

Chambert-Loir, Henri, ed. *Cerita Asal Bangsa Jin dan Segala Dewa-Dewa* (Bandung: Penerbit Angkasa & Ecole français d'Extrême Orient, 1985).

Chambert-Loir, Henri, ed., *Syair Kerajaan Bima* (Jakarta: Ecole français d'Extrême Orient, 1982). Naskah dan dokumen Nusantara III.

Chambert-Loir, Henri. "Les Sources Malaises de l'histoire de Bima," *Archipel*, 20 (1980): 269–280.

Chambert-Loir, Henri, and Claude Guillot. *Le Culte des Saints dans le Monde Musulman* (Paris: EFEO, 1995).

Chandler, James. "On the Face of the Case: Conrad, Lord Jim, and the Sentimental Novel," *Critical Inquiry*, 33 (2007): 837–864.

Chaudhuri, K. N. *Trade and Civilisation in the Indian Ocean: An Economic History from the Rise of Islam to 1750* (Cambridge: Cambridge University Press, 1985).

Cherif, Ahmed. *Le Pelerinage de la Mecque: Essai d'Histoire, de Psychologie et d'hygiene sur le Voyage Sacre de l'Islam* (Beirut: Angelil, 1930).

Che-Ross, Raimy. "Munshi Abdullah's Voyage to Mecca: A Preliminary Introduction and Annotated Translation," *Indonesia and the Malay World*, 28/81, 2000: 173–212.

Chew, Daniel. "Oral History Methodology: The Life History Approach," in P. Lim Pui Huen, James Morrison, and Kwa Chong Guan, eds., *Oral History in Southeast Asia: Theory and Method* (Singapore: National Archives of Singapore and the Institute of Southeast Asian Studies, 1998), pp. 47–54.

Ching, Stephanie Po Yin. "Western Law in Asian Customs: Legal Disputes on Business Practices in India, British Malaya and Hong Kong, 1850s–1930s," *Asia Europe Journal*, 1, 1993: 527–529.

Cholifah, Hajja Saida. *Ibu Rumah Tangga Naik Haji* (Yogyakarta, Indonesia: Pustaka Marwa, 2006).

Chulan bin Hamid, Raja. *Misa Melayu*, ed. R. O. Winstedt (Kuala Lumpur: Pustaka Antara, 1962).

Cirakman, Asli. *From the "Terror of the World" to the "Sick Man of Europe": European Images of Ottoman Empire and Society from the Sixteenth Century to the Nineteenth* (New York: Peter Lang, 2002).

Clarence-Smith, William. "Hadhramaut and the Hadhrami Diaspora in the Modern Colonial Era: An Introductory Survey," in Ulrike Frietag and William Clarence-Smith, eds., *Hadhrami Traders, Scholars, and Statesmen in the Indian Ocean, 1750s–1960s* (Leiden: E. J. Brill, 1997), pp. 1–18.

Clarence-Smith, William Gervase. "The Spread of Coffee Cultivation in Asia, from the Seventeenth to the Early Nineteenth Century," in Michel Tuchscherer, ed., *Le Commerce du Café Avant l'ère des Plantations Coloniales* (Cairo: Institut Français d'Archéologie Orientale, 2001).

Clift, Jean Dalby, and Wallace Clift. *The Archetype of Pilgrimage* (New York: Paulist, 1996).

Coates, W. H. *The Old Country Trade of the East Indies* (London: Imray, Laurie, Nurie, and Wilson, 1911).

Coedes, Georges. *The Indianized States of Southeast Asia* (Honolulu: University of Hawai'i Press, 1968).

Cohen, Erik. "Pilgrimage and Tourism: Convergence and Divergence," in Alan Morinis, ed., *Sacred Journeys: The Anthropology of Pilgrimage* (Westport, CT: Greenwood, 1992), pp. 47–64.

Cohn, Bernard. "History and Anthropology: The State of Play," in Bernard Cohn, *An Anthropologist among the Historians* ((New Delhi: Oxford University Press, 1990).

Cole, Juan. "Rival Empires of Trade and Imami Shi'ism in Eastern Arabia, 1300–1800," *IJMES*, 19/2, 1987: 177–204.

Coleman, Simon, and John Elsner. *Pilgrimage: Past and Present in the World Religions* (Cambridge, MA: Harvard University Press, 1995).

Collier, Kit. "The Philippines," in Greg Fealy and Virginia Hooker, eds., *Voices of Islam in Southeast Asia: A Contemporary Sourcebook* (Singapore: ISEAS, 2006), pp. 63–70.

Collins, William. *The Chams of Cambodia* (Phnom Penh: Interdisciplinary Research on Ethnic Groups in Cambodia, Center for Advanced Study, 1996).

Collits, Terry. "Imperialism, Marxism, Conrad: A Political Reading of Victory," *Textual Practice*, 3, 1989: 313–322.

Condominas, Georges. *We Have Eaten the Forest: The Story of a Montagnard Village in the Central Highlands of Vietnam* (New York: Hill and Wang, 1977).

Conrad, Joseph. *Lord Jim* (edited by Cedric Watts) (Peterborough, ON: Broadview Literary Texts, 2001).

Conway, Jill. *When Memory Speaks: Reflections on Autobiography* (New York: Knopf, 1998).

Cooke, Miriam, and Bruce Lawrence. "Introduction," in Miriam Cooke and Bruce Lawrence, eds., *Muslim Networks from Hajj to Hip Hop* (Chapel Hill: University of North Carolina Press, 2005).

Coolhaas, W. Ph., ed., *Generale Missiven van Gouverneurs-Generaal en Raden aan Heren XVII der Verenigde Oostindische Compagnie* ('s Gravenhage: Martinus Nijhoff, 1960).

Cordier, G. "Un Voyage à La Mecque," *Revue du Monde Musulman*, 14, 1911: 510–513.

Cornell, Vincent. "Ibn Battuta's Opportunism: The Networks and Loyalties of a Medieval Muslim Scholar," in Miriam Cooke and Bruce Lawrence, eds., *Muslim Networks from Hajj to Hip Hop* (Chapel Hill: University of North Carolina Press, 2005), pp. 31–50.

Corso, R. "Per l'Etnografica delle Nostre Colonie," *La Rivista d'Orientale*, 1934, p. 73.

Cortesi, F. "Le Piante da Profumo, da Aroma e da Essenza delle Nostre Colonie," *Riv. Coloniale*, 1919.

Costa, P. M. "Il Ruolo dell'Arabica nel Commercio delle Spezie e dell'incenso: da Elio Gallo a Vasco da Gama" in Avanzini, Alessandra, ed., *Profumi d'Arabia: Atti del Convegno* (Roma: L'Erma di Bretschneider, 1997): 437.

Couvy, L. *Le Choléra et le Pèlerinage Musulman au Hedjaz* (Paris, 1934).

Crellin, J. K. "The Dawn of Germ Theory: Particles, Infection and Biology," in F. N. L. Poynter, *Medicine and Science in the 1860s* (London: Wellcome Institute, 1968), pp. 61–66.

Crone, Patricia. *Meccan Trade and the Rise of Islam* (Princeton, NJ: Princeton University Press, 1986).

Curle, Richard. "Conrad in the East," *Yale Review*, 12, 1923: 497–508.

Curtin, Philip. "Field Techniques for Collecting and Processing Oral Data," *Journal of African History*, 9/3, 1968: 367–385.

Daghfous, Radhi. "Des Sources de l'Histoire Médiévale du Yemen," *Cahiers de Tunisie*, 28/113, 1980: 201–227.

Daguenet, Roger. *Aux Origines de l'Implantation Française en Mer Rouge: Vie et Mort d' Henri Lambert Consul de France a Aden, 1859* (Paris: L'Harmattan, 1992).

Daguenet, Roger. *Histoire de la Mer Rouge* (Paris: L'Harmattan, 1997).

Dalziel, N. R. "British Maritime Contacts with the Persian Gulf and Gulf of Oman, 1850–1900" (PhD Dissertation, University of Lancaster, England, 1989).

Danarto. *Catatan Perjalanan Haji Danarto, Orang Jawa Naik Haji* (Pengantar Taufiq Ismail), (Jakarta: Penerbit PT Grafiti, 1984).

Dandeker, Christopher. *Surveillance, Power and Modernity: Bureaucracy and Discipline from 1700 to the Present Day* (New York: St. Martin's Press, 1990).

Darwis, Ir. H. Avicenia. *40 Hari Mencari Cinta: Kisah Nyata Berhaji di Tanah Suci* (Bogor, Indonesia: Ar-Rahmah, 2005).

Das Gupta, Ashin. "Gujarati Merchants and the Red Sea Trade, 1700–1725," in B. B. Kling and M. N. Pearson, eds., *The Age of Partnership* (Honolulu: University of Hawai'i Press, 1979), p. 124.

Das Gupta, Ashin. *Indian Merchants and the Decline of Surat, c. 1700–1750* (Wiesbaden: Harrasowitz Verlag, 1979).

Das Gupta, Ashin. "Indian Merchants and the Trade in the Indian Ocean," in *Cambridge Economic History of India*, vol. 1 (Cambridge: Cambridge University Press, 1982), p. 430.

Daud, Haja Maimunah Haji. "The Haj—A Personal Experience," *Sarawak Gazette*, 119, #1521, 1992: 22–29.

d'Avril, A. *L'Arabie Contemporaine, avec la Description du Pelerinage a La Mecque* (Paris, 1868).

Defert, Gabriel. "Les Musulmans en Birmanie. Une Minorite 'Para-Nationale,'" in Michel Gilquin, ed., *Atlas des minorités musulmanes en Asie méridionale et orientale* (Paris: CNRS éditions, 2010), pp. 125–158.

Delden, E. Th. van. "Mekkagangers," *TNI*, 2, 1898: 639–661.

Dharma, S. Satya. *Haji Kita: Fakta dan Problema Penyelenggaraan Haji di Indonesia 1990–2000* (Jakarta: AWAM, 2000).

Dhofier, Zamakhsyari. "Dampak Ekonomi Ibadah Haji di Indonesia," *Prisma*, 12/4, 1984: 52–53.

Dhofier, Zamakhsyari. "The Economic Effect of the Indonesian Hajj," *Prisma*, 36, 1985.

Dijk, Kees van. "Indonesische Hadji's op Reis," in Willy Jansen and Huub de Jonge, eds., *Islamitische Pelgrimstochten* (Muiderberg, Netherlands: Coutinho, 1991), pp. 37–56.

Dinet, E., and S. Baamer. *Le Pélerinage à la Maison Sacrée d'Allah* (Paris, 1930).

Djajadiningrat. "Critisch Overzicht van de in Maleisch Werken Vervatte Gegevens over de Geschiedenis van het Soeltanaat van Atjeh," *BKI*, 65, 1911: 135–269.

Donovan, Stephen. "Figures, Facts, Theories: Conrad and Chartered Company Imperialism," *The Conradian*, 24/2, 1999: 31–60.

Douwes, Dick, and Nico Kaptein, eds. *Indonesia dan Haji* (Jakarta: INIS, 1997).

Drewes, G. W. J. "New Light on the Coming of Islam to Indonesia?" *Bijdragen tot de Taal-, Land- en Volkenkunde*, 124 (1968): 433–459.

Drewes, G. W. J. *Directions for Travellers on the Mystic Path*. Verhandelingen van het Koninklijk Instituut voor Taal-, Land- en Volkenkunde, 81 (The Hague: Nijhoff, 1977).

Drewes, G. W. J., and L. F. Brakel. *The Poems of Hasmzah Fansuri* (Dordrecht: Foris, 1986).

Dudd, Ross. *The Adventures of Ibn Battuta, a Muslim Traveler of the Fourteenth Century* (Berkeley: University of California Press, 1986).

Duguet, F. *Le Pélerinage de La Mecque au Point de Vue Religieux, Social et Sanitaire* (Paris, 1932).

Dunia, H. Gazali. "Hanya GBpounds 60," in E. Syarief Nurdin and E. Kosasih, *100 Keajaiban di Tanah Suci Pengalaman Unik Jamaah Haji* (Bandung: Pustaka Hidayah, 1996), pp. 183–184.

Durand, R. P. "Les Chams Bani," *BEFEO*, 3/1, 1903: 54–62.

Echenberg, Myron. *Plague Ports: The Global Bubonic Plague of 1906* (New York: New York University Press, 2007).

Eckart, Wolfgang. "Medicine and German Colonial Expansion in the Pacific: The Caroline, Mariana and Marshall Islands," in Roy Macleod and Milton Lewis, eds., *Disease, Medicine, and Empire* (London: Routledge, 1988), pp. 81–91.

Eickelman, Dale, and James Piscatori, eds. *Muslim Travellers: Pilgrimage, Migration and the Religious Imagination* (Berkeley: University of California Press, 1990).

Eisenberger, Johan. "Indie en de Bedevaart naar Mekka" (PhD Dissertation, Leiden University, 1928).

El-Amrousi, Mohamed. "Beyond Muslim Space: Jeddah, Muscat, Aden and Port Said" (PhD Dissertation, University of California, Los Angeles, 2001).

Elias, Norbert. *The Civilizing Process: Sociogenetic and Psychogenetic Investigations* (Oxford: Blackwell, 1994).

Erkal, Mehmed. "The Pilgrimage Organization in Turkey," in Zafarul-Islam Khan and Yaqub Zaki, eds., *Hajj in Focus* (London: Open Press, 1986), pp. 137–150.

Errington, Shelly. *A Study of Genre: Meaning and Form in the Malay Hikayat Hang Tuah* (PhD Thesis, Cornell University, 1975).

Esmara, Hendra. *Aku Datang Memenuhi Panggilanmu Ya, Allah* (Jakarta: Penerbit PT Gramedia, 1993).

Facey, Roy. "The Development of the Port of Aden," *British-Yemeni Society Journal*, 6, 1998: 5–9.

Farah, Caesar. "Smuggling and International Politics in the Red Sea in the Late Ottoman Period," in G. Rex Smith et al., eds., *New Arabian Studies* (Exeter, England: University of Exeter Press, 2000).

Farah, Cesar. *The Sultan's Yemen: Nineteenth-Century Challenges to Ottoman Rule* (London: Tauris, 2002).

Farah, Cesar. "Anglo-Ottoman Confrontation in the Persian Gulf in the Late Nineteenth and Early Twentieth Centuries," *Proceedings of the Seminar for Arabian Studies*, 33, 2003.

Farooqhi, Suraiya. *Pilgrims and Sultans: The Hajj under the Ottomans, 1517–1683* (London: I. B. Tauris, 1994).

Farouk, Omar. "The Re-Organization of Islam in Cambodia and Laos," in Omar Farouk and Hiroyuki Yamamoto, eds., *Islam at the Margins: The Muslims of Indochina* (Kyoto: CIAS, 2008), pp. 70–85.

Fauvel, A. "Note sur l'épidémic de Choléra Observée Parmi les Pélerins à leur Retour de la Meque," in *Recuiel des Travaux du Comité Consultatif d'Hygiène Publique de France et des Actes Officiels de L'Administration Sanitaire* 7 (Paris, 1878), pp. 1–9.

Fealy, Greg, and Virginia Hooker, eds. *Voices of Islam in Southeast Asia: A Contemporary Sourcebook* (Singapore: ISEAS, 2006).

Feener, Michael. "Hybridity and the Hadhrami Diaspora in the Indian Ocean Muslim Networks," *Asian Journal of Social Science*, 32/3, 2004: 353–372.

Feener, Michael, and Michael Laffan. "Sufi Scents across the Indian Ocean: Yemeni Historiography and the Earliest History of Southeast Asian Islam," *Archipel*, 70, 2005: 185–208.

Feener, Michael, and Terenjit Sevea, eds. *Islamic Connections: Muslim Societies in South and Southeast Asia* (Singapore: ISEAS, 2009).

Fernando, Lloyd. "Conrad's Eastern Expatriates: A New Version of His Outcasts," *Proceedings of the Modern Language Association*, 91/1, 1976: 79–90.

Filesi, Cesira. *L'Archivio del Museo Africano in Roma: Presentazione e Inventario del Documento* (Roma: Istituto Italiano per l'Africa e'Oriente, 2001).

Fletcher, Ian. "Rhythm and Pattern in Autobiographies," in Denis Donoghue and J. R. Mulryne, eds., *An Honored Guest: New Essays on W. B. Yeats* (New York: St. Martin's Press, 1966).

Fogel, Aaron. *Coercion to Speak: Conrad's Poetics of Dialogue* (Cambridge, MA: Harvard University Press, 1985).

Folkenflik, Robert, ed. *The Culture of Autobiography: Constructions and Self-Representation* (Stanford, CA: Stanford University Press, 1993).

Forbes, Andrew. "The Crescent in Laos," *Saudi Aramco World*, 48/3, 1997: 36–39.

Forbes, Andrew, and David Henley. *The Haw: Traders of the Golden Triangle* (New Zealand: Asia Film House Editions, 1997).

Foster, William, ed. *The Journal of John Jourdain, 1608–1617* (London: Hakluyt Society, 1905), series II, vol. 16.

Foster, William, ed. *The Red Sea and Adjacent Countries at the Close of the Seventeenth Century* (London: Hakluyt, 1949).

Foster, William. *Early Travels in India* (Delhi: S. Chan, 1968).

Foucault, Michel. *The Archaeology of Knowledge* (translated by A. M. Sheridan Smith) (London: Routledge, 2002).

Fraser, Gail. *Interweaving Patterns in the Works of Joseph Conrad* (Ann Arbor: UMI Research Press, 1988).

Freitag, Ulrieke. "Hadhramis in International Politics, 1750–1967," in Ulrike Frietag and William Clarence-Smith, eds., *Hadhrami Traders, Scholars, and Statesmen in the Indian Ocean, 1750s–1960s* (Leiden: E. J. Brill, 1997), p. 130.

Freitag, Ulrike. "Hadhrami Migration in the 19th and 20th Centuries," *British-Yemeni Society Journal*, 7, 1999: 25–32.

Freitag, Ulrike. *Indian Ocean Migrants and State Formation in Hadhramaut: Reforming the Homeland* (Leiden: Brill, 2003).

Freitag, Ulrike. "From Golden Youth in Arabia to Business Leaders in Singapore: Instructions of a Hadrami Patriarch," in Eric Tagliacozzo, *Southeast Asia and the Middle East: Islam, Movement, and the Longue Duree* (Palo Alto, CA: Stanford University Press, 2009), pp. 235–249.

Freitag, Ulrike, and William Clarence-Smith, eds. *Hadhrami Traders, Scholars, and Statesmen in the Indian Ocean, 1750s–1960s* (Leiden: Brill, 1997).

Funston, John. "Thailand," in Greg Fealy and Virginia Hooker, eds., *Voices of Islam in Southeast Asia: A Contemporary Sourcebook* (Singapore: ISEAS, 2006), pp. 77–88.

Gade, Anna. *The Qur'an: An Introduction* (Oxford: Oneworld, 2010).

Gaerlan, Kristina, et al., eds. *Rebels, Warlord and Ulama: A Reader on Muslim Separatism and the War in the Southern Philippines* (Manila: Institute for Popular Democracy, 2000).

Gallop, Annabel Teh. *Golden Letters: Writing Traditions of Indonesia* (London: British Library, 1993).

Gallop, Annabel Teh. *The Legacy of the Malay Letter* (London: British Library, 1994).

Gallop, Annabel Teh. "Malay Sources for the History of the Sultanate of Brunei in the Early Nineteenth Century: Some Letters from the Reign of Sultan Muhammad Kanzul Alam," in Victor T. King and A. V. M. Horton, eds., *From Buckfast to Borneo: Essays Presented to Father Robert Nicholl on the 85th Anniversary of His Birth, 27 March 1995* (Hull: University of Hull, 1995), pp. 207–235.

Garbolino, F. "Carta del Mar Rosso e Teatro di Guerra in Africa" (Firenze: Benelli, 1885).

Garnett, Edward. *Letters from Joseph Conrad* (Indianapolis, IN: Bobbs-Merrill, 1928).

Gasim Zaman, Muhamad. "The Scope and Limits of Islamic Cosmopolitanism and the Discursive Language of the 'Ulama,'" in Miriam Cooke and Bruce Lawrence, eds., *Muslim Networks from Hajj to Hip Hop* (Chapel Hill: University of North Carolina Press, 2005), pp. 84–104.

Gaudefroy-Demombynes, M. "Notes sur la Mekke at Medine," *Revue de l'Histoire des Religions*, 77, 1918: 316–344.

Gavin, R. J. *Aden under British Rule, 1839–1967* (New York: Harper and Row, 1975).

Gelder, Geert Jan van. "Pelgrims, Passie en Poezie," in Willy Jansen and Huub de Jonge, eds., *Islamitische Pelgrimstochten* (Muiderberg, Netherlands: Coutinho, 1991), pp. 69–73.

Gervaise-Smith, William C. "Hadhrami Entrepeurs in the Malay World, 1750–1940," in Ulrike Frietag and William Clarence-Smith, eds., *Hadhrami Traders, Scholars, and Statesmen in the Indian Ocean, 1750s–1960s* (Leiden: E. J. Brill, 1997), p. 301.

Giddens, Anthony. *Modernity and Self-Identity: Self and Society in the Late Modern Age* (Cambridge: Polity, 1991).

Gilmartin, David. "A Networked Civilization?" in Miriam Cooke and Bruce Lawrence, eds., *Muslim Networks from Hajj to Hip Hop* (Chapel Hill: University of North Carolina Press, 2005), p. 54.

Gilquin, Michel, ed. *Atlas des Minorites Musulmanes en Asia Meridionale et Orientale* (Paris: CNRS Editions, 2010), pp. 125–158.

Gilquin, Michel. "Musulmans et Malais de Thailande," in Michel Gilquin, ed., *Atlas des Minorites Musulmanes en Asia Meridionale et Orientale* (Paris: CNRS Editions, 2010), pp. 159–182.

Gilsenan, Michael. *Recognizing Islam: Religion and Society in the Modern Middle East* (London: Tauris, 2005).

Gilsenan, Michael. "Topics and Queries for a History of Arab Families in Inheritance in Southeast Asia: Some Preliminary Thoughts," in Eric Tagliacozzo, *Southeast Asia and the Middle East: Islam, Movement, and the Longue Duree* (Palo Alto, CA: Stanford University Press, 2009), pp. 199–234.

Gobee, E., and C. Adriaanse, eds. *Ambtelijke Adviezen van C. Snouck Hurgronje* (The Hague: Martinus Nijhoff, 1959).

Goffman, Erving. *The Presentation of Self in Everyday Life* (Edinburgh: University of Edinburgh Social Sciences Research Centre, 1959).

Goitein, S. D. "From Aden to India: Specimens of the Correspondence of India Traders of the Twelfth Century," *JESHO*, 23/1–2, 1980: 43–66.

Goody, Jack. *The Interface Between the Written and the Oral* (Cambridge: Cambridge University Press, 1987).

Gopal, Surenda. "Coffee Traders of Western India in the Seventeenth Century," in Michel Tuchscherer, ed., *Le Commerce du Café Avant l'ere des Plantations Coloniales* (Cairo: Institut Francais d'Archeologie Orientale, 2001), p. 299.

Goubert, Jean-Pierre. *The Conquest of Water: The Advent of Health in the Industrial Age* (Princeton, NJ: Princeton University Press, 1989).

Gowing, Peter. *Muslim Filipinos: Heritage and Horizon* (Quezon City, Philippines: New Day, 1979).

Gowing, Peter. "Moros and Khaek: The Position of Muslim Minorities in the Philippines and Thailand," in Ahmad Ibrahim et al., eds., *Readings on Islam in Southeast Asia* (Singapore: ISEAS, 1990), pp. 180–192.

Graf, L. I. "Christiaan Snouck Hurgronje en Zijn Critici," *De Gids*, 9/10, 1980: 807–830.

Gran, Peter. "Political Economy as a Paradigm for the Study of Islamic History," *IJMES*, 1980: 511–526.

Green, Anthony. *Our Journey: Thirty Years of Haj Services in Singapore* (Singapore: Majlis Ugama Islam Singapura, 2006).

Griffiths, John. *Joseph Conrad and the Anthropological Dilemma* (Oxford: Clarendon, 1995).

Groom, Nigel. "The Northern Passes of Qataban," *Proceedings of the Seminar for Arabian Studies*, 6, 1976: 69–80.

Groom, Nigel. *Frankincense and Myrrh: A Study of the Arabian Incense Trade* (London: Longman, 1981).

Groom, Nigel. "The Island of Two Moons: Kamaran 1954," *British-Yemeni Society Journal*, 10, 2002: 29–37.

Guba, Egon, and Yvonne Lincoln. "Competing Paradigms in Qualitative Research: Theories and Issues," in Sharlene Hesse-Biber and Patricia Levy, eds., *Approaches to Qualitative Research: A Reader on Theory and Practice* (New York: Oxford University Press, 2004).

Guerin, Mathieu. "Cambodge—Les Cham et leur 'veranda sur la Mecque'—l'influence des Malais de Patani et du Kelantan su l'islam des Cham du Cambodge," *Aseanie*, 14/1, 2004: 29–67.

Gullick, J. M. *Indigenous Political Systems of Western Malaya* (London: Athlone, 1958).

Habermas, Jürgen. *The Structural Transformation of the Public Sphere* (Cambridge: Polity, 1962).

Hadiluwih, RM. H. Subanindyo. *Ibadah Haji: Perjalanan Spiritual 40 Hari* (Medan, Indonesia: Penerbit Dhian-Doddy, 1990).

Hadler, Jeffrey. "A Historiography of Violence and the Secular State in Indonesia: Tuanku Imam Bondjol and the Uses of History," *JAS*, 67/3, 2008: 971–1010.

Hadler, Jeffrey. *Muslims and Matriarchs: Cultural Resilience in Indonesia through Jihad and Colonialism* (Ithaca, NY: Cornell University Press, 2008).

Halliday, Fred. "Oman and Yemen: An Historic Re-Encounter," *British-Yemeni Society Journal*, 8, 2000: 41–52.

Hamid, A. *Petundjuk Petundjuk Tjara Menunaikan Ibadah Hadji* (Jakarta: Departemen Agama, 1962).

Hamid, Abdul Wahab Haji. *Panduan Sistematik Haji dan Umrah* (Kuala Lumpur: K Publishing, 1990).

Hamid, Abu. *Syekh Yusuf Makassar: Seorang Ulama, Sufi dan Pejuang* (Jakarta: Yayasan Obor Indonesia, 1994).

Hamilton, Alastair, et al., eds. *Friends and Rivals in the East: Studies in Anglo-Dutch Relations in the Levant from the Seventeenth Century to the Early Nineteenth Century* (Leiden: Brill, 2000).

Hamka, H. M. Jusuf. *Engkoh Bun Naik Haji* (Jakarta: Penerbit Pustaka Panjimas, 1985).

Hammoudi, Abdellah. *A Season in Mecca: Narrative of a Pilgrimage* (New York: Hill and Wang, 2006).

Hamner, Robert. *Joseph Conrad: Third World Perspectives* (Washington, DC: Three Continents, 1990).

Hansman, John. *Julfar, an Arabian Port: Its Settlement and Far Eastern Ceramic Trade from the Fourteenth to the Eighteenth Centuries* (London: RASGB and Ireland, 1985), pp. 25–65.

Hardy-Guilbert, Claire, and Axelle Rougeulle, "Archaeological Research into the Islamic Period in Yemen: Preliminary Notes on the French Expedition," *Proceedings of the Seminar on Arabian Studies*, 25, 1995: 29–44.

Harrington, Richard. "On the Frankincense Road in Yemen," *Canadian Geographic Journal*, 95/3, 1978: 14–21.

Hart, Francis. "Notes for an Anatomy of Modern Autobiography," *New Literary History*, 1/3 (1970): 485–511.

Harun, Jelani, ed. *Bustan al-Salatin (I and II)* (Kuala Lumpur: Dewan Bahasa dan Pustaka, 2004).

Hasan, Haji Usman Muqim. *Bimbingan Ibadat Haji, Umrah dan Ziarah* (Selangor, Malaysia: Pustaka ILMI, 1994).

Hasan, Wan Hasnan. "Ajal dan Bertemu Jodoh di Atas Kapal," *Tabung Haji*, December 27, 2003, pp. 15–17.

Hasbullah, Haji Ali Haji. *Soal-Jawab Haji dan Umrah* (Kuala Lumpur: Penerbitan Pustaka Antara Malaysia, 1993).

Hasjim, K. H. A. Wahid. *Menudju Perbaikan Perdjalanan Hadji* (Jakarta: Departemen Agama, n.d).

Hasjmy, A. *Surat Surat dari Tanah Suci* (Jakarta: Penerbit Bulan Bintang, 1979).

Hassan, Fuad. *Pengalaman Seorang Haji* (Perlawatan ke Haramain) (Jakarta: Bulan Bintang, 1975).

Hassan, Hamdan, ed. *Surat al-Anbiya'* (Kuala Lumpur: Dewan Bahasa dan Pustaka, 1992).

Hassan, Zaini, and Helmi Mohamad Foad, "Menjala Udang: Tampung Simpanan ke Mekah," *Tabung Haji*, December 27, 2003, pp. 29–30.

Hasyim, K. H. Yusuf. "Inikah Akhir Hidup Saya?" in Anonymous, *Haji, Sebuah Perjalanan Air Mata* (Yogyakarta, Indonesia: Bentang, 1993), p. 233.

Hattox, Ralph. *Coffee and Coffeehouses: The Origins of a Social Beverage in the Medieval Near East* (Seattle: University of Washington Press, 1985).

Hawkins, Clifford. *The Dhow: An Illustrated History of the Dhow and Its World* (Lymington, England: Hampshire Nautical, 1977).

Hawkins, Hunt. "Conrad and the Psychology of Colonialism," in Ross Murfin, ed., *Conrad Revisited: Essays for the Eighties* (Huntsville: University of Alabama Press, 1985).

Hayase, Shinzo. *Mindanao Ethnohistory beyond Nations: Maguindanao, Sangir, and Bagobo Societies in East Maritime Southeast Asia* (Quezon City, Philippines: Ateneo de Manila, 2007).

Hayat, Amir Hamzah. *Petundjuk Djalan ke Tanah Stji* (Bandung: Penerbit Tarate, 1962).

Headley, Stephen. "Afterword: The Mirror in the Mosque," in David Parkin and Stephen Headley, eds., *Islamic Prayer across the Indian Ocean: Inside and Outside the Mosque* (London: Curzon, 2000), pp. 213–238.

Hefner, Robert. *Hindu Javanese: Tengger Tradition and Islam* (Princeton, NJ: Princeton University Press, 1985).

Hefner, Robert, ed. *Making Modern Muslims: The Politics of Islamic Education in Southeast Asia* (Honolulu: University of Hawai'i Press, 2009).

Hefner, Robert, and Patricia Horvatich, eds. *Islam in an Era of Nation-States: Politics and Religious Renewal in Muslim Southeast Asia* (Honolulu: University of Hawai'i Press, 1997).

Helmi, Mohamad Foad. "Apam Balik: Jejakkan Kaki Pak Omar ke Mekah," *Tabung Haji*, December 27, 2003, pp. 28–29.

Henderson, P. M. *The Transformation of Fact into Fiction in the Historical Novels of Joseph Conrad and Upton Sinclair, and the Relation of These Novels to the Genre of Reportage* (Zurich: Zentralstelle der Studentenschaft, 1992).

Herwerden, J. D. van. *Toenemende Bedevaart naar Mekka* (The Hague: J. A. de la Vieter, 1875).

Heywood, Colin. *Writing Ottoman History: Documents and Interpretations* (Aldershot, England: Ashgate, 2002).

Hickey, Gerald. *Sons of the Mountains: Ethnohistory of the Vietnamese Central Highlands to 1954* (New Haven, CT: Yale University Press, 1982).

Hill, A. H. "Hikayat Raja-Raja Pasai, a Revised Romanised Version," *JMBRAS*, 33/2, 1960: 109–166.

Hill, A. H. *Hikayat Abdullah: An Annotated Translation* (Kuala Lumpur: Oxford University Press, 1970).

Hill, Ann Maxwell. *Merchants and Migrants: Ethnicity and Trade among Yunnanese Chinese in Southeast Asia* (New Haven, CT: Yale Southeast Asia Studies, 1998).

Hindess, Barry. *Discourses of Power: From Hobbes to Foucault* (London: Blackwell, 1996).

Ho, Eng Seng. *The Graves of Tarim* (Berkeley: University of California Press, 2006).

Ho, Engseng. "Hadhramis Abroad in Hadhramaut: The Muwalladin," in Ulrike Frietag and William Clarence-Smith, eds., *Hadhrami Traders, Scholars, and Statesmen in the Indian Ocean, 1750s–1960s* (Leiden: E. J. Brill, 1997), p. 131.

Honda, Gisho, Wataru Miki, and Saito Mitsuko. *Herb Drugs and Herbalists in Syria and North Yemen* (Tokyo: Institute for the Study of Languages and Cultures of Asia and Africa, 1990).

Hooker, M. B., ed. *Islam in South-East Asia* (Leiden: E. J. Brill, 1983).

Hourani, Albert. "How Should We Write the History of the Middle East?" *IJMES*, 23, 1991: 125–136.

Hourani, G. F. *Arab Seafaring in the Indian Ocean in Ancient and Early Medieval Times* (New York: Octagon, 1975).

Huber, Valeska. "The Unification of the Globe by Disease? The International Sanitary Conferences on Cholera, 1851–1894," *Historical Journal*, 49/2, 2006: 453–476.

Hunter, Allan. *Joseph Conrad and the Ethics of Darwinism* (London: Croom Helm, 1983).

Hussain, Khalid M. *Bukhari al-Jauhari, Taj al-Salatin* (Kuala Lumpur: Dewan Bahasa dan Pustaka, 1992).

Husson, Laurence. "Les Indonésiens en Arabie Saoudite pour la foi et le travail," *Revue Européene des Migrations Internationales*, 13/1, 1997: 125–147.

Hutch, Richard. *The Meaning of Lives: Biography, Autobiography and the Spiritual Quest* (London: Cassell, 1997).

Ibrahim, Mahmood. "Social and Economic Conditions in Pre-Islamic Mecca," *IJMES*, 14/3, 1982: 343.

Ileto, Reynaldo. "Cholera and the Origins of the American Sanitary Order in the Philippines," in David Arnold, ed., *Imperial Medicine and Indigenous Societies* (Manchester, England: Manchester University Press, 1988), p. 131.

Ishino, Iwao. "Memories and Their Unintended Consequences," in Marea Teski and Jacob Climo, eds., *The Labyrinth of Memory: Ethnographic Journeys* (Westport, CT: Bergin & Garvey, 1995), pp. 185–201.

Iskandar, Amat. *Ketika Haji Kami Kerjakan* (Semarang, Indonesia: Dahara Prize, 1994).

Iskandar, Teuku, ed., *De Hikajat Atjéh* ('s-Gravenhage: Nijhoff, 1958). Verhandelingen van het Koninklijk Instituut voor Taal-, Land en Volkenkunde, deel 26.

Izzedine, C. *Le Choléra el l'hygiène à la Mecque* (Paris, 1909).

Jansen, Willy, and Huub de Jonge. "Islamitische Pelgrimstochten: Inleiding," in Willy Jansen and Huub de Jonge, eds., *Islamitische Pelgrimstochten* (Muiderberg, Netherlands: Coutinho, 1991), pp. 7–10.

Jarcho, Saul. *The Concept of Contagion in Medicine, Literature, and Religion* (Malabar, FL: Krieger, 2000).

Jauhari, Muhammad Taufiq. *Rahsia Ka'bah dan Masjid Nabawi* (Kuala Lumpur: Jasmine Enterprise, 2004).

Johnson, S. W. "Cholera and the Meccan Pilgrimage," *British Medical Journal*, 1, 1895: 1218–1219.

Jones, Russell, ed. *Nuru'd-din ar-Raniri, Bustan al-Salatin Bab IV Fasal I (A Critical Edition of the First Part of Fasal I, Which Deals with Ibrahim ibn Adam)* (Kuala Lumpur: Dewan Bahasa dan Pustaka, 1974).

Jones, Russell. "The Texts of the Hikayat Raja Pasai, a Short Note," *JMBRAS*, 53/1 (1980: 167–171).

Jones, Russell, ed. *Hikayat Raja Pasai* (Kuala Lumpur: Fajar Bakti, 1987).

Jones, Russell. *Hikayat Sultan Ibrahim ibn Adham: An Edition of an Anonyomous Malay Text with Translation and Notes* (Berkeley: Center for South and Southeast Asia Studies, University of California, 1985). Monograph series No. 27.

Jonge, Huub de. "Heiligen, Middelen en Doel: Ontwikkeling en Betekenis van Twee Islamitische Bedevaartsoordelen op Java," in Willy Jansen and Huub de Jonge, eds., *Islamitische Pelgrimstochten* (Muiderberg, Netherlands: Coutinho, 1991), pp. 81–100.

Jonge, Huub de. "Dutch Colonial Policy Pertaining to Hadhrami Immigrants," in Ulrike Frietag and William Clarence-Smith, eds., *Hadhrami Traders, Scholars, and Statesmen in the Indian Ocean, 1750s–1960s* (Leiden: E. J. Brill, 1997), p. 99.

Jonge, Huub de. "Contradictory and against the Grain: Snouck Hurgronje on the Hadramis in the Dutch East Indies, 1889–1936," in Huub de Jonge and Nico Kaptein, eds., *Transcending Borders: Arabs, Politics, Trade, and Islam in Southeast Asia* (Leiden: KITLV, 2002), pp. 219–234.

Jonge, Huub de, and Nico Kaptein, eds. *Transcending Borders: Arabs, Politics, Trade and Islam in Southeast Asia* (Leiden: KITLV, 2002).

Julius, M. *Kenangan Rohani Perjalanan Haji* (Malang, Indonesia: Rumah Sakit Islam Aisyiyah, 1994).

Jumsari, Jusuf, Tuti Munawar, Retnadi Geria, and Amin Fukri Hoesin, eds. *Antologi Syair Simbolik dalam Sastra Indonesia Lama* (Jakarta: Proyek Pembangunan Media Kebudayaan, Departemen Pendidikan dan Kebudayaan, Republik Indonesia, 1978), part 4.

Junker, Laura. *Raiding, Trading, and Feasting: The Political Economy of Philippine Chiefdoms* (Honolulu: University of Hawai'i Press, 1999).

Jutin, H. A. *712 Mudjahid Gambela Jang Menggemparkan* (Malang, Indonesia: Penerbit UB Milan, n.d.).

Kalus, L., and C. Guillot. "Réinterprétion des plus anciennes stèles funéraires islamiques nousantariennes: I. Les deux inscriptions du 'Champa,'" *Archipel*, 64, 2003: 63–90.

Kalus, L., and C. Guillot. "Réinterprétion des plus anciennes stèles funéraires islamiques nousantariennes: II. La stèle de Leran (Java) datée de 475/1082 et les stèles associées," *Archipel*, 67, 2003: 17–36.

Kamajaya, H. Karkono. "Tidak Awur-awuran Atau Asal Haji-hajian," in Anonymous, *Haji Sebuah Perjalanan Air Mata* (Yogyakarta, Indonesia: Bentang, 1993), pp. 111–117.

Kane, Solomon. "Les Musulmans des Philippines," in Michel Gilquin, ed., *Atlas des Minorites Musulmanes en Asia Meridionale et Orientale* (Paris: CNRS Editions, 2010), pp. 243–262.

Kapferer, Bruce, and Angela Hobart, eds. *Aesthetics in Performance: Formations of Symbolic Construction and Experience* (New York: Berghahn, 2005).

Kaptein, Nico. "Meccan Fatwas from the End of the Nineteenth Century on Indonesian Affairs," *Studia Islamika*, 2/4, 1995: 141–159.

Kaptein, Nico. *The Muhimmat al-Nafa'is: A Bilingula Meccan Fatwa Collection for Indonesian Muslims from the End of the Nineteenth Century* (Jakarta; INIS, 1997).

Kaptein, Nico, and Dick Douwes, eds. *Indonesia dan Haji: Empat Karangan* (Jakarta: INIS, 1997).

Karl, Frederick, and Laurence Davies, eds. *The Collected Letters of Joseph Conrad*, vol. 2 (Cambridge: Cambridge University Press, 1986).

Kassim, Ahmad, ed. *Kisah Pelayaran Abdullah* (Kuala Lumpur: Oxford University Press, 1964).

Kassim, Ahmad. *Hikayat Hang Tuah* (Kuala Lumpur: Yayasan Karyawan dan Dewan Bahasa dan Pustaka, 1997).

Kassim, Ahmad Syahir. "Lapan Kali: Pak Mad Sayur ke Tanah Suci," *Tabung Haji*, December 27, 2003, p. 31.

Kastama, Emo. *Catatan Harian Seorang Jemaah Haji* (Jakarta: Cita Putra Bangsa, 1997), pp. 318–319.

Katianda, H. A. Gozali. "Tiba-tiba Tangan Saya Ada yang Membimbing," in E. Syarief Nurdin and E. Kosasih, *100 Keajaiban di Tanah Suci Pengalaman Unik Jamaah Haji* (Bandung: Pustaka Hidayah, 1996), pp. 67–68.

Kawashima, Midori. "The Islamic Reform Movement at Lanao in the Philippines during the 1930s: The Founding of the Kamilol Islam Society," *Journal of Sophia Asian Studies*, 27, 2009: 141–154.

Kazem, Zadeh H. "Relation d'un Pélerinage à La Mecque," *Revue du Monde Musulman*, 19, 1912: 144–227.

Keall, Edward. "The Evolution of the First Coffee Cups in Yemen," in Michel Tuchscherer, ed., *Le Commerce du Café Avant l'ère des Plantations Coloniales* (Cairo: Institut Français d'Archéologie Orientale, 2001), pp. 35–50.

Keijzer, S. *De Bedevaart der Inlanders naar Makka: Volledeige Beschrijving van Alles wat op de Bedevaart-gangers uit Nederlandsch-Indie Betrekking Heeft* (Leiden: Gualt, Kolff, 1871).

Kerr, Douglas. "Crowds, Colonialism and Lord Jim," *The Conradian*, 18/2, 1994: 49–64.

Khalidi, Omar. "The Hadhrami Role in the Politics and Society of Colonial India," in Ulrike Frietag and William Clarence-Smith, eds., *Hadhrami Traders, Scholars, and Statesmen in the Indian Ocean, 1750s–1960s* (Leiden: E. J. Brill, 1997), p. 67.

Khamis, Muhammad 'Attiyah. *Fiqh Wanita Haji* (Kuala Lumpur: Penerbit Hizbi, 1987), pp. 36–40.

Khan, Sameen. "Carrying One's Own Food and Water on Haj," *Haj and Umra*, 57/4, 2002: 14–15.

Khan, Zafarul-Islam, and Yakub Zaki, eds. *Hajj in Focus* (London: Open Press, 1986).

Kiefer, Thomas. *The Tausug: Violence and Law in a Philippine Moslem Society* (Prospect Heights, IL: Waveland, 1986).

Kiernan, Ben. *How Pol Pot Came to Power* (London: Zed, 1985).

Kiernan, Ben. "Chams" *Encyclopedia of Islam*, 3rd ed. (Leiden: Brill, 2010, pp. 173–180.

Kimon, D. *La Pathologie de l'Islam et les Moyens de le Detruire. Étude Psychologique* (Paris, 1897).

King, David. *Mathematical Astronomy in Medieval Yemen: A Bibliographical Survey* (Cairo: American Research Center in Egypt, 1983).

Klinkert, H. A. "Verhaal eener Pelgrimsreis van Singapoera naar Mekah, door Abdoellah bin Abdil Kadir Moensji, gedaan in het jaar 1854," *BKI*, 2, 1867: 384–410.

Knowles, Owen, and Gene Moore, eds. *Oxford Reader's Companion to Conrad* (Oxford: Oxford University Press, 2000), pp. 77–80.

Koningsveld, P. Sj. Van. "Snouck Hurgronje Zoals Hij Was," *De Gids*, 9/10, 1980: 763–784.

Koningsveld, P. Sj. Van. *Orientalism and Islam: The Letters of C. Snouck Hurgronje to Th. Noldeke from the Tubingen University Library* (Leiden: Leiden University Press, 1985).

Koningsveld, P. Sj. Van. "Izharu 'l-Islam Snouck Hurgronje: Segi Sejarah Kolonial yang Diabaikan," in P. Sj. Van Koningsveld, *Snouck Hurgronje dan Islam: delapan karangan tentang hidup dan karya seorang orientalis zaman kolonial* (Jakarta: Girimukti Pusaka, 1989).

Koningsveld, P. Sj. van. "Raden Jusuf di Bandung Mengakhiri Kebungkamannya sekitar Pernika-han-Pernikahan Islam Ayahnya, Christian Snouck Hurgronje," in P. Sj. van Koningsveld, *Snouck Hurgronje dan Islam: delapan karagan tentang hidup dan karya seorang orientalis zaman kolonial* (Jakarta: Girimukti Pusaka, 1989): 164–165.

Koningsveld, P. Sj. van. "Orientalistik sebagai Ilmu-Bantu Kolonial: 'Masuk' Islamnya Snouck Hurgronje," in P. Sj. Van Koningsveld, *Snouck Hurgronje dan Islam: delapan karangan tentang hidup dan karya seorang orientalis zaman kolonial* (Jakarta: Girimukti Pusaka, 1989).

Koningsveld, P. Sj. Van. "Snouck Hurgronje alias Abdul-Ghaffar. Beberapa Catatan-Pinggir Kritik Sejarah," in P. Sj. Van Koningsveld, *Snouck Hurgronje dan Islam: delapan karangan tentang hidup dan karya seorang orientalis zaman kolonial* (Jakarta: Girimukti Pusaka, 1989).

Koningsveld, P. Sj. Van. "Penulisan Sejarah Suatu Perang Ekspansi Kolonial. Lima Puluh Tahun Setelah Kematian Snouck Hurgronje," in P. Sj. Van Koningsveld, *Snouck Hurgronje dan Islam: delapan karangan tentang hidup dan karya seorang orientalis zaman kolonial* (Jakarta: Girimukti Pusaka, 1989), p. 261.

Koningsveld, P. Sj. Van. "Sisa-sisa Kolonial dalam Kebijaksanaan Negeri Belanda Dewasa ini men-genai Islam," in P. Sj. Van Koningsveld, *Snouck Hurgronje dan Islam: delapan karangan tentang hidup dan karya seorang orientalis zaman kolonial* (Jakarta: Girimukti Pusaka, 1989).

Kosasih, E., *100 Keajaiban di Tanah Suci Pengalaman Unik Jamaah Haji* (Bandung: Pustaka Hidayah, 1996).

Koster, G. L. "Making It New in 1884: Lie Kim Hock's Syair Siti Akbari," *BKI*, 154/1, 1998: 95–115.

Kratz, E. Ulrich, and Adriyetti Amir, eds. *Surat Keterangan Syeikh Jalaluddin karangan Fakih Saghir* (Kuala Lumpur: Dewan Bahasa dan Pustaka, 2002).

Krenn, Heliena. *Conrad's Lingard Trilogy: Empire, Race, and Women in the Malay Novels* (New York: Garland, 1990).

Krieken, G. S. van. *Snouck Hurgronje en het Panislamisme* (Leiden: Brill, 1985).

Kroef, J. M. van der. "The Arabs in Indonesia," *Middle East Journal*, 7/3, 1953: 300–323.

Kuehn, Robert. "Introduction," in Robert Kuehn, *Twentieth Century Interpretations of Lord Jim: A Collection of Critical Essays* (Englewood Cliffs, NJ: Prentice Hall, 1969), p. 1.

Kumar, Ann. *The Diary of a Javanese Muslim: Religion, Politics, and the Pesantren, 1883–1886* (Canberra: Faculty of Asian Studies Monographs, 1985).

Kuneralp, S. "Pilgrimage and Choelra in Ottoman Hedjaz," *Turkish-Arab Relations*, 4, 1989: 69–81.

Kwa Chong Guan. "The Value of Oral Testimony: Text and Orality in the Reconstruction of the Past," in P. Lim Pui Huen, James Morrison, and Kwa Chong Guan, eds., *Oral History in Southeast Asia: Theory and Method* (Singapore: National Archives of Singapore and the Institute of Southeast Asian Studies, 1998), pp. 19–32.

Labrousse, Henri. "L'Arabie du Suud et L'Europa a l'aube des Temps Modernes," in Joseph Chel-hod, ed., *L'Arabie du Suud: Histoire et Civilisation*, vol. 1 (Paris: G.P. Maisonneuve et Larose, 1984), pp. 91–109.

Labussiere, A. "Rapport sur les Chams et les Malais de L'Arrondissment de Chaudoc," *Excursions et Reconnaissance*, 6, 1880: 373–380.

Laffan, Michael. "Raden Aboe Bakar: An Introductory Note Concerning Snouck Hurgronje's Informant in Jeddah, 1884–1912," *BTLV*, 155/4, 1999: 517–542.

Laffan, Michael. "A Watchful Eye: The Meccan Plot of 1881 and Changing Dutch Perceptions of Islam in Indonesia," *Archipel*, 63, 2002: 79–108.

Laffan, Michael. *Islamic Nationhood and Colonial Indonesia: The Umma below the Winds* (London: Routledge, 2003).

Laffan, Michael. "Finding Java: Muslim Nomenclature of Insular Southeast Asia from Srivijaya to Snouck Hurgronje," in Eric Tagliacozzo, ed., *Southeast Asia and the Middle East: Islam, Movement, and the Longue Duree* (Palo Alto, CA: Stanford University Press, 2009), pp. 17–64.

Laffan, Michael. *The Making of Indonesian Islam: Orientalism and the Narration of a Sufi Past* (Princeton, NJ: Princeton University Press, 2011).

Lafont, Pierre-Bernard. "Contribution a l'Etude des Structures Sociales des Cham du Vietnam," *BEFEO*, 52, 1964: 157–171.

Lambourn, Elizabeth. "From Cambay to Samudera-Pasai and Gresik: The Export of Gujerati Grave Memorials to Sumatra and Java in the Fifteenth Century C.E.," *Indonesia and the Malay World*, 31/90, 2003: 221–289.

Lambourn, Elizabeth. "Tombstones, Texts, and Typologies: Seeing Sources for the Early History of Islam in Southeast Asia," *JESHO*, 51, 2008: 252–286.

Lambrecht, Curtis. "Burma (Myanmar)," in Greg Fealy and Virginia Hooker, eds., *Voices of Islam in Southeast Asia: A Contemporary Sourcebook* (Singapore: ISEAS, 2006), pp. 22–29.

Lang, William, and Laurie Mercier. "Getting It Down Right: Oral History's Reliability in Local History Research," *Oral History Review*, 12, 1984: 81–99.

Lanzing, Fred. "Snouck Hurgrnje, Schrijver," *Indische Letteren*, 16/4, 2001: 154–169.

Lay, Maung Maung. "The Emergence of the Panthay Community at Mandalay," in *Studies in Myanma History* (Yangon, Myanmar: Thein Htike Yadana, 1999), p. 93.

Leeuwen, Marianne van. "Politieke Geweld in Mekka," in Willy Jansen and Huub de Jonge, eds., *Islamitische Pelgrimstochten* (Muiderberg, Netherlands: Coutinho, 1991), pp. 57–68.

Lekon, Christian. "The Impact of Remittances on the Economy of Hadhamaut, 1914–1967," in Ulrike Frietag and William Clarence-Smith, eds., *Hadhrami Traders, Scholars, and Statesmen in the Indian Ocean, 1750s-1960s* (Leiden: E. J. Brill, 1997).

Leman, Ida. "Allah Mengundang Hajiku dengan Tiba-tiba," in Anonymous, *Haji, Sebuah Perjalanan Air Mata* (Yogyakarta, Indonesia: Bentang, 1993), pp. 94–95.

Lester, John. *Conrad and Religion* (London: Macmillan, 1988).

Lesure, Michel. "Un Document Ottoman de 1525 sur L'Inde Portugaise et les Pays de la Mer Rouge," *Mare Luso-Indicum*, 3, 1976: 137–160.

Lewis, Archibold. "Maritime Skills in the Indian Ocean, 1368–1500," *JESHO*, 16/2–3, 1973: 238–239.

Liaw, Yock Fang. *Sejarah Kesusasteraan Melayu Klasik* (Jakarta: Erlangga, 1993).

Licata, G. B. "L'Italia nel Mar Rosso," *Boll. Sez. Fiorentina della Soc. Africana d'Italia*, March 1885, p. 5.

Lieberman, Victor. *Strange Parallels* (Cambridge; Cambridge University Press, 2003).

Lim, How Seng. "Interviewing the Business and Political Elite of Singapore: Methods and Problems," in P. Lim Pui Huen, James Morrison, and Kwa Chong Guan, eds., *Oral History in Southeast Asia: Theory and Method* (Singapore: National Archives of Singapore and the Institute of Southeast Asian Studies, 1998), pp. 55–65.

Lippe, Hans. "Lord Jim: Some Geographic Observations," *The Conradian*, 10/2, 1985: 135–138.

Lippe, Hans. "Reconsidering the Patna Inquiry in Lord Jim," *The Conradian*, 15/1, 1990: 59–69.

Liverani, M. "Beyond Deserts, beyond Oceans" in Alessandra Avanzini, ed., *Profumi d'Arabia: Atti del Convegno* (Roma: L'Erma di Bretschneider, 1997), p. 560.

Lobo, Jeronimo. *The Itinerary of Jerinomo Lobo*, trans. Donald M. Lockhart (London: Hakluyt, 1984).

Lombard, Denys. "Le Campa vu du Sud," *BEFEO*, 76, 1987: 311–317.

Lombard, Denys. *Le Sultanat d'Atjeh au Temps d'Iskandar Muda, 1607–1636* (Paris: EFEO, 1967).

Lombard, Denys. *Le Carrefour Javanais: Essai d'Histoire Globale* (Paris: Editions de l'Ecole des Hautes Etudes en Sciences Sociales, 1990).

Long, David. *The Hajj Today: A Survey of the Contemporary Mekkah Pilgrimage* (Albany: State University of New York Press, 1979).

Loos, Tamara. *Subject Siam* (Ithaca, NY: Cornell University, 2006).

Lorimer, J. G. *Gazeteer of the Persian Gulf, Oman, and Central Arabia* (Calcutta: Government Printers, 1915).

Low, Michael. "Empire and the Hajj: Pilgrims, Plagues, and Pan-Islam under British Surveillance, 1965–1908," *International Journal of Middle Eastern Studies*, 40, 2008: 269–290.

Lyons, Maryinez. "Sleeping Sickness, Colonial Medicine and Imperialism: Some Connections in the Belgian Congo," in Roy Macleod and Milton Lewis, eds., *Disease, Medicine, and Empire* (London: Routledge, 1988), p. 247.

Lysa, Hong. "Ideology and Oral History Institutions in Southeast Asia," in P. Lim Pui Huen, James Morrison, and Kwa Chong Guan, eds., *Oral History in Southeast Asia: Theory and Method* (Singapore: National Archives of Singapore and the Institute of Southeast Asian Studies, 1998), pp. 33–46.

Maaten, K. van der. *Snouck Hurgronje en de Atjeh Ooorlog*, vol. 1 (Rotterdam: Oostersch Instituut te Leiden, 1948).

Machfudz, Drg. H. Ircham. "Saya Menangis, Nikmat Sekali," in Anonymous, *Haji, Sebuah Perjalanan Air Mata* (Yogyakarta, Indonesia: Bentang, 1993), p. 105.

Madale, Nagasure. "The Resurgence of Islam and Nationalism in the Philippines," in Taufik Abdullah and Sharon Siddique, eds., *Islam and Society in Southeast Asia* (Singapore: ISEAS, 1986), pp. 289–310.

Mahmoud, H. E. "Communications sur le Choléra. Le Choléra et le Haddj," *Union Medical*, 2/28, 1865: 260–264.

Mahmud, H. Junus. *Manasik Hadji* (Bandung: P.T. Alma'arif, 1967).

Maier, H. M. J. *In the Center of Authority: The Malay Hikayat Merong Mahawangsa* (Ithaca, NY: Cornell University Southeast Asia Program, 1988).

Maier, Hendrik. "Tales of Hang Tuah—In Search of Wisdom and Good Behavior," *BKI*, 155, 1999: 342–361.

Maier, Hendrik. "Sedjarah Melayu—Maleise Geschiedenissen," in *Oosterse Omzwervingen— Klassieke Teksten over Indonesia uit Oost en West* (Leiden: KITLV, 2000), pp.153–184.

Maier, Hendrik. *We Are Playing Relatives: A History of Malay Writing* (Leiden: KITLV, 2004).

Majid, Haji Abdul. "A Malay's Pilgrimage to Mecca," *Journal of the Malaysian Branch of the Royal Asiatic Society*, 4/2, 1926: 269–287.

Majid, M. Dien. "Berhaji Tempo Dulu dengan Kapal Laut," in Edi Sedyawati and Susanto Zuhdi, eds., *Arung Samudra: Persembahan Memperingati Sembilan Windu A. B. Lapian* (Depok, Indonesia: Pusat Penelitian dan Budaya Lembaga Penelitian UI, 2001).

Majul, Cesar. *Muslims in the Philippines* (Quezon City: University of the Philippines Press, 1973).

Makky, Ghazy Abdul Wahed. *Mecca: The Pilgrimage City: A Study of Pilgrim Accommodation* (London: Croom Helm, 1978).

Malik, Camelia. "Ada yang Menakut-nakuti Saya," in Anonymous, *Haji Sebuah Perjalanan Air Mata* (Yogyakarta, Indonesia: Bentang, 1993), p. 83.

Maman, M. S. *Orang Sunda Munggah Haji* (Bandung: Penerbit Kiblat, 2004).

Mandal, Sumit. "Natural Leaders of Native Muslims: Arab Ethnicity and Politics in Java under Dutch Rule," in Ulrike Frietag and William Clarence-Smith, eds., *Hadhrami Traders, Scholars, and Statesmen in the Indian Ocean, 1750s–1960s* (Leiden: E. J. Brill, 1997), p. 186.

Mangano, G. "Relazione Riassuntiva di un Viaggio di Studi nell 'A.O., India, Ceylon, Malacca, e Giava," *L'Agricoltura Coloniale* 4/5, 1909: 272, 313.

Manguin, Pierre Yves. "Etudes Cam II: L'Introduction de l'Islam au Campa," *Bulletin de l'Ecole Francaise d'Extreme-Orient*, 66 (1979): 255–287.

Marcovich, Anne. "French Colonial Medicine and Colonial Rule: Algeria and Indochina," in Roy Macleod and Milton Lewis, eds., *Disease, Medicine, and Empire* (London: Routledge, 1988), pp. 105–109.

Marcus, Luara. *Auto/biographical Discourses: Theory, Criticism, Practice* (Manchester, UK: Manchester University Press, 1994).

Markasan, Suratman. *Perempuan Kerudang Hitam* (Kuala Lumpur: Dewan Bahasa dan Pustaka Kementerian Pendidikan Malaysia, 1991).

Marle, Hans van. "Conrad and Richard Burton on Islam," *Conradiana*, 17 (1985): 139.

Marle, Hans van, and Pierre Lefranc. "Ashore and Afloat: New Perspectives on Topography and Geography in Lord Jim," *Conradiana*, 20, 1988: 109–135.

Marston, Thomas. *Britain's Imperial Role in the Red Sea Area, 1800–1878* (Hamden, CT: Shoe String, 1961).

Maspero, Georges. *Le Royaume de Champa* (Paris: Van Oest, 1928).

Massara, E. "Islamismo e Confraternite in Eritrea: I Morgani," *L'Ilustraz. Colon.* 8, 1921: 306.

Ma'sum, H. Sumarmo. *Kesehatan Haji* (Jakarta: Badan Koordinasi Ikatan Persaudraan Haji Indonesia, 1991).

Matheson, V., and M. B. Hooker. "Jawi Literature in Patani: The Maintenance of a Tradition," *JMBRAS*, 41/1, 1988: 6.

Matheson, V., and A. C. Milner. *Perceptions of the Haj: Five Malay Texts* (Singapore: ISEAS, 1984).

Matheson, Virginia, and Barbara Watson Andaya, eds. and trans. *The Precious Gift, Tuhfat al-Nafis* (Kuala Lumpur: Oxford University Press, 1982).

Mattei, G. E. "Studi sulla Flora della Colonie Italiane," *Bell. Soc. Africana d'Italia*, 1911: 131–173.

Maxwell, Allen. "Recording Oral Traditions and Language," *Borneo Research Bulletin*, 21/2 (1989): 97–142.

Maxwell, W. E. "Notes on Two Perak Manuscripts," *JSBRAS*, 2, 1871: 181–191.

Mayjen. (Purn.) H. Basofi Sudirman. "Semuanya Merupakan Paket," in Anonymous, *Haji, Sebuah Perjalanan Air Mata* (Yogyakarta, Indonesia: Bentang, 1993), pp. 64–72.

Mazzoni, S. "Complex Society, Urbanization and Trade: The Case of Eastern and Western Arabia" in Alessandra Avanzini, ed., *Profumi d'Arabia: Atti del Convegno* (Roma: L'Erma di Bretschneider, 1997), p. 24.

McCargo, Duncan. *Tearing Apart the Land: Islam and Legitimacy in Southern Thailand* (Ithaca, NY: Cornell University Press, 2008).

McDonnell, Mary Byrne. "The Conduct of the Hajj from Malaysia and Its Socio-Economic Impact on Malay Society: A Descriptive and Analytical Study, 1860–1981" (PhD Dissertation, Columbia University, 1986).

McGraw, Fred. "Mecca's Food Supplies and Muhammad's Boycott," *JESHO*, 20/3, 1977: 249–250.

McNair, Frederick. *Perak and the Malays* (London: Tinsley Brothers, 1878).

McPherson, Kenneth. *The Indian Ocean: A History of People and the Sea* (Delhi: Oxford University Press, 1993).

Mees, C. A., ed. *De Kroniek van Kutai* (PhD Dissertation, Universiteit te Leiden, Santpoort, 1935).

Metzger, Laurent. "Politiques d'Integration de la Minorite Musulman de Singapour," in Michel Gilquin, ed., *Atlas des Minorites Musulmanes en Asia Meridionale et Orientale* (Paris: CNRS Editions, 2010), pp. 217–242.

Meulen, Daniel van der. "The Revival of the Pilgrimage to Mecca," *Niewsblad voor de Residentien Palembang, Djambi, en Banka*, September 14, 1937.

Meulen, Daniel van der. "The Revival of the Pilgrimage to Mecca," *De Telegraaf*, October 2, 1937.

Meulen, Daniel van der. "The Mecca Pilgrimage," *Palembanger*, 1938 (n.d., clipping).

Meulen, Daniel van der. "The Pilgrimage to Mecca," *Palembanger*, June 18, 1938.

Meulen, Daniel van der. "The Return of the Mecca Pilgrims to the Dutch East Indies," *Deli Courant*, March 25, 1938.

Meulen, Daniel van der. "The Mecca Pilgrimage and Its Importance to the Netherlands Indies," *The Moslem World*, 31, 1941: 48–60.

Meulen, Daniel van der. "De Bedevaart naar Mekka en haar beteekenis voor Nederlands-Indie," *Zendingstijdschrift De Opwekker*, 86/1, 1942: 474–486.

Miller, A. G., and T. A. Cope. *Flora of the Arabian Peninsula and Socotra*, vol. 1 (Edinburgh: Edinburgh University Press, 1996).

Miller, J. Hillis. "Heart of Darkness Revisited," in Ross Murfin, ed., *Joseph Conrad, Heart of Darkness: A Case Study in Contemporary Criticism* (New York: St. Martin's Press, 1989).

Miller, Michael. "Pilgrims' Progress: The Business of the Hajj," *Past and Present*, 191, 2006: 189–228.

Milner, A. "Islam in the Muslim State," in M. B. Hooker, ed., *Islam in South-East Asia* (Leiden: Brill, 1988), pp. 23–49.

Mintz, Sidney. "The Anthropological Interview and the Life History," *Oral History Review*, 7 (1979): 18–26.

Mitchell, Timothy. *Colonising Egypt* (Cambridge: Cambridge University Press, 1988).

Mobini-Kesheh, Natalie. "Islamic Modernism in Colonial Java: The Al-Irshad Movement," in Ulrike Frietag and William Clarence-Smith, eds., *Hadhrami Traders, Scholars, and Statesmen in the Indian Ocean, 1750s–1960s* (Leiden: E. J. Brill, 1997), p. 231.

Mobini-Kesheh, Natalie. *The Hadrami Awakening: Community and Identity in the Netherlands East Indies, 1900–1942* (Ithaca, NY: SEAP, 1999).

Moereels, A. J. P. *Chr. Snouck Hurgronje* (Rijswijk, Netherlands: V. A. Kramers, 1938).

Mokhzani, Azixah. "The Writing of the Biography of Tan Sri Fatimah Hashim," in P. Lim Pui Huen, James Morrison, and Kwa Chong Guan, eds., *Oral History in Southeast Asia: Theory and Method* (Singapore: National Archives of Singapore and the Institute of Southeast Asian Studies, 1998), pp. 140–152.

Mongia, Padmini. "Empire, Narrative, and the Feminine in *Lord Jim* and *Heart of Darkness*," in Keith Carabine et al., eds., *Contexts for Conrad* (New York: Columbia University Press, 1993).

Mongia, Padmini. "Ghosts of the Gothic: Spectral Women and Colonized Spaces in Lord Jim," *The Conradian*, 17/2, 1993: 1–16.

Moore, Gene. "The Missing Crew of the Patna," *The Conradian*, 25/1, 2000: 83–98.

Moore, Gene. "Joseph Conrad in Indonesia," in Gene Moore, ed., *A Joseph Conrad Archive: The Letters and Papers of Hans van Marle, Conradian*, 30/2, 2005.

Morf, Gustav. *The Polish Heritage of Joseph Conrad* (Marston, England: Sampson Low, 1930).

Mori, A. "Le Nostre Colonie del Mar Rosso Giudicate dalla Stanley," *Boll. Sez. Fiorentina della Soc. Africana d'Italia*, May 1886, p. 84.

Mori, A. "Il Problema Coloniale nei suoi Rapporti con le Scienze Geografiche e l'Attivita dell'Istituto Coloniale Italiano nei Primi Quattro Anni di Vita," in *Congresso Geografico Italiano Palermo 1910* (Palermo, 1911), p. 478.

Morinis, Alan. "Introduction," in Alan Morinis, ed., *Sacred Journeys: The Anthropology of Pilgrimage* (Westport, CT: Greenwood, 1992), pp. 10–13.

Morris, M. "The Harvesting of Frankincense in Dhofar, Oman," in Alessandra Avanzini, ed., *Profumi d'Arabia: Atti del Convegno* (Roma: L'Erma di Bretschneider, 1997), p. 232.

Moser, Thomas, ed. *Joseph Conrad Lord Jim: Authoritative Text, Backgrounds, Sources, Criticism* (New York: Norton, 1996).

Muchtar, K. H. A. Latif. "Haji Bukan Ibadah Puncak," in Anonymous, *Haji, Sebuah Perjalanan Air Mata* (Yogyakarta, Indonesia: Bentang, 1993), pp. 130–133.

Mukherjee, Arun. *Crime and Public Disorder in Colonial Bengal, 1861–1912* (Calcutta: K. P. Bagchi, 1995).

Mundy, Rodney. *Narrative of Events in Borneo and Celebes, Down to the Occupation of Labuan: From the Journals of James Brooke, Esq., Rajah of Sarawak*, 2 vols. (London: Murray, 1848), vol 1.

Musa, Mohamad Zain Bin. "Dynamics of Faith: Imam Musa in the Revival of Islamic Teaching in Cambodia," in Omar Farouk and Hiroyuki Yamamoto, eds., *Islam at the Margins: The Muslims of Indochina* (Kyoto: CIAS, 2008), pp. 59–69.

Mutalib, Hussin. "The Islamic Malay Polity in Southeast Asia," in Mohamed Taib Osman, ed., *Islamic Civilization in the Malay World* (Kuala Lumpur: Dewan Bahasa dan Pustaka, 1997), pp. 1–48.

Naarding, Jan Willem. *Het conflict Snouck Hurgronje-van Heutsz-van Daalen: een onderzoek naar de verantwoordelijkheid* (Utrecht: A. Oosthoek, 1938).

Nakamura, Rie. "Cham in Vietnam: Dynamics of Ethnicity" (PhD Thesis, Anthropology Department, University of Washington, Seattle, 1999).

Nasron, Haji Mazlan. *Air Mata: Di Pintu Baitullah* (Kuala Lumpur: Progressive, 2002).

Nasution, H., et al., eds. *Ensiklopedi Islam Indonesia* (Jakarta: Jambatan, 1992).

Navis, A. A. *Surat dan Kenangan Haji* (Jakarta: Penerbit PT Gramedia Pustaka Utama, 1994).

Navis, H. A. A. "Penampilan Ego yang Tak Bertuah," in E. Syarief Nurdin and E. Kosasih, eds., *100 Keajaiban di Tanah Suci Pengalaman Unik Jamaah Haji* (Bandung: Pustaka Hidayah, 1996), pp. 92–93.

Ner, Marcel. "Les Musulmans de l'indochine francaise," *Bulletin de l'ecole Francaise d'extreme orient*, 2, 1941: 151–202.

Ngah, Haji Mohamad Daud bin Che'. *Panduan Haji dan Umrah* (Kuala Lumpur: Pustaka Al-Mizan, 1989).

Nicolini, Beatrice. "Little Known Aspects of the History of Muscat and Zanzibar during the First Half of the Nineteenth Century," *Proceedings of the Seminar for Arabian Studies*, 27, 1997: 193–198.

Noer, H. Arifin C. "Tuhan Menidurkan Saya," in E. Syarief Nurdin and E. Kosasih, eds., *100 Keajaiban di Tanah Suci Pengalaman Unik Jamaah Haji* (Bandung: Pustaka Hidayah, 1996), pp. 63–64.

Nomani, Farhad, and Ali Rahnema. *Islamic Economic Systems* (London: Zed, 1994).

Norman, Henry. "The Globe and the Island," *Cosmopolis*, 7/19, 1897: 79–92.

Nutton, Vivian. "The Contact between Civilizations," in Mario Gomes Marques and John Cule, eds., *The Great Maritime Discoveries and World Health* (Lisbon: Escola Nacional Saude Publica Ordem dos Medicos, 1991), p. 77.

O'Connor, Richard. *A Theory of Southeast Asian Urbanism* (Singapore: ISEAS Research Monograph No. 38, 1983).

Odirizzi, D. "Studio Storico della Provincia Arabica dello Jemen e Sulle Relazioni Etniche con l'Eritrea e l'Etiopia," *Atti Congresso Coloniale Italiano di Asmara* (Asmara: 1905), p. 323.

Odirizzo, D. *Note Storiche sulla Religione Mussulmana e Sulle Divisioni dell'Islam in Eritrea* (Asmara: Tip. Fioretti, 1916).

O'Hanlon, Redmund. *Joseph Conrad and Charles Darwin: The Influence of Scientific Thought on Conrad's Fiction* (Edinburgh: Salamander, 1984).

Olney, James. *Metaphors of Self: The Meaning of Autobiography* (Princeton, NJ: Princeton University Press, 1972).

Oslchanjetzki, D. "Souvenirs de l'epidemie de choléra au Hedjaz en 1893," in F. Daguet, *Le pelerinage de la Mecque* (Paris, 1932), p. 297.

Osman, Mohamad Taib. *Manual for Collecting Oral Tradition with Special Reference to South East Asia* (Kuala Lumpur: Dewan Bahasa dan Pustaka, 1982).

Osman, Mohamad Taib, ed. *Islamic Civilization in the Malay World* (Kuala Lumpur: Dewan Bahasa dan Pustaka, 1997).

Osman, Mohamed Taib. "Introduction," in Mohamed Taib Osman, ed., *Islamic Civilization in the Malay World* (Kuala Lumpur: Dewan Bahasa dan Pustaka, 1997), pp. 1–24.

Osterrieth, Anne. "Pilgrimage, Travel and Existential Quest," in Robert Stoddard and Alan Morinis, eds., *Sacred Places, Sacred Spaces: The Geography of Pilgrimages* (Baton Rouge, LA: Geoscience, 1997), p. 27.

Othman, Mohammad. "Hadhramis in the Politics and Administration of the Malay States in the Late Eighteenth and Late Nineteenth Centuries," in Ulrike Frietag and William Clarence-Smith, eds., *Hadhrami Traders, Scholars, and Statesmen in the Indian Ocean, 1750s–1960s* (Leiden: E. J. Brill, 1997), pp. 85–88.

Othman, Mohammad Rezuan. "The Role of Makka-Educated Malays in the Development of Early Islamic Scholarship and Education in Malaysia," *Journal of Islamic Studies*, 9/2, 1998: 146–157.

Ovington, John. *A Voyage to Surat in the Year 1689* (London: Hakluyt, 1929).

Owen, J. "Do Anchors Mean Ships? Underwater Evidence for Maritime Trade along the Dhofar Coast, Southern Indian Ocean," in Alessandra Avanzini, ed., *Profumi d'Arabia: Atti del Convegno* (Roma: L'Erma di Bretschneider, 1997), p. 351.

Pamuk, Sevket. *A Monetary History of the Ottoman Empire* (Cambridge: Cambridge University Press, 2000).

Pamuk, Sevket. "Prices in the Ottoman Empire," *IJMES*, 36, 2004: 451–467.

Panzac, Daniel. "International and Domestic Maritime Trade in the Ottoman Empire during the 18th Century," *IJMES*, 24/2, 1992: 189–206.

Parkin, David. "Inside and Outside the Mosque: A Master Trope," in David Parkin and Stephen Headley, eds., *Islamic Prayer across the Indian Ocean: Inside and Outside the Mosque* (London: Curzon, 2000).

Parkin, David, and Stephen Headley, eds. *Islamic Prayer across the Indian Ocean* (London: Curzon, 2000).

Parry, Benita. *Conrad and Imperialism: Ideological Boundaries and Visionary Frontiers* (London: Macmillan, 1983).

Pearson, M. N. *Pious Passengers: The Hajj in Earlier Times* (Dhaka, Bangladesh: University Press Limited, 1994).

Pearson, Michael N. *Pilgrimage to Mecca: The Indian Experience 1500–1800* (Princeton, NJ: Markus Weiner, 1996).

Pearson, Michael. *The Indian Ocean* (London: Routledge, 2003).

Peletz, Michael. *Islamic Modern: Religious Courts and Cultural Politics in Malaysia* (Princeton, NJ: Princeton University Press, 2002).

Peters, F. E. *Jerusalem and Mecca: The Typology of the Holy City in the Near East* (New York: New York University Studies in Near Eastern Civilization #11, 1986).

Peters, F. E. *The Hajj: The Muslim Pilgrimage to Mecca and the Holy Places* (Princeton, NJ: Princeton University Press, 1994).

Petet, Didi. "Allah Sekana Mengundang Saya ke Makah Setiap Tahun," in Anonymous, *Haji, Sebuah Perjalanan Air Mata* (Yogyakarta, Indonesia: Bentang, 1993), pp. 87–93.

Phu, Trung. "Bani Islam Cham in Vietnam," in Omar Farouk and Hiroyuki Yamamoto, eds., *Islam at the Margins: The Muslims of Indochina* (Kyoto: CIAS, 2008), pp. 24–33.

Pijper, G. F. *Studien over de Geschiedenis van de Islam in Indonesia, 1900–1950* (Leiden: E. J. Brill, 1977).

Pirotta, R. "Contribuzioni alla Conoscenza della Flora dell'Africa Orientale," *Annuario del. R. Istituto Botanico di Roma*, 5, 1894; and 9, 1902.

Pirzio Biroli, A. "Il Mar Rosso e l'A. O. I.," *Rivista delle Colonie Italiane*, 1936, p. 1426.

Piscatori, James. "Asian Islam: International Linkages and Their Impact on International Relations," in John Esposito, ed., *Islam in Asia: Religion, Politics, and Society* (New York: Oxford University Press, 1987), p. 251.

Plate, S. Brent. *Walter Benjamin, Religion and Aesthetics* (London: Routledge, 2004).

Poggi, Gianfranco. *Durkheim* (Oxford: Oxford University Press, 2000).

Portelli, Alessandro. *The Death of Luigi Trastulli and Other Stories: Form and Meaning in Oral History* (Albany: State University of New York Press, 1991).

Porter, Venetia. "The Ports of Yemen and the Indian Ocean Trade during the Tahirid Period, 1454–1517," in J. F. Healey and V. Porter, eds., *Studies on Arabia in Honour of Professor G. Rex Smith* (Oxford: Oxford University Press, 2002), pp. 171–190.

Powers, D. S. "The Islamic Endowment (Waqf)," *Vanderbilt Journal of Transnational Law*, 32, 1999: 4.

Prakash, Om. *Precious Metals and Commerce: The Dutch East India Company in the Indian Ocean Trade* (Aldershot, UK: Variorum, 1994).

Preston, James. "Spiritual Magnetism: An Organizing Principle for the Study of Pilgrimage," in Alan Morinis, ed., *Sacred Journeys: The Anthropology of Pilgrimage* (Westport, CT: Greenwood, 1992), pp. 33–35.

Priestly, Harry. "The Outsiders," *The Irrawaddy*, 14/1, 2006: 16–19.

Proust, A. "Le choléra de la Mer Rouge en 1890," *Bulletin Acad. de Med.*, 3S/25, 1891: 421–445.

Puccioni, N. "L'esplorazione Antropologica delle Colonie Italiane," *Atti I Congr. Studi Colon.*, vol. 3 (Firenze, 1931), p. 309.

Purchas, Samuel. *Purchas, His Pilgrimes* (Glasgow: Hakluyt, 1905–1907).

Putuhena, Shaleh. *Historiografa Haji Indonesia* (Yogyakarta: LKIS, 2007).

Rafael, Vincente, ed. *Figures of Criminality in Indonesia, the Philippines and Colonial Vietnam* (Ithaca, NY: Southeast Asia Program Publications, 1999).

Raffles, Thomas Stamford. *The History of Java*, part 2 (1817).

Rahman, Mohamad Jajuli A. *The Malay Law Text* (Kuala Lumpur: Dewan Bahasa dan Pustaka, 1995).

Rais, Amien. "Saya Mina Keturunan, Dikabulkan Allah," in Anonymous, *Haji Sebuah Perjalanan Air Mata* (Yogyakarta, Indonesia: Bentang, 1993), pp. 30–37.

Ramali, Ahmad. *Perdjalanan Hadji: Naik Hadji dan Hubungan sebagai Dokter Djemaah Hadji* (Jakarta: Tintomas, 1969).

Ras, J. J. *Hikajat Bandjar: A Study in Malay Historiography* (The Hague: Nijhoff, Koninklijk Insititunut voor Taal-, Land- en Volkenkunde, 1968).

Reid, Anthony. "Nineteenth Century Pan-Islam in Indonesia and Malaysia," *JAS*, 26/2, 1967: 267–283.

Reid, Anthony. "Sixteenth Century Turkish Influence in Western Indonesia," *Journal of South East Asian History*, 10/3, 1969: 395–414.

Reid, Anthony. *Southeast Asia in the Age of Commerce: The Lands beneath the Winds*, 2 vols. (New Haven, CT: Yale University Press, 1988, 1993).

Reid, Anthony. *An Indonesian Frontier: Acehnese and Other Histories of Sumatra* (Singapore; Singapore University Press, 2005).

Remlinger, P. *Police Sanitaire: Les Conditions Sanitaires du Pelérinage Musulman* (Paris: 1908).

Resink, G. J. "The Eastern Archipelago under Joseph Conrad's Western Eyes," in G. J. Resink, ed., *Indonesia's History's between the Myths* (The Hague: van Hoeve, 1968), pp. 307–308.

Ricklefs, M. C. *Mystic Synthesis in Java: A History of Islamization from the Fourteenth to the Early Nineteenth Centuries* (Norwalk, CT: Eastbridge, 2006).

Ricklefs, M. C. *Polarising Javanese Society: Islamic and Other Visions, 1830–1930* (Singapore: Singapore University Press, 2007).

Ricklefs, Merle. *A History of Modern Indonesia* (Stanford, CA: Stanford University Press, 1993), pp. 78–79.

Riddell, Peter. *Transferring a Tradition: `Abd Al-Ra'ûf Al-Singkili's Rendering into Malay of the Jalalâyn Commentary*, monograph 31 (Berkeley: Centers for South and Southeast Asia Studies, University of California, 1990).

Riddell, Peter. "Religious Links between Hadhramaut and the Malay-Indonesian World, 1850–1950," in Ulrike Frietag and William Clarence-Smith, eds., *Hadhrami Traders, Scholars, and Statesmen in the Indian Ocean, 1750s–1960s* (Leiden: E. J. Brill, 1997), p. 230.

Riddel, Peter. *Islam and the Malay-Indonesian World: Transmission and Responses* (Honolulu: University of Hawai'i Press, 2001).

Ridhwan, Cuk Hudoro. "Haji Mandiri: Kasus Lima Keluarga Asy Syifa" (MS Thesis, Universitas Indonesia, 1998).

Rinkes, D. A. *Nine Saints of Java* (Kuala Lumpur: Malaysian Sociological Research Institute, 1996).

Risso, Patricia. "Muslim Identity in Maritime Trade: General Observations and Some Evidence from the Eighteenth Century Persian Gulf/Indian Ocean Region," *IJMES*, 21/3, 1989: 381–392.

Risso, Patricia. *Merchants and Faith: Muslim Commerce and Culture in the Indian Ocean* (Boulder, CO: Westview, 1995).

Robin, C. J. "Arabie Meridionale: L'État et les Aromates," in Alessandra Avanzini, ed., *Profumi d'Arabia: Atti del Convegno* (Roma: L'Erma di Bretschneider, 1997), pp. 37–56.

Robin, Christian. "The Mine of ar-Radrad: Al-Hamdani and the Silver of Yemen," in Werner Daum, ed., *Yemen: 3000 Years of Art and Civilisation in Arabia Felix* (Innsbruck: Pinguin-Verlag, 1987), pp. 123–124.

Robinson, J. Brian. *Coffee in Yemen: A Practical Guide* (Sana'a: Ministry of Agriculture and Water Resources, 1993).

Robson, Stuart. "Java at the Crossroads," *Bijdragen tot de Taal-, Land- en Volkenkunde*, 137/2–3 (1981): 259–292.

Roff, William. *Autobiography and Biography in Malay Historical Studies* (Singapore: ISEAS, 1972).

Roff, William. *The Origins of Malay Nationalism* (Kuala Lumpur: Penerbit Universiti Malaya, 1974).

Roff, William. "The Conduct of the Hajj from Malaya, and the First Malay Pilgrimage Officer," in Anonymous, *Sari Terbitan Tak Berkala: Occasional Papers* (Kuala Lumpur: Institute of Malay Language and Culture, University of Malaya, 1975), pp. 81–112.

Roff, William. "Sanitation and Security: The Imperial Powers and the Haj in the Nineteenth Century," *Arabian Studies*, 6, 1982: 143–160.

Roff, William. "The Meccan Pilgrimage: Its Meaning for Southeast Asian Islam," in Raphael Israeli and Anthony Johns, eds., *Islam in Asia* (II) (Boulder, CO: Westview, 1984), pp. 238–245.

Roff, William, ed. *Islam and the Political Economy of Meaning: Comparative Studies of Muslim Discourse* (Berkeley: University of California Press, 1987).

Roff, William. "Sociological Interpretations of Religious Practice: The Case of the Hajj," in Virginia Hooker and Noraini Othman, eds., *Malaysia, Islam, Society and Politics: Essays in Honor of Clive Kessler* (Singapore: ISEAS, 2002), pp. 37–54.

Rogan, Eugene. *Frontiers of the State in the Late Ottoman Empire* (Cambridge: Cambridge University Press, 1999).

Roham, A. *Abujamin, Aku Pergi Haji* (Jakarta: Media Da'wah, 1992).

Romanis, F. de. "Tus e Murra: Aromi Sudarabici nella Roma Arcaica," in Alessandra Avanzini, ed., *Profumi d'Arabia: Atti del Convegno* (Roma: L'Erma di Bretschneider, 1997), p. 230.

Roolvink, R. "The Variant Versions of the Malay Annals," *BKI*, 123/3 (1967): 301–324.

Rosaldo, Renato. *Ilongot Headhunting 1883–1974: A Study in Society and History* (Stanford, CA: Stanford University Press, 1980).

Rosenberg, Charles. *Explaining Epidemics and Other Studies in the History of Medicine* (Cambridge: Cambridge University Press, 1992).

Rosenthal, Franz. *History and Muslim Historiography* (Leiden: Brill, 1968).

Rossetti, C. "Gomma Arabica," *Atti a Congr. Ital. all'Estero*, 1, 1911.

Rossi, E. "Il Hedjaz, il Pellegrinaggio e il cholera," *Gior. D. Soc. Ital*, ig., 4, 1882: 549–578.

Rouaud, Alain. "Remarques sur Quelques Aspects de l'Emigration Hadrami en Insulinde," in *Migrations, Minorités et Échanges en Ocean Indien, XIX–XX Siècle* (Aix, France: Université de Provence, 1978), pp. 68–92.

Rougeulle, Axelle. "Coastal Settlements in Southern Yemen: The 1996–1997 Expeditions on the Hadhramawt and Mahra Coasts," *Proceedings of the Seminar for Arabian Studies*, 29, 1999: 123–136.

Rousseau, Jerome. "Response to Rubenstein," *Borneo Research Bulletin*, 21/2 (1989): 95–96.

Rousydiy, T. A. Lathief. *Manasil Haji dan 'Umrah Rasulullah S.A.W.* (Medan, Indonesia: Penerbit Firma Rainbow, 1989).

Rowley, Gwyn. "The Pilgrimage to Mecca and the Centrality of Islam," in Robert Stoddard and Alan Morinis, eds., *Sacred Places, Sacred Spaces: The Geography of Pilgrimages* (Baton Rouge, LA: Geoscience, 1997), pp. 141–160.

Rubenstein, Carol. "Oral Literature Research and Review," *Borneo Research Bulletin*, 21/2 (1989): 83–94.

Rutter, Eldon. *The Holy Cities of Arabia*, vol. 1 (London: G. P. Putnam's Sons, 1928).

Saddik, M. "Voyage à La Mecque," *Bulletin de la Société Khediviale de Géographie du Caire*, 1, 1881: 5–40.

Said, Edward. *Joseph Conrad and the Fiction of Autobiography* (Cambridge, MA: Harvard University Press, 1966).

Said, H. A. Fuad. *Adab Manasik Haji dan Umrah* (Kuala Lumpur: Penerbitan Kintan, 1994).

Saleh, H. Ismail. "Balasan Setelah Mati," in E. Syarief Nurdin and E. Kosasih, eds., *100 Keajaiban di Tanah Suci Pengalaman Unik Jamaah Haji* (Bandung: Pustaka Hidayah, 1996), pp. 114–115.

Saleh, Ismail. *Pengalaman sebagai Amirul Haji* (Jakarta: Pustaka Kartini, 1990).

Salleh, Al-Ustaz Haji Hassan. *Konsep Ibadat Haji dalam Islam* (Kuala Lumpur: Dewan Ulama PAS Wilayah Persekuan, 1988).

Salleh, Awang Had. "Modern Concept of Hajj Management," in Z. Sardar and M. A. Zaki Badawi, eds., *Hajj Studies*, vol. 1 (London: Croom Helm, 1979), pp. 73–86.

Salleh, Muhammad Haji, ed. *Syair Tantangan Singapura Abad Kesembilan Belas* (Kuala Lumpur: Dewan Bahasa dan Pustaka, 1994).

Salleh, Siti Hawa. *Hikayat Merong Mahawangsa* (Kuala Lumpur: Penerbit Universiti Malaya, 1991).

Samman, Omar. "Jeddah: Gateway to the Ultimate Way," *Haj and Umra*, 58/2, 2003: 15.

Santagata, F. "La Colonia Eritrea nel Mar Rosso Davanti all'Abissinia," in *Libreria Internazionale Treves di Leo Lupi* (Napoli, 1935), p. 229.

Santasombat, Yos. "Oral History and Self-Portraits: Interviewing the Thai Elite," in P. Lim Pui Huen, James Morrison, and Kwa Chong Guan, eds., *Oral History in Southeast Asia: Theory and Method* (Singapore: National Archives of Singapore and the Institute of Southeast Asian Studies, 1998), pp. 66–85.

Satha-Anand, Chaiwat. "Spiritualising Real Estate, Commoditising Pilgrimage: The Muslim Minority in Thailand," in Joseph Camilleri and Chandra Muzzafar, eds., *Globalisation: The Perspectives and Experiences of the Religious Traditions of Asia Pacific* (Selangor, Malaysia: International Movement for a Just World, 1998), pp. 135–146.

Satia, Priya. *Spies in Arabia: The Great War and the Cultural Foundations of Britain's Covert Empire in the Middle East* (Oxford: Oxford University Press, 2008).

Schnepp, B. *Le Pèlerinage de La Mecque* (Paris, 1865).

Schroeder, F. "Orientalistische Retoriek: Van Konongsveld over de Vuile Handen van Snouck Hurgronje," *De Gids*, 9/10, 1980: 785–806.

Schulze, Fritz. "Islamizing Malay Culture: The Evidence of Malay Court Chronicles," in Fritz Schulze and Holger Warnk, eds., *Insular Southeast Asia: Linguistic and Cultural Studies in Honour of Bernd Nothofer* (Wiesbaden: Harrassowitz Verlag, 2006), pp. 131–140.

Schuman, Lein Oebele. "Political History of the Yemen at the Beginning of the Sixteenth Century: Abu Makhama's Account (1500–1521)" (PhD Dissertation, University of Groningen, 1960).

Searight, Sarah. "Jiddah in the Nineteenth Century: The Role of European Consuls," in Janet Starkey, ed., *People of the Red Sea* (Oxford: British Archeological Reports Series, 2005), pp. 109–116.

Sears, Laurie. "The Contingency of Autonomous History," in Laurie Sears, ed., *Autonomous Histories, Particular Truths: Essays in Honor of John R. W. Small* (Madison: Wisconsin Monographs on Southeast Asia, 1993).

Serjeant, R. B. *The Portuguese off the South Arabian Coast: Hadrami Chronicles, with Yemeni and European Accounts* (Beirut: Librairie du Liban, 1974).

Serjeant, R. B. "Historians and Historiography of Hadramawt," in R. B. Serjeant, *Studies in Arabian History and Civilisation* (London: Variorum, 1981), pp. 240–257.

Serjeant, R. B. "Pottery and Glass Fragments from the Aden Littoral, with Historical Notes," in R. B. Serjeant, *Studies in Arabian History and Civilisation* (London: Variorum, 1981), pp. 108–133.

Serjeant, R. B. "The Ports of Aden and Shihr (Medieval Period)," in R. B. Serjeant, *Studies in Arabian History and Civilisation* (London: Variorum, 1981), pp. 207–224.

Serjeant, R. B. "Early Islamic and Medieval Trade and Commerce in Yemen," in Werner Daum, ed., *Yemen: 3000 Years of Art and Civilisation in Arabia Felix* (Innsbruck: Pinguin-Verlag, 1987), pp. 163–166.

Sergeant, R. B. "The Hadhrami Network," in R. B. Sargeant, *Society and Trade in South Arabia* (Aldershot, UK: Variorum, 1996), pp. 147–149.

Sergeant, R. B. "Yemeni Merchants and Trade in Yemen, 13th–16th Centuries," in R. B. Sargeant, *Society and Trade in South Arabia* (Aldershot, UK: Variorum, 1996), pp. 61–82.

Shaikh, Habib. "IDB's Haj Services," *Haj and Umra*, 57/6, 2002: 28–29.

Sherry, Norman. *Conrad's Eastern World* (Cambridge: Cambridge University Press, 1966).

Shiddieqy, T. M. Hasbi Ash. *Pedoman Haji* (Johore Bahru, Malaysia: P. T. Bulan Bintang, 1986).

Shin, Ba. "The Coming of Islam to Myanma Down to 1700 AD," in *Asian History Congress* (New Delhi: Azad Bhavan, 1961).

Shipman, J. G. T. "The Hadhramaut," *Asian Affairs*, 15, 1984: 154–162.

Shiraishi, Saya. "A Study of Bustanu's Salatin (The Garden of the Kings)," in Takashi Shiraishi et al., eds., *Reading Southeast Asia: Translations of Contemporary Scholarship on Southeast Asia* (Ithaca, NY: Cornell Southeast Asia Program, 1990), pp. 41–55.

Sidel, John. "Other Schools, Other Pilgrimages, Other Dreams: The Making and Unmaking of 'Jihad' in Southeast Asia," in James T. Siegel and Audrey R. Kahin, eds., *Southeast Asia over*

Three Generations: Essays Presented to Benedict R. O'G. Anderson (Ithaca, NY: Cornell University Southeast Asia Program, 2003), pp. 347–382.

Sidel, John. "Jihad and the Specter of Transnational Islam in Southeast Asia: A Comparative Historical Perspective," in Eric Tagliacozzo, ed., *Southeast Asia and the Middle East: Islam, Movement, and the Longue Durée* (Palo Alto, CA: Stanford University Press, 2008), pp. 275–318.

Siegel, James. *The Rope of God* (Berkeley: University of California Press, 1969).

Siegel, James. *Shadow and Sound: The Historical Thought of a Sumatran People* (Chicago: University of Chicago Press, 1979).

Silverman, D. *Qualitative Methodology and Sociology* (Hants, UK: Gower, 1985).

Singh, R. P. B. "Time and Hindu Rituals in Varanasi: A Study of Sacrality and Cycles," in S. M. Bhardwaj, G. Rinschede, and A. Sievers, eds., *Pilgrimage in the Old and New World* (Berlin: Dietrich Reimer Verlag, 1994).

Situmorang, T. D., and A. Teeuw. *Sedjarah Melaju, Menurut Terbitan Abdullah bin Abdulkadir Munsji* (Jakarta/Amsterdam: Penerbit Djambatan, 1952).

Sjafruddin, Prawiranegara H. *Djangan Mempersulit Ibadah Hadji* (Jakarta: D. P. P. Husmai, 1970).

Sjihab, H. Abdurrahman. *Penuntun Hadji Tjara Mengerdjakan Hadji Dengan Praktis* (Medan, Indonesia: Forma Islamyah, 1963).

Skinner, C., ed. *Ahmad Rijaluddin's Hikayat Perintah Negeri Benggala* (Leiden: Martinus Nijhoff, 1982).

Skinner, C., ed. *The Battle for Junk Ceylon: The Syair Sultan Maulana, Text, Translation and Notes* (Dordrecht: Foris, for the Koninklijk Instituut voor Taal-, Land- en Volkenkunde, 1985).

Skinner, Cyril. *The Civil War in Kelantan in 1839* (Kuala Lumpur: Monographs of the Malaysian Branch, Royal Asiatic Society, 1965).

Smail, John. "On the Possibility of an Autonomous History of Southeast Asia," *Journal of Southeast Asian History*, 2/2, 1961: 72–102.

Smith, G. R. "Ibn al-Mujawir's 7th/13th Century Arabia—The Wondrous and the Humorous," in A. K. Irvine, R. B. Serjeant, and G. Rex Smith, eds., *Miscellany of Middle Eastern Articles in Memoriam Thomas Muir Johnstone 1924–83* (Harlow, England: Longman, 1988), pp. 111–124.

Smith, G. Rex. "Have You Anything to Declare? Maritime Trade and Commerce in Ayyubid Aden, Practices and Taxes," *Proceedings of the Seminar for Arabian Studies*, 25, 1995: 127–140.

Smith, G. Rex. "More on the Port Practices and Taxes of Medieval Yemen," in G. Rex Smith, *Studies in the Medieval History of the Yemen and South Arabia* (Aldershot, UK: Variorum, 1997), pp. 208–218.

Smith, G. Rex. "The Political History of the Islamic Yemen down to the First Turkish Invasion, 622–1538," in G. Rex Smith, *Studies in the Medieval History of the Yemen and South Arabia* (Aldershot, UK: Variorum, 1997), pp. 129–139.

Snouck Hurgronje, C. "Het Mekkaansche Feest" (PhD Dissertation, Leiden University, 1880).

Snouck Hurgronje, C. "Nieuwe Bijdragen tot de Kennis van de Islam," *BTLV*, 4/6, 1882: 357–421.

Snouck Hurgronje, C. *De beteekenis van den Islam voor zijne belijders in Ost-Indië* (Leiden: E. J. Brill, 1883).

Snouck Hurgronje, C. "Le Droit Musulman," *Revue de l'Histoire des Religions*, 19/37, 1898: 1–22, 174–203.

Snouck Hurgronje, C. "Hadji Politiek?" *Java-Bode*, March 6–8, 1899: 353–368.

Snouck Hurgronje, C. *Het Gajoland en Zijne Bewoners* (Batavia, Indonesia: Landsdrukkerij, 1903).

Snouck Hurgronje, C. "De Hadji-Politiek der Indische Regeering," *Onze Eeuw*, 1909: 331–360.

Snouck Hurgronje, C. "Het Mohammedanisme," in H. Colijn, ed. *Neerlands Indie*, vol. 1 (Amsterdam: 1911), pp. 243–265.

Snouck Hurgronje, C. "Notes sur le Mouvement du Pélerinage de la Mecque aux Indies Néerlan-daises," in *Collection de la Revue du Monde Musulman* #15 (Paris, 1911), pp. 397–413.

Snouck Hurgronje, C. "Politique Musulmane de la Hollande," in *Collection de la Revue du Monde Musulman* #14 (Paris, 1911).

Snouck Hurgronje, C. *De Islam in Nederlandsch-Indie* (Baarn, Netherlands: Hollandia, 1913).

Snouck Hurgronje, C. "De Islam," *De Gids*, 2, 1886: 239–273, 454–498; 3, 1886: 90–134.

Snouck Hurgronje, C. "De Mekkagangers en de Oorlog," *Nieuwe Rotterdamsche Courant*, November 24–25, 1915: 299–310.

Snouck Hurgronje, C. *De Islam en het Rassenprobleem* (Leiden: E. J. Brill, 1922).

Snouck Hurgronje, C. "Vergeten Jubile's," *De Gids*, 87/7, 1923: 61–81.

Snouck Hurgronje, C. *Mekka in the Latter Part of the 19th Century: Daily Life, Customs and Learning, the Moslims of the East-Indian-Archipelago* (Leiden: E. J. Brill, 1931).

Sobary, Mohamad. *Tamu Allah* (Jakarta: Pustaka Firdaus, 1996).

Soonthornpasuch, Suthep. "Islamic Identity in Chiengmai City: A Historical and Structural Comparison of Two Communities" (PhD Thesis, University of California, Berkeley, 1977).

Soubhy, S. "Pélerinage à La Mecque et à Medine," *Bulletin de la Societé Khediviale de Géographie du Caire*, 4, 1894: 45–88, 105–144.

Spaan, Ernst. "Taikong's and Calo's: The Role of Middlemen and Brokers in Javanese International Migration," *International Migration Review*, 28/1, 1994: 93–128.

Speece, Mark. "Aspects of Economic Dualism in Oman, 1830–1930," *IJMES*, 21/4, 1989: 495–515.

Spengermann, William. *The Forms of Autobiography: Episodes in the History of a Literary Genre* (New Haven, CT: Yale University Press, 1980).

St. John, Spencer. *Life in the Forests of the Far East*, vol. 1 (Kuala Lumpur: Oxford in Asia Historical Reprints, Oxford University Press, 1974).

Stape, J. H. "Lord Jim," in *The Cambridge Companion to Joseph Conrad* (Cambridge: Cambridge University Press, 1996), pp. 63–80.

Stape, J. H., and Gene Moore. "The Stone of the Sultan of Succadana: Another Source for Lord Jim," *The Conradian*, 27/1, 2002: 44–50.

Stauth, Georg. "Slave Trade, Multiculturalism and Islam in Colonial Singapore: A Sociological Note on Christian Snouck Hurgronje's 1891 Article on Slave Trade in Singapore," *Southeast Asian Journal of Social Science*, 20/1, 1992: 67–79.

Steenbrink, Karel. *Dutch Colonialism and Indonesian Islam: Contacts and Conflicts, 1596–1950* (Amsterdam: Radopi, 1993).

Stock, Emiko. "Les Communautes Musulmanes du Cambodge: Un Apercu," in Michel Gilquin, ed., *Atlas des Minorites Musulmanes en Asia Meridionale et Orientale* (Paris: CNRS Editions, 2010), pp. 183–216.

Stoddard, Robert. "Pilgrimage along Sacred Paths," in R. L. Singh and Rana Singh, eds., *Trends in the Geography of Pilgrimages* (Varanasi, India: National Geographic Society of India, 1987).

Stoddardt, W. *Le Soufisme* (Lausanne, Switzerland: Trois Continentes, 1979).

Stokhof, Malte. "The Baweans of Ho Chi Minh City," in Omar Farouk and Hiroyuki Yamamoto, eds., *Islam at the Margins: The Muslims of Indochina* (Kyoto: CIAS, 2008), pp. 34–58.

Strauss, A. L. *Qualitative Analysis for Social Scientists* (New York; Cambridge University Press, 1987).

Straver, Hans, Chris van Fraassen, and Jan van der Putten, eds. *Ridjali: Historie van Hitu. Een Ambonse geschiedenis uit de zeventiende eeuw* (Utrecht: LSEM (Landelijk Steunpunt Educatie Molukkers), 2004).

Subandi. "Pengaruh Pelatihan terhadap Produktivitas Kerja Suatu Studi terhadap Tim Pembimbang Haji Indonesia Non Kelompok Terbang" (MS Thesis, Universitas Indonesia, 1995).

Subrahmanyam, Sanjay. *Improvising Empire: Portuguese Trade and Settlement in the Bay of Bengal* (Delhi: Oxford University Press, 1990).

Subrahmanyman, Sanjay. *The Career and Legend of Vasco da Gama* (Cambridge: Cambridge University Press, 1997).

Sudjiman, Panuti H. M., ed. *Adat Raja-Raja Melayu* (Jakarta: Penerbit Universitas Indonesia, 1983).

Sukarsono, H. *Liku-Liku Perjalanan ke Tanah Suci* (Jakarta: P. T. Pranadaya, 1975).

Sumarni, Hj. Sri. "Bayangan Putih di Balik Tragedi Mina," in E. Syarief Nurdin and H. Aqib Suminto, eds., *Politik Islam Hindia Belanda: Het Kantoor voor Inslandsche Zaken* (Jakarta: Lembaga Penelitian Pendidikan dan Penerangan Ekonomi dan Sosial, 1985).

Suryadi, *Syair Sunur; Teks dan Konteks 'otobiografi'Seorang Ulama Minangkabau Abad ke-19* (Padang, Indonesia: YDIKM & Citra Budaya, 2004).

Swanson, Jon. *Emigration and Economic Development: The Case of the Yemen Arab Republic* (Boulder, CO: Westview, 1979).

Swanson, Jon. "Histoire et Conséquences de l'émigration hors de la République Arabe du Yemen," in Paul Bonnenfant, ed., *La Péninsule Arabique D'Aujourd'hui* (Paris: CNRS, 1982), p. 108.

Sweeney, Amin. *Karya Lengkap Abdullah bin Abdul Kadir Munsyi, Jilid 1* (Jakarta: Kepustakaan Populer Gramedia/École française d'Extrême-Orient, 2005).

Syair Makkah al-Musyarrafah Madinah al-Munawwarat (Singapore: Publisher Ibrahim, Kampung Gelam, 1886).

Syair Mekah Madinah (Singapore: Tuan Syaikh Haji Muhammad Ali b. Haji Mustafa bala(d) Berbalingga Makam Cahaya, Lorong Masjid, Kampung Gelam, 1869).

Syair Mekah Madinah; Syair Mekah Syair Madinah (Singapore: Tuan Haji Muhammad Nuh b. Haji Ismail ahl al-Jawi bil(d) Juwana namanya tempat Dusun Kajian, 1873).

Syair Mekah Madinah Jiddah Araafat dan Sekalian Tanah Arab dan Menyatakan Peri Hal Ihwal Orang yang Pergi Haj dan Keelokan (Singapore: Ofis Cap Haji Sirat, 1885).

Syair Negeri Makkah al-Musyarrafah dan Madinah al-Munawwarat (Singapore: Haji Muhammad Sidik, 1889).

Syair Negeri Makkah al-Musyarrafah dan Madinah al-Munawwarat; Syair Macam Baru peri menyatakan Orang yang Pergi Haj dari Negeri Bawah Angin sampai kepada Negeri Atas Angin seperti Jiddah dan Mekah dan Madinah dan seperti lain-lainnya (Singapore: Tuan Haji Muhammad Taib, 1888).

Tagliacozzo, Eric. *Secret Trades, Porous Borders: Smuggling and States along a Southeast Asian Frontier, 1865–1915* (New Haven, CT: Yale University Press, 2005).

Tagliacozzo, Eric. "Underneath the Indian Ocean: A Review Essay," *Journal of Asian Studies*, 67/3, 2008: 1–8.

Tagliacozzo, Eric, ed. *Southeast Asia and the Middle East: Islam, Movement, and the Longue Duree* (Palo Alto, CA: Stanford University Press, 2009).

Tan, Samuel. *Internationalization of the Bangsomoro Struggle* (Quezon City: University of the Philippines, 1995).

Tangban, O. E. "The Hajj and the Nigerian Economy, 1960–1981," *Journal of Religion in Africa*, 21/3, 1991: 241–167.

Tanner, Tony. *Lord Jim*. Studies in English Literature 12 (London: Edward Arnold, 1963).

Taylor, Philip. *Cham Muslims of the Mekong Delta: Place and Mobility in the Cosmopolitan Periphery* (Singapore: NUS, 2007).

Teeuw, A., ed. *Shair Ken Tambuhan* (Kuala Lumpur: University of Malay Press, 1966).

Teski, Marea, and Jacob Climo, eds. *The Labyrinth of Memory: Ethnographic Journeys* (Westport, CT: Bergin & Garvey, 1995).

Thomas, Brook. "Preserving and Keeping Order by Killing Time in Heart of Darkness," in Ross Murfin, ed., *Joseph Conrad, Heart of Darkness: A Case Study in Contemporary Criticism* (New York: St. Martin's Press, 1989).

Tibbetts, G. R. *Arab Navigation in the Indian Ocean before the Coming of the Portuguese* (London: RASGB, 1981).

Tibbetts, G. R. *A Study of the Arabic Texts Containing Material on South-East Asia* (Leiden: Brill, 1979),

Tiro, Tengku Hasan M. de. "Indonesian Nationalism: A Western Invention to Contain Islam in the Dutch East Indies," in M. Ghayasuddin, ed., *The Impact of Nationalism on the Muslim Word* (London: Muslim Institute, 1986), pp. 61–73.

Tolibas-Nunez, Rosalita. *Muslims, Christian and the Mindanao Struggle* (Makati City, Philippines: Asian Institute of Management, 1997).

Tonnies, Ferdinand. *Community and Society: Gemeinschaft und Gesellschaft*, Charles Loomis, trans. and ed. (East Lansing: Michigan State Press, 1957).

Tracy, James, ed. *The Political Economy of Merchant Empires* (Cambridge: Cambridge University Press, 1991).

Turner, Bryan. *For Weber: Essays on the Sociology of Fate* (London: Sage, 1996).

Turner, Victor. "The Center Out There: The Pilgrims Goal," *History of Religions*, 12/3, 1973: 191–230.

Turner, Victor. "Pilgrimages as Social Processes," in Victor Turner, ed., *Dramas, Fields, and Metaphors* (Ithaca, NC: Cornell University Press, 1974), pp. 167–230.

Turner, Victor. "Death and the Dead in the Pilgrimage Process," in F. E. Reynolds and E. Waugh, eds., *Religious Encounters with Death* (University Park: Pennsylvania State University Press, 1976), pp. 24–39.

Turner, Victor, and Edith Turner. *Image and Pilgrimage in Christian Culture: Anthropological Perspectives* (New York: Columbia University Press, 1978).

Um, Nancy Ajung. "A Red Sea Society in Yemen: Architecture, Urban Form and Cultural Dynamics in the Eighteenth-Century Port City of al-Mukha" (PhD Dissertation, University of California, Los Angeles, 2001).

Vansina, Jan. *Oral Tradition as History* (Madison: University of Wisconsin Press, 1985).

Veer, Peter van der. "De Orientalist en de Dominee," in Peter van der Veer, ed., *Modern Orientalisme* (Amsterdam: Meulenhoff, 1995), pp. 167–202.

Verleun, Jan. *Patna and Patusan Perspectives: A Study of the Function of the Minor Characters in Joseph Conrad's Lord Jim* (Groningen, Netherlands: Bert Hagen Castricum, 1979).

Veth, P. J. *Java: Geographisch, Ethnologisch, Historisch*, vol. 4 (Haarlem, Netherlands: De Erven F. Bohn, 1907), pp. 128–167.

Villier, Allan. *Sons of Sinbad* (New York: Scribners, 1969).

Voll, John Obert. *Islam: Continuity and Change in the Modern World* (Syracuse, NY: Syracuse University Press, 1982).

Vredenbregt, Jacob. "The Hadj: Some of Its Features and Functions in Indonesia," *Bijdragen tot de Taal-, Land-, en Volkenkunde*, 118, 1962: 91–154.

Wakeman, Frederic. *Policing Shanghai, 1927–1937* (Berkeley: University of California Press, 1995).

Wallace, Alfred Russel. *The Malay Archipelago*, vol. 2 (London: Macmillan, 1869).

Warnk, Holger. "Some Notes on the Malay Speaking Community in Cairo at the Turn of the Nineteenth Century," in Fritz Schulze and Holger Warnk, *Insular Southeast Asia: Linguistic and Cultural Studies in Honour of Bernd Nothofer* (Wiesbaden: Harrassowitz Verlag, 2006), pp. 141–152.

Warren, J. F. "Joseph Conrad's Fiction as Southeast Asian History: Trade and Politics in East Borneo in the Late Nineteenth Century," in James Warren, ed., *At the Margins of Southeast Asian History* (Quezon City, Philippines: New Day, 1987), pp. 15–19.

Warren, James Francis. *The Sulu Zone* (Singapore: University of Singapore Press, 1981).

Watson, C. W. *Of Self and Nation: Autobiography and the Representation of Modern Indonesia* (Honolulu: University of Hawai'i Press, 2000).

Watt, W. Montgomery. *Muhammad's Mecca: History and the Qur'an* (Edinburgh: Edinburgh University Press, 1988).

Watts, C. T., ed. *Joseph Conrad's Letters to R. B. Cunningham Graham* (Cambridge: Cambridge University Press, 1969).

Weintraub, Karl. *The Value of the Individual: Self and Circumstance in Autobiography* (Chicago: University of Chicago Press, 1978).

Weiringa, E. P. *Catalogue of Malay and Minangkabau Manuscripts in the Library of Leiden University and Other Collections in the Netherlands. Volume I, Comprising the Acquisitons of Malay Manuscripts in Leiden University up to the Year 1896*, ed. Joan de Lijster-Streef and Jan Just Witkam (Leiden: Legatum Warnerianum, 1998).

Wertheim, W. F. "Counter-Insurgency Research at the Turn of the Century—Snouck Hurgronje and the Aceh War," in W. F. Wertheim, *Dawning of an Asian Dream: Selected Articles on Modernization and Emancipation* (Amsterdam: University of Amsterdam Press, 1973), pp. 136–148.

White, Andrea. *Joseph Conrad and the Adventure Tradition: Constructing and Deconstructing the Imperial Subject* (Cambridge: Cambridge University Press, 1993).

Widayat, H. "Saya Bertemu Malaikat," in Anonymous, *Haji Sebuah Perjalanan Air Mata* (Yogyakarta, Indonesia: Bentang, 1993), pp. 225–231.

Wilson, R. T. O. "The Tihama from the Beginning of the Islamic Period to 1800," in Francine Stone, ed., *Studies on the Tihama* (Essex, England: Longman, 1985), pp. 31–35.

Winder, R. Bayly. *Saudi Arabia in the Nineteenth Century* (New York: St. Martin's Press, 1965).

Winstedt, R. O. "The Malay Annals, or Sejarah Melayu," *JMBRAS*, 16/3, 1938: 1–222.

Winstedt, R. O., ed. *Hikayat Bayan Budiman* (Kuala Lumpur: Oxford University Press, 1966).

Witkam, Jan Just, "Introduction," in C. Snouck Hurgronje, *Mecca in de Tweede Heift van de Negentiends Eevw: Schetse vit het Dagelijks Leven* (Amsterdam: Atlas, 2007).

Witlox, Marcel. "Met Gevaar voor Lijf en Goed: Mekkagangers uit Nederlands-Indie in de 19de Eeuw," in Willy Jansen en Huub de Jonge, eds., *Islamitische Pelgrimstochten* (Muiderberg, Netherlands: Coutinho, 1991).

Wolfe, Michael. *One Thousand Roads to Mecca: Ten Centuries of Travelers Writing about the Muslim Pilgrimage* (New York: Grove, 1997).

Wolluston, A. "The Pilgrimmage to Mecca," *Asiatic Quarterly Review*, 1, 1886.

Wong, H. Johnny. "Ingin Seperti Presiden," in E. Syarief Nurdin and E. Kosasih, *100 Keajaiban di Tanah Suci Pengalaman Unik Jamaah Haji* (Bandung: Pustaka Hidayah, 1996), pp. 45–46.

Wood, J. R. *A Handbook of the Yemen Flora* (Kew, England: Royal Botanic Gardens, 1997).

Yamazaki, Tomoko. *Sandakan Brothel #8: An Episode in the History of Lower-Class Japanese Women* (Armonk, NY: Sharpe, 1999).

Yang, Anand, ed. *Crime and Criminality in British India* (Tucson: University of Arizona Press, 1985).

Yaron, Perry, and Efraim Lev. *Modern Medicine in the Holy Land: Pioneering British Medical Services in Late Ottoman Palestine* (London: Tauris Academic Studies, 2007).

Yassin, Suhaimee. *Panduan Haji* (Kuala Lumpur: Bahagian Hal Ehwal Islam Jabatan Perdana Menteri, 1995).

Yegar, Moshe. *The Muslims of Burma: A Study of a Minority Group* (Wiesbaden: Harrassowitz Verlag, 1972).

Yegar, Moshe. *Islam and Islamic Institutions in British Malaya: Policies and Implementation* (Jerusalem: Magnes Press, 1979).

Yegar, Moshe. *Between Integration and Secession: The Muslim Communities of the Southern Philippines, Southern Thailand, and Western Burma/Myanmar* (Lanham, MD: Lexington, 2002).

Yeni. "Burma's Muslim Hero," *The Irrawaddy*, 14/1, 2006: 19.

Yeni. "Stateless in Arakan," *The Irrawaddy*, 14/1, 2006: 22–23.

Yeoh, Brenda. *Municipal Sanitary Surveillance, Asian Resistance and the Control of the Urban Environment in Colonial Singapore* (Oxford: Oxford Geography Research paper 47, 1991).

Yeoh, Brenda. *Contesting Space in Colonial Singapore: Power Relations and the Urban Built Environment* (Oxford: Oxford University Press, 1996).

Yoshimoto, Yasuko. "Is Cham Bani Indigenized Islamic Cham? A Study on Islamization and Religious Syncretism." Unpublished Paper.

Yule, Henri, and Henri Cordier. *The Book of Ser Marco Polo* (Amsterdam: Philo, 1975).

Yunus, A. "Pengaruh Optimalisasi Koordinasi dan Komunikasi terhadap Efektivitas Pelayanan Ibadah Haji di Kebupaten Sumedang" (MS Thesis, Univeristas Satyyagama, Jakarta, 1999).

Zaini, H. Azkarmin. *Pengalaman Haji di Tanah Suci: Sebuah Reportase Lengkap tentang Menunai-kan Ibadah Haji* (Jakarta: P. T. Gramedia, 1975).

Zaman, Muhammad Qasim. "The Scope and Limits of Islamic Cosmopolitanism and the Discursive Language of the 'Ulama,'" in Miriam Cooke and Bruce Lawrence, eds., *Muslim Networks from Hajj to Hip Hop* (Chapel Hill: University of North Carolina Press, 2005), pp. 84–104.

Zehner, Edward. "Muslims in Thailand: The State of the Field." Unpublished Paper Presented to the Comparative Muslim Societies Program, Cornell University, February 2009.

Zoppi, V. "Civiltà Fascista," *Il Mar Rosso*, 1935, p. 321.

INDEX